# Handbook of Evidence-Based Substance Abuse Treatment in Criminal Justice Settings

## Issues in Children's and Families' Lives

*Series Editors:*
**Thomas P. Gullotta**, *Child and Family Agency of Southeastern Connecticut, New London, Connecticut*
**Herbert J. Walberg**, *University of Illinois at Chicago, Chicago, Illinois*
**Roger P. Weissberg**, *Univeristy of Illinois at Chicago, Chicago, Illinois*

---

For other titles published in this series, go to
http://www.springer.com/series/6110

---

A Continuation Order Plan is available for this series. A continuation order will bring delivery of each new volume immediately upon publication. Volumes are billed only upon actual shipment. For further information please contact the publisher.

Carl Leukefeld · Thomas P. Gullotta ·
John Gregrich
Editors

Jessica M. Ramos
Research Assistant

# Handbook of Evidence-Based Substance Abuse Treatment in Criminal Justice Settings

Springer

Child & Family Agency of Southeastern Connecticut, Inc.
It's About Children

UIC University of Illinois at Chicago Great Cities Institute
College of Urban Planning & Public Affairs

*Editors*
Carl Leukefeld
Department of Behavioral Science
Center on Drug & Alcohol Research
University of Kentucky
Lexington, KY 40506, USA
cleukef@uky.edu

Thomas P. Gullotta
Child and Family Agency of Southeastern Connecticut
New London, CT 06320, USA
tpgullotta@aol.com

John Gregrich
Columbia, MD 21044, USA
jbgregrich@comcast.net

ISSN 1572-1981
ISBN 978-1-4419-9469-1 e-ISBN 978-1-4419-9470-7
DOI 10.1007/978-1-4419-9470-7
Springer New York Dordrecht Heidelberg London

Library of Congress Control Number: 2011934028



Printed on acid-free paper

Springer is part of Springer Science+Business Media (www.springer.com)

# Preface

This is a book about the interplay between two issues that dominate the evening news – drugs and criminal behavior. Neither issue is new. Both have plagued American society from its beginning. What is different is our response to these issues. To illustrate, before there was cocaine, heroin, and prescription drugs there was alcohol and tobacco. The fermentation of apples pressed into cider each fall insured American colonists that their daily nutritional needs for fruit would be met by an ample supply of that amber liquid stored in wooden casks and found in cellar holes throughout the colonies. In those casks small microbes ingested sugar and excreted by way of a byproduct alcohol. When the percentage of alcohol climbed to 6, the little critters died in their own waste. With time, later immigrant groups would bring the necessary knowledge to brew beer (considered by many Europeans to be less a beverage and more a food) and to distill grains and berries into even more potent intoxicating beverages.

The mind-altering effect of alcohol on the behavior of colonists was a concern from the beginning with efforts to control its misuse dating to the earliest establishment of settlements in New England. Interestingly and this is the point, the majority of those efforts focused on the control of those intoxicating beverages more than on the individual psychological weaknesses of the individual. Mind you, the misbehaving consumer was urged, pleaded with, entreated, and beseeched to stop his/her destructive behavior but the "Demon" was rum not the individual! It was believed that the individual was not a personality-disordered miscreant but rather a person poisoned by the consumed beverage and not "in his/her right mind." The phrase "not in their right mind" implies that the formerly inebriated person was or could be a contributing member to society and not a parasite. Thus, across the colonies and later the United States one sees local evidence of the rigid regulation of taverns to feed, house, and serve beverages to the traveler and local citizenry. Tavern operators were chosen on the basis of public standing and licensed by the community to operate an "ordinary" that complied with the moral standards of the area. In the minds, writings, and initiatives of these first substance abuse specialists when these early community controls loosened due to the growth of urban areas (seaports), the rising immigrant population (the first wave being the Irish), and the emergence of businesses solely intended to serve alcohol (saloons), more vigorous actions were necessary. Again, the anti-saloon movement and the prohibition of the commercial manufacturing, distribution, and sale of alcoholic beverages were societal and not deviant individual approaches.

Tobacco did not enjoy the European reputation of being considered a nutritious food and from its earliest introduction into Europe and other areas encountered strong religious and governmental opposition. True, tobacco was assumed to possess certain medicinal qualities to treat ailments such as snake bites, fever, exhaustion, and the Black Plague. Indeed, the great diarist Samuel Pepy recorded

> This day... I see in Drury Lane houses marked with a red cross [denoting the presence of the Plague]... which was a sad sight to me... It put me into an ill conception of myself and of my smell, so I was forced to buy some roll tobacco to smell an[d] chaw, which took away the apprehension (Gullotta, 2009, p. 5).

As tobacco's medicinal purposes quickly evaporated into thin smoke and the meaning of, "blowing smoke up one's ass," lost its original curative meaning to represent instead hoodwinkery for a period of time lasting from the mid-1800s to America's entry into the World War I, anti-tobacco movements were as vocal and nearly as successful as the anti-saloon movement. The anti-tobacco league saw this weed as noxious in its odor, filthy in its waste products of smoke, ash, and spittle, and debilitating to the health of its user.

For the careful reader who questions the use of spittle in the previous sentence, you are correct – tobacco does not spit but it does create copious amounts of saliva in those like Pepy who choose to chew or "chaw" it. Whether America during the 1700s and 1800s had a shortage of spittoons or good shots is a question still awaiting study but this we do know – travelers to the states were awestruck, perhaps the better word is shocked, by how Americans disposed of their saliva. Consider, for example, Charles Dickens's impression of visiting the US Congress in session:

> The Senate is a dignified and decorous body, and its proceedings are conducted with much gravity and order. Both Houses are handsomely carpeted; but the state to which these carpets are reduced by the universal disregard of the spittoon with which every member is accommodated, and the extraordinary improvements on the pattern which are squirted and dabbled upon it in every direction, do not admit of being described. I will merely observe, that I strongly recommend all strangers not to look at the floor; and if they happen to drop anything, though it be their purse, not to pick it up with an ungloved hand on any account (Dickens, 1898, pp. 176–177).

Was Congress the only setting in which spit and fur flew? Apparently not, as this English traveler through the American frontier observed:

> We discussed these important questions [in the Tavern] until my companions paired themselves off into their respective beds. I selected the cleanest corner of the [room] that had been least spat upon [not wanting to share a bed with another person] – and lay down on the floor with my carpetbag for a pillow (Anonymous, 1863, p. 499).

Lastly, picture Dickens after a busy day of sightseeing and speaking being visited by several gentlemen in his hotel room, "who in the course of conversation frequently missed the spittoon at five paces; and one (but he was certainly short-sighted) mistook the closed sash for the open window at three (Dickens, 1898, p. 177)." Ah, the image of Dickens staring at his hotel window as a copious slow-moving brownish yellow mass descended to the window sill is priceless.

The practice of saw dusting floors in public eating and drinking establishments offered a practical but no more sanitary solution to the messy practice.[1] As the public health movement gathered momentum in the late 1800s and into the progressive era that marked the beginning of the last century, laws were passed discouraging the use of the common tin drinking cup to be found by the well pump and spitting on sidewalks. Success in tightening controls on alcohol and tobacco grew during this time period culminating in the prohibition of the public manufacturing and sale of alcoholic beverages except for medicinal and religious purposes. Interestingly, an individual's production of beer and wine for his or her own consumption was exempted from the Volstead Act. Tobacco usage escaped a similar fate thanks to the outbreak of hostilities in Europe in 1914. Tobacco usage, especially the use of cigarettes, was encouraged by American generals like Black Jack Pershing who saw the tranquilizing effects of tobacco as necessary to men before and after battle. As he bluntly stated, "You ask me what we need to win this war? I answer tobacco as much as bullets" (Black Jack Pershing cited in Burns, 2006, p. 158).

During WWII, draft deferments were extended to tobacco growers to insure that an adequate supply of this weed was available to servicemen and women. It would not be until 1964 that the words found in King James' 1604 anonymously published *Counter-Blaste to Tobacco* gained new credence, "[tobacco is] hateful to the nose, harmful to the brain, [and] dangerous to the lungs (King James 1604/1932, pp. 34–35).

Importantly and presently, the majority of efforts devoted to the reduction of tobacco use in America are focused more on the control of this noxious weed than on the individual psychological weaknesses of the individual. Mind you, again, the misbehaving consumer is urged, pleaded with, entreated, and beseeched to stop his/her destructive behavior but the "Demon" is nicotine not the individual! Thus, while smoking cessation programs, patches, and gum exist there is seemingly a consensus that higher taxes, regulating usage in public locations, and establishing age-to-purchase laws are more useful approaches.

Why dwell on both these legal addictive substances? The answer is found in a series of papers published nearly 40 years ago by Denise Kandel and her associates (Kandel, 1981; Kandel & Faust, 1975; Kandel, Kessler, & Margulies, 1978; Kandel, Yamaguchi, & Chen, 1992) that have never been refuted. Kandel proposed that the gateway or, if you prefer "stepping stones" to illegal substance abuse begins with the use of tobacco and alcohol. Delay the onset of their use and the likelihood that other mind-altering substances will be tried drops dramatically. Thus, recent efforts to more tightly regulate

---

[1] For those who might think that this unhealthy behavior was solely American, Freud (1950) reveals that he spat on the stairs of a client when the need arouse and a spittoon was not available much to the consternation of the women's servant. Interestingly, Freud took offense at the servant's anger viewing it as disrespectful of his stature as a doctor.

the distribution of alcohol and tobacco products should have over time a positive effect in reducing drug use by the greater US population. Still, there will be that population subset who despite the barriers erected to discourage drug use will abuse drugs, commit criminal offenses, and end up in the justice system. Followers of Durkheim would sigh and remark that this is inevitable. Society, every society, needs deviants committing acts that violate the standards of acceptable community behavior. These violations serve to unite the rest of the community in outrage and define good law-abiding folk from bad law-breaking folk. Readers of Kai Erikson's (1966) classic *Wayward Puritans* or students of the "Red Scare" episode in America after WWII recognize that many times the rules (laws) a society establishes at one time will be seen as ludicrous at some future date. Mind you, we are not suggesting that drug abuse should be ignored or that stealing and assault should be tolerated. What intrigues us is that prior to the arrival of the first immigrants (Irish Catholics) who were neither British nor Protestant to the States in the early 1800s what little crime existed was handled in a manner that expulsion from the community was a rare occurrence. This leads us to the conclusion that when the substance is stigmatized the reentry of the user into mainstream society is less fraught with difficulty than when the individual is stigmatized.

How so? Simply put, to have membership in a group one must belong, be valued, and be able to make a meaningful contribution to the group. In most of American society, the criminal drug user is not viewed as a part of society. The drug-using criminal is simply put – dirt. This criminal drug user is not valued. The drug-using criminal should be locked away – forever. This criminal drug user is not able to make a meaningful contribution to society. Employ an ex-con, a junkie – never. Unable to escape the past, criminals embrace the underground culture that does accept, value, and enable them to contribute to their culture. The challenge for society is balancing individual responsibility for missteps in one's life with our collective responsibility for reintegrating the criminal into our society. Our laws suggest that this is the intention but the editors of this volume over a lifetime have grown suspicious that those laws were never intended for everyone. Thus, we begin this book with skepticism that what society wants it really does not say, and the successful evidence-based interventions that emerge from the failures that surround us are too often ignored for the old ways.

With this cautionary comment in place, in Chapter 1 Weinman reminds us that criminal drug abusers can be effectively treated using social behavioral interventions. Importantly, the use of this methodology can be employed successfully with resistant individuals reminding us of the earlier discussion in this preface that the "Demon" was found in the substance and not the person. Remove the substance and the probability that improvement will occur increases. The difficulty of successfully treating this population is made clear in the second chapter by Samenow whose description of addicted personalities reminds us of the story about the woman whose purse was stolen twice in one week – once by a wino who felt guilty about it, and then by a drug user who helped her look for it. The point of this dark humor is that many substance-abusing criminals possess personality disorders. In these instances it is not the misuse of drugs that brings out deviant behavior; rather those behavioral tendencies existed prior to drug use. Samenow echoes the observation made earlier and throughout this volume that behavioral interventions offer the greatest likelihood of success. In Chapter 3 Heffron and his associates examine several substances including alcohol and tobacco for their impact on the brain in-utero, in childhood, and adolescence. These three chapters provide the reader with an overview of the subject area leading to the next set of chapters that examine the individual through the system.

In Chapter 4 Hiller and his associates discuss the importance of screening and the proper assessment of drug-abusing criminals. The appropriate assessment should lead to the application of the correctional intervention most likely to succeed. Chapter 5 by Paparozzi and Guy is a logical extension of the previous work focusing as it does on the growing technology to monitor substance abusers as the criminal justice system seeks alternatives to incarceration.

Staton-Tindall and her colleagues in Chapter 6 provide a statistical backdrop enabling the reader to discern the correlation between drug abuse and criminal behavior. She and her fellow writers then examine several interventions to ascertain what works, what might work, and what doesn't work with this population. Chapter 7 is an extension of the previous chapter with Chodrow and Hora addressing the issue of impaired driving.

The next four chapters take the reader on a journey through the criminal justice system. Beginning with Chapter 8 by Marlowe on drug courts, the reader understands the absolute importance of structure in this setting and that the evidence suggests that for adults they can be effective. Unfortunately, the same encouraging statement cannot be made for with juveniles. Chapter 9 examines probation. Carey draws the reader's attention to the correlation between caseload and success. Success is measured by staying out of the justice system. Proper caseloads and appropriate supervision encouraging behavioral change can mean a decline in recidivism of up to 30%. In Chapter 10 Rodriguez extends this discussion to include the importance of case management. The next chapter discusses drug treatment in prison facilities. MacKenzie and her colleagues share the results of a meta-analysis that provides cautious preliminary evidence about those programs that may work. Therapeutic communities, self-help efforts like AA, and behavioral approaches reached the authors level of statistical acceptance ($p \leq 0.10$). Chapter 12 on parole by Taxman shares the reality that the literature on this practice is fraught with difficulties. From the pessimism emerges a reoccurring theme appearing in this volume that behavioral approaches are most likely to demonstrate success.

The remaining five chapters address special issues and populations within the justice system. The first of these is women within the correctional system. In Chapter 13 Zweben examines the dramatic increase of women in the system and the reality that many have children. In Chapter 14 Magaletta and Leukefeld take a look at the importance of self-help in the transformation of the drug-abusing criminal to reformed citizen. They observe that self-help is an integral part of most rehabilitation programs, that it contains a behavioral element, and they caution that arbitrarily insisting that individuals enter self-help programs like AA is no guarantee of a successful outcome. In Chapter 15 the appropriate use of pharmacological agents is discussed. Schwartz and his co-authors discuss the growth of psychopharmacology in recent years and the reality that for many these drugs offer drug-abusing criminals an opportunity to change the pathway their lives have taken. Chapter 16 focuses on co-occurring disorders. It should not be surprising that with the appropriate closure of many in-patient mental health facilities and the inadequate funding of community mental healthcare that the correctional system would soon become the dumping ground for individuals whose mental health issues would eventually lead them into circumstances that were illegal. Lurigio discusses the stigmatization these inmates experience and suggests that integrated treatment approaches are preferable to either sequential or parallel treatment plans. The final chapter in this sequence examines the reality that drug-abusing inmates are at special risk for having contracted or contracting HIV. Oser and her colleagues examine those interventions that presently appear most useful. This volume concludes with the editors' assessment of the current relationship between evidence-based knowledge and customary field practice.

We conclude this preface with a special thanks to the talented authors with whom we have had the privilege to work with over the past 2 years. Their contributions provide those in the criminal justice system with a useful assessment of the value of the practices currently being employed to rehabilitate offenders. For students, drug treatment professionals, and policy makers, this volume suggests those directions in monitoring and treatment that hold the greatest promise for reducing recidivism. Whether the will to pursue those evidence-based pathways exists remains to be seen.

New London, CT Thomas P. Gullotta

## References


Anonymous. (1863). A run through the southern states. *Cornhill Magazine, 7*(4), 495–515.

Burns, E. (2006). *The smoke of the gods: A social history of tobacco*. New York: Temple University Press.

Dickens, C. (1898). *American notes*. Boston, MA: Samuel E. Cassino.

Erikson, K. (1966). *Wayward puritans*. New York: Wiley.

Freud, S. (1950). *Interpretation of dreams*. New York: Modern Library.

Gullotta, T. P. (2009). A selected social history of the stepping-stone drugs. In C. G. Leukefeld, T. P. Gullotta, & M. Staton-Tindall (Eds.), *Adolescent substance abuse: Evidence-based approaches to prevention and treatment* (pp. 1–13). New York: Springer.

King James (1604/1932). *A counter-blaste to tobacco*. Cincinnati, OH: Antioch Press.

Kandel, D. B. (1981). Drug use by youth: An overview. In D. J. Lettieri & J. P. Lundford (Eds.), *Drug abuse and the American adolescent* (NIDA Research Monograph No. 38, # ADM 81-1166) (pp. 1–24). Washington, DC: U.S. Government Printing Office.

Kandel, D. B., & Faust, R. (1975). Sequence and stages in patterns of adolescent drug use. *Archives of General Psychiatry, 32*, 923–932.

Kandel, D. B., Kessler, R., & Margulies, R. (1978). Adolescent initiation into stages of drug use: A developmental analysis. In D. B. Kandel (Ed.), *Longitudinal research on drug use: Empirical findings and methodological issues* (pp. 5–19). Washington, DC: Hemisphere-Wiley.

Kandel, D. B., Yamaguchi, K., & Chen, K. (1992). Stages of progression in drug involvement from adolescence to adulthood: Further evidence for the gateway theory. *Journal of Studies on Alcohol, 53*, 447–457.

# Contents

# Contributors

**Shanna Babalonis** Department of Behavioral Science, College of Medicine, University of Kentucky, Lexington, KY 40503, USA, babalonis@uky.edu

**Steven Belenko** Department of Criminal Justice, Temple University, Philadelphia, PA 19122, USA, sbelenko@temple.edu

**Mary Carroll Burnett** University of Kentucky, Lexington, KY 40506, USA, mary.burnett@uky.edu

**Mark Carey** The Carey Group, White Bear Lake, MN 55110, USA, mark@thecareygroup.com

**Brian Chodrow** Impaired Driving Division, National Highway Traffic Safety Administration, Washington, DC 20590, USA, Chodrow@mindspring.com

**Michael S. Gordon** Friends Research Institute, Baltimore, MD 21201, USA, mgordon@friendsresearch.org

**John Gregrich** Retired from Office of National Drug Control Policy (ONDCP), Washington, DC 20503, USA, jbgregrich@comcast.net

**Thomas P. Gullotta** Child and Family Agency of Southeastern Connecticut, New London, CT 06320, USA, tpgullotta@aol.com

**Roger Guy** Department of Sociology and Criminal Justice, University of North Carolina, Pembroke, NC 28372, USA, roger.guy@uncp.edu

**Kathi L. Harland Harp** Department of Sociology, Center on Drug and Alcohol Research, University of Kentucky, Lexington, KY 40506, USA, kathi.harp@gmail.com

**Jennifer R. Havens** Department of Behavioral Science, Center on Drug and Alcohol Research, University of Kentucky, Lexington, KY 40504, USA, jennifer.havens@uky.edu

**William M. Heffron** Mental Health Services, Frankfort, KY 40601, USA, billm.heffron@ky.gov

**Matthew L. Hiller** Department of Criminal Justice, Temple University, Philadelphia, PA 19122, USA, mhiller@temple.edu

**Hon. Peggy Fulton Hora** Superior Court of California (Ret.), Walnut Creek, CA 94596, USA, peggyhora@sbcglobal.net

**Katie House** Psychiatry Research Center, University of Kentucky, Lexington, KY 40509, USA, klhous2@uky.edu

**Alessandra N. Kazura** Center for Tobacco Independence Maine Health, Portland, ME 04102, USA, kazura@mmc.org

**Timothy W. Kinlock** Friends Research Institute, Baltimore, MD 21201, USA, tkinlock@friendsresearch.org

**Carl Leukefeld** Department of Behavioral Science, Center on Drug and Alcohol Research, University of Kentucky, Lexington, KY 40506, USA, cleukef@uky.edu

**Karen M. Lommel** Department of Psychiatry, University of Kentucky, Lexington, KY 40509, USA, kmlomm2@email.uky.edu

**Arthur J. Lurigio** College of Arts and Sciences, Loyola University, Chicago, IL 60656, USA, alurigi@luc.edu

**Doris Layton MacKenzie** Department of Sociology, Crime, Law and Justice Program, Justice Center for Research, College of the Liberal Arts, University Outreach, University Park, PA 16802, USA, dlm69@psu.edu

**Philip R. Magaletta** Federal Bureau of Prisons, Psychology Services Branch, Washington, DC 20534, USA, pmagaletta@bop.gov

**Douglas B. Marlowe** Treatment Research Institute, University of Pennsylvania, Philadelphia, PA 19106, USA, dmarlowe@tresearch.org

**Catherine A. Martin** Department of Psychiatry, College of Medicine, University of Kentucky, Lexington, KY 40509, USA, cmartin@uky.edu

**Ojmarrh Mitchell** Department of Criminology, University of South Florida, Tampa, FL 33620, USA, ojmarrh@gmail.com

**Shannon Gwin Mitchell** Friends Research Institute, Baltimore, MD 21201, USA, sgwinmitchell@hotmail.com

**Lori Molenaar** University of Kentucky, Lexington, KY 40506, USA; University Health Service, Lexington, KY 40536, USA, molenaa@uky.edu

**Carrie B. Oser** Department of Sociology, Center on Drug and Alcohol Research, University of Kentucky, Lexington, KY 40506, USA, cboser0@uky.edu

**Mario A. Paparozzi** Department of Sociology and Criminal Justice, University of North Carolina, Pembroke, NC 28372, USA, mario.paparozzi@uncp.edu

**Roger H. Peters** Louis de la Parte Florida Mental Health Institute (FMHI), University of South Florida (USF), Tampa, FL 33612, USA, peters@fmhi.usf.edu

**Pamela F. Rodriguez** TASC, Inc., Chicago, IL 60642, USA, prodriguez@tasc-il.org

**Stanton E. Samenow** Clinical Psychology, Alexandria, VA 22311, USA, samenow@cox.net

**Robert P. Schwartz** Friends Research Institute, Baltimore, MD 21201, USA, rschwartz@friendsresearch.org

**Michele Staton-Tindall** College of Social Work, Center on Drug and Alcohol Research, University of Kentucky, Lexington, KY 40506, USA, mstindall@uky.edu

**Faye S. Taxman** Criminology, Law & Society, Fairfax, VA 22030, USA, ftaxman@gmu.edu

**Beth Weinman** Federal Bureau of Prisons, National Drug Abuse Programs, Correctional Programs Division, Psychology Services Branch, Washington, DC 20534, USA, bweinman@bop.gov

**Wayne N. Welsh** Department of Criminal Justice, Temple University, Philadelphia, PA 19122, USA, wwelsh@temple.edu

**David B. Wilson** Department of Criminology, Law and Society George Mason University, Fairfax, VA 22030, USA, dwilsonb@gmu.edu

**Gary Zajac** Justice Center for Research, College of the Liberal Arts and University Outreach, The Pennsylvania State University, University Park, PA 16802, USA, gxz3@psu.edu

**Joan E. Zweben** Department of Psychiatry, University of California, San Francisco, CA 94143, USA, joan.zweben@ucsf.edu

# A Historical Perspective on Offender Drug Abuse Treatment

1

Beth Weinman

**Abstract**

The nexus between substance abuse and crime has its roots in the nineteenth century when alcohol was seen as a problem that contributed to crime. In the twenty-first century, there is a need to continue to seek magical solutions that will "break the cycle" of substance abuse and crime. The research conducted and collected from programs and interventions has been established over the years and indicates there is evidence that what works, and what does not work with the offender population has been proven. A historical review of what has been done throughout the years to reduce the impact of the drug abusing offender underscores this knowledge. This review demonstrates that "effective" programs have been developed, and redeveloped under different names throughout the last quarter of a century. Today there is the opportunity to bring together researchers, programmers and funders to develop evidence-based program infrastructures, implementation plans, performance standards, training and evaluation knowledge to develop strong, evidence-based foundations for designing future operations, programs and interventions.

**Keywords**

Harrison act • *Robinson v. California* • the Narcotic addict rehabilitation act • Comprehensive drug abuse prevention and control act • Drug policy • Coerced treatment • Special Action Office of Drug Abuse Prevention (SAODAP) • Federal Bureau of Prisons • National Institute on Drug Abuse (NIDA) • Office of Justice Programs • Treatment Alternatives for Safer Communities (TASC) • In-Prison treatment • Drug courts • Reentry • the Second Chance Act

## Introduction

The United States continues to experience the effects of the drug/crime nexus. For example, on June 30, 2008, 2,310,984 prisoners were held in federal or state prisons and in local jails;

B. Weinman (✉)
Federal Bureau of Prisons, National Drug Abuse Programs, Correctional Programs Division, Psychology Services Branch, Washington, DC 20534, USA
e-mail: bweinman@bop.gov

C. Leukefeld et al. (eds.), *Handbook of Evidence-Based Substance Abuse Treatment in Criminal Justice Settings*, Issues in Children's and Families' Lives 11,
DOI 10.1007/978-1-4419-9470-7_1, 

1,540,805 sentenced prisoners were under state or federal jurisdiction; and 53% of State prisoners as well as 45% of Federal prisoners met the Diagnostic and Statistical Manual of Mental Disorders, Fourth Edition, Text Revision (DSM IV-TR) criteria for a drug use disorder (American Psychiatric Association, 2000). In addition, about half of jail inmates meet the criteria for substance dependence (Karberg & James, 2005), and two-thirds of arrestees in major US cities test positive for drugs (National Institute of Justice, 2003). In addition, almost 70% of probationers reported using drugs or alcohol (Mumola & Karberg, 2006). These high rates of drug use are exacerbated by the increased number of state prisoners and parolees. However, clients "...referred from the criminal justice system have been shown to stay in treatment longer than other clients. Their longer retention leads to an expectation that these criminal justice system clients will have better treatment outcomes than other clients" (Hubbard et al., 1989).

This chapter reviews criminal justice drug treatment interventions and treatment approaches. Programs that enable offenders to reenter their communities without returning to the cycle of drug use and crime are emphasized.

Offender treatment has its roots in the late nineteenth century when alcohol was seen as a problem that contributed to crime and other miscreant behaviors. At that time asylums, sanatoriums, hospitals, and jails "locked away" alcoholics who were "treated" by psychiatrists, lay therapists, and medical personnel (White, 1998). By the turn of the century, asylum directors were lobbying state legislatures to pass laws for legal commitment of inebriates. In 1903, for example, the State of Pennsylvania passed the "inebriate law" whereby inebriates could be legally committed for up to 1 year in an asylum, after a legal hearing in which two physicians certified the need for such action (White, 1998).

More commonly discussed is that offender treatment began soon after the passage of the Harrison Narcotic Act of 1914 which criminalized physicians dispensing narcotics. After the constitutionality of the Harrison Act was established in 1919, physicians became reluctant to maintain patients on opiates for fear of prosecution (Campbell, 2007). Also in 1914, the State of New York was the first state to enact a statute that allowed "...upon complaint to a magistrate and after due notice and hearing, the magistrate shall, if the person is found to be addicted to the use of a habit-forming drug, commit such person to a state, county or city hospital" (Hafemeister & Amirshahi, 1992). Thus, civil commitment, which is also known as compulsory treatment or mandatory treatment, began. The philosophical basis of civil commitment for drug abusers appears to be sound. The theory of civil commitment holds that while some heroin and other substance abusers are motivated for treatment, most are not. Therefore, there must be a way to order those into treatment who ordinarily would not volunteer.

In 1919, the US Treasury Department's Narcotics Unit urged Congress to set up federal "narcotics farms" where heroin users could be incarcerated and treated for their addiction. The first of these "farms" was the United States Public Health Service (USPHS) Hospital established in Lexington, Kentucky in 1935, with a second hospital in Fort Worth, Texas in 1938. Treatment was provided for incarcerated federal prisoners, although voluntary patients were also accepted. The Lexington/Fort Worth approach provided treatment for drug users within an institutional setting, to free them of their psychological dependence on drugs, their immaturities, and personality problems. After treatment patients would return to their communities to resume their lives (Inciardi, 1988).

Because these hospitals served federal prisoners, they became more prison-like than most hospitals, but less prison-like than most prisons (Maddux, 1978). The first annual report from the USPHS Hospital in Lexington noted that "treatment of voluntary patients had not been very effective because most of them left before treatment was completed" (Maddux, 1988). Lexington/Fort Worth follow-up studies emphasized that addicts treated under legal coercion had better outcomes than others, but prisoners without compulsory post-institution supervision and treatment did no better than voluntary patients overtime (Maddux, 1978). It should be noted that post-institution supervision and treatment is known today as reentry.

The legislation creating these hospitals was predicated on the premise that narcotic addiction was not a problem of public morals, but rather public health and treatment could be completed within the confines of a hospital, ignoring the need for aftercare support and guidance. The then Director of the Bureau of Prisons, James Bennett suggested that this failure to include aftercare was the greatest barrier to the success of the Lexington and Fort Worth Hospitals (Bennett, 1963).

## Civil Commitment

Civil commitment has been legally tested in the US Courts and upheld on three occasions. The first test before the United States Supreme Court was *Robinson v. California, 370 U.S. 660* (1962), which established that addiction was not in and of itself a crime and that a state could use its coercive power to compel addicts into treatment. This landmark civil commitment case also defined addiction as an illness rather than a crime. It held that the state could force an addict to submit to treatment and could impose criminal sanctions for failure to comply with the treatment program. The California Supreme Court upheld Robinson in *De La O, U.S. 856* in 1963, which found that a state could coerce addicts into treatment, and again in two New York Court of Appeals cases in the late 1960s by the Narcotic Addiction Control Commission (NACC); *NACC v. James* and *People v. Fuller* that followed the *De La O* decision. In those contexts, when coercion was disavowed as an effective way to get addicts into treatment and community-based treatment for substance abuse was only slowly gaining acceptability and credibility, alternatives to routine criminal justice system processing for drug-dependent offenders were initiated (Weinman, 1992).

A number of programs using Civil Commitment began in the 1960s with varying degrees of success including the 1961 California Civil Addict Program (CAP), New York State's Narcotic Addiction Control Commission (NACC) in 1966, and later in 1966, the passage of Public Law 89-793 which created the federal Narcotic Addict Rehabilitation Act (NARA) which was the largest and most evaluated civil commitment offender program.

*The California Civil Addict Program* (CAP) – Patients received treatment in an institution for up to 7 years, with 3 years of supervision and outpatient treatment follow-up. CAP patients were not convicted of a crime but were mandated to participate in drug abuse treatment. Initially, CAP required inmates to spend an average of 18 months incarcerated in unit-based treatment programs, followed by release to aftercare, or outpatient treatment where they were closely monitored. If a person was found to be using drugs, he/she was returned to the institution. Evaluations found Civil Commitment had the important effect of suppressing daily narcotic use and reducing criminal behavior (Anglin & McGlothlin, 1988). However, as program criteria became less stringent over time, evaluation results indicated that shorter treatment duration and the lack of certain negative sanctions reduced its beneficial effects.

*The Narcotic Addiction Control Commission (NACC)* – NACC was a Civil Commitment program in which individuals could be judicially "certified" to treatment for 3–5 years. Individuals eligible for NACC certification included those arrested for drug-related crimes, volunteers, and others whose friends, family members, or relatives petitioned the court for commitment. The treatment process included a period of institutional commitment followed by *community aftercare*. The NACC program was determined to be a failure largely due to rapid and incomplete development including NACC's mission not being fully developed, staff not being fully trained, and appropriate reporting and violation sanctions not being used (Inciardi, 1988). NACC was initiated in response to an overwhelming public outburst of concern surrounding the then growing epidemics of heroine use and drug-related street crime. However, NACC was criticized for overwhelming expenditure of tax dollars, faulty offender supervision, and skewed data (Inciardi, 1988).

*The Narcotic Addict Rehabilitation Act (NARA)* – NARA (Public Law 89-793) provided compulsory treatment for drug users charged with nonviolent federal crimes as well as drug users not involved in the criminal justice system. NARA established a close connection between the health care system and the criminal justice system to provide treatment for drug abusers who commonly would not seek treatment voluntarily. The NARA act included three titles which authorized federally managed treatment and Title IV which provided funds to establish treatment programs in states and municipalities. In brief, the treatment titles were as follows:

> *Title I* permitted pre-trial Civil Commitment to treatment (i.e., diversion) instead of prosecution for addicts charged with specific federal crimes and was administered by the US Public Health Service;
>
> *Title II* authorized sentencing to treatment certain addicts convicted of specific federal crimes and was administered by the Federal Bureau of Prisons; and
>
> *Title III* allowed for voluntary Civil Commitment to treat addicts not charged with any criminal violation and was administered by the US Public Health Service.

After an examination period of 30 days, individuals who were considered addicts and suitable could be civilly committed for institutional treatment and aftercare. Many NARA civil committees had previously been admitted to other facilities under separate legal authority (Lindblad, 1988). NARA demonstrated that Civil Commitment can provide a way of bringing addicts who might not otherwise be treated into treatment. Civilly committed addicts who entered treatment appeared to do as well as, or better than, addicts receiving care in noncompulsory treatment. While the NARA treatment data are limited, it is clear that Civil Commitment resulted in less drug use, less criminal activity, and more productive behavior for addicts who were civilly committed (Kitchener & Teitelbaum, 1986).

*State Civil Commitment* – While many states had specific statutory authority or indirect authority to commit drug-dependent individuals to treatment, few actually utilized Civil Commitment. Civil Commitment of drug offenders was based on the experience of commitment for mental health reasons, which established commitment criteria that drug users did not meet and provided for treatment that drug offenders did not need. Other obstacles included a lack of secure treatment facilities and other treatment resources, reluctance of mental health personnel to treat drug users and/or to participate in coerced treatment, difficulties between the justice and mental health systems regarding responsibility and regular communications, and legal/procedural barriers.

Civil Commitment led to the creation of a community-based treatment system, and with this increase in community drug treatment the criminal justice system now utilizes "coerced treatment" more readily. Coerced treatment systems, such as those used by TASC and Drug Courts, find the defense, the prosecution and the judge, working together in a nonadversarial way that simply focuses on the offender's recovery.

Today we know that coerced treatment is effective. Coerced treatment reduces relapse into drug use and criminal behavior and reduces the adverse social effects associated with it. Over the years, many of the early barriers have dropped away as criminal justice and community mental health and treatment personnel have learned to work together. However, of greatest import is the finding that coerced treatment works to get drug-dependent offenders into treatment when they refuse to enter voluntarily (Anglin & Hser, 1990).

## Drug Policy and US Drug Wars

In the late 1960s the rise of the drug use counterculture, growing opiate use in US inner cities, and the war in Viet Nam contributed to an increase in the number of heroin addicts. Few trained drug abuse treatment professionals and limited drug abuse treatment capacity were available to counter this drug abuse surge. Along with the rise in heroin use, the nation's crime rate doubled. Richard Nixon, elected president in 1968, was adamant about reducing the nation's crime rate and was advised that he could do so by lowering the incidence of drug abuse

(Baum, 1996). Consequently, in 1969, Nixon presented a drug budget of $81 million with about $43 million for treatment, mostly overseen by the National Institute of Mental Health (NIMH). Remaining drug funds went to the Customs Bureau, which patrolled US borders, and the Bureau of Narcotics and Dangerous Drugs (BNDD) to reduce drug trafficking.

The NIMH conducted a broad interagency study on drug treatment in which traditional psychotherapy for drug abusers was supported. The report noted that creating systems for "...delivering psychiatric care to drug abusers should have high priority" in national treatment and expressed strong doubts about methadone maintenance treatment, despite research findings which reported marked reductions in heroin use, unemployment, and criminal activity among those treated with methadone (Massing, 1998).

At the time of the NIMH report, Jerome Jaffee, a psychiatrist who promoted methadone treatment for heroin addicts, came to the attention of the White House. He was asked to convene a group of experts to develop suggestions for US drug treatment. The Jaffee report, in contrast to the NIMH report, called heroin addiction a serious national problem requiring "bold government action." The report cited unsuccessful attempts to treat narcotic addition and alcoholism with psychotherapy, with unanimous agreement that "addictive states" were curiously resistive to psychotherapy. The report called for $15 million over 2 years to create 14,000 methadone slots and to establish a national drug office.

President Nixon proposed that Congress reduce the confusion over federal policy and duplication by combining disparate regulations into a single statute. Congress agreed by enacting the Comprehensive Drug Abuse Prevention and Control Act of 1970 that included the Controlled Substances Act which became effective on May 1, 1971. The legislation proposed a balanced approach to the nation's drug problem, including education, treatment, and rehabilitation. In March 1972, Congress authorized the creation of the Special Action Office of Drug Abuse Prevention (SAODAP), with Jerome Jaffee as the first Drug Czar, for 3 years after which duties would be given to the National Institute on Drug Abuse (NIDA). By March 1973 federal spending for treatment and prevention increased to $420 million: more than eight times the amount when Nixon took office (Massing, 1998).

SAODAP expanded methadone treatment. A methadone versus long-acting methadone (LAMM) comparison study was initiated, drug testing was utilized, and a national system to counter addiction was created. Crime began to decrease, heroin addicts were receiving treatment, and veterans returning home from Viet Nam were treated. Nixon's drug strategy was the first, and possibly the only effective drug treatment strategy.

Other federal administrations were not as aggressive or supportive. For example, President Ford decreased methadone treatment funding and increased support for incarceration. President Carter did not increase treatment funding, which in the period's high inflation resulted in a reduction. Illicit drug use continued to increase and 11 states decriminalized marijuana during Carter's presidency. President Reagan emphasized enforcement, and federal spending for treatment decreased by 75%. Nancy Reagan as first lady attended antidrug events telling people to "Just Say No." In response to a poll which indicated that 64% of Americans named drug abuse as the number one problem in the country with the increased crime and crack/cocaine epidemic, President George Bush established the Office of National Drug Control Policy (ONDCP) in the Executive Office of the President with the passage of the Anti-Drug Abuse Act of 1988. President Clinton elevated the Drug Czar to a cabinet member, increased the antidrug budget tenfold and named Lee Brown and then General Barry McCaffrey to lead the war on drugs. President George W. Bush targeted marijuana use, prescription drug abuse, and drug abuse among the elderly while the United States came in a close second to Russia in the rate of incarceration. President Obama moved ONDCP out of the cabinet and appointed Gil Kerlikowske as Drug Czar and his Deputy, Thomas McLellan, to bring leadership, experience, and treatment expertise to drug policy.

Wars require knowledgeable leaders and expert lieutenants, not political ideologues. According to a Carnevale Associates (2008) Policy Brief, a Zogby/Inter-American Dialogue Survey reported that three of four Americans thought that the nation's drug war was failing. Congress continues to under-fund treatment and prevention, with two-thirds of the current Federal drug budget supporting enforcement.

## Offender Treatment

The following federal programs have been used to support offender drug abuse treatment:

*Treatment Alternatives to Street Crime* – By the early 1970s, a Nixon-appointed Special Study Commission on Drugs established a definite link between drugs, particularly narcotics, and crime. The report emphasized that a small number of addicts were responsible for a large percentage of crimes, and a disproportionate share of criminal justice system resources was being absorbed by their recidivism. Discussions on how to link treatment with the judicial process and interrupt the drugs and property crimes relationship led Federal officials to develop an initiative, modeled after earlier diversion programs and demonstration projects in New York City and Washington, DC. This federal initiative was called Treatment Alternatives to Street Crime, today it is called Treatment Alternatives for Safer Communities (TASC).

TASC combines the influence of legal sanctions for probable or proven crimes with dispositions, such as deferred prosecution, creative community sentencing, diversion, pretrial intervention, and probation or parole supervision. TASC's goal is to motivate substance abuser treatment cooperation. Through treatment referral, drug testing, closely supervised community reintegration, monitoring, and reporting to the courts or supervising authority, TASC can effectively interrupt the cycle of addiction, criminality, arrest, prosecution, conviction, incarceration, release, readdiction, criminality, and rearrest (Cook et al., 1988). A 1996 evaluation of five TASC programs reported that TASC was more effective with high-risk offenders than with first-time offenders (Anglin et al., 1996).

Declining support for offender drug abuse treatment continued in the United States until July 1986 when Leonard Kevin "Len" Bias, the University of Maryland basketball star, suffered a fatal cardiac arrhythmia from a cocaine overdose fewer than 48 hours after being selected second overall by the Boston Celtics in the NBA Draft. Len Bias's death, so near the beltway, led the Congress to pass a "tough on crime/tough on drugs" bill. *The Anti-Drug Abuse Act of 1986*, created laws against money laundering, reinstated mandatory prison sentences for drug possession, and established mandatory minimum sentences for drug crimes. The act also established the Edward Byrne Memorial State and Local Law Enforcement Assistance Program. Byrne grants provided assistance to states which in turn provided sub-grant funds to local agencies in 11 and later (1988) 26 broad areas. Bureau of Justice Assistance (BJA) also made available limited discretionary funds to state and local governments to fund treatment in jails and prisons, and reinstated federal funding for TASC, pretrial identification and drug testing programs, drug testing technology programs, and cross training for treatment/criminal justice staff. These Bureau of Justice Assistance Discretionary Programs created lasting treatment advances which include the following:

*Projects REFORM and RECOVERY* led to a major paradigm shift in how prisons conducted substance abuse treatment to a structured and proven effective therapeutic community model with many of the programs still operational (Wexler & Lipton, 1993).

*Drug Abuse Treatment in Jails* – The American Jail Association completed a survey of jail drug abuse treatment which included a finding that "treatment" in jails was varied and that treatment personnel were not professionals (Peters & May, 1992). In addition, demonstration program findings indicated that relatively short-term interventions (6–8 weeks) provided inmates with coping skills for high-risk situations; increased knowledge about recovery; increased understanding of relapse prevention principles;

and that *cognitive behavioral treatment* was appropriate for reducing recidivism (Peters & May, 1992).

*Defining TASC* – The National Association of State Alcohol and Drug Abuse Directors (NASADAD) received cooperative agreement funding from BJA to survey TASC programs and to describe TASC by developing a program brief with 10 critical elements to be used as an implementation guide and training manual to develop a national identity for TASC Programs. The elements still provide a strong implementation and program review tool for TASC programs.

*Drug Testing Technology* – The Pre-Trial Services Resource Center developed a drug testing guide to identify arrestees who need treatment. The Drug Testing Manual included guidance on chain of custody, testing technologies, confirmatory testing, pretrial interventions, and treatment options. This drug testing technology was instrumental in the National Institute of Justice's (NIJ) development of the Drug Use Forecasting (DUF) system, renamed Arrestee Drug Abuse Monitoring (ADAM) program, which collected data on drug use at arrest, treatment involvement, and drug market participation among recently booked arrestees (within 48 hours) in 40 US communities. ADAM data helped policy makers and practitioners monitor drug use and make responsive decisions (NIJ, 2003).

*Drug Courts* – Federal funding was provided for the first US drug court which responded to a growing cocaine problem in Miami, Florida. Chief Judge Gerald Wetherington, Judge Herbert Klein, then State Attorney Janet Reno, and Public Defender Bennett Brummer designed the court in 1989 for nonviolent offenders to receive treatment for their drug addiction. Drug Courts quickly became popular for the ever-increasing number of drug offenders. For example, in 1999 there were 472 US drug courts and by 2005 there were 1,262 with another 575 drug courts being planned. There are about 120,000 people treated annually in drug courts (Curtis, Fox, Deutsch, & Foster, 2009) with other specialized courts including mental health courts, juvenile courts, and veteran's courts. Drug courts reduce rearrest rates by 8–24%, according to meta-analyses conducted in 2005 and 2006 (National Institute of Drug Abuse, 2008). Drug courts also increase the time drug abusers stay in treatment. For example, an average of 60% of drug court clients complete at least 12 months of treatment, while only 10% of probationers and parolees typically remain for a year in drug treatment.

Alan Leshner, then NIDA Director, cautioned the Urban Institute by saying that "Courts need access to an array of effective treatment modalities and they have to be able to bring to bear an array of support services simultaneously. Judges and drug courts are not treatment providers; they are not treatment workers. They have to have around them people who can make sure that treatment in the broadest sense is available and can be tailored to the situation of the individual" (Leshner, 2003).

*Residential Substance Abuse Treatment (RSAT)* began with the Violent Crime Control and Law Enforcement Act of 1994 to assist states and local governments in developing residential substance abuse treatment in state and local correctional and detention facilities. RSAT programs provided individual and group treatment for 6–12 months as separate residential treatment, focusing on inmate substance abuse problems, and developing the inmates' cognitive, behavioral, social, vocational, and other skills. A national evaluation reported that RSAT programs included three treatment modalities: therapeutic community, cognitive behavioral, and/or 12-step programs (e.g., Alcoholics Anonymous or Cocaine Anonymous). A meta-analysis of RSAT evaluations found positive outcomes from in-prison substance abuse treatment (Bureau of Justice Assistance, 2005). Inmates who completed treatment were less likely to be rearrested or placed into a higher custody institution. Aftercare treatment was associated with decreased recidivism and relapse. RSAT programs also increased offenders' self-esteem, prosocial decision making, and self-efficacy which reduced anxiety, depression, risk taking, and hostility. Cognitive distortions (e.g., self-centeredness, blaming others, minimizing problems, assuming the worst) were also significantly reduced (BJA, 2005).

*Reentry* – Continuity of treatment and supervision from an institutional setting to the community is crucial for treatment success. Although TASC programs provide reentry services by managing and supervising offenders for paroling authorizes, only a few prison therapeutic communities (TC) offered continued TC treatment when offenders were paroled, including Donovan State Prison in California, and the Delaware State Prison for men. In addition, the Bureau of Prisons designed their residential drug abuse programs to incorporate reentry. However, it wasn't until 1999 that attention was paid to reentry after Attorney General Janet Reno asked what the Justice Department was doing about prisoners who were returning home (Travis, 2005).

To address recidivism, the US Departments of Justice, Labor, Housing and Urban Development, and Health and Human Services established the Serious and Violent Offender Reentry Initiative (SVORI). This program provided over $100 million to 69 grantees to develop community programming, training, and state-of-the-art reentry strategies. These programs focused on reducing recidivism in addition to improving employment, housing, and health outcomes of participating released offenders. Early evaluations indicated that SVORI participants were more likely to receive services; received more services prerelease than post-release; and had better overall outcomes following release from prison. Although SVORI served only a small numbers of offenders, it provided communities with the opportunity to develop more offender resources and provided significant but small increases in employment, education, health and basic living skills services (Lattimore et al., 2004).

At the same time, the National Institute of Corrections developed the Transition from Prison to Community (TPC) reentry model which encouraged strategic system changes to reduce recidivism and future victimization, to enhance public safety, and to improve the lives of community victims as well as offenders. This reentry model focused on building and mobilizing interdisciplinary teams as well as planning and continuity through the criminal justice system with noncorrectional stakeholders (e.g., health professionals and educators). Convincing the drug abuse community and criminal justice practitioners about the importance of community reentry would not seem to be a problem. However, reentry is complicated by confidentiality laws, regulations, and practices that continue to enforce determinate sentencing and long prison terms, and an increasing number of incarcerated and reentering drug abusing prisoners (Leukefeld et al., 2009).

The Federal Bureau of Prisons, as the largest US correctional system with an inmate population of more than 207,000 in July, 2009, begins community reentry preparation on the first day of incarceration. This preparation includes identifying and measuring skill deficits for community reentry; targeting resources to inmates with the greatest skill deficits as well as the greatest risk of reoffending; and strengthening community collaborative relationships to ensure the inmates receive treatment.

The Second Chance Act of 2007 was designed to improve reentry outcomes for employment assistance, substance abuse treatment, housing, family support, mentoring, victim support, and other services to reduce recidivism. The Act included demonstration grants to nonprofit organizations to mentor adult offenders or offer community transitional services; substance abuse treatment; family drug treatment; and family-based treatment programs for Native American tribes. The Act also included a Federal initiative to enhance reentry planning and research by the National Institute of Corrections, Bureau of Justice Statistics, and the National Adult and Juvenile Offender Reentry Resource Center.

## Lessons from History

> There is an old parable that has made the rounds about the grasshopper who decided to consult the hoary consultant of the animal kingdom, the owl, about a personal problem. The problem concerned the fact that the grasshopper suffered each winter from severe pains due to the savage temperature.

> After a number of these painful winters, in which all of the grasshopper's known remedies were of no avail, he presented his case to the venerable and wise owl. The owl, after patiently listening to the grasshopper's misery, as the story goes, prescribed a simple solution. "Simply turn yourself into a cricket and hibernate during the winter." The grasshopper jumped joyously away, profusely thanking the owl for his wise advice. Later however, after discovering that this important knowledge could not be transformed into action, the grasshopper returned to the owl and asked him how he could perform metamorphosis. The owl replied rather curtly, "Look, I gave you the principle. It's up to you to work out the details!" (Bennis, Benne, Chin, & Corey, 1976).

Program implementation is critical. Implementation is a specific set of actions designed to put into practice an activity or program of known dimensions (Fixxen, Naoom, Blase, Friedman, & Wallace, 2005). Implementation processes must be purposeful and described in sufficient detail to allow independent observers to detect the presence and strength of the specific actions required for implementation. Observers must clearly see two sets of activities (intervention-level activity and implementation-level activity) and two sets of outcomes (intervention outcomes and implementation outcomes).

Consequently, offender program implementation should

1. Be based on a treatment theory that has been found effective. For the offender, that treatment theory is behavioral;
2. Have a stated goal, such as a reduction in antisocial peer associations; an increase in positive relationships; an increase in self-control, improved self-management, and improved problem-solving skills; ending drug use, replacing lying and aggression with prosocial alternatives; and/or reduced recidivism;
3. Target a specific offender population, at least initially;
4. Be implemented slowly and deliberately;
5. Be implemented with defined data collection, including a process evaluation to measure implementation fidelity, outcome measures, and program management data;
6. Obtain the support of the executive staff of the system and the support of the staff who will implement the program. From top to bottom, staff must own the program;
7. Employ staff trained in behavioral treatment and offender treatment; and
8. Provide staff with ongoing clinical supervision. (Cullen & Gendreau, 2000).

Several approaches have been developed to meet the requirements of evidence-based offender treatment. The implementation literature generally agrees on how to implement evidence-based programs (Center for Substance Abuse Treatment, 2009; Fixxen et al., 2005). One example of a practical implementation strategy includes the BJA series of "Program Briefs," developed for TASC, Offender Drug Testing, and Pre-Trial Diversion to provide program implementation guidance and orthodoxy. Each brief provided an outline and program roadmaps. A program brief also described how a program could gain permanency by demonstrating its value. The specific roadmap, developed by the field (ownership), partitioned the program into specific elements and provided performance standards. A similar approach was used in 1998 by the Institute of Behavioral Science at the University of Colorado, Boulder, to develop Blueprints for Violence Prevention. The objective was to identify outstanding programs, and to describe these interventions in a series of "Blueprints." Each program selected for the blueprint had to meet a set of evaluation standards: (1) an experimental design, (2) evidence of a statistically significant deterrent (or marginal deterrent) effect, (3) replication at multiple sites with demonstrated effects, and (4) evidence that the deterrent effect was sustained for at least 1 year post treatment. This high standard reflects what we now call "evidence based programming" (Elliott, Botivin, Mihalic, & Grotpeter, 1998).

## Conclusions

Offender treatment research presents information about what works which indicates that (1) coerced treatment can work; (2) the longer an individual stays in treatment the more likely treatment will be successful; (3) treatment engagement is crucial for effectiveness, and "induction" strategies can increase treatment engagement; (4) treatment readiness comes from offender commitment, confidence, and rapport and offender-counselor rapport contributes to treatment success; (5) incentives and sanctions, when used correctly, foster compliance; (6) setting, duration, and staff training are important in establishing intensive treatment; (7) medication-assisted treatment (MAT) shows promising results; (8) appropriate placement and matching increases treatment effectiveness and efficiency; and (9) participation in transitional aftercare is essential for lasting treatment success.

Treating the drug-involved offender requires a carefully designed array of processes with specific elements and stages. The offender does not have to want treatment. Offender treatment requires multimodal, behaviorally based strategies including cognitive behavioral therapy, motivational interviewing, and relapse prevention. When resources and services are focused on the high-risk offender, there can be a greater reduction in recidivism that translates to a higher level of community safety. Program implementation is a process, not an event. Fidelity to program design must be continually reviewed, and staff must be involved at the beginning, recruited, trained, and clinically supervised to ensure that effective treatment methods are employed.

"Effective" programs have been developed, and redeveloped under different names. What makes TASC effective is what makes Drug Courts effective and, in turn, the "newer and better" diversion programs, such as "Operation Ceasefire" in Boston or "Project Hope" in Hawaii (Rosen, 2010). Practitioners and researchers can join efforts to develop, not simply evidence-based interventions, but evidence-based program infrastructures, elements, implementation plans, training, performance standards, and process evaluations. Research can assist program developers to implement interventions and/or programs within complex systems in their organizational structure and to develop strong, evidence-based foundations for designing future programs. Funding streams should also be changed. Specifically, funding that flows to an evidence-based infrastructure, operation, and implementation plan, rather than a specific program, will generate a "library" of evidence-based interventions and programs, which criminal justice and treatment professionals may draw upon. Our continuing challenge, in effectively treating the offender, is to integrate knowledge and develop a more collaborative and structured treatment services system.

## References


American Psychiatric Association. (2000). *Diagnostic and statistical manual of mental disorders* (4th ed., text revision). Washington, DC: American Psychiatric Association.

Anglin, M. D. (1988). The efficacy of civil commitment in treatment narcotics addiction. *Journal of Drug Issues, 18*, 527–545.

Anglin, M. D., & Hser, Y. (1990). Legal coercion and drug abuse treatment: Research findings and social policy implications. In J. Inciardi (Ed.), *Handbook of drug control in the United States* (pp. 151–176). Westport, CT: Greenwood Press.

Anglin, M. D., Longshore, D., Turner, T., McBride, D., Inciardi, J. A., & Pendergast, M. (1996). *Studies of the functioning and effectiveness of treatment alternatives to street crime (TASC) programs – Final report.* Reported and funded by the National Institute on Drug Abuse (N01DA-1-8408). Unpublished.

Anglin, M. D., & McGlothlin, W. H. (1988). Outcomes of narcotic addict treatment in California. In F. Tims & N. Ruchman (Eds.), *Drug abuse treatment evaluation: Strategies, progress and prospects* (pp. 1–89). National Institute of Drug Abuse Research Monograph 51. Washington, DC: U.S. Government Printing Office.

Baum, D. (1996). *Smoke and mirrors: The war on drugs and the politics of failure.* Boston: Little Brown and Company.

Bennett, J. V. (1963). A prison administrator views today's narcotic problem. In R. B. Livingston (Ed.), *Narcotic drug problems* (pp. 159–173). Washington, DC: U.S. Government Printing Office.

Bennis, W. G., Benne, K. D., Chin, R., & Corey, K. E. (Eds.). (1976). *The planning of change.* New York: Holt, Rinehart, & Winston.

Bureau of Justice Assistance. (2005). *Residential substance abuse treatment for state prisoners (RSAT) program.* Program update (NCJ Publication No. 06269). Washington, DC: U.S. Department of Justice.

Campbell, N. D. (2007). *Discovering addiction – The science and politics of substance abuse research.* Ann Arbor, MI: The University of Michigan Press.

Carnevale Associates, LLC. (2008). Back to basics: Principles of an effective national drug policy. *Policy Brief: Fixing national drug control policy*. Gaithersburg, MD: Carnevale Associates.

Center for Substance Abuse Treatment. (2009). *Implementing change in substance abuse treatment programs*. Technical Assistance Publication (TAP) Series 31 [HHS Publication No. (SMA) 09-4337]. Rockville, MD: Substance Abuse and Mental Health Services Administration.

Cook, L. F., Weinman, B. A., Cook, P., Fontain, M., Heaps, M., & Zugor, B., et al. (1988). Treatment alternatives to street crime. In C. G. Leukefeld & F. M. Tims (Eds.), *Compulsory treatment of drug abuse: Research and clinical practice* (pp. 99–105). National Institute of Drug Abuse Research Monograph 86 [DHHS No. (ADM 89-1578)]. Washington, DC: U.S. Government Printing Office. (Over 300 authors from the TASC field, the National Association of State Alcohol and Drug Abuse and the Bureau of Justice Assistance contributed to this chapter).

Cullen, F. T., & Gendreau, P. (2000). Assessing correctional rehabilitation: Policy, practice, and prospects. In J. Horney (Ed.), *Criminal justice 2000, Volume 3: Policies, processes, and decisions of the criminal justice system* (pp. 109–175). Washington, DC: U.S. Department of Justice, National Institute of Justice.

Curtis, K., Fox, C., Deutsch, C., & Foster, R. (Eds.). (2009). Twentieth anniversary of Drug Courts Honored in Miami, Florida. *All rise: The magazine of the national association of drug court professionals* [National Association of Drug Court Professionals (*NADCP*), p. 9]. Alexandria, VA: NADCP.

Elliott, D. S., Botivin, G. J., Mihalic, S. F., & Grotpeter, J. K. (Eds.). (1998). *Blueprint for violence prevention: Life skills training*. Golden, CO: Venture Publishing/Denver, CO: C & M Press.

Fixxen, D. L., Naoom, S. F., Blase, K. A., Friedman, R. M., & Wallace, F. (2005). *Implementation research: A synthesis of the literature* (pp. 2–55). The National Implementation Research Network (FMHI Publication No. 231). Tampa, FL: University of South Florida, Louis de la Parte Florida Mental Health Institute.

Hafemeister, T. L., & Amirshahi, A. J. (Eds.). (1992). Civil commitment for drug dependency: The judicial response. *Loyola of Los Angeles Law Review, 26*(1), 39–104.

Hubbard, R. L., Marsden, M. E., Rachel, V. J., Harwood, H. J., Cavanaugh, E. R., & Ginsburg, H. M. (1989). *Drug abuse treatment: A national study of effectiveness*. Chapel Hill, NC: University of North Carolina Press.

Inciardi, J. A. (1988). Compulsory treatment in New York: A brief narrative history of misjudgment, mismanagement, and misrepresentation. *Journal of Drug Issues, 18*, 547–560.

Karberg, J. C., & James, D. J. (2005). *Substance dependence, abuse and treatment of jail inmates, 2005*. Bureau of Justice Statistics, Special report (NCJ Publication No. 209588). Washington, DC: Department of Justice.

Kitchener, H. L., & Teitelbaum, H. (1986). *A review of research on the implementation of NARA Title II in the Bureau of Prisons*. Washington, DC: Federal Bureau of Prisons.

Lattimore, P. K., Brumbaugh, S., Visher, C., Lindquist, C., Winterfield, L., Salas, M., et al. (2004). *National portrait of SVORI: Serious and violent reentry initiative*. Washington, DC: The Urban Institute.

Leshner, A. (2003, April 1). *Speech at the Urban Institute, First Tuesday Session*, Washington, DC. Retrieved February 3, 2010, from www.urban.org

Leukefeld, C. G., Oser, C. B., Havens, J., Tindel, M. S., Mooney, J., Duval, J., et al. (2009). Drug abuse treatment beyond prison walls. *Addiction Science & Clinical Practice, 5*(1), 24–30.

Lindblad, R. (1988). Civil commitment under the federal narcotic addict rehabilitation act. *Journal of Drug Issues, 18*(4), 595–624.

Maddux, J. F. (1978). History of the hospital treatment programs 1935–1974. In W. Martin & H. Isbell (Eds.), *Drug addiction and the U.S. Public Health Service* (pp. 217–250). Department of Health, Education and Welfare (DHEW Pub. No. 77-434). Washington, DC: U.S. Government Printing Office.

Maddux, J. F. (1988). Clinical experience with civil commitment. In C. G. Leukefeld & F. M. Tims (Eds.), *Compulsory treatment of drug abuse: Research and clinical practice* (pp. 35–56). National Institute of Drug Abuse Research Monograph 86 [DHHS Pub No. (ADM) 89-1578]. Washington, DC: U.S. Government Printing Office.

Massing, M. (1998). *The fix: Under the Nixon administration, America had an effective drug policy. We should restore it*. New York: Simon & Shuster.

Mumola, C. J., & Karberg, J. C. (2006). *Drug use and dependence, State and federal prisoners 2004*. Bureau of Justice Statistics, Special report (NIC Publication No. 213530). Washington, DC: Department of Justice.

National Institute of Drug Abuse. (2008). High-risk drug offenders do better with close judicial supervision. *NIDA Notes, 22*(2), 1.

National Institute of Justice. (2003). *2000 Arrestee drug monitoring report*. U.S. Department of Justice, Office of Justice Programs. Washington, DC: National Institute of Justice.

Peters, R. H., & May, R. (1992). Drug treatment services in jail. In C. G. Leukefeld & F. M. Tims (Eds.), *Drug abuse treatment in prisons and jails* (pp. 38–50). National Institute of Drug Abuse Research Monograph 118 [DHHS No. (ADM) 92-1884]. Washington, DC: U.S. Government Printing Office.

Rosen, J. (2010, January 10). Prisoners of parole. *The New York Times Magazine* (pp. 17–19). New York: New York Times.

Travis, J. (2005). *But they all come back: Facing the challenges of prisoner reentry*. Washington, DC: Urban Institute Press.

Weinman, B. (1992). *Mandatory treatment*. Washington, DC: Unpublished manuscript, on file with the Federal Bureau of Prisons.

Wexler, H. K., & Lipton, D. S. (1993). From REFORM to RECOVERY: Advances in prison dug treatment. In J. A. Inciardi (Ed.), *Drug treatment and criminal justice* (pp. 209–227). Newberry Park, CA: Sage.

White, W. L. (1998). *Slaying the dragon – The history of addictions treatment and recovery in America*. Bloomington, IL: Chestnut Health Systems/ Lighthouse Institute.

# Individual Characteristics Associated with Crime and Substance Misuse

# 2

Stanton E. Samenow

**Abstract**

This chapter focuses primarily on people who are habitual drug users. In other words, their use of mind-altering substances is a regular and ongoing aspect of their lives. Clearly, the extent of use of any mind-altering substance, legal or not, varies along a continuum from a person who refuses to take even an aspirin to the individual who uses mind-altering substances whenever he can obtain them. To gain an understanding of the personality of the frequent or habitual drug user is fraught with difficulty. This is because, when asked about behavior that one is trying to hide, the user's self-report is likely to be unreliable. The user scopes out whoever is asking for information, seeking to avoid incriminating himself and feed his questioner only what he thinks will satisfy him. Even in requesting a response to a confidential research protocol with no legal ramifications, one encounters a variety of tactics from drug users who may minimize or, in some instances, exaggerate their drug use.

**Keywords**

Errors in thinking • Drugs as facilitators • Phenomenological approach • Cognitive patterns

The user is unlikely to reveal his state of mind before, during, and after any behavior for which he might be held accountable. Questioning a user about *why* he uses drugs is also likely to be an exercise in futility. Responses are laced with justification and rationalization. Psychologists, sociologists, criminologists, and physicians have attributed drug use to almost anything imaginable – the individual's attempt to cope with social ills, a dysfunctional family, peer pressure, identification with celebrities who use drugs, and so forth. The list is never ending as experts point to factors external to the individual user (Brecher & The Editors of Consumer Reports, 1972; Freedman, 1972; Starratt, 1971).

Drug use is ascribed to so many different factors that are cited again and again that the user comes to half believe some of them himself. One savvy drug-using offender remarked, "If I didn't

S.E. Samenow (✉)
Clinical Psychology, Alexandria, VA 22311, USA
e-mail: samenow@cox.net

C. Leukefeld et al. (eds.), *Handbook of Evidence-Based Substance Abuse Treatment in Criminal Justice Settings*, Issues in Children's and Families' Lives 11,
DOI 10.1007/978-1-4419-9470-7_2, © Springer Science+Business Media, LLC 2011

have enough excuses before psychiatry, I have more than enough now."

A review of the literature reveals a range of opinion as to whether drug abuse can be ascribed to identifiable aspects of personality. Almost every psychological condition has been linked with drug abuse – e.g., chronic anxiety, pathological narcissism, depression, obsessive-compulsive disorders. The contention is that a person turns to drugs to help him cope with psychological distress. However, little by way of explanation is offered as to why some people with a given psychological condition use drugs but others with the same condition do not.

Drug abuse can induce symptoms that then are seen as causal to the drug abuse itself. For example, a person may become more anxious or depressed after using drugs. Then a conclusion is reached that he was using drugs because he was anxious or depressed.

Some writers caution that drug use should not necessarily be considered as indicative of pathology since it may appear as "normative behavior" during adolescence (National Commission on Marijuana and Drug Abuse, 1973). They point out that drug experimentation may be part of a youth's quest to establish his independence and identity. It is certainly true that many people who try illegal drugs use them very briefly and never again. Experimentation does not a pattern make. However, it may be useful to identify what is different about experimenters who quit and those who continue to use drugs. Some researchers have linked the latter to seeking novelty and taking risks. But such an explanation is of limited value. There are many forms of risk taking, some legal and not destructive, others illegal and very destructive. To say that a person looks for adventure or seeks new sensations reveals little about whether he will become a drug abuser.

A search of the literature shows that some researchers have cited particular aspects of personality as giving rise to drug use. For example, it has been observed that people who turn to drugs have extreme difficulty coping with daily life (Krystal & Raskin, 1970). Drugs free them from fear and other painful emotional states by enabling them to feel active and powerful. However, there is no differentiation between those who cope with such difficulties by using drugs and those who cope in more responsible ways. Stymied by why some people use drugs and others don't when there are no discernable differences between the groups they are studying, some clinicians have concluded that drug use is a result of unconscious motives, a proposition that is virtually impossible to defend or refute. Others who are baffled by the difficulty of explaining why people with comparable life experiences differ with regard to drug usage invoke as explanatory the fuzzy concept of having an "addictive personality."

There are writers who point to the high incidence of personality disorders, especially antisocial personality disorder, among drug users (The Monitor, 1990). Drug use is seen as one of a number of manifestations of this preexisting personality disorder. Conducting one of the few longitudinal studies of its type, Jonathan Shedler and Jack Block (1990) found that children who became frequent drug users were already having significant interpersonal difficulties in elementary school. They were not getting along with others and had little concern about moral issues such as treating others fairly. In short, Shedler and Block noted that adolescents who became frequent drug users were already maladjusted as children. The authors of the study dismissed as inadequate an explanation that these youngsters came to use drugs because of peer pressure in their teens.

For every individual who latches onto environmental adversity that drove him to use drugs, there are others in his family and neighborhood enduring the same or worse hardships who did not use drugs. Drug users come from all segments of society. Critical is not the environment from which the person comes but how he chooses to cope with whatever circumstances life hands him. In neighborhoods where drugs are as easy to acquire as candy, most residents are not addicts, and many have no desire whatsoever even to experiment with illegal substances. Many individuals who are economically well off and grew up in stable families use drugs regularly. All youngsters have to deal with peer pressure. The issue is not whether peer pressure exists, but whom the youth selects as his peers. “My friends turned me on to drugs,” explained a 15-year-old boy. Further discussion revealed that he sought out these youngsters because they were exciting, far more so than what he called contemptuously “the puny–eyed bookworms.” He sought their acceptance; they did not recruit him.

The environment in which a person lives can make access to drugs easy or difficult depending on the deterrents. Drug users gravitate to particular areas, and the person in quest of drugs learns precisely where to go. A person who wants drugs that are not readily available will persevere and travel a considerable distance in their pursuit. A heroin user who lived in the suburbs with his parents talked about how he would “gear himself up” and go downtown when he needed a new supply.

Part of the lingo picked up by the user to explain drug-seeking behavior is to claim that he is “self-medicating” – a term heard often in the realm of drug treatment. A girl friend dumped him. His boss fired him. A relative died suddenly. His car was repossessed, and he had no transportation. To seek relief from stress, he “medicates” himself. Much of the stress cited by users is self-created because of their own irresponsibility. An examination of the user's contention that he was “self-medicating” translates into his failure to cope responsibly with life's challenges. Users latch onto this phrase to make their behavior appear more socially acceptable.

## Drugs as Facilitators

Abusers of mind-altering substances often say that drugs offer “escape” from the problems they are facing. This is the case no matter what environment the person is in. If he lives in poverty, he is escaping hardship. A person may cite drug use as a response to his lack of a job, mounting unpaid bills, pressures from family. If he is wealthy, he may complain about a marriage going downhill, too much pressure at work, or difficulties with his children or other family members. Individuals face all sorts of adversities in life but do not resort to drugs. They endeavor to address their problems in a more constructive fashion. Regardless of circumstance, habitual users of drugs are restless, irritable, and dissatisfied. They seek excitement that living responsibly does not offer.

The concept of drugs as escape distracts from understanding the thinking and behavior of the user. More important than escape is what the individual seeks by using drugs. Drugs bring out only what already resides in the individual. If 10 men get drunk, not all will rape or kill. Those unused to drinking may become sleepy. Some may become silly or tell crude jokes. A few may become boisterous, the life of the party. Perhaps one may become hostile to the point of engaging in an assault. And one person may jump into his car and drive off. The crime does not reside in the bottle, the pill, or the powder. Criminality resides within the user. Drugs knock out deterrents or fears and thereby facilitate whatever the user wants – an enhanced sense of power and control, an emboldened approach to a woman for sex, or illegal activity that requires more daring than he could otherwise muster.

## Thought Processes – A Phenomenological Approach

Behavior is a product of thinking. What is written in this chapter is a result of what the author is thinking as he writes. People who habitually abuse drugs share in common thought processes or “errors in thinking.” They are not “errors” from the standpoint of the person doing the thinking. But if these patterns are prevalent and habitual, in combination with one another, they result in emotional, physical, or financial injury to others. The errors in thinking were present before drug use was part of the user's life. The use of mind-altering substances compounded the frequency and seriousness of the thinking errors.

The concept of “thinking errors” was first introduced by Samuel Yochelson, a psychiatrist who, during a long-term research-treatment study of offenders at St. Elizabeth's Hospital in Washington, D.C., developed a phenomenological approach after abandoning more traditional and unproductive methods (Yochelson & Samenow, 1994, 1995a, 1995b). Dr. Yochelson found that, because of the prevalence of thinking errors, these individuals have a radically different view of human existence than do responsible people who make such errors far less frequently. Dr. Yochelson studied and treated both drug using offenders and those who seldom used mind-altering substances.

We all make thinking errors; they are not limited to criminals. The failure to put oneself in the place of others is one example. Many individuals who are highly responsible occasionally fail to be empathetic because they are focused so intently on their own point of view. Consequently, they may hurt someone's feelings or, if the situation is egregious, permanently alienate that person. On the other hand, an individual who is self-centered to the point that he seldom considers the needs of others leaves a trail of injury behind.

To understand the mental makeup of the drug user requires seeing the world from his point of view. A phenomenological approach allows the clinician, researcher, or student to do this without being distracted by explanations and theories about causes. The focus then is on phenomena of mind almost as if one had a computer printout of thinking as it occurs.

This chapter focuses on cognitions – thinking errors – of habitual substance abusers. Drug use did not create or cause the thinking errors. Rather it intensified those that already were present. The discussion here highlights errors in thinking as manifested by individuals who use mind-altering substances habitually and frequently.

## Control for Its Own Sake

The drug user wants to control others for the sake of control. If he is talented, bright, and creative, others are likely to admire him and rarely challenge his take-charge approach, even if they are uncomfortable with it. For drug users, controlling others is a critical component of their self-esteem. They approach life like a chessboard, regarding people as their pawns. This applies not just to users of illegal drugs but also to many who abuse alcohol or prescribed drugs. They have controlling personalities but are far more controlling when they are on drugs. For this person, any means to an end is acceptable, and, to gain the upper hand, they employ intimidation, deception, or brute force. This is far different from the legitimate control exercised by a person who has authority and uses it to benefit others – e.g., a police officer, a teacher, a parent.

Perpetrators of domestic violence are controllers. Such an individual regards a female as "his" woman who is obligated to fulfill his desires or whim of the moment. Domineering when sober, the abusive spouse becomes more so when using mind-altering substances. His shift in moods is more frequent, his temper more volatile. An angry, impatient, demanding individual without drugs, he may be more so on drugs. Marriage counselors frequently hear a spouse complain that she walks on eggshells living with such an individual.

## Lying

The drug user is a chronic liar. Those who live with him reluctantly stop believing anything he says. It is not just the stories he concocts to cover his tracks that are distressing, but his lies of omission and the later unwelcome surprises that make life with him so trying. This individual is very crafty. Perfectly capable of telling the truth, he will look someone in the eye and tell him 20% of the truth while pretending to be 100% truthful. When using drugs, lies roll off his tongue as automatically as he breathes. Failing to keep track of the myriad of different lies he has told, he occasionally trips himself up and others catch him out in a lie.

Drugs do not compel the user to lie. However, because of the life he is living, he has a great deal to lie about. He wants to conceal his use from his family. He does not want others to know the places he goes, the people with whom he associates, the risks that he takes. His life is shrouded in secrecy. Yet, he still may function well enough to do a good job at work and accomplish other things that are expected of him. A cocky individual to begin with, he is even more arrogant when he uses drugs.

## Sense of Uniqueness

Each of us is unique physically, psychologically, and experientially. The drug user believes himself to be unique in a far different manner. He thinks he is truly exceptional in the sense of being better than others – cleverer, savvier, slicker, and more powerful. He is certain that no one can penetrate his façade and discover what he is up to. If nine drug users formed a baseball team, each would consider himself the captain because he believes he knows more, has exceptional skills, and is more qualified to take charge. Such individuals seldom function as team members. They expect others to work for them but not with them.

Accompanying a belief in his uniqueness is a sense of entitlement. Many a drug user believes that he can do a job far better than anyone else. Even when he lacks skills or credentials, he expects to acquire whatever position he seeks or obtain a promotion where he works. Walking into a fast food restaurant, he thinks he should be the regional manager, not the person who flips burgers. In the mentality of the drug user, thinking something makes it so. He does not entertain possibilities. If he expects something, it has to come to pass because he is entitled. Running late to meet his girl friend, he speeds onto the interstate only to have to slam on his brakes for a traffic jam. It is not incumbent upon him to creep along with all the other "suckers," and so he lurches onto the lane restricted to high-occupancy vehicles. He is furious when a police officer pulls him over and writes a ticket. Indignant at being delayed further, he gets back onto the highway tailgating the driver in front. He finds it intolerable to creep along like all the others. What applies to others does not apply to him.

## Lack of Empathy

From what has been said thus far, it is probably no surprise that drugs abusers are seldom inclined to put themselves in the place of others. They look at their fellow human beings mostly as means to an end.

Observers sometimes are confused by the sentimentality displayed by some drug users. Many appear to be highly cultured individuals, appreciative of art, aficionados of music, and devotees of theater. They may be involved in community and charitable organizations. Their good deeds may be well known. They are outraged at others' cruelty to animals. However, when they have an objective in mind, they are ruthless. Maudlin sentiment and savage brutality exist side by side within the same individual. Nursing a wounded animal back to health by no means precludes knocking an elderly lady to the ground and snatching her purse.

Experiencing empathy would constitute a barrier to the pursuit of the objectives of the drug abuser. He has no concept of what a victim is. In fact, he considers himself the victim if someone thwarts his plans or holds him accountable. Said one man about a burglary when he searched for jewelry and electronics to sell for drugs, "I know the guy misses his stuff, but I'm the one who has to do time." The perpetrator of the crime is oblivious to the broader impact of his crime. Life is never the same for his victim and his family whose sense of security is shattered.

The irritable, impatient drug user wants what he wants instantly. His family members perpetually are on edge, worried that any misstep might unleash an explosive reaction with no warning. A late dinner, an off-the-cuff remark, a particular look sets off the drug user who takes things very personally. Rarely does he consider the impact of his hair-trigger temper even on those whom he claims to love.

## Lack of Effort

Most chronic substance abusers lack a concept of effort. They do not struggle and see things through. For many, dropping out becomes a way of life. They leave school, become dissatisfied with organizations and activities, and disenchanted with jobs. This is not due to lack of ability. Rather, they expect immediate success and for others to operate on their terms. Their enthusiasms are quick, but just as rapidly the luster or novelty of an activity wears off and they become disenchanted, then quit.

Even those who use drugs and excel in school and rise to prominence in a career are short on effort when it comes to managing many challenges that arise. They may perform well on the job especially if they are in positions of authority and others depend on them. But in many other aspects of life, they are short-distance sprinters, not long-distance runners. When they encounter a disagreeable situation, they take shortcuts or ignore whatever problem has arisen. Though, in some respects, they may be high achievers, drug users take a toll on those who are close to them, burdening families and demoralizing work colleagues. Relationships are treated as one-way streets. Takers, but rarely givers, they demand that others capitulate to their wishes. Resolving conflicts is not something they do readily or willingly. From their standpoint, there is nothing to "work out."

Drug users are remarkably self-indulgent, having the attitude, "If I like it, I'll do it; if not, the heck with it." If one defines effort as not doing what you want to do and doing what you don't want to do, the drug user does neither!

Users will tell others that they use drugs in order to "escape" stress. If one examines what this is really about, it becomes clear that what the user wants to avoid are the requirements that responsible living imposes on others. By defaulting on responsibilities, they create stress. A user says, "My old lady wants to throw me out if I don't get a job." Bill collectors are knocking at the door. His children are asking that he spend time with them. This is the "escape" he seeks rather than meet the requirements that everyday living imposes.

## Changeability

Drug users appear extremely changeable in their demeanor, attitude, and intentions. Drugs destabilize an already unstable personality. The user may seem affable, even magnanimous, then quickly become enraged and self-righteous without any indication as to what precipitated the dramatic change. Chronic substances abusers are creatures of extremes. And because of this, their families, colleagues, and acquaintances seldom know what to expect. A sunny disposition may turn to rage for no obvious reason. Even when life appears to be going well for these individuals, they are restless, irritable, and dissatisfied.

Use of mind-altering substances in and of itself can precipitate upheavals within the user's personality. But even before drugs were in the picture, the individual experienced emotional peaks and swamps, depending upon whether his demands were met. The changes may be more dramatic when he is on drugs and still more so during periods when the drug supply is interrupted and he is forced to face life as it is.

## Quick to Anger

Any aspect of life that does not meet the drug user's expectations gives rise to anger. If a driver behaves erratically, the user takes it as a personal affront and retaliates as though to teach the other guy a lesson. Road rage arises from such events. The drug user reacts personally to events that others shrug off or ignore altogether. He'll dish out harsh criticism but bridles at even a minor constructive suggestion directed at him. His entire self-esteem is on the line when the least little thing does not go as he expects.

With such hypersensitivity, the chronic substance abuser is chronically angry at a world that he thinks does not give him his due. No one could anticipate what might be the one stress too much that ignites an outburst of temper. This individual does not usually show that he is angry. He seethes and simmers before erupting. Like a cancer, anger festers and then may turn lethal.

## An Intense Fear of Fear

For the drug user, fear is a dirty word. To acknowledge that he is afraid amounts to showing that he is "lame," "weak," or a "sissy." Without drugs, the user may lack the "heart" or daring to undertake what he is contemplating. With drugs, he overcomes fear of consequences – arrest, imprisonment, injury, or death. As one user commented, "Drugs knock off my caution." What he contemplated doing without drugs, he now is emboldened to do and takes risks that, otherwise, he would not take.

Some users participate in drug treatment programs so they can reduce or completely stop drug use. This is because they realize that, on drugs, they become too reckless and jeopardize their freedom if not their lives.

Fears emanating from conscience are reduced or eliminated when the perpetrator of a crime is on drugs. Knowing right from wrong, capable of experiencing remorse (however temporary or shallow), on drugs, the user obliterates considerations of conscience long enough to execute his plan.

As to whether drugs successfully help the individual overcome fears of getting caught or of conscience depends on the substances and the circumstances in which they are used. Users have tastes and preferences in their selection of drugs (often dictated by availability). For the chronic user, if one substance is not available, he will substitute another.

## A Good Person

However nefarious his activities, the user considers himself a good person. If his plans do not work out and, unintentionally someone gets hurt, he may blame the drug, claiming the substance did the deed, that it was not his choice. If held accountable, he maintains that he is a person who never intended to cause harm to anyone. He will assert that the drug "made" him act as he did causing unintended consequences.

Incarcerated, many drug users assert that they are not like the other inmates. They are not "criminals" because, if it were not for drugs, they would not be locked up. Such a statement is patently false. People who used drugs as a way of life were irresponsible, if not frankly arrestable, *before* drug use was a pattern.

The errors described above occur on occasion in the thinking processes of people who are neither drug users nor criminals. For example, a person who is otherwise responsible may be so intent on achieving a particular responsible objective that he is blind to the inconvenience that he is causing others. Substance abusers and other offenders who regularly make the errors of thinking described above leave a long trail of injury and exact an enormous toll. If one were assessing such individuals utilizing DSM IV-TR criteria, their personality makeup would include a co-occurring disorder along with substance abuse such as narcissistic, antisocial, and borderline personality disorders.

Attaching a diagnostic label is less important than understanding the overall mental makeup of the individual. Mind-altering substances potentiate the thinking errors mentioned above. A person who is a chronic liar becomes even more dishonest when he uses drugs. Although drug users may claim that they become more sensitive to others when on drugs, this is rarely true. They are likely to show little genuine empathy and become more self-centered.

As indicated above, drugs facilitate whatever the user seeks. In as much as drugs knock out deterrents, some individuals think they are freer to commit crimes that they might only fantasize about while sober. A man who considered using a firearm to rob a convenience store, after injecting heroin, carried out the crime with a sense of invulnerability. Some offenders become less vigilant on drugs, misgauging potential consequences and are apprehended. As one man commented retrospectively, "Drugs knocked off my caution."

Drugs may facilitate sexual activity. Fear of rejection, self-consciousness over impotence, or anticipation of premature ejaculation dissipates when the individual is on drugs. A "maybe" becomes a sure thing as the individual approaches a potential partner. On drugs, other apprehensions fade, and the user grows less concerned about pregnancy or contacting a sexually transmitted disease. The conquest and buildup are more important than the sexual act. If the user is on a high dose of drugs, he may have no sexual interest at all. Users have sought drug treatment solely for the purpose of recovering sexual desire.

Offenders who use drugs may not intend to commit more daring crimes but they do experience an enhanced sense of power. Drug users articulate this in their own language: "Drugs make me feel 10 feet tall. On drugs, I feel like I can do anything. Drugs make me feel like Hercules." The perception of the world as their own personal chessboard, which they have when sober, becomes magnified. Sometimes, the heightened experience is a sense of gaining unique insights and enhancing creativity.

If the user seeks a religious experience, he may find what he seeks especially when using so-called hallucinogenic drugs. However, rather than being "in touch with" a supreme being, he experiences himself as having godlike powers.

Since the drug user discovers that drugs facilitate whatever he has in mind, it is also the case that, if he becomes extremely depressed, drugs can facilitate suicidal thinking and even the commission of suicide. Consumed with self-pity and blazing anger at a world that is unsatisfactory, he is fed up. He despairs about continuing to live when people do not give him what he thinks he deserves.

The excitement of engaging in risky and illicit activities constitutes the "oxygen" of the user's life. When a person contends, "Drugs are my problem," he may truly believe this. However, if he were to remain drug-free, there remain thinking errors that still must be identified and corrected if he is to become a responsible human being. Therein lies the problem. As one user commented, "If you take my crime away, you take my world away. What do you have to offer that compares with cocaine?" He and others like him have three alternatives, each of which seems unacceptable. He can continue on the path he has traveled of drugs and crime with consequences that inevitably will be disagreeable. Or he can do what many have done for a limited period of time – embrace a drug-free life that he has experienced as intolerably tedious. Finally, there is the option of not living at all. Drug users, from time to time, have opted for a fourth possibility – playing both "sides of the street." They give an appearance of being responsible while "cheating" on the side. Ultimately, the user invariably returns to a criminal lifestyle with its disastrous consequences for himself, the people who care about him, and the community at large.

It is possible to help even the hardened offender who is a long-term drug user, under certain circumstances, to give up drugs and become a responsible person. Cognitive behavioral therapy that focuses on identifying and correcting errors in thinking can be a potent approach in helping drug users turn around their lives in a significant and enduring manner.

Many treatment programs address detoxification, drug education, and encourage responsible behavior through various processes, including the use of "therapeutic communities." Cognitive Therapy, long applied to such maladaptive behavior as anxiety, depression, and phobias, has also been recognized as providing effective intervention in working with substance abusers. However, all cognitive therapy is not alike. In working with offenders who are also substance abusers, an essential ingredient that all too often is missing is a focus on cognitive "errors" that dominate their thinking. Unless these errors are known to the therapist or counselor, it is not possible to address the core thought patterns that invariably give rise to substance abuse and other irresponsible behavior.

Even if the drug user were to be completely abstinent, the thinking errors of a lifetime that resulted in substance abuse do not vanish. The user relapses not just because he "craves" a particular mind-altering substance, but mainly because he finds responsible living unsatisfactory (in his words "dull" or "boring"). Expecting that others accommodate him, the substance abuser has not been especially accommodating of others. The abstinent alcoholic or "dry drunk" remains controlling, dishonest, and insensitive. The abstinent illegal drug user still shows evidence of what A.A. terms "stinking thinking."

If a person wants to change in an enduring manner, he needs to be aware of the thinking that precedes and follows the behavior at issue. A drug user can best be helped by participating in a process that guides him first to be cognizant of a particular thought, i.e., to become an observer of his own thinking. Having "caught" the thought before acting on it, he needs to consider what such undeterred thinking has resulted in and invariably will result in again – consequences injurious to others (including those whom he says he cares about) and disagreeable to him. Developing an inner dissatisfaction with his thinking errors is essential to motivating him to abandon them and learn correctives. The process entails focusing on a specific thought, placing the thought under a magnifying glass to examine its ramifications, then teaching a corrective concept that can apply to similar situations. This goes beyond solving specific problems one at a time. The objective is to help the user learn new ways of thinking so that he can live without hurting himself or others (Yochelson & Samenow, 1994, 1995a, 1995b).

Examples of corrective concepts are using the past as a guide to the present and the future, putting oneself in the place of others, dealing with adversity in a constructive fashion, focusing on a long-term gain rather than an immediate gratification and, most of all, becoming realistic in terms of what one expects of other people.

This type of cognitive behavioral work can be undertaken intensively in residential drug treatment programs. However, such work must continue once the user is residing in the community. For it is in the community where he will encounter the usual array of temptations and many more arenas in which to implement change. Self-help and Twelve Step groups can facilitate and reinforce abstinence and other changes. But, in addition, there must be counseling that is dedicated to helping users identify and correct errors in thinking. There is no quick fix! Cognitive patterns that have existed for years, often decades, do not disappear quickly, if at all.

This type of cognitive-behavioral treatment offers considerable hope in helping substance abusers become responsible human beings.

## References

Brecher, E. M., & The Editors of Consumer Reports. (1972). *Licit and illicit drugs*. San Francisco: Jossey-Bass.

Freedman, A. M. (1972). Drugs and society: An ecological approach. *Comprehensive Psychiatry, 13*, 411–420.

Krystal, H., & Raskin, H. (1970). *Drug dependence*. Detroit, MI: Wayne State University Press.

National Commission on Marijuana and Drug Abuse. (1973). *Drug use in America: Problem in perspective*. Washington, DC: Government Printing Office.

Shedler, J., & Block, J. (1990). Adolescent drug use and psychological health. *American Psychologist, 45*, 612–618.

Starratt, A. B. (1971). Drugs and the new morality. In C. C. Brown & C. Savage (Eds.), *The drug abuse controversy* (pp. 77–86). Baltimore: National Educational Consultants.

The Monitor. (1990, February). *Drug abuse risk linked with antisocial disorder*, Washington, DC: The American Psychological Association.

Yochelson, S., & Samenow, S. E. (1994). *The criminal personality, Volume 3: The drug user*. Livingston, NJ: Roman and Littlefield.

Yochelson, S., & Samenow, S. E. (1995a). *The criminal personality, Volume 1: A profile for change*. Livingston, NJ: Roman and Littlefield.

Yochelson, S., & Samenow, S. E. (1995b). *The criminal personality, Volume 2: The change process*. Livingston, NJ: Roman and Littlefield.

# 3 Evidence-Based Practice in Criminal Justice Settings

## A Biological/Genetic Perspective: The Addicted Brain

William M. Heffron, Shanna Babalonis, Michele Staton-Tindall, Lori Molenaar, Karen M. Lommel, Alessandra N. Kazura, Katie House, and Catherine A. Martin

**Abstract**

The role of substance use and fetal exposure to substances of abuse is reviewed from the viewpoint of what role it may play in current or future criminal behavior. Fetal exposure to Alcohol, Nicotine and Marijuana does have long term consequences in terms of problems with learning, planning and analyzing situations. These effects can lead to impaired school performance and increased impulsivity in the classroom. Having problems in school is a risk factor for later delinquent behavior. There is some association with later criminal behavior in youth with fetal Nicotine exposure. Current use of Alcohol, Cannabis, Cocaine, Methamphetamine, Opiates and high levels of Caffeine is associated with increased criminal and violent behavior. Appropriate screening, assessment of prenatal substance abuse exposure and adolescent substance abuse is recommended in order to minimize delinquent behavior.

**Keywords**

Alcohol • Cannabis • Marijuana • Cocaine • Methamphetamine • Opiates • Inhalants • Caffeine • Nicotine • Stimulants • Dopamine • GABA • Fetal Exposure • Substance Abuse • Delinquency • Criminal Behavior • Violence • Risk Factors • Screening • Assessment • Treatment • Reclaiming Futures

Teen drug and alcohol use is a serious issue for the juvenile justice system. Studies show that nearly 60% of delinquent youth were under the influence of alcohol or drugs at the time of their arrest (Dennis, Dawoud-Noursi, Muck, & McDermett, 2002). The National Center on Addiction and Substance Abuse (CASA) found that at least 80% of arrested youth had one or more of the following characteristics (CASA, 2004):

- Positive test for drug use
- Took drugs or alcohol before committing their crime
- Admitted to substance abuse
- Committed a drug or alcohol related crime

W.M. Heffron (✉)
Mental Health Services, Frankfort, KY 40601, USA
e-mail: billm.heffron@ky.gov

C. Leukefeld et al. (eds.), *Handbook of Evidence-Based Substance Abuse Treatment in Criminal Justice Settings*, Issues in Children's and Families' Lives 11,
DOI 10.1007/978-1-4419-9470-7_3, 

In addition, rearrests are related to substance use (Cuellar, McReynolds, & Wasserman, 2006).

The most commonly used drugs are tobacco, alcohol, and marijuana High lifetime rates of other drugs have also been observed including inhalants (39%); amphetamines (32%); opiates (32%); tranquilizers (32%); cocaine (23%); hallucinogens (23%); diverted prescription drug use (21%); and ecstacy/MDMA (20%) (Vaughn, Howard, Foster, Dayton, & Zelner, 2005). Nearly half of the detainees have one or more substance use disorders with half having two or more (not including nicotine dependence; McClelland, Elkington, Teplin, & Abram, 2004).

In this chapter, we examine the relationship between substance abuse and exposure and risk factors for later adolescent violence and serious offending. Serious offending can be defined as having committed one or more of the following offenses – violent offenses, felony larceny/theft, auto theft, fraud, dealing in stolen property, burglary, breaking and entering, carjacking, extortion, forgery and counterfeiting, embezzlement, drug trafficking, arson, weapons violations, or violation of firearms statutes or regulations (Loeber, Farrington, & Waschbusch, 1998). Particular attention is given to examining the association between prenatal and family drug exposure, and more recent drug use by youth and delinquent behavior. We examine how substance use is associated with the risk factors that predict and are part of current juvenile offenses. For the purpose of this chapter we target drugs of abuse that have been more closely tied to adolescents who end up in the juvenile justice system. These substances include nicotine, alcohol, marijuana, stimulants (methamphetamine, diverted, therapeutic stimulants, cocaine), inhalants, and opiates. We also comment briefly on ubiquitous caffeine.

Many of the risk factors for delinquency and substance abuse are similar and overall the greater number of risk factors imports a greater risk for delinquency and substance abuse. Examples of critical risk factors include gang membership, family substance abuse history, family legal problems, family violence, violence by the child, associating with substance abusing, and/or antisocial peers and adults, and impulsivity. It is important to add that school factors have been associated with delinquency including poor academic achievement (Maguin & Loeber, 1996). In addition, high truancy rates in early adolescence predict violence in adolescence and adulthood (Farrington, 1989; Henry & Huizinga, 2007).

## The Reciprocal Relationship of Substance Abuse and Impulse Disorders

A pattern of early initiation of aggression, violence, and delinquency predicts later serious chronic violent behavior. In males, early involvement with stealing, destruction of property, tobacco smoking, early sexual intercourse, and drug selling predicts later violent behavior. Caspi, Moffitt, Newman, and Silva (1996) found that undercontrolled behavior (defined as impulsivity, restlessness, and distractibility) at age 3 was associated with having a diagnosis of antisocial personality disorder or having committed a violent crime by age 21. The use of cognitive distortions is related positively to indicators of undersocialized aggressive conduct disorder, reactive aggression, and commission of violent crimes in a sample of highly aggressive juvenile offenders (Dodge, Price, Bachorowski, & Newman, 1990). Further the combination of family history of substance abuse, poor cognitive constructive thinking, and cognitive distortions predicted a much higher level of delinquent behavior in 16-year-old adolescent males (Gudonis, Giancola, & Tarter, 2007).

There is evidence that early and more frequent drug use predicts drug abuse and dependence. Kandel has long suggested that use of tobacco and alcohol contributes to a trajectory to marijuana and harder drugs (Kandel, Yamaguchi, & Chen, 1992). In addition, cannabis use even when accounting for other risk factors is a gateway drug to other drug abuse (Fergusson, Boden, & Horwood, 2008).

There is compelling evidence that attention and conduct problems predict use and abuse of a range of drugs (Mannuzza, Klein, & Moulton, 2008; Molina et al., 2007; Putņinŝ, 2006).

It is clear that the origins of delinquent behavior and substance abuse are linked (Vaughn et al., 2005). The relationship between substance use and delinquency is reciprocal with substance abuse predicting delinquent behavior and interpersonal crime, delinquent behavior predicting future substance abuse (D'Amico, Edelen, Miles, & Morral, 2007; Mason & Windle, 2002). Recently, Helstrom, Bryan, Hutchison, Riggs, and Blechman (2004) found that alcohol use and smoking behaviors emerged as mediators between externalizing behaviors and marijuana and hard drug use. However there are continued unanswered questions regarding directionality and the mechanism of influence.

## Prenatal Exposure

Examination of the relationship of intrauterine drug exposure to later drug-related delinquent activity is challenging. First many of the studies of the neonatal impact of drug use do not address polysubstance abuse which should include ATOD (alcohol, tobacco, and other drugs of abuse). Second, the complications of "host" factors such as lack of family support, poverty, poor nutrition, lack of education and skilled job, poor nutrition, and high stress frequently associated with drug abuse in pregnancy are rarely accounted for when examining these relationships (Schempf, 2007). Third, when examining the relationship between prenatal exposure, risk factors that could impact the pregnancy are likely important in impacting later child behavioral outcomes (Dixon, Kurtz, & Chin, 2008). Despite these complexities, there are certain drugs that with intrauterine exposure have a clear impact on future behavior and these are addressed with specific drugs to follow.

## Family Exposure

The Center on Addiction and Substance Abuse (CASA, 2005) reports that nearly half of all children in the United States live with at least one parent or caregiver who uses alcohol, illicit substance, or tobacco. These estimates are based on 27 million children living in homes where tobacco is used, 17 million with a parent/caregiver binge drinking, and 9.2 million living in homes where illicit substances are used (CASA, 2005). With the well-documented link between drug use and crime (e.g., Leukefeld, Tims, & Farabee, 2002), it is likely that a number of these children have also been affected by parental or caregiver arrest.

Parents who misuse alcohol and drugs are often characterized as ineffective caregivers due to (1) physical and mental impairments during intoxication and withdrawal states which are often associated with ineffective parenting strategies and harsh discipline and punishment; (2) using limited funds on substances instead of food, shelter, and other basic household needs; and (3) spending time seeking, procuring, and using drugs and alcohol instead of caring for their children (Hien & Honeyman, 2000; Kolar, Brown, Haertzen, & Michaelson, 1994; Office of Applied Studies, 2003).

While cases of neglect are common among children of substance users, substance use is also a powerful predictor of child maltreatment severity (Sprang, Clark, & Bass, 2005). In fact, research spanning the last two decades has consistently shown that there is a link between parental substance use, child maltreatment, and severity of child trauma exposure (Drapela & Mosher, 2007; Magura & Laudet, 1996). Chaffin, Kelleher, and Hollenberg (1996) reported that substance-using parents were nearly three times more likely to abuse and neglect their children than a case-controlled comparison group, even when demographic and other social variables were considered. The relationship between parental substance use and child maltreatment has been attributed to a number of theoretical explanations including (1) intergenerational transmission of substance use and violent behavior (McCloskey & Bailey, 2000); (2) the bond between parents and adolescents at risk or a protective factor of child deviant acts (Drapela & Mosher, 2007); (3) the parent's ability to nurture their children negatively impacted by parental substance users' high levels of disorganization and avoidant behavior (Edwards, Eiden, & Leonard, 2004; Goodman, Hans, & Cox, 1999).

Work by Fellitti et al. (1998) through the Adverse Childhood Experience studies indicated that children's health and mental health can be significantly affected by exposure to parental substance use, violence, and maltreatment. Parental substance use has also been associated with social consequences including increased likelihood of children and adolescents engaging in substance use (Drapela & Mosher, 2007), developing adult patterns of addiction (Widom, White, Czaja, & Marmorstein, 2007), experiencing adult victimization and/or perpetration of violence (Haller & Miles, 2003), and becoming involved with the criminal justice system (Huebner & Gustafson, 2007).

### Neuropharmacology

Most drugs of abuse have direct or indirect effects on dopamine neurons throughout the brain. The dopamine reward pathway consists of the following regions rich in dopamine receptors: caudate/putamen, nucleus accumbens, tuberculum olfactoreum, prefrontal cortex, and frontal cortex. Caffeine attaches to adenosine receptors and blocks them. This prevents sedation and causes increased alertness. Adenosine receptors also inhibit dopamine release and gamma-aminobutyric acid (GABA) neuron activation. Blocking adenosine receptors and inhibiting GABA activation results in enhanced dopamine release. Nicotine binds to acetylcholine receptors which modulate dopamine function. So nicotine indirectly acts to release more dopamine. Alcohol has actions on a variety of cell systems including GABA and n-methyl-D-aspartate (NMDA). By inhibiting their activation, alcohol indirectly causes more dopamine release. Stimulants act by preventing monoamine reuptake and by enhancing monoamine release. The effect is to increase the amount of epinephrine and dopamine between neurons. The dopamine effect seems to be greater at sites in the dopamine reward pathway. Methamphetamine and cocaine act in a similar fashion (Kelly, Kazura, Lommel, Babalonis, & Martin, 2008). Cannabinoids in marijuana attach to cannabinoid receptors which inhibit the release of glutamate and GABA. The effect is to release more dopamine. The mechanism of action of most inhalants is not very clear (Luscher, 2009).

## Specific Drugs

### Caffeine

There is evidence that heavy caffeine use is associated with drug use and other problem behaviors in children and adolescents (Tennant & Detels, 1976). High levels of caffeine consumption in early and mid adolescents are associated with cigarette use and aggressive behavior, conduct problems, social problems, and attention/ADHD problems, as reported by adolescents and their parents (Martin et al., 2008). It is not known whether behavioral problems in children and adolescents who consume large amounts of caffeine are due to caffeine, or whether children and adolescents with these problems consume large amounts of caffeine in order to self-medicate their symptoms (Leviton, 1992).

Caffeine may interact with and enhance the effects of other drugs of abuse. For example, caffeine has been found to enhance the reinforcing and stimulant subjective effects of nicotine in adult cigarette smokers (Jones & Griffiths, 2003). It is not known if this interaction occurs among children and adolescents, and further research is required to examine whether caffeine use increases sensitivity to the pharmacological effects of other drugs of abuse during development.

Given the association of caffeine with aggression and its ubiquitous use several issues need to be considered. First restriction of caffeine products during structured treatment settings may be advised. However possible caffeine withdrawal with associated headache, depression, anxiety, fatigue, feelings of rejection may need to be considered (Griffiths & Mumford, 1995). One study found that children who had consumed 150 mg/day of caffeine for 13 days had decreased functioning on a vigilance task 24 hours after discontinuing their daily dose and again 1 week later (Bernstein et al., 1998). A tapered caffeine exposure might be considered in the juvenile justice system.

## Tobacco

Approximately 23% of pregnant women report smoking during the 3 months prior to pregnancy, with 13% continuing to smoke throughout pregnancy (Centers for Disease Control & Prevention [CDCP], 2002). This frequency is likely to be an underestimate of true rates since it is based on survey data. Rates of smoking identified with surveys are generally lower than those identified when quantitative measures of smoking (e.g., salivary cotinine) are used to determine smoking rates (Walsh, Redman, & Adamson, 1996).

In utero exposure to nicotine has important implications for behavioral development. Prenatal nicotine exposure is associated with the development of altered patterns of behavior during early postnatal life (Law et al., 2003). For example, toddlers exposed in utero are more likely to be impulsive, hyperactive, and oppositional and to have lower language skills than their unexposed peers (Wakschlag, Leventhal, Pine, Pickett, & Carter, 2006). Multiple studies suggest that these effects continue to be expressed during adolescence. Furthermore, in utero exposure increases the risk of developing both internalizing and externalizing disorders (e.g., mood disorders, conduct disorder) known to be risk factors for the emergence of adolescent experimental and persistent smoking (Fried & Watkinson, 2001; Upadhyaya, Deas, Brady, & Kruesi, 2002). Postnatal environmental tobacco smoke exposure may also have an impact on child and adolescent brain and behavioral development (Okoli, Kelly, & Hahn, 2007), although disentangling postnatal and prenatal associations is methodologically difficult (Eskenazi & Castorina, 1999).

By age 10, nicotine-exposed offspring are more likely to have tried smoking, and smoking rates among the prenatally exposed remain higher during adolescence (Cornelius, Leech, Goldschmidt, & Day, 2000). Adult women exposed to tobacco in utero are four times more likely to be smokers than those who were not exposed (Kandel, Wu, & Davies, 1994). It is clear that there are multiple environmental, biological, and genetic factors that contribute to tobacco use, and many of these factors may contribute to multigenerational tobacco use.

Adolescents endorse more symptoms of dependence than adults smoking the same number of cigarettes per day, suggesting that adolescents may be more sensitive to the effects of nicotine (Kandel & Chen, 2000). In cross-sectional studies, withdrawal symptoms have been reported earlier in the course of tobacco use among adolescents than adults, and may precede regular or daily use among adolescent smokers (DiFranza et al., 2007).

In juvenile delinquents Helstrom et al. (2004) demonstrated that tobacco and alcohol use mediated the relationship between externalizing behaviors to heavier drug use.

When considering treatment of nicotine-dependent adolescents in the juvenile justice system several issues need to be considered. First whether or not to use nicotine replacement is controversial. One of the better-studied pharmacologic interventions for adolescent smokers is buproprion (Killen et al., 2004; Upadhyaya, Brady, & Wang, 2004).

Clinical reasoning suggests the importance of considering psychiatric comorbidity with any decisions to use tobacco treatment medications for nicotine-dependent adolescent smokers. For example, bupropion might be considered for potential dual benefits with a youth with both nicotine dependence and ADHD. However, given the absence of a clear evidence base for medication for adolescent tobacco treatment, healthcare providers need to be careful to avoid overestimation of the tobacco treatment benefits.

## Alcohol

Fetal and infantile alcohol exposure is predictive of subsequent alcohol use during adolescence, which is associated with excessive alcohol use later in life (Spear & Molina, 2005). Alcohol use during adolescence is associated with elevated risks for liver disease and adverse endocrine and metabolic effects (National Institute on Alcohol Abuse and Alcoholism [NIAAA], 2004/2005).

In utero rates of alcohol exposure are estimated to occur with 13% of all pregnancies and with 3% of pregnant women reporting frequent (7 or more drinks/week) or binge drinking (5 or more drinks in one setting; Bertrand et al., 2004).

De Bellis and colleagues (2005) found reduced prefrontal cortex volume in adolescents with early onset alcohol use and comorbid mental health conditions, although the study design was not able to differentiate that acquired from preexisting volume decrements. Another study by De Bellis and colleagues (2001) found reduced hippocampal volumes in individuals with early onset alcohol use disorders, and age of onset was inversely associated with total volume, suggesting that hippocampal development and associated memory processes may be particularly vulnerable to the impairing effects of alcohol during adolescence.

Adolescents using alcohol are at risk for cognitive impairments thought to be associated with the toxic effects of the alcohol on brain development. Brown and Tapert (2004) found visuospatial deficits and information retrieval deficits 3 weeks after adolescents detoxified from heavy drinking patterns. Among adolescents, the presence of an alcohol use disorder has been associated with changes in working memory tasks in functional neuroimaging studies (Sher, 2006). Changes such as these may contribute to a dynamic negatively spiraling interaction between biological and environmental risk factors. For example, students with low school connectedness are at increased risk of problematic use of alcohol, and if cognitive impairments develop with use, then the likelihood of a negative trajectory of poor academic achievement and further disconnection with school is more likely, intensifying the risk for continued heavy alcohol use and dependence.

The association of violence and alcohol use is well established in adults and there are some studies that support the association in delinquent adolescents. Evans, Mezey, and Ehlers (2009) found an association between high alcohol intake and amnesia for extremely violent crime (grievous bodily harm, murder). In a study of Russian delinquents, Fritz, Wiklund, Koposov, af Klinteberg, and Ruchkin (2008) found that delinquents with higher levels of violence reported more problems related to alcohol use as measured by the Adolescent Alcohol Involvement Scale (Mayer & Filstead, 1979). Finally this may be exacerbated by the observation that exposure to traumatic experiences, such as violence, is a well-known risk factor for adolescent alcohol use (Vermeiren, Scwa-Stone, Deboutte, Leckman, & Ruchkin, 2003).

## Marijuana

The effects of prenatal marijuana exposure (PME) have been studied primarily by two groups. The Ottawa Prenatal Prospective Study (OPPS) has followed the offspring of a sample consisting of low-risk, white, and primarily middle-class families (Fried & Smith, 2001). The Maternal Health Practices and Child Development Study (MHPCD) has studied the offspring of a sample consisting of high-risk and low socioeconomic families. Half of the group is African–American (Goldschmidt, Day, & Richardson, 2000). In both groups, some mothers smoked marijuana during pregnancy. Their children were studied over time to see if there were differences with unexposed children.

The OPPS group found several differences in PME infants in the first week, at 9 days, and at 30 days after delivery. They primarily demonstrated exaggerated startle responses. At less than 1 week of age, they showed poorer habituation to visual but not auditory stimuli. There were no group differences thereafter until 48 months of age.

Both groups began using neuropsychological batteries when their subjects were toddlers and continued to do so through adolescence. Overall IQ scores were not impaired but consistently children and adolescents seemed to have some difficulty in analytical or integrative tasks. They had adequate basic abilities but some difficulty with executive functioning especially in tasks requiring visual analysis (Fried, Watkinson, & Gray, 2003).

The OPPS group used fMRI to study PME effects on 18–22-year-old young adults. Increasing exposure resulted in increased neural activity in the bilateral prefrontal cortex and right premotor cortex during response inhibition. There was also attenuation of activity in the left cerebellum. The authors concluded that neural changes continued until young adulthood (Smith, Fried, Hogan, & Cameron, 2004).

Both groups also studied the effects of PME on hyperactivity, impulsivity, and inattention. In the MHPCD, 6-year-olds had increasing inattention and impulsivity related in a dose-response fashion to maternal marijuana use during pregnancy (Leech, Richardson, Goldschmidt, & Day, 1999). The OPPS group looked at 6–9-year-olds. Children with PME were rated as more distractible by their mothers. On the Continuous Performance Test (CPT) they made more errors of commission. They also had delayed response times and a lower rate of correct responses (reviewed in Fried & Watkinson, 2001). The MHPCD group looked at 10-year-olds with PME. They continued to be rated overactive, impulsive, and inattentive by their mothers (Goldschmidt et al., 2000). The OPPS group looked at 13–16-year-old adolescents with PME and found that they had impaired stability of attention on the CPT (Fried & Watkinson, 2001).

Both groups also looked at the effect of PME on later marijuana use. The MHPCD group looked at 14-year-old adolescents and concluded that PME was associated with greater marijuana usage (Day, Goldschmidt, & Thomas, 2006). The OPPS group looked at adolescents and young adults aged 16–21. They found increased marijuana use in the PME subjects with a dose-response effect. The larger the exposure, the more subjects used marijuana (Porath & Fried, 2005).

Use of marijuana during adolescence has also been studied to look for any effects related to delinquency or further substance abuse. Juvenile detention center studies in Florida have shown that youth testing positive for marijuana reported higher rates of marijuana or hashish use and also had twice as many juvenile court referrals for nondrug felonies. The same pattern also held true for youth who tested negative for marijuana but still reported recent use (Dembo, Washburn, Wish, Yeung, et al., 1987; Dembo, Washburn, Wish, Schmeidler, et al., 1987). Youth testing positive for marijuana also had more drug delinquency referrals to juvenile court (Dembo et al., 1990). In a self-report study of tenth graders in California and Oregon, adolescents who admitted to marijuana use also admitted to engaging in more deviant behavior (Hays & Ellickson, 1996). In the longitudinal Dunedin, New Zealand study, adolescents with a history of conduct disorder accounted for most of the violence committed by individuals with marijuana dependence. Individuals with marijuana dependence and violent behavior had a longstanding involvement with crime (Arseneault, Moffitt, Caspi, Taylor, & Silva, 2000). In a 5-year followup of youth probated to the South Carolina Department of Juvenile Justice, individuals who used marijuana frequently and had comorbid mental health disorders continued to use marijuana as young adults. Those who used marijuana and alcohol as young adults were more likely to engage in criminal behavior (Clingempeel, Henggeler, Pickrel, & Brondino, 2005). National Youth Survey data showed that adolescents who used marijuana were also more likely to use other illicit drugs (Rebellon & Van Gundy, 2006). In a sample of youth from the National Household Surveys on Drug Abuse, individuals with multiple and serious behavior problems had the highest rates of drug use especially inhalants and marijuana (Storr, Accornero, & Crum, 2007). In a sample of French high-school students, marijuana use was a significant predictor of delinquency (Chabrol & Saint-Martin, 2009).

## Stimulants

### Methamphetamine

Methamphetamine (MA), also known as crystal meth, is a synthetic stimulant which affects the brain and central nervous system (National Institute on Drug Abuse [NIDA], 2002). The most common route of administration of MA is smoking, followed by injection. It produces a powerful initial rush, lasting for a couple of minutes followed by a prolonged high resulting in an extended state of euphoria (Klasser & Epstein, 2005). The half-life of MA ranges from 10 to 30 hours, which can vary according to the purity of the drug, urine pH, and the amount consumed (NIDA, 2002).

MA produces physiological and psychological effects similar to cocaine. It stimulates the release of dopamine, norepinephrine, and serotonin, blocking their reuptake (NIDA, 2002; Sulzer, Sanders, Paulsen, & Galli, 2005). MA is produced quickly, reasonably simply, and inexpensively using legal, readily available ingredients such as ephedrine, pseudoephedrine, red phosphorous, iodine, ammonia, paint thinner, lye, camping fuel, drain cleaner, and lithium (Klasser & Epstein, 2005). Many of the chemicals used in MA production are explosive and the waste products generated are corrosive and toxic (Parks & Jack, 2005). Ingredients and cooking tools for MA can be purchased at local drug and hardware stores; recipes can be found on the Internet (Royal Canadian Mounted Police K Division: Methamphetamine Strategy, 2005). It is thus easy to understand why MA is the fastest growing illicit drug in the United States (Scott, Fleming, Bennett, & Graves, 2005). In 2004, the US National Survey on Drug Use and Health surveyed persons over the age of 11, finding that 1.4 million people (0.6% of the population) had used MA in the past 12 months (Office of Applied Studies, 2005). A large-scale multisite investigation (the IDEAL Study) found 5.2% of 1,632 drug-abusing pregnant women had used MA at some point during their pregnancies (Arria et al., 2006a).

Prenatal exposure to MA has deleterious effects on intrauterine growth, birth weight, and neonatal behavior. The IDEAL Study found MA-exposed neonates were 3.5 times more likely to be small for gestational age compared with unexposed controls (Arria et al., 2006b). Neurobehavioral effects of prenatal MA exposure were also assessed by the IDEAL Study. The NICU Network Neurobehavioral Scale was administered within the first 5 days of life to 74 MA-exposed neonates. Exposure to MA was associated with increased physiological stress, with heavier use related to lower arousal, more lethargy, and increased physiological stress, particularly CNS stress. First trimester use of MA was related to elevated stress abstinence, and third trimester use to poorer quality of movement (Arria et al., 2006b). Smith et al., also found an increased incidence of small for gestational age term infants with MA exposure, and also reported 4% of infants in the study required pharmacologic intervention for withdrawal (Smith et al., 2003).

There have been several small-scale MRI and/or PET scan studies of children with prenatal MA exposure. Most find smaller striatal volumes in the MA exposed groups, with decreased size also found in the putamen bilaterally, smaller hippocampal volume, and small caudate. There were also increased levels of creatinine found in the striatum (Chang, Alicata, Ernst, & Volkow, 2007). The meth-exposed children scored lower on measures of visual motor integration, attention, verbal memory, and long-term spatial memory. The smaller putamen, globus pallidus, hippocampal volume, and caudate were associated with poorer performance on sustained attention and delayed verbal memory (Chang et al., 2003).

More longitudinal research is indicated to ascertain if effects of prenatal MA exposure are persistent into adolescence. It is interesting that prenatal MA exposure in children is linked to smaller striatal volume; in adult MA abusers, the opposite is true. It is hypothesized that the greater striatal volume is a compensatory mechanism for depletion of dopamine terminals. This does not seem to occur in utero (Berman, O'Neill, Fears, Bartzokis, & London, 2008). A 2001 PET scan study by Volkow of adult detoxified MA abusers showed the expected decrease in dopamine transporters, associated with motor slowing and memory impairment. A second study, conducted on MA abusers who had been abstinent for 12–17 months showed a 19% improvement in caudate dopamine transporter performance, and a 16% increase in putamen dopamine transporter activity. This was not statistically significant, but appears to indicate remaining viable terminals increase synaptic arborization. Neuropsychologic testing of the subjects did not improve to the same extent (Volkow, Chang, Wang, Farber, et al., 2001; Volkow, Chang, Wang, Fowler, et al., 2001). It is not yet clear whether children with prenatal MA exposure will also show evidence of recovery over time. There is some controversy about whether "meth babies" will be unfairly stigmatized prematurely, especially if they show the same tendency to outgrow cognitive or behavioral dysfunction seen in children with prenatal cocaine exposure (Glantz and Chambers, 2006). At this point, it is not possible to predict with any accuracy due to the lack of controlled studies.

## Cocaine

An estimated 8.3 million children under the age of 18 lived with a parent who was dependent on or abused an illicit drug or alcohol in the past year, with 2.1 million of those children living with a parent abusing or dependent on an illicit drug (Substance Abuse and Mental Health Services Administration [SAMHSA], 2009).

In 2002–2003 4.3% of pregnant women aged 15–44 reported using illicit drugs in the past month, with the 15–25 age group at the highest risk (SAMHSA, 2005a). According to a 1999 report, 27% of pregnant women were seeking treatment for cocaine, compared with 20% of those women who were not pregnant (SAMSHA, 2002). One group estimates that approximately 375,000 cocaine-exposed children are born every year (U.S. General Accounting Office, 1990). With these alarming trends, it is important to understand the impact of prenatal cocaine exposure on children's learning, behavior, brain structure, and any potential predisposition to drug use.

Cocaine use during pregnancy can complicate the pregnancy by inducing maternal cardiac complications and risk for adverse pregnancy events (e.g., hypertension, tachycardia). However, the degree to which neonates, infants, and children are affected by maternal cocaine use is unclear.

Overall, reports detailing the health of human neonates and infants exposed to cocaine in utero have been largely inconsistent. Some reports of intrauterine growth indices (birth weight, length, and head circumference) have shown little to no effect of prenatal cocaine exposure (Schempf & Strobino, 2008; Schempf, 2007), while other research has shown significant effects (Bada et al., 2005; Singer et al., 2002). Research on changes in brain structure and function as a result of prenatal cocaine exposure is also inconsistent. Preclinical research using animal models of prenatal cocaine exposure produce clear results, with effects observed in brain development and structure, neurochemical composition, motor and cognitive skills, and social behavior (Trksak, Glatt, Mortazavi, & Jackson, 2007; Magalhães et al., 2006). However, equivocal results have emerged in clinical research that addresses similar topics such as spatial skills and IQ measures (Singer et al., 2004), working memory (Hurt et al., 2008), brain activation during a working memory task (Hurt et al., 2008), global cerebral blood flow (Rao et al., 2007), structural deficits (Avants et al., 2007; Hurt et al., 2008), and social skills (Dixon et al., 2008). Factors that may contribute to these discrepancies may include concomitant cigarette smoking and poly-drug use, and differences in maternal socioeconomic status, maternal stress, overall maternal health, access to prenatal care, and child rearing.

Cocaine use in adolescence is a significant problem. SAMSHA data indicates that 61.8% of adolescents ages 12–17 who used cocaine also were involved in violent behavior in the past year (SAMHSA, 2006). In addition, adolescent cocaine use also increases the likelihood of adult cocaine use and abuse (Fergusson et al., 2008). Both clinical and preclinical research suggests that chronic cocaine administration during adolescence increases aggressive behavior (Moeller et al., 1994) through modulation of the serotonin receptor system (Ricci, Grimes, & Melloni, 2004). Thus, cocaine use during adolescence affects brain neurochemistry that may alter inhibitory control and aggressive behavior.

## Nonmedical Prescription Stimulant Use

Nonmedical prescription stimulant use (i.e., diversion of prescription medication) appears to be on the rise. Significant numbers of college-aged individuals who have received prescriptions for stimulant medication report misusing their own or other prescription medication (Arria et al., 2008). Many of those who misuse prescription medication meet the criteria for Conduct Disorder and Substance-Use Disorder (Wilens, Gignac, Swezey, Monuteaux, & Biederman, 2006).

Diversion of prescription stimulant medication in college-aged students who initiated treatment in grade school is no greater than that of the general population, but diversion escalates among college-aged students who were first prescribed stimulant medication after completing grade school (McCabe, Teter, & Boyd, 2006). Nonmedical stimulant use is also increasing among high-school-aged adolescents, particularly among those with lower grade point averages. Poulin (2007) reported that about 26% of junior and senior high-school students who were receiving prescribed stimulants had given or sold their medication to others. Illicit stimulant medication use among high-school students has been linked with the use of other drugs, including tobacco cigarette smoking, heavy episodic drinking, marijuana and cocaine use, as well as peer drug use (Poulin, 2007).

It is important to balance the risk of prescription stimulant misuse with the potential clinical benefits of the medication. It is somewhat ironic, for example, that while there is risk for the misuse of prescription stimulants, these medications may also be protective for other forms of drug abuse, with the possible exception of tobacco. The interval of time between initial use of a drug and the development of abuse or dependence is significantly shorter for adolescents with ADHD than for age-matched normals (Biederman et al., 1997), even when controlling for comorbid conditions, such as Conduct Disorder (Wilens, Biederman, Mick, Faraone, & Spencer, 1997). However rates of drug abuse and dependence are actually lower in ADHD adolescents who are treated effectively with stimulants as compared to ADHD adolescents who are not treated (Wilens, Faraone, Biederman, & Gunawardene, 2003).

It is possible, however, that stimulant medication may actually exacerbate the risk of tobacco use. ADHD is a risk factor for early initiation of tobacco use (Milberger, Biederman, Faraone, Chen, & Jones, 1997). Stimulant medications increase tobacco-smoking behavior in healthy adults (e.g., Henningfield & Griffiths, 1981; Rush et al., 2005). Among ADHD patients who are treated effectively with stimulants, tobacco-smoking rates are higher than among than those who are not taking prescription stimulants (Lambert & Hartsough, 1998). It is possible that the severity of ADHD symptoms was higher among those receiving stimulant medications in this study, so additional research is required to determine whether stimulant medication use alters the risk of tobacco smoking among individuals with ADHD.

Despite escalating use of stimulant medications, few clinical studies have examined their potential teratogenic effects. Several studies examining the potential teratogenic effects of nonmedical stimulant use (cocaine, methamphetamine) have been conducted and found growth restrictive effects on the fetus (Smith et al., 2006).

## Opiates

The examination of the relationship between opiate use and birth outcomes is complicated by studies concerns including absence of biological measures of drug use; and lack of control for impact of other drug use and psychosocial variables including prenatal care and poverty. In studies that have included controls for at least some of these variables the findings are mixed. For example, Zuckerman et al. (1989) controlled for use of tobacco, alcohol, marijuana, and cocaine and did not find a relationship between opiate use and fetal growth parameters. Hulse, Milne, English, and Holman (1997) also observed no difference in head circumference or birth link in opiate-exposed infants when controlling for tobacco, prenatal care, and maternal education. Similarly Messinger et al. (2004) reported no growth factor differences associated with maternal opiate exposure when controlling for prenatal care, medical risk, and other drug use. In contrast Jacobson et al. (1994) found a decrease in infant head circumference when controlling for other drug use, prepregnancy weight, and prenatal care.

We are currently in the midst of an epidemic of opioid misuse in adolescents (Sung, Richter, Vaughan, Johnson, & Thom, 2005) with dramatically increased rates of use and emergency department visits related to opiate misuse. Those adolescents who misuse opiates are more likely to be engaged in delinquent activity and involved in the mental health system, and over one-third have been engaged in selling illicit drugs (Sung et al., 2005). Kraus (1981) observed that there were associations between type of drug and offense. For example opiate users had higher numbers of criminal convictions. While there is limited information on adolescents addicted to heroin there is evidence that they are delinquent and are likely abusing multiple substances (Hopfer, Mikulich, & Crowley, 2000). Simonds (1980) reported that amphetamine, cocaine, barbiturates, benzodiazepine, and PCP use was associated with person offenses. Further they reported that many of the delinquents reported taking drugs to give them courage to commit the act of violence.

## Inhalants

Inhalant use is one of the most prevalent forms of adolescent substance abuse (Wu & Ringwalt, 2006), with 17.3% of eighth graders reporting inhalant use in 2004 (Johnston, O'Malley, Bachman, & Schulenberg, 2004) and inhalants being the most commonly used illicit drug among adolescents ages 12 and 13, with approximately 3.4% of 12-year-olds and 4.8% of 13-year-olds using the drug in the past year (SAMHSA, 2008). The most frequent categories of inhalants used by adolescents ages 12–17 included glue, shoe polish, and toluene (29.6%), gasoline or lighter fluid (25.7%), spray paint (24.4%), and nitrous oxide or whippets (22.7%) (SAMHSA, 2008).

The effects of inhalants are quite rapid and include effects that resemble alcohol intoxication (e.g., slurred speech, euphoria, impaired motor coordination) (Rosenberg & Sharp, 1997). Prenatal exposure syndromes resulting from inhalant use during pregnancy cannot be readily distinguished from fetal alcohol syndrome primarily because the two substances are typically abused concomitantly (Rosenberg & Sharp, 1997).

Inhalant use is also correlated with delinquent behavior and other drug use in adolescents. Inhalant users ages 12 and 13 were twice as likely to have been in a serious fight in the past year and six times as likely to have stolen an item valued at $50 or more (SAMHSA, 2005b). In addition, 35% of 12- and 13-year-old inhalant users report using at least one other illicit drug, compared to 7.5% of their noninhalant using counterparts (SAMHSA, 2005b). Youth in the criminal justice system are at very high risk for inhalant abuse (Howard & Jenson, 1999). Lifetime inhalant use estimates range from 34 to 40% of adolescents in residential rehabilitation facilities and those on probation (Howard, Balster, Cottler, Wu, & Vaughn, 2008; Howard & Jenson, 1999). In a recent study, approximately 20% of adolescents residing in a residential rehabilitation facility met DSM-IV abuse criteria for inhalants, while an additional 29% met inhalant abuse criteria (Howard & Perron, 2009). There have also been reports of inhalant withdrawal, with 11% of inhalant-using adolescents reporting this symptom (Ridenour, Bray, & Cottler, 2007).

Inhalant use is correlated with other illicit drug use. Adolescents using inhalants prior to age 16 were nine times as likely to use heroin by age 32 (Johnson, Schütz, Anthony, & Ensminger, 1995) and those using inhalants prior to age 14 were twice as likely to use opiates by early adulthood (Storr, Westergaard, & Anthony, 2005). In addition, adults with inhalant-use histories were three times more likely to be intravenous drug users (Dinwiddie, Reich, & Cloninger, 1991).

## Implications for Treatment of the Addicted Brain

### Screen for Substance Abuse and Mental Health Issues in Adolescents in Juvenile Justice Settings

A variety of substance-abuse screening tools have been tried in Juvenile Justice settings. Several large states have also developed their own systems that are integrated into their databases. The Reclaiming Futures Project sites have tried various instruments which were found to be acceptable (Bidmon et al., 2007). All of these screening tools were relatively easy to use. The CRAFFT is a 6-item questionnaire developed at Children's Hospital in Boston (www.ceasar-boston.org). The GAIN SS is a 20 = item questionnaire developed by Chestnut Health Systems (www.chestnut.org). The MAYSI-2 is a 52-item screening instrument developed at the University of Massachusetts used in juvenile justice settings for a variety of mental health issues including substance use (http://www.prpress.com/books/maysi2.html).

## Nonmedical Intervention for Drug Dependence in Adolescents

In the last decade much more research has been focused on effective treatment methods for adolescent substance abuse. Interventions that seem to be most promising revolve around several areas. Family involvement in the treatment process is effective (Henggeler, Clingempeel, Brondino, & Pickrel, 2002). In addition, motivational enhancement and cognitive behavioral approaches are ingredients that are effective (Webb, Burleson, & Ungemack, 2002). Since 2002, The Robert Wood Johnson Foundation has funded the Reclaiming Futures Initiative to effect system change in order to develop more effective treatment for adolescents involved in the Justice System. There are currently 23 sites in the United States involved in the project. The model has six steps: Initial Screening, Initial Assessment, Service Coordination between agencies and the family, Initiation of Treatment (as soon as possible), developing Engagement (more than three visits monthly assists retention), and Completion of treatment (with consequent increased community involvement) (Dishongh et al., 2007).

## Medical Intervention for Comorbid Substance Abuse and Mental Health Issues

While it is well recognized that substance abuse and mental health issues are comorbid in general and in particular in adolescents in the juvenile justice system they are no well-accepted algorithms for treatment. There are several overriding principles for clinicians however. The first is that patient safety is foremost. Any concerns about therapeutic drugs potentiating the drug of abuse have to be considered. Second, drug screening and biological monitoring for drugs of abuse have to be a central part of clinical management (Winters, 1999). Third, the interaction of psychotropics and risk for drug abuse is complex. For example in the case of ADHD and tobacco smoking, there is evidence that stimulants decrease overall risk for drug abuse except in the case of tobacco smoking. Whether or not stimulants increase smoking behaviors in adolescents with ADHD is still under consideration.

Developmental issues also impact on therapeutic interventions. For example, in addition to affecting the development of dependence, the age of initial alcohol use may have an impact on response to treatment. Ondansetron decreases alcohol craving by reducing serotonin receptor activity. Subjects with onset of alcohol dependence before the age of 25 years were found to have a more robust therapeutic response to ondansetron than those exhibiting alcohol-related problems at a later age (Johnson et al., 2000).

Table 3.1 presents a summary of disorders that are commonly comorbid with substance abuse in addition to pharmacological treatment strategies. It is important to emphasize that treating psychiatric disorders alone has not been associated with significant improvement in substance use and that psychiatric medications are not the first line of treatment but should be considered part of treatment (Riggs, Hall, Mikulich-Gilbertson, Lohman, & Kayser, 2004). How these pharmacologic interventions particularly apply to the delinquent with comorbid psychiatric disorders

**Table 3.1** Psychiatric disorders, substance use and promising pharmacological treatment strategies (Leukefeld, Smiley McDonald, Stoops, Reed, & Martin, 2005)

| Comorbidity | Medication | Impact on psychiatric symptoms | Changes in substance use |
|---|---|---|---|
| **Mood disorders** | | | |
| Bipolar, aggression | Lithium | Stabilizes mania | Decreases substance abuse (Geller et al., 1998) |
| Major depression, dysthymia | Fluoxetine SSRIs | Decreases depression, good safety profile (Deas, Randall, Roberts, & Anton, 2000; Deas & Thomas, 2001; Riggs, Mikulich, Coffman, & Crowley, 1997; Riggs et al., 2007) | |
| **Anxiety** | | | |
| PTSD | SSRIs | Assists with sleep difficulties, depressive symptoms, intrusive memories, hyperarousal (March & Wells, 2002) | |
| Social anxiety | SSRIs Paxil | Decreases social anxiety in adults (Liappas, Paparrigopoulos, Tzavellas, & Christodoulou, 2003; Randall et al., 2001) | |
| **Disruptive disorders** | | | |
| ADHD | Pemoline | Pemoline has been associated with decreased ADHD symptoms at the same level as adolescents who were not abusing stimulants but with no accompanying decrease in substance use<br>Note: Concerns regarding liver toxicity require careful selection of patients and liver enzyme monitoring (Riggs, Mikulich, & Hall, 2001; Riggs, Thompson, Mikulich, Whitmore, & Crowley, 1996; Safer, Zito, & Gardner, 2001) | None |
| ADHD | Stimulants | Stimulant use (methylphenidate, dexedrine short and long acting) are associated with decreases in inattention and impulsivity | Decreased use of all substance abuse other than nicotine. Increases nicotine use in laboratory setting (Henningfield & Griffiths, 1981; Wilens et al., 2003) |
| ADHD + Depression | Bupropion | Since bupropion is effective for both depression and ADHD it may be considered when the disorders occur together. Has good safety profile in substance users. There is an increased risk for seizure in patients with bulimia and bulimia is associated with alcohol abuse<br>Note: Tricyclics are contraindicated in adolescents using substances because of potential for interactions with drugs of abuse and lethality associated with a tricyclic overdose. (Riggs & Davies, 2002; Riggs, Leon, Mikulich, & Pottle, 1998; Wilens et al., 1997) | |
| Bulimia nervosa | Antidepressants | Antidepressants (tricyclic), serotonergic uptake inhibitors, monoamine oxidase inhibitors were effective in decreasing bulimia nervosa (Ahu & Walsh, 2002; Bacaltchuk & Hay, 2003) | |
| CD | Stimulants | Decreases CD symptoms (Klein et al., 1997) | |

**Table 3.2** Drugs of abuse: medically significant acute effects and withdrawal symptoms (Friedman, Hyman, Roberts, & Fleming, 1996; Leukefeld et al., 2005)

| Drug | Pharmacological effects | Withdrawal symptoms | Management |
|---|---|---|---|
| Nicotine | Euphoria, increased heart rate, and blood pressure, weak analgesia, nausea and vomiting, increased attention | Anxiety, irritability, decreased concentration, restlessness, hunger, tremor, heart racing, sweating, craving, insomnia, drowsiness, headaches, depression, digestive disturbances | NRT, bupropion |
| Alcohol/sedative hypnotics | 100 mg/ml blood alcohol level (BAL): mild sedation and intoxication (slurred speech; staggering gait; slowed reflexes)<br>100–200 mg/ml: impairment of visual-motor skills and integration of sensory information<br>>200 mg/ml: severe intoxication and sedation<br>>450 mg/ml: stupor and coma<br>Personality change (belligerence, irritability, dysphoria, social disinhibition) | *Acute*: Increased heart rate and blood pressure, agitation, tremors, increased reflexes, auditory and visual hallucinations<br>12–14 hours: seizures (infrequent)<br>72–96 hours: delirium tremens with confusion, disorientation, severe agitation, visual and tactile hallucinations, severe autonomic hyperactivity with hyperthermia, medical emergency requiring hospitalization | Withdrawal: hospitalization is often required; sedative-hypnotics such as diazepam (Valium); thiamine, and multivitamins<br>*Major health risk*: delirium tremens: hospitalization as this may be life threatening |
| Marijuana | Euphoria, relaxation, and disinhibition; impaired problem-solving skills and difficulty organizing thoughts, and conversing; impaired cognitive function and motor coordination | Irritability, restlessness, nervousness, loss of appetite, weight loss, insomnia, chills, tremors, and sleep disturbance<br>Amotivational syndrome; depression in some | |
| Stimulants (Amphetamines) | Restlessness, dizziness, tremor, irritability, insomnia, weakness, headache, chills, flushing, excessive sweating, palpitations, increased blood pressure and heart rate, anorexia, nausea and vomiting, diarrhea<br>Acute toxicity: paranoid symptoms and panic, hyperactive reflexes, hyperthermia, and seizures | Crash (9 hours to 4 days): acute sadness leading to agitation, depression, and drug craving followed by fatigue and exhaustion<br>Withdrawal (1–10 weeks): less drug craving, more normal sleep, depressed or anxious mood<br>Extinction (indefinite): mood normalizes but episodic drug craving persists, especially with certain cues (i.e., alcohol use) | Intoxication: support and benzodiazepines such as diazepam (Valium) to calm; if psychotic and agitated neuroleptics may be indicated. Seizures are also treated with benzodiazepines<br>Chronic use: hospitalization may be required because of withdrawal depression |
| Cocaine | (See stimulants) More risk for cardiac complications | (See stimulants) | (See stimulants)<br>*Major health risk*: hospitalization for medical conditions if necessary |
| Opiates | Decreased respirations, slow heart rate, decrease in blood pressure, death | Increased heart rate and blood pressure, muscle and stomach cramps, nausea and vomiting | Methadone, clonidine for acute withdrawal<br>Narcotic antagonist such as naloxone for acute overdose |
| **Drugs of abuse without withdrawal symptoms** | | | |
| Inhalants (glues, aerosols, solvents) | Disinihibition, disorientation, dizziness, headache, red watery eyes, respiratory problems<br>High dose: confusion, impaired judgment, memory difficulties, seizure, coma, slowed heart rate<br>*Major health risk*: sudden death (either via cardiopulmonary arrest or respiratory depression). Acute toxicity to brain, heart, liver, and kidneys | | Acute effects: delirium requiring hospitalization with supportive care. Liver, renal, and cardiac function need to be monitored |

has received limited attention and primarily by Riggs (2003).

## Medical Intervention for Acute Intoxication or Acute Withdrawal

Acute drug effects and withdrawal have not received rigorous laboratory assessments in adolescents. Although drug withdrawal symptoms may be less frequent in adolescents when compared to chronic adult users, withdrawal symptoms and syndromes should be assessed and treated in the same way as recommended for adults (Bukstein, 1997). An exception may be nicotine dependence since there is no evidence that nicotine substitution is effective in maintaining abstinence among adolescent smokers (Hanson, Allen, Jensen, & Hatsukami, 2003). However, the use of adolescent nicotine substitution is in the early stages of evaluation. Table 3.2 presents a summary of acute effects and withdrawal symptoms associated with drugs of abuse.

**Conclusion**

The addicted brain has multiple influences on adolescents who end up in the juvenile justice system. Prenatal exposure leads to altered brain function that increases the risk for impulsivity and poor judgment and future drug use which further exacerbates impulsivity and poor judgment. Having an addicted parent and the associated malfunction of parenting increases the chances that the adolescent will end up in the juvenile justice system. Acute drug effects and drug withdrawal can impair impulsivity and judgment. Generally, as adolescents get more involved with drug usage, they begin to get involved with a peer group that has poor impulse control and is more likely to get into legal difficulty. Further, adolescents can engage in illegal activity to support their drug habit.

Prenatal exposure to drugs does have implications for the juvenile justice system. Prenatal exposure to tobacco, alcohol, and marijuana increases the risk for use of each of these drugs in adolescents. In addition, there is evidence for biological changes in brain anatomy and behavior associated with prenatal drug exposure. Prenatal exposure to tobacco can result in impulsiveness, oppositional behavior, and learning difficulties in children which persist into adolescence. Prenatal exposure to alcohol is associated with decreased brain volumes, learning difficulties, and the more serious issues of fetal alcohol syndrome and fetal alcohol effects. Prenatal exposure to marijuana is associated with long-term impaired visual analysis and impulsivity. Prenatal methamphetamine use is associated with smaller corpus striatum volumes and attention problems in children but long-term effects are unclear.

Drug usage during adolescence is clearly relevant to the juvenile justice system. Heavy use of caffeine is associated with other drug use and problematic behavior. Youth withdrawing from caffeine score lower on tests of vigilance. Alcohol and marijuana are two of the drugs most commonly used by adolescents in the juvenile justice system. Alcohol use is associated with criminal behavior and learning difficulties while marijuana use is associated with criminal behavior and violence. Cocaine use and inhalant use are both associated with use of other drugs, criminal behavior, and violence. Opiate use is also associated with criminal behavior.

Addressing substance abuse issues must be a priority for the juvenile justice system. Reducing some of the causes of poor impulse control, learning difficulties, and violent behavior will improve public safety and improve the lives of youth caught up in a criminal lifestyle.

## References

Ahu, A. J., & Walsh, B. T. (2002). Pharmacologic treatment of eating disorders. *Canadian Journal of Psychiatry, 47*, 227–234.

Arria, A. M., Caldeira, K. M., O'Grady, K. E., Vincent, K. B., Johnson, E. P., & Wish, E. D. (2008). Nonmedical use of prescription stimulants among college students:

Associations with attention-deficit-hyperactivity disorder and polydrug use. *Pharmacotherapy, 28*(2), 156–169.

Arria, A., Derauf, C., La Gasse, L., Grant, P., Shah, R., Smith, L., et al. (2006a). Methamphetamine and substance abuse during pregnancy: Preliminary estimates from the infant development, environment and lifestyle (IDEAL) study. *Maternal and Child Health Journal, 10*(3), 293–302.

Arria, A., Derauf, C., La Gasse, L., Grant, P., Shah, R., Smith, L., et al. (2006b). The infant development, environment and lifestyle study: Effects of prenatal methamphetamine exposure, polydrug exposure and poverty on intrauterine growth. *Pediatrics, 118*(3), 1149–1156.

Arseneault, L., Moffitt, T. E., Caspi, A., Taylor, P. J., & Silva, P. A. (2000). Mental disorders and violence in a total birth cohort: Results from the Dunedin study. *Archives of General Psychiatry, 57*, 979–986.

Avants, B. B., Hurt, H., Giannetta, J. M., Epstein, C. L., Shera, D. M., Rao, H., et al. (2007). Effects of heavy in utero cocaine exposure on adolescent caudate morphology. *Pediatric Neurology, 37*(4), 275–279.

Bacaltchuk, J., & Hay, P. (2003). Antidepressants versus placebo for people with bulimia nervosa. *Cochrane Database System Review, 4*, CD003391.

Bada, H. S., Das, A., Bauer, C. R., Shankaran, S., Lester, B. M., Gard, C. C., et al. (2005). Low birth weight and preterm births: Etiologic fraction attributable to prenatal drug exposure. *Journal of Perinatology, 25*(10), 631–637.

Berman, S., O'Neill, J., Fears, S., Bartzokis, G., & London, E. D. (2008). Abuse of amphetamines and structural abnormalities in the brain. *Annals of the New York Academy of Science, 1141*, 195–220.

Bernstein, G. A., Carroll, M. E., Dean, N. W., Crosby, R. D., Perwien, A. R., & Benowitz, N. L. (1998). Caffeine withdrawal in normal school-age children. *Journal of the American Academy of Child and Adolescent Psychiatry, 37*, 858–865.

Bertrand, J., Floyd, R. L., Weber, M. K., O'Connor, M., Riley, E. P., Johnson, K. A., et al. (2004). *National task force on FAS/FAE. Fetal alcohol syndrome: Guidelines for referral and diagnosis*. Atlanta, GA: Centers for Disease Control and Prevention.

Bidmon, J., Cadue, P. Y. E., Enniss, K., Heffron, W. M., Moffitt, L., Nguyen, T., et al. (2007). *Juvenile probation officers call for a new response to teen drug and alcohol use and dependency*. A Reclaiming Futures National Fellowship report. Portland, OR: Reclaiming Futures National Program Office, Portland State University.

Biederman, J., Wilens, T., Mick, E., Faraone, S. V., Weber, W., Curtis, S., et al. (1997). Is ADHD a risk factor for psychoactive substance use disorders? Findings from a four-year prospective follow-up study. *Journal of the American Academy Child Adolescent Psychiatry, 36*(1), 21–29.

Brown, S. A., & Tapert, S. F. (2004). Adolescence and the trajectory of alcohol use: Basic to clinical studies. *Annals of the New York Academy of Sciences, 1021*, 234–244.

Bukstein, O. (1997). Practice parameters for the assessment and treatment of children and adolescents with substance use disorders. *Journal of the America Academy of Child and Adolescent Psychiatry, 36*(10 Suppl), 140S–156S.

Caspi, A., Moffitt, T. E., Newman, D. L., & Silva, P. A. (1996). Behavioral observations at age 3 years predict adult psychiatric disorders: Longitudinal evidence from a birth cohort. *Archives of General Psychiatry, 53*, 1033–1030.

Centers for Disease Control & Prevention. (2002). *PRAMS surveillance report*. Retrieved December 11, 2007, from http://www.cdc.gov/prams/2002PRAMSSurvReport/

Chabrol, H., & Saint-Martin, C. (2009). Cannabis use and delinquent behaviors in high-school students. *Addictive Behaviors, 34*, 187–189.

Chaffin, M., Kelleher, K., & Hollenberg, J. (1996). Onset of physical abuse and neglect: Psychiatric, substance abuse, and social risk factors from prospective community data. *Child Abuse & Neglect, 20*, 191–203.

Chang, L., Alicata, D., Ernst, T., & Volkow, N. (2007). Structural and metabolic brain changes in the striatum associated with methamphetamine abuse. *Addiction, 102*(Supplement 1), 16–32.

Chang, L., Smith, L. M., Lo Presti, C., Yonekura, M. L., Kuo, J., Walot, I., et al. (2003). Smaller subcortical volume and cognitive deficits in children with prenatal methamphetamine exposure. *Psychiatry Resources, 132*(2), 95–106.

Clingempeel, W. G., Henggeler, S. W., Pickrel, S. G., & Brondino, M. J. (2005). Beyond treatment effects: Predicting emerging adult alcohol and marijuana use among substance-abusing delinquents. *American Journal of Orthopsychiatry, 75*, 540–552.

Cornelius, M. D., Leech, S. L., Goldschmidt, L., & Day, N. L. (2000). Prenatal tobacco exposure: Is it a risk factor for early tobacco experimentation? *Nicotine and Tobacco Research, 2*(1), 45–52.

Cuellar, A. E., McReynolds, L. S., & Wasserman, G. A. (2006). A cure for crime: Can mental health treatment diversion reduce crime among youth? *Journal of Policy Analysis and Management, 25*(1), 197–214.

D'Amico, E. J., Edelen, M. O., Miles, J. N., & Morral, A. R. (2007). The longitudinal association between substance use and delinquency among high-risk youth. *Drug and Alcohol Dependence, 93*(1–2), 85–92.

Day, N. L., Goldschmidt, L., & Thomas, C. A. (2006). Prenatal marijuana exposure contributes to the prediction of marijuana use at age 14. *Addiction, 101*, 1313–1322.

Deas, D., Randall, C. L., Roberts, J. S., & Anton, R. F. (2000). A double-blind, placebo-controlled trial of sertraline in depressed adolescent alcoholics: A pilot study. *Human Psychopharmaocology, 15*(6), 461–469.

Deas, D., & Thomas, S. E. (2001). An overview of controlled studies of adolescent substance abuse treatment. *American Journal on Addictions, 10*(2), 178–189.

De Bellis, M. D., Clark, D. B., Beers, S. R., Soloff, P. H., Boring, A. M., Hall, J., et al. (2001). Hippocampal volume in adolescent-onset alcohol use disorders. *American Journal of Psychiatry, 158*(5), 820–821.

De Bellis, M. D., Narasimhan, A., Thatcher, D. L., Keshaven, M. S., Soloff, P., & Clark, D. B. (2005). Prefrontal cortex, thalamus, and cerebellar volumes in adolescents and young adults with adolescent-onset alcohol use disorders and comorbid mental disorders. *Alcoholism, Clinical and Experimental Research, 29*(9), 1590–1600.

Dembo, R., Washburn, M., Wish, E. D., Schmeidler, J., Getreu, A., Berry, E., et al. (1987). Further examination of the association between heavy marijuana use and crime among youths entering a juvenile detention center. *Journal of Psychoactive Drugs, 19*, 361–373.

Dembo, R., Washburn, M., Wish, E. D., Yeung, H., Getreu, A., Berry, E., et al. (1987). Heavy marijuana use and crime among youths entering a juvenile detention center. *Journal of Psychoactive Drugs, 19*, 47–56.

Dembo, R., Williams, L., Wish, E. D., Berry, E., Getreu, A., Washburn, M., et al. (1990). Examination of the relationships among drug use, emotional/psychological problems, and crime among youths entering a juvenile detention center. *The International Journal of the Addictions, 25*, 1301–1340.

Dennis, M. L., Dawoud-Noursi, S., Muck, R. D., & McDermett, M. (2002). The need for developing and evaluating adolescent treatment models. In S. J. Stevens & A. A. Morat (Eds.), *Adolescent substance abuse treatment in the United States: Exemplary models from a national evaluation study* (pp. 3–36). Binghamton, NY: Haworth Press.

DiFranza, J. R., Savageau, J. A., Fletcher, K., O'Loughlin, J., Pbert, L., Ockene, J., et al. (2007). Symptoms of tobacco dependence after brief intermittent use: The development and assessment of nicotine dependence in youth-2 study. *Archives of Pediatric and Adolescent Medicine, 161*, 704–710.

Dinwiddie, S. H., Reich, T., & Cloninger, C. R. (1991). Solvent use as a precursor to intravenous drug abuse. *Comprehensive Psychiatry, 32*(2), 133–140.

Dishongh, D., Eltman, C., Goris, J., Landry, S., Manov, B., Noto, J., et al. (2007). *Improved care for teens in trouble with drugs, alcohol, and crime: Reclaiming Futures Treatment Providers advocate for change.* A Reclaiming Futures National Fellowship report. Portland, OR: Reclaiming Futures National Program Office, Portland State University.

Dixon, D. R., Kurtz, P. F., & Chin, M. D. (2008). A systematic review of challenging behaviors in children exposed prenatally to substances of abuse. *Research in Developmental Disabilities, 29*(6), 483–502.

Dodge, K., Price, J., Bachorowski, J., & Newman, J. (1990). Hostile attributional biases in severely aggressive adolescents. *Journal of Abnormal Psychology, 99*, 385–392.

Drapela, L. A., & Mosher, C. (2007). The conditional effect of *parental drug use* on *parental* attachment and adolescent *drug use*: Social control and social development model perspectives. *Journal of Child & Adolescent Substance Abuse, 16*, 63–87.

Edwards, E. P., Eiden, R. D., & Leonard, K. E. (2004). Impact of fathers' alcoholism and associated risk factors on parent-infant attachment stability from 12 to 18 months. *Infant Mental Health Journal, 25*, 556–579.

Eskenazi, B., & Castorina, R. (1999). Association of prenatal maternal or postnatal environmental tobacco smoke exposure and neurodevelopmental and behavioral problems in children. *Environmental Health Perspectives, 107*, 991–1000.

Evans, C., Mezey, G., & Ehlers, A. (2009). Amnesia for violent crime among young offenders. *Journal of Forensic Psychiatry Psychology, 20*(1), 85–106.

Farrington, D. P. (1989). Early predictors of adolescent aggression and adult violence. *Violence and Victims, 4*, 79–100.

Fellitti, V. J., Anda, R. F., Nordenberg, D., Williamson, D. F., Spitz, A. M., Edwards, V., et al. (1998). Relationship of childhood abuse and household dysfunction to many of the leading causes of death in adults: The Adverse Childhood Experiences (ACE) study. *American Journal of Preventative Medicine, 14*(4), 245–258.

Fergusson, D. M., Boden, J. M., & Horwood, L. J. (2008). The developmental antecedents of illicit drug use: Evidence from a 25-year longitudinal study. *Drug and Alcohol Dependence, 96*(1–2), 165–177.

Fried, P. A., & Smith, A. M. (2001). A literature review of the consequences of prenatal marihuana exposure: An emerging theme of a deficiency in aspects of executive function. *Neurotoxicology and Teratology, 23*, 1–11.

Fried, P. A., & Watkinson, B. (2001). Differential effects on facets of attention in adolescents prenatally exposed to cigarettes and marihuana. *Neurotoxicology and Teratology, 23*, 421–430.

Fried, P. A., Watkinson, B., & Gray, R. (2003). Differential effects on cognitive functioning in 13- to 16-year olds prenatally exposed to cigarettes and marihuana. *Neurotoxicology and Teratology, 25*, 427–436.

Friedman, L., Hyman, S. E., Roberts, D. H., & Fleming, N. F. (1996). *Source book of substance abuse and addiction*. Balitmore, MD: Lippincott Williams & Wilkins.

Fritz, M. V., Wiklund, G., Koposov, R. A., af Klinteberg, B., & Ruchkin, V. V. (2008). Psychopathy and violence in juvenile delinquents: What are the associated factors? *International Journal of Law and Psychiatry, 31*, 272–279.

Geller, B., Cooper, T. B., Sun, K., Zimerman, B., Frazier, J., Williams, M., et al. (1998). Double-blind and placebo-controlled study of lithium for adolescent bipolar disorders with secondary substance dependency. *Journal of the American Academy of Child and Adolescent Psychiatry, 37*(2), 171–178.

Glantz, M. D., & Chambers, J. C. (2006). Prenatal drug exposure effects on subsequent vulnerability to drug abuse. *Development and Psychopathology, 18*, 893–922.

Goldschmidt, L., Day, N. L., & Richardson, G. A. (2000). Effects of prenatal marijuana exposure on child behavior problems at age 10. *Neurobehavioral Toxicology, 22*, 325–336.

Goodman, G., Hans, S. L., & Cox, S. M. (1999). Attachment behavior and its antecedents in offspring born to methadone-maintained women. *Journal of Clinical Child Psychology, 28*, 58–69.

Griffiths, R. R., & Mumford, G. K. (1995). Caffeine – A drug of abuse? In F. E. Bloom & D. J. Kupfer (Eds.), *Psychopharmacology: The fourth generation of progress* (pp. 535–580). New York: Raven Press.

Gudonis, L. C., Giancola, P. R., & Tarter, R. E. (2007). A 3-year longitudinal investigation of the relation between nonintellective cognitive skills and delinquency in adolescent boys with a family history of substance abuse disorder. In H. C. Sentowski (Ed.), *Cognitive disorder research trends* (pp. 183–194). New York: Nova Science Publishers, Inc.

Haller, D. L., & Miles, D. R. (2003). Victimization and perpetration among perinatal substance abusers. *Journal of Interpersonal Violence, 18*, 760–780.

Hanson, K., Allen, S., Jensen, S., & Hatsukami, D. (2003). Treatment of adolescent smokers with the nicotine patch. *Nicotine and Tobacco Research, 5*(4), 515–526.

Hays, R. D., & Ellickson, P. L. (1996). Associations between drug use and deviant behavior in teenagers. *Addictive Behaviors, 21*, 291–302.

Helstrom, A., Bryan, A., Hutchison, K., Riggs, P. D., & Blechman, E. A. (2004). Tobacco and alcohol use for the association between externalizing behavior and illicit drug use among delinquent adolescents. *Prevention Science, 5*(4), 267–277.

Henggeler, S. W., Clingempeel, W. G., Brondino, M. J., & Pickrel, S. G. (2002). Four-year follow-up of multisystemic therapy with substance-abusing and substance-dependent juvenile offenders. *Journal of American Academy of Child Adolescent Psychiatry, 41*, 868–874.

Henningfield, J. E., & Griffiths, R. R. (1981). Cigarette smoking and subjective response: Effects of d-amphetamine. *Clinical Pharmacology and Therapeutics, 30*, 497–505.

Henry, K. L., & Huizinga, D. H. (2007). Truancy's effect on the onset of drug use among urban adolescents placed at risk. *Journal of Adolescent Health, 40*(4), 358.e9–358.e17.

Hien, D., & Honeyman, T. (2000). A closer look at the drug abuse-maternal aggression link. *Journal of Interpersonal Violence, 15*, 503–522.

Hopfer, C. J., Mikulich, S. K., & Crowley, T. J. (2000). Heroin use among adolescents in treatment for substance use disorders. *Journal of American Academy of Child & Adolescent Psychiatry, 39*(10), 1316–1323.

Howard, M. O., Balster, R. L., Cottler, L. B., Wu, L. T., & Vaughn, M. G. (2008). Inhalant use among incarcerated adolescents in the United States: Prevalence, characteristics, and correlates of use. *Drug and Alcohol Dependence, 93*(3), 197–209.

Howard, M. O., & Jenson, J. M. (1999). Inhalant use among antisocial youth: Prevalence and correlates. *Addictive Behaviors, 24*(1), 59–74.

Howard, M. O., & Perron, B. E. (2009). A survey of inhalant use disorders among delinquent youth: Prevalence, clinical features, and latent structure of DSM-IV diagnostic criteria. *BMC Psychiatry, 8*(9), 8.

Huebner, B. M., & Gustafson, R. (2007). The effect of maternal incarceration on adult offspring involvement in the criminal justice system. *Journal of Criminal Justice, 35*, 283–296.

Hulse, G. K., Milne, E., English, D. R., & Holman, C. D. (1997). The relationship between maternal use of heroin and methadone and infant birth weight. *Addiction, 92*(11), 1571–1579.

Hurt, H., Giannetta, J. M., Korczykowski, M., Hoang, A., Tang, K. Z., Betancourt, L., et al. (2008). Functional magnetic resonance imaging and working memory in adolescents with gestational cocaine exposure. *The Journal of Pediatrics, 152*(3), 371–377.

Jacobson, J. L., Jacobson, S. W., Sokol, R. J., Martier, S. S., Ager, J. W., & Shankaran, S. (1994). Effects of alcohol use, smoking, and illicit drug use on fetal growth in black infants. *Journal of Pediatrics, 124*(5 Pt 1), 757–764.

Johnson, B. A., Roache, J. D., Javors, M. A., DiClemente, C. C., Cloninger, C. R., Prihoda, T. J., et al. (2000). Ondansetron for reduction of drinking among biologically predisposed alcoholic patients: A randomized controlled trial. *Journal of the American Medical Association, 284*(8), 963–971.

Johnson, E. O., Schütz, C. G., Anthony, J. C., & Ensminger, M. E. (1995). Inhalants to heroin: A prospective analysis from adolescence to adulthood. *Drug and Alcohol Dependence, 40*(2), 159–164.

Johnston, L. D., O'Malley, P. M., Bachman, J. G., & Schulenberg, J. E. (2004). *Monitoring the future national results on adolescent drug use: Overview of key findings, 2003* (NIH Publication No. 04-5506). Bethesda, MD: National Institute on Drug Abuse.

Jones, H. E., & Griffiths, R. R. (2003). Oral caffeine maintenance potentiates the reinforcing and stimulant subjective effects of intravenous nicotine in cigarette smokers. *Psychopharmacology, 165*, 280–290.

Kandel, D. B., & Chen, K. (2000). Extent of smoking and nicotine dependence in the United States: 1991–1993. *Nicotine and Tobacco Research, 2*(3), 263–274.

Kandel, D. B., Wu, P., & Davies, M. (1994). Maternal smoking during pregnancy and smoking by adolescent daughters. *American Journal of Public Health, 84*(9), 1407–1413.

Kandel, D. B., Yamaguchi, K., & Chen, K. (1992). Stages of progression in drug involvement from adolescence to adulthood: Further evidence for the gateway theory. *Journal of Studies on Alcohol, 53*(5), 447–457.

Kelly, T. H., Kazura, A. N., Lommel, K. M., Babalonis, S., & Martin, C. A. (2008). A biological/genetic perspective: The addicted brain. In C. G. Leukefeld, T. P. Gullotta, & M. Staton-Tindall (Eds.), *Handbook on the prevention and treatment of substance abuse in adolescence* (pp. 15–43). New York: Springer.

Killen, J. D., Robinson, T. N., Ammerman, S., Hayward, C., Rogers, J., Stone, C., et al. (2004). Randomized clinical trial of the efficacy of bupropion combined with nicotine patch in the treatment of adolescent smokers. *Journal of Consulting and Clinical Psychology, 72*(4), 729–735.

Klasser, G. D., & Epstein, J. (2005). Methamphetamine and its impact on dental care. *Journal of the Canadian Dental Association, 71*(10), 759–762.

Klein, R. G., Abikoff, H., Klass, E., Ganeles, D., Sees, L. M., & Pollack, S. (1997). Clinical efficacy of methlyphenidate in conduct disorder with and without attention deficit hyperactivity disorder. *Archives of General Psychiatry, 54*(12), 1073–1080.

Kolar, A. F., Brown, B. S., Haertzen, C. A., & Michaelson, B. S. (1994). Children of substance abusers: The life experiences of children of opiate addicts in methadone maintenance. *American Journal of Drug & Alcohol Abuse, 20*, 159–171.

Kraus, J. (1981). Juvenile drug abuse and delinquency: Some differential associations. *British Journal of Psychiatry, 139*, 422–430.

Lambert, N. M., & Hartsough, C. S. (1998). Prospective study of tobacco smoking and substance dependencies among samples of ADHD and non-ADHD participants. *Journal of Learning Disabilities, 31*(6), 533–544.

Law, K. L., Stroud, L. R., LaGasse, L. L., Niaura, R., Liu, J., & Lester, B. M. (2003). Smoking during pregnancy and newborn neurobehavior. *Pediatrics, 111*(6 Pt 1), 1318–1223.

Leech, S. L., Richardson, G. A., Goldschmidt, L., & Day, N. L. (1999). Prenatal substance exposure: Effects on attention and impulsivity of 6-year-olds. *Neurotoxicology and Teratology, 21*, 109–118.

Leukefeld, C. G., Smiley McDonald, H., Stoops, W. W., Reed, L., & Martin, C. (2005). Substance misuse and abuse. In T. P. Gullotta & G. Adams (Eds.), *Handbook of adolescent behavioral problems: Evidence-based approaches to prevention and treatment* (pp. 439–465). New York: Kluwer Academic Publishing.

Leukefeld, C. G., Tims, F. M., & Farabee, D. (Eds.). (2002). *Treatment of drug offenders: Policies and issues*. New York: Springer.

Leviton, A. (1992). Behavioral correlates of caffeine consumption by children. *Clinical Pediatrics (Phila), 31*(12), 742–750.

Liappas, J., Paparrigopoulos, T., Tzavellas, E., & Christodoulou, G. (2003). Alcohol detoxification and social anxiety symptoms: A preliminary study of the impact of mirtazapine administration. *Journal of Affective Disorders, 76*, 279–284.

Loeber, R., Farrington, D. P., & Waschbusch, D. A. (1998). Serious and violent juvenile offenders. In R. Loeber & D. P. Farrington (Eds.), *Serious & violent juvenile offenders: Risk factors and successful interventions* (pp. 13–29). Thousand Oaks, CA: Sage.

Luscher, C. (2009). Section V. Drugs that act in the central nervous system. Chapter 32 Drugs of abuse. In B. Katzung (Ed.), *Basic and clinical pharmacology* (11th ed., pp. 511–526). New York: McGraw-Hill. http://online.statref.com/Document.aspx?docAddress=roOzOiyvU9h221OcpN0-A%3d%3d&offset=7&SessionId=10B7B80OHSSTLWPJ. Accessed October 21, 2009.

Magalhães, A., Summavielle, T., Melo, P., Rosa, R., Tavares, M. A., & De Sousa, L. (2006). Prenatal exposure to cocaine and enriched environment: Effects on social interactions. *Annals of the New York Academy of Sciences, 1074*, 620–631.

Maguin, E., & Loeber, R. (1996). Academic performance and delinquency. In M. Tonry (Ed.), *Crime and justice: A review of research* (Vol. 20, pp. 145–264). Chicago: University of Chicago Press.

Magura, S., & Laudet, A. B. (1996). Parental substance abuse and child maltreatment: Review and implications for intervention. *Children and Youth Services Review, 18*, 193–220.

Mannuzza, S., Klein, R. G., & Moulton, J. L. (2008). Lifetime criminality among boys with attention deficit hyperactivity disorder: A prospective follow-up study into adulthood using official arrest records. *Psychiatry Research, 160*, 237–246.

March, J., & Wells, K. (2002). Combining medications and psychotherapy. In J. F. Leckman, L. Schill, & D. S. Charney (Eds.), *Pediatric psychopharmacology: Principles and practice* (pp. 426–444). London: Oxford University Press.

Martin, C. A., Cook, C., Woodring, J. H., Burkhardt, G., Guenthner, G., Omar, H. A., et al. (2008). Caffeine use: Association with nicotine use, aggression, and other psychopathology in psychiatric and pediatric outpatient adolescents. *The Scientific World Journal: Child Health and Human Development, 8*, 512–516.

Mason, W. A., & Windle, M. (2002). Reciprocal relations between adolescent substance use and delinquency: A longitudinal latent variable analysis. *Journal of Abnormal Psychology, 111*(1), 63–76.

Mayer, J., & Filstead, W. J. (1979). The adolescent alcohol involvement scale. An instrument for measuring adolescents' use and misuse of alcohol. *Journal of Studies on Alcohol, 40*(3), 291–300.

McCabe, S. E., Teter, C. J., & Boyd, C. J. (2006). Medical use, illicit use, and diversion of abusable prescription drugs. *Journal of American College of Health, 54*(5), 269–278.

McClelland, G. M., Elkington, K. S., Teplin, L. A., & Abram, K. M. (2004). Multiple substance use disorders in juvenile detainees. *Journal of the American Academy of Child and Adolescent Psychiatry, 43*(10), 1215–1224.

McCloskey, L. A., & Bailey, J. A. (2000). The intergenerational transmission of risk for child sexual abuse. *Journal of Interpersonal Violence, 15*, 1019–1035.

Messinger, D. S., Bauer, C. R., Das, A., Seifer, R., Lester, B. M., Lagasse, L. L., et al. (2004). The maternal lifestyle study: Cognitive, motor, and behavioral outcomes of cocaine-exposed and opiate-exposed infants through three years of age. *Pediatrics, 113*, 1677–1685.

Milberger, S., Biederman, J., Faraone, S. V., Chen, L., & Jones, J. (1997). ADHD is associated with early initiation of cigarette smoking in children and adolescents. *Journal of American Academy of Child & Adolescent Psychiatry, 36*(1), 37–44.

Moeller, F. G., Steinberg, J. L., Petty, F., Fulton, M., Cherek, D. R., Kramer, G., et al. (1994). Serotonin and impulsive/aggressive behavior in cocaine dependent subjects. *Progress in Neuropsychopharmacology and Biological Psychiatry, 18*, 1027–1035.

Molina, B. S., Flory, K., Hinshaw, S. P., Greiner, A. R., Arnold, L. E., Swanson, J. M., et al. (2007). Delinquent behavior and emerging substance use in the MTA at 36 months: Prevalence, course, and treatment effects. *Journal of American Academy of Child & Adolescent Psychiatry, 46*(8), 1028–1040.

National Center on Addiction and Substance Abuse (CASA). (2004). *Criminal neglect: Substance abuse, juvenile justice and the children left behind*. New York: National Center on Addiction and Substance Abuse, Columbia University.

National Center on Addiction and Substance Abuse (CASA). (2005). *National Center on Addiction and Substance Abuse (CASA) Family matters: Substance abuse and the American family*. CASA White Paper, Columbia University, New York. Retrieved March 3, 2008, from http://www.casacolumbia.org/Absolutenm/articlefiles/380-family_matters_report.pdf

National Institute on Alcohol Abuse and Alcoholism. (2004/2005). Alcohol and development in youth – A multidisciplinary overview. *Alcohol Research & Health, 28, 3*.

National Institute on Drug Abuse. (2002). *Methamphetamine abuse and addiction*. Research report series. Rockville, MD: U.S. Department of Health and Human Services, National Institutes of Health, National Institute on Drug Abuse.

Office of Applied Studies. (2003). *The NDSDA report: Children living with substance-abusing or substance-dependent parents*. Washington, DC: SAMHSA.

Office of Applied Studies. (2005). *National Survey on Drug Use and Health report: Methamphetamine use, abuse, and dependence: 2002, 2003, and 2004*. Rockville, MD: Substance Abuse and Mental Health Services Administration (SAMHSA).

Okoli, C. T. C., Kelly, T. H., & Hahn, E. L. (2007). Secondhand smoke and nicotine exposure: A brief review. *Addictive Behaviors, 32*, 1977–1988.

Parks, L., & Jack, M. (2005). *Methamphetamine in Alberta: A focus on children, youth and families*. Alberta Centre for Child, Family and Community Research, Edmonton, Alberta, Canada. Retrieved September 9, 2009, from http://www.research4children.org/public/data/documents/ACF46E.pdf

Porath, A. J., & Fried, P. A. (2005). Effects of prenatal cigarette and marijuana exposure on drug use among offspring. *Neurotoxicology and Teratology, 27*, 267–277.

Poulin, C. (2007). From attention-deficit/hyperactivity disorder to medical stimulant use to the diversion of prescribed stimulants to non-medical stimulant use: Connecting the dots. *Addiction, 102*(5), 740–751.

Putniņŝ, A. L. (2006). Substance use among young offenders: Thrills, bad feelings, or bad behavior? *Substance Use and Misuse, 41*(3), 415–422.

Randall, C. L., Johnson, M. R., Thevos, A. K., Sonne, S. C., Thomas, S. E., Willard, S. L., et al. (2001). Paroxetine for social anxiety and alcohol use in dual-diagnosed patients. *Depression and Anxiety, 14*(4), 255–262.

Rao, H., Wang, J., Giannetta, J., Korczykowski, M., Shera, D., Avants, B. B., et al. (2007). Altered resting cerebral blood flow in adolescents with in utero cocaine exposure revealed by perfusion functional MRI. *Pediatrics, 120*(5), e1245–e1254.

Rebellon, C. J., & Van Gundy, K. (2006). Can social psychological delinquency theory explain the link between marijuana and other illicit drug use? A longitudinal analysis of the gateway hypothesis. *The Journal of Drug Issues, 36*, 515–539.

Ricci, L. A., Grimes, J. M., & Melloni, R. H., Jr. (2004). Serotonin Type 3 receptors modulate the aggression-stimulating effects of adolescent cocaine exposure in Syrian hamsters (Mesocricetus auratus). *Behavioral Neuroscience, 118*, 1097–1110.

Ridenour, T. A., Bray, B. C., & Cottler, L. B. (2007). Reliability of use, abuse, and dependence of four types of inhalants in adolescents and young adults. *Drug and Alcohol Dependence, 91*(1), 40–49.

Riggs, P. D. (2003). Treating adolescents for substance abuse and comorbid psychiatric disorders. *Scientific & Practice Perspectives, 2*(1), 18–29.

Riggs, P. D., & Davies, R. D. (2002). A clinical approach to integrating treatment for adolescent depression and substance abuse. *Journal of the American Academy of Child and Adolescent Psychiatry, 41*(10), 1253–1255.

Riggs, P. D., Hall, S. K., Mikulich-Gilbertson, S. K., Lohman, M., & Kayser, A. (2004). A randomized controlled trial of pemoline for attention-deficit/hyperactivity disorder in substance-abusing adolescents. *Journal of the American Academy of Child and Adolescent Psychiatry, 43*(4), 420–429.

Riggs, P. D., Leon, S. L., Mikulich, S. K., & Pottle, L. C. (1998). An open trial of bupropion for ADHD in adolescents with substance use disorders and conduct disorder. *Journal of the American Academy of Child and Adolescent Psychiatry, 37*(12), 1271–1278.

Riggs, P. D., Mikulich, S. K., Coffman, L. M., & Crowley, T. J. (1997). Fluoxetine in drug-dependent delinquents with major depression: An open trial. *Journal of Child and Adolescent Psychopharmacology, 7*(2), 87–95.

Riggs, P. D., Mikulich, S. K., & Hall, S. (2001). *Effects of Pemoline on ADHD, antisocial behaviors and substance use in adolescents with conduct disorder and substance use disorder*. Proceedings of the 63rd annual scientific meeting of the College on Problems of Drug Dependence. Rockville, MD: National Institute on Drug Abuse.

Riggs, P. D., Mikulich-Gilbertson, S. K., Davies, R. D., Lohman, M., Klein, C., & Stover, S. K. (2007). A randomized controlled trial of fluoxetine and cognitive behavioral therapy in adolescents with major depression, behavior problems, and substance use disorders. *Archives of Pediatric and Adolescent Medicine, 161*(11), 1026–1034.

Riggs, P. D., Thompson, L. L., Mikulich, S. K., Whitmore, E. A., & Crowley, T. J. (1996). An open trial of pemoline in drug-dependent delinquents with attention-deficit hyperactivity disorder. *Journal of the American Academy of Child and Adolescent Psychiatry, 35*(18), 1018–1024.

Rosenberg, N. L., & Sharp, C. W. (1997). Solvent toxicity: A neurological focus. *Substance Use & Misuse, 32*(12 & 13), 1859–1864.

*Royal Canadian Mounted Police K Division: Methamphetamine Strategy*. (2005). Edmonton, Alberta, Canada. Retrieved September 11, 2009, from http://www.rcmp-grc.gc.ca/ab/prog_serv/meth_e.htm

Rush, C. R., Higgins, S. T., Vansickel, A. R., Stoops, W. W., Lile, J. A., & Glaser, P. E. (2005). Methlyphenidate increases cigarette smoking. *Psychopharmacology (Berl), 181*(4), 781–789.

Safer, D. J., Zito, J. M., & Gardner, J. F. (2001). Pemoline hepatotoxicity and post marketing surveillance. *Journal of the American Academy of Child and Adolescent Psychiatry, 40*(6), 622–629.

Schempf, A. H. (2007). Illicit drug use and neonatal outcomes: A critical review. *Obstetrical and Gynecological Survey, 62*(11), 749–757.

Schempf, A. H., & Strobino, D. M. (2008). Illicit drug use and adverse birth outcomes: Is it drugs or context? *Journal of Urban Health, 85*(6), 858–873.

Scott, P., Fleming, M., Bennett, K., & Graves, C. (2005). Methamphetamine use during pregnancy. *American Journal of Obstetrics and Gynecology, 193*(6 Pt 1), 587.

Sher, L. (2006). Functional magnetic resonance imaging studies of neurocognitve effects of alcohol use on adolescents and young adults. *International Journal of Adolescent Medicine and Health, 18*(1), 3–7.

Simonds, J. R. (1980). Specific drug use and violence in delinquent boys. *American Journal of Drug and Alcohol Abuse, 7*(3 & 4), 305–322.

Singer, L. T., Arendt, R., Minnes, S., Farkas, K., Salvator, A., Kirchner, H. L., et al. (2002). Cognitive and motor outcomes of cocaine-exposed infants. *Journal of the American Medical Association, 287*(15), 1952–1960.

Singer, L. T., Minnes, S., Short, E., Arendt, R., Farkas, K., Lewis, B., et al. (2004). Cognitive outcomes of preschool children with prenatal cocaine exposure. *Journal of the American Medical Association, 291*(20), 2448–2456.

Smith, A. M., Fried, P. A., Hogan, M. J., & Cameron, I. (2004). Effects of prenatal marijuana on response inhibition: An fMRI study of young adults. *Neurotoxicology and Teratology, 26*, 533–542.

Smith, L. M., LaGasse, L. L., Derauf, C., Grant, P., Shah, R., Arria, A., et al. (2006). The infant development, environment, and lifestyle study: Effects of prenatal methamphetamine exposure, polydrug exposure, and poverty on intrauterine growth. *Pediatrics, 118*(3), 1149–1156.

Smith, L., Yonekura, M. L., Wallace, T., Berman, N., Kuo, J., & Berkowitz, C. (2003). Effects of prenatal methamphetamine exposure on fetal growth and drug withdrawal symptoms on infants born at term. *Journal of Developmental and Behavioral Pediatrics, 24*(1), 17–23.

Spear, N. E., & Molina, J. C. (2005). Fetal or infantile exposure to ethanol promotes ethanol ingestion in adolescence and adulthood: A theoretical review. *Alcoholism, Clinical and Experimental Research, 29*(6), 909–929.

Sprang, G., Clark, J., & Bass, S. (2005). Predicting the severity of child maltreatment using multidimensional assessment and measurement approaches. *Child Abuse and Neglect: An International Journal, 29*, 335–350.

Storr, C. L., Accornero, V. H., & Crum, R. M. (2007). Profiles of current disruptive behavior: Association with recent drug consumption among adolescents. *Addictive Behaviors, 32*, 248–264.

Storr, C. L., Westergaard, R., & Anthony, J. C. (2005). Early onset inhalant use and risk for opiate initiation by young adulthood. *Drug and Alcohol Dependence, 78*(3), 253–261.

Substance Abuse and Mental Health Services Administration. (2002). *The Drug and Alcohol Services Information System report: Pregnant women in substance abuse treatment*. Rockville, MD: Office of Applied Studies.

Substance Abuse and Mental Health Services Administration. (2005a). *National Survey on Drug Use and Health report: Substance use during pregnancy: 2002 and 2003 update*. Rockville, MD: Office of Applied Studies.

Substance Abuse and Mental Health Services Administration. (2005b). *National Survey on Drug Use and Health report: Inhalant use and delinquent behaviors among young adolescents*. Rockville, MD: Office of Applied Studies.

Substance Abuse and Mental Health Services Administration. (2006). *National Survey on Drug Use and Health report: Youth violence and illicit drug use*. Rockville, MD: Office of Applied Studies.

Substance Abuse and Mental Health Services Administration. (2008). *National Survey on Drug Use and Health report: Inhalant use adolescent years*. Rockville, MD: Office of Applied Studies.

Substance Abuse and Mental Health Services Administration. (2009). *National Survey on Drug Use*

*and Health report: Children living with substance-dependent or substance-abusing parents: 2002 to 2007*. Rockville, MD: Office of Applied Studies.
Sulzer, D., Sanders, M. S., Paulsen, N. W., & Galli, A. (2005). Mechanisms of neurotransmitter release by amphetamines: A review. *Progressive Neurobiology, 75*(6), 406–433.
Sung, H. E., Richter, L., Vaughan, R., Johnson, P. B., & Thom, B. (2005). Nonmedical use of prescription opioids among teenagers in the United States: Trends and correlates. *Journal of Adolescent Health, 37*, 44–51.
Tennant, F. S., & Detels, R. (1976). Relationship of alcohol, cigarette, and drug abuse in adulthood with alcohol, cigarette and coffee consumption in childhood. *Preventive Medicine, 5*, 70–77.
Trksak, G. H., Glatt, S. J., Mortazavi, F., & Jackson, D. (2007). A meta-analysis of animal studies on disruption of spatial navigation by prenatal cocaine exposure. *Neurotoxicology and Teratology, 29*(5), 570–577.
Upadhyaya, H. P., Brady, K. T., & Wang, W. (2004). Bupropion SR in adolescents with comorbid ADHD and nicotine dependence: A pilot study. *Journal of the American Academy of Child and Adolescent Psychiatry, 43*(2), 199–205.
Upadhyaya, H. P., Deas, D., Brady, K. T., & Kruesi, M. (2002). Cigarette smoking and psychiatric comorbidity in children and adolescents. *Journal of the American Academy of Child and Adolescent Psychiatry, 41*(11), 1294–1305.
U.S. General Accounting Office. (1990). *Drug exposed infants: A generation at risk* (GAO/HRD-90-138). Washington, DC: U.S. Government Printing Office.
Vaughn, M. G., Howard, M. O., Foster, K. A., Dayton, M. K., & Zelner, J. L. (2005). Substance use in a state population of incarcerated juvenile offenders. *Journal of Evidence-Based Social Work, 2*(1/2), 155–173.
Vermeiren, R., Scwa-Stone, M., Deboutte, D., Leckman, P. E., & Ruchkin, V. (2003). Violence exposure and substance use in adolescents: Findings from three countries. *Pediatrics, 111*, 535–540.
Volkow, N. D., Chang, L., Wang, G. J., Farber, J. S., Franceschi, D., Sedler, M., et al. (2001). Loss of dopamine transporters in methamphetamine abusers: Recovers with protracted abstinence. *Journal of Neuroscience, 21*(23), 9414–9418.
Volkow, N. D., Chang, L., Wang, G. J., Fowler, J. S., Leonido-Yee, M., Franceschi, D., et al. (2001). Association of dopamine transporter reduction with psychomotor impairment in methamphetamine abusers. *American Journal of Psychiatry, 158*(3), 377–382.
Wakschlag, L. S., Leventhal, B. L., Pine, D. S., Pickett, K. E., & Carter, A. S. (2006). Elucidating early mechanisms of developmental psychopathology: The case of prenatal smoking and disruptive behavior. *Child Development, 77*(4), 893–906.
Walsh, R. A., Redman, S., & Adamson, L. (1996). The accuracy of self-report of smoking status in pregnant women. *Addictive Behaviors, 21*(5), 675–679.
Webb, C. P. M., Burleson, J. A., & Ungemack, J. A. (2002). Treating juvenile offenders for marijuana problems. *Addiction, 97*(Supp. L), 15–45.
Widom, C. S., White, H. R., Czaja, S. J., & Marmorstein, N. R. (2007). Long-term effects of child abuse and neglect on alcohol use and excessive drinking in middle adulthood. *Journal of Studies on Alcohol and Drugs, 68*(3), 317–326.
Wilens, T. E., Biederman, J., Mick, E., Faraone, S. V., & Spencer, T. (1997). Attention deficit hyperactivity disorder (ADHD) is associated with early onset substance use disorders. *Journal of Nervous and Mental Disease, 185*(8), 475–482.
Wilens, T. E., Faraone, S. V., Biederman, J., & Gunawardene, S. (2003). Does stimulant therapy of attention-deficit hyperactivity disorder beget later substance abuse? A meta-analytic review of literature. *Pediatrics, 111*(1), 179–185.
Wilens, T. E., Gignac, M., Swezey, A., Monuteaux, M. C., & Biederman, J. (2006). Characteristics of adolescents and young adults with ADHD who divert or misuse their prescribed medications. *Journal of the American Academy of Child & Adolescent Psychiatry, 45*(4), 408–414.
Winters, K. C. (1999). *Treatment of adolescents with substance use disorders*. Treatment improvement protocol series 32. Rockville, MD: Center for Substance Abuse Treatment.
Wu, L. T., & Ringwalt, C. L. (2006). Inhalant use and disorders among adults in the United States. *Drug and Alcohol Dependence, 85*(1), 1–11.
Zuckerman, B., Frank, D. A., Hingson, R., Amaro, H., Levenson, S. M., Kayne, H., et al. (1989). Effects of maternal marijuana and cocaine use on fetal growth. *New England Journal of Medicine, 320*(12), 762–768.

# Screening and Assessment: An Evidence-Based Process for the Management and Care of Adult Drug-Involved Offenders

4

Matthew L. Hiller, Steven Belenko,
Wayne N. Welsh, Gary Zajac, and Roger H. Peters

**Abstract**

Valid and reliable assessment of risk and needs is a cornerstone of evidence-based practices with offenders who use and abuse drugs. They provide the needed clinical information upon which the case planning and services referral and delivery processes observed in criminal justice settings are based. However, recent surveys of nationally representative samples shows critical gaps remain, with many criminal justice programs either forgoing assessment of risks and needs or using instruments that have not be externally validated. To encourage more widespread use of risk and substance abuse instruments that have been shown to be reliable and valid, the current chapter reviews a number instruments within the context of the Risk-Need-Responsivity (R-N-R) model for assessment and services planning. Descriptions of these instruments as well as their reliability and validity when used with offender samples are presented. Discussion focuses on the need to adhere to evidence-based practices and processes when assessing and managing offenders with drug abuse problems.

**Keywords**

Criminogenic risk • Substance abuse • Assessment • Review of instruments

## Introduction

Based on the time-tested medical model for screening and assessing patients for disease, in order to refer and triage cases into appropriate care, the screening and assessment of criminogenic risk and needs represent an evidence-based process to guide the care and management of drug-involved offenders in correctional institutions and in the community. Several recent studies and monographs illustrate the need for such evidence-based procedures.

For example, guidelines from the National Institute of Corrections (Clawson, Bogue, &

M.L. Hiller (✉)
Department of Criminal Justice, Temple University,
Philadelphia, PA 19122, USA
e-mail: mhiller@temple.edu

C. Leukefeld et al. (eds.), *Handbook of Evidence-Based Substance Abuse Treatment in Criminal Justice Settings*, Issues in Children's and Families' Lives 11,
DOI 10.1007/978-1-4419-9470-7_4, © Springer Science+Business Media, LLC 2011

Joplin, 2005) identify the development and maintenance of a system for ongoing offender risk screening/triage and needs assessments as its first evidence-based principle for effective correction-based treatment. Further, the National Institute on Drug Abuse (NIDA; 2006) indicates that "assessment is the first step in (the) treatment (of drug-involved offenders)" (p. 2).

Indeed, the development and testing of screening and assessment tools for use with criminal justice samples was a major focus of the recently completed NIDA-funded Criminal Justice Drug Abuse Treatment Studies (CJDATS; Simpson & Knight, 2007).

Despite such national leadership, a recent national representative survey, the National Criminal Justice Treatment Practices Survey (NCJTPS) (also completed as a part of the CJDATS research cooperative) found that although 58.2% of correctional facilities (including prisons, jails, and probation, parole, and community corrections agencies) used at least one standardized tool to screen for substance abuse problems, 10% reported using nonstandardized and/or internally developed screens, and 31.8% reported no use of a substance abuse screening tool (Taxman, Cropsey, Young, & Wexler, 2007; Taxman, Young, Wiersema, Rhodes, & Mitchell, 2007). Findings from a national survey of adult drug court programs, implemented as a part of the eCourt project of the CJ-DATS research cooperative, were similar (Taxman, Perdoni, Young, Belenko, Hiller, in press). Specifically, 68% of drug courts surveyed reported using a standardized substance abuse screening tool, while 21% used a standardized risk assessment, but only 4% used a standardized mental health screen. Taxman and colleagues (in press) noted, "Survey results demonstrate that 'legal criteria' (e.g., type and severity of charge and whether the defendant has a history of violent offenses) rather than clinical criteria (e.g., drug dependence severity, risk) are the most determinative factors in deciding who is allowed entry into drug courts and who is not." Ninety-two percent of drug courts involve members of the "legal team" (including the judge, prosecutor and defense attorney) in the admission process and nearly 80% of courts involve coordinators and case managers, while 48% of drug courts involve treatment providers." (p. 14).

Given that substantial gaps are evident in how existing practice conforms to evidence-based guidelines for screening offenders and that research shows that standardized screening and assessment information often is not used to inform services delivery, the focus of the current chapter is on a commonly cited model, Risk-Need-Responsivity (R-N-R; Andrews, Bonta, & Hoge, 1990), for offender assessment and rehabilitation. Commonly used instruments in the criminal justice system are reviewed regarding how they complement the R-N-R framework, and promising instruments, recently developed as a part of the CJDATS research collaborative, are reviewed regarding their potential to improve offender assessment and care.

The perspective taken here, regarding the assessment of offenders with drug and alcohol problems, is that assessment is an ongoing and iterative process. It begins when brief screening instruments are administered to offenders to identify those who may have problems and who are in need of more in-depth assessment and diagnosis. In turn, when diagnostic assessments identify significant clinical problems, this information is used to develop an individualized treatment plan. Subsequent to the initial treatment plan, ongoing assessment monitors treatment progress and identifies any needed modification to the treatment plan (Knight, Simpson, & Hiller, 2002; Roberts, Contois, Willis, Worthington, & Knight, 2007; Simpson & Knight, 2007). Unfortunately, ongoing assessment is not often accomplished in the criminal justice system (Peters & Wexler, 2005), particularly for those offenders moving between different points in the system (e.g., courts, jails, prisons, community corrections). Programs often fall short in the provision of initial assessments, making subsequent reassessments impossible and jeopardizing any possibility of continuity of care as the offender progresses through the criminal justice system. Indeed, systematic program reviews have found that the lack of rigorous assessment is often one of the greatest weaknesses within offender programs (Hubbard,

Travis, & Latessa, 2001; Latessa & Holsinger, 1998; Lowenkamp, Latessa, & Smith, 2006).

## Risk-Need-Responsivity: An Evidence-Based Model for Offender Assessment

One conceptual model used to guide offender assessment and rehabilitation, Risk-Need-Responsivity (R-N-R; Andrews et al., 1990; Andrews, Bonta, & Wormith, 2006; Bonta & Andrews, 2007; Ogloff & Davis, 2004), provides a framework for focusing on specific offender attributes in relation to planning services for rehabilitation and for preventing recidivism. Developed by Andrews and colleagues (1990), and grounded in general personality and social psychology theory, this model was introduced in the late 1980s and early 1990s as a set of evidence-based guidelines to direct the implementation of treatment services in correctional settings. This approach ran counter to the prevailing antirehabilitation sentiment of that time. Incorporating elements of differential association, operant conditioning, and social learning theory, R-N-R is specifically interested in the assessment of individual characteristics (like criminal history and antisocial attitudes) predictive of criminal behavior, "making it a particularly useful guide for both assessing the risk of recidivism and planning rehabilitation attempts" (Ogloff & Davis, 2004, p. 230). It provides several empirically based principles for matching services to an offender's assessed risks and needs (e.g., the Risk Principle, the Needs Principle; Andrews & Dowden, 2007).

The empirical literature on the prediction of recidivism provides the evidence-base for the assessment of an individual's risk (Andrews et al., 1990; Andrews & Dowden, 2007; Andrews et al., 2006). Risk factors may be either static or dynamic characteristics, with the latter representing the best possible targets for rehabilitation. Andrews and Bonta (2006) and Andrews and Dowden (2007) highlight the "Big 8" risk factors that account for the largest amount of variance in the prediction of recidivism. These include a history of antisocial behavior, antisocial personality patterns, antisocial cognitions, antisocial associates, family problems, low levels of performance in school/work, low levels of involvement with noncriminal leisure activities, and substance abuse. The level of an individual's assessed risk (i.e., high versus low) informs the application of the "Risk Principle," which indicates that more intensive services should be reserved for those at high risk, while those with lower risk levels receive either minimal or no intervention (Andrews et al., 1990; Taxman, Thanner, & Weisburd, 2006; Thanner & Taxman, 2003). This principle also suggests that placing low-risk offenders in a very intensive intervention may have unintended harmful effects.

Needs (also referred to as treatment needs, Ogloff & Davis, 2004) are comprised of two sets of dynamic characteristic, criminogenic and noncriminogenic. Criminogenic needs are a specific subset of dynamic (modifiable) risk factors that are predictive of recidivism. In particular, these include antisocial attitudes, antisocial feelings, substance abuse, poor parental bonding and parenting skills, and antisocial peers (Dowden & Andrews, 2000). Noncriminogenic needs are not directly related to the probability of reoffending, and include poor self-esteem, anxiety, psychological distress, feelings of alienation, and socially disorganized neighborhoods (Ogloff & Davis, 2004). Because correctional and other criminal justice interventions are expected to reduce recidivism, the "Need Principle" states that criminogenic needs should be the primary treatment targets. Although the Need Principle does not specifically discourage addressing noncriminogenic needs, it cautions researchers and clinicians that expected outcomes related to addressing these should not include recidivism. Some evidence exists that programs that primarily target criminogenic needs, as opposed to noncriminogenic needs, and that target *more* criminogenic needs, have better outcomes (Latessa & Lowenkamp, 2006; Lowenkamp & Latessa, 2002). Ongoing assessment of criminogenic needs during treatment is recommended to monitor change.

Responsivity refers to characteristics of the services delivered (general) and attributes of the individual offender (specific) that can modify the impact of treatment. For example, with respect to specific responsivity, one's level of motivation for treatment has been shown to affect engagement in treatment (Hiller, Knight, Leukefeld, & Simpson, 2002) as well as treatment outcome (Broome, Knight, Knight, Hiller, & Simpson, 1997). Other offender characteristics that may affect treatment effectiveness include intellectual ability, learning styles, and self-esteem (Ogloff & Davis, 2004). General responsivity refers to factors related to the treatment episode, such as intensity and types of services received, therapeutic relationships, and interactions with counselors (Andrews et al., 1990; Broome, Flynn, Knight, & Simpson, 2007; Ogloff & Davis, 2004; Simpson, Joe, & Broome, 2002).

Specific application of R-N-R clearly indicates that the most important targets for assessment are the dynamic risk factors (needs) of individual offenders. Treatment plans should specifically address these needs, reserving the highest levels of treatment for those with the highest risk and greatest needs. Beyond initial assessment of the individual, R-N-R highlights the need for ongoing assessment of changes in criminogenic needs, to provide feedback on how treatment plans should be modified to improve the likelihood of favorable outcomes (i.e., reduced recidivism). For example, the Level of Service Inventory-Revised, LSI-R, includes versions for baseline and followup administrations. In addition, assessment also should include measurement of both individual differences and characteristics of the services provided to identify ways to improve the offender's response to these services.

## Screening and Assessment in the Criminal Justice System

A wide variety of screening and assessment instruments is available to guide custody and treatment decisions for offenders with drug problems in the criminal justice system but, as discussed below, only a few of these are in common use. These instruments can be placed into two broad categories, risk assessment and substance abuse assessment, with the former tending to focus on a wider spectrum of the "Big 8" and the latter on a more narrowly defined subset, typically only on substance abuse problems. Substance abuse assessments, unlike risk assessments, typically focus on measuring symptoms, based on a diagnostic standard like the *Diagnostic and Statistical Manuals* of the American Psychiatric Association.

As noted by Andrews et al. (2006), risk assessment has evolved over the past several decades, beginning with first-generation (1G) assessments, which emphasized unstructured professional judgments in rating an individual's risk for recidivism. These ratings were shown to be inconsistent across practitioners and ineffective for accurately quantifying risk. To address this, a second generation (2G) of instruments adopted an "actuarial approach" whereby static risk factors for recidivism (offender characteristics like age and prior offense history which predicted recidivism but were not amenable to change) were aggregated into summative indices as an objective prediction of the extent to which one was at risk for recidivism. Because 2G instruments focused on aspects of the person that could not be changed through therapeutic interventions, third- generation (3G) instruments were developed to include dynamic risk factors, including many of the "Big 8" (described above), that could be specifically targeted for change. The most well known of these is the Level of Services Inventory – Revised (LSI-R), which is described in more depth below.

Recently, fourth-generation (4G) instruments have emerged, which extend the collection of assessments beyond initial baseline measures to include case planning and management and responsivity assessment. Because of their newness, relatively little empirical information is available and, thus, these will not be a focus of the current chapter. One example of a 4G instrument that is currently being studied and shows promise is the Correctional Offender Management Profile for Alternative Sanctions (COMPAS) tool (Brennan, Dieterich, & Ehret, 2009; Fass, Heilbrun, DeMatteo, & Fretz, 2008). Another is the Level of Service/Case Management Inventory (LS/CMI; Andrews, Bonta, & Wormith, 2004; Andrews & Bonta, 2006), which is based on the 3G LSI-R.

There are numerous instruments for screening risk and substance abuse in the criminal justice system and a comprehensive review of all of these is beyond the scope of this chapter. Instead, the chapter reviews specific instruments that constitute "common practice" (i.e., are the most commonly used) among criminal justice programs (including drug courts) and discussess the evidence base for each. As will be shown below, not all instruments commonly used in the criminal justice system have a strong body of empirical research that supports their use with these populations. Most notable among these is the commonly used Substance Abuse Subtle Screening Inventory (SASSI), for which empirical research has failed to confirm the validity of the parts of the instrument related to the subtle assessment of drug problems.

Whether an assessment is viewed as being a part of "common practice" is based on findings from recent surveys of treatment practices (including screening and assessment) on national samples of correctional programs and drug courts (see Taxman, Cropsey et al., 2007; Taxman et al., under review). As shown in Table 4.1, despite the availability of best practices standards from NIC and NIDA, which include screening and assessment as central components, a majority of agencies and programs do not use a structured risk assessment instrument, and many do not use a standardized substance abuse tool. For structured risk instruments, the LSI-R is in most common use (e.g., 25.3% of the NCJTPS and 17.7% of the eCourt sample) followed by the Wisconsin Risk/Needs Assessment (WRN). With respect to substance abuse, the Addiction Severity Index (ASI) is the most commonly used assessment in both correctional systems and drug courts (46.4 and 44.7%, respectively) followed by the Substance Abuse Subtle Screening Inventory in 42.3 and 23.4% of programs respectively. Other substance abuse screening instruments in common use in the criminal justice system are the Texas Christian University Drug Screen (TCUDS), the Michigan Alcohol Screening Test (MAST), and the Drug Abuse Screening Test (DAST).

**Table 4.1** Use of screening and assessment instruments reported in National System Surveys of Institutional and Community Corrections and Drug Courts

| Instrument | NCJTPS[a] | eCourt[b] |
|---|---|---|
| *Risk-needs* | | |
| Use no standardized risk tool | 65.8 | 79.0 |
| LSI-R | 25.3 | 17.7 |
| WRN | 12.7 | 4.3 |
| *Substance abuse* | | |
| Use no standardized substance abuse tool | 42.8 | 32.0 |
| ASI | 46.4 | 44.7 |
| SASSI | 42.3 | 23.4 |
| TCUDS | 22.0 | 5.0 |
| MAST | 20.8 | 9.9 |
| DAST | 17.9 | 5.7 |

[a]Based on Taxman, Cropsey et al. (2007).
[b]Based on Taxman et al. (in press).

The most commonly used risk assessments (i.e., the LSI-R and WRN) are reviewed next, followed by screening and assessment tools for substance abuse problems (i.e., ASI, SASSI, TCUDS, MAST, and DAST), presented in the order of most to least commonly used. An instrument's being commonly used does not necessarily mean it is evidence-based; and special emphasis is placed on describing the evidence base (i.e., reliability/validity) of each instrument. Screening and assessment tools must be valid and reliable in order for them to be useful for informing clinical planning and practice (Knight, Simpson, & Hiller, 2002; Peters, Greenbaum, & Edens, 1998; Peters et al., 2000). In addition, information is provided on whether each is in the public domain, requires specialized training, is interviewer- or self-administered, and an estimate is provided of the length of time required to complete each. These reviews are followed by a description of a number of instruments that were recently developed and tested in NIDA's CJDATS research cooperative.

## Risk Assessments

*Level of Supervision Inventory-R (LSI-R)*. The Level of Service Inventory-Revised (LSI-R; Andrews & Bonta, 1995), a 3G instrument, has become a popular assessment for the classification and management of offenders both within correctional institutions and in the community. As an objective, actuarial instrument that is based on theory (i.e., the R-N-R principles of effective correctional intervention described above) and empirically validated on diverse samples of offenders, the LSI-R attempts to meet the dual task of managing offenders and assessing their needs (Bonta, 2002).

The LSI-R is a 54-item instrument comprised of subscales measuring 10 different risk/need areas: criminal history, education and employment, financial circumstances, family and marital situation, accommodations/housing, leisure and recreation, companions, drug and alcohol abuse, emotional and personal characteristics, and attitudes and orientations. The 10 domains, taken individually, allow correctional agents to identify and target areas of criminogenic need. For example, if the offender scores high on the alcohol and drug problem subscale, this should trigger a referral to substance abuse treatment programming in prison, the community, or both.

The instrument has been validated on a wide range of offender groups including probationers (Andrews, Kiessling, Mickus, & Robinson, 1986), male inmates (Bonta & Motiuk, 1987, 1990; Lowenkamp, Hodsinger, & Latessa, 2001; Loza & Simourd, 1994; Simourd, 2004), female inmates (Coulson, Ilacqua, Nutbrown, Giulekas, & Cudjoe, 1996), juvenile offenders (Shields & Simourd, 1991), and sexual offenders (Simourd & Malcolm, 1998). A meta-analysis summarizing 30 predictive studies of the LSI-R (Gendreau, Goggin, & Smith, 2002) found that LSI-R total scores were significantly correlated with both general and violent recidivism. Although fewer studies have examined the predictive validity of individual subscales, Kelly and Welsh (2008) found that both the drug and alcohol subscale and the LSI-R total score significantly predicted reincarceration in a sample of drug-dependent adult offenders released from prison. The LSI-R and its subscales have been shown to be both reliable and valid (Simourd, 2006). There are costs associated with the training for, and use of, this instrument. The LSI-R is not in the public domain, requires special training, and is most commonly administered as an interview. It takes between 45 minutes and 2 hours to complete.

*Wisconsin Risk/Needs Assessment (WRN)*. Among the first 2G actuarial risk assessments to be developed, it has experienced a renewed interest (Baird, 2009; Eisenberg, Bryl, & Fabelo, 2009). It focuses primarily on static risk factors like age at first conviction, number of probation/parole supervision periods and revocations, and number of address changes in the previous 12 months (Baird, Heinz, & Bemus, 1979, 1981; Eisenberg et al., 2009). Typically scored by staff using information from an individual's Presentencing Investigation Report, the instrument represents an efficient alternative to lengthy interviews. However, the evidence base for this instrument, including descriptions of validity and reliability, comes primarily from published reports from Department of Corrections researchers, including Wisconsin and Texas, with only a few examples evident in the scientific literature (e.g., Clear & Gallagher, 1983; Knight, Simpson, & Hiller, 1999). Overall, findings show that the scale is reliable and valid, and can make adequate predictions regarding risk for recidivism. It is in the public domain and can therefore be used at no cost.

## Substance Abuse Instruments

*Addiction Severity Index (ASI)*. Perhaps the most well-researched psychosocial assessment instrument for use with substance abusers both in the community and within criminal justice treatment settings, the ASI was originally developed in the early 1980s and has since undergone several revisions (McLellan, Luborsky, Cacciola, & Griffith, 1985; McLellan, Luborsky, Woody, & O'Brien, 1980; McLellan et al., 1992). It is organized into seven assessment areas, including medical problems, employment, alcohol use, drug use, legal problems, family/social relationships, and psychiatric problems. A set of interviewer severity ratings (ISRs) and composite scores (CSs) can be calculated from the information collected during this interview, which can be compared to those typical for clients in the program, to help inform treatment planning. Several of the ASI assessment areas clearly map into the "Big 8" criminogenic needs (see Table 4.2), including a history of antisocial behavior, disorganized family/marital relationships, low performance in education/work, and substance abuse. In addition, other assessment areas capture information relevant for identifying noncriminogenic needs (e.g., mental health). The ASI CS scores have been found to be highly reliable and valid for numerous populations, including those in the criminal justice system (Alterman, Bovasso, Cacciola, & McDermott, 1994; Hanlon, O'Grady, & Bateman, 2000; Leonhard, Mulvey, Gastfriend, & Shwartz, 2000; Mäkelä, 2004). The ISR scores have been found to be less reliable and valid, varying with the level of interviewer training (Alterman et al., 2001; Mäkelä, 2004). Recent research shows that ASI CS scores are highly predictive of DSM-IV alcohol and drug dependence diagnoses (Rikoon, Cacciola, Carise, Alterman, & McLellan, 2006). The ASI is in the public domain, should be completed in an interview, and specialized training is available. When administered by a trained interviewer, it takes approximately 40 minutes to complete.

*Substance Abuse Subtle Screening Inventory (SASSI)*. Originally released in 1985 and revised twice (Miller, 1985; Miller & Lazowski, 1999; Swartz, 1998), the SASSI is a 93-item paper-and-pencil self-report screening instrument that includes a total of nine direct and indirect scales for identifying individuals, who may have substance abuse disorders, as candidates for more in-depth assessment. Direct scales for measuring substance abuse problems include the face-valid alcohol, face-valid other drug, and symptoms scales. Reflecting the belief that some individuals, like offenders, have a vested interest in lying about their drug use, scales that are purported to be indirect measures of substance abuse problems (i.e., obvious attributes, subtle attributes, and defensiveness) also are included to detect substance abuse problems among those who have a vested interest in concealing it. Two other scales, family versus control subjects and corrections, are also indirect measures of substance abuse problems because they measure its correlates (family problems, criminal history). A final scale, random answering pattern, is included as a validity scale. As shown in Table 4.2, the three direct substance abuse scales and the family and correctional scales relate most closely to the criminogenic risk factors of the R-N-R model and, thus, measure domains relevant to reducing recidivism.

A comparative analysis of the SASSI and several other screening instruments that are used with offenders determined that the SASSI was the least effective in identifying substance dependence disorders (Peters et al., 2000). Furthermore, a recent monograph, reviewing the literature on screening and assessment among offenders, published by the National GAINS Center (Peters, Bartoi, & Sherman, 2008) indicates that the SASSI is significantly less effective than other instruments in detecting substance use disorders among offenders. The monograph recommends that the SASSI should be avoided for use in criminal justice settings due to concerns about its validity. The common use of the SASSI, in the criminal justice system, underscores the importance of knowing whether the instrument being used has an adequate evidence base: especially because best practices emphasize the need to use instruments that are both reliable and valid for the population for which they are being used (Knight, Simpson, & Hiller, 2002).

Recent meta-analyses (Feldstein & Miller, 2007; Miller, Woodson, Howell, & Shields, 2009) examining SASSI's use among primarily nonoffender populations, have also focused on the psychometric properties (i.e., reliability and validity) of this inventory. The general finding of these meta-analyses is that the direct scales and the corrections scale are the most reliable and valid parts of the SASSI but the indirect scales have poor measurement properties. Feldstein and Miller (2007, p. 40) conclude "We found no evidence

**Table 4.2** Mapping of screening and assessment instruments to the R-N-R framework

| Instrument | Screen or assessment | "Big 8" Risk/Needs (Andrews & Dowden, 2007) | | | | | | | | |
|---|---|---|---|---|---|---|---|---|---|---|
| | | Antisocial behavior | Antisocial personality | Antisocial cognitions | Antisocial associates | Family/marital status | School/work | Leisure activities | Substance abuse | Other risks/responsivity |
| LSI-R | Assessment | Yes | Yes | Yes | Yes | Yes | Yes | Yes | Yes | Yes |
| WRN | Screen | Yes | No | No | No | No | Yes | No | Yes | No |
| ASI | Assessment | Yes | No | No | No | Yes | Yes | No | Yes | Yes |
| SASSI | Screen | Yes | No | No | No | Yes | No | No | Yes | No |
| TCUDS | Screen | No | No | No | No | No | No | No | Yes | Yes |
| MAST | Screen | No | No | No | No | No | No | No | Yes | No |
| DAST | Screen | No | No | No | No | No | No | No | Yes | No |
| IPASS | Assessment | Yes | No | No | No | No | Yes | No | Yes | Yes |
| CODSI | Screen | No | No | No | No | No | No | No | Yes | Yes |
| CEST | Assessment | No | Yes | Yes | Yes | No | No | No | No | Yes |
| TCU CTS | Assessment | No | Yes | Yes | No | No | No | No | No | No |
| CAI | Assessment | No | Yes | Yes | No | No | Yes | No | Yes | Yes |

to support claims that the indirect scales of the SASSI offer a unique or additive advantage to correctly detecting current substance use disorders." In addition, Feldstein and Miller (2007) indicate an average false positive rate of 38%. The authors of both meta-analyses suggest that it may be more cost effective to use other screening instruments (like the MAST, see below) that are "shorter, have equal or better reliability, and are in the public domain". The SASSI is not in the public domain, is typically completed as a self-administered instrument in less than an hour, and requires specialized training to hand score. Computerized scoring programs are available for purchase.

*Texas Christian University Drug Screen (TCUDS)*. Although, when compared to the ASI, SASSI, MAST, and DAST, the TCU Drug Screen is a relative newcomer to the field, it is implemented in some large correctional systems, including the Texas Department of Criminal Justice and the Pennsylvania Department of Corrections (Knight, Simpson, & Hiller, 2002). This screen includes a face-valid measure with items that closely map to the Diagnostic and Statistical Manual IV (American Psychiatric Association, 1994) as well as additional questions for assessing the extent to which the individual has used 11 substances (including alcohol, marijuana, hallucinogens, crack, cocaine, heroin, heroin and cocaine mixed, street methadone, other opiates, methamphetamine, and tranquilizers) (Knight, Simpson, & Morey, 2002). As such, the majority of this instrument measures substance abuse as a criminogenic risk/need. However, two supplemental questions ask respondents to indicate whether they have ever been in substance abuse treatment and the extent to which they feel they currently need treatment. These items fit more closely with specific responsivity in the R-N-R model (see Table 4.2).

Perhaps related to its relative newness, the TCUDS has been subjected to less empirical investigation than the other measures covered in this section, and most of what has been done is not published in the peer-reviewed literature (e.g., Hiller & Narevic, 2005; Knight, Simpson, & Hiller, 2002; Knight, Simpson, & Morey, 2002). One notable exception is a study conducted by Peters and colleagues (2000). This study administered eight different substance abuse screening instruments to 400 inmates, including the drug use scales from the ASI, the Alcohol Dependence Scale, DAST, MAST, SASSI-2, TCUDS, and the Simple Screening Instrument. The clinical assessment "gold standard" against which the performance of these screens was judged was provided by the substance use disorders module of the Structured Clinical Interview for the DSM-IV. Findings showed that the ADS, SSI, and TCUDS were the most effective for identifying substance use disorders. The TCUDS had the highest sensitivity (.85) and overall accuracy (.82) among the screening instruments examined, and also had good specificity (.78). Studies also indicate that the TCUDS has very good test-retest reliability among offenders (.89–.95; Knight, Simpson, & Morey, 2002; Peters et al., 2000). That is, the TCUDS is a valid, reliable instrument that is at least as accurate as, and in some cases more accurate than, other commonly available measures. It is typically self-administered, requires fewer than 10 minutes to complete, and is publically available at no charge.

*Michigan Alcohol Screening Test (MAST)*. One of the first brief screening questionnaires ever developed (Selzer, 1971), the MAST is a 25-item scale that is used to identify individuals who may have an alcohol use disorder. A shorter form, the SMAST, includes 13 of the original 25 items from the full version of the questionnaire (Selzer, Vinokur, & van Rooijen, 1975). Because it measures only problematic alcohol use, it is only relevant to the substance abuse criminogenic risk factor in the R-N-R model. Several meta-analyses have confirmed that it has good measurement properties, representing both a reliable and a valid test of problem alcohol use (Shields, Howell, Potter, & Weiss, 2007; Storgaard, Nielsen, & Gluud, 1994; Teitelbaum & Mullen, 2000). However, like most screeners and assessments, the MAST does not perform uniformly well across all samples relevant to criminal justice planning. For example, Shields and colleagues (2007) note that samples with higher proportions of females yield lower levels of reliability, while clinical samples yield higher reliability than do nonclinical ones. Teitelbaum and Mullen (2000) noted that the validity of the scores on the MAST is also influenced by gender and type of clinical problem. Specifically, in studies with proportionally higher numbers of women, validity estimates were higher than in samples with fewer women. Also, samples from alcoholism treatment programs yield scores with higher levels of validity than those from psychiatric settings. Both studies conclude that characteristics of the clients to whom, as well as the setting in which, the MAST is administered should be considered prior to actual use of the instrument. One concern in using the MAST with offenders is that it tends to have greater sensitivity than specificity (Peters et al., 2000), and thus is more likely than other screeners to misidentify, as alcohol abusers, offenders who do not have alcohol use disorders. Importantly, a review of the literature provided in these meta-analyses and other reviews included few references to studies of the MAST in criminal justice settings (the vast majority of which were offenders arrested for Driving While Intoxicated). This suggests more study is needed to determine the extent to which different types of criminal justice samples and settings affect the performance of the MAST. The MAST is publicly available, self-administered, and hand-scored easily by staff. It typically takes fewer than 10 minutes to complete.

*Drug Abuse Screening Test (DAST)*. The DAST was first published in 1982 as a 28-item brief screening instrument for identifying those who may have drug problems. It was developed by rewording questions from the MAST to refer to drugs instead of alcohol (Skinner, 1982). Since it was introduced, two shorter versions have been published, including one that comprises a subset of 20 of the original items and an even shorter one that includes 10 of the original items. Although it is copyrighted, releases for not-for-profit research and clinical applications are usually granted (Yudko, Lozhkina, & Fouts, 2007). As shown in Table 4.2, it measures only one of the "Big 8" criminogenic needs. Research on it with criminal justice samples has been limited, with only one study identified in an extensive review of this instrument, in which it was used with women in jail or on probation (Saltstone, Halliwell, & Hayslip, 1994). Each version of the DAST was observed to have good measurement properties and was shown to produce reliable and valid measures of problem drug use (Yudko et al., 2007); but, as with the MAST, its reliability and validity estimates vary across different groups. With only limited research on its application to the criminal justice system, more empirical work is needed to determine whether the type of offender and/or the specific setting (e.g., prison vs. community corrections) affects the reliability and validity of its scores. Like the MAST, the DAST is publicly available, self-administered and easily hand-scored by staff. It typically takes fewer than 10 minutes to complete.

## Screening and Assessment Instruments Developed During CJDATS

Seeking to call national attention to the need to use evidence-based practices in substance abuse treatment, NIDA, in 2002, funded nine research centers under a cooperative agreement known as Criminal Justice Drug Abuse Treatment Studies (CJDATS; Fletcher, 2003). CJDATS conducted multisite research to improve drug treatment services for drug-involved offenders and develop and test system-level drug treatment models, with a goal of building new evidence-based interventions for criminal justice populations. One particular focus of CJDATS was the development of new screening and assessment instruments, to improve substance abuse treatment for offenders with drug and alcohol programs. Several instruments were developed and tested during this project, showed promise, and were found deserving of additional research (Simpson & Knight, 2007). All of these instruments, discussed below, are in the public domain, are self-administered, and require no specialized training to use. Because they are so new, estimates of the amount of time to complete are not yet available for discussion.

*Inmate Prerelease Assessment* (*IPASS*). The IPASS is a prerelease assessment designed and tested under CJDATS (Farabee, Knight, Garner, & Calhoun, 2007) with a focus on identifying the risk and needs of prisoners in drug abuse treatment nearing parole. Its primary intent is to identify the types of additional treatment needed by the offender, upon release, as well as each offender's amenability for continuing treatment in the community. Specifically, it consists of four major parts including a general background risk index (GBRI), Texas Christian University Drug Use Scale (TCUDS, described above), the Client Evaluation of Treatment (CET), and the Counselor Evaluation of Client (CEC). The GBRI, based on the Salient Factor Score, a well-validated 2G risk assessment (Hoffman, 1983), provides an actuarial measure for determining an offender's risk for recidivism through analysis of their preincarceration criminal behavior, including arrest and incarceration history, revocation history, and their age at first arrest. As already noted, the TCUDS is a brief assessment based on the Diagnostic and Statistical Manual (DSM) criteria for substance dependence. The CET is composed of several items that measure an offender's perceptions of his/her in-prison treatment experience, and the CEC is the primary counselor's appraisal of the offender. Each of these four different assessments are scored as composite measures, with the combined sum of the GBRI and TCUDS (representing risk and need for additional treatment) ranging from 0 to 18 and the combined score of the CET and CES (representing amenability to additional treatment) ranging from 0 to 18. A final index is created by subtracting the scores on the GBRI/TCUDS from the CET/CEC which can range from –18 to 18. Within the R-N-R framework, IPASS specifically addresses antisocial behavior and drug abuse as criminogenic risk factors and taps specific responsivity, through an offender's self-report and the primary counselor's report of his/her amenability to treatment. Analyses reported by Farabee and colleagues (2007) show the instrument has sound measurement properties, having high levels of validity and reliability. Although IPASS is promising, additional research is needed to replicate these findings with other samples, to establish a larger body of research on this instrument and determine whether it has a broad evidence base supporting its use with offender samples.

*Co-occurring Disorders Screening Instruments* (*CODSIs*). Sacks and colleagues (2007a) discuss the development of two brief screening instruments for use in the criminal justice system. These instruments, the Co-occurring Disorders Screening Instrument – Mental Disorder (CODSI-MD) and the Co-occurring Disorders Screening Instrument – Severe Mental Disorder (CODSI-SMD), were created by taking six items (CODSI-MD) and three items (CODSI-SMD) from three commonly used mental health screening instruments that had the highest correlation with diagnoses provided by the Structured Clinical Interview for the DSM-IV (SCID-IV) and combining them with TCUDS (described above) (Sacks et al., 2007a). Each measures one of the "Big 8" criminogenic needs, substance abuse, and also measures mental illness, considered a noncriminogenic need in the R-N-R model, which can affect an individual's responsiveness to treatment. Psychometric analyses show that the CODSI-MD and CODSI-SMD have good reliability and are valid for use with criminal justice populations. In addition, when compared with other standardized mental health assessments, the CODSI-SMD showed the highest overall accuracy rate and required the least amount of time to administer among the instruments studied (Duncan et al., 2008; Sacks et al., 2007a, 2007b).

*TCU Criminal Thinking Styles Scales* (*TCU CTS*). Based on Glenn Walters's (1995) work and developed in collaboration with the Bureau of Prisons with funding from the National Institute on Corrections, the TCU CTS is a brief self-report assessment (36 items, estimated to take between 5 and 10 minutes to complete) that assesses dynamic risk factors including antisocial attitudes and cognitions (Knight, Simpson, & Morey, 2002). It contains six scales, representing entitlement, justification, personal irresponsibility, power orientation, cold heartedness, and criminal rationalization (Knight, Garner, Simpson, Morey, & Flynn, 2006). As shown in Table 4.2, these six scales fit squarely within the antisocial personality and antisocial cognitions areas of the "Big 8" criminogenic risks and needs. This instrument is designed to be administered at repeated intervals during an offender's tenure in a treatment program to assess changes in these dynamic criminogenic factors. To date, however, there is no published peer-reviewed literature on this specific intended application. However, psychometric data are available from a cross-sectional application of the TCU CTS to a large sample of offenders in 26 residential programs during CJDATS. Findings reported by Knight et al. (2006) shows the measure is reliable, but, to date, has not been examined for validity. Although the TCU CTS shows promise, additional research is needed to determine whether it also is a valid instrument, especially for the monitoring of offender progress during treatment.

*TCU Client Evaluation of Self and Treatment (TCU CEST)*. Compared to the TCU CTS, a relatively large amount of research has been accomplished with the TCU Client Evaluation of Self and Treatment. Earlier versions of this instrument (referred to at different times as the TCU Motivational Scales, the TCU Self-Rating Form, and the TCU Evaluation of Self and Treatment) were developed for application in outpatient community-based drug treatment programs, and numerous studies showed it was reliable and valid in this setting (see Joe, Broome, Rowan-Szal, & Simpson, 2002; Simpson & Joe, 1993; Simpson, Joe, Rowan-Szal, & Greener, 1995). It was adapted and renamed the Resident Evaluation of Self and Treatment (REST; Hiller, Knight, Leukefeld et al., 2002; Hiller, Knight, Rao, & Simpson, 2002; Hiller, Knight, Saum, & Simpson, 2006; Welsh, 2006; Welsh & McGrain, 2008) for use with drug-involved offenders in correctional settings. Subsequent to this, it was renamed the TCU Client Evaluation of Self and Treatment (TCU-CEST) and was tested during CJDATS (Garner, Knight, Flynn, Morey, & Simpson, 2007; Saum et al., 2007; Staton-Tindall et al., 2007). The TCU-CEST contains 130 self-administered statements on which the respondents rate the extent to which they agree or disagree (1 = strongly disagree, 5 = strongly agree) with each. A total of 15 scales in three major domains (i.e., treatment motivation, psychosocial functioning, and treatment engagement) are scored, and this questionnaire may also be combined with the TCU CTS, described above (see Garner et al., 2007). Subscales for the treatment motivation domain include desire for help, treatment readiness, treatment needs, and pressures for treatment. The psychosocial functioning domain includes anxiety, depression, self-esteem, decision making, hostility, and risk taking. Finally, the treatment engagement domain includes treatment participation, treatment satisfaction, counseling rapport, peer support, and social support. When considered within the context of the R-N-R framework, the scales from the TCU CEST map to some of the "Big 8" criminogenic needs. For example the hostility, risk taking, and decision making scales measure antisocial cognitions and attitudes (see Table 4.2) while peer support reflects prosocial peer networks. The remaining scales examine noncriminogenic needs (e.g., anxiety, depression) as well as specific responsivity (e.g., desire for help, treatment readiness, treatment participation). The reliability and validity of this scale (as well as previous versions) are good, and it shows a great deal of promise for measuring changes in criminogenic risk and needs as well as in other needs and responsivity factors. The recommended use for this instrument is as a monitoring tool administered repeatedly throughout an offender's tenure in treatment to assess change in these areas and inform the revision of treatment plans (Garner et al., 2007).

*Client Assessment Inventory (CAI)*. Like the TCU CEST, the CAI was first developed for application to community-based substance abuse treatment programs and was modified and tested within CJDATS for use with criminal justice samples (Kressel, De Leon, Palij, & Rubin, 2000; Sacks, McKendrick, & Kressel, 2007). Based on the theoretical work of De Leon (2000) on therapeutic communities (TC), the

CAI is a 103-item self-administered questionnaire that includes 14 scales in four general domains (i.e., developmental, socialization, psychological, and program participation). Scales for the developmental domain include maturity, responsibility, and values. For the socialization dimension, scales include drug/criminal lifestyle, maintaining images, work attitude, and social skills. The psychological domain comprises scales for cognitive skills, emotional skills, and self-esteem/self-efficacy. Finally, the program participation dimension includes philosophy/understands program rules, engagement, attachment/investment, and role model. Within the context of R-N-R, the CAI measures antisocial personality and cognitions, drug/criminal lifestyle, and employment as criminogenic needs (see Table 4.2). Specific responsivity also is measured by several scales (e.g., emotional skills, self-esteem/self-efficacy). Scores on it have been shown to be reliable among offenders in correctional substance abuse treatment (TC and non-TC; Sacks et al., 2007), but to date no validity data have been published. Like the TCU CEST, its intended use is to monitor treatment progress, which requires repeated administration throughout an offender's time in treatment.

## Conclusions

Wide variation exists in screening and assessment practices implemented within the criminal justice system, particularly for those offenders with substance use and other related disorders (Taxman, Cropsey et al., 2007). Standardized instruments are not used in many criminal justice settings, and when used are often deficient with respect to reliability and validity. As indicated in this review, most substance abuse screening and assessment instruments have not been extensively validated for use with offenders. Thus, it is unclear whether the observed reliability and validity of these instruments are generalizable to criminal justice settings. Many settings do not employ an integrated set of screening and assessment instruments to address the wide range of psychosocial needs among offenders (Belenko, 2006). Also of concern is that most settings do not routinely compile information regarding offenders' risk levels.

Even when the level of offender risk and need is assessed, there are challenges in developing evidence-based approaches to translate this information into triage/placement decisions that affect the level of rehabilitative services and supervision provided. This referral and service delivery gap is particularly problematic during reentry to probation or parole. Supervision priorities favor security and monitoring over rehabilitation, community supervision officers are not trained to make service referrals, and supervision requirements make it difficult for offenders to access services (Belenko, 2006; Marlowe, 2003; Taxman, Young, & Byrne, 2004).

The Risk-Needs-Responsivity (R-N-R) model provides a useful framework to address these deficiencies in offender screening and assessment, and has proven to be effective in the United States and internationally in guiding assessment and treatment among offenders who have substance abuse and other psychosocial problems (Bonta & Andrews, 2007; Taxman & Marlowe, 2006). At the core of this model, the risk principle asserts that criminal behavior can be reliably predicted through assessment of key static and dynamic variables and that treatment interventions should focus on the dynamic variables presented by those assessed as higher-risk offenders. The R-N-R model identifies "criminogenic" needs empirically linked to recidivism and its psychosocial antecedents (e.g., antisocial beliefs, substance use disorders, self-control/management, criminal peers) as the cornerstone for both assessment and subsequent treatment interventions. This model is ideally suited to guide the development and implementation of screening, assessment, and triage/service matching within the criminal justice system, and also to help organize offender treatment, supervision, and community reentry (Dowden & Andrews, 2004).

At least five evidence-based screening and assessment principles flow from the R-N-R model. First, assuming reduced recidivism is the most important outcome, each offender's risk should be assessed. Second, more intensive services should be provided to offenders with the highest assessed risk. Third, screening and assessment instruments should be designed to calibrate offender risks and needs. Screens should lead to more extensive assessment and not be used as primary means for making treatment referral decisions. Fourth, assessments would optimally address multiple areas of criminogenic risk and need (e.g., criminal history, substance abuse, criminal peers, maladaptive belief systems). Finally, assessment based on the R-N-R model is an ongoing process and results should be used at each sequential point in the criminal justice system to inform institutional and community placement, involvement in rehabilitative services, and supervision approaches.

There are five decades of research indicating that objective, actuarial assessment is a key component of any human services intervention (Grove & Meehl, 1996). Moreover, there is evidence that offender programs that use risk and needs assessment information produce greater reductions in recidivism than programs that do not (Lowenkamp et al., 2006). Thus, increased attention to the psychometric adequacy of commonly used substance abuse assessment instruments is critical for both researchers and criminal justice practitioners, and should be a priority agenda.

A number of screening and assessment instruments have been developed and are reviewed here, that can be integrated to examine the level of offenders' risk and needs. For offender populations, these include evidence-based screens for substance abuse (TCUDS) and co-occurring disorders (CODSI), substance abuse assessment instruments (ASI), prerelease instruments (IPASS), and specialized instruments to evaluate offenders' risk level (LSI-R). As indicated previously, additional research will help determine the psychometric properties of instruments designed to evaluate offender risk and needs, and to determine how the results of screening and assessment can best be integrated to formulate decisions related to community placement, treatment, and supervision. Improvements in assessment instruments and the use of these assessments for appropriate supervision and treatment planning for offenders are needed to enhance both public safety and public health.

## References


Alterman, A. I., Bovasso, G. B., Cacciola, J. S., & McDermott, P. A. (1994). A comparison of the predictive validity of four sets of baseline ASI summary indices. *Psychology of Addictive Behavior, 15*, 159–162.

Alterman, A. I., Mulvaney, F. D., Cacciola, J. S., Cnaan, A., McDermott, P. A., & Brown, L. S. (2001). The validity of the interviewer severity ratings in groups of ASI interviewers with varying training. *Addiction, 96*, 1297–1305.

American Psychiatric Association. (1994). *Diagnostic and statistical manual of mental disorders* (4Th Ed.). Washington, DC: Author.

Andrews, D. A., & Bonta, J. (1995). *The LSI-R: The level of service inventory-revised*. Toronto, ON: Multi-Health Systems, Inc.

Andrews, D. A., & Bonta, J. (2006). *The psychology of criminal conduct* (4th ed.). Newark, NJ: Lexis Nexis/Matthew Bender.

Andrews, D. A., Bonta, J., & Hoge, R. D. (1990). Classification for effective rehabilitation: Rediscovering psychology. *Criminal Justice and Behavior, 17*, 19–52.

Andrews, D. A., Bonta, J., & Wormith, S. J. (2004). *The level of service/Case management inventory (LS/CMI)*. Toronto, ON: Multi-Health Systems.

Andrews, D. A., Bonta, J., & Wormith, S. J. (2006). The recent past and near future of risk and/or need assessment. *Crime and Delinquency, 52*, 7–27.

Andrews, D. A., & Dowden, C. (2007). The risk-need-responsivity model of assessment and human service in prevention and corrections: Crime-prevention jurisprudence. *Canadian Journal of Criminology and Criminal Justice, 49*(4), 439–464.

Andrews, D. A., Kiessling, J. J., Mickus, S., & Robinson, D. (1986). The construct validity of interview based risk assessment in corrections. *Canadian Journal of Behavioral Science, 18*, 460–470.

Baird, C. (2009). *A question of evidence: A critique of risk assessment models used in the justice system*. Oakland, CA: National Council on Crime and Delinquency.

Baird, C., Heinz, R., & Bemus, B. (1979). *The Wisconsin case classification/staff deployment project*. Madison, WI: Wisconsin Division of Corrections.

Baird, C., Heinz, R., & Bemus, B. (1981). *The Wisconsin case classification staff deployment project: Two year follow-up report*. Madison, WI: Wisconsin Division of Corrections.

Belenko, S. (2006). Assessing released inmates for substance-abuse related service needs. *Crime and Delinquency, 52*, 94–113.

Bonta, J. (2002). Offender risk assessment: Guidelines for selection and use. *Criminal Justice and Behavior, 29*, 355–379.

Bonta, J., & Andrews, D. A. (2007). *Risk-need-responsivity model for offender assessment and rehabilitation*. Ottawa, ON: Public Safety Canada.

Bonta, J., & Motiuk, L. L. (1987). The diversion of incarcerated offenders to correctional halfway houses. *Journal of Research in Crime and Delinquency, 24*, 302–323.

Bonta, J., & Motiuk, L. L. (1990). Classification to correctional halfway houses: A quasi-experimental evaluation. *Criminology, 28*, 497–506.

Brennan, T., Dieterich, W., & Ehret, B. (2009). Evaluating the predictive validity of the COMPAS risk and needs assessment system. *Criminal Justice and Behavior, 36*, 21–40.

Broome, K. M., Flynn, P. M., Knight, D. K., & Simpson, D. D. (2007). Program structure, staff perceptions, and client engagement in treatment. *Journal of Substance Abuse Treatment, 33*, 149–158.

Broome, K. M., Knight, D. K., Knight, K., Hiller, M. L., & Simpson, D. D. (1997). Peer, family, and motivational influences on drug treatment process and recidivism for probationers. *Journal of Clinical Psychology, 53*, 387–397.

Clawson, E., Bogue, B., & Joplin, L. (2005). *Implementing evidence-based practices in corrections*. Washington, DC: National Institute on Corrections.

Clear, T. R., & Gallagher, K. W. (1983). Screening devices in probation and parole: Management problems. *Evaluation Review, 7*, 217–234.

Coulson, G., Ilacqua, G., Nutbrown, V., Giulekas, D., & Cudjoe, F. (1996). Predictive validity of the LSI for incarcerated female offenders. *Criminal Justice and Behavior, 23*, 427–439.

De Leon, G. (2000). *The therapeutic community: Theory, model & method*. New York: Springer.

Dowden, C., & Andrews, D. A. (2000). Effective correctional treatment and violent re-offending: A meta-analysis. *Canadian Journal of Criminology, 42*, 449–467.

Dowden, C., & Andrews, D. A. (2004). The importance of staff practices in delivering effective correctional treatment: A meta-analysis of core correctional practices. *International Journal of Offender Therapy and Comparative Criminology, 48*, 203–214.

Duncan, A., Sacks, S., Melnick, G., Cleland, C. M., Pearson, F. S., & Coen, C. (2008). Performance of the CJDATS Co-Occurring Disorders Screening Instruments (CODSIs) among minority offenders. *Behavioral Sciences and the Law, 26*, 351–368.

Eisenberg, M., Bryl, J., & Fabelo, T. (2009). *Validation of the Wisconsin department of corrections risk assessment instrument*. New York: Council of State Governments Justice Center.

Farabee, D., Knight, K., Garner, B. R., & Calhoun, S. (2007). The inmate prerelease assessment for reentry planning. *Criminal Justice and Behavior, 34*, 1188–1197.

Fass, T. L., Heilbrun, K., DeMatteo, D., & Fretz, R. (2008). The LSI-R and the COMPAS: Validation data on two risk-needs tools. *Criminal Justice and Behavior, 35*, 1095–1108.

Feldstein, S. W., & Miller, W. R. (2007). Does subtle screening for substance abuse work? A review of the Substance Abuse Subtle Screening Inventory (SASSI). *Addiction, 102*, 41–50.

Fletcher, B. W. (2003). The national criminal justice drug abuse treatment studies (CJ-DATS). *Offender Substance Abuse Report, 3*, 1–5.

Garner, B. R., Knight, K., Flynn, P. M., Morey, J. T., & Simpson, D. D. (2007). Measuring offender attributes and engagement in treatment using the client evaluation of self and treatment. *Criminal Justice and Behavior, 34*, 1113–1130.

Gendreau, P., Goggin, C., & Smith, P. (2002). Is the PCL-R really the "unparalleled" measure of offender risk? A lesson in knowledge cumulation. *Criminal Justice and Behavior, 29*, 397–426.

Grove, W. M., & Meehl, P. E. (1996). Comparative efficiency of informal (subjective, impressionistic) and formal (mechanical, algorithmic) prediction procedures: The clinical-statistical controversy. *Psychology, Public Policy and Law, 2*, 293–323.

Hanlon, T. E., O'Grady, K. E., & Bateman, R. W. (2000). Using the Addiction Severity Index to predict treatment outcome among substance abusing parolees. *Journal of Offender Rehabilitation, 31*, 67–79.

Hiller, M. L., Knight, K., Leukefeld, C., & Simpson, D. D. (2002). Motivation as a predictor of treatment engagement in mandated residential substance abuse treatment. *Criminal Justice and Behavior, 29*, 56–75.

Hiller, M. L., Knight, K., Rao, S. R., & Simpson, D. D. (2002). Assessing and evaluating mandated correctional substance abuse treatment. In C. G. Leukefeld, F. Tims, & D. Farabee (Eds.), *Treatment of drug offenders: Policies and issues* (pp. 41–56). New York: Springer.

Hiller, M. L., Knight, K., Saum, C. A., & Simpson, D. D. (2006). Social functioning, treatment dropout, and recidivism of probationers mandated to a modified therapeutic community. *Criminal Justice and Behavior, 33*, 738–759.

Hiller, M. L., & Narevic, E. (2005). Evaluating brief substance abuse screening instruments for drug-involved offenders. *Offender Substance Abuse Report, 5*(3), 35–37, 48.

Hoffman, P. B. (1983). Screening for risk: A revised salient factor score. *Journal of Criminal Justice, 11*, 539–547.

Hubbard, D. J., Travis, L. F., & Latessa, E. J. (2001). *Case classification in community corrections: A national survey of the state of the art*. Washington, DC: National Institute of Justice.

Joe, G. W., Broome, K. M., Rowan-Szal, G. A., & Simpson, D. D. (2002). Measuring patient attributes and engagement in treatment. *Journal of Substance Abuse Treatment, 22*, 183–196.

Kelly, C. E., & Welsh, W. N. (2008). The predictive validity of the level of service inventory-revised for drug-involved offenders. *Criminal Justice and Behavior, 35*, 819–831.

Knight, K., Garner, B., Simpson, D. D., Morey, J. T., & Flynn, P. M. (2006). An assessment of criminal thinking. *Crime and Delinquency, 52*, 159–177.

Knight, K., Simpson, D. D., & Hiller, M. L. (1999). Three-year reincarceration outcomes for in-prison therapeutic community treatment in Texas. *Prison Journal, 79*(3), 337–351.

Knight, K., Simpson, D. D., & Hiller, M. L. (2002). Screening and referral for substance-abuse treatment in the criminal justice system. In C. G. Leukefeld, F. Tims, & D. Farabee (Eds.), *Treatment of drug offenders: Policies and issues* (pp. 259–272, 373–376). New York: Springer.

Knight, K., Simpson, D. D., & Morey, J. T. (2002). *TCU-NIC cooperative agreement: Final report*. Fort Worth, TX: Texas Christian University, Institute of Behavioral Research.

Kressel, D., De Leon, G., Palij, M., & Rubin, G. (2000). Measuring client clinical progress in therapeutic community treatment: The therapeutic community client assessment inventory, client assessment summary, and staff assessment. *Journal of Substance Abuse Treatment, 19*, 267–272.

Latessa, E. J., & Holsinger, A. (1998). The importance of evaluating correctional programs: Assessing outcome and quality. *Corrections Management Quarterly, 2*, 22–29.

Latessa, E. J., & Lowenkamp, C. (2006). What works in reducing recidivism? *University of St. Thomas Law Journal, 3*, 521–535.

Leonhard, C., Mulvey, K., Gastfriend, D. R., & Shwartz, M. (2000). The Addiction Severity Index: A field study of internal consistency and reliability. *Journal of Substance Abuse Treatment, 18*, 129–135.

Lowenkamp, C., Hodsinger, S., & Latessa, E. (2001). Risk/need assessment, offender classification, and the role of child abuse. *Criminal Justice and Behavior, 28*, 543–563.

Lowenkamp, C. T., & Latessa, E. J. (2002). *Evaluation of Ohio's community based correctional facilities and halfway house programs*. Cincinnati, OH: University of Cincinnati.

Lowenkamp, C. T., Latessa, E. J., & Smith, P. (2006). Does correctional program quality really matter? The impact of adhering to the principles of effective intervention. *Criminology & Public Policy, 5*, 575–594.

Loza, W., & Simourd, D. J. (1994). Psychometric evaluation of the Level of Supervision Inventory (LSI) among male Canadian federal offenders. *Criminal Justice and Behavior, 21*, 468–480.

Mäkelä, K. (2004). Studies of the reliability and validity of the Addiction Severity Index. *Addiction, 99*, 398–410.

Marlowe, D. B. (2003, August). *Integrating substance abuse treatment and criminal justice supervision*. Science and practice perspectives. Rockville, MD: National Institute on Drug Abuse.

McLellan, A. T., Kushner, H., Metzger, D., Peters, R., Smith, I., Grissom, G., et al. (1992). The fifth edition of the Addiction Severity Index. *Journal of Substance Abuse Treatment, 9*, 199–213.

McLellan, A. T., Luborsky, L., Cacciola, J., & Griffith, J. E. (1985). New data from the Addiction Severity Index: Reliability and validity in three centers. *Journal of Nervous and Mental Disease, 173*, 412–423.

McLellan, A. T., Luborsky, L., Woody, G. E., & O'Brien, C. P. (1980). An improved diagnostic evaluation instrument for substance abuse patient, the Addiction Severity Index. *Journal of Nervous and Mental Disease, 168*, 26–33.

Miller, C. S., Woodson, J., Howell, R. T., & Shields, A. L. (2009). Assessing the reliability of scores produced by the substance abuse subtle screening inventory. *Substance Use and Misuse, 44*, 1090–1100.

Miller, F. G. (1985). *The substance abuse subtle screening inventory manual*. Bloomington, IN: Glenn A. Miller.

Miller, F. G., & Lazowski, L. E. (1999). *The adult SASSI-3 manual*. Springville, IN: SASSI Institute.

National Institute on Drug Abuse. (2006). *Principles of drug abuse treatment for criminal justice populations*. Rockville, MD: Author.

Ogloff, J. R. P., & Davis, M. R. (2004). Advances in offender assessment and rehabilitation: Contributions of the risk-needs-responsivity approach. *Psychology, Crime, and Law, 10*, 229–242.

Peters, R. H., Bartoi, M. G., & Sherman, P. B. (2008). *Screening and assessment of co-occurring disorders in the justice system*. Delmar, NY: The National GAINS Center.

Peters, R. H., Greenbaum, P. E., & Edens, J. F. (1998). Prevalence of *DSM-IV* substance abuse and dependence disorders among prison inmates. *American Journal of Drug and Alcohol Abuse, 24*, 573–587.

Peters, R. H., Greenbaum, P. E., Steinberg, M. L., Carter, C. R., Ortiz, M. M., Fry, B., et al. (2000). Effectiveness of screening instruments in detecting substance abuse disorders among prisoners. *Journal of Substance Abuse Treatment, 18*, 349–358.

Peters, R. H., & Wexler, H. K. (Eds.). (2005). *Substance abuse treatment for adults in the criminal justice system*. Treatment improvement protocol (TIP) series 44. Rockville, MD: Substance Abuse and Mental Health Services Administration, Center for Substance Abuse Treatment.

Rikoon, S. H., Cacciola, J. S., Carise, D., Alterman, A., & McLellan, A. T. (2006). Predicting DSM-IV dependence diagnoses with the Addiction Severity Index composite scores. *Journal of Substance Abuse Treatment, 31*, 17–24.

Roberts, E. A., Contois, M. W., Willis, J. C., Worthington, M. R., & Knight, K. (2007). Assessing offender needs and performance for planning and monitoring criminal justice drug treatment. *Criminal Justice and Behavior, 34*, 1179–1187.

Sacks, J. Y., McKendrick, K., & Kressel, D. (2007). Measuring offender progress in treatment using the Client Assessment Inventory. *Criminal Justice and Behavior, 34*, 1131–1142.

Sacks, S., Melnick, G., Coen, C., Banks, S., Friedmann, P. D., Grella, C., et al. (2007a). CJDATS Co-occurring disorders screening instrument for mental disorders (CODSI-MD): A pilot study. *The Prison Journal, 87*, 86–110.

Sacks, S., Melnick, G., Coen, C., Banks, S., Friedmann, P. D., Grella, C., et al. (2007b). CJDATS Co-occurring disorders screening instrument for mental disorders: A validation study. *Criminal Justice and Behavior, 34*, 1198–1215.

Saltstone, R., Halliwell, S., & Hayslip, M. A. (1994). A multivariate evaluation of the Michigan Alcohol Screening Test and the Drug Abuse Screening Test in a female offender population. *Addictive Behaviors, 19*, 455–462.

Saum, C. A., O'Connell, D. J., Martin, S. S., Hiller, M. L., Bacon, G. A., & Simpson, D. D. (2007). Tempest in a TC: Changing treatment providers for in-prison therapeutic communities. *Criminal Justice and Behavior, 37*, 1168–1178.

Selzer, M. L. (1971). The Michigan Alcoholism Screening Test: The quest for a new diagnostic instrument. *American Journal of Psychiatry, 127*, 1653–1658.

Selzer, M. L., Vinokur, A., & van Rooijen, L. (1975). A self-administered Short Michigan Alcoholism Screening Test (SMAST). *Journal of Studies on Alcohol, 36*, 117–126.

Shields, A. L., Howell, R. T., Potter, J. S., & Weiss, R. D. (2007). The Michigan Alcoholism Screening Test and its shortened form: A meta-analytic inquiry into score reliability. *Substance Use and Misuse, 42*, 1783–1800.

Shields, I. W., & Simourd, D. J. (1991). Predicting predatory behavior in a population of young offenders. *Criminal Justice and Behavior, 18*, 180–194.

Simourd, D. (2004). Use of dynamic risk/need assessment instruments among long-term incarcerated offenders. *Criminal Justice and Behavior, 31*, 306–323.

Simourd, D. (2006, May). *Validation of risk/needs assessments in the Pennsylvania Department of Corrections*. Interim report. Collingswood, NJ: Volunteers of America-Delaware Valley.

Simourd, D. J., & Malcolm, P. B. (1998). Reliability and validity of the Level of Service Inventory-Revised among federally incarcerated offenders. *Journal of Interpersonal Violence, 13*, 261–274.

Simpson, D. D., & Joe, G. W. (1993). Motivation as a predictor of early dropout from drug abuse treatment. *Psychotherapy, 30*, 357–368.

Simpson, D. D., Joe, G. W., & Broome, K. M. (2002). A national 5-year follow-up of treatment outcomes for cocaine dependence. *Archives of General Psychiatry, 59*, 538–544.

Simpson, D. D., Joe, G. W., Rowan-Szal, G. A., & Greener, J. M. (1995). Client engagement and change during substance abuse treatment. *Journal of Substance Abuse Treatment, 7*, 117–134.

Simpson, D. D., & Knight, K. (2007). Offender needs and functioning assessments from a national cooperative research program. *Criminal Justice and Behavior, 34*, 1105–1112.

Skinner, H. A. (1982). The Drug Abuse Screening Test. *Addictive Behaviors, 7*, 363–371.

Staton-Tindall, M., Garner, B. R., Morey, J. T., Leukefeld, C., Krietemeyer, J., Saum, C. A., et al. (2007). Gender differences in treatment engagement among a sample of incarcerated substance abusers. *Criminal Justice and Behavior, 34*, 1143–1156.

Storgaard, H., Nielsen, S. D., & Gluud, C. (1994). The validity of the Michigan Alcohol Screening Test (MAST). *Alcohol and Alcoholism, 29*, 493–502.

Swartz, J. A. (1998). Adapting and using the Substance Abuse Subtle Screening Inventory-3 with criminal justice offenders: Preliminary results. *Criminal Justice and Behavior, 25*, 344–365.

Taxman, F. S., Cropsey, K. L., Young, D. W., & Wexler, H. (2007). Screening, assessment, and referral practices in adult correctional settings: A national perspective. *Criminal Justice and Behavior, 34*, 1216–1234.

Taxman, F. S., & Marlowe, D. B. (2006). Risk, needs, responsivity: In action or inaction? *Crime and Delinquency, 52*(1), 3–6.

Taxman, F. S., Perdoni, M., Young, D., Belenko, S., & Hiller, M. (in press). Twenty years of drug treatment courts: The current state of drug courts. In D. K. Shaffer (Ed.). *Drug Courts and the Criminal Justice System*. Boulder, CO: Lynne Rienner Publishers.

Taxman, F. S., Thanner, M., & Weisburd, D. (2006). Risk, need, and responsivity (RNR): It all depends. *Crime and Delinquency, 52*, 28–51.

Taxman, F., Young, D., & Byrne, J. (2004). Transforming offender reentry into public safety: Lessons from OJP's Reentry Partnership Initiative. *Justice Policy and Research, 5*, 101–128.

Taxman, F. S., Young, D., Wiersema, B., Rhodes, A., & Mitchell, S. (2007). The National criminal justice treatment practices survey: Methods and procedures. *Journal of Substance Abuse Treatment, 32*, 225–238.

Teitelbaum, L., & Mullen, B. (2000). The validity of MAST in psychiatric settings: A Meta-analytic integration. *Journal of Studies on Alcohol, 61*, 254–261.

Thanner, M., & Taxman, F. S. (2003). Responsivity: The value of providing intensive services to high-risk offenders. *Journal of Substance Abuse Treatment, 24*, 137–147.

Walters, G. D. (1995). The psychological inventory of criminal thinking styles: Part I. Reliability and preliminary validity. *Criminal Justice and Behavior, 22*, 307–325.

Welsh, W. N. (2006). *Evaluation of drug treatment programs at the State Correctional Institution (SCI) at Chester: A partnership between the Pennsylvania Department of Corrections, Gaudenzia Inc., and Temple University.* (Final Report to the National Institute of Justice 2002-RT-BX-1002). Retrieved October 9, 2009, from the PADOC Web site http://www.cor.state.pa.us/stats/lib/stats/ChesterReporttoNIJ-Final-November2006.pdf

Welsh, W. N., & McGrain, P. N. (2008). Predictors of therapeutic engagement in prison-based drug treatment. *Drug and Alcohol Dependence, 96*, 271–280.

Yudko, E., Lozhkina, O., & Fouts, A. (2007). A comprehensive review of the psychometric properties of the Drug Abuse Screening Test. *Journal of Substance Abuse Treatment, 32*, 189–198.

# Substance Abuse Technology: A Primer for Community Corrections Practitioners

5

Mario A. Paparozzi and Roger Guy

**Abstract**

Community corrections practitioners generally conceptualize "substance abuse technologies" to mean those things that are used to detect the use of some substance that an offender is prohibited from using as a condition of pretrial release, probation, parole, work release, or any other correctional options that involve an alternative to traditional incarceration (e.g., day reporting programs, electronic monitoring, or community-based residential and treatment programs for inmates reentering the community after a period of incarceration). In this chapter, we broaden the focus of "technologies" in order to give due diligence to substance abuse *testing* technologies from their traditionally narrow focus on detection to include technologies associated with delivering *services* that produce reductions in substance abuse and ultimately in individual offender recidivism.

**Keywords**

Probation • Parole • Community corrections • Urine testing technology • Monitoring

## Introduction

Community corrections practitioners generally conceptualize "substance abuse technologies" to mean those things that are used to detect the use of some substance that an offender is prohibited from using as a condition of pretrial release, probation, parole, work release, or any other correctional options that involve an alternative to traditional incarceration (e.g., day reporting programs, electronic monitoring, or community-based residential and treatment programs for inmates reentering the community after a period of incarceration). In this chapter, we broaden the focus of "technologies" in order to give due diligence to substance abuse *testing* technologies from their traditionally narrow focus on detection to include technologies associated with delivering *services*

M.A. Paparozzi (✉)
Department of Sociology and Criminal Justice,
University of North Carolina, Pembroke, NC 28372,
USA
e-mail: mario.paparozzi@uncp.edu

C. Leukefeld et al. (eds.), *Handbook of Evidence-Based Substance Abuse Treatment in Criminal Justice Settings*, Issues in Children's and Families' Lives 11,
DOI 10.1007/978-1-4419-9470-7_5, 

that produce reductions in substance abuse and ultimately in individual offender recidivism.

The notion that technology should incorporate the inclusion of "gadgets," "mechanical devices," "automated management information systems," and "programmatic services" that are grounded in scientific findings is not new (Travis, 1997). Moreover, Travis convincingly argues that the use of technology to support evidence-based substance abuse intervention services is a necessary condition for maximizing the potential to reduce individual offender recidivism.

Conceptualizing as "technologies" to include those services and programs that are designed to ameliorate substance abuse and recidivism can be confusing to practitioners and even more so to the general public and elected officials charged with policy making. The confusion derives from a simplistic, narrow, and erroneous view of technology as being limited to physical objects. We posit that such a conceptualization impedes the development of theoretically relevant and empirically driven policies, programs, and practices. Finally, we discuss the importance of technology transfer as the conveyance of knowledge from the world of research and academic scholarship to that of corrections practitioners. We close by offering some suggestions that might lead to a building of that ever-elusive bridge between the "ivory towers" of universities and the stark realities of "the streets."

Before turning to a discussion about substance abuse technologies, it is helpful to examine the scholarly and social frameworks that have spurred and shaped the implementation of substance abuse technologies within a variety of criminal justice system components, specifically community correctional environments.

Within the social and legal contexts of the past 40 years, many scholars have intensely debated whether or not criminal behavior causes substance abuse or whether substance abuse causes criminal behavior. For example, Bean and Wilkinson (1988), Burr (1987), Matthews and Trickey (1996), and Mott and Taylor (1974) found that criminality predates substance abuse. Others have found evidence supporting the notion that the temporal ordering is that substance abuse precedes crime (Goldstein, 1985; Massing, 2000; Parker, Bakx, & Newcombe, 1988; Parker & Bottomley, 1996; Parker & Newcombe, 1987). Lastly, there is research indicating that the type of illegal substances used has varying effects on influencing criminal behavior (Klee & Morris, 1995).

Research on the relationships between substance abuse, criminality, and crimes of choice is a work in progress. Notwithstanding the fluid nature of knowledge cumulation with regard to the link between substance abuse and crime, there is no dispute that a correlation exists. It is essential, therefore, that treatment technologies that derive from a variety of research findings be fully understood and transferred to community corrections practitioners for use and ongoing evaluation of their effectiveness in breaking the vicious cycle of drug use and crime.

The 1960s and early 1970s was a period of considerable social upheaval. Due to a variety of events (e.g., civil rights protests, Kent State, Vietnam War, and Watergate), the view that government, with all its bureaucracy, could continue to function as a benevolent godfather and "do good" was called into serious question (Paparozzi & Gendreau, 2005). These turns of events ushered in a more punitive and controlling societal view of substance abusers including a renewed emphasis on coerced treatment.[1] One notable early example of coerced treatment that was incorporated into the criminal justice process was California's Civil Addict Program (CAP). The CAP merged civil with criminal court processing by permitting sentencing courts to order civil commitment (i.e., compulsory treatment) for substance abusers convicted of a felony or misdemeanor (Henry & Clark, 1999). The underlying authority for CAP came from a US Supreme Court decision that authorized states to establish programs of compulsory treatment for criminals

[1] Coerced treatment in the United States had its beginnings in the 1920s, albeit in limited fashion. For example, several states had morphine maintenance facilities (Waldorf, Orlick, & Reinarman, 1974).

convicted of substance abuse offenses (*Robinson v. California*, 1962).

Ultimately, the emergence of the law and order agenda initiated by President Nixon in the late 1960s provided significant funds to fight America's first "War on Drugs" (Frontline, 2007). As part of the war effort, criminal justice agencies were encouraged, through financial support, to develop methods for swift detection and response to illegal substance abuse (Courtright, 1982; Massing, 2000).

With the support of federal funds, programs like the Treatment Alternatives to Street Crime (TASC) were established. TASC was implemented for the specific purpose of breaking the link between substance abuse and crime. These programs typically provide substance abuse treatment services and urine testing for the purpose of holding offenders accountable to "remain clean." Within corrections, pretrial services as well as probation and parole use TASC programs to procure substance abuse treatment services (Henry & Clark, 1999). In many instances, the TASC programs were used to conduct urine monitoring so that local community corrections agencies did not have to do so. Eventually, and largely due to the need for expanded drug testing for a burgeoning community corrections caseload, community corrections agencies like pretrial, probation, and parole began to implement in-house urine testing protocols.

## Substance Abuse Testing Technologies – A Brief History and Current Trends

### Urine Testing Technology

Within community corrections, testing for the use of illegal substances began to take hold in 1972 (Henry & Clark, 1999). The earliest forms of testing involved sending urine specimens to laboratories where they were screened for drugs using immunoassay technology. A detailed discussion of immunoassay techniques is well beyond the scope of this chapter.[2] Suffice to say that immunoassay techniques involve the measurement of the level of interaction between a chemical (commonly referred to as the reagent) and an enzyme in the urine specimen being tested. The interactive effect detects the presence of a drug.[3]

### Thin Layer Chromatography

While it was a state-of-the-art methodology at the time, laboratory testing was expensive, imprecise, time consuming, and required skilled laboratory technicians to conduct the tests. Also problematic was the fact that the earliest tests used a technology known as thin layer chromatography (TLC). As the science of urine testing advanced, it was determined that TLC tests were subject to significant error, in particular with regard to false negatives (Visher, 1991).[4] In short, many offenders who actually used illegal substances went undetected.

False negative test results, of course, do not trigger a second confirmatory test as would a false positive test. Moreover, an unreasonable number of false negative tests undermines the addiction recovery process as well as the justice and public safety functions of community corrections because of the following: (a) therapeutic interventions require breaking the cycle of denial; (b) offenders are not held accountable for the terms of their conditional liberty; and (c) unchecked substance abuse is associated with criminal behavior (Belenko & Peugh, 1998;

[2] The most commonly used immunoassays are the enzyme immunoassay, the radio immunoassay, and the fluorescence polarization immunoassay. All three tests work on the same basic principle: they use binding antibodies capable of recognizing drugs or drug groups. When urine or hair containing the drug is mixed in solution with the drugs antibody, it binds to the antibody.

[3] For a detailed explanation of how reagents are used to conduct TLC tests, see Touchstone (1992, pp. 1–6).

[4] False positive test results lead to the incorrect conclusion that the person tested used drugs when in fact he/she did not. False negative tests lead to the incorrect conclusion that the person tested did not use drugs when in fact he/she did.

Office of National Drug Control Policy, 2000).[5] Finally, second confirmatory tests for false positives incur unnecessary financial costs and diversion of limited human resources that could be better dedicated to the supervision of offenders actually using illegal drugs. On the other hand, confirmatory tests assure that offenders who are subjected to crude initial testing techniques, such as TLC, are given due process of law by avoiding being falsely accused and violated, based upon a testing technology with questionable accuracy.

It has always been the case that initial positive urine tests required confirmation either by an admission from the offender tested or by a confirmatory test. In fact, in correctional settings, a drug test cannot be treated as positive without an admission from the person tested, or a confirmatory test. Prior to conducting a confirmatory test on a positive initial test, the urine specimen is generally tested for *validity* to determine if it has been adulterated or replaced by a different specimen. If a specimen tests positive for adulteration, a second confirmatory test for adulterants is recommended.

In community corrections, there are numerous accepted methods for conducting confirmatory tests on positive urine specimens. Historically, confirmatory tests were performed using a variety of drug testing technologies, including the same technology that was used for the initial test (Meyer, 2008). The only limitation was that the confirmatory test used an independent test on the same specimen that was used for the initial test (Meyer, 2008).

This strategy permitted confirmatory tests to be conducted using less expensive, albeit less reliable, technologies. For many years, there was no requirement that confirmatory tests be conducted using what was, and remains acknowledged to be, the most accurate substance abuse testing technology available – gas chromatography/mass spectrometry (GC/MS). Currently, virtually all community corrections agencies use GC/MS for confirmatory testing of positive urine specimens because it is widely recognized among practitioners to be the "gold standard" for test result accuracy.

As an example, the US Administrative of the Courts (AOC), following the United States Administrative Code (the Code), established policies that require that GC/MS be used for confirmatory tests. The Code does permit occasional alternative methods of confirmatory testing provided the Director of the AOC, after consultation with the Secretary of the Department of Health and Human Services, determines that the alternative confirmatory testing technology is at least as accurate as GC/MS (US Code, 2008).

## Enzyme Multiple Immunoassay Technique

Testing for illegal drugs using urine samples has progressed significantly since the early days of TLC laboratory testing. Subsequent to the TLC test technology, a urine screening method known as enzyme multiple immunoassay technique (EMIT) was developed. The EMIT technology was much more accurate than TLC technology, and it could be conducted on-site by corrections staff with minimal training.

One of the first uses of EMIT in the community corrections arena occurred in 1977 in a Texas probation department (Lozito, 1979). The EMIT technology, for the first time, permitted community corrections practitioners the ability to obtain immediate – typically within 15 minutes – and more accurate results when screening for illegal substances. Depending on the desires and financial limitations of the users of the EMIT technology, tests could be conducted for virtually any illegal drug. Earlier laboratory testing technologies took days or, very often, weeks for results to be returned to community corrections agencies. This time lag seriously impeded the ability of community corrections agencies to fulfill their drug interdiction and public safety objectives through timely detection of an offender's illegal drug use.

The use of EMIT has waned considerably since the mid-1980s with the development of noninstrument-based on-site test cup technologies. Before turning to a discussion of these

[5] For an alternative view of the link between drugs and crime, see Seddon (2000).

**Fig. 5.1** Viva-E® drug testing system, used to process Syva® Emit® tests

newer technologies, a discussion of how EMIT actually works follows.

To conduct a typical EMIT urine test in a community corrections setting, an instrument provided by the manufacturer is used. The instruments vary in size; however, they can be easily accommodated in a small office: see Figs. 5.1 and 5.2 of the Viva-E® Drug Testing System that is used to process Syva® Emit® tests, and the V-Twin for Siemens Healthcare Diagnostics, respectively.

The EMIT test instruments measure changes in the amount of light that the urine specimen absorbs. More light absorption indicates the presence of illegal drugs, less light indicates an absence. The specimen being tested is subjected to measurement against a known amount of the drug contained in the testing instrument. This comparison is then interpreted and reported with regard to the presence or absence of illegal drugs.

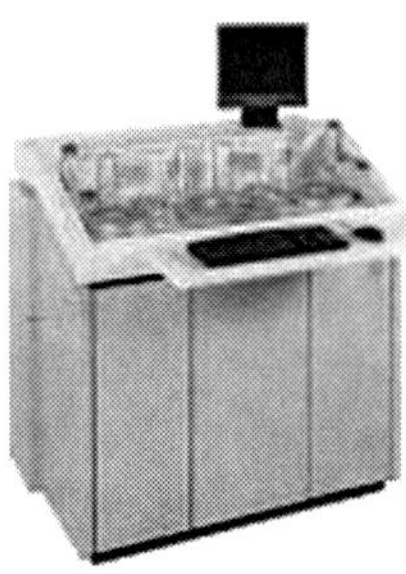

**Fig. 5.2** V-Twin for Siemens Healthcare Diagnostics

While EMIT affords community corrections practitioners greater case management flexibility and cost savings than laboratory testing technologies, newer technologies have evolved that are noninstrument based, more immediate, and less costly. The most prominent examples of noninstrument-based testing technology involve test strips, handheld testing cassettes, and test cups (Jenkins & Goldberg, 2002).

## Portable Urine Testing Technology

Portable urine testing technology (PUTT) has, in our opinion, become the screening test of choice in community corrections. Portable urine tests offer several distinct advantages over off-site laboratory or on-site mechanical testing techniques (e.g., EMIT). Some of the benefits of PUTT include (a) reduced costs; (b) immediate results; (c) flexibility for testing in a variety of locations; (d) simplified chain of custody; and (e) minimal staff training to conduct and interpret tests. The three most common types of PUTT are (a) test strip; (b) handheld cassette; and (c) test cup.

Depending on the type of PUTT selected by a community corrections agency, these tests are capable of screening for a single drug or multiple drugs simultaneously. While PUTT provides many important benefits in a community corrections environment, there are some potential problems that are often overlooked in the literature about drug testing but are well known to community corrections practitioners. For example, portable testing technologies have the potential of producing a net widening effect because they are easy to use and readily available. Some officers with a law enforcement orientation (Paparozzi & Gendreau, 2005), for example, might be inclined to test most or all offenders more frequently than necessary. Moreover, when PUTT is available for conducting multiple simultaneous tests, community corrections officers with a law enforcement professional orientation might be inclined to test for multiple drugs each and every time that an offender is tested. There are ways to control for the potential net widening effects of PUTT; the failure to do so could actually lead to increased costs for drug testing while not producing any value added in terms of offender accountability.

When using PUTT, it is essential that community corrections agencies adopt policies that are designed to effectively *and* efficiently accomplish the desired result. The result sought, of course, is the ability to detect use in order to interdict drug use and enhance public safety. Policies and procedures for case assessment and random testing can be very effective in minimizing the tendency of line staff to overuse PUTT. In this regard, thorough case assessments by a supervising community corrections officer provide important information about an offender's drug(s) of choice. Once the offender's drug profile is known, supervising officers should be required to reasonably target these illegal "drug(s) of choice" rather than screen for a wide variety of drugs each time a test is conducted. Supervising officers can also be guided by policy to randomly test for other illegal substances as case needs dictate during the course of ongoing supervision of the offender. The following example illuminates this point:

> An initial case assessment indicates that methamphetamine is an offender's drug of choice. During the course of supervision, the offender's mother advises that she suspects marijuana use by the offender. This information justifies the introduction of tests for drugs other than the known drug(s) of choice.

Random testing, both in terms of timing of tests and drug choice, gives the supervising officer the element of surprise. This policy strategy effectively obviates the need to spend money needlessly on more frequent testing as well as testing for multiple drugs each time an offender is tested. In the end, the policy consideration should focus on two competing portable urine testing strategies: (1) test frequently for all drugs every time a test is conducted; (2) test randomly with a focus on drug(s) of choice and occasionally introduce tests for other drugs. The latter of these two policy strategies is the preferred choice both in terms of its effectiveness (because it fosters offender accountability) and efficiency (because it saves money through the judicious use of test kits).

## Single and Multiple Test Strip and Cassette Testing Technology

This type of PUTT involves a test strip or a cassette that tests for one drug, or multiple drugs, by immersing the strip or a cassette into a urine specimen. Single test strip technology is inexpensive and can be used effectively when policies and procedures require thorough case assessments, active supervision of offenders, and truly random conduct of tests. Multiple test strips are more costly; however, they are effective supervision tools only when the totality of circumstances surrounding the supervision of an offender justifies their use.

Figure 5.3 depicts a test strip technology typically used in community corrections settings.

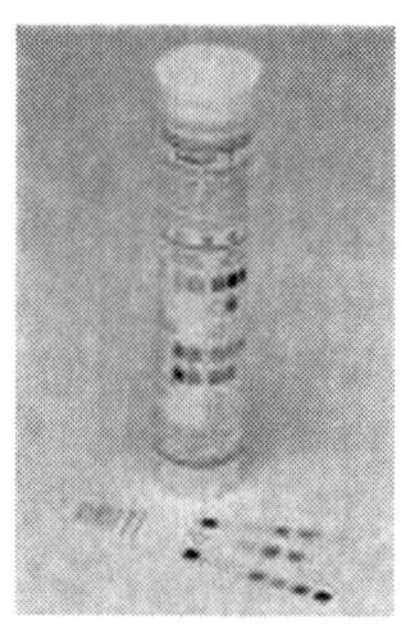

**Fig. 5.3** Typical test strip technology (The Intect® 7)

## Cassette Testing Technology

Like the test strip technology, cassette testing can also be used to conduct single or multiple drug tests. Manufacturers of this technology have developed a variety of ways to conduct these tests. The two most common technologies involve the use of either a multiple panel cassette the size of a small cell phone or the individual panel pipette that can be as small as a USB flash drive.

This type of PUTT involves a cassette that tests for multiple drugs or one drug, either by immersing the entire cassette into a urine specimen or by using a pipette to deposit a specimen onto the cassette. Similar to the test strip, this technology is less expensive when used to test for one drug versus multiple drugs during a single test. Cassette technology is also effective when policies and procedures require thorough case assessments, active supervision of offenders, and truly random conduct of tests. Figure 5.4 depicts cassette testing technology typically used in community corrections settings.

## Test Cup Technology

Test cup technology has the capability to test for single drugs; however it is most common for this type of PUTT to test for between 3 and 10 drugs during a single test. As with other portable urine testing methods, testing for fewer drugs during a single test reduces costs. A significant advantage of test cup technology is that it involves less contact with a urine specimen. Unlike the test strip and cassette technology, there is no need to dip a test stick or a cassette into a specimen, nor is there a need to use a pipette to suction urine from a specimen and place it onto a panel to complete the test. Test cups also provide the added advantage of enhanced amenability to chain of custody concerns. A test cup revealing a positive specimen can easily be capped, sealed, and sent to a laboratory for confirmatory testing.

The matter of the amount of staff contact with urine specimens should be taken seriously. In many instances, individuals responsible for conducting tests have resisted the use of on-site testing methods claiming that such testing increases occupational health hazards. Health hazard concerns are certainly not to be overlooked, but they should not be used as a basis to avoid performing critical public safety and treatment functions that are universally accepted as primary goals of community corrections. Urine testing is one of these critical functions since it facilitates short-term risk management of offenders while working toward their long-term behavior reform. Basic safeguards such as wearing protective gloves and thorough hand washing virtually eliminate health hazards. Figure 5.5 depicts a typical test cup technology used in community corrections settings.

## Transdermal Testing Technology (Sweat Patch Perspiration Technology)

This type of perspiration or sweat patch testing technology relies on an adhesive patch that

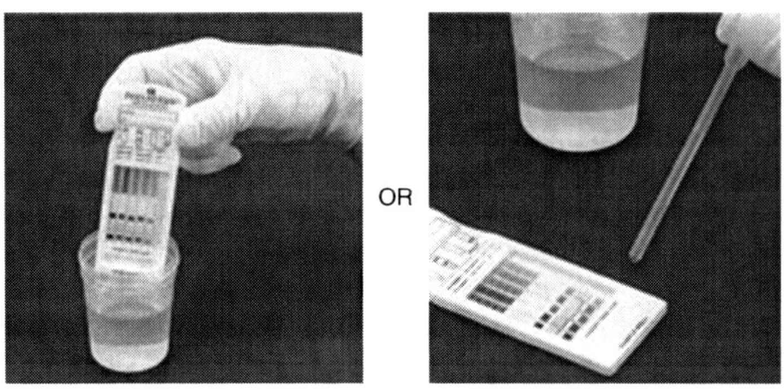


**Fig. 5.4** Cassette testing technology (Copyright 2009; AlcoPro)

**Fig. 5.5** Test cup (On-Site® CupKit™)

is applied to the skin, usually the upper arm, of the person being tested. The patch itself is made of a gauze-like material, and it is covered when affixed to the skin by using a tape similar to small adhesive bandage. Typically, the patch remains affixed to the offender for 7–10 days. The claim of the manufacturer, PharmChem, Inc., is that the patch is tamper evident. However, there have been reports that the sweat patch can come loose as a result of vigorous activity and excessive perspiration as opposed to tampering by the wearer (U.S. v. Snyder. F.Supp. 2d. 2002 WL 257381 N.D.N.Y., 2002).

The patch, like the other portable technologies already discussed in this chapter, uses an immunoassay technology. During the time the patch is worn, the gauze pad captures secreted perspiration. Once the patch is removed, it must be sent to the manufacturer for analysis; on-site analysis is not possible.

An advantage of the sweat patch is that it expands the drug detection window to the entire time that the patch is worn. In addition, the patch is not as intrusive as on-site urine testing, and it avoids problems associated with the need for having a member of the same sex as the offender conduct the test. Another advantage is that secretion of drugs by the wearer is not affected by consumption of water or other liquids, as is the case with urine testing. The sweat patch, however, is not without its problems.

Perhaps one of the most notable problems is the excessive rates of false positive results due to environmental contamination in which drugs or other substances that yield positive results penetrate the external membrane of sweat patch. Sweat patches have also been associated with higher rates of false positives than urine tests and have been subjected to considerable scrutiny following a Supreme Court decision in 2002 in which the Court rejected the use of the sweat patch to revoke the defendant's supervised release. In this case, there was evidence that the manufacturer's (PharmChem) own tests of the sweat patch technology confirm that false positive results are problematic (Long & Kidwell, 2002; U.S. v. Snyder. F.Supp. 2d. 2002 WL 257381 N.D.N.Y., 2002). These problems render patches less reliable than other testing technologies.

While transdermal testing technology is readily available to community corrections agencies, it has not been widely used (Mieczkowski & Lersch, 1997). Possible reasons for its limited use include (a) problems arising from the inability to immediately detect illegal substance abuse because sweat patches require time for a sufficient amount of perspiration to accumulate on the patch; (b) the questionable accuracy of results; and (c) the fact that the patch is not reliably tamper evident.

With regard to cost, transdermal testing technologies cost more than portable urine testing technologies; however, the increased cost is negated by the fact that fewer tests may be required. Figure 5.6 depicts a typical sweat/perspiration patch technology used in community corrections settings.

## Hair Analysis

Hair analysis is regarded as perhaps the most advanced and accurate technique for detecting drugs. Because hair growth is supported by nutrients from the bloodstream, drug molecules are deposited and remain indefinitely in body hair. The testing relies on obtaining and screening a small sample of hair from the scalp for drug

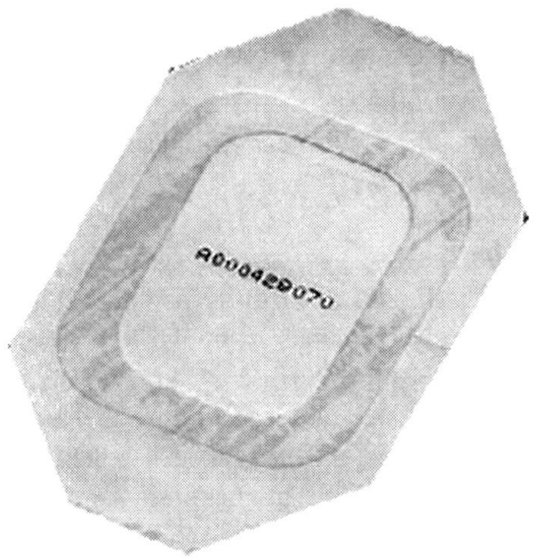

Fig. 5.6 Perspiration/sweat patch

metabolites contained in the shaft. If no scalp hair is available, body hair may be used.

If the initial screening is positive, a gas chromatography/mass spectrometry (GC/MS) is the accepted standard for confirmatory testing. Compared to the methods of substance abuse testing previously discussed, hair analysis is superior in several respects. First, there is a longer detection window. Whereas urinalysis typically detects the presence of substances in a 2–3-day window, hair analysis is able to detect the presence of drugs for up to 12 months because each half-inch of hair provides a 30-day window of drug use. In this way, historical patterns of usage are able to be established. Also, unlike urine testing, analyzing hair samples virtually eliminates false positives, it is tamper proof, and chain of custody concerns are minimal. Finally, foreign substances such as shampoo, bleach, or contaminants such as smoke from cannabis have not been shown to affect the results, and hair analysis is not complicated by the invasiveness or healtn concerns associated with urine tests.

Currently, a large number of commercial laboratories offer hair analysis services for psychoactive drugs, and a large number of corporations, some government agencies, and a number of criminal justice agencies use hair testing to identify potential drug abuse (Mieczkowski, 2001). While the hair analysis has been used in probation and parole since the 1980s, the expense incurred by the necessity of laboratory analysis for both initial and confirmatory testing has limited its widespread adoption in criminal justice agencies (Baer, Baumgartner, & Werner, 1991). Research has shown that while hair analysis provides more accurate data on the use of heroin, cocaine, and amphetamines than does urine testing, it has proven to be less accurate for marijuana. Using data from the Arrestee Drug Abuse Monitoring (ADAM) Program, Mieczkowski (2002) found that hair testing was more effective than urine analysis in identifying less recent drug use. However, there is some dispute regarding the environmental contamination of hair and the relative absence of a universal standard for the preparation of hair prior to analysis.

## Pupillometry

Following the trend toward noninvasive methods of drug detection, physiological methods to detect illegal substance abuse continue to emerge. One such technology is the pupillometry detection method. In its simplest form, pupillometry means measurement of the diameter or width of the pupil of the eye. Research has shown that an alteration in pupils is associated with the presence of drugs or alcohol (Kosnoski, Yolton, Citek, Hayes, & Evans, 1998; Linzmayer, Fischer, & Grunberger, 1997; Tennant, 1988). This type of testing technology detects impairment (i.e., whether an individual is under the influence of a controlled dangerous substance, a legally prescribed narcotic, or alcohol).

Pupil scanning relies on infrared scanning to detect the presence of controlled substances or alcohol by using sophisticated technology to measure the dilation of pupils. A pupillometer, which resembles a pair of binoculars, flashes a beam of light onto the subject's eyes and records his pupillary response. From this response, the device uses a series of algorithms to determine if a subject is under the influence of a prohibited substance.

There is, of course, a difference between the presence of measurable impairment through pupil scans and the presence of chemical substances, both legal and illegal, which are not detectable through urine testing. Whereas urine testing is able to detect the use of a prohibited substance, it is not able to detect actual impairment at the time of the test or the amount of the substance present. Therefore, it is possible to have a positive urine test result without actually being under the influence of a prohibited substance at the time of the test (Richman & Noriega, 2002). On the other hand, urine tests permit a broader detection window than does a pupil scan. An offender under supervision, for example, could test with normal pupils only a short time after the ingestion of a prohibited substance. In such cases, the ability of community corrections officers to detect substance use is impeded.

A typical use of pupil scanning for substance abuse incorporates another technology known as kiosks. Kiosks are used to automate an office reporting check-in protocol for offenders under community supervision. With kiosk reporting, the offender inserts one or more finger into/on a kiosk. The kiosk takes a fingerprint scan to verify the reporting of a specific offender. While this verification process is taking place, it is possible to conduct a pupil scan in order to detect whether or not the offender is impaired by some substance. If the pupil scan reveals impairment, the common protocol is to require that the offender submit to a urine test (Hillyer, 2008). This method of monitoring substance abuse is problematic because of the short detection window provided by pupil scans. An offender could have used a prohibited substance the day before a pupil scan, reported to a kiosk instead of a trained professional who could probe well beyond the ability of a kiosk and pupillometer, and remained undetected and unaccountable for using prohibited substances while under supervision.

Pilot programs in San Diego County Department of Probation have revealed that pupil scanning is more efficient and less costly than urine testing. For example, if the pupillometry test reveals no impairment, the presumption is that the person tested is not under the influence of any legal or illegal substance. In such instances, no further testing is required. The San Diego County Probation Department found that the use of pupil scanning reduced the need for the number of urine tests by 56%. The result was a cost savings to the county of approximately $150,000 (Russo, 2003). Currently, federal probation officers in two states have begun to use remote pupil scanning to detect drug usage (Hillyer, 2008).

### Saliva Testing

Saliva testing is a relatively new technology. It is generally marketed as an alternative to urine and blood testing. As discussed previously, alternative substance abuse testing technologies are based on detecting the chemical breakdown of a drug as opposed to the drug itself. Unlike these alternative methods, saliva samples contain the parent drug rather than the metabolized compound of the drug.

Community corrections agencies have begun to employ saliva testing technology because of its ease of use, reliability, and because samples are difficult to adulterate. If conducted correctly, saliva tests accurately predict the concentration of illegal substances with the same level of accuracy as blood and urine testing technologies. Saliva testing is currently being used as a roadside method of detecting drugs during traffic stops and also in numerous community corrections settings (Thatcher, 2007). Saliva testing technology shows promise for use in prison and jails (Fatah & Cohn, 2003).

Saliva testing is by far one of the simplest substance abuse technologies to use in community corrections. The need for the use of syringes to collect blood samples, the need to watch the voiding of a urine sample in the case of urine testing, and the minimal contact with body fluids make saliva testing the more preferable technology. Saliva is a relatively clean liquid (compared to urine), and it is easy to collect by a swab on the end of a plastic stick. The swab used is a flat collection pad. In conducting a saliva test, the swab is placed between the cheek and gum. The swabbed sample is then inserted into a companion analysis device in order to detect the use of prohibited substances. Figure 5.7 shows a typical saliva swab testing device. If a sample tests positive, the swab testing often requires the voiding of another sample for confirmatory testing due to the small sample collected during the swabbing

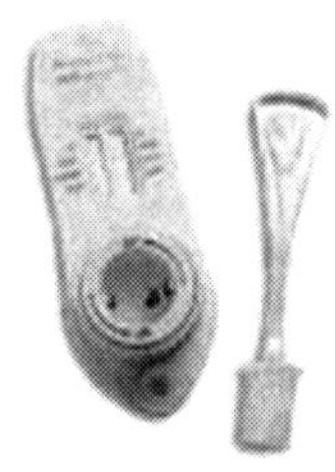

Fig. 5.7 Saliva swab testing device

procedure. Even when the initial sample is of a sufficient size for confirmatory testing, the swab must be removed from the end of the test stick, placed into a container, and sealed. For these reasons, collecting spit samples (discussed below) is preferable to swabbing for samples to be tested.

Another method of collection of a saliva sample involves having the person being tested simply spit into a spit specimen container. The specimen container has a separate chamber where the spit specimen can be suctioned into and then analyzed for prohibited substances. The test results are reported on the side of the container, similar to the manner in which on-site urine test cups report results. If a sample is positive, the container can be sealed and sent to a laboratory for confirmatory testing. Figure 5.8 shows the spit specimen container.

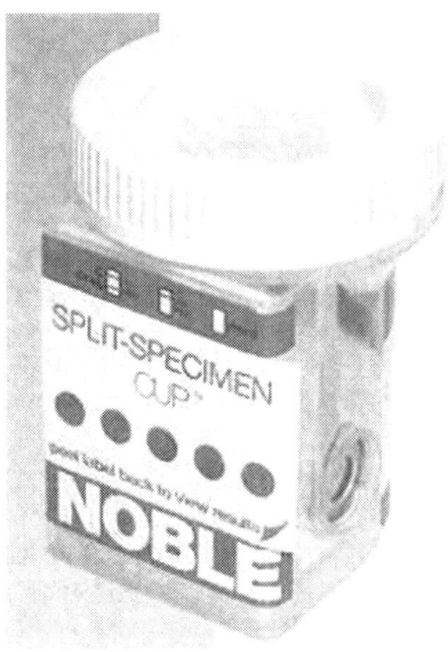


Fig. 5.8 Spit test cup container

One drawback with saliva testing is that the detection window is relatively short compared to other technologies (e.g., hair analysis, urine testing, and blood sample analysis). For example, the detection window is typically reported to be no more than 24 hours after ingestion of a prohibited substance.

## Breathe Analysis Technology

For the layperson, breathalyzers are probably the most common and one of the oldest known methods of alcohol testing (Bogen, 1927). While blood tests are more accurate than breathalyzers, the portability and convenience of breathalyzers make them the preferred device for use in field sobriety tests in making determinations of arrests, prosecution, and conviction of driving while intoxicated (DWI) or driving under the influence (DUI) (Simon, 2000). Breathalyzers estimate the blood alcohol content (BAC) by having the person being tested exhale into a handheld or desktop device. In community corrections, handheld devices are the overwhelming choice due to the need to monitor offenders in a variety of settings, obtain immediate results, and also minimize costs. Desktop devices are typically used by police at police stations. Desktop breathalyzers are extremely expensive compared to handheld testing devices.

Breath-testing equipment measures the amount of alcohol in a specific amount of lung air and estimates a person's BAC, which is done by converting the breath test results to a blood alcohol concentration. The conversion factor for breath to blood is 1–2,100 – 1 unit of alcohol in a tested subject's breath is equal to 2,100 units of alcohol in the blood. This conversion rate is the primary basis for appealing DUI convictions because it represents an average, rather than the actual blood alcohol content which can vary from 1 to 1,150 and 1 to 3,000 (Dubowski, 1986). The actual conversion ratio for an individual lies somewhere between the range which makes the average subject to legal challenges for the use of the 1 to 2100 conversion ratio especially when there is evidence of a low alcohol concentration. This has led some state legislatures to amend drunk- driving statutes to include impairment as measured by the blood, urine, and breath (Simon, 2000).

In community corrections, however, the matter of average conversion rates is not as critical as it is for police and prosecutors addressing driving-while-impaired offenses. When an offender supervised under some form of community corrections has a requirement to abstain from alcohol use, the prohibition is absolute. In others words, it is the determination of the use of alcohol, and not the amount, that is important.

Breathalyzer results are not without problems. Some common mouthwashes that contain alcohol have been shown to interfere with testing results because breathalyzers cannot distinguish between alcohol in the mouth and alcohol coming from the lungs. Alcohol in the mouth may only raise a breathalyzer reading by a small amount and therefore cause problems with prosecution for a DUI offense. The problem with detection of even a small amount of alcohol contained in items like mouthwash is critical, however, to community corrections. This is because the breathalyzer result may falsely predict that an offender under community corrections supervision consumed alcohol and therefore faces reincarceration. Figure 5.9 shows the handheld breathalyzer testing device.

## Testing Technologies Available But Not Typical in Community Corrections Settings

There are several additional technologies available to test for the use of illegal substances. Some of these technologies are NIR absorption spectroscopy, actigraphy, and blood testing. These technologies require expensive equipment and may require highly skilled technicians to administer them. At the time of this writing, their use is so rare in community corrections that they are not presented in detail in this chapter. Instead, only a brief definition of each is provided.

Near-infrared (NIR) absorption spectroscopy testing is used to detect alcohol use. This technology is more expensive than standard breathalyzer tests, and it involves the shining of a light on the skin, usually the underside of the forearm of the person being tested. The person being tested places a forearm onto a flat panel and the test is conducted. The light is absorbed into the skin and unique "absorption signatures" are established. These "absorption signatures" are able to identify alcohol use, but the current state of the technology does not permit reliable testing for controlled dangerous substances. In fact, the alcohol testing aspects of this technology are reported to be fairly accurate, and the detection window for alcohol use is about the same as it would be using blood testing.[6]

Actigraphy testing involves the measurement of sleep patterns in order to detect substance abuse. Through a mechanical device worn by the person being tested, body motions over a period of several nights are recorded and reported.

Blood testing technology requires trained clinicians and laboratory tests. The use of this type of substance abuse testing technology in community corrections is rare.

**Fig. 5.9** Handheld breathalyzer testing device

## Applying Substance Abuse Technology in Community Corrections Programs

The substance abuse testing technologies discussed in this chapter are only as effective as the programs in which they are used. Over the past three decades, much has been learned

[6] For a detailed explanation of the NIR absorption spectroscopy, see Pollard, Nadler, and Stearns (2007).

about best practices for reducing instances of drug use among offender populations. Abstinence and accountability are cornerstones of effective substance abuse programs. The use of modern technologies to monitor the use of prohibited substances by offenders under supervision has significantly enhanced the ability of community corrections to monitor and respond to substance abuse.

There are three major reasons for monitoring for substance abuse of offenders under community corrections supervision:

1. To manage short-term risk to public safety posed by drug- and alcohol-abusing offenders.
2. To facilitate assessment of the existence and extent of substance abuse by offenders under supervision.
3. To support treatment and recovery of substance-abusing offenders in an effort to break the cycle of abuse and addiction and foster long-term prosocial behavioral change.

In addressing substance abuse by offenders under some form of community correctional supervision, it is essential to remember that drug and alcohol abuse involve a complex array of emotional and physical interactions with abusers. These emotional and physical components of substance abuse must be balanced with the legal requirements imposed as conditions of community release. In some instances, judges, parole boards, and departments of corrections, for example, impose conditions requiring abstinence from alcohol – at all times. The use of illegal drugs is prohibited since it is a crime (i.e., *mala prohibita*). Conditions of community release also often include zero tolerance for substance abuse, whether alcohol or illegal drugs. When zero tolerance approaches are employed, they require an immediate response to all instances of substance abuse. Zero tolerance for substance abuse does not mean that one instance of substance abuse should result in an offender being violated and returned to jail or prison. Instead, it infers that offenders will be held accountable for their use and that the community corrections system will respond to each instance of use through a range of sanctions (counseling, enhanced supervision, referral for treatment, etc.).

Because substance abuse involves a complex array of emotional and physical interactions, there is a need for flexibility throughout the period of community-based supervision. Simply put, ordering an abuser to stop using drugs is not likely to work. Relapse has long been acknowledged to be normal within the abuse and recovery process. Therefore, zero-tolerance approaches, while they may appeal to simplistic and erroneous notions of deterrence, rarely are justified in community corrections supervision when they demand reincarceration. If the goal is to ameliorate an offender's substance abuse problems, then zero-tolerance approaches requiring a return to custody are ineffective. Finally, there is no research evidence supporting the notion that zero-tolerance approaches to substance abuse by offenders under supervision have any positive effect.

When substance abuse technologies are used to support zero-tolerance supervision strategies, they specify revocation and reincarceration of the abuser, in other words, a deterrence approach to reducing instances of substance abuse. As such, they amount to nothing more than a "pee 'em and see 'em" model of community corrections supervision (Cullen, Eck, & Lowenkamp, 2002). This type of supervision strategy is premised on elementary understanding of punishment, "... a common-sense faith in vague and uncertain threats, and a disregard for the vast literature on punishment and persuasion" (Cullen et al., 2002; Gendreau, 1996; Gendreau, Goggin, Cullen, & Paparozzi, 2002).

Substance abuse technologies are designed to make detection of drug or alcohol use more effective and efficient, enable community corrections practitioners to hold offenders accountable, and implement appropriate risk management and behavioral reform responses with celerity. Effective interdiction of substance abuse by offenders under community corrections supervision is not a linear process that proceeds from abuse to cessation. It is, however, a process that demands rigorous accountability. After approximately 40 years of development and application, there now exists a wide range of technologies that makes unrelenting offender accountability for substance abuse possible. This is perhaps the most significant contribution that substance abuse testing technologies have made over the past four decades. It is the responsibility of community corrections practitioners to apply these technologies in ways that manage risk and ultimately reform behavior. Technology applied in a context devoid of evidence-based policies, programs, and practices accomplishes little, if anything.

Programs that have been found to reduce substance abuse include therapeutic communities, behavior-oriented counseling supplemented by peer support groups, and family-oriented counseling (National Institute on Drug Abuse, 2009a, 2009b). All of the foregoing examples of substance abuse intervention treatment modalities include ongoing monitoring for the purpose of detecting drug or alcohol use.[7] It is also critically important to respect the fact that not all offenders are equally responsive to the same treatment modality or counseling styles. Programs that do not pay attention to this well-documented fact are not likely to reduce instances of substance abuse and promote overall behavioral reform. Matching offenders to appropriate treatment modalities and styles of counseling has been found to enhance success of offenders in the community (Andrews & Bonta, 2006).

Within community corrections settings, substance abuse testing technologies are best understood as tools that support evidence-based intervention. When these technologies are used primarily to detect and react to the prohibited use of a substance, their behavioral reform effectiveness is seriously diminished.

[7] For more information on substance abuse treatment interventions that are supported by program evaluation research, see Mathias (2000), National Institute on Drug Abuse (2009b), and Tims and Ludford (1983).

## Bridging Research, Theory, and Practice: Obstacles to Technology Transfer

Bridging gaps between academia and practice has been talked about in community corrections quarters for well over three decades. While there has been some progress in bridging the academia/practitioner gap, there remains much more that needs to be done. One of the reasons for this lack of progress has to do with the politics of policy making in community corrections. This can be summed up as the seemingly endless debate by internal and external stakeholders involved with community corrections about whether it is better to get tough on criminals versus offender rehabilitation approaches. There is scant research evidence supporting the former and a plethora of evidence supporting the latter. The opposing points made in this debate frequently inform the application of substance abuse technologies in community corrections.

Under a "get tough" rubric, the primary purpose of substance abuse testing is to "trail 'em, nail 'em, and jail 'em." Under an offender rehabilitation framework, substance abuse technologies are applied in a treatment/service and graduated sanctioning and rehabilitation-oriented context. The rehabilitative approach, however, does not comport with zero-tolerance practices that require violation of community release and return to custody. Many policy makers are extremely sensitive about being tagged with the "soft on crime" scarlet label. When this concern prevails, the transfer of evidence-based knowledge about how best to apply substance abuse technologies to community corrections practice is impeded.

In addition to the politics of policy making with regard to the application of substance abuse technologies in community corrections, organizational culture is often an obstacle to effective application of substance abuse testing technologies. Organizational culture, for example, might not favor having community corrections practitioners involved with testing techniques that involve potential health hazards. As noted previously, the health hazard risks associated with the application of substance abuse technologies are minimal. Nevertheless, it might be necessary to change organizational cultures in order to implement any substance abuse technology.[8]

An additional factor that can impede the application of substance abuse technologies has to do with the workload of staff. This impediment to implementation rests on two prongs: (a) administering substance abuse testing takes time (in fact, many community corrections workers are already overburdened with high caseloads and increased administrative tasks); and (b) the information efficiently provided to community corrections officers by dint of a positive test result must be addressed. Unfortunately, these workload issues have remained largely unaddressed. The result has been that urine testing is, more often than not, used as a tool to catalog violations of conditions of release more than it used as a mechanism to ameliorate substance abuse problems.

It is indeed true that there are many community corrections jurisdictions that have adopted a graduated sanctions approach when responding to positive results obtained through substance abuse testing technologies. However, the reality is that the availability of treatment services for offenders under community corrections supervision is woefully inadequate and often of questionable quality. Under such a scenario, substance abuse testing technologies cannot reach their full potential as facilitators of evidence-based practices in community corrections.

Substance abuse testing technology does not make more efficient that which was not effective in the first place (unrealistically high staff to client caseload ratios, establishing policies based more on political rather than professional concerns, shortage of high-quality treatment services, etc.).

[8] The first author worked as a community corrections practitioner for approximately 30 years and was involved with the implementation of urine monitoring protocols. Initially, staff strongly resisted taking on the responsibility of urine testing because it involved additional work. Staff also argued that being involved in urine testing constituted a health hazard under OSHA (Occupational Safety and Health Hazard Administration) regulations. The workload issue was legitimate, but no accommodations for the additional work required were ever made. The OSHA argument was neutralized through the implementation of certain procedures that reduced the risk of a health hazard (issuance of gloves, procedures for community correction involvement in specimen collection, sealing the specimen, etc.).

## References


Andrews, D., & Bonta, J. (2006). *The psychology of criminal conduct*. Cincinnati, OH: Anderson Publishing.

Baer, J. D., Baumgartner, W. A., & Werner, A. (1991). Hair analysis for the detection of drug use in pretrial, probation, and parole populations. *Federal Probation, 55*(1), 3–10.

Bean, P., & Wilkinson, C. (1988). Drug taking, crime and the illicit supply system. *British Journal of Addiction, 83*, 533–539.

Belenko, S., & Peugh, J. (1998). Fighting crime by treating substance abuse. *Issues in Science and Technology, Fall*, 53–60.

Bogen, E. (1927). The diagnosis of drunkenness – A quantitative study of acute alcohol intoxication. *California and Western Medicine, 27*(6), 778–783.

Burr, A. (1987). Chasing the dragon: Heroin misuse, delinquency and crime in the context of south London culture. *British Journal of Criminology, 27*(4), 333–357.

Courtright, D. T. (1982). *Dark paradise: A history of opiate use in America*. Boston: Harvard University Press.

Cullen, F. T., Eck, J. E., & Lowenkamp, C. (2002). Environmental corrections: A new paradigm of effective probation and parole supervision. *Federal Probation, 66*, 28–37.

Dubowski, K. (1986, April–June). Recent developments in alcohol analysis. *Alcohol, Drugs, and Driving, 2*(2), 13–46.

Fatah, A., & Cohn, J. (2003). Developments in drug testing: Saliva as an alternative to urine and blood. *Corrections Today, 65*(6), 3–4.

Frontline. (2007). *Timeline: America's war on drugs*. Retrieved August 27, 2009, from http://www.npr.org/templates/story/story.php?storyId=9252490

Gendreau, P. (1996). The principles of effective interventions with offenders. In A. T. Harland (Ed.), *Choosing correctional options that work: Defining demand and evaluating the supply* (pp. 117–130). Thousand Oaks, CA: Sage.

Gendreau, P., Goggin, C., Cullen, F. T., & Paparozzi, M. (2002). The common sense revolution and correctional policy. In J. McGuire (Ed.), *Offender rehabilitation and treatment: Effective programs and policies to reduce re-offending* (pp. 360–386). Chichester, UK: Wiley.

Goldstein, P. J. (1985). The drugs/violence nexus: A tripartite conceptual framework. *Journal of Drug Issues, 15*(4), 493–506.

Henry, D. A., & Clark, J. (1999). *Pretrial drug testing: An overview of issues and practices*. Washington, DC: United States Department of Justice, Bureau of Justice Assistance.

Hillyer, B. (2008). *Regarding drug testing, the eyes don't lie*. Retrieved November 2, 2009 from http://www.hawaiinewsnow.com/Global/story.asp?S=7096034

Jenkins, A. J., & Goldberg, B. A. (Eds.). (2002). *On-site drug testing*. Totowa, NJ: Humana Press.

Klee, H., & Morris, J. (1995). Factors that characterize street injectors. *Addiction, 90*, 837–841.

Kosnoski, E. M., Yolton, R. L., Citek, K., Hayes, C. E., & Evans, R. B. (1998). The drug evaluation classification program: Using ocular and other signs to detect drug intoxication. *Journal of the American Optometric Association, 69*(4), 211–227.

Linzmayer, L., Fischer, G., & Grunberger, J. (1997). Pupillary diameter and pupillary reactions in heroin dependent patients and in patients participating in a methadone and morphine replacement program. *Wiener Medizinische Wochenschrif, 147*(3), 67–69.

Long, M., & Kidwell, D. A. (2002). *Improving the PharmChek sweat patch: Reducing false positives from environmental contamination and increasing drug detection*. Unpublished final report, U.S. Department of Justice Document No. 196030, Award No. 2000-RD-CX-A038.

Lozito, F. (1979). Operating a urine screening program in a probation department. In D. V. Babst (Ed.), *Drug abuse testing: Successful models for treatment and control in correctional programs* (pp. 8–10). College Park, MD: American Correctional Association.

Massing, M. (2000). *The fix*. Los Angeles: University of California Press.

Mathias, R. (2000). Putting science-based drug abuse prevention programs to work in communities. *NIDA Notes, 14*(6). Retrieved November 10, 2009, from http://www.drugabuse.gov/NIDA_Notes/NNVol14N6/Putting.html

Matthews, R., & Trickey, J. (1996). *Drugs and crime: A study amongst young people in Leicester*. Leicester, England: Centre for the Study of Public Order, University of Leicester.

Meyer, W. G. (2008, September 3–5). *Constitutional and other legal issues in problem-solving courts*. Paper delivered at the Wyoming Drug Court conference, Cheyenne.

Mieczkowski, T. (2001, October). The effect of color and curvature on the concentration of morphine in hair analysis. *Forensic Science Communications* [Online]. Retrieved November 18, 2009 from http://www.fbi.gov/hq/lab/fsc/backissu/oct2001/index.htm

Mieczkowski, T. (2002). Does Adam need a haircut? A pilot study of self-reported drug use and hair analysis in an arrestee sample. *Journal of Drug Issues, 32*(1), 97–118.

Mieczkowski, T. M., & Lersch, K. M. (1997). Drug testing in criminal justice: Evolving uses, emerging technologies. *National Institute of Justice Journal, 234*, 9–15.

Mott, J., & Taylor, M. (1974). *Delinquency amongst opiate users* (Home Office Research Study No. 23, 1–29). London: HMSO.

National Institute on Drug Abuse. (2009a). *Principles of drug addiction treatment: A research-based guide* (Publication No. 9-4180). Washington, DC: Author.

National Institute on Drug Abuse. (2009b). *Treatment approaches for drug addiction: Info-facts*. Washington, DC: U.S. Department of Health and Human Services, National Institute on Drug Abuse.

Office of National Drug Control Policy. (2000). *Drug related crime*. Washington, DC: Executive office of the President, Office of National Drug Control Policy.

Paparozzi, M., & Gendreau, P. (2005). An ISP that worked. *The Prison Journal, 84*(4), 445–466.

Parker, H. J., Bakx, K., & Newcombe, R. (1988). *Living with heroin*. Philadelphia: Open University Press.

Parker, H., & Bottomley, T. (1996). *Crack cocaine and drugs – crime careers* (Monograph No. 34). London: Home Office Research Findings, Home Office RDS Directorate.

Parker, H., & Newcombe, R. (1987). Heroin use and acquisitive crime in an English community. *British Journal of Sociology, 38*(3), 331–350.

Pollard, J. K., Nadler, E. D., & Stearns, M. D. (2007). *Review of technology to prevent alcohol-impaired crashes*. Springfield, VA: National Technical Information Service.

Richman, J., & Noriega, R. S. (2002, December 12–15). *The sensitivity and specificity of infrared pupillometry measurements in identifying drug impairment in a county probation program*, Scientific program American Academy of Optometry, San Diego, CA.

Robinson v. California. (1962). (370 US 660). U.S. Supreme Court, No. 554, Argued April 17, 1962, Decided June 25, 1962, 370 U.S. 660. Retrieved December 15, 2009, from: http://supreme.justia.com/us/370/660/

Russo, J. (2003). Use of existing technology for new purposes. *Proceedings from the Large Jail network meeting* (pp. 41–46). Washington, DC: National Institute of Corrections.

Seddon, T. (2000). Explaining the drug crime link: Theoretical policy and research issues. *Journal of Social Policy, 29*(1), 95–107.

Simon, S. (2000, September). Evidence of alcohol and drug impairment obtained after arrest. *Issues and methods in the detection of alcohol and other drugs*. Washington, DC: National Research Council Number E-C020. Retrieved December 2, from onlinepubs.trb.org/onlinepubs/circulars/ec020.pdf

Tennant, F. (1988). The rapid eye test to detect drug abuse. *Postgraduate Medicine, 84*(1), 108–114.

Thatcher, J. (2007). ROSITA II Project: Evaluation of on-site saliva drug testing devices in Washington State. Retrieved December 1, 2009, from:www.icadts2007.org/print/80rosita_salivascreen.pdf

Tims, F. M., & Ludford, J. P. (1983). *NIDA Research Monograph 51a RAUS review report*. Rockville, MD: Department of Health and Human Services, Public Health Service Alcohol, Drug Abuse, and Mental Health Administration.

Touchstone, J. C. (1992). *Practice of thin layer chromatography*. Hoboken, NJ: Wiley.

Travis, J. (1997, March 13). *Technology in criminal justice: Creating the tools for transformation*. Address of Jeremy Travis Director, National Institute of Justice Academy of Criminal Justice Sciences. Retrieved August 27, 2009, from: http://www.ojp.usdoj.gov/nij/speeches/acjs.htm

U.S. v. Snyder. (2002). *Memorandum – Decision and order*. United States District Court Northern District of New York, 187 F. Supp. 2d 52, N.D.N.Y., Retrieved December 10, 2009 from http://74.125.47.132/search?q=cache%3Av_WoKHALEesJ%3Awww.drugpolicy.org%2FdocUploads%2Fusv_snyder.pdf+http%3A%2F%2Fwww.drugpolicy.org%2FdocUploads%2Fusv_snyder.pdf&hl=en&gl=us. United States Code (January 8, 2008). Title 18, Part II, Chapter 227, subchapter 8, Section 3563.

Visher, C. (1991). *A comparison of urinalysis technologies for drug testing in criminal justice* (Research report). Washington, DC: U.S. Department of Justice, Office of Justice Programs, National Institute of Justice.

Waldorf, D., Orlick, M., & Reinarman, C. (1974). *Morphine maintenance: The Shreveport Clinic 1919–1923*. Washington, DC: The Drug Abuse Council, Inc.

# 6 Substance Use Prevalence in Criminal Justice Settings

Michele Staton-Tindall, Jennifer R. Havens, Carrie B. Oser, and Mary Carroll Burnett

**Abstract**
Since the mid-1970s, research studies in the United States have focused on the drug-crime connection. Federal drug abuse efforts in the early 1980s targeted controlling the supply of drugs, determinate sentencing for drug offenders, and long prison terms. With the growing number of substance users involved in the criminal justice system, this chapter overviews recent prevalence studies on substance use among individuals involved in differing levels of the criminal justice system from prison and jail to community corrections, including a discussion of special populations of offenders. This chapter also overviews the theoretical underpinnings of the relationship between drug use and crime as it relates to the development of treatment approaches for this population. Finally, the chapter concludes with an overview of evidence-based interventions and promising approaches for substance abuse for the criminal justice population and future directions.

**Keywords**
Drug offenders • Jail inmates • Prison inmates • Community supervision

*Many of those with the underlying disease of addiction commit crimes and thus, frequently come into contact with the criminal justice system. We can no longer afford to simply incarcerate them, while leaving their addiction untreated and their problems unaddressed.*
*Gil Kerlikowske, Director Office of National Drug Control Policy Statement from the 2009 World Drug Report, June 24, 2009*

## Introduction

Since the mid-1970s, research studies in the United States have focused on the drug-crime connection. Federal drug abuse efforts in the early 1980s targeted controlling the supply of

M. Staton-Tindall (✉)
College of Social Work, Center on Drug and Alcohol Research, University of Kentucky, Lexington, KY 40506, USA
e-mail: mstindall@uky.edu

C. Leukefeld et al. (eds.), *Handbook of Evidence-Based Substance Abuse Treatment in Criminal Justice Settings*, Issues in Children's and Families' Lives 11,
DOI 10.1007/978-1-4419-9470-7_6, © Springer Science+Business Media, LLC 2011

drugs, determinate sentencing for drug offenders, and long prison terms. As expected, these efforts were followed by rapid increases in the number of incarcerated drug abusers and drug abusers with criminal justice system referrals in community treatment. For example, US drug abuse treatment admission data in the late 1990s indicated that over one-third (37%) of client admissions are directly referred from the criminal justice system (Substance Abuse and Mental Health Services Administration [SAMHSA], 2001). By 2004, 59% of referrals to community substance abuse treatment were from the criminal justice system (McLellan, 2009).

With this shift in federal drug abuse efforts in the 1980s, trends in national statistics demonstrated an increase in the number of incarcerated drug abusers. This increase was substantiated by a special report from the Bureau of Justice Statistics (Scalia, 2001) showing that the number of defendants charged with drug offenses in federal courts increased 147% between 1984 and 1999. This report noted that 62% of convicted drug defendants were subject to minimum prison terms. In addition, two-thirds of defendants with drug offenses in US District Courts had prior arrests. Of this group, 44% had been arrested more than five times.

Further demonstrating the drug/crime nexus, a survey of both state and federal inmates found that 83.2% of state and 78.7% of federal prisoners reported lifetime use of an illicit substance (Mumola & Karberg, 2006). These data are consistent with an early report stating that 83% of state inmates had been drug-involved before incarceration, but reflect a considerable increase from the 52% of federal inmates that were drug-involved during the late 1990s (Mumola, 1999). In addition, arrestee data from the Arrestee Drug Abuse Monitoring (ADAM) system indicated that about two-thirds of arrestees in 10 major US urban cities test positive for drugs at the time of their arrest (Office of National Drug Control Policy [ONDCP], 2009), which has remained fairly consistent over the last decade.

With the growing number of substance users involved in the criminal justice system, this chapter overviews recent studies on substance use among individuals involved in differing levels of the criminal justice system from prison and jail to community corrections, including a discussion of special populations of offenders. Since substance use is typically measured at admission or intake into a criminal justice setting and is considered illegal while under correctional and community supervision, this chapter focuses more on the prevalence of substance use rather than the incidence or number of newly occurring cases. This chapter also overviews the theoretical underpinnings of the relationship between drug use and crime as it relates to the development of treatment approaches for this population. Finally, the chapter concludes with an overview of evidence-based interventions and promising approaches for substance abuse for the criminal justice population and future directions.

## Substance Use Among Prison Inmates

The most highly cited resource for prevalence data among correctional populations is the Bureau of Justice Statistics (BJS). Starting in 1926, Congress mandated statistical data collection on all prisoners at midyear and yearend through the National Prisoner Statistics (NPS) program (West & Sabol, 2009). The Bureau of Justice Statistics compiles the data through semiannual and annual reports, as well as special topics on the offender population such as drug use and mental health issues. A recent BJS report indicated that more than 1.6 million individuals in the United States are currently serving time in a state or federal prison (West & Sabol, 2009), and an estimated one out of five of these individuals in state prisons and one of two inmates in federal prisons are currently serving time for a drug-related offense (Mumola & Karberg, 2006), which does not account for the number of individuals who committed other crimes (like property offenses) while under the influence of drugs.

Prevalence data from the BJS on prison inmates includes the number of individuals who reported using substances in their lifetime, regular use, use in the month before their offense, and use at the time of their offense. In addition, the most recent special report from BJS on substance use and dependence also includes those who are incarcerated that meet the criteria for drug and alcohol abuse and dependence as outlined by the Diagnostic and Statistical Manual of Mental Disorders, Fourth Edition (DSM-IV) (American Psychiatric Association, 1994). This report compared trends in the data over a 7-year period from 1997 to 2004 to find that rates of substance use are high and largely consistent over time. As shown in Table 6.1, approximately 80% of state (83.2%) and federal prisoners (78.7%) reported lifetime use of an illicit substance. About two-thirds reported regular use, more than half reported use in the month before their offense, and more than a quarter reported being under the influence at the time of their current offense (Mumola & Karberg, 2006).

These findings are consistent with previous survey findings about the prevalence of substance use among US prisoners which indicated that 80% of state and 70% of federal prisoners reported prior illicit drug use (Mumola, 1999). In examining trends in use over the past 7 years, with the exception of methamphetamine use, trends in use of marijuana, cocaine/crack, and heroin and other opiates remained fairly consistent between 1997 and 2004 (Mumola & Karberg, 2006). This report did indicate that reported use of methamphetamine increased from 19% in 1997 to 23% in 2004.

In addition to the rates of lifetime use of illicit substances, the most recent BJS survey on drug and alcohol abuse included measures to estimate the number of inmates meeting the abuse and dependence criteria based on the DSM-IV. Findings indicated that about half of state (53%) and federal (45%) prisoners met DSM-IV criteria for drug dependence or abuse (Mumola & Karberg, 2006). Thus, not only is the prevalence of lifetime substance use considerable, the number of individuals using substances to the level of abuse or dependence is five times higher than identified in the general population (SAMHSA, 2008).

In addition to the rates of abuse and dependence in the US prison population, as shown in

**Table 6.1** Prevalence of substance use among prisoners in 2004

| Type of drug | Ever used? | | Used regularly? | | Used in month before current offense | | Used at the time of the current offense | |
|---|---|---|---|---|---|---|---|---|
| | State (%) | Federal (%) | State (%) | Federal (%) | State (%) | Federal (%) | State (%) | Federal (%) |
| Any drug | 83.2 | 78.7 | 69.2 | 64.3 | 56.0 | 50.2 | 32.1 | 26.4 |
| Marijuana | 77.6 | 71.2 | 59.0 | 53.0 | 40.3 | 36.2 | 15.4 | 14.0 |
| Cocaine/crack | 46.8 | 43.3 | 30.0 | 27.5 | 21.4 | 18.0 | 11.8 | 7.4 |
| Heroin/opiates | 23.4 | 17.9 | 13.1 | 9.2 | 8.2 | 5.8 | 4.4 | 3.2 |
| Depressants | 21.3 | 16.9 | 9.9 | 8.6 | 5.4 | 4.4 | 2.0 | 1.4 |
| Stimulants | 28.6 | 21.0 | 17.9 | 14.8 | 12.2 | 10.8 | 6.7 | 7.4 |
| Hallucinogens | 32.9 | 25.9 | 13.3 | 11.9 | 5.9 | 5.8 | 2.0 | 1.9 |

Source: Mumola and Karberg (2006).

**Table 6.2** Prevalence of substance use among prisoners in 2004 by type of offense

| Type of offense | Used in month before current offense | | Used at the time of the current offense | | Met DSM criteria for abuse or dependence | |
|---|---|---|---|---|---|---|
| | State (%) | Federal (%) | State (%) | Federal (%) | State (%) | Federal (%) |
| Drug offenses | 71.9 | 57.3 | 43.6 | 32.3 | 63.1 | 51.9 |
| Property offenses | 64.0 | 27.7 | 38.5 | 13.6 | 63.2 | 27.3 |
| Violent offenses | 49.6 | 49.1 | 27.7 | 24.0 | 46.7 | 41.6 |
| Public-order offenses | 49.9 | 41.2 | 25.4 | 18.7 | 50.2 | 41.2 |

Source: Mumola and Karberg (2006).

Table 6.2 among the general prison population, about one-third (32%) of state prisoners and one-quarter (26%) of federal prisoners indicated that their current offense was committed while under the influence of drugs (Mumola & Karberg, 2006). Not surprising, among those serving time in a state prison for a drug offense, nearly three-quarters (71.9%) reported use in the past month before their offense, nearly half (43.6%) indicated that their crime was committed while under the influence of drugs, and almost two-thirds met DSM criteria for substance abuse or dependence (see Table 6.2).

As expected, rates of substance use are higher among offenders serving time for drug-related crimes. Rates of substance use are also higher among prisoners who have been identified as having a mental health problem. In a separate national report focused on state and federal prisoners, mental health problems were profiled based on the inmate identifying a recent history of mental health issues (clinical diagnosis or treatment provided by a mental health professional) or self-reported symptoms based on DSM-IV criteria (James & Glaze, 2006). Among state prisoners who were identified as having a mental health problem, about three quarters (74%) also met criteria for substance use and dependence compared to 56% of other state prisoners who did not report a mental health problem. This finding suggests that the high rates of reported substance use among state prisoners are also likely coupled with high rates of co-occurring mental health disorders.

## Substance Use Among Jail Inmates

Similar to prison prevalence data, Bureau of Justice Statistics (BJS) is a widely used resource for estimating the characteristics of jail populations. In conjunction with the US Census Bureau as data collectors, BJS conducts the Annual Survey of Jails to provide a nationwide profile of inmates serving time in local jail facilities (Minton & Sabol, 2009). BJS then compiles the data through semi-annual and annual reports, as well as special topics on the offender population such as drug use and mental health issues. A recent BJS report indicated that more than 785,000 individuals in the United States are currently serving time in a local jail facility (Minton & Sabol, 2009), and more than 13 million offenders were admitted to jails between 2007 and 2008 (Office of Justice Programs, 2009). These numbers differ considerably from the prison numbers because inmates detained in jails are either there following an arrest, awaiting trial or sentencing, or completing a short sentence (i.e., usually less than 1 year).

Consistent with prevalence data reported on prison inmates, a 2005 BJS report provided the most recent estimate of substance use and dependence among jail inmates including the number of individuals who reported using substances in their lifetime, regular use, use in the month before their offense, use at the time of their offense, and prevalence of jail inmates meeting DSM-IV criteria for drug and alcohol abuse and dependence. As shown in Table 6.3, 82.2% of jail

**Table 6.3** Prevalence of substance use among jail inmates in 2002

| Type of drug | Ever used? | Used regularly? | Used in month before current offense[a] | Used at the time of the current offense[a] |
|---|---|---|---|---|
| Any drug (%) | 82.2 | 68.7 | 54.6 | 28.8 |
| Marijuana (%) | 75.7 | 58.5 | 37.5 | 13.6 |
| Cocaine/crack (%) | 48.1 | 30.9 | 20.7 | 10.6 |
| Heroin/opiates (%) | 20.7 | 12.0 | 7.8 | 4.1 |
| Depressants (%) | 21.6 | 10.7 | 6.1 | 2.4 |
| Stimulants (%) | 27.8 | 17.1 | 11.4 | 5.2 |
| Hallucinogens (%) | 32.4 | 13.4 | 5.9 | 1.6 |

Source: Karberg and James (2005).

[a]Note: Data for illicit substance use in the month before the current offense and at the time of the current offense was collected from jail inmates who had a current or prior conviction only.

inmates reported lifetime use of an illicit substance. Similar to prevalence rates reported for prison inmates, about two-thirds reported regular use, more than half reported use in the month before their offense, and more than a quarter reported being under the influence at the time of their current offense (Karberg & James, 2005). In addition to the rates of lifetime use of illicit substances, 85.4% of jail inmates reported lifetime alcohol use, and two-thirds (66%) reported regular alcohol use. In addition, 40% reported binge drinking and one-third reported using alcohol at the time of their offense (Karberg & James, 2005).

The BJS survey on drug and alcohol abuse among jail inmates included measures to estimate abuse and dependence criteria based on the DSM-IV. Findings indicated that more than two-thirds (68%) of jail inmates met DSM-IV criteria for alcohol and/or drug dependence or abuse (Karberg & James, 2005). This rate is higher than that reported for state (53%) and federal (45%) prisoners (Mumola & Karberg, 2006), which may possibly be explained by incorporating *alcohol* abuse and dependence into the measurement.

Similar to prison-based studies, jail inmates serving time for drug-related charges had higher rates of both drug and alcohol use. As shown in Table 6.4, among those serving time in a local jail facility for a drug offense, nearly half (43.2%) indicated that their crime was committed while under the influence of drugs, and two-thirds met DSM criteria for substance abuse or dependence (see Table 6.4).

Similar to data reported for state prisoners, rates of substance use are higher among jail inmates who have been identified as having a mental health problem. In the same national report focused on mental health problems among prison and jail inmates, among those who were identified as having a mental health problem, slightly more than three-quarters (76%) met DSM-IV criteria for substance use and dependence compared to 53% of other jail inmates who did not report a mental health problem (James & Glaze, 2006). This finding suggests there are high rates of co-occurring substance use and mental health disorders among jail inmates.

## Substance Use Among Community Offenders

The Bureau of Justice Statistics maintains prevalence data on offenders under community supervision. Data from 2007 annual surveys of probationers and parolees indicated that more than 5.1 million adults in the United States are being supervised in the community (Glaze & Bonczar, 2008). The majority of individuals (84%) on community supervision are on probation, which means that they have been formally sentenced to a period of correctional supervision in the community for their crime rather than serving time in a correctional institution (Glaze & Bonczar, 2008). The remaining individuals on community supervision (16%) are on parole, which is a time of conditional supervised release following release from prison. It is estimated that more than 800,000 US adults are being supervised on parole and more than 4.2 million are on probation (Glaze & Bonczar, 2008).

Among individuals under community supervision, the BJS 2007 report indicates that 27% of probationers committed drug law violations and 37% of parolees served their prison sentence

**Table 6.4** Prevalence of drug use among jail inmates in 2002 by type of offense

| Type of offense | Used at the time of the current offense | | Met DSM criteria for abuse or dependence | |
|---|---|---|---|---|
| | Drugs (%) | Alcohol (%) | Drugs (%) | Alcohol (%) |
| Drug offenses | 43.2 | 22.4 | 66.6 | 40.1 |
| Property offenses | 32.5 | 28.5 | 61.8 | 48.4 |
| Violent offenses | 21.8 | 37.6 | 47.9 | 52.0 |
| Public-order offenses | 19.5 | 26.2 | 48.2 | 45.8 |

Source: Karberg and James (2005).

for a drug offense. The most recent BJS report released on the prevalence of substance use among community-supervised offenders focused on probationers in 1995 (Mumola & Bonczar, 1998), which is more than 10 years old at the time of chapter preparation. No recent data on the prevalence of substance use among parolees could be located, likely because they are reentering the community from prison and prevalence rates would be based on their use patterns prior to incarceration because use of illicit substances while on parole is a violation of their conditions of supervision. As shown in Table 6.5, this report indicated that 69.4% of probationers reported lifetime use of an illicit substance. In addition, nearly one-third of probationers indicated that they used drugs during the month before their offense, and about 14% reported being under the influence at the time of their current offense.

As shown in Table 6.6, probationers who committed violence offenses and public-order offenses (such as public intoxication) reported higher rates of both drug and alcohol use at the time of their offense compared to drug and property offenders. This is different from trends shown for populations of prison and jail inmates in that those serving time for drug-related offenses reported higher rates of drug and alcohol use at the time of their offense. Measures to assess drug and alcohol dependence based on DSM-IV criteria were not available in this early report. However, as shown in Table 6.6, more than a third of public-order offenders met criteria for alcohol abuse or dependence based on endorsement of three or more CAGE screening questions.

Since recent prevalence data for community offenders was not available, analyses were conducted using the 2007 National Survey on Drug Use and Health (NSDUH) to estimate substance use prevalence among community offenders. The NSDUH incorporates a stratified, multistage sampling approach to generate a random sample of noninstitutionalized persons residing in the United States. To determine criminal justice involvement, survey respondents were asked, "Were you on parole, supervised release, or other

**Table 6.5** Prevalence of substance use among probationers in 1995

| Type of drug | Ever used? | Used in month before current offense | Used at the time of the current offense |
|---|---|---|---|
| Any drug (%) | 69.4 | 31.8 | 13.5 |
| Marijuana (%) | 66.5 | 25.3 | 9.5 |
| Cocaine/crack (%) | 31.0 | 9.2 | 3.8 |
| Heroin/opiates (%) | 8.1 | 1.5 | 0.9 |
| Depressants/Barbiturates (%) | 15.4 | 2.0 | 0.6 |
| Stimulants (%) | 25.3 | 4.8 | 1.8 |
| Hallucinogens (%) | 19.7 | 2.7 | 0.6 |

Source: Mumola and Bonczar (1998).

**Table 6.6** Prevalence of substance use among probationers in 1995 by type of offense

| Type of offense | Used at the time of the current offense | | | Met criteria for alcohol abuse or dependence[a] (%) |
|---|---|---|---|---|
| | Drugs (%) | Alcohol (%) | Alcohol or drugs (%) | |
| Drug offenses | 31.7 | 16.3 | 38.4 | 15.7 |
| Property offenses | 9.8 | 18.5 | 23.0 | 18.3 |
| Violent offenses | 10.7 | 40.7 | 43.5 | 21.8 |
| Public-order offenses | 6.4 | 75.1 | 77.0 | 36.1 |

Source: Mumola and Bonczar (1998).

[a]Note: Abuse or dependence based on CAGE screening score of three or more items endorsed.

conditional release from prison at any time during the past 12 months?" If they had been on community supervision in the past 12 months, they were coded as 1 for the current analysis and if they had not, were coded as 0. This definition of community supervision excludes probationers. Lifetime and past 12-month drug use were then examined by supervision status to determine whether community residents on probation or parole were significantly more likely than those not involved in the criminal justice system to use licit and illicit drugs.

Less than 1% (0.7%) of NSDUH survey respondents reported that they had been on community supervision during the past 12 months. Those who were on criminal justice supervision were significantly more likely to be younger, African American or Hispanic, and had fewer years of education. When comparing substance use prevalence, there were no statistically significant differences in lifetime substance use among those who were and were not under criminal supervision (see Table 6.7). However, more than three-quarters of those who were on supervision reported lifetime illicit substance use compared to only half of those who were not on supervision. For both cigarettes and alcohol, there were no differences in the prevalence of lifetime use; however, for each illicit substance examined, those who had been under community supervision in the past 12 months were significantly more likely to report use than those with no recent criminal involvement. Lifetime marijuana use was most prevalent among both groups (63.4% versus 42.9%, $p < 0.001$), followed by nonmedical use of prescription analgesics (39.2% versus 13.5%, $p < 0.001$), and cocaine use (35.1% versus 15.6%, $p < 0.001$).

The prevalence of past 12-month substance use proved similar to lifetime use, apart from past 12-month use of any substance or illicit substance (results not shown). Respondents who were recently criminally involved were significantly more likely to report any past 12-month use (85.9% versus 75.0%, $p = 0.008$) and past 12-month illicit use (37.0% versus 13.4%, $p < 0.001$). Among the illicit substances, marijuana use was reported by one in five respondents who were under criminal supervision and less than 10% of those who were not ($p < 0.001$). In addition, nonmedical users of prescription analgesics were four times more likely to be under criminal justice supervision ($p < 0.001$).

Another strategy for estimating patterns of substance use among community offenders was examined through utilization of the 2007 Treatment Episode Data Set (TEDS, 2007). Community substance abuse treatment providers that receive any state funding must collect admissions data that are submitted for inclusion in TEDS. To determine criminal justice involvement, two variables from TEDS were utilized. The first variable determined the principle source of treatment referral. If it was determined to be a criminal justice referral, another variable further delineated the source of the criminal justice referral (state/federal court, probation/parole/prison, DUI/DWI and diversionary program/other). The criminal justice variable that was created for the current analysis was based on increasing levels of criminal justice involvement. If the referral source did not include any of the criminal justice categories, the client was assigned a 0. If the client had been referred from court, DUI/DWI, or a diversion program, they were assigned a 1, and if they had been referred from parole or prison, they were assigned a 2. Within TEDS, the intake instrument asks the client to list up to three problem substances for which they are seeking treatment.

More than 1.8 million records were contained in the TEDS dataset. However, once those under 18 years of age and those with missing data for referral source were removed from the data, a little under 1 million (987,006) data points were available for analysis. Almost three-quarters of those initiating substance abuse treatment in 2007 were referred from noncriminal justice sources, whereas 13.2% of clients were referred from court, DUI/DWI, or diversion programs, and 12.7% from probation/parole/prison. Those who were referred from the criminal justice system were significantly more likely to be male, younger, African American or Hispanic, and had fewer years of education.

**Table 6.7** Substance use prevalence among offenders on community criminal justice supervision compared to general population

| | Under criminal justice supervision (%) | Non-criminal justice supervision (%) | *p*-value |
|---|---|---|---|
| Any lifetime substance use | 93.3 | 91.2 | 0.467 |
| Any past 12-month substance use | 85.9 | 75.0 | 0.008 |
| Any lifetime illicit substance use* | 75.8 | 47.9 | <0.001 |
| Any past 12-month illicit substance use* | 37.0 | 13.4 | <0.001 |
| Lifetime cigarette use | 73.6 | 69.9 | 0.484 |
| Past 12-month cigarette use | 59.2 | 29.5 | <0.001 |
| Lifetime alcohol use | 88.1 | 87.3 | 0.826 |
| Past 12-month alcohol use | 64.7 | 68.8 | 0.326 |
| Lifetime marijuana use | 63.4 | 42.9 | <0.001 |
| Past 12-month marijuana use | 21.7 | 9.6 | <0.001 |
| Lifetime cocaine use | 35.1 | 15.6 | <0.001 |
| Past 12-month cocaine use | 6.6 | 2.2 | <0.001 |
| Lifetime crack use | 18.1 | 3.6 | <0.001 |
| Past 12-month crack use | 6.7 | 0.5 | <0.001 |
| Lifetime methamphetamine use | 7.6 | 1.6 | <0.001 |
| Past 12-month methamphetamine use | 3.0 | 0.4 | <0.001 |
| Lifetime heroin use | 7.6 | 1.6 | <0.001 |
| Past 12-month heroin use | 0.6 | 0.1 | 0.002 |
| Lifetime hallucinogen use | 29.6 | 14.8 | <0.001 |
| Past 12-month hallucinogen use | 5.3 | 1.3 | <0.001 |
| Lifetime inhalant use | 16.3 | 9.0 | 0.004 |
| Past 12-month inhalant use | 1.9 | 0.4 | 0.002 |
| Lifetime nonmedical analgesic use | 39.2 | 13.5 | <0.001 |
| Past 12-month nonmedical analgesic use | 16.6 | 4.6 | <0.001 |
| Lifetime nonmedical sedative use | 11.4 | 3.5 | <0.001 |
| Past 12-month nonmedical sedative use | 3.0 | 0.3 | <0.001 |
| Lifetime nonmedical stimulant use | 20.5 | 8.9 | <0.001 |
| Past 12-month nonmedical stimulant use | 3.8 | 1.0 | <0.001 |
| Lifetime nonmedical tranquilizer use | 26.2 | 8.6 | <0.001 |
| Past 12-month nonmedical tranquilizer use | 6.8 | 2.0 | 0.003 |

Source: National Survey on Drug Use and Health (2007).
*Does not include cigarettes or alcohol.

As shown in Table 6.8, there were statistically significant differences between the criminal justice groups for all of the primary, secondary, and tertiary problematic substances reported, which may be attributed to the large sample size. However, those who were criminally involved did not report greater problematic use on all substances. Not surprisingly, for alcohol, the highest proportion of those reporting problematic use were in the group referred from DUI/DWI, whereas for marijuana, the highest problematic use rates were in the prison/parole-referred group. For cocaine, nonmedical methadone, heroin, prescription opiates, benzodiazepines, other sedatives/hypnotics, and tranquilizers, those referred to treatment from a noncriminal source were significantly more likely to report problematic use compared to the criminally referred groups. For methamphetamine, hallucinogens, and prescription stimulants, the

**Table 6.8** Problematic drug use among TEDS clients referred from criminal and noncriminal sources

| Type of drug mentioned as either primary, secondary or tertiary drug of abuse | Noncriminal treatment referral (%) | Criminal justice treatment referral (%) | Prison or parole treatment referral (%) | *p*-value |
|---|---|---|---|---|
| Alcohol | 61.1 | 71.6 | 62.5 | <0.001 |
| Marijuana | 27.9 | 43.7 | 53.8 | <0.001 |
| Cocaine | 42.1 | 28.6 | 32.7 | <0.001 |
| Nonmedical methadone | 1.1 | 0.4 | 0.3 | <0.001 |
| Methamphetamine | 3.5 | 5.3 | 6.3 | <0.001 |
| Amphetamines | 0.7 | 1.2 | 1.2 | <0.001 |
| Heroin | 26.7 | 9.1 | 11.1 | <0.001 |
| Hallucinogens | 0.4 | 0.5 | 0.6 | <0.001 |
| Inhalants | 0.08 | 0.1 | 0.08 | <0.001 |
| Other opiates (Rx) | 11.7 | 5.4 | 5.2 | <0.001 |
| Benzodiazepines | 4.4 | 2.4 | 1.8 | <0.001 |
| Other sedatives/ hypnotics | 0.7 | 0.6 | 0.4 | <0.001 |
| Stimulants | 0.2 | 0.2 | 0.3 | <0.001 |
| Tranquilizers | 0.1 | 0.09 | 0.06 | <0.001 |

Source: Treatment Episode Dataset (TEDS, 2007).

prison/parole group had the greatest rates of problematic use; and for amphetamines, a similar proportion of both of the criminal justice referral and prison/parole referral groups (1.2% each) indicated problematic use. Finally, among those referred to substance abuse treatment from non-prison/parole criminal justice sources, these clients reported significantly greater problematic use for inhalants. Given that illicit drug use is a criminal offense, we would hypothesize that those referred from criminal justice sources would report greater use of illicit substances, which was not the case. However, the sample used for this analysis is also biased by those who enter community treatment. It is possible that despite significant patterns of use and indicators of serious addictions, substance users in the criminal justice system may be less likely to enter community treatment when it is not mandated or required. Therefore, it is possible that the group of criminal justice offenders represented in this analysis are more representative of those who are mandated into treatment than those who voluntarily enter and complete treatment, thus explaining possible differences in the direction of drug use findings.

## Substance Use Among Special Populations of Offenders

This section overviews prevalence data on two special populations of offenders who are disproportionately impacted by the consequences of substance use – women offenders and African-American offenders.

### Women

Women represent the fastest growing segment of the criminal justice system increasing 757% between 1977 and 2004, a rate nearly twice the percent increase in the male offender population (Frost, Greene, & Pranis, 2006). The number of women involved in the US criminal justice system has doubled since 1990, compared to a 27% increase in the number of men (Beck, 2000). Nearly 100,000 women were incarcerated in 2002, with an estimated one in every 109 US women involved in some way with the criminal justice system (Harrison & Beck, 2003). During 2002, the rate of women under the jurisdiction of state or federal prison authorities increased 4.9% compared to 2.4% for men.

The increasing number of women offenders in state custody has implications for reentry planning and service initiatives because the majority of female offenders in prison will be returning to the community. Estimates show that 95% of state inmates will be released, and about 80% of those will be released to state parole. Female offenders represent 23% of individuals on community supervision, which is an increase of 21% from 1995 (Glaze & Bonczar, 2006). With the increasing number of women offenders who are incarcerated and subsequently released to the community, there is increasing need to develop services which enhance community reentry. A major gap exists at community reentry because a number of women offenders face obstacles to accessing services including availability of treatment, transportation, family and caretaking responsibilities, and financial constraints (O'Brien, 2001).

Studies have shown that being able to access substance abuse services is a primary concern for women offenders reentering the community (O'Brien, 2001; Parsons & Warner-Robbins, 2002; Staton-Tindall, Duvall, Leukefeld, & Oser, 2007). Substance use and abuse have been consistently reported as major contributing factors in the increasing population of women offenders (e.g., Greenfeld & Snell, 1999; Henderson, 1998). In fact, a large number of women offenders, reported as high as 98%, have a history of substance abuse, and nearly half of incarcerated women indicate that they were under the influence of alcohol or drugs at the time of their offense (Brewer, Marquart, Mullings, & Crouch, 1998; Cotton-Oldenburg, Jordan, Martin, & Kupper, 1999; Greenfeld & Snell, 1999). A survey of male and female offenders indicated that a higher percentage of females reported drug use (including ever used, using regularly, and using at the time of the offense) compared to male offenders (Greenfeld & Snell, 1999). In this survey, one-third of female offenders self-reported that they committed their crime in order to obtain drugs or money to buy drugs.

Substance abuse can have deleterious consequences for women compared to men. For example, one study showed that women are more susceptible than men to the adverse effects of alcohol due to a decreased level of the metabolizing enzyme, gastric alcohol dehydrogenase (Lieber, 1993). The physical health consequences of alcohol and drug use are often more severe for women than for men. Frequently cited health concerns among substance-using women are HIV, hepatitis, severe headaches, dental problems, hypertension, emphysema, and asthma (Ingram-Fogel, 1991; Ross & Lawrence, 1998). Other studies indicate that women in drug treatment programs tend to report co-occurring mental health issues including high levels of psychological distress, increased incidence of trauma and abuse, and a propensity for diagnosable disorders, including post-traumatic stress disorder (PTSD) (Hall, 1998; Sacks, 2004). Given the severity of these health and mental health issues, there is a critical need for establishing community reentry substance abuse treatment services for women offenders.

## African Americans

At midyear 2008, there were 4,777 African-American male inmates per 100,000 African-American males held in state and federal prisons and local jails, compared to 727 white male inmates per 100,000 white males (Sabol & Couture, 2008). According to the recent PEW Center on the States 2008 report, while 1 in 30 men between the ages of 20 and 34 is behind bars, the figure is one in nine among African-American males in that age group. The Bureau of Justice Statistics (BJS) (Sabol & Couture, 2008) reports that in 2007, African-American males ages 30–34 had the highest custody incarceration rate of any race, age, or gender group and while African-American men represent 14% of the population of young men in the United States, they represent over 40% of the prison population (Harrison & Beck, 2005).

This rise in incarceration, especially among African-American males, has been well documented in the literature with drug-related offenses as significant contributors to the increase due to more punitive US drug policies (Blankenship, Smoyer, Bray, & Mattocks, 2005). The number of sentenced inmates in federal prisons for drug offenses increased an overwhelming 64.8% between 1995 and 2003 (Harrison & Beck, 2005). With regard to ethnicity, about 33% of African-American males between the ages of 18 and 40 are involved in the criminal justice system (Mayer, 1999). It is imperative to examine African-American male offenders because rates of drug use have not necessarily been shown to be different between whites and African Americans, although data shows arrests for drug charges to be proportionally higher among African Americans (Uniform Crime Reports [UCR], 2002). Reasons for the higher arrest rate among African Americans has been examined and may include that African Americans are more likely than whites to purchase drugs in the open outdoors, more likely to buy from a stranger, and more likely to buy drugs away from their homes (Ramchand, Pacula, & Iguchi, 2006). In addition, some researchers indicate that African Americans have been stigmatized by the United States Constitution, and have been subjected to racial profiling in policing and punitive policies that mandate minimum sentencing – all of which might be factors in the disproportionate arrests and incarceration rates for African Americans (Brockett, 2000; Ramchand et al., 2006). For example, there is an irrefutable link between the increase in the number of African Americans incarcerated in the United States and the emergence of crack cocaine use in the 1980s (Belenko, Shedlin, & Chaple, 2005; Chitwood, Rivers, & Inciardi, 1996; De La Rosa, Lambert, & Gropper, 1990). US policies that increased the incidence of arrest and incarceration include mandatory minimum sentencing, penalty enhancements for the use or sale of drugs in drug-free zones, inequality in penalties associated with crack (versus powder cocaine), and limitations on the availability of syringes (Smoyer & Blankenship, 2004).

## Underlying Theories and Research

### The Relationship Between Drug Use and Crime

Prevalence data on substance use across criminal justice settings demonstrates that there is a strong association between drug use and the consequences of crime. The association of chronic drug abuse and crime has been the focus of a number of research studies in the United States (see Leukefeld, Tims, & Farabee, 2002). For example, heavy drug users are more likely to engage in more diverse criminal activity (Farabee, Joshi, & Anglin, 2001). Drug use usually leads to involvement in the criminal justice system through one or more of the following avenues: (1) possession or sales of an illicit substance, (2) illegal activity (such as stealing) to support a drug addiction, or (3) illegal activity associated with the drug-using lifestyle (National Institute on Drug Abuse [NIDA], 2006).

Research shows that there is a strong correlation between the *type* of crime committed and the type of drug used. For example, in their meta-analysis of 30 studies, Bennett, Holloway, and Farrington (2008) found that the odds of committing a crime were highest among crack users (6 times greater); second highest among heroin users (about 3 times greater), and third highest among cocaine users (about 2.5 times greater). Additionally, the relationship between drug use and property crime tends to be much stronger than the relationship between drug use and violent crime (De Li, Priu, & MacKenzie, 2000). However, drug dealers tend to be engaged more heavily in violent crime than do drug users alone. In an early study, Inciardi (1979) reported that a cohort of 239 male heroin addicts from Miami committed 80,644 criminal acts during the 12 months prior to being interviewed. Ball, Lawrence, Flueck, and Nurco (1982) found that over an 11-year period a Baltimore cohort of 243 heroin addicts committed 248 crime days per year while addicted. When not addicted, the same cohort committed only 40.8 crime days per year. Theft followed by drug sales was the most frequent type of crime committed. While drug use and drug dealing are not mutually exclusive phenomena, it is important to be able to compare their drug use and criminal behavior trends (De Li et al., 2000).

Among both male and female prisoners, it has been consistently shown that drug use intensifies criminal involvement (Leukefeld et al., 2002). While there seems to be some discrepancy in the literature about the causal relationships between drug use and crime, studies have demonstrated that an early onset of substance use likely precedes increased criminal involvement (van Kammen & Loeber, 1994), and more intense involvement in the criminal lifestyle among adolescents is often characterized by drug dealing and trading drugs (Inciardi & Pottieger, 1991).

Missing from theoretical discussions around drug use and crime is an explanation for high rates of use across criminal justice setting. Given the understanding that there is a robust, positive relationship between drug use and increased criminal activity, it would seem likely that those who report the most harmful levels of use or are in more severe stages of addiction also face more serious legal consequences. This can possibly be observed from trends in this chapter with community offenders reporting less use overall than inmates in jail and prison. However, the distinction between offenders in jail and inmates in prison with regard to substance use is minimal. This raises the question whether – despite the well-documented link between drug use and crime – the relationship is robust enough to sustain other factors that may influence someone's criminal justice status (i.e., SES and poverty; race, etc.). The answer to this question may have important implications for understanding the role of substance use as a contributing factor to criminal justice involvement.

## The Development of Interventions

Much of the theoretical models on drug use and crime have wrestled with the question of which came first – a person's drug use which led to the engagement in criminal behaviors, or a person's lifestyle of illegal activity that involved the use of substances (Inciardi, 1981). These questions can lead to divergence in the theoretical models which guide intervention development. If you adhere to the medical model which suggests that addiction is a disease of the brain and body, you likely support the development of treatment approaches to target substance use as the primary factor contributing to deleterious consequences such as criminal involvement. If you adhere to the public safety model which suggests that addiction is an unfortunate consequence of a criminal lifestyle, you likely support the development of increased sanctioning efforts to promote a safe society by removing criminals from the street. This debate is less pronounced in the theoretical underpinnings of traditional substance abuse treatment because, when substance-using criminals are involved, there may be more perceived risk to society if interventions are not effective. However, treatment interventions designed for substance-using offenders in the criminal justice system have shown promise. In addition to cost savings, substance abuse treatment in criminal justice settings can help reduce crime as well as the spread of HIV/AIDS, hepatitis, and other infectious diseases (NIDA, 2006), as well as improving the housing, employment, and family situations of offenders with prior substance abuse addictions.

The next section overviews the guiding principles of effective treatment of substance-using offenders, as well as treatment modalities and interventions which have been used with success with substance-using offenders. The section concludes with an overview of emerging interventions which show promising results for the future.

## Interventions That Work

The financial impact of substance abuse has been reported to be in excess of $467 billion state and federal government spending – more than 95% of which was in dealing with the consequences of drug and alcohol addiction rather than in treatment programs (Center on Addiction and

Substance Abuse [CASA], 2009). The National Institute on Drug Abuse has estimated that for every dollar spent on drug and alcohol treatment, there is a $4–$7 reduction in the cost of drug-related crimes (NIDA, 1999). Therefore, the question is not *IF* we should invest resources into the development of effective interventions for substance-using offenders; the question is *HOW* do we develop and tailor the most effective interventions for this population?

## Guiding Principles of Substance Abuse Treatment with Offenders

In 2006, the National Institute on Drug Abuse published *Principles of Drug Abuse Treatment for Criminal Justice Populations*. This publication was based on the latest state of knowledge in effective treatment approaches for substance-using offenders involved in the criminal justice system. The following 13 principles (Table 6.9) were developed based on what we know "works" with this population, and should be integrated into treatment for criminal justice-involved substance users, regardless of the specific modality of treatment or treatment intervention.

## Therapeutic Communities

One of the most widely researched modalities of treatment for incarcerated substance users is the therapeutic community. Therapeutic communities began in the mid 1940s to treat returning WWII veterans struggling with former combat experiences (Lipton, 1998). The modality expanded in the 1950s in psychiatric hospitals (DeLeon, 2000), and was first used in a US prison setting in 1969 in a federal prison in Marion, IL (Lipton, 1998). Therapeutic communities (or TCs) operate on the philosophy that drug use is one behavior that is part of a holistic behavior disorder, and that behavioral change depends on the learning and adoption of prosocial behaviors (Deitsch, Carlton, Koutsenok, & Marsolais, 2002). TCs depend on the community – or peers, role models – as the change agent (DeLeon, 2000; Lipton, 1998).

Research on the effectiveness of corrections-based therapeutic communities (TCs) has consistently shown reductions in new arrests and recidivism following prison release. For example, graduates from a TC program in Texas were less likely than dropouts to be rearrested at 6 months (Knight, Simpson, Chatham, & Camacho, 1997).

**Table 6.9** NIDA principles of drug treatment for criminal justice populations

| | |
|---|---|
| 1 | Drug addiction is a brain disease that affects behaviour |
| 2 | Recovery from drug addiction requires effective treatment, followed by management of the problem over time |
| 3 | Treatment must last long enough to produce stable behavioral changes |
| 4 | Assessment is the first step in treatment |
| 5 | Tailoring services to fit the needs of the individual is an important part of effective drug abuse treatment for criminal justice populations |
| 6 | Drug use during treatment should be carefully monitored |
| 7 | Treatment should target factors that are associated with criminal behaviour |
| 8 | Criminal justice supervision should incorporate treatment planning for drug-abusing offenders, and treatment providers should be aware of correctional supervision requirements |
| 9 | Continuity of care is essential for drug abusers reentering the community |
| 10 | A balance of rewards and sanctions encourages prosocial behavior and treatment participation |
| 11 | Offenders with co-occurring drug abuse and mental health problems often require an integrated treatment approach |
| 12 | Medications are an important part of treatment for many drug-abusing offenders |
| 13 | Treatment planning for drug-abusing offenders who are living in or reentering the community should include strategies to prevent and treat serious, chronic medical conditions, such as HIV/AIDS, hepatitis B and C, and tuberculosis |

Source: NIDA (2006).

These trends were also observed in a therapeutic community in Delaware, and supported the idea that while recidivism is reduced for the TC group, findings are even more positive when TC treatment is followed by community aftercare (Inciardi, Martin, Butzin, Hooper, & Harrison, 1997). In addition, in a 3-year followup study in Texas, TC graduates who also completed aftercare were the least likely to be reincarcerated (25%) compared to 64% of TC treatment/aftercare dropouts, and 42% of the control group (Knight, Simpson, & Hiller, 1999). A similar study for a TC program in California reported consistent 3-year outcome findings with 27% of TC graduates who completed aftercare being reincarcerated compared to 75% of the control group (Wexler, Melnick, Lowe, & Peters, 1999). The California study reported similar trends in their 5-year outcome study with a smaller percentage of the treatment group being reincarcerated than the control group, and among those who were reincarcerated, the treatment group spent significantly more days on the street than the control group (Prendergast, Hall, Wexler, Melnick, & Cao, 2004). These findings suggest that the effects of therapeutic community treatment are promising over time.

Therapeutic community outcome studies have also demonstrated that substance-abusing offenders who complete treatment are less likely to use drugs following release from prison. For example, a longitudinal followup of substance-abusing offenders found that participation in a therapeutic community was the largest predictor of staying drug free at followup 42 months and 60 months after release from prison (Inciardi, Martin, & Butzin, 2004). This study showed that participants in the prison-based therapeutic community program were more than four times more likely to stay drug free at 42 months post-release compared to the control group. In addition, treatment participants were more than three times more likely than the control group to stay drug free at 60 months post-release (Inciardi et al., 2004). Additional analyses in this study compared those offenders who did not participate in the TC, program dropouts, program graduates, and program graduates who also attended aftercare. Overall, when compared with the no-treatment group, those participants in the treatment groups were 15–20 times more likely to remain drug free at followup. Among these groups, those who completed treatment reported the best overall outcomes, and those who completed in-prison treatment followed by community aftercare were the least likely to have engaged in drug use (Inciardi et al., 2004).

These research findings suggest that therapeutic communities are effective modalities for reducing recidivism and relapse among substance-using offenders, particularly when combined with community aftercare treatment following release.

## Cognitive Behavioral Interventions

Within treatment programs for offenders, infusion of evidence-based practices for treating substance abuse behaviors is also recommended. Cognitive behavioral approaches were recognized in the NIDA (2006) publication as an evidenced-based practice for drug users involved in the criminal justice system. Cognitive behavioral therapy (CBT) assumes that thinking and learning processes are critical in the initiation and continued use of substances, and that changing those thinking patterns to recognize, avoid, and cope with substance use triggers is therefore critical to stopping drug use (Carroll, 2000). CBT approaches have shown consistent success in reducing drug use behavior across different treatment modalities (i.e., Carroll & Onken, 2005; Maude-Griffin et al., 1998).

CBT approaches for substance-using offenders in the criminal justice system are challenged by addressing not only the relationship between "thinking" and "behavior," but also having to address criminal thinking errors common among this population. This is a unique dimension of substance abuse treatment programs that integrate CBT approaches which serve offenders, because the absence of attention and focus on criminal thinking as related to behaviors can compromise treatment success (Prendergast, 2009). Cleckley (1988) identified manipulative characteristics used by criminals in 1941 which were described later as Criminal Thinking Errors by Yochelson and Samenow (1976). Their work described patterns and qualities of criminal thinking errors that emerged during clinical experiences with individuals being evaluated for competency to stand trial or being treated in lieu of incarceration (Yochelson & Samenow, 1976), many of which have been adapted and incorporated into the clinical literature (Gorski, 1984; Leukefeld et al., 2002; Wanberg & Milkman, 1999). These thinking errors were called "automatic perceptions of self and the world." Through this focus on the uniqueness of CBT approaches with offenders, an emergence of a number of CBT approaches has been specialized for use with substance-using offenders in the criminal justice system (Prendergast, 2009).

## Motivational Enhancement Therapy

Motivational Enhancement Therapy (MET) was also recognized in the recent NIDA (2006) publication as a recommended treatment approach for drug users involved in the criminal justice system. MET is a manualized therapeutic approach grounded in key principles of motivational interviewing with the overall goal of motivating a client to draw upon her own internal resources for change (Miller, 1995). Therapists aid the participant in achieving change by utilizing an empathic therapeutic style associated with motivational interviewing and creating an environment in which resistance and argumentation are avoided and self-efficacy is supported (Carroll et al., 2006). Because the approach can be tailored to the individual needs of the client and the client's own motivation for change, MET can be used at different stages of treatment or in different stages of the criminal justice process from prison to the community.

Studies which included MET have shown positive outcomes for decreased substance use including marijuana (Stephens, Roffman, Fearer, Williams, & Burke, 2007), smoking (Huang, Svikis, & Diclemente, 2004), alcohol (Donovan, Kadden, DiClemente, & Carroll, 2002), and cocaine (Rohsenow et al., 2004). In addition, MET has shown promise to engage clients in substance abuse services and is currently being tested in three NIDA-funded Clinical Trials Network (CTN) protocols including one study to test the therapeutic usefulness of incorporating MET into the standard community drug abuse treatment entry process in order to improve treatment engagement, retention, and outcome (Carroll et al., 2002).

# Interventions That Might Work

## Contingency Management

Contingency management approaches were also recognized in the NIDA (2006) publication as an evidenced-based practice for drug users involved in the criminal justice system. Contingency management (CM) has historical roots in the theory of operant conditioning (Bigelow & Silverman, 1999). This approach suggests that drug use is influenced by the environmental context, and that rewards or incentives for not using drugs can override rewards or incentives to use drugs provided the appropriate context (Prendergast, Podus, Finney, Greenwell, & Roll, 2006; Roll, Prendergast, Sorensen, Prakash, & Chudzynski, 2005). Much like the CBT and MET approaches, CM has shown positive benefits for sustained abstinence, but the current state of research suggests that the positive effects of CM tend to diminish over time following treatment (Prendergast, 2009).

Research on the use of CM approaches with substance users in the criminal justice system is emerging. It has been suggested that the use of CM may be even more beneficial for substance users who are involved with the criminal justice system who enter treatment under legal pressures because positive reinforcement in the form of incentives may be more motivating than the threat of punishment, and perhaps reincarceration, for noncompliance (Prendergast, 2009). Roll et al. (2005) reported findings from two CM trials with substance users in community treatment using voucher-based incentives, one group of substance users was involved in the criminal justice system and the other was a group not involved in the criminal justice system. Results indicated that participants in the criminal justice group found the incentives to be helpful for paying court fines and related legal charges. Outcome data on the long-term effectiveness of the model in reducing drug use was not available. Similarly, a trial conducted as part of the NIDA-funded Criminal Justice Drug Abuse Treatment Studies (CJ-DATS) focused on the use of community vouchers and incentives for parolees to stay clean during the transition from prison to the community (Friedmann, 2005). Outcome data is not yet available. In summary, building on the literature on the effectiveness of CM in treating substance use, CM is considered a promising approach given the state of long-term outcome studies on the effectiveness of CM with substance-using offenders in the criminal justice system.

### Pharmacotherapy

Along with developing evidence on behavioral interventions for substance-using offenders, new research is emerging in the United States and internationally on the promise of pharmacological treatments for substance-using offenders (Cropsey, Villalobos, & St. Clair, 2005). Typically, pharmacological treatment is used for individuals who are addicted to opiates and commonly include treatment drugs such as methadone, buprenorphine, and naltrexone (Prendergast, 2009). One of the first pharmacotherapies is no longer used was done using Levo-alpha-acetylmethadonl (LAAM) alongside weekly drug education counseling while individuals were incarcerated, followed by community use of methadone (Kinlock, Battjes, & Schwartz, 2005). At the 9-month followup, reincarceration rates were low (29%) but rearrests were similar to the control group (33%). Further, 53% of the treatment group entered community treatment and continued treatment for at least 6 months, with 37% of the treatment group still in community treatment at the time of followup (which was not the case for any of the participants in the control group). Pharmacological treatment has been found to be effective; however due to a number of limitations in the existing clinical trials specific to retrospective reporting, sample sizes, and lack of generalizability (Cropsey et al., 2005) as well as the noted resistance to this type of treatment from the criminal justice system and treatment providers (Prendergast, 2009), continued research is needed with this population.

## Interventions That Do Not Work

In 1979, a publication by Robert Martinson suggested that "Nothing Works" for substance users involved in the criminal justice system, an unsubstantiated belief at the time which became a point of media attention (Field, 2002). This sparked 2 decades of outcome studies focused on offender-based treatment interventions which complemented the emerging body of research from community substance abuse treatment during this time period. Meta-analyses on the effectiveness of corrections-based treatment have indicated that the least effective forms of treatment in reducing relapse and recidivism (usual targeted outcomes of corrections-based treatment) include boot camps and group counseling sessions (Mitchell, Wilson, & Mackenzie, 2007; Pearson & Lipton, 1999). Boot camps are intensive treatment programs modeled after military training that include physical training, hard labor, and general drug education (Mackenzie & Herbert, 1996). Group counseling sessions usually consist of 8–10 members and meet 1–2 days per week. In the traditional sense of group counseling, it is likely that these are less effective in correction facilities because the group dynamic may be tempered by the presence of a correction officer, and the inmates returning to communal living following group sessions may make confidentiality and openness difficult (Lipton, Falkin, & Wexler, 1992).

## Future Directions

This chapter highlights the prevalence of substance use across criminal justice settings from prison to jail to community offenders. Data suggests that more than 80% of offenders in both state prisons and local jails reported lifetime use of illicit substances. In addition, more than two-thirds of offenders in prisons (69.2%) and jails (68.7%) reported regular use. The numbers are also strikingly similar for offenders in prisons and jails who reported use of any illicit substance in the month before the arrest (56% of prisoners and 55% of jail inmates), as well as the number who reported using during the time of their offense (32.2% of prisoners, 28.8% of jail inmates). The prevalence of substance use is slightly less among community offenders, which is largely driven by a sampling frame of probationers rather than parolees who were formerly incarcerated. Slightly more than 69.4% of community offenders reported lifetime substance use, nearly a third (31.8%) reported use during the previous month, and only 13.5% reported using at the time of their current offense.

Comparing prevalence rates across criminal justice settings may imply that the frequency and intensity of substance use may be associated with degree of criminal justice involvement: more involved substance use associated with more involved criminal careers. However, it is also possible that these prevalence rates are captured at one point in time – meaning that those who are on probation may be new to the criminal justice system – and in the absence of effective treatment interventions targeted at this population that address both their substance use and their criminal thinking and criminal careers may proceed into longer term involvement with the criminal justice system through jail and/or prison incarceration. Therefore, it is critical that the current state of knowledge on the effectiveness of substance abuse treatment and interventions be modified and tailored for use with the criminal justice population. These interventions should also be sensitive to the correctional environment and the offender's transition from stages of incarceration, community reentry, and community treatment so that the context serves to enhance treatment rather than serve as a barrier to the treatment process.

The next 10 years hold considerable promise for advancing research and treatment of substance use among individuals involved in the criminal justice system. A NIDA-funded research initiative currently underway has the potential to shape the future of substance abuse research and treatment for offenders during the transition from prison to the community. The first round of cooperative studies as part of the CJ-DATS involved 11 different research centers focused on individual-level interventions to reduce the risks for substance abuse at reentry (www.cjdats.org). CJDATS concluded in 2008, and followup studies are continuing to be released on the outcomes of new interventions. CJDATS 2 was funded in the fall of 2008 to support organizational and systems level studies to examine the processes associated with implementation of evidence-based practices and other interventions during the continuum of care from institution to community. The first round of CJDATS 2 studies is slated for implementation in fall 2009.

Another area of promise for addiction research and treatment with offenders is an increased reliance on neuroscience and neurobiology research. A growing body of research has developed in recent years to help understand the neurologic basis of addictive behavior (see summary of research findings in Chandler, Fletcher, & Volkow, 2009). While a number of these studies have targeted brain structures of adults, a number of studies about the impact of substance use on the developing brain have also emerged to suggest that substance use can have a tremendous impact because children who are prenatally exposed to substance use can have lifetime neural consequences (Cornelius, Goldschmidt, Day, & Larkby, 2002; Cornelius, Leech, & Larkby, 2007; Covington, Nordstrom-Klee, Ager, Sokol, & Delaney-Black, 2002) and that environmental stress and stimuli associated with growing up in a substance-using environment shape neurological development (Sprang et al., 2009). Thus, an increased reliance on neuroscience has three important implications for clinical and empirical science on treating substance-using offenders: (1) A better understanding of the neurological functions affected by repeated drug and alcohol use provides avenues for expanded medication development and behavioral interventions; (2) Identifying factors associated with the biological basis of behaviors associated with addiction can change policies associated with treatment – and coerced treatment – for individuals; and (3) A recognition of the impact of substance use on neurological and biological functioning can help addicts understand their own recovery (Chandler et al., 2009). Through integration of these important elements of neuroscience research, as well as increased research involving more rigorous designs for testing promising interventions with substance-using offenders, the future looks promising for advancing treatment opportunities for this at-risk group of substance users.

**Acknowledgments** The authors would like to recognize Brandy Jones and Nikki Stanaitis for their contributions to the literature review for this chapter.

## References

American Psychiatric Association. (1994). *Diagnostic and statistical manual of mental disorders* (4th ed.). Washington, DC: American Psychiatric Association.

Ball, J. C., Lawrence, R., Flueck, J. A., & Nurco, D. N. (1982). Lifetime criminality of heroin addicts in the United States. *Journal of Drug Issues, Summer*, 225–239.

Beck, A. J. (2000). *Prisoners in 1999* (Publication No. 183476). Washington, DC: Bureau of Justice Statistics, US Department of Justice.

Belenko, S., Shedlin, M., & Chaple, M. (2005). HIV risk behaviors, knowledge, and prevention service experiences among African American and other offenders. *Journal of Health Care for the Poor and Underserved, 16*, 108–129.

Bennett, T., Holloway, K., & Farrington, D. (2008). The statistical association between drug misuse and crime. *Aggression and Violent Behavior, 13*, 107–118.

Bigelow, G., & Silverman, K. (1999). Theoretical and empirical foundations of contingency management treatments for drug abuse. In S. T. Higgins & K. Silverman (Eds.), *Motivating behavior change among illicit drug abusers: Research on contingency management intervention* (pp. 15–31). Washington, DC: American Psychological Association.

Blankenship, K. M., Smoyer, A. B., Bray, S. J., & Mattocks, D. (2005). Black-white disparities in HIV/AIDS: The role of drug policy in the corrections system. *Journal of Health Care for the Poor and Underserved, 16*, 140–156.

Brewer, V. E., Marquart, J. W., Mullings, J. L., & Crouch, B. N. (1998). AIDS-related risk behaviors among female prisoners with histories of mental impairment. *Prison Journal, 78*, 101–118.

Brockett, R. (2000). Conceptual incarceration: A thirteenth-amendment look at African Americans and policing. In M. W. Markowitz & D. D. Jones-Brown (Eds.), *The system in black and white: Exploring the connections between race, crime, and justice* (pp. 109–124). Westport, CT: Praeger Publishers.

Carroll, K. M. (2000). *A cognitive-behavioral approach: Treating cocaine addiction* (Publication No. 0-4308). Bethesda, MD: National Institute on Drug Abuse.

Carroll, K. M., Ball, S. A., Nich, C., Martino, S., Frankforter, T. L., Farentinos, C., et al. (2006). Motivational interviewing to improve treatment engagement and outcome in individuals seeking treatment for substance abuse: A multisite effectiveness study. *Drug and Alcohol Dependence, 81*, 301–312.

Carroll, K. M., Farentinos, C., Ball, S. A., Crits-Christoph, P., Libby, B., Morgenstern, J., et al. (2002). MET meets the real world: Design issues and clinical strategies in the Clinical Trials Network. *Journal of Substance Abuse Treatment, 23*, 73–80.

Carroll, K. M., & Onken, L. S. (2005). Behavioral therapies for drug abuse. *American Journal of Psychiatry, 162*, 1452–1460.

Center on Addiction and Substance Abuse (CASA). (2009). *Shoveling up II: The impact of substance abuse on federal, state, and local budgets*. The National Center of Addiction and Substance Abuse at Columbia University. Retrieved August 4, 2009, from www.casacolumbia.org/su2report

Chandler, R. K., Fletcher, B. W., & Volkow, N. D. (2009). Treating drug abuse and addiction in the criminal justice system: Improving public health and safety. *Journal of the American Medical Association, 301*(2), 183–190.

Chitwood, D. D., Rivers, J. E., & Inciardi, J. A. (Eds.). (1996). *The American pipe dream: Crack and the inner city*. Fort Worth, TX: Harcourt Brace.

Cleckley, H. (1988). *The mask of sanity* (5th ed.). Atlanta, GA: C.V. Mosby Co.

Cornelius, M. D., Goldschmidt, L., Day, N. L., & Larkby, C. (2002). Alcohol, tobacco, and marijuana use among pregnant teenagers: 6-year follow-up of offspring growth effects. *Neurotoxicology and Teratology, 24*(6), 703–710.

Cornelius, M. D., Leech, S., & Larkby, C. (2007). Prenatal substance exposure: Growth outcomes among 10-year-old offspring of teenage mothers. *Neurotoxicology & Teratology, 29*(3), 409.

Cotton-Oldenburg, N. U., Jordan, K., Martin, S. L., & Kupper, L. (1999). Women inmates' risky sex and

drug behaviors: Are they related? *American Journal of Drug and Alcohol Abuse, 25*, 129–149.
Covington, C. Y., Nordstrom-Klee, B., Ager, J., Sokol, R., & Delaney-Black, V. (2002). Birth to age 7 growth of children prenatally exposed to drugs: A prospective cohort study. *Neurotoxicology and Teratology, 24*(4), 489–496.
Cropsey, K. L., Villalobos, G. C., & St. Clair, C. L. (2005). Pharmacotherapy treatment in substance-dependent correctional populations: A review. *Substance Use & Misuse, 40*, 1983–1999.
De La Rosa, M., Lambert, E. Y., & Gropper, B. (Eds.). (1990). *Drugs and violence: Causes, correlates, and consequences* (NIDA Research Monograph 103). Rockville, MD: NIDA, U.S. Department of Health and Human Services.
De Li, S., Priu, H. D., & MacKenzie, D. L. (2000). Drug involvement, lifestyles, and criminal activities among probationers. *Journal of Drug Issues, 30*(3), 593–620.
DeLeon, G. (2000). *The therapeutic community: Theory, model, and method*. New York: Springer.
Deitsch, D. A., Carlton, S., Koutsenok, I. B., & Marsolais, K. (2002). Therapeutic community treatment in prisons. In C. Leukefeld, F. Tims, & D. Farabee (Eds.), *Treatment of drug offenders* (pp. 127–137). New York: Springer.
Donovan, D. M., Kadden, R. M., DiClemente, C. C., & Carroll, K. M. (2002). Client satisfaction with three therapies in the treatment of alcohol dependence: Results from project MATCH. *The American Journal on Addictions, 11*, 291–307.
Farabee, D., Joshi, V., & Anglin, M. (2001). Addiction careers and criminal specialization. *Crime and Delinquency, 47*, 196–220.
Field, G. (2002). Historical trends of drug treatment in the criminal justice system. In C. Leukefeld, F. Tims, & D. Farabee (Eds.), *Treatment of drug offenders* (pp. 9–21). New York: Springer.
Friedmann, P. (2005). *CJDATS brief report: Step'n out*. Retrieved August 15, 2009 from www.cjats.org
Frost, N. A., Greene, J., & Pranis, K. (2006). *Hard hit: The growth in the imprisonment of women, 1977–2004*. The Punitiveness report, Institute on Women & Criminal Justice. Retrieved October 22, 2009 from http://www.wpaonline.org/institute/hardhit/foreword.htm
Glaze, L. E., & Bonczar, T. P. (2006). *Probation and parole in the United States, 2005* (Publication No. 215091). Washington, DC: Bureau of Justice Statistics, US Department of Justice.
Glaze, L. E., & Bonczar, T. P. (2008). *Probation and parole in the United States, 2007 statistical tables* (Publication No. 224707). Washington, DC: Bureau of Justice Statistics, US Department of Justice.
Gorski, T. (1984). *Relapse prevention therapy with chemically dependent criminal offenders: The relapse prevention workbook for the criminal offender*. Independence, MO: Independence Press.
Greenfeld, L. A., & Snell, T. L. (1999). *Women offenders* (Publication No. 175688). Washington, DC: Bureau of Justice Statistics, US Department of Justice.
Hall, S. (1998). Drug abuse treatment. In E. A. Blechman & K. D. Brownell (Eds.), *Behavioral medicine & women: A comprehensive handbook* (pp. 420–424). York, PA: Guilford Press.
Harrison, P. M., & Beck, A. J. (2003). *Prisoners in 2002* (Publication No. 200248). Washington, DC: Bureau of Justice Statistics, US Department of Justice.
Harrison, P. M., & Beck, A. J. (2005). *Prisoners in 2004* (Publication No. 210677). Washington, DC: Bureau of Justice Statistics, US Department of Justice.
Henderson, D. J. (1998). Drug abuse and incarcerated women. *Journal of Substance abuse Treatment, 15*, 579–587.
Huang, N. A., Svikis, D. S., & Diclemente, C. (2004). Motivational enhancement therapy for nicotine dependence in methadone-maintained pregnant women. *Psychology of Addictive Behaviors: Journal of the Society of Psychologists in Addictive Behaviors, 18*, 289–292.
Inciardi, J. A. (1979). Heroin use and street crime. *Crime Delinquency, 25*, 335–346.
Inciardi, J. A. (1981). Drug use and criminal behavior: Major research issues. In J. A. Inciardi (Ed.), *The drugs-crime connection*. Beverly Hills, CA: Sage.
Inciardi, J. A., Martin, S. S., & Butzin, C. A. (2004). Five-year outcomes of therapeutic community treatment of drug-involved offenders after release from prison. *Crime and Delinquency, 50*(1), 88–107.
Inciardi, J. A., Martin, S. S., Butzin, C. A., Hooper, R. M., & Harrison, L. D. (1997). An effective model of prison-based treatment for drug-involved offenders. *Journal of Drug Issues, 27*(2), 261–278.
Inciardi, J. A., & Pottieger, A. E. (1991). Kids, crack, and crime. *Journal of Drug Issues, 21*(2), 257–271.
Ingram-Fogel, C. (1991). Health problems and needs of incarcerated women. *Journal of Prison & Jail Health, 10*, 43–57.
James, D. J., & Glaze, L. E. (2006). *Mental health problems of prison and jail inmates* (Publication No. 213600). Washington, DC: Bureau of Justice Statistics, US Department of Justice.
Karberg, J. C., & James, D. J. (2005). *Substance dependence, abuse, and treatment of jail inmates, 2002* (Publication No. 209588). Washington, DC: Bureau of Justice Statistics, US Department of Justice.
Kinlock, T. W., Battjes, R. J., & Schwartz, R. P. (2005). A novel opioid maintenance program for prisoners: Report of post-release outcomes. *American Journal of Drug and Alcohol Abuse, 31*(3), 433–454.
Knight, K., Simpson, D. D., Chatham, L. R., & Camacho, L. M. (1997). An assessment of prison-based drug treatment: Texas' in-prison therapeutic community program. *Journal of Offender Rehabilitation, 24*(3/4), 75–100.
Knight, K., Simpson, D. D., & Hiller, M. L. (1999). Three-year reincarceration outcomes for in-prison

therapeutic community treatment in Texas. *The Prison Journal, 79*(3), 337–351.

Leukefeld, C., Tims, F., & Farabee, D. (Eds.). (2002). *Treatment of drug offenders*. New York: Springer.

Lieber, C. S. (1993). Women and alcohol: Gender differences in metabolism and susceptibility. In E. S. L. Gomberg & T. D. Nirenberg (Eds.), *Women and substance abuse* (pp. 1–17). Westport, CT: Ablex Publishing.

Lipton, D. S. (1998, October). Therapeutic communities: History, effectiveness and prospects. *Corrections Today*. Retrieved August 10, 2009, from http://findarticles.com/p/articles/mi_hb6399/is_n6_v60/ai_n28712553/

Lipton, D. S., Falkin, G. P., & Wexler, H. K. (1992). Correctional drug abuse treatment in the United States: An overview. In C. G. Leukefeld & F. M. Tims (Eds.), *Drug abuse treatment in prisons and jails* (NIDA Research Monograph 118, pp. 8–30). Washington, DC: US Department of Health and Human Services.

MacKenzie, D. L., & Herbert, E. E. (1996). *Correctional boot camps: A tough intermediate sanction*. National Institute of Justice Research Report. Washington, DC: US Department of Justice.

Maude-Griffin, P. M., Hohenstein, J. M., Humfleet, G. L., Reilly, P. M., Tusel, D. J., & Hall, S. M. (1998). Superior efficacy of cognitive-behavioral therapy for crack cocaine abusers: Main and matching effects. *Journal of Consulting & Clinical Psychology, 66*, 832–837.

Mayer, M. (1999). *Race to incarcerate: The sentencing project*. New York: The New Press.

McLellan, T. (2009, April 20). *What's wrong with addiction treatment: What could help?* Paper presentation, Robert Straus Distinguished Speaker Lecture, University of Kentucky, Lexington, KY.

Miller, W. R. (1995). *Motivational enhancement therapy with drug abusers*. The University of New Mexico, Department of Psychology and Center on Alcoholism, Substance Abuse, and Addictions (CASAA). Retrieved August 25, 2007, from http://motivationalinterview.org/clinical/METDrugAbuse.PDF

Minton, T. D., & Sabol, W. J. (2009). *Jail inmates at midyear 2009 – Statistical tables* (Publication No. 225709). Washington, DC: Bureau of Justice Statistics, US Department of Justice.

Mitchell, O., Wilson, D. B., & MacKenzie, D. L. (2007). Does incarceration-based drug treatment reduce recidivism? A meta-analytic synthesis of the research. *Journal of Experimental Criminology, 3*, 352–375.

Mumola, C. J. (1999). *Substance abuse and treatment, state and federal prisoners, 1997* (Publication No. 172871). Washington, DC: Bureau of Justice Statistics, US Department of Justice.

Mumola, C. J., & Bonczar, T. (1998). *Substance abuse and treatment of adults on probation, 1995* (Publication No. 166611). Washington, DC: Bureau of Justice Statistics, US Department of Justice.

Mumola, C. J., & Karberg, J. C. (2006). *Drug use and dependence, state and federal prisoners, 2004* (Publication No. 213530). Washington, DC: Bureau of Justice Statistics, US Department of Justice.

National Institute on Drug and Alcohol Abuse. (1999). *Principles of drug addiction treatment: A research-based guide* (Publication No. 0-4180). Washington, DC: National Institutes of Health, National Institute on Drug Abuse, U.S. Department of Health and Human Services.

National Institute on Drug Abuse. (2006). *Principles of drug abuse treatment for criminal justice populations: A research-based guide* (Publication No. 6-5316). Washington, DC: US Department of Health and Human Services.

National Survey on Drug Use and Health. (2007). *National survey on drug use and health* [Computer file]. ICPSR23782-v2 (United States Department of Health and Human Services. Substance Abuse and Mental Health Services Administration. Office of Applied Studies). Ann Arbor, MI: Inter-University Consortium for Political and Social Research [distributor], 2009-08-12. doi:10.3886/ICPSR23782.

O'Brien, P. (2001). *Making it in the "free world."* Albany, NY: State University of New York Press.

Office of Justice Programs. (2009). *Growth in prison and jail populations slowing: 16 states report declines in the number of prisoners*. Bureau of Justice Statistics, US Department of Justice (Press release). Retrieved August 9, 2009, from www.ojp.usdoj.gov/bjs

Office of National Drug Control Policy. (2009). *ADAMII: 2008 Annual report: Arrestee drug abuse monitoring program*. Washington, DC: Abt Assoicates, Inc. Retrieved October 22, 2009, from http://www.whitehousedrugpolicy.gov/publications/pdf/adam2008.pdf

Parsons, M. L., & Warner-Robbins, C. (2002). Factors that support women's successful transition to the community following jail/prison. *Health Care for Women International, 23*, 6–18.

Pearson, F. S., & Lipton, D. S. (1999). A meta-analytic review of the effectiveness of corrections-based treatment for drug abuse. *The Prison Journal, 79*, 384–410.

Prendergast, M. (2009). Intervention to promote successful re-entry among drug-abusing parolees. *Addiction Science & Clinical Practice, 5*(1), 4–13.

Prendergast, M. L., Hall, E. A., Wexler, H. K., Melnick, G., & Cao, Y. (2004). Amity prison-based therapeutic community: 5-year outcomes. *The Prison Journal, 84*(1), 36–60.

Prendergast, M., Podus, D., Finney, J., Greenwell, L., & Roll, J. (2006). Contingency management for treatment of substance use disorders: A meta analysis. *Addiction, 101*, 1546–1560.

Ramchand, R., Pacula, R. L., & Iguchi, M. Y. (2006). Racial differences in marijuana-users' risk of arrest in the United States. *Drug and Alcohol Dependence, 84*, 264–272.

Rohsenow, D. J., Monti, P. M., Martin, R. A., Colby, S. M., Myers, M. G., Gulliver, S. B., et al. (2004). Motivational enhancement and coping skills training for cocaine abusers: Effects on substance use outcomes. *Addiction, 99*, 862–874.

Roll, J. M., Prendergast, M. L., Sorensen, K., Prakash, S., & Chudzynski, J. E. (2005). A comparison of voucher exchanges between criminal justice involved and noninvolved participants enrolled in voucher based contingency management drug abuse treatment programs. *The American Journal of Drug and Alcohol Abuse, 31*, 393–401.

Ross, P. H., & Lawrence, J. E. (1998). Health care for women offenders. *Corrections Today, 60*, 122–127.

Sabol, W. J., & Couture, H. (2008). *Prison inmates at midyear 2007* (Publication No. 221944). Washington, DC: Bureau of Justice Statistics, US Department of Justice.

Sacks, J. Y. (2004). Women with co-occurring substance use and mental disorders (COD) in the criminal justice system: A research review. *Behavioral Sciences & The Law, 22*, 449–466.

Scalia, J. (2001). *Federal drug offenders, 1999* (Publication No. 187285). Washington, DC: Bureau of Justice Statistics, US Department of Justice.

Smoyer, A., & Blankenship, K. M. (2004). *Drug policy: Definition, discussion, and state variation.* New Haven, CT: Center for Interdisciplinary Research on AIDS.

Sprang, G., Kaak, H. O., Staton-Tindall, M., Clark, J., Hubbard, K., Whitt-Woosley, A., et al. (2009). A response from the field: Perspectives on translating neuroscience to clinical practice. *Journal of Loss and Trauma, 14*(4), 315–346.

Staton-Tindall, M., Duvall, J. L., Leukefeld, C., & Oser, C. B. (2007). Health, mental health, substance use, and service utilization among rural and urban incarcerated women. *Women's Health Issues, 17*, 183–192.

Stephens, R. S., Roffman, R. A., Fearer, S. A., Williams, C., & Burke, R. S. (2007). The Marijuana check-up: Promoting change in ambivalent marijuana users. *Addiction, 102*, 947–957.

Substance Abuse and Mental Health Services Administration. (2001). *The DASIS report*. Substance Abuse and Mental Health Services Administration. Retrieved August 4, 2009, from http://www.dasis.samhsa.gov.99ufds/Resource-556/t35.htm

Substance Abuse and Mental Health Services Administration. (2008). *Results from the 2007 National survey on drug use and health: National findings* (NSDUH Series H-34, DHHS Publication No. SMA 08-4343). Rockville, MD: Substance Abuse and Mental Health Services Administration, Office of Applied Studies.

Treatment Episode Dataset. (2007). *Treatment episode data set – Admissions (TEDS-A), 2007* [Computer file]. ICPSR24280-v3 (United States Department of Health and Human Services. Substance Abuse and Mental Health Services Administration. Office of Applied Studies). Ann Arbor, MI: Inter-University Consortium for Political and Social Research [distributor], 2009-09-15. doi:10.3886/ICPSR24280.

Uniform Crime Reports. (2002). *Crime in the United States, 2002*. Washington, DC: U.S. Department of Justice, Federal Bureau of Investigation.

van Kammen, W. B., & Loeber, R. (1994). Are fluctuations in delinquent activities related to the onset and offset in juvenile illegal drug use and drug dealing? *Journal of Drug Issues, 24*(1/2), 9–25.

Wanberg, K. W., & Milkman, H. B. (1999). *Criminal conduct and substance abuse treatment: Strategies for self-improvement and change: The participant's workbook*. Thousand Oakes, CA: Sage.

West, H. C., & Sabol, W. J. (2009). *Prison inmates at midyear 2008 – Statistical tables* (Publication No. 225619). Washington, DC: Bureau of Justice Statistics, US Department of Justice.

Wexler, H. K., Melnick, G., Lowe, L., & Peters, J. (1999). Three-year reincarceration outcomes for Amity in-prison therapeutic community and aftercare in California. *The Prison Journal, 79*(3), 321–336.

Yochelson, S., & Samenow, S. E. (1976). *The criminal personality, Volume I: A profile for change*. New York: Jason Aronson.

# DWI/DUI Interventions

# 7

Brian Chodrow and Hon. Peggy Fulton Hora

**Abstract**

Attitudes about drinking and driving have changed dramatically over the past few decades due to a combination of factors. Initiatives to address impaired driving have varied from harsher penalties to substance abuse treatment responses. This article reviews what works, what doesn't, what is inconclusive, and what looks promising for the future including traditional police responses such as sobriety checkpoints and vehicle or license sanctions. Victim Impact Panels and other more innovative initiatives have mixed reviews. Knowing that severity of sentences does not affect long term change, the criminal justice system has initiated robust programs that look promising. Courts are using new technologies and pharmacological responses to monitor offenders and reduce recidivism. Over the past ten years, Driving While Impaired (DWI) courts have sprung up throughout the United States and look to be an important part of the goal of reduced impaired driving and resulting crashes.

**Keywords**

Alcohol • Drunk driving • Driving under the influence • DWI • Impaired driving • Vehicle impoundment • Drivers' license restrictions • Drivers' license revocation • Drivers' license suspension • NHTSA • Victim impact panels • Victim advocacy • Drug courts • Drug treatment courts • Repeat offenders • Sobriety courts • Driving while impaired courts • Problem-solving courts

B. Chodrow (✉)
Impaired Driving Division, National Highway Traffic Safety Administration, Washington, DC 20590, USA
e-mail: Chodrow@mindspring.com

This work was written by the author in his individual capacity and is not a work of the US Government, Department of Transportation or the National Highway Traffic Safety Administration. It represents his views alone.

C. Leukefeld et al. (eds.), *Handbook of Evidence-Based Substance Abuse Treatment in Criminal Justice Settings*, Issues in Children's and Families' Lives 11,
DOI 10.1007/978-1-4419-9470-7_7, © Springer Science+Business Media, LLC 2011

## Introduction

It was not all that long ago that a good host or hostess saw to it that the guests' cocktail or wine glasses were never empty and the last duty of the evening was to ask, "Will you have one for the road?" Fortunately, we have changed our attitudes toward alcohol and driving, primarily through public education, victim advocacy, and legislation. This cultural shift is reflected in the number of traffic fatalities in 2008 that reached its lowest level since 1961. There was a 9.7% decline in the number of people killed in motor vehicle crashes in the United States, from 41,259 in 2007 to 37,261 in 2008, according to the National Highway Traffic Safety Administration (NHTSA, as cited in National Center for Statistics and Analysis, 2009a). This decline of almost 4,000 deaths is the largest annual reduction in terms of both number and percentage since 1982 (NHTSA, as cited in National Center for Statistics and Analysis, 2009a). One reason for this decrease in alcohol-related deaths may be the fact that, since 2005, all 50 states, the District of Columbia and Puerto Rico have established the blood alcohol concentration (BAC) of 0.08 g/dL as the level of impairment. Of the 11,773 people who died in alcohol-impaired-driving crashes in 2008, 8,027 (68%) were drivers with a BAC of 0.08 or higher. Sentencing has also become more severe for defendants convicted of driving while impaired (DWI). Finally, technology and pharmacology have improved to the point where they can be applied to prevent people from driving while impaired, and the criminal justice system has initiated robust changes that look promising.

There are lingering myths, however, about drinking and driving that need to be dispelled. In general, DWI offenders are not party guests who have had a bit too much of the bubbly; rather, they are often repeat offenders. The challenge for traffic safety is the prevention of impaired driving, particularly by those drivers who are arrested multiple times. We have sufficient data to know what works, what doesn't, what is inconclusive, and what looks promising for the future. To be successful, a combination of responses, including better targeting of offenders and effective criminal and civil policies, must be implemented.

## What Is the Estimated Number of DWI/DUI Identified Individuals Needing Interventions and Treatment Each Year?

The person who is detained for driving while impaired by alcohol has, on average, driven impaired 400 times before being caught for the "first time." Since few states provide screening and assessment for those convicted of DWI, it is quite difficult to estimate how many people would benefit from treatment; however, substance abuse disorders are found in 85–90% of multiple DWI offenders and in 40–50% of "first-time" offenders. Of DWI probationers, 31% report drinking daily as do 40% of those in jail for the offense. Most people arrested for DWI have a BAC of 0.16, twice the "legal limit." FBI statistics show that 1.2 million people were arrested for DWI in 2003 but that 30.7 million drivers, aged 21 or older, admit to alcohol use before driving. About one-third of young adults, those aged 21–25, drive while impaired and more men than women (4% vs. 1%) commit this offense. In self-reports, about 4.4% of white males, 3.1% of Latinos, and 2.8% of African American men admit to driving while impaired. Overall almost 10% of all arrests in the United States have been for DWI over the past decade (Jones & Lacey, 2002).

## What Abused Drugs Are Most Common in DWI?

Obviously, alcohol is the drug for which most people are arrested for DWI. However, "drugged driving," as it has come to be called, is receiving increasing attention. Detection of impaired driving without the odor of alcohol, bloodshot eyes, slurred speech, and other indicia of alcohol consumption is difficult for a traffic safety officer. Further, less research has been done on the effects of drugs other than alcohol, most importantly on the potential for impaired motor skills, reaction time, and judgment.

In 2007, NHTSA conducted the National Roadside Survey of Alcohol and Drug Use by Drivers. While the estimates are not conclusive regarding the nature and scale of the drug-impaired driving problem, they are an important part of ongoing research. Subjects were provided an option to be tested (saliva in most cases, blood in others) for prescription, over-the-counter, and illicit drug use. The results showed more nighttime drivers (14.4%) were drug positive than daytime drivers (11.0%). And overall, 13.8% of the nighttime drivers were found to be drug-positive when administered the, more reliable, blood test (NHTSA as cited in National Center for Statistics and Analysis, 2009b).

## Are There Specific Treatments for Specific Drugs?

Although a significant number of impaired drivers are poly-drug users, we are still dealing with alcohol as the primary drug of abuse. Therefore, we rely heavily on the treatment protocols defined as evidence based by the National Institute of Alcoholism and Alcohol Abuse (NIAAA), for the vast majority of offenders. Research now being conducted on the subject, at the UCLA Integrated Substance Abuse Program (2009), is "looking at the effects of therapist interventions on patients during and after their participation in three psycho-social treatments for alcoholism" (*ISAP News*, 2009 cited in UCLA Integrated Substance Abuse Programs, 2009).

Drugged driving laws have lagged behind alcohol legislation, in part because of limitations in current technology for determining drug levels and resulting impairment. For alcohol, detection of its blood concentration (BAC) is relatively simple and concentrations greater than 0.08% have been shown to impair driving performance in all subjects. Thus, 0.08% is the legal limit in this country although individual impairment may occur at lower BAC levels. For illicit drugs, there is no agreement on the limit at which impairment has been reliably demonstrated, and determining current drug levels can be difficult because some drugs linger in the body for a period of days or weeks after initial ingestion. Some states have made driving with any amount of any illicit drug illegal, without the necessity to show individual impairment, while others require a showing of impairment to convict for drugged driving.

## What Are the Principal Interventions Used?

### Traditional Approaches to DWI Enforcement

The goal of DWI enforcement is to reduce the number of automotive crashes and fatalities caused by impaired driving. Enforcement of DWI laws serves as an intake system for the courts that are tasked to impose sanctions that will keep offenders from drinking and driving in the future. In carrying out this mission, law enforcement officers use tools such as the standardized field sobriety test (SFST) and they have access to a number of technological devices, used with varying success, that measure breath alcohol.

DWI enforcement serves as both a general and specific deterrent. Zero-tolerance arrest policies increase the perceived risk of arrest if one drives while impaired. If the perceived risk is high, the incidence of the behavior is reduced and safer highways result. The community learns about DWI enforcement in two ways: (1) observing actual enforcement as a driver or passenger, and (2) reports from others as well as news coverage. Thus, highly visible and frequent enforcement is observed by drivers as they travel on roadways; publicity, either planned or spontaneous, increases public awareness. A sobriety checkpoint over the weekend, for instance, leads to discussions about DWI around the water cooler on Monday.

### Dedicated Patrols

Federal funding for DWI enforcement has increased dramatically since 1975 (Borkenstein, 1975) and many law enforcement agencies have established special DWI patrols dedicated to impaired driving detection, particularly on weekends. Consequently, the number of DWI arrests in the United States has increased from 1 to 1.5 million in just 10 years (1995–2005) (FBI crime statistics), making the odds of being arrested if over the limit substantially higher today. Experience in the Alcohol Safety Action Program (ASAP) program indicated that one or two dedicated patrols would double the annual number of DWI arrests in a jurisdiction (Levy, Voas, Johnson, & Klein, 1978; Voas, 1981).

### Sobriety Checkpoints

Sobriety checkpoints are an enforcement operation in which law enforcement officers stop all vehicles, or a systematic selection of vehicles, to evaluate drivers for signs of alcohol or other drug impairment. To minimize public concern about the activity and comply with court rulings, checkpoints typically are publicized in advance and signs are posted at the approaches to warn drivers. Uniformed officers approach drivers and identify themselves, state the purpose of the stop, and ask drivers questions designed to elicit responses that will permit the officer to observe the drivers' general demeanor. Drivers who do not appear impaired are immediately waved on; drivers who show signs of impairment are usually detained in a safe enforcement area where they are investigated further, and either arrested or released.

Several studies in the early 1980s found significant decreases in alcohol-related crashes associated with sobriety checkpoint programs in Arizona (Epperlein, 1987); in Clearwater and Largo, Florida (Lacey, Rudisill, Popkin, & Stewart, 1986); and, in Charlottesville, Virginia (Voas, Rhodenizer, & Lynn, 1985). Later studies confirmed those results, by demonstrating that checkpoint programs reduced alcohol-related crashes by 10–20% in locations such as New Jersey (Levy, Asch, & Shea, 1990; Levy, Shea, & Asch, 1988) and Binghamton, New York (Wells, Preusser, & Williams, 1992).

## Interventions That Work

### Deterrence

Classical deterrence theory seeks to explain the influence of punishment on personal behavior. It holds that three factors – risk of detection, severity of the sanction, and the speed with which the sanction is applied – determine the response to laws. Ross (1982) provides perhaps the clearest explanation of deterrence, emphasizing that it is the perception of each of the three factors, rather than the reality, that controls behavior. The basic concept of the theory has been demonstrated in the many evaluations of traffic safety programs that have been conducted in the last half century. The relative influence of each of the elements of the theory, however, has been less studied. Ross and Klette (1995), who looked at Scandinavian laws, concluded that the perceived probability of arrest was a more significant factor than the severity of the penalty (Ross, 1992). Some evidence for this position was developed from studies of DWI enforcement in the United States as well (Ross, McCleary, & LaFree, 1990; Ross & Voas, 1990).

### Driver's License Sanctions

For the last century, license suspension has been the most widely used and most effective sanction for impaired driving. Studies on the effect of state administrative license revocation or administrative license suspension laws have shown them to be a general deterrent (Klein, 1989; Voas, Tippetts, & Fell, 2000; Zador, 1991). Since DWI offenders are high-risk drivers, these laws also have been effective as a specific deterrent in reducing the recidivism and crash involvement of drivers apprehended and convicted of impaired driving (Coppin & Oldenbeek, 1965; McKnight & Voas, 1991; Peck, 1991; Peck, Sadler, & Perrine, 1985; Williams, Hagen, & McConnell, 1984). Voas, Tippetts, and Taylor (2000) found that the DWI reoffense rates were approximately 40% lower for suspended DWI offenders compared to reinstated DWI offenders. Based on the Fatal Accident Reporting System (FARS), 7.4% of all drivers in fatal crashes have suspended or revoked licenses, and 20%

of drivers in fatal crashes in the United States are improperly licensed (Griffin & DeLaZerda, 2000). DeYoung, Peck, and Helander (1997) found that in California suspended or revoked drivers were 3.7 times more likely to be at fault in a two-vehicle crash.

### Substance Abuse Treatment

There is substantial evidence that substance abuse treatment programs are effective in reducing crashes in which alcohol plays a role (McKnight & Voas, 1991; Peck et al., 1985). DeYoung (1997a) and Peck et al. (1985) have shown that the effect of routine punishments for repeat offenders can be enhanced if combined with alcohol treatment. Wells-Parker, Bangert-Drowns, McMillen, and Williams (1995) conducted a meta-analysis of 215 evaluations of drinking-and-driving remediation (treatment) programs. The conclusion of that analysis was that the best designed studies indicate that treatment can produce an additional 7–9% reduction in drinking-and-driving recidivism and alcohol-related crashes when compared with control groups that largely received only license restrictions. The reported rate of reduction in recidivism may be conservative, in that a number of the less well-designed studies produced results indicating larger reductions.

Recent evaluation studies have found remedial interventions (e.g., treatment and educational programs) to be more effective than traditional punitive sanctions (e.g., jail terms and fines), in reducing recidivism and alcohol-related crashes. This is particularly the case when remedial interventions are combined with license restrictions (DeYoung, 1997a; Green, French, Haberman, & Holland, 1991; Jones & Lacey, 1998; Jones, Wiliszowski, & Lacey, 1996; Kunitz et al., 2002; Martell, Stewart, & Jamburajan, 1998; Nochajski, Miller, Wieczorek, & Whitney, 1993; Tashima & Helander, 2000). Wells-Parker and Williams (2002), commenting on their review of court-mandated treatment, noted that, "In general, research has consistently shown that treatment has a modest effect on reducing drinking-driving and alcohol-impaired crashes among offenders who are mandated to attend and who actually receive the intervention" [emphasis added]. Mann et al. (1994) found that offenders who received treatment had lower mortality rates when compared to similar members of a comparison group. And Dill and Wells-Parker (2006), in their review of mandated treatment, indicated that such programs have shown less effectiveness in reducing the severity of alcohol-related problems other than impaired driving.

Research conducted on the efficacy of psychosocial and pharmacological alcohol treatments in non-DWI contexts have identified several interventions that are effective in reducing alcohol use (Irvin, Bowers, Dunn, & Wang, 1999; Miller & Wilbourne, 2002; Moyer, Finney, Swearingen, & Vergun, 2002; Project MATCH Research, 1998; Swearingen, Moyer, & Finney, 2003). These interventions emphasize abstinence or reduced drinking and consider individual social support systems and social contexts.

*Motivational enhancement therapy (MET)* assumes that individuals have the inherent skills necessary to change their drinking with the help of a professional who provides support and encouragement throughout the process (Donovan et al., 1994). MET relies on an individual's ability to develop his or her own coping mechanisms and internal agents of change to stop drinking. The therapist provides feedback, reviews progress, and reinforces the client's motivation and commitment.

*Cognitive-behavioral coping skills training* assumes that when individuals learn to address their broader problems, rather than their drinking problem specifically, they will be less likely to rely on alcohol as a coping mechanism. The goal is to help people improve their skills in dealing with the stress of high-risk situations that might otherwise lead to heavy drinking. Core therapy sessions focus on "understanding the importance of coping skills to prevent relapse, coping with cravings and urges to drink, managing thoughts about alcohol and drinking, general problem-solving skills, drink refusal skills, seemingly irrelevant decisions that lead the person closer to drinking, and development of plans to help cope with emergencies and relapse if they occur" (Donovan et al., 1994).

*Twelve Step peer support groups* are based on the disease model of alcoholism (i.e., that the individual has lost control over alcohol due to changes in brain chemistry). Twelve-step programs focus on (a) getting the individual to accept his or her powerlessness over alcohol and the unmanageability of his or her life because of uncontrollable drinking; (b) incorporating the program's belief system into the individual's life and living the principles of the 12 steps; and (c) recognizing that abstinence requires working the 12 steps and participating in the fellowship of Alcoholics Anonymous or similar groups with other alcoholics in recovery who turn to a "higher power" for support.

### Ignition Interlock

The most direct and specific method for preventing impaired driving by DWI offenders is to require that they place a device on their vehicles that prevents the engine from starting if the prospective driver has been drinking. As of 2004, 43 states had enacted laws providing for interlock programs, but only a small proportion of DWI offenders have actually installed devices despite the strong evidence for their effectiveness.

When the device is attached to a vehicle, the operator is required to provide a breath sample for analysis each time the engine is started. If alcohol is present, the car will not start. A log is kept to reflect these false starts and the device is also tamper proof. There are also precautions in place to prevent someone else from starting the car such as a camera that shows the subject. Generally, a state-licensed service provider must install the unit, inspect it regularly, and provide a report on any attempt to circumvent the device to the court, a probation officer, or a department of motor vehicles driver analyst as specified in each state's law. Such monitoring systems, with substantial consequences for tampering with the device, are essential for the integrity of the program.

Recently, some states (such as Michigan, Colorado, and Florida) have enacted legislation requiring the installation of an interlock on second offenders' vehicles for up to a year in addition to the suspension of the privilege to drive. As of mid-2011, 14 states have enacted legislation requiring the ignition interlock installation after a first offense. Interlock installation is a prerequisite for reinstatement of the offender's license because recidivism is highest early in the reinstatement period. In some states, this legislation permits the offender to avoid the interlock reinstatement requirement simply by delaying application for reinstatement beyond the period to which the interlock requirement applies (Tashima & Helander, 1999; Voas, McKnight, & Tippetts, 2006).

Several states have passed laws requiring the installation of an interlock no matter how long offenders delay reinstatement of their licenses. For instance, since 2004 in Florida, second DWI offenders can never reinstate their privilege to drive unless they install an interlock for a period of a year. That law was the subject of a 2-year study (Voas et al., 2006). Between 2004 and 2006, the Florida Department of Motor Vehicles and Driver Licensing sent 51,043 notices to multiple offenders informing them of their eligibility to reinstate their licenses if they installed an interlock. Of those, 13,413 or 26.3% responded to the invitation by installing the devices. The remainder continued to have their licenses suspended. Of those who agreed to install the device, 5.1% (689) dropped out of the program before completing the required period on the interlock. In addition, another 13.6% (1,822) of the interlock program participants were referred to treatment based on recorded high-level BAC attempts to start the vehicle. The effectiveness of the Florida program remains to be determined, but it is clear that its effectiveness will be limited because only one in four offenders offered the opportunity to reinstate with an interlock are choosing to do so.

## Drug/DWI Treatment Courts

Drug treatment courts (DTCs) take a rehabilitative approach to justice that is usually applied to nonviolent, addicted offenders. The number of DTCs in the United States has grown from 1 in 1989, to 12 in 1994, to 1,100 in 2003, to more than 2,500 today. Additionally there are another 1,200 problem-solving courts as they have come to be called. DTCs provide coordination of the judiciary, prosecution, probation, defense bar, law enforcement, social services, mental health, and the treatment community to intervene with chronic offenders to break the cycle of substance abuse, addiction, and criminal activity. Offenders undergo an intensive regimen of substance abuse treatment, case management, drug testing, probation supervision, and consistent monitoring. They are subject to periodic court reviews with a judge who has special expertise in the DTC model (Fox & Huddleston, 2003). In a critical review of 120 evaluations of numerous drug court programs, the National Center on Addiction and Substance Abuse at Columbia University concluded that drug courts lower recidivism, reduce drug use, and reduce both direct and indirect costs of investigating and adjudicating drug-related crime (Belenko, 1998; also Belenko, 2001). An evaluation of six drug courts in New York State – Bronx, Brooklyn, Queens, Suffolk, Syracuse, and Rochester – showed that they reduced offender recidivism by an average of 29% over the 3-year post-arrest period when compared to similar offenders receiving standard sentences (Rempel et al., 2003). Drug treatment courts appear to succeed because they engage offenders and retain them in rehabilitation programs. In a survey conducted by the American University Drug Court Clearinghouse and Technical Assistance Project (2000), drug court jurisdictions reported retention rates ranging from 67 to 71%.

Based on the effectiveness of drug treatment courts, DWI courts (also called Driving Under the Influence (DUI) and Sobriety Courts) emerged around 2005. Modeled after drug treatment courts and addressing offenders post-conviction, DWI courts monitor probation conditions that typically include frequent interaction with the DWI court judge, intensive supervision by probation officers, an appropriate level of evidence-based treatment, random alcohol and other drug testing, community service, lifestyle changes, positive reinforcement for successful performance in the program, and jail time and other sanctions for noncompliance. Mostly nonviolent offenders who have had two or more prior DWI convictions or "first time" offenders with high blood alcohol content are assigned to a DWI court, if one exists in the jurisdiction.

DWI courts reportedly have held offenders accountable for their actions, changed offenders' behavior to end recidivism, reduced alcohol abuse, treated the victims of DWI offenders in a fair and just way, and protected the public (Freeman-Wilson & Wilkosz, 2002; Tauber & Huddleston, 1999). Breckenridge, Winfree, Maupin, and Clason (2000) reported that a DWI court program significantly reduces recidivism among alcoholic DWI offenders. Other studies of this type of program are currently underway and DWI courts are being implemented in numerous states. As of June 2009, there were a total of 526 DWI courts; 166 courts that focus exclusively on DWI and 360 "hybrid" drug courts that fold in DWI defendants. One report on a DWI court in Bernalillo County, New Mexico indicated that recidivism was reduced by more than 50% for 341 offenders who completed the DWI court program compared to similar offenders not assigned to the DWI court (Guerin & Pitts, 2002). Those results, however, were preliminary and the study did not adhere strictly to established drug court evaluation criteria. A study funded by the Michigan Office of Highway Safety Planning and conducted by NPC Research (Fuller, Carey, & Kissick, 2007) found that offender participation in a DWI court dramatically reduced recidivism, with offenders sentenced to traditional probation rearrested nearly six times more often in the first year. The study also found that participation in a DWI Court led to lower recidivism rates, with traditional court defendants being three times more likely to be rearrested for any charge and 19 times more likely to be arrested for a DWI charge. Furthermore, time to rearrest was increased in DWI Court. Offenders under probation, without DWI Court participation, were rearrested two times sooner after starting probation. The study went on to find that DWI courts reduced levels of substance abuse and were successful in bringing program participants to completion and graduation in their program.

### Zero Tolerance for Under 21

Zero tolerance for alcohol or other drugs is a policy created to reduce the high level of crash involvement by young drivers, both the 16- and 17-year-old novice drivers and the 18- to 20-year-old drivers. In 1984, the US Congress adopted measures to sanction states that did not adopt 21 as their minimum legal drinking age and by 1988 all had done so as had the District of Columbia. This trend continued in 1995 when the US Congress passed a law requiring states to adopt zero-tolerance laws for drivers younger than 21 years. By 1998, all states and the District of Columbia had passed such laws. Zero-tolerance and "sort of" zero-tolerance laws ranging from 0.00 to 0.02 g/dL for youth have proved effective in reducing the number of fatal crashes involving underage drinking drivers (Fell & Voas, 2006a). Also see Blomberg (1992), Lacey, Jones, and Wiliszowski (2000) and Hingson, Howland, Heeren, and Winter (1992). In a follow-up study, Hingson, Heeren, and Winter (1994) compared 12 states that adopted zero tolerance for youth before 1991 with 12 comparison states that did not lower their BAC levels. The study suggests that those states dropping the BAC level to 0.00 the true zero-tolerance laws, or 0.02 g/dL, send a strong drinking and driving message to youth, rather than the mixed and confusing message sent to youth by states setting a higher limit. Zwerling and Jones (1999) conducted a systematic review of zero-tolerance laws and their effect on alcohol-related injuries and fatalities. The six studies that met their strict selection criteria showed reductions in injuries and fatalities associated with the implementation of zero-tolerance laws, and in three studies, the reductions were statistically significant. Voas, Tippetts, and Fell (2003) used data on all US drivers younger than 21 involved in fatal crashes from 1982 through 1997. After accounting for differences among the states in various background factors, changes in economic and demographic factors within states over time, and the effects of other related laws, results indicated a significant 24.4% reduction associated with the zero-tolerance laws for alcohol-positive drivers younger than 21 who were involved in fatal crashes.

## Interventions That Might Work

### Vehicle Sanctions

Because of the large number of suspended DWI offenders driving illegally and the limited enforcement resources available to deal with the problem, many states have begun to enact legislation directed at the vehicles used by offenders in an attempt to limit illicit driving. In addition to ignition interlock discussed above, two other vehicle sanctions are (1) programs that confiscate or impound the vehicle and (2) programs that confiscate the vehicle plates and vehicle registration and/or require special plates on the vehicles of DWI offenders. None of these vehicle controls is foolproof; each one can be circumvented if the offender drives a vehicle registered in someone else's name. Nevertheless, as with license suspension, several of the vehicle sanctions have been found to have a specific deterrent effect of reducing recidivism for DWI offenders (Beck, Rauch, Baker, & Williams, 1999; DeYoung, 1997b, 2000; Voas & DeYoung, 2002; Voas & Tippetts, 1995; Voas, Tippetts, & Taylor, 1997; Voas, Tippetts, & Taylor, 1998). The only study of the general deterrent effect of vehicle impoundment was conducted in California by DeYoung (1998) who found no evidence that impoundment had a general deterrent effect on the driving public as a whole.

### Registration Suspension and License Plate Actions

A number of states have laws requiring the registration of an offender-owned vehicle be suspended for the same period as the driver's license. In concept, offenders should surrender their registration document and license plates to the DMV; however, there is weak followup to this requirement. In some jurisdictions, the courts require theses documents be submitted at the time of sentencing. In others, Departments of Motor Vehicles must depend upon local enforcement agencies to apprehend drivers operating vehicles with suspended registrations. Because most local enforcement officers are overwhelmed with more serious tasks, seizing the license plates and registrations of suspended DWI offenders has generally proven to be unlikely. There have been no evaluations of the provisions for canceling registrations at the time of suspension (Voas, 1992).

Although the traditional programs canceling the offender's registration have not been evaluated, two other applications of registration cancellation and license plate forfeiture have been shown to be effective. Washington and Oregon laws allow officers, who apprehend an unlicensed driver, to seize the vehicle registration and mark the license plate with a "suspended" sticker. Voas, Tippetts, and Lange (1997) studied the before-and-after effects of this law, considering alcohol-related offenses, Driving While Suspended (DWS) offenses, moving traffic violations, and crashes among drivers suspended for DWI. Their results showed a significant general deterrent effect in Oregon but not in Washington which had a similar but more limited law and a weaker enforcement effort.

Minnesota implemented license plate seizure at the point of arrest for drivers who had BAC levels of 0.20 g/dL or higher. When the seizure was dependent on court actions, few plates were confiscated but when the law changed to DMV administrative enforcement, plate seizures increased and were demonstrated to have a specific deterrent effect. Leaf and Preusser (2011) compared first offenders who were affected by the DMV plate seizure law with first-time DWI offenders, who had lower BAC levels of 0.17–0.19 g/dL, and were not subject to plate impoundment. During the first year after the offense, when sanction differences were greatest, the drivers subject to plate impoundment (BACs $> = 0.20$ g/dL) had a recidivism rate 25% lower than the drivers who were not subject to plate impoundment (BACs = 0.17–0.19 g/dL). Beyond the first year, the two groups of offenders experienced no significant differences in recidivism rates. Leaf and Preusser (2011) concluded that the plate impoundment was effective, at least in the short term while the sanctions were in place. Ohio and Minnesota provide for the suspension of the registration of vehicles owned by DWI offenders for the period of the driver's license suspension. These states also provide for a special license plate (a "family plate") for the DWI offender's vehicle to permit family members to use the vehicle while the offender-owner is suspended. The license plate is marked so that law enforcement can stop the vehicle and determine whether the suspended offender is driving illegally. No evaluations of family plate laws have been conducted.

*Forfeiture*: Unlike the temporary holding of the offender's vehicle involved in impoundment actions, forfeiture involves seizing and selling the offender's vehicle. The state of knowledge regarding the usefulness of forfeiture remains sketchy. Nonetheless, a fairly strong quasi-experimental study has been conducted on the forfeiture program in Portland, Oregon resulting in some interesting anecdotal evidence that sheds some light on forfeiture programs including those in New York City and California.

The city of Portland enacted a civil forfeiture program in 1989 that focused not on the behavior of the offender, but rather, on the unlawful use of the vehicle irrespective of the culpability of the owner. Thus, in Portland, vehicles are seized for forfeiture as a public nuisance when drivers have lost their driving privilege because of a DWI conviction or when the driver is arrested as a habitual traffic offender. Crosby (1995) conducted a study in which all offenders whose vehicles were seized for forfeiture between 1990 and 1995 were compared with all offenders, arrested for the same offense, whose vehicles were not seized. The results showed that the rearrest rate was about 50% lower for offenders whose vehicles were seized than the comparison group. The study also found that offenders whose vehicles were forfeited had about the same rearrest rate as offenders whose vehicles were simply impounded.

Safir, Grasso, and Messner (2000) reported on a forfeiture program in New York City. Beginning in February 1999, the city police seized the vehicles of DWI offenders under three circumstances: (1) when the impaired driver owned the vehicle; (2) when the impaired driver was not the owner but the owner knew or should have known of the criminal use of the vehicle; and (3) when the impaired driver was the "beneficial owner" or registered owner of the vehicle. In 10 months

1,458 vehicles were seized in connection with DWI arrests and 827 forfeiture actions were commenced. During that period, the police department instituted a pilot project that returned the vehicle upon successful completion of an authorized alcohol treatment program and the payment of administrative and litigation costs. To qualify for that program, the driver had to have an arrest BAC level of less than 0.20 g/dL and no previous DWI offenses. This allowed some first offenders to avoid having their vehicles forfeited. Although the authors reported anecdotal evidence showing that, while the ordinance was in effect, DWI arrests and DWI crashes decreased, no scientific evaluation was conducted.

*Impoundment/immobilization*: Impoundment and immobilization laws are similar in that they are designed to deny the offender the use of a vehicle for a span of time to help ensure that suspended individuals will not drive illegally. Immobilization provides a low-cost alternative to having the vehicle stored by a commercial towing service, a cost absorbed by the public when an offender fails to retrieve the vehicle. Several studies of impoundment laws have been conducted. Beirness, Simpson, Mayhew, and Jonah (1997) evaluated both the general and specific deterrent effects of Manitoba's program. Although the analysis did show a decline in both measures contemporaneous with the introduction of impoundment, the results are ambiguous because Manitoba introduced the administrative license suspension (ALS) law at the same time as the impoundment law. Concurrent with the implementation of a 30-day vehicle impoundment law for first-time DWS offenders, California also implemented a vehicle forfeiture law for repeat DWS offenders. Although the first offender impoundment law was widely applied throughout the state, with more than 100,000 vehicles impounded in the first year of the legislation, the companion forfeiture law was implemented in only two communities. Peck and Voas (2002) surveyed police departments receiving state grants to conduct impoundment programs to determine why they did not use the forfeiture provisions of the law. They identified five factors that accounted for the low application of forfeiture: (1) lack of support from the prosecutor's office because of attendant costs; (2) cumbersome administrative procedures; (3) poor cost recovery in that proceeds from the sale of vehicles did not exceed the cost of seizure; (4) a high percentage of third-party owners to whom forfeiture does not apply, and (5) the 30-day impoundment was often equivalent to forfeiture because half of the offenders did not retrieve their vehicles. Despite the failure of most California communities to implement forfeiture programs, those that did (Santa Barbara and San Diego) found the process relatively straightforward and easy to apply. Because of the limited use of the second DWS offender forfeiture law, there has been no effectiveness evaluation of that legislation.

### Victim Impact Panels

A widely used offender program – the victim impact panel (VIP) – is designed to increase the offender's empathy for victims of DWI and appreciation for the damage that impaired driving can cause. At the VIP, victims describe their injuries and the problems they have experienced as a result of their involvement in an alcohol-related crash (Shinar & Compton, 1995). VIPs are provided to an estimated 400,000 DWI offenders per year by more than 200 Mothers Against Drunk Driving (MADD) chapters in the United States. The empirical evidence regarding the effectiveness of VIPs is mixed and inconclusive. Anecdotal reports indicate that DWI offenders are often moved by victims' stories and vow to reform their ways. Decreased DWI recidivism, however, did not result when VIPs were used (Shinar & Compton, 1995). Polacsek et al. (2001) examined the efficacy of MADD VIPs specifically compared to a 10- to 12-hour DWI school. Results showed no significant difference in movement through the stages of change or in recidivism over the 2-year followup period. Wheeler, Rogers, Tonigan, and Woodall (2004) reported similar findings with little difference between VIP attendees and nonattendees on alcohol consumption, drinking-and-driving behavior, or recidivism. In fact, some research suggests that VIPs may actually have an effect on recidivism opposite to that desired. One study, deBaca, Lapham, Liang, and Skipper (2001), examined rearrest rates of 6,702 first-time and repeat offenders in New Mexico between 1989 and 1994 following referral to VIPs. Results showed that, after controlling for multiple risk factors, VIP referral was not statistically associated with recidivism for first offenders. When gender was taken into account however, female repeat offenders referred to VIPs were significantly more likely to be rearrested compared with those not referred. Possible reasons for these inconsistent results may lie in the research designs that were quasi-experimental or the fact that they lacked randomization and equivalent groups.

## BAC Monitoring

Another method of controlling impaired driving by DWI offenders is monitoring their alcohol consumption. Some courts implemented closely supervised Antabuse® (disulfiram); naltrexone hydrochloride (daily oral tabs marketed as Revia® and long acting injections marketed as Vivitrol®) administration. Others have implemented intensive supervision programs in which probation officers make surprise visits to the homes of offenders and conduct breath tests. DWI courts also generally provide for intensive monitoring of abstinence. Some conduct liver panels (ethyl glucuronide (EtG) and ethyl sulfate (EtS) tests) to see if the defendant has been drinking; some send probation officers on "bottle checks" where even the garbage cans are searched for evidence of drinking. Such systems are labor intensive and expensive for the courts. In the last couple of decades, innovative technological methods for collecting BAC data have received considerable attention. One of these systems has been in use for some time by providers of electronically supervised home confinement programs. It involves electronic remote breath test systems through a telephone thus allowing frequent monitoring of the BAC level while the offender is at home. A more direct monitoring system is worn on the body to constantly monitor (or check) the BAC level. Two devices currently available are the SCRAM™ ankle bracelet and the WrisTAS™ which is about the size of a large wrist watch. The SCRAM™ incorporates a system for detecting attempts to circumvent the system. There are at least 10,000 units currently in use by courts in the United States and Canada according to the AMS Company, the developer of SCRAM™. These systems provide the promise of monitoring abstinence with a minimum of limitations on the offender's other behaviors. Experimental evidence appears to confirm that these devices estimate BAC levels with acceptable accuracy. Neither class of devices has attained anything close to perfection; both experiencing some problems and peculiarities. Overall, the idea of measuring alcohol at the skin surface is valid: both devices can do it, and with further developments, alcohol monitoring of this type is likely to be more widely used.

## Interventions That Do Not Work

### Risk of Apprehension for Driving While Suspended Is Low

License suspension is supposed to incapacitate the driver but because up to 75% of suspended offenders drive illicitly, its effectiveness is limited (Ross & Gonzales, 1988). Early in the twentieth century when there were more horse-drawn carriages than motor vehicles, it was general knowledge when a person had his or her privilege to drive suspended or revoked. Thus, driving while suspended (DWS) was relatively rare. Today, with approximately 231 million motor vehicles on the roadways, it is difficult for law enforcement to adequately enforce the laws against DWS. It would be unconstitutional to stop a driver just to check license status; however if a law enforcement officer stops a vehicle for another traffic offense, the officer can require the driver to produce his or her driver's license. Suspended, but careful, drivers can continue to drive with very little risk, if they avoid committing traffic violations.

Because suspended drivers do not believe they will be caught, there are high rates of illicit driving as reported by Ross and Gonzales (1988). Despite this, there is evidence that strong sanctions against DWI and DWS can reduce illicit driving. McCartt, Geary, and Nissen (2002) found that 88% of the DWI offenders in Milwaukee, Wisconsin, where the penalties for DWI and DWS were perceived to be relatively low drove illicitly compared to 36% of offenders in Bergen County, New Jersey, where the penalties were perceived to be relatively high. Both of these studies reported that suspended offenders reported considerable concern about being apprehended for DWS and indicated that they limit or manage their driving to avoid detection.

*DWI offenders delay reinstatement.* A further indication that DWI offenders find it possible to drive while suspended with relatively little risk of apprehension is the large number of suspended drivers who do not reinstate their licenses when they are first eligible. Early studies of the effect of license suspension noted that the reduced rate of repeat offenses demonstrated by suspended DWI offenders compared to those who avoided suspension continued beyond the end of the suspension period (Hagen, 1977). Later, followup studies reported that up to 50% of the suspended DWI offenders were not reinstating their licenses when eligible. Consequently, those offenders continued to have a reduced rate of recidivism for all traffic offenses (Sadler & Perrine, 1984; Tashima & Helander, 1999). In a study funded by NHTSA in Washington state, Voas and McKnight (1989) evaluated the relative efficacy of limited vocational licensing (allowing the offender to drive to and from work as well as in the course of employment) versus full suspension for DWI. They found that only one-third of first DWI offenders reinstated their licenses when eligible to do so after 90 days. Another third reinstated during the following year, and the last third remained suspended after 2 years.

## Education Programs for DWI Offenders

For the "social drinkers" among DWI offenders whose screening results indicate that they do not have an Alcohol Use Disorders (AUD), a short (8- to 10-hour) educational program may be a sufficient court mandate (Voas & Fisher, 2001). These are usually modeled on the "DWI Phoenix" program developed by Stewart and Malfetti (1970). Results indicate that such programs may be successful in increasing intermediate goals, such as readiness to change, but have little effect on DWI recidivism. Rider, Voas, Kelley-Baker, Grosz and Murphy (2007) described the Preventing Alcohol-Related Convictions (PARC) program, a novel educational curriculum for first-caught DWI offenders, with the specific goal of reducing DWI recidivism. It differs from traditional DWI education and prevention programs in that it does not suggest to DWI offenders that they must abstain from alcohol entirely or that they must control their drinking to prevent a future DWI; rather, it teaches students to prevent a future DWI by not driving their motor vehicles to drinking events. Thus, the emphasis of the curriculum is on controlling driving rather than controlling drinking to avoid future DWI convictions. The program has been tested in a random clinical trial with 43,000 first offenders in Florida. The initial study of the program (Rider et al., 2006) involved the use of a readiness to change the questionnaire (Prochaska, DiClemente, & Norcross, 1992) to gauge the extent to which the first offenders accepted the contrasting traditional "control drinking" approach to the PARC "control driving" approach. This first study demonstrated that the PARC program was effective in moving participants toward more readiness for change and toward a strategy of planning to avoid driving to any venue in which drinking may occur. A followup study compared the recidivism of 10,000 of the offenders in the study based on a full year of exposure to recidivism training with the PARC system. That study (Rider et al., 2007) demonstrated that the first DWI offenders exposed to the PARC curriculum were associated with a 42% reduction in recidivism when compared to the traditional curriculum.

There is some evidence that the effectiveness of an education program when compared to jail may vary according to whether the DWI was a citation for a first or a multiple offender. Socie, Wagner, and Hopkins (1997) selected drivers convicted of their first offence who were sentenced either to jail or to a certified driver intervention program (DIP) in Franklin County, Ohio, in 1987. Although random assignment to treatment was apparently not possible, the authors claimed that because each impaired-driving charge was assigned to one of a pool of 15 judges with widely varying sentencing patterns, there was no apparent bias in subject allocation to jail or the DIP program. The study compared the likelihood of subsequent impaired driving of 124 jailed offenders with 218 DIP offenders over 4 years following conviction. After controlling for potentially important covariates (such as gender, age, race, BAC, additional charges filed at the time of arrest, and driving history), they derived logistic regression results indicating that DIP attendees had significantly lower rates of subsequent impaired driving. Drivers who had no prior history of an alcohol-related offense and were jailed were significantly more likely to again drive while impaired when compared to those enrolled in a DIP. Furthermore, it should be noted that drivers younger than 21 years of age are at elevated risk for recidivism, regardless of the program involved. Finally, DIPs appear most effective when used for people who have not had previous alcohol-related crashes or driving offenses.

## Traditional Sanctions for DWI Offenses

### Imprisonment

In the decade between 1910 and 1920, the states began to pass laws to incarcerate impaired drivers. Despite the early and continuous use of this sanction for over a century, the evidence for its effectiveness in reducing impaired driving is limited. One problem in evaluating its utility is that it potentially has both a general and specific deterrent effect, so it can be evaluated in two ways: by its overall affect on alcohol-related crashes and by its specific effect on the crashes of DWI offenders. Wagenaar, Zobeck, Hingson, and Williams (1995) and Zobeck and Williams (1994) reviewed 87 evaluation studies of laws providing mandatory jail and minimum fines covering the 31-year period from 1960 to 1991 and found only limited evidence for the effectiveness of jail sanctions. One reason that the jail sanction may not have as strong a general deterrent effect as might be expected has been proposed by Ross, who argued that the low probability of apprehension is more salient than the severity of the sanction (Ross & Voas, 1990). The economic costs of jail space and its limited availability present additional problems. The response to these barriers has been the diversion of offenders (who would normally be jailed) into community service programs or electronically monitored home confinement. Efforts by advocate groups such as MADD to mandate jail time for first offenders (Fell & Voas, 2006b) have generally failed because of the cost and jail overcrowding issues (Voas, 1986).

Adding to the complexity is the fact that other court-imposed conditions on the DWI offender provide the threat of incarceration for violations of probation. Independent of its direct effect on recidivism and/or crashes, through its incapacitating effect, the threat of jail time reinforces participation in requirements such as treatment programs, house arrest, and the installation of interlock devices.

In a study under review at the time of this writing, Wagenaar et al. (2007) surveyed the literature between 1991 and 2006 and found 20 studies on the effectiveness of jail penalties. Nine of the studies evaluated the effect of jail sanction on traffic fatalities. Two of those found a significant reduction in alcohol-related crashes but five similar studies failed to find a reduction. Wagenaar et al. (2007) concluded from this review that the evidence for the effectiveness of jail was, at best, mixed. They followed up that review with their own analysis of 18 states that implemented mandatory minimum jail sentences for first-time DWI offenders between 1976 and 2002. In that analysis, they found five states with decreases and two with significant increases in single-vehicle nighttime crashes. They concluded that evidence for the efficacy of mandatory jail penalties is weak.

In summary, incarceration of DWI offenders is a controversial issue. It is not clear whether it has a general deterrent effect, but it does have a specific deterrent effect on DWI offenders, as it temporarily keeps them from driving. Unless it is combined with a strong treatment program however, jail time does not reduce the likelihood of impaired driving after the offender is released and it is costly to the community (Kunitz et al., 2002). Typical DWI incarceration periods are brief and studies show that long sentences are no more of a deterrent than short ones (Voas, 1986). Nevertheless, the threat of a substantial jail sanction can motivate offenders to participate in treatment programs and to comply with interlock and other sanction requirements. In particular, drug treatment courts and DWI courts use a structured series of incentives and sanctions, including jail time, to gain compliance with the courts' orders and have higher rates of treatment completion than traditional courts. Coerced treatment works and ultimately it is the best tool for reducing recidivism when dealing with an alcoholic/addict (Breckenridge et al., 2000; Freeman-Wilson & Wilkosz, 2002; Tauber & Huddleston, 1999).

### Severity of Punishment

The sanctions for DWI have generally been increasing since 1980 when citizen advocacy groups against impaired driving were formed (Fell & Voas, 2006b). Either the maximum penalties have changed or been strengthened, or mandatory minimum penalties have been introduced. There is limited evidence to support the positive influence of the severity of DWI sanctions on general deterrence (Nichols & Ross, 1990; Ross & Voas, 1989). More severe sanctions can be counterproductive if they motivate defendants to demand more jury trials in an already overburdened judicial system. However increased sanctions may result in increased plea bargaining and the use of diversion programs (Little, 1975; Robertson & Simpson, 2002; Ross & Voas, 1989). Severe punishments do not appear to produce fewer crashes than less severe penalties (Ross, 1992). Conversely, Falkowski (1984) and Cleary and Rodgers (1986), in their studies of a judicial policy to impose a 48-hour jail sentence for first DWI offenders in Minnesota, found a 20% reduction in nighttime fatal crashes. This result was somewhat clouded by an overall increase in the arrest rate in that state during the same period, suggesting that the reduction in fatal crashes may have resulted from a general increase in enforcement. Severe sanctions appear to have a limited role in creating general deterrence. As noted by Voas and Fisher (2001) and Voas (2001), however, these sanctions play a significant role in specific deterrence programs aimed at convicted offenders where tough penalties, such as imprisonment, can have beneficial indirect effects by providing a sanction of last resort to motivate repeat offenders to participate in more constructive programs, such as probation coupled with substance abuse treatment.

## Treatment Recommendations

### Evidence-Based Sentencing Initiatives

Over one million felony offenders are sentenced in state courts annually, accounting for 94% of all felony convictions in the United States (PEW, May 2009 cited in Warren, 2007); 60 to 80% of state felony defendants are placed on probation, fined, or incarcerated in their communities. Although the United States has the highest incarceration rate in the world, there are nearly three times as many offenders on probation as there are in state prisons. Judges share the goals of reducing the number of people who drive impaired on our nation's roadways and reducing needless deaths. How can the courts effectively sentence offenders so that DWI deaths and injuries are reduced within our communities? One effort is known as "Evidence-based Sentencing" using cost-effective evidence-based practices. The Pew Center on the States published "Arming the Courts with Research: 10 Evidence-Based Sentencing Initiatives to Control Crime and Reduce Costs" in 2009 as set forth below:

1. Establish recidivism reduction as an explicit sentencing goal. Those states with sentencing commissions should explicitly adopt this objective. The failure of mainstream sentencing policies to address offender drug abuse and addiction, mental illness, domestic violence, and low-level "quality of life" crime has motivated many state judges, prosecutors, and corrections officials to establish specialized "problem-solving" courts, such

as DWI courts, discussed earlier. The goal of recidivism reduction is to reduce crime, not to just rehabilitate offenders. It includes both effective substance abuse and mental health treatment services which have been proven to reduce reoffending and swift and effective use of graduated incentives and sanctions to extract behavioral change.

2. Provide sufficient flexibility to consider recidivism reduction options. State sentencing statutes, rules, and guidelines should provide sufficient flexibility so that sentencing judges can craft orders designed to reduce the risk of recidivism in appropriate cases, and should avoid overly broad, strict, or arbitrary sentencing mandates that interfere with more appropriate sentencing options. Research indicates that whether a particular offender is an appropriate candidate for recidivism reduction cannot accurately be assessed relying solely on the type of offense committed, BAC level, and offender's prior criminal history. Individual offender characteristics must also be taken into consideration including criminogenic risks.
3. Base sentencing decisions on risk/needs assessment. Actuarial risk/needs assessment tools use hard data to identify the offender characteristics most closely associated with the likelihood of future criminality. When these tests are validated through known correctional populations, they will be much more accurate than human judgment in predicting the risk of an offender's recidivism.
4. Require evidence-based community corrections programs. In many communities, there is a barrier to effective sentencing in the absence of state policy or financial or technical support for the development and operation of evidence-based treatment programs. Policy makers can obtain a review of existing programs in their communities and use this to identify the types of offenders for which the programs were designed and assessing whether the programs have the intended types of offenders in them. Evidence-based programs are available through the Department of Health and Human Services, Substance Abuse and Mental Health Services Administration (SAMHSA) on their National Registry of Evidence-based Programs and Practices website (http://nrepp.samhsa.gov/).
5. Integrate services, incentives, and sanctions. Research has shown that in the absence of effective treatment, traditional criminal sanctions such as incarceration and intensive supervision do not reduce recidivism beyond the period of the offenders' confinement, restraint, or surveillance. Of course, such sanctions may be appropriate to achieve other sentencing objectives, such as punishment, general deterrence, or incapacitation. The most powerful outcomes use both incentives (e.g., a reduction in the time of a license suspension) and sanctions (e.g., community service work) as well as needed services to change the behavior of the offender.
6. Ensure courts know about available sentencing options. Any recidivism reduction strategies require that sentencing judges, prosecutors, and defense attorneys have access to reliable data and information, not only about the offender, but community corrections, treatment, and other programs that are available and suitable. This information should include the types of offenders accepted, levels of risk, and specific criminal risk factors that the programs are intended to address.
7. Train court officers on evidence-based practice. No program will work unless sentencing judges, prosecutors, defense attorneys, and probation officers are knowledgeable about the research on evidence-based practices and are skilled in applying its principles in day-to-day sentencing and corrections decision making. All of the major players in this process should be educated about the principles and practices on an annual basis and the curricula should emphasize the importance of the roles of each principal.
8. Encourage swift and certain responses to violations of probation. Any violation of probation should be acted upon immediately, whether by the court or the probation agency, and should be certain, consistent, and fair. Sanctions should vary depending

on the severity of the violation, the probationer's adjusted level of risk in light of the infraction, and the extent of the motivation, cooperation, and success the probationer has demonstrated in complying with the other terms and conditions of probation.

9. Use of hearings and incentives to motivate offender behavior change. The ultimate goal is to develop the offender's intrinsic motivation to change. As such, it is not only the content of the sentencing decision that matters in the reduction of recidivism, but also the manner in which the court interacts with the offender. The motivation is strongly influenced by the offender's interpersonal relationships, especially with probation officers, judges, and others in the criminal justice system.
10. Promote effective collaboration among criminal justice agencies. In order to reduce recidivism, it requires the effective implementation of state and local sentencing and corrections policies. It also requires cooperation between the court, probation agencies, and treatment providers, as well as collaboration between the prosecution and defense. The local criminal justice system should evaluate their charging, plea negotiation, and probation violation policies to maximize the effectiveness of sentencing outcomes in reducing recidivism (PEW Foundation, 2009 http://www.pewcenteronthestates.org/uploadedFiles/Final_EBS_Brief.pdf).

## Conclusion

From the DWI perspective, there appears to be a myriad of dynamics that come into play when a person elects to drink and drive. There is the deterrence theory that law enforcement will arrest you if you drive impaired, whether it is during an individualized stop or if it is at a sobriety checkpoint or saturation patrol. Once convicted, significant theories and practices have been tried, but the most positive theory is using evidence-based practices such as DWI courts to enforce the conditions of probation that lead to reduced recidivism.

## References


American University Drug Court Clearinghouse and Technical Assistance Project. (2000). *Adult drug court treatment provider survey, January–March 2000* (pp. 28–29). Washington, DC: Author.

Beck, K., Rauch, W., Baker, E., & Williams, A. (1999). Effects of ignition interlock license restrictions on drivers with multiple alcohol offenses: A random trial in Maryland. *American Journal of Public Health, 89*, 1696–1700.

Beirness, D. J., Simpson, H. M., Mayhew, D. R., & Jonah, B. J. (1997). The impact of administrative license suspension and vehicle impoundment for DWI in Manitoba. In C. Mercier-Guyon (Ed.), *Proceedings of the 14th international conference on Alcohol, drugs and traffic safety* (pp. 919–925). Annecy, France: Centre d'Etudes et de Recherches en Medecine du Trafic.

Belenko, S. (1998). Research on drug courts: A critical review. *National Drug Court Institute Review, 1*(1), 1–42.

Belenko, S. (2001, May). *Research on drug courts: A critical review*. New York: The National Center on Addiction and Substance Abuse, Columbia University.

Blomberg, R. (1992). *Lower BAC limits for youth: Evaluation of the Maryland. 02 law* (DOT HS 806 807). Washington, DC: U.S. Department of Transportation.

Borkenstein, R. F. (1975). Problems of enforcement, adjudication and sanctioning. In S. Israelstam & S. Lambert (Eds.), *Proceedings of the 6th international conference on Alcohol, drugs and traffic safety*, September 8–13, 1974 (pp. 655–662). Toronto, ON: Addiction Research Foundation of Ontario.

Breckenridge, J. F., Winfree, L. T., Maupin, J. R., & Clason, D. L. (2000). Drunk drivers, DWI "Drug Court" treatment, and recidivism: Who fails? *Justice Research and Policy, 2*(1), 87–105.

Cleary, J., & Rodgers, A. (1986). *Analysis of the effects of recent changes in Minnesota's DWI laws: Part III. Longitudinal analysis of policy impacts*. St. Paul, MN: Minnesota House of Representatives, Research Department.

Coppin, R. S., & Oldenbeek, G. (1965). *Driving under suspension and revocation: A study of suspended and revoked drivers classified as negligent operators*. Sacramento, CA: California Department of Motor Vehicles.

Crosby, I. B. (1995). *Portland's asset forfeiture program: The effectiveness of vehicle seizure in reducing rearrest among "problem" drunk drivers*. Portland, OR: Reed College Public Policy Workshop.

deBaca, J. C., Lapham, S. C., Liang, H. C., & Skipper, B. J. (2001). Victim impact panels: Do they impact drunk drivers? A follow-up of female and male first-time and repeat offenders. *Journal of Studies on Alcohol, 62*, 615–620.

DeYoung, D. J. (1997a). An evaluation of the effectiveness of alcohol treatment driver license actions and jail terms in reducing drunk driving recidivism in California. *Addiction, 92*(8), 989–997.

DeYoung, D. J. (1997b, November). *An evaluation of the specific deterrent effect on vehicle impoundment on suspended, revoked, and unlicensed drivers in California* (DOT HS 808 727). Washington, DC: Department of Transportation, National Highway Traffic Safety Administration.

DeYoung, D. J. (1998). *An evaluation of the general deterrent effects of vehicle impoundment on suspended and revoked drivers in California* (RSS-98-180). Sacramento, CA: California Department of Motor Vehicles.

DeYoung, D. J. (2000). An evaluation of the general deterrent effects of vehicle impoundment on suspended and revoked drivers in California. *Journal of Safety Research, 31*(2), 51–59.

DeYoung, D. J., Peck, R. C., & Helander, C. J. (1997). Estimating the exposure and fatal crash rates of suspended/revoked and unlicensed drivers in California. *Accident Analysis and Prevention, 29*(1), 17–23.

Dill, P. L., & Wells-Parker, E. (2006). Court-mandated treatment for convicted drinking drivers. *Alcohol Research and Health, 29*(1), 41–48.

Donovan, D. M., Kadden, R. M., DiClemente, C. C., Carroll, K. M., Longabaugh, R., Zweben, A., et al. (1994). Issues in the selection and development of therapies in alcoholism treatment matching research. *Journal of Studies on Alcohol Supplement, 12*, 138–148.

Epperlein, T. (1987). Initial deterrent effects of the crackdown on drunken drivers in the state of Arizona. *Accident Analysis and Prevention, 19*(4), 271–283.

Falkowski, C. L. (1984). *The impact of two-day jail sentences for drunk drivers in Hennepin County, Minnesota* (DOT HS 806 839). Washington, DC: National Highway Traffic Safety Administration.

Fell, J. C., & Voas, R. (2006a). The effectiveness of reducing illegal blood alcohol concentration limits for driving: Evidence for lowering the limit to .05 BAC. *Journal of Safety Research, 37*, 233–243.

Fell, J. C., & Voas, R. B. (2006b). Mothers Against Drunk Driving (MADD): The first 25 years. *Traffic Injury Prevention, 7*(3), 195–212.

Fox, C., & Huddleston, W. (2003). Drugs in the U.S. *Issues of Democracy, 8*(1), 13–19.

Freeman-Wilson, K., & Wilkosz, M. P. (2002). *Drug court publications resource guide* (4th ed.). Alexandria, VA: National Drug Court Institute.

Fuller, B., Carey, S., & Kissick, K. (2007). *Michigan DUI Courts outcome evaluation: Final report.* Portland, OR: NPC Research.

Green, R. E., French, J. F., Haberman, P. W., & Holland, P. W. (1991). The effects of combining sanctions and rehabilitation for driving under the influence: An evaluation of the New Jersey Alcohol Countermeasures Program. *Accident Analysis and Prevention, 23*(6), 543–555.

Griffin, L. I., III, & DeLaZerda, S. (2000). *Unlicensed to kill.* Washington, DC: AAA Foundation for Traffic Safety.

Guerin, P., & Pitts, W. J. (2002). *Evaluation of the Bernalillo County Metropolitan DWI/Drug Court: Final report.* Albuquerque, NM: University of New Mexico, Center for Applied Research and Analysis.

Hagen, R. E. (1977). *Effectiveness of license suspension or revocation for drivers convicted of multiple driving-under-the-influence offenses.* Sacramento, CA: Department of Motor Vehicles.

Hingson, R., Heeren, T., & Winter, M. (1994). Lower legal blood alcohol limits for young drivers. *Public Health Reports, 109*(6), 739–744.

Hingson, R., Howland, J., Heeren, T., & Winter, M. (1992). Reduced BAC limits for young people (impact on night fatal) crashes. *Alcohol, Drugs and Driving, 7*(2), 117–127.

Irvin, J. E., Bowers, C. A., Dunn, M. E., & Wang, M. C. (1999). Efficacy of relapse prevention: A meta-analytic review. *Journal of Consulting and Clinical Psychology, 67*(4), 563–570.

Jones, R. L., & Lacey, J. H. (1998, December). *Evaluation of an individualized sanctioning program for DWI offenders* (DOT HS 808 842). Washington, DC: National Highway Traffic Safety Administration.

Jones, R. K., & Lacey, J. H. (2002, November). *Alcohol and highway safety 2001: A review of the state of knowledge* (Final Report DOT HS 809 383). Washington, DC: National Highway Traffic Safety Administration.

Jones, R. K., Wiliszowski, C. H., & Lacey, J. H. (1996). *Evaluation of alternative programs for repeat DWI offenders* (DOT HS 808 493). Washington, DC: Office of Program Development and Evaluation, National Highway Traffic Safety Administration.

Klein, T. M. (1989). *Changes in alcohol-involved fatal crashes associated with tougher state alcohol legislation* (DOT HS 807 511). Washington, DC: National Highway Traffic Safety Administration.

Kunitz, S. J., Woodall, W. G., Zhao, H., Wheeler, D. R., Lillis, R., & Rogers, E. (2002). Rearrest rates after incarceration for DWI: A comparative study in a southwestern U.S. county. *American Journal of Public Health, 92*(11), 1826–1831.

Lacey, J. H., Jones, R. K., & Wiliszowski, C. H. (2000, June). *Zero-tolerance laws for youth: Four states' experience* (DOT HS 809 053). Washington, DC: U.S. Department of Transportation, National Highway Traffic Safety Administration.

Lacey, J. H., Rudisill, L. C., Popkin, C. L., & Stewart, J. R. (1986). Education for drunk drivers: How well has it worked in North Carolina? *Popular Government, 51*(3), 44–48.

Leaf, W. A., & Preusser, D. F. (2011, January). *Evaluation of Minnesota's vehicle plate impoundment law for impaired drivers,* (DOT HS 811 351). Washington, DC: National Highway Traffic Safety Administration.

Levy, D., Asch, P., & Shea, D. (1990). An assessment of county programs to reduce driving while intoxicated. *Health Education Research, 5*, 247–255.

Levy, D., Shea, D., & Asch, P. (1988). Traffic safety effects of sobriety checkpoints and other local DWI programs in New Jersey. *American Journal of Public Health, 79*, 291–293.

Levy, P., Voas, R. B., Johnson, P., & Klein, T. M. (1978). An evaluation of the Department of Transportation's alcohol safety action projects. *Journal of Safety Research, 10*(4), 162–176.

Little, J. W. (1975). *Administration of justice in drunk driving cases*. Gainesville, FL: The University Presses of Florida.

Mann, R. E., Anglin, L., Wilkins, K., Vingilis, E. R., MacDonald, S., & Sheu, W. J. (1994). Rehabilitation for convicted drinking drivers (second offenders): Effects on morality. *Journal of Studies on Alcohol, 55*(3), 372–374.

Martell, C. A., Stewart, J. R., & Jamburajan, S. (1998). *DWI evaluation and query system: Final report*. Chapel Hill, NC: University of North Carolina Highway Safety Research Center.

McCartt, A. T., Geary, L. L., & Nissen, W. J. (2002, August). *Observational study of the extent of driving while suspended for alcohol-impaired driving* (DOT HS 809 491). Washington, DC: National Highway Traffic Safety Administration.

McKnight, A. J., & Voas, R. B. (1991). The effect of license suspension upon DWI recidivism. *Alcohol, Drugs and Driving, 7*(1), 43–54.

Miller, W. R., & Wilbourne, P. L. (2002). Mesa grande: A methodological analysis of clinical trials of treatments for alcohol use disorders. *Addiction, 97*(3), 265–277.

Moyer, A., Finney, J. W., Swearingen, C. E., & Vergun, P. (2002). Brief interventions for alcohol problems: A meta-analytic review of controlled investigations in treatment-seeking and non-treatment-seeking populations. *Addiction, 97*(3), 279–292.

National Center for Statistics and Analysis. (2009a). *Traffic safety facts: 2008 Traffic safety annual assessment – Highlights* (DOT HS 811 172). Washington, DC: National Highway Traffic Safety Administration.

National Center for Statistics and Analysis. (2009b). *Traffic safety facts: Results of the 2007 National roadside survey of alcohol and drug use by drivers* (DOT HS 811 175). Washington, DC: National Highway Traffic Safety Administration.

Nichols, J. L., & Ross, H. L. (1990). The effectiveness of legal sanctions in dealing with drinking drivers. *Alcohol, Drugs and Driving, 6*(2), 33–55.

Nochajski, T. H., Miller, B. A., Wieczorek, W. F., & Whitney, R. (1993). The effect of a drinker-driver treatment program: Does criminal history make a difference? *Criminal Justice and Behavior, 20*(2), 174–189.

Peck, R. C. (1991). General and specific deterrent effects of DUI sanctions: A review of California's experience. *Alcohol, Drugs and Driving, 7*(1), 13–42.

Peck, R. C., Sadler, D. D., & Perrine, M. W. (1985). The comparative effectiveness of alcohol rehabilitation and licensing control actions for drunk driving offenders: A review of the literature. *Alcohol, Drugs and Driving: Abstracts and Reviews, 1*(4), 15–40.

Peck, R., & Voas, R. (2002). Forfeiture programs in California: Why so few? *Journal of Safety Research, 33*(2), 245–258.

Polacsek, M., Rogers, E. M., Woodall, W. G., Delaney, H., Wheeler, D., & Nagesh, R. (2001). MADD victim impact panels and stages-of-change in drunk-driving prevention. *Journal of Studies on Alcohol, 62*, 344–350.

Prochaska, J. O., DiClemente, C. C., & Norcross, J. C. (1992). In search of how people change: Applications to addictive behaviors. *American Psychologist, 47*, 1102–1114.

Project MATCH Research. (1998). Matching patients with alcohol disorders to treatments: Clinical implications from Project MATCH. *Journal of Mental Health 7*(6), 589–602.

Rempel, M., Fox-Kralstein, D., Cissner, A., Cohen, R., Labriola, M., Farole, D., et al. (2003). *The New York State adult drug court evaluation: Policies, participants and impacts*. New York: Center for Court Innovation.

Rider, R., Kelley-Baker, T., Voas, R., Murphy, B., McKnight, A. J., & Levings, C. (2006). The impact of a novel educational curriculum for first-time DUI offenders on intermediate outcomes relevant to DUI recidivism. *Accident Analysis and Prevention, 38*(3), 482–489.

Rider, R. P., Voas, R. B., Kelley-Baker, T., Grosz, M., & Murphy, B. (2007). Preventing alcohol-related convictions (PARC): The impact of a novel curriculum for first-time offenders on DUI recidivism. *Traffic Injury Prevention, 8*(2), 147–152.

Robertson, R. D., & Simpson, H. M. (2002, June). *DWI system improvements for dealing with hard core drinking drivers: Prosecution*. Ottawa, ON: Traffic Injury Research Foundation.

Ross, H. L. (1982). Prevention and deterrence: The international experience. *Alcohol Health and Research World, 7*(1), 26–30, 39–43.

Ross, H. L. (1992). Are DWI sanctions effective? *Alcohol, Drugs and Driving, 8*(1), 61–69.

Ross, H., & Gonzales, P. (1988). The effect of license revocation on drunk-driving offenders. *Accident Analysis and Prevention, 20*(5), 379–391.

Ross, H. L., & Klette, H. (1995). Abandonment of mandatory jail for impaired drivers in Norway and Sweden. *Accident Analysis and Prevention, 27*(2), 151–157.

Ross, H. L., McCleary, R., & LaFree, G. (1990). Can mandatory jail laws deter drunk driving? The Arizona case. *Journal of Criminal Law and Criminology, 81*(1), 156–170.

Ross, H. L., & Voas, R. B. (1989). *The New Philadelphia story: The effects of severe penalties for drunk driving*. Washington, DC: AAA Foundation for Traffic Safety.

Ross, H. L., & Voas, R. B. (1990). The New Philadelphia story: The effects of severe punishment for drunk driving. *Law and Policy, 12*(1), 51–79.

Sadler, D. D., & Perrine, M. W. (1984). *The long-term traffic safety impact of a pilot alcohol abuse treatment as an alternative to license suspensions, Volume 2. An evaluation of the California drunk driving countermeasure system*. Sacramento, CA: Department of Motor Vehicles.

Safir, H., Grasso, G., & Messner, R. (2000, May 22–26). The New York City police department DWI forfeiture initiative – Prevention section. In H. Laurell & F. Schlyter (Eds.), *Proceedings of the 15th international conference on Alcohol, drugs and traffic safety – T 2000* (Vol. 3, pp. 837–840). Stockholm: ICADTS.

Shinar, D., & Compton, R. (1995). Victim impact panels: Their impact on DWI recidivism. *Alcohol, Drugs and Driving, 11*(1), 73–87.

Socie, E. M., Wagner, S. A., & Hopkins, R. S. (1997). The relative effectiveness of sanctions applied to first-time drunken driving offenders. *American Journal of Preventive Medicine, 10*(2), 85–90.

Stewart, E. I., & Malfetti, J. L. (1970). *Rehabilitation of the drunken driver: A corrective course in Phoenix, Arizona, for persons convicted of driving under the influence of alcohol*. New York: Teachers College Press.

Swearingen, C. E., Moyer, A., & Finney, J. W. (2003). Alcoholism treatment outcome studies, 1970–1998. An expanded look at the nature of the research. *Addictive Behaviors, 28*(3), 415–436.

Tashima, H. N., & Helander, C. J. (1999, January). *1999 annual report of the California DUI Management Information System* (CAL-DMV-RSS-99-179). Sacramento, CA: California Department of Motor Vehicles, Research and Development Section.

Tashima, H. N., & Helander, C. J. (2000). *Annual report of the California DUI Management Information System*. Sacramento, CA: California Department of Motor Vehicles.

Tauber, J., & Huddleston, C. W. (1999). *DUI/drug courts: Defining a national strategy*. Alexandria, VA: National Drug Court Institute.

UCLA Integrated Substance Abuse Programs. (2009, December). Mechanisms of action in alcoholism treatment. *ISAP News 7*(Issue 2).

Voas, R. B. (1981). Results and implications of the ASAPs. In L. Goldberg (Ed.), *Proceedings of the 8th international conference on Alcohol, drugs and traffic safety – T80*, June 15–19, 1980, Stockholm (Vol. 3, pp. 1129–1144). Göteborg, Sweden: Graphic Systems.

Voas, R. B. (1986). Evaluation of jail as a penalty for drunken driving. *Alcohol, Drugs and Driving: Abstracts and Reviews*, 2(2), 47–70.

Voas, R. B. (1992, June). *Assessment of impoundment and forfeiture laws for drivers convicted of DWI. Phase I report: Review of state laws and their application* (DOT HS 807 870). Washington, DC: Department of Transportation, National Highway Traffic Safety Administration.

Voas, R. B. (2001). Have the courts and the motor vehicle departments adequate power to control the hard-core drunk driver? *Addiction, 96*(12), 1701–1707.

Voas, R. B., & DeYoung, D. J. (2002). Vehicle action: Effective policy for controlling drunk and other high-risk drivers? *Accident Analysis and Prevention, 34*(3), 263–270.

Voas, R. B., & Fisher, D. A. (2001). Court procedures for handling intoxicated drivers. *Alcohol Research and Health World, 25*(1), 32–42.

Voas, R. B., & McKnight, A. J. (1989). *An evaluation of hardship licensing for DWIs* (Contract No. DTNH22-34-C-07292). Washington, DC: U.S. Department of Transportation, National Highway Traffic Safety Administration.

Voas, R., McKnight, A. S., & Tippetts, A. S. (2006, May). *DWI offenders' failure to reinstate driver's licenses: Volume 1 – Summary* (Draft final report). Washington, DC: National Highway Traffic Safety Administration.

Voas, R. B., Rhodenizer, A. E., & Lynn, C. (1985). *Evaluation of Charlottesville checkpoint operations* (Final Report DOT HS 806 989). Washington, DC: (Available in hard copy format only from the National Technical Information Service, Springfield, VA): National Highway Traffic Safety Administration.

Voas, R. B., & Tippetts, A. S. (1995). Evaluation of Washington and Oregon license plate sticker laws. *Proceedings of the 39th annual proceedings of the Association for the Advancement of Automotive Medicine (AAAM)* (pp. 29–44). Des Plaines, IL: Association for the Advancement of Automotive Medicine.

Voas, R. B., Tippetts, A. S., & Fell, J. C. (2000). The relationship of alcohol safety laws to drinking drivers in fatal crashes. *Accident Analysis and Prevention, 32*(4), 483–492.

Voas, R. B., Tippetts, A. S., & Fell, J. (2003). Assessing the effectiveness of minimum legal drinking age and zero tolerance laws in the United States. *Accident Analysis and Prevention, 35*(4), 579–587.

Voas, R. B., Tippetts, A. S., & Lange, J. E. (1997). Evaluation of a method for reducing unlicensed driving: The Washington and Oregon license plate sticker laws. *Accident Analysis and Prevention, 29*(5), 627–634.

Voas, R. B., Tippetts, A. S., & Taylor, E. P. (1997). Temporary vehicle immobilization: Evaluation of a program in Ohio. *Accident Analysis and Prevention, 29*(5), 635–642.

Voas, R. B., Tippetts, A. S., & Taylor, E. P. (1998). Temporary vehicle impoundment in Ohio: A replication and confirmation. *Accident Analysis and Prevention, 30*(5), 651–655.

Voas, R. B., Tippetts, A. S., & Taylor, E. P. (2000, October). *Effectiveness of the Ohio vehicle action and administrative license suspension laws* (Final Report DOT HS 809 000). Washington, DC: National Highway Traffic Safety Administration.

Wagenaar, A. C., Maldonado-Molina, M. M., Erickson, D. J., Ma, L., Tobler, A. L., & Komro, K. A. (2007,

September). General deterrence effects of U.S. statutory DUI fine and jail penalties: Long-term follow-up in 32 states. *Accident Analysis and Prevention, 39*(5), 982–994.

Wagenaar, A. C., Zobeck, T. S., Hingson, R., & Williams, G. D. (1995). Studies of control efforts: A meta-analysis from 1960 through 1991. *Accident Analysis and Prevention, 27*, 1–16.

Warren, R. K. (2007). *Arming the Courts with research: 10 Evidence-based sentencing initiatives to control crime and reduce costs*. PEW Foundation Public Policy Brief, May 2009. Washington, DC: The PEW Charitable Trusts. (Originally published in the 2007 issue of the Indiana Law Journal)

Wells, J. K., Preusser, D. F., & Williams, A. F. (1992). Enforcing alcohol-impaired driving and seat belt use laws, Binghamton, New York. *Journal of Safety Research, 23*, 63–71.

Wells-Parker, E., Bangert-Drowns, R., McMillen, R., & Williams, M. (1995). Final results from a meta-analysis of remedial interventions with drink/drive offenders. *Addiction, 90*(7), 907–926.

Wells-Parker, E., & Williams, M. (2002). Enhancing the effectiveness of traditional interventions with drinking drivers by adding brief individual intervention components. *Journal of Studies on Alcohol, 63*(6), 655–664.

Wheeler, D. R., Rogers, E. M., Tonigan, J. S., & Woodall, W. G. (2004). Effectiveness of customized Victim Impact Panels on first-time DWI offender inmates. *Accident Analysis and Prevention, 36*(1), 29–35.

Williams, R. L., Hagen, R. E., & McConnell, E. J. (1984). A survey of suspension and revocation effects on the drinking-driver offender. *Accident Analysis and Prevention, 16*(5/6), 339–350.

Zador, P. L. (1991). Alcohol-related relative risk of fatal driver injuries in relation to driver age and sex. *Journal of Studies on Alcohol, 52*(4), 302–310.

Zobeck, T. S., & Williams, G. D. (1994). *Evaluation synthesis of the impacts of DWI laws and enforcement methods: Final report* (Contract No. ADM-281-89-0002). Rockville, MD: Office of Policy Analysis, National Institute on Alcohol Abuse and Alcoholism (NIAAA).

Zwerling, C., & Jones, M. P. (1999). Evaluation of the effectiveness of low blood alcohol concentration laws for younger drivers. *American Journal of Preventive Medicine, 16*(1 Suppl), 76–80.

# Adult and Juvenile Drug Courts

# 8

Douglas B. Marlowe

**Abstract**

Drug courts provide judicially supervised substance abuse treatment and other needed services in lieu of prosecution or incarceration. Two decades of research confirms that adult drug courts reduce crime and substance abuse, improve family relationships, and return average net cost savings that are two to three times the initial investment. The optimal target population for adult drug courts has been identified and fidelity to key components of the model has been demonstrated to be necessary for favorable outcomes. Less can be confidently concluded about juvenile drug courts, but recent studies suggest the programs are becoming more effective with increasing experience. Future directions are considered for bringing this blended public health/public safety model to scale.

**Keywords**

Drug court • Criminal justice • Therapeutic jurisprudence • Offenders • Antisocial personality disorder • Addiction • Drug abuse • Drug dependence

## Introduction

Drug courts are judicially supervised programs that provide certain nonviolent, drug-abusing or addicted offenders with a mandatory regimen of substance abuse treatment and other indicated services in lieu of criminal prosecution or incarceration (National Association of Drug Court Professionals, 1997). Participants undergo random weekly drug testing and attend regular status hearings in court, during which the judge reviews their progress in treatment and may impose a range of consequences contingent upon their performance. These consequences may include punitive sanctions (e.g., writing assignments, community service, or brief jail detention), desired rewards (e.g., verbal praise,

D.B. Marlowe (✉)
Treatment Research Institute, University of Pennsylvania, Philadelphia, PA 19106, USA
e-mail: dmarlowe@tresearch.org

C. Leukefeld et al. (eds.), *Handbook of Evidence-Based Substance Abuse Treatment in Criminal Justice Settings*, Issues in Children's and Families' Lives 11,
DOI 10.1007/978-1-4419-9470-7_8, 

reduced supervision requirements, or token gifts) or modifications to the participant's treatment plan (e.g., transfer to a more intensive modality of care).

The consequences are often administered by the judge in open court, after the drug court team has met privately in a staff meeting to review the case and reach a tentative determination about the appropriate course of action. The various team members – often representatives of the court, prosecution, defense bar, treatment providers, case managers, and probation officers – contribute information from their perspectives about participants' progress in the program, and may offer recommendations for suitable responses; however, the judge is legally and ethically required to make the final decision about what consequences to impose, after giving due consideration to all of the relevant information and discussing the matter with the participant in court.

In preadjudication drug courts, successful graduates have the charge(s) dropped, and may also have an opportunity to have the offense expunged from their record. Although the record is not literally erased from criminal justice databases, record expungement ordinarily entitles the individual to respond truthfully on an employment application or similar document that the arrest or conviction did not occur (e.g., Festinger, DeMatteo, Marlowe, & Lee, 2005). In post-adjudication drug courts, graduates may avoid incarceration, reduce the conditions of their probation, or consolidate multiple probationary sentences.

In recent years, the drug court model has been applied with some modifications to juvenile offenders in delinquency proceedings. Considerably less research has been published, to date, on the effects of juvenile drug courts as compared to their adult counterparts. This chapter begins by reviewing the large body of research data on adult drug courts, and concludes with a brief review of the available evidence on juvenile drug courts.

## Effectiveness of Adult Drug Courts

### Criminal Recidivism

Meta-analysis is an advanced statistical procedure that yields a conservative and rigorous estimate of the average effects of an intervention. This process involves systematically reviewing the research literature, selecting only those studies that are scientifically defensible according to standardized criteria, and statistically averaging the effects of the intervention across the acceptable studies (e.g., Lipsey & Wilson, 2001).

Five meta-analyses have been performed, to date, on the effects of adult drug courts (Aos, Miller, & Drake, 2006; Latimer, Morton-Bourgon, & Chretien, 2006; Lowenkamp, Holsinger, & Latessa, 2005; Shaffer, 2006; Wilson, Mitchell, & MacKenzie, 2006). These meta-analyses included several randomized controlled trials (e.g., Gottfredson, Najaka, & Kearley, 2003; Turner, Greenwood, Fain, & Deschenes, 1999) and dozens of quasi-experimental studies. In each case, the results indicated that adult drug courts significantly reduced criminal recidivism (typically measured by rearrest rates) by an average of approximately 8–14 percentage points.

Because these figures reflect averages, they mask substantial variability in the performance of individual drug courts. On the positive side, approximately three quarters of the drug courts (78%) were determined to have significantly reduced recidivism (Shaffer, 2006), with the best drug courts reducing recidivism by as much as 35% (Lowenkamp et al., 2005; Shaffer, 2006). In well-controlled studies, the reductions in recidivism were found to last at least 3 years post entry (Gottfredson, Kearley, Najaka, & Rocha, 2005; Turner et al., 1999) and in one study the effects lasted an astounding 14 years (Finigan, Carey, & Cox, 2007).

The positive findings were, however, by no means universal. A substantial minority (22%) of the drug courts was found to have had minimal impact on recidivism (Shaffer, 2006) and in a few instances some drug courts were associated with increases in recidivism by as much as 15% (Lowenkamp et al., 2005). These latter findings underscore the importance of identifying the best practices for drug courts that can minimize harms and optimize positive impact. The critical task facing the drug court field is to determine what distinguishes effective drug courts from ineffective or harmful ones. As discussed later in this chapter, evidence suggests that some of the poorer performing drug courts may have been providing ineffective services, or may have been targeting their services at the wrong types of drug-involved offenders. Research is beginning to identify the optimal target population for drug courts and the treatment and supervisory practices that are associated with more favorable results.

## Cost Effectiveness

In line with their generally positive effects on crime reduction, drug courts have also proven to be cost effective (Belenko, Patapis, & French, 2005). A recent cost-related meta-analysis concluded that drug courts produced an average of $2.21 in direct benefits to the criminal justice system for every $1.00 invested (Bhati, Roman, & Chalfin, 2008). These savings reflected measurable cost offsets to the criminal justice system stemming from reduced rearrests, law enforcement contacts, court hearings, use of jail or prison beds, and tangible impact of crime victimization. When more distal cost offsets were also taken into account, such as savings from reduced foster care placements or healthcare service utilization, studies have reported economic benefits ranging from approximately $2.00–$27.00 for every $1.00 invested (Barnoski & Aos, 2003; Carey, Finigan, Crumpton, & Waller, 2006; Finigan et al., 2007; Loman, 2004). The result has been net economic benefits to local communities ranging from approximately $3,000–$13,000 per drug court participant (Aos et al., 2006; Barnoski & Aos, 2003; Carey et al., 2006; Finigan et al., 2007; Logan et al., 2004; Loman, 2004).

## Other Outcomes

In 2005, the US Government Accountability Office (U.S. GAO, 2005) concluded that adult drug courts reduce criminal recidivism and save significant money for taxpayers as a consequence of their impact on crime. However, the GAO concluded that relatively little was known about their effects on other important outcomes, such as substance abuse, employment, family functioning, and mental health.

In response to the GAO Report, the National Institute of Justice (NIJ) sponsored a national study of adult drug courts, entitled the Multisite Adult Drug Court Evaluation (MADCE). The MADCE is comparing outcomes for participants in 23 adult drug courts located in seven geographic clusters around the country ($n = 1,156$) to those of matched comparison drug offenders drawn from six nondrug court sites in four geographic clusters ($n = 625$). The participants were interviewed at baseline and at 6- and 18-month followups and provided oral fluid specimens at the 18-month follow-up. Their official criminal records are also being examined up to 24 months.

The results have not been published as of this writing; however, 6- and 18-month findings were recently presented at the 2009 Annual Conference of the American Society of Criminology (Rempel & Green, 2009; Rossman, Green, & Rempel, 2009). In addition to reporting significantly less involvement in criminal activity, the drug court participants reported significantly less use of illegal drugs and heavy use of alcohol (defined as $\geq$ 4 drinks per day for women or $\geq$ 5 drinks per day for men) at the 6- and 18-month followups. These self-report findings were confirmed by saliva drug tests, which revealed significantly fewer positive results for the drug court participants at the 18-month assessment (29% vs. 46%, $p < 0.01$). The drug court participants also reported significantly greater improvements in their family relationships, and nonsignificant trends favoring higher employment rates and school enrollment. These findings must be viewed as preliminary until the final peer-reviewed report is published; however, the data suggest that drug courts may elicit improvements in outcome domains other than criminal recidivism and cost.

## Target Population for Adult Drug Courts

### The Risk Principle

According to the criminological theory of the *Risk Principle*, intensive programs such as drug courts are hypothesized to exert the greatest effects for high-risk offenders who have more severe antisocial propensities or treatment-refractory histories; however, such programs may be unnecessary or counterproductive for low-risk offenders (Andrews & Bonta, 1998; Taxman & Marlowe, 2006). Low-risk offenders are less likely to be on a fixed antisocial trajectory, and are apt to improve their conduct following a run-in with the law. Therefore, intensive interventions may offer smaller incremental benefits for these individuals, but at a substantial cost (DeMatteo, Marlowe, & Festinger, 2006). Worse still, low-risk offenders may learn antisocial attitudes and behaviors from associating with high-risk offenders, which can make their outcomes worse (e.g., Petrosino, Turpin-Petrosino, & Finckenauer, 2000). In contrast, high-risk offenders have a generally poor prognosis for success in standard interventions, and often require intensive and sustained interventions to dislodge their entrenched, negative behavioral patterns.

Among drug-abusing offenders, the most reliable and robust risk factors for failure in standard interventions include a younger age (especially prior to age 25), male gender, early onset of substance abuse or delinquency, prior felony convictions, previously unsuccessful attempts at treatment or rehabilitation, a coexisting diagnosis of antisocial personality disorder (APD), or a preponderance of antisocial peers or associates (e.g., Butzin, Saum, & Scarpitti, 2002; Gendreau, Little, & Goggin, 1996; Hiller, Knight, & Simpson, 1999; Marlowe, Patapis, & DeMatteo, 2003; Peters, Haas, & Murrin, 1999; Roll, Prendergast, Richardson, Burdon, & Ramirez, 2005). Individuals with these high-risk characteristics often respond poorly to standard treatment interventions and require substantial structure and accountability in order to succeed.

The Risk Principle has been validated in a wide range of correctional rehabilitation programs (e.g., Lowenkamp, Latessa, & Holsinger, 2006) and recent research confirms its applicability to drug courts as well. Consistent with the predictions of the Risk Principle, drug courts have been shown to have the largest effects for high-risk drug offenders who were relatively younger, had more prior felony convictions, were diagnosed with antisocial personality disorder or had previously failed in less intensive dispositions (Festinger et al., 2002; Fielding, Tye, Ogawa, Imam, & Long, 2002; Lowenkamp et al., 2005; Marlowe, Festinger, Dugosh, Arabia, & Kirby, 2007; Marlowe, Festinger, Lee, Dugosh, & Benasutti, 2006). In one meta-analysis, the effect size (ES) for drug court was found to be twice the magnitude for high-risk offenders than for low-risk offenders (Lowenkamp et al., 2005). In a countywide evaluation in Los Angeles, virtually all of the positive effects of the drug courts were determined to have been attributable to the higher-risk offenders (Fielding et al., 2002).

### Reaching the Target Population

There is reason to question whether some drug courts are serving their appropriate target population. A small number of studies have reported that low-risk participants comprised roughly 30% of the sample in felony drug courts (Fielding et al., 2002) and more than 60% of the sample in misdemeanor drug courts (Marlowe et al., 2006; Marlowe, Festinger, Arabia et al., 2008).

There is a further question whether all drug court participants require formal substance abuse treatment services. A few studies have found that approximately one-half of misdemeanor drug court participants (Marlowe, Festinger et al., 2003) and one-third of felony drug court participants (Marlowe, Festinger, & Lee, 2004a) produced subthreshold Drug Composite scores on the Addiction Severity Index (ASI; McLellan et al., 1992), which were not significantly different from a community sample of individuals who had not identified as substance abusers. In another study, roughly one-third (34%) of misdemeanor drug court participants provided a nearly unbroken string of drug-negative urine specimens during the first 4 months after entering the program (DeMatteo, Marlowe, Festinger, & Arabia, 2009). This raises the question of whether many of these individuals had a substance abuse problem to begin with. Some of these individuals may have been drug experimenters, or low-level abusers, who were not clinically impaired or predisposed to continue or escalate their drug usage.

If, in fact, drug courts are treating substantial numbers of low-risk or nonimpaired offenders, the success rates for the programs could be difficult to interpret. Graduation rates in drug courts average approximately 50–70% (e.g., Belenko, 1998; Marlowe, DeMatteo, & Festinger, 2003), which is unusually high for offender populations. If, however, these high completion rates are partially capitalizing on cases that had a good prognosis to begin with, then the positive outcomes may not all be attributable to the effects of programs. This phenomenon, referred to as creaming or skimming, is one of the major remaining criticisms of the research findings on drug courts.

Fortunately, it appears that drug courts may be evolving over time to better serve their optimal target population. In the early years of drug courts, many of the programs followed a preplea model for relatively low-level offenders. In some programs, the offenders were not required to enter a formal plea as a condition of entry. In the event of unsuccessful termination from the program, the offenders were merely placed back in the same legal position that they had been in at the time of arrest. Needless to say, prosecutors are unlikely to offer such purely diversionary opportunities to serious offenders.

This preplea model is becoming increasingly rare in drug court practice. The most rapidly developing drug court programs follow a post-adjudication or post-conviction model for offenders who are facing the realistic prospect of substantial jail or prison time, or for repeat probation violators facing a probation revocation (Huddleston, Marlowe, & Casebolt, 2008). In addition, reentry drug courts for parolees or inmates conditionally released from custody are developing at an increasing rate, especially in the federal system. Because these newer models require a formal plea or conviction as a condition of entry, and have the realistic threat of jail or prison as leverage for noncompliance, prosecutors are more willing to admit serious offenders into the programs. Thus, drug courts show promise for serving higher-risk drug offenders as they expand their coverage to additional segments of the criminal justice system.

## Fidelity to the Adult Drug Court Model

In fiscally challenging times, there is always the pressure to do more with less. This raises the critical question of whether certain components of the drug court model can be dropped or the dosage decreased without eroding the effects. The "key components" of drug courts are hypothesized to include an ongoing schedule of judicial status hearings, a multidisciplinary team approach to managing cases, weekly drug testing, contingent sanctions and incentives, and a standardized regimen of substance abuse treatment (NADCP, 1997). Each of these hypothesized key components has been studied to some degree by researchers or evaluators to determine whether it is, in fact, required for effective results.

Fidelity to the key components of adult drug courts has been studied in two general categories of research. The first category of studies experimentally manipulated specific components of the drug court model to determine whether those components contributed to effective results. For example, components such as judicial status hearings have been removed from the program on a random basis to determine whether this influenced outcomes. This type of study, called a *dismantling study*, yields the strongest evidence for the relative contribution of a particular element of a program.

The second category of research is what is commonly referred to as studies of *best practices*. These studies compared the characteristics of drug courts that had significant positive outcomes with those that had poor or insignificant outcomes. Presumably, services that are provided by effective programs and not provided by ineffective programs are likely to be important ingredients of an effective intervention. However, one must place less confidence in the reliability of such findings, because the services were not under experimental control. There is always the possibility that the programs differed, by chance, on dimensions that were not responsible for the differences in outcomes. Regardless, in the absence of more definitive evidence from controlled studies, it makes logical sense to emulate the practices of effective programs and avoid the practices of ineffective or harmful programs.

With funding from NIJ, Carey, Finigan, and Pukstas (2008) performed best-practice analyses on a sample of 18 adult drug courts. Outcomes for each drug court were compared to a respective quasi-experimental or matched comparison sample, resulting in an average effect size (ES) for each drug court. The investigators then determined whether differences in the magnitude of the ESs were related to differences in the operations of the programs, such as the schedule of court hearings or urine drug testing. More recently, these best-practice analyses were completed on an expanded sample of 25 adult drug courts (Carey, Waller, & Weller, in press) and still newer analyses are being conducted on more than 60 drug courts. Because these studies are being performed by the same research team on an expanding sample of programs, confidence in the results remains somewhat attenuated until comparable analyses can be replicated by new investigators on an independent sample of programs.

## Judicial Status Hearings

Judicial status hearings are the defining ingredient of a drug court (e.g., Marlowe et al., 2004a). Many correctional programs offer substance abuse treatment, drug testing, and sanctions and rewards for drug-involved offenders; however, only drug courts are primarily supervised by a judge and require frequent court appearances. The research evidence is exceptionally strong that judicial status hearings are a critical ingredient for effective outcomes in drug courts – assuming that the programs are treating their appropriate target population of high-risk drug offenders.

In a systematic program of experimental research, investigators randomly assigned drug court participants either to appear before the judge every 2 weeks for a status hearing, or to be monitored instead by their clinical case managers and brought to court only in response to repetitive rule violations. The results revealed that for high-risk drug offenders – those who were diagnosed with antisocial personality disorder (APD) or had previously failed substance abuse treatment – outcomes were significantly better in terms of greater counseling attendance, drug abstinence, and graduation rates when the participants were required to appear frequently before the judge (Festinger et al., 2002). This finding was replicated in misdemeanor and felony drug courts serving both urban and rural communities (Marlowe et al., 2004a, 2004b) and was subsequently confirmed in a prospective matching study, in which participants were assigned at entry to the optimal schedule of court hearings based upon their assessed risk level (Marlowe et al., 2006, 2007).

Research on best practices has uncovered highly similar findings. Drug courts that required participants to appear in court for status hearings on at least a biweekly basis during the first phase of the program (roughly the first 2–3 months) had significantly better outcomes than those that held their status hearings less frequently (Carey, Finigan et al., 2008). In that same study, it was further learned that holding status hearings at least once per month during the latter phases of the program was also associated with better outcomes, and with nearly three times greater cost savings resulting primarily from lower recidivism.

Outcomes have also been reported to be significantly better for drug courts in which the judges served on the drug court bench for at least 2 years, and thus had greater seniority and experience (Carey, Finigan et al., 2008; Finigan et al., 2007). Finally, outcomes were better when the judges spent an average of at least 3 minutes interacting with the participants in court (Carey, Finigan et al., 2008).

These findings are very much in line with the perceptions of the drug court participants themselves. A consistent theme emerging from interviews and focus groups with drug court participants is that they generally perceived their contacts with the judge to be critical to their success in the program (Drug Court Clearinghouse & Technical Assistance Project, 1999; Farole & Cissner, 2007; Goldkamp, White, & Robinson, 2002; National Institute of Justice, 2006; Satel, 1998; Saum et al., 2002; Turner et al., 1999). Taken together, the results from these dismantling studies, best-practice studies and focus-group studies yield strong empirical evidence that the judge is an active ingredient of adult drug courts.

## Multidisciplinary Team Approach

One of the more controversial features of drug courts is the practice of having professionals from various disciplines meet regularly to coordinate their functions as a team (NADCP, 1997). Traditionally, judges, prosecutors, defense counsel, and treatment providers did not sit down together to decide how best to respond to offenders' behaviors. This practice has raised concerns among some commentators about whether drug court professionals might be sacrificing their ethical obligations of neutrality, objectivity, confidentiality, or zealous representation (e.g., Bozza, 2007; Hoffman, 2000; National Association of Criminal Defense Lawyers, 2009). Although anecdotal arguments abound on both sides of the debate, at this juncture no empirical evidence has been garnered to indicate whether such ethical concerns are justified (Hora & Stalcup, 2008).

Evidence is beginning to emerge, however, to indicate whether a multidisciplinary team approach may be necessary to improve outcomes. Drug courts require a substantial investment of time and effort from professional team members, in part because they must attend frequent staff meetings and status hearings. It is important to determine whether this intensity of team involvement is truly necessary for effective outcomes, and thus worth the investment costs.

Research on best practices indicates that the more effective drug courts do require ongoing attendance by defense counsel, prosecutors, treatment providers, and law enforcement officers at staff meetings and status hearings (Carey, Finigan et al., 2008). When any one of these professional disciplines was regularly absent from team discussions, the programs tended to have outcomes that were, on average, approximately 50% less favorable (Carey et al., in press). In other words, if any one professional discipline walks away from the table, there is reason to anticipate that the effectiveness of a drug court could be reduced by as much as 50%.

Because staff attendance at the team meetings was not under experimental control, it is certainly possible that this correlation was not responsible for the differences in outcomes. Nevertheless, the finding makes intuitive sense for drug court practice. Addiction and associated crime are severe and chronic conditions that require an intensive and coordinated response (e.g., McLellan, Lewis, O'Brien, & Kleber, 2000). No one profession should be expected to have the knowledge, expertise, and authority to deal effectively with this intransigent social problem. It would not be surprising if a coordinated team approach, involving the continuous input of several professional disciplines, was required to intervene effectively with high-risk drug offenders.

## Drug Testing

The success of any program for drug offenders depends, ultimately, on the reliable monitoring of participants' behaviors. If the drug court team does not have accurate information about whether a participant is being compliant or noncompliant in the program, there is no possible way to apply incentives or sanctions correctly, or to adjust treatment and supervision services accordingly (e.g., Marlowe & Kirby, 1999; Marlowe, 2007, 2008).

Research on best practices indicates that the most effective drug courts perform urine drug testing at least twice per week during the first several months of the program (Carey, Finigan et al., 2008). Because the metabolites of most common drugs of abuse remain detectable in human bodily fluids for only about 1–4 days (e.g., Auerbach, 2007), testing less frequently leaves an unacceptable time gap, during which participants can use drugs and evade detection. In addition, urine drug testing is most effective when it is performed on a random basis (e.g., McIntire, Lessenger, & Roper, 2007). If participants know in advance when they will be drug tested, they can simply adjust their usage accordingly. They can also front-load on water consumption or take other counter measures in an effort to beat the tests.

Although urine testing is the most common procedure in drug courts, other technologies which can extend the time window for detection are becoming more commonplace. For example, the Secure Continuous Remote Alcohol Monitor (SCRAM©) is an anklet device that detects alcohol vapors in sweat and transmits signals wirelessly to a remote monitoring station. Recent research suggests that SCRAM© monitoring may be effective in deterring alcohol consumption among recidivist offenders in drug courts or DWI courts when it is worn for at least 90 days (Flango & Cheesman, 2009).

## Graduated Sanctions and Rewards

Drug courts administer gradually escalating sanctions for infractions and rewards for accomplishments (NADCP, 1997). Common examples of sanctions include verbal reprimands, writing assignments, community service, and brief intervals of jail detention (e.g., Arabia, Fox, Caughie, Marlowe, & Festinger, 2008). Common examples of rewards include verbal praise, reduced supervision requirements, and token gifts (e.g., Marlowe & Wong, 2008).

The general perception among both staff members and participants (e.g., Goldkamp et al., 2002; Harrell & Roman, 2001; Lindquist, Krebs, & Lattimore, 2006) is that sanctions and incentives are strong motivators of behavioral change in drug courts. Relatively little research, however, has examined the actual impact of sanctions or rewards on participants' behaviors in drug courts. A handful of studies have sought to correlate the imposition of sanctions or rewards with outcomes; however, those results must be discounted as quite likely to be seriously biased. Sanctions are imposed, by design, on individuals who are performing poorly in the program, and rewards are granted, by design, to those who are performing well. Therefore, the imposition of sanctions should be positively correlated with worse outcomes, and the granting of rewards should be positively correlated with more favorable outcomes. This could lead to the unwarranted conclusion that sanctions cause poor outcomes and rewards cause good outcomes, when the opposite is more likely to be true – poor outcomes tend to elicit sanctions and good outcomes tend to elicit rewards.

Two controlled experiments have examined whether imposing gradually escalating sanctions for drug-positive urine specimens or other infractions significantly reduced substance use and crime among drug-involved offenders (Harrell, Cavanagh, & Roman, 1999; Hawken & Kleiman, 2007). These studies were not conducted in drug courts, but rather in comparable pretrial supervision or probation programs. In both studies, drug-involved offenders were randomly assigned either to receive escalating sanctions, including brief intervals of jail detention, for infractions, or to attend probation or pretrial supervision as usual. Results revealed that outcomes for the sanctioning regimens were two to three times better than for the comparison conditions.

The use of jail sanctions, in particular, is a highly controversial matter in drug courts. Although some commentators have argued that the realistic threat of a jail sanction provides the necessary leverage for drug courts to retain recalcitrant offenders in treatment (e.g., Snavely, 2000), research on this issue remains sparse for understandable reasons. It is very difficult, if not impossible, to study the question in a controlled experiment. Few participants or staff members (or research ethics boards, for that matter) would be willing to permit jail to be imposed in a nonindividualized and randomized manner.

The most practical way to study this issue is to compare outcomes between similarly matched drug court participants who did or did not face the realistic possibility of receiving a jail sanction. So far, such studies have yielded mixed findings. One study reported better outcomes when drug court participants faced the prospect of jail (Carey, Pukstas, Waller, Mackin, & Finigan, 2008) whereas another study found no differences in outcomes regardless of whether or not jail could be imposed (Hepburn & Harvey, 2007).

A second practical method for addressing this question is to interview the drug court participants. A consistent finding from focus group studies is that drug court participants viewed the threat of jail to be a highly motivating factor to keep them engaged in treatment and committed to their sobriety (Farole & Cissner, 2007; Goldkamp et al., 2002).

In addition to examining the influence of sanctions, two experimental studies have investigated the effects of enhancing the positive rewards that were available to participants for desired achievements in drug courts (Marlowe, Festinger, Dugosh, Arabia, & Kirby, 2008; Prendergast, Hall, Roll, & Warda, 2008). The enhanced rewards were delivered in the form of payment vouchers or gift certificates for drug-negative urine samples and other desired accomplishments. Neither study found significantly improved outcomes, apparently due to a statistical ceiling effect. The outcomes were generally so good for both of those drug courts that it was difficult to improve any further upon those outcomes.

In one of the studies, however, a preplanned interaction analysis revealed a nonsignificant trend ($p = 0.08$), in which high-risk offenders with more serious criminal histories may have performed better in the enhanced rewards conditions (Marlowe, Festinger, Dugosh et al., 2008). This preliminary finding could suggest that when drug courts treat the most incorrigible types of drug offenders, positive rewards may make significant additive contributions to outcomes. More research is needed to confirm this interaction effect and gain a better understanding of this issue.

## Substance Abuse Treatment

Substance abuse treatment forms the core of a drug court program. The basic assumption underlying drug courts is that drug abuse or addiction fuels criminal activity. Therefore, it is believed to be essential to treat this pathology in order to reduce crime and improve the psychosocial functioning of offenders (NADCP, 1997). It is surprising, therefore, that relatively little attention has been paid to the quality and impact of substance abuse treatment within drug court programs (e.g., Belenko, 2002).

It is no secret that substance abuse treatment is sparsely available and of notoriously uneven quality in the criminal justice system generally (Friedmann, Taxman, & Henderson, 2007; Taxman, Perdoni, & Harrison, 2007) and these problems may extend to some drug courts as well. Treatment services within certain drug courts have been characterized as nonevidence-based, lacking in a coherent focus or structure, and delivered by inadequately trained staff (Taxman & Bouffard, 2003). The services also tend to be indistinguishable from those that are routinely provided to noncriminal justice populations, and thus may not adequately address the unique needs and risk factors presented by offenders (Lutze & van Wormer, 2007). It remains unclear, however, whether these problems are endemic to many drug courts, or limited to certain programs or geographic regions.

The degree to which substance abuse treatment influences positive outcomes in drug courts is also unclear. Although evidence is convincing that substance abuse treatment can reduce criminal reoffense as a general matter (Gossop, Tradaka, Stewart, & Witton, 2005; Holloway, Bennett, & Farrington, 2006), the additive value of treatment above and beyond the other elements of the drug court model – court hearings, urine monitoring, probation supervision, sanctions, and incentives – is unknown. Some commentators have argued that formal treatment may be dispensed with, at least for certain types of drug offenders, so long as the offenders are closely monitored and held meaningfully accountable for misbehavior (Bozza, 2007; Hoffman, 2000; Kleiman et al., 2003).

Much of the evidence for the contribution of treatment in drug courts is inferential. Longer tenure in substance abuse treatment predicts better outcomes (Simpson, Joe, & Brown, 1997) and drug courts retain offenders in treatment considerably longer than most other correctional programs (Belenko, 1998; Lindquist, Krebs, Warner, & Lattimore, 2009; Marlowe, DeMatteo et al., 2003). Arguably, therefore, treatment would seem to be responsible for at least some of the positive effects of drug courts. It is equally plausible, however, that more obedient or higher-functioning individuals are simply more likely to attend treatment and to refrain from further misconduct. Thus, better treatment attendance could merely be an indicator of better compliance with supervision conditions, rather than the cause of improved outcomes. Nevertheless, the evidence is clear that receiving more treatment in drug courts is a marker or predictor of a better prognosis for the future, irrespective of the precise mechanism of cause and effect (Gottfredson, Kearley, Najaka, & Rocha, 2007; NIJ, 2006; Shaffer, 2006).

Treatment quality also appears to be important in drug courts. Better results have been achieved when drug courts adopted standardized evidence-based treatments, including Moral Reconation Therapy (MRT; Heck, 2008; Kirchner & Goodman, 2007), the MATRIX Model (Marinelli-Casey et al., 2008), and Multisystemic Therapy (MST; Henggeler et al., 2006) as well as culturally proficient services (Vito & Tewksbury, 1998). Very briefly, MRT focuses on altering antisocial cognitions and attitudes, the MATRIX Model teaches strategies for managing cravings and other triggers for substance use, and MST trains caregivers to assist in managing the offender's behavior. What these treatments all share in common is that they are highly structured, clearly specified in a manual or workbook, incorporate behavioral or cognitive-behavioral interventions, and take the offenders' community of origin into account. If adopting such evidence-based practices can enhance drug court outcomes, then logically treatment must be capable of making an additive contribution to the drug court model.

Research on best practices indicates that outcomes were better for drug courts that contracted with a single coordinating agency (e.g., Treatment Accountability for Safer Communities [TASC]) to serve as the primary case manager for treatment services (Carey, Finigan et al., 2008). The coordinating agencies did not necessarily provide all of the clinical services, but rather were responsible for assessing the participants, referring them to the appropriate treatment programs and providing routine progress reports to the judge and drug court team. This arrangement appears to be superior to sending all participants to the same treatment provider (Shaffer, 2006), perhaps because the absence of market competition can lead to greater complacency in the provision of services. It also appears to be superior to referring participants to a myriad of different treatment programs, without engaging a primary agency to coordinate the referrals. It can be exceedingly difficult to remain abreast of participants' progress when they have been referred to numerous providers. Designating a primary case manager to coordinate the referrals may be essential for maintaining an accurate flow of up-to-date information, and administering consistent and timely consequences for participants' performance in treatment.

In sum, although the specific contribution of treatment to drug court outcomes is yet to be established, the available findings do suggest that treatment is likely to play a meaningful role. It is probably safe to assume that high quality, evidence-based treatment can make a unique and valuable contribution to drug court outcomes, and, therefore, that drug court outcomes can be improved upon to the extent that such treatments are presently lacking.

## Mechanisms of Action in Adult Drug Courts

There has been considerable speculation about how or why adult drug courts may exert positive effects. Some commentators have theorized that drug courts can apply the techniques of behavioral modification known as *operant conditioning* in a more effective manner than many other criminal justice programs. By closely monitoring offenders and administering immediate and certain consequences for their performance, drug courts may be more likely to reduce undesired behaviors and increase adaptive behaviors (e.g., Marlowe & Wong, 2008).

Other investigators have hypothesized that the due process requirements of a court proceeding might contribute to greater perceptions of *procedural fairness* or *procedural justice* (e.g., Burke & Leben, 2007). Evidence from cognitive psychology reveals that offenders are more likely to respond favorably to an adverse judgment or punitive disposition if they believe the professionals were following the rules, avoiding favoritism and treating participants with respect and dignity (e.g., Tyler, 1994). This could explain why drug courts tend to elicit larger effects than interventions that are not delivered in a courtroom setting.

Still other commentators hypothesize that the development of a positive relationship between the participant and the judge may be partly responsible for the positive effects of drug courts. Sometimes referred to as the "symbolic impact of the black robe" (Satel, 1998, p. 47), the judge may take on the role of a powerful authority figure or parental figure who can compete more forcefully and effectively against the antisocial peer influences that are often predominant in participants' lives. Few individuals in our society have prestige and authority comparable to a judge. Offenders may respond especially well to encouragement and praise from the bench, and may work especially hard to avoid disappointing or offending the powerful magistrate figure.

Unfortunately, little research has uncovered the mechanisms of action that explain the positive effects of drug courts. There is correlational evidence that participation in drug court does lead to improvements on short-term, proximal measures that could support several of the theories being proposed. For example, participation in drug court has been associated with improvements in perceptions of procedural justice, motivation for change, engagement in prosocial activities, and positive attachments to staff members, including the judge. In a small number of studies, these short-term improvements were further found to mediate, or contribute to, longer-term reductions in substance use and recidivism (Gottfredson et al., 2007). These early findings must be replicated before they can be relied upon, and ideally should be confirmed in controlled research studies. For example, it would be informative to evaluate the effects of interventions specifically designed to enhance perceptions of procedural justice in a drug court program. Until such studies are completed, the mechanism(s) of action of adult drug courts remain open to debate and speculation.

## Adaptive Programming in Adult Drug Courts

It is estimated that adult drug courts currently serve only about 5–10% of the roughly 1.5 million adults arrested each year in the United States who meet criteria for substance abuse or dependence (Bhati et al., 2008). If drug courts extend their reach to the larger at-risk population, it may no longer be feasible for team members to meet regularly in staff meetings to review all of the cases. It will become necessary to model how well-functioning drug courts typically respond to various presentations by participants, and to routinize or standardize that process so that it can be reliably implemented with a large number of drug offenders (Farole, Puffett, Rempel, & Byrne, 2004). In the treatment literature, this process is referred to as *adaptive programming* and the responses are referred to as adaptive interventions.

Adaptive programs adjust the dose or type of services that are administered to participants in response to their clinical presentation or performance in treatment (e.g., Collins, Murphy, & Bierman, 2004; Murphy, Lynch, McKay, Oslin, & TenHave, 2007). The decision rules or algorithms are specified a priori, that is, before treatment has been initiated. In this way, decisions are guided primarily by the research evidence rather than by individual professional judgment, which can be negatively influenced by such factors as time pressure, insufficient expertise, or personal bias. Professionals always retain the authority to override or alter an indicated adaptive response. However, they are typically requested to articulate the rationale for doing so in the participant's record.

## Noncompliance Versus Nonresponsiveness

Selecting suitable adaptive interventions can be complicated when dealing with offender populations, who are jointly supervised by the criminal justice system and the substance abuse treatment system. Criminal justice professionals are primarily charged with protecting public safety and are empowered to respond to misconduct with enhanced supervision or punitive sanctions. Treatment professionals, in contrast, are primarily charged with improving the health of their clients and may intensify a client's treatment plan in furtherance of these goals. This requires a distinction to be drawn between *noncompliance* with supervision requirements and *nonresponsiveness* to the clinical interventions (Marlowe, 2008).

If, for example, a drug court participant fails to show up for counseling sessions or to deliver urine specimens when directed to do so, he or she is arguably engaged in willful noncompliance, assuming that the absences were unexcused and avoidable. Under such circumstances, it might be appropriate to apply a punitive sanction or to increase the participant's supervision requirements as a consequence for the infraction. On the other hand, if the participant is meeting his or her obligations in the program, but is not responding to the clinical interventions, the fault might lie not with the participant but with the treatment plan. Rather than apply a punitive sanction, it would be preferable to alter the treatment plan. For example, the participant might require intensive clinical case management services to address a co-occurring psychiatric disorder.

Distinguishing between noncompliance and nonresponsiveness addresses an important problem that is commonly encountered in drug courts. Some judges or probation officers may increase treatment requirements as a consequence for misconduct in the program. For example, a participant who misses several counseling sessions or is rearrested might be "sanctioned" with a more restrictive modality of treatment, such as residential treatment. This practice not only risks wasting scarce treatment slots, it may also give the inadvertent message to participants that treatment is aversive and thus something to be avoided. It would be preferable for the judge to order a clinical reevaluation of the case, and to solicit recommendations from the treatment professionals about the best course to pursue.

## Stepped Care Versus Branching Models

There are two general models of adaptive programs. The *stepped care* model intensifies treatment after less intensive interventions have proven to be insufficient. For example, some studies have reported superior outcomes by beginning substance abuse clients in drug-free outpatient counseling, and then referring those who failed to respond to more intensive counseling or medication (Sobell & Sobell, 2000). This model has the obvious benefit of conserving scarce treatment resources while placing the least burden on participants commensurate with their needs.

However, evidence among offender populations suggests that each treatment failure may increase the likelihood of continued failure in future treatment episodes (e.g., Rothbard et al., 1999). A history of prior drug abuse treatment has been associated in several research studies with negative outcomes in correctional rehabilitation (Marlowe, Patapis et al., 2003). Each disappointing episode may undermine offenders' confidence in treatment or generate counterproductive feelings of pessimism or despondency. Worse still, failure on an initial treatment regimen might lead a judge or other criminal justice professionals to impose a punitive sanction on the participant, such as incarceration. Judges might, correctly or incorrectly, interpret a poor response to treatment as evidence of low motivation or incorrigibility. Because judges are responsible for protecting public safety, it may be unrealistic to expect them to abide multiple treatment failures before symptom remission can be achieved. It may be preferable to begin drug offenders on the proper treatment regimen from the outset, rather than risk unanticipated negative repercussions from trial-and-error treatment planning. This approach is referred to as a *branching* model, because participants are sorted into the most appropriate interventions at each branch or decision-point in the adaptive algorithm.

## Pilot Study of an Adaptive Intervention

Marlowe and colleagues (Marlowe, Festinger, Arabia et al., 2008; Marlowe et al., 2009) pilot tested a branching adaptive algorithm in a misdemeanor drug court. The algorithm distinguished between noncompliance with the supervisory conditions of the program (e.g., failing to attend counseling sessions) and nonresponsiveness to the clinical interventions (e.g., providing drug-positive urine specimens). Increased judicial supervision was specified as the consequence for noncompliance, and enhanced clinical case management was specified as the consequence for nonresponsiveness (see Fig. 8.1).

The first branch in the adaptive algorithm assigned participants to different schedules of judicial status hearings based upon their assessed risk levels. This baseline-matching procedure was derived from research findings described earlier (Marlowe et al., 2006, 2007), which indicated that high-risk drug offenders required biweekly status hearings to succeed in drug court. Subsequently, participants were assessed at monthly intervals to determine how they were progressing in the program. Those who had two or more unexcused absences from counseling sessions or unexcused failures to provide a valid urine specimen were determined to be noncompliant with the conditions of the program. For those individuals, the schedule of court hearings was increased. If they were previously on an as-needed schedule, they were reassigned to biweekly hearings. If they were already on a biweekly schedule, they were placed on a jeopardy contract. A jeopardy contract involves "zero tolerance" for further violations of the rules of the program. Any further violation leads to a termination hearing, also known as a show-cause hearing. At the termination hearing, the participant is terminated from the program and sentenced on the original charge(s), unless he or she can provide a good-cause reason to be given another chance.

Participants who provided two or more drug-positive urine specimens were determined to be nonresponsive to the clinical interventions. Those individuals were referred to an intensive clinical case-management program administered by the local Treatment Accountability for Safer Communities (TASC) Office. Participants in the TASC program are required to meet twice weekly with an intensive clinical case manager who provides individual substance abuse counseling with an emphasis on motivational enhancement, relapse prevention, and cognitive restructuring techniques.

Consenting participants were randomly assigned at entry to drug court as-usual ($n = 14$) or to the adaptive intervention ($n = 16$). This small pilot study was not intended to be statistically powered to detect small effects. The aims were limited to determining whether the adaptive algorithm was feasible to implement in a real-world drug court and whether it showed sufficient promise to justify the cost and effort of a fully powered trial.

Results revealed that the adaptive algorithm was implemented with 88% fidelity, was acceptable to both participants and staff, and showed substantial promise for improving outcomes. The estimated effect sizes ranged from 0.40 to 0.60 (in the moderate to large range) across various dependent measures, including drug-negative urine specimens and on-time graduation rates (Marlowe, Festinger, Arabia et al., 2008). It took

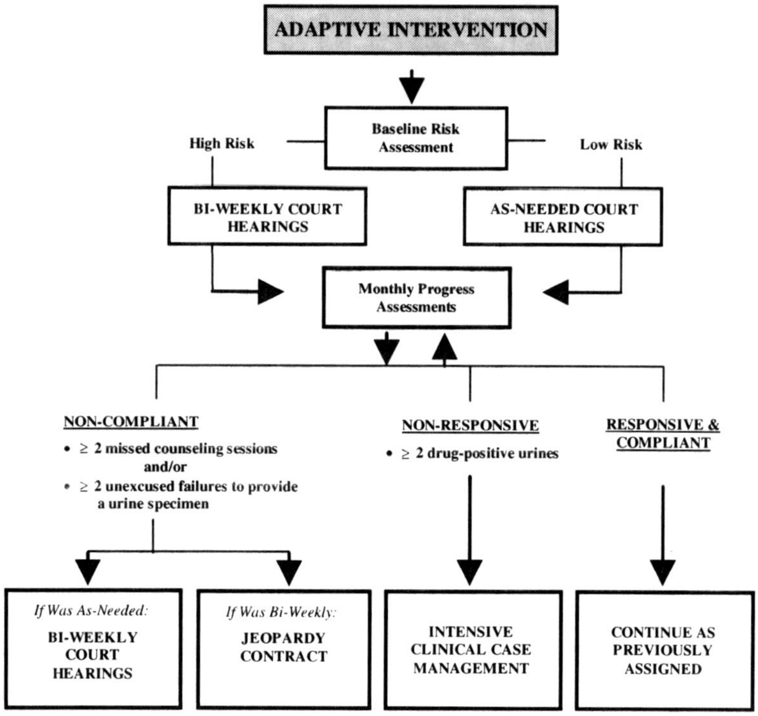


**Fig. 8.1** Adaptive Programming Algorithm in a Misdemeanor Drug Court. Reprinted with permission from Marlowe, Festinger, Arabia et al. (2008)

an average of approximately 4 fewer months for participants in the adaptive condition to graduate from the program or to reach a final resolution of the case (Marlowe et al., 2009). Given that the average annual cost of a drug court is estimated to be approximately \$4,000 per participant, plus treatment costs which may average an additional \$7,000 for outpatient counseling (\$11,000 total) (Bhati et al., 2008), reducing the time to case resolution by 4 months could be expected to save approximately \$3,700 per participant. This could help to conserve scarce resources and permit drug court programs to treat a larger number of needy offenders who might otherwise be facing jail or prison sentences for their crimes.

Data from the pilot study also suggested a possible mechanism of action for the adaptive program. Employing the same criteria for noncompliance and nonresponsiveness as in the adaptive condition, participants in the as-usual condition were much less likely to receive a response for inadequate performance. Consequences were imposed only 31% of the time when they were indicated for the as-usual participants, as opposed to 88% of the time for the adaptive condition. It also took the drug court team considerably longer to respond to instances of noncompliance and nonresponsiveness in the as-usual condition (mean $\pm$ SD $= 89.67 \pm 79.61$ days vs. $16.25 \pm 24.66$ days).

These findings suggest that the adaptive algorithm may have focused the drug court team's attention more readily on poorly performing individuals, thus allowing the team to "nip problems in the bud" before they developed too fully. It should not be surprising that outcomes were less impressive in the as-usual condition, because there was only about a 1 in 3 chance of receiving a consequence for infractions, and the consequences were imposed after an average delay of nearly 3 months. The primary contribution of adaptive algorithms may be to increase the probability that infractions (and perhaps achievements as well) are recognized and responded to, and to shorten the time delay before the responses are imposed. This could permit greater numbers of offenders to be treated in drug courts with equivalent or superior results.

## Juvenile Drug Courts

As was noted earlier, the drug court model has been applied with some modifications to the treatment of juvenile offenders in delinquency proceedings. Like adult drug courts, participants in juvenile drug courts attend frequent status hearings in court, undergo weekly drug testing, complete a mandatory regimen of substance abuse treatment and other indicated services, and receive escalating rewards for achievements and sanctions for infractions (e.g., Rossman, Butts, Roman, DeStefano, & White, 2004). However, juvenile drug courts are more likely to reach out to family members and the schools when rendering services, and they attempt to tailor their interventions to the cognitive and maturational levels of the participants.

### Effectiveness of Juvenile Drug Courts

Two meta-analyses of juvenile drug court evaluations, published in 2006, analyzed the results of studies through the early to mid 2000s. Both concluded that the average effect of juvenile drug court was not reliably better than that of juvenile probation (Shaffer, 2006; Wilson et al., 2006). Although a few quasi-experimental studies had reported superior outcomes for juvenile drug courts over conventional juvenile probation (e.g., Rodriguez & Webb, 2004), others had found no differences in outcomes (e.g., Anspach, Ferguson, & Phillips, 2003).

Since that time, promising findings have been emerging more decidedly in favor of juvenile drug courts. In a well-controlled experimental study, Henggeler et al. (2006) randomly assigned juvenile drug offenders to traditional family court services, juvenile drug court, or juvenile drug court augmented with multisystemic therapy (MST) and/or contingency management (CM). As was described earlier, MST is a manualized intervention that trains parents, teachers, and other caregivers to assist in managing the juvenile's behavior. In the CM procedure, the juveniles received gradually escalating payment vouchers for drug-negative urine specimens. The results revealed significantly lower rates of substance use and delinquency for the juvenile drug court participants as compared to the family court participants, and these effects were further enhanced through the addition of MST and CM, alone or in combination.

A multisite quasi-experimental study was recently completed in Ohio, which compared outcomes between juvenile drug court participants and those of matched comparison samples of juvenile drug offenders (Shaffer, Listwan, Latessa, & Lowenkamp, 2008). The results revealed that participants in the juvenile drug courts had significantly lower rearrest rates than the comparison juvenile offenders.

### Mechanisms of Action in Juvenile Drug Courts

Preliminary evidence is beginning to identify the processes by which juvenile drug courts may elicit superior effects over traditional programs. Several risk factors have been reliably associated with adolescent delinquency and substance abuse by numerous research studies. These risk factors include ineffective supervision and inconsistent disciplinary practices on the part of the juveniles' parents or guardians, frequent associations with deviant peers, and low engagement in prosocial activities, such as school or sports (Dishion & Patterson, 2006; Mayes & Suchman, 2006). In the experimental study described above (Henggeler et al., 2006), the investigators found that the juvenile drug court did a significantly better job than the traditional family court of improving parental supervision and discipline of the juveniles, as well as reducing the juveniles' associations with deviant peers (Schaeffer et al., 2010). More importantly, these short-term improvements were found, in turn, to predict longer-term reductions in substance use and delinquency.

These early findings suggest that juvenile drug courts may have the potential to outperform conventional juvenile probation and family court services; however, this may only be true to the extent that they use their leverage over both the juveniles and their guardians to enhance parental supervision, improve parental disciplinary practices, and reduce the juveniles' associations with delinquent peers. If juvenile drug courts do not focus their attention and efforts on these key risk processes, they may be unlikely to achieve significant improvements in outcomes.

## Conclusion

Success comes rather infrequently to the criminal justice system. Most correctional rehabilitation programs for drug-involved offenders have minimal or short-lasting effects (e.g., Marlowe, 2003) or are associated with negative side effects and worse outcomes (e.g., McCord, 2003). Drug courts offer a glimpse of what is possible for improving the lives of drug offenders, protecting public safety and saving money in the process.

Five meta-analyses involving randomized, controlled studies and dozens of quasi-experimental studies have concluded that adult drug courts significantly reduce crime, and cost/benefit analyses have estimated net dollar savings from drug courts that are several times the initial investments. The optimal target population for adult drug courts has been identified, and fidelity to several key components of the drug court model has been demonstrated to be necessary for favorable results. Less can be confidently concluded about the effects of juvenile drug courts; however, recent studies are tending to show better effects than older studies, suggesting that the programs may be getting better with increasing experience.

The challenge now is to extend the reach of drug courts without diluting the intervention below effective levels. Any program can be made cheaper simply by lowering the dosage and providing fewer services to more participants. The difficult task is to maintain the effectiveness of the program in the process. Many interventions show efficacy on a small scale, only to have the quality of implementation drift unacceptably downward when they are applied on a large scale in day-to-day practice.

Adaptive programming shows early promise for extending the reach of drug courts without interfering with the effects of the intervention. Rather than drop essential components of the program, the better course of action appears to be to standardize the best practices so that they can be reliably implemented by a larger number of programs, each serving a larger census of clients.

Addiction and associated crime are severe and chronic conditions that require an intensive, sustained, and coordinated response. It is naïve to think that one-dimensional approaches emphasizing either treatment alone or punishment alone should be effective. An integrated strategy that combines treatment with close monitoring and strict behavioral accountability appears to be the minimum intervention necessary to break the stubborn cycle of drugs and crime. The goal now is to find ways to apply this blended model on a grand enough scale to have a meaningful impact on the drug/crime problem in this country.

## References


Andrews, D. A., & Bonta, J. (1998). *The psychology of criminal conduct* (2nd ed.). Cincinnati, OH: Anderson.

Anspach, D. F., Ferguson, A. S., & Phillips, L. L. (2003). *Evaluation of Maine's statewide juvenile drug treatment court program*. Portland, ME: University of Southern Maine, Department of Sociology.

Aos, S., Miller, M., & Drake, E. (2006). *Evidence-based public policy options to reduce future prison construction, criminal justice costs, and crime rates*. Olympia, WA: Washington State Institute for Public Policy.

Arabia, P. L., Fox, G., Caughie, J., Marlowe, D. B., & Festinger, D. S. (2008). Sanctioning practices in an adult felony drug court. *Drug Court Review, 6*(1), 1–31.

Auerbach, K. (2007). Drug testing methods. In J. E. Lessenger & G. F. Roper (Eds.), *Drug courts: A new approach to treatment and rehabilitation* (pp. 215–233). New York: Springer.

Barnoski, R., & Aos, S. (2003, March). *Washington State's drug courts for adult defendants: Outcome evaluation and cost-benefit analysis*. Olympia, WA: Washington State Institute for Public Policy.

Belenko, S. (1998). Research on drug courts: A critical review. *National Drug Court Institute Review, 1*, 1–42.

Belenko, S. (2002). Drug courts. In C. G. Leukefeld, F. Tims, & D. Farabee (Eds.), *Treatment of drug offenders: Policies and issues* (pp. 301–318). New York: Springer.

Belenko, S., Patapis, N., & French, M. T. (2005, February). *Economic benefits of drug treatment: A critical review of the evidence for policy makers.* St. Louis, MO: National Rural Alcohol & Drug Abuse Network. Available at www.tresearch.org. Retrieved January 27, 2010.

Bhati, A. S., Roman, J. K., & Chalfin, A. (2008, April). *To treat or not to treat: Evidence on the prospects of expanding treatment to drug-involved offenders.* Washington, DC: The Urban Institute.

Bozza, J. A. (2007). Benevolent behavior modification: Understanding the nature and limitations of problem-solving courts. *Widener Law Journal, 17*, 97–143.

Burke, K., & Leben, S. (2007). Procedural fairness: A key ingredient in public satisfaction. *Court Review, 44*, 4–24.

Butzin, C. A., Saum, C. A., & Scarpitti, F. R. (2002). Factors associated with completion of a drug treatment court diversion program. *Substance Use and Misuse, 37*, 1615–1633.

Carey, S. M., Finigan, M., Crumpton, D., & Waller, M. (2006). California drug courts: Outcomes, costs and promising practices: An overview of phase II in a statewide study. *Journal of Psychoactive Drugs, SARC Supplement, 3*, 345–356.

Carey, S. M., Finigan, M. W., & Pukstas, K. (2008). *Exploring the key components of drug courts: A comparative study of 18 adult drug courts on practices, outcomes and costs.* Portland, OR: NPC Research. Available at www.npcresearch.com. Retrieved January 27, 2010.

Carey, S. M., Pukstas, K., Waller, M. S., Mackin, R. J., & Finigan, M. W. (2008). *Drug courts and state mandated drug treatment programs: Outcomes, costs and consequences.* Portland, OR: NPC Research. Available at www.npcresearch.com. Retrieved January 27, 2010.

Carey, S. M., Waller, M., & Weller, J. (in press). *California drug court cost study – Phase III: Statewide costs and promising practices, final report.* Portland, OR: NPC Research.

Collins, L. M., Murphy, S. A., & Bierman, K. A. (2004). A conceptual framework for adaptive preventive interventions. *Prevention Science, 5*, 185–196.

DeMatteo, D. S., Marlowe, D. B., & Festinger, D. S. (2006). Secondary prevention services for clients who are low risk in drug court: A conceptual model. *Crime and Delinquency, 52*, 114–134.

DeMatteo, D. S., Marlowe, D. B., Festinger, D. S., & Arabia, P. L. (2009). Outcome trajectories in drug court: Do all participants have serious drug problems? *Criminal Justice and Behavior, 36*, 354–368.

Dishion, T. J., & Patterson, G. R. (2006). The development and ecology of antisocial behavior in children and adolescents. In D. Cicchetti & D. J. Cohen (Eds.), *Developmental psychopathology, Volume 3: Risk, disorder, and adaptation* (2nd ed., pp. 503–541). Hoboken, NJ: Wiley.

Drug Court Clearinghouse & Technical Assistance Project. (1999). *Looking at a decade of drug courts* (NCJ 171140). Washington, DC: Office of Justice Programs, U.S. Department of Justice.

Farole, D. J., & Cissner, A. B. (2007). Seeing eye to eye: Participant and staff perspectives on drug courts. In G. Berman, M. Rempel, & R. V. Wolf (Eds.), *Documenting results: Research on problem-solving justice* (pp. 51–73). New York: Center for Court Innovation.

Farole, D. J., Puffett, N., Rempel, M., & Byrne, F. (2004). *Can innovation be institutionalized? Problem-solving in mainstream courts.* New York: Center for Court Innovation. Available at http://www.courtinnovation.org. Retrieved January 27, 2010.

Festinger, D. S., DeMatteo, D. S., Marlowe, D. B., & Lee, P. A. (2005). Expungement of arrest records in drug court: Do clients know what they're missing? *Drug Court Review, 5*, 1–21.

Festinger, D. S., Marlowe, D. B., Lee, P. A., Kirby, K. C., Bovasso, G., & McLellan, A. T. (2002). Status hearings in drug court: When more is less and less is more. *Drug and Alcohol Dependence, 68*, 151–157.

Fielding, J. E., Tye, G., Ogawa, P. L., Imam, I. J., & Long, A. M. (2002). Los Angeles County drug court programs: Initial results. *Journal of Substance Abuse Treatment, 23*, 217–224.

Finigan, M., Carey, S. M., & Cox, A. (2007). *The impact of a mature drug court over 10 years of operation: Recidivism and costs.* Portland, OR: NPC Research. Available at www.npcresearch.com. Retrieved January 27, 2010.

Flango, V. E., & Cheesman, F. L. (2009). The effectiveness of the SCRAM alcohol monitoring device: A preliminary test. *Drug Court Review, 6*, 109–134.

Friedmann, P. D., Taxman, F. S., & Henderson, C. E. (2007). Evidence-based treatment practices for drug-involved adults in the criminal justice system. *Journal of Substance Abuse Treatment, 32*, 267–277.

Gendreau, P., Little, T., & Goggin, C. (1996). A meta-analysis of the predictors of adult offender recidivism: What works! *Criminology, 34*, 575–596.

Goldkamp, J. S., White, M. D., & Robinson, J. B. (2002). An honest chance: Perspectives on drug courts. *Federal Sentencing Reporter, 6*, 369–372.

Gossop, M., Tradaka, K., Stewart, D., & Witton, J. (2005). Reductions in criminal convictions after addiction treatment: 5-year follow-up. *Drug and Alcohol Dependence, 79*, 295–302.

Gottfredson, D. C., Kearley, B. W., Najaka, S. S., & Rocha, C. M. (2005). The Baltimore City Drug Treatment Court: 3-year outcome study. *Evaluation Review, 29*, 42–64.

Gottfredson, D. C., Kearley, B. W., Najaka, S. S., & Rocha, C. M. (2007). How drug treatment courts work: An analysis of mediators. *Journal of Research on Crime and Delinquency, 44*, 3–35.

Gottfredson, D. C., Najaka, S. S., & Kearley, B. (2003). Effectiveness of drug treatment courts: Evidence from a randomized trial. *Criminology and Public Policy, 2*, 171–196.

Harrell, A., Cavanagh, S., & Roman, J. (1999). *Final report: Findings from the evaluation of the*

*D.C. Superior Court Drug Intervention Program.* Washington, DC: The Urban Institute.

Harrell, A., & Roman, J. (2001). Reducing drug use and crime among offenders: The impact of graduated sanctions. *Journal of Drug Issues, 31*, 207–232.

Hawken, A., & Kleiman, M. (2007). H.O.P.E. for reform. *The American Prospect*, available at http://www.prospect.org/cs/articles?article=hope_for_reform. Retrieved August 9, 2008.

Heck, C. (2008). MRT: Critical component of a local drug court program. *Cognitive Behavioral Treatment Review, 17*(1), 1–2.

Henggeler, S. W., Halliday-Boykins, C. A., Cunningham, P. B., Randall, J., Shapiro, S. B., & Chapman, J. E. (2006). Juvenile drug court: Enhancing outcomes by integrating evidence-based treatments. *Journal of Consulting and Clinical Psychology, 74*, 42–54.

Hepburn, J. R., & Harvey, A. N. (2007). The effect of the threat of legal sanction on program retention and completion: Is that why they stay in drug court? *Crime and Delinquency, 53*, 255–280.

Hiller, M. L., Knight, K., & Simpson, D. D. (1999). Risk factors that predict dropout from corrections-based treatment for drug abuse. *The Prison Journal, 79*, 411–430.

Hoffman, M. B. (2000). The drug court scandal. *North Carolina Law Review, 78*, 1437–1534.

Holloway, K. R., Bennett, T. H., & Farrington, D. P. (2006). The effectiveness of drug treatment programs in reducing criminal behavior. *Psicothema, 18*, 620–629.

Hora, P. F., & Stalcup, T. (2008). Drug treatment courts in the twenty-first century: The evolution of the revolution in problem-solving courts. *Georgia Law Review, 42*, 717–811.

Huddleston, C. W., Marlowe, D. B., & Casebolt, R. (2008, May). *Painting the current picture: A national report card on drug courts and other problem solving court programs in the United States* (Vol. II, No. 1). Alexandria, VA: National Drug Court Institute and Bureau of Justice Assistance.

Kirchner, R. A., & Goodman, E. (2007). Effectiveness and impact of Thurston County, Washington drug court program. *Cognitive Behavioral Treatment Review, 16*(2), 1–4.

Kleiman, M. A. R., Tran, T. H., Fishbein, P., Magula, M. T., Allen, W., & Lacy, G. (2003). *Opportunities and barriers in probation reform: A case study of drug testing and sanctions.* Berkeley, CA: University of California, Policy Research Center.

Latimer, J., Morton-Bourgon, K., & Chretien, J. (2006). *A meta-analytic examination of drug treatment courts: Do they reduce recidivism?* Canada: Department of Justice, Research & Statistics Division.

Lindquist, C. H., Krebs, C. P., & Lattimore, P. K. (2006). Sanctions and rewards in drug court programs: Implementation, perceived efficacy, and decision making. *Journal of Drug Issues, 36*, 119–146.

Lindquist, C. H., Krebs, C. P., Warner, T. D., & Lattimore, P. K. (2009). An exploration of treatment and supervision intensity among drug court and non-drug court participants. *Journal of Offender Rehabilitation, 48*, 167–193.

Lipsey, M. W., & Wilson, D. B. (2001). *Practical meta-analysis.* Thousand Oaks, CA: Sage.

Logan, T. K., Hoyt, W., McCollister, K. E., French, M. T., Leukefeld, C., & Minton, L. (2004). Economic evaluation of drug court: Methodology, results, and policy implications. *Evaluation and Program Planning, 27*, 381–396.

Loman, L. A. (2004). *A cost-benefit analysis of the St. Louis City Adult Felony Drug Court.* St. Louis, MO: Institute of Applied Research.

Lowenkamp, C. T., Holsinger, A. M., & Latessa, E. J. (2005). Are drug courts effective? A meta-analytic review. *Journal of Community Corrections, Fall*, 5–28.

Lowenkamp, C. T., Latessa, E. J., & Holsinger, A. M. (2006). The risk principle in action: What have we learned from 13,676 offenders and 97 correctional programs? *Crime and Delinquency, 52*, 77–93.

Lutze, F. E., & van Wormer, J. G. (2007). The nexus between drug and alcohol treatment program integrity and drug court effectiveness: Policy recommendations for pursuing success. *Criminal Justice Policy Review, 18*, 226–245.

Marinelli-Casey, P., Gonzales, R., Hillhouse, M., Ang, A., Zweben, J., Cohen, J., et al. (2008). Drug court treatment for methamphetamine dependence: Treatment response and post-treatment outcomes. *Journal of Substance Abuse Treatment, 34*, 242–248.

Marlowe, D. B. (2003). Integrating substance abuse treatment and criminal justice supervision. *NIDA Science & Practice Perspectives, 2*(1), 4–14.

Marlowe, D. B. (2007). Strategies for administering rewards and sanctions. In J. E. Lessenger & G. F. Roper (Eds.), *Drug courts: A new approach to treatment and rehabilitation* (pp. 317–336). New York: Springer.

Marlowe, D. B. (2008). Application of sanctions. In C. Hardin & J. N. Kushner (Eds.), *Quality improvement for drug courts: Evidence-based practices* (pp. 107–114) [Monograph Series No. 9]. Alexandria, VA: National Drug Court Institute.

Marlowe, D. B., DeMatteo, D. S., & Festinger, D. S. (2003). A sober assessment of drug courts. *Federal Sentencing Reporter, 16*, 153–157.

Marlowe, D. B., Festinger, D. S., Arabia, P. L., Dugosh, K. L., Benasutti, K. M., Croft, J. R., et al. (2008). Adaptive interventions in drug court: A pilot experiment. *Criminal Justice Review, 33*, 343–360.

Marlowe, D. B., Festinger, D. S., Arabia, P. L., Dugosh, K. L., Benasutti, K. M., & Croft, J. R. (2009). Adaptive interventions may optimize outcomes in drug courts: A pilot study. *Current Psychiatry Reports, 11*, 370–376.

Marlowe, D. B., Festinger, D. S., Dugosh, K. L., Arabia, P. L., & Kirby, K. C. (2008). An effectiveness trial of contingency management in a felony pre-adjudication drug court. *Journal of Applied Behavior Analysis, 41*, 565–577.

Marlowe, D. B., Festinger, D. S., Dugosh, K. L., Lee, P. A., & Benasutti, K. M. (2007). Adapting judicial supervision to the risk level of drug offenders: Discharge and six-month outcomes from a prospective matching study. *Drug and Alcohol Dependence, 88*(Suppl 2), S4–S13.

Marlowe, D. B., Festinger, D. S., & Lee, P. A. (2004a). The judge is a key component of drug court. *Drug Court Review, 4*(2), 1–34.

Marlowe, D. B., Festinger, D. S., & Lee, P. A. (2004b). The role of judicial status hearings in drug court. In K. Knight & D. Farabee (Eds.), *Treating addicted offenders: A continuum of effective practices* (pp. 11-1–11-10). Kingston, NJ: Civic Research Institute.

Marlowe, D. B., Festinger, D. S., Lee, P. A., Dugosh, K. L., & Benasutti, K. M. (2006). Matching judicial supervision to clients' risk status in drug court. *Crime and Delinquency, 52*, 52–76.

Marlowe, D. B., Festinger, D. S., Lee, P. A., Schepise, M. M., Hazzard, J. E. R., Merrill, J. C., et al. (2003). Are judicial status hearings a key component of drug court? During-treatment data from a randomized trial. *Criminal Justice and Behavior, 30*, 141–162.

Marlowe, D. B., & Kirby, K. C. (1999). Effective use of sanctions in drug courts: Lessons from behavioral research. *National Drug Court Institute Review, 2*, 1–31.

Marlowe, D. B., Patapis, N. S., & DeMatteo, D. S. (2003). Amenability to treatment of drug offenders. *Federal Probation, 67*, 40–46.

Marlowe, D. B., & Wong, C. J. (2008). Contingency management in adult criminal drug courts. In S. T. Higgins, K. Silverman, & S. H. Heil (Eds.), *Contingency management in substance abuse treatment* (pp. 334–354). New York: Guilford Press.

Mayes, L. C., & Suchman, N. E. (2006). Developmental pathways to substance abuse. In D. Cicchetti & D. J. Cohen (Eds.), *Developmental psychopathology, Volume 3: Risk, disorder, and adaptation* (2nd ed., pp. 599–619). Hoboken, NJ: Wiley.

McCord, J. (2003). Cures that harm: Unanticipated outcomes of crime prevention programs. *Annals of the American Academy of Political and Social Science, 587*, 16–30.

McIntire, R. L., Lessenger, J. E., & Roper, G. F. (2007). The drug and alcohol testing process. In J. E. Lessenger & G. F. Roper (Eds.), *Drug courts: A new approach to treatment and rehabilitation* (pp. 234–246). New York: Springer.

McLellan, A. T., Cacciola, J., Kushner, H., Peters, R., Smith, I., & Pettinati, H. (1992). The fifth edition of the Addiction Severity Index: Cautions, additions and normative data. *Journal of Substance Abuse Treatment, 9*, 461–480.

McLellan, A. T., Lewis, D. C., O'Brien, C. P., & Kleber, H. D. (2000). Drug dependence, a chronic medical illness: Implications for treatment, insurance, and outcomes evaluation. *Journal of the American Medical Association, 284*, 1689–1695.

Murphy, S. A., Lynch, K. G., McKay, J. R., Oslin, D., & TenHave, T. (2007). Developing adaptive treatment strategies in substance abuse research. *Drug and Alcohol Dependence, 88*(2), S24–S30.

National Association of Criminal Defense Lawyers. (2009). *America's problem-solving courts: The criminal costs of treatment and the case for reform*. Washington, DC: Author.

National Association of Drug Court Professionals. (1997). *Defining drug courts: The key components*. Washington, DC: Office of Justice Programs, U.S. Department of Justice.

National Institute of Justice. (2006). *Drug courts: The second decade* (NCJ 211081). Washington, DC: Office of Justice Programs, U.S. Department of Justice.

Peters, R. H., Haas, A. L., & Murrin, M. R. (1999). Predictors of retention and arrest in drug court. *National Drug Court Institute Review, 2*, 33–60.

Petrosino, A., Turpin-Petrosino, C., & Finckenauer, J. O. (2000). Well-meaning programs can have harmful effects! Lessons from experiments such as Scared Straight. *Crime and Delinquency, 46*, 354–379.

Prendergast, M. L., Hall, E. A., Roll, J., & Warda, U. (2008). Use of vouchers to reinforce abstinence and positive behaviors among clients in a drug court treatment program. *Journal of Substance Abuse Treatment, 35*, 125–136.

Rempel, M., & Green, M. (2009, November). *Do drug courts reduce crime and produce psychosocial benefits?* Paper presentation at the 2009 annual conference of the American Society of Criminology, Philadelphia.

Rodriguez, N., & Webb, V. J. (2004). Multiple measures of juvenile drug court effectiveness: Results of a quasi-experimental design. *Crime and Delinquency, 50*, 292–314.

Roll, J. M., Prendergast, M., Richardson, K., Burdon, W., & Ramirez, A. (2005). Identifying predictors of treatment outcome in a drug court program. *American Journal of Drug and Alcohol Abuse, 31*, 641–656.

Rossman, S. B., Butts, J. A., Roman, J., DeStefano, C., & White, R. (2004). What juvenile drug courts do and how they do it. In J. A. Butts & J. Roman (Eds.), *Juvenile drug courts and teen substance abuse* (pp. 55–106). Washington, DC: Urban Institute Press.

Rossman, S. B., Green, M., & Rempel, M. (2009, November). *Substance abuse findings from the Multi-Site Adult Drug Court Evaluation (MADCE)*. Paper presentation at the 2009 annual conference of the American Society of Criminology, Philadelphia.

Rothbard, A., Alterman, A., Rutherford, M., Liu, F., Zelinski, S., & McKay, J. (1999). Revisiting the effectiveness of methadone maintenance treatment on crime reductions in the 1990s. *Journal of Substance Abuse Treatment, 16*, 329–335.

Satel, S. (1998). Observational study of courtroom dynamics in selected drug courts. *National Drug Court Institute Review, 1*, 43–72.

Saum, C. A., Scarpitti, F. R., Butzin, C. A., Perez, V. W., Jennings, D., & Gray, A. R. (2002). Drug court participants' satisfaction with treatment and the court experience. *Drug Court Review, 4*, 39–81.

Schaeffer, C. M., Henggeler, S. W., Chapman, J. E., Halliday-Boykins, C. A., Cunningham, P. B., Randall, J., et al. (2010). Mechanisms of effectiveness in juvenile drug court: Altering risk processes associated with delinquency and substance abuse. *Drug Court Review, 7*, 57–94.

Shaffer, D. K. (2006). *Reconsidering drug court effectiveness: A meta-analytic review* (Doctoral dissertation). Las Vegas, NV: Department of Criminal Justice, University of Nevada.

Shaffer, D. K., Listwan, S. J., Latessa, E. J., & Lowenkamp, C. T. (2008). Examining the differential impact of drug court services by court type: Findings from Ohio. *Drug Court Review, 6*, 33–66.

Simpson, D. D., Joe, G. W., & Brown, B. S. (1997). Treatment retention and follow-up outcomes in the drug abuse treatment outcome study (DATOS). *Psychology of Addictive Behaviors, 11*, 294–307.

Snavely, K. R. (2000). *The critical need for jail as a sanction in the drug court model* (Practitioner Fact Sheet Vol. II(3)). Alexandria, VA: National Drug Court Institute.

Sobell, M. B., & Sobell, L. C. (2000). Stepped care as a heuristic approach to the treatment of alcohol problems. *Journal of Consulting and Clinical Psychology, 68*, 573–579.

Taxman, F. S., & Bouffard, J. A. (2003). Substance abuse counselors' treatment philosophy and the content of treatment services provided to offenders in drug court programs. *Journal of Substance Abuse Treatment, 25*, 75–84.

Taxman, F. S., & Marlowe, D. B. (Eds.). (2006). Risk, needs, responsivity: In action or inaction? [Special Issue]. *Crime and Delinquency, 52*(1), 3–6.

Taxman, F. S., Perdoni, M. L., & Harrison, L. D. (2007). Drug treatment services for adult offenders: The state of the state. *Journal of Substance Abuse Treatment, 32*, 239–254.

Turner, S., Greenwood, P., Fain, T., & Deschenes, E. (1999). Perceptions of drug court: How offenders view ease of program completion, strengths and weaknesses, and the impact on their lives. *National Drug Court Institute Review, 2*, 61–85.

Tyler, T. R. (1994). Psychological models of the justice motive: Antecedents of distributive and procedural justice. *Journal of Personality and Social Psychology, 67*, 850–863.

U.S. Government Accountability Office. (2005). *Adult drug courts: Evidence indicates recidivism reductions and mixed results for other outcomes* (No. GAO-05-219). Washington, DC: Author.

Vito, G. F., & Tewksbury, R. A. (1998). The impact of treatment: The Jefferson County (Kentucky) drug court program. *Federal Probation, 62*, 46–51.

Wilson, D. B., Mitchell, O., & MacKenzie, D. L. (2006). A systematic review of drug court effects on recidivism. *Journal of Experimental Criminology, 2*, 459–487.

# 9 Probation

Mark Carey

**Abstract**

Probation is the most commonly used correctional sanction, covering nearly 60% of all adults under supervision in the United States. The field has undergone tremendous changes over the years and more recently has been applying research knowledge to improve services. The research indicates that probation can have a profound impact on rearrest rates if it applies proper interventions and techniques. Meta-analysis has identified the principles of risk, need, and responsivity as having the most influence on risk reduction. As a result, probation agencies are discovering the need to apply actuarial assessment tools, motivational interviewing techniques, case plans that address criminogenic needs, cognitive behavioral programs, and effective behavioral management strategies.

**Keywords**

Probation • Community corrections • Risk reduction • Research-based • Criminogenic • Social learning • Risk • Big Four • Responsivity • Cognitive behavioral • Assessments • Actuarial • Case plan • Intervention

Probation has been a mainstay in American criminal and juvenile justice policy for over 100 years, set in motion by John Augustus, a boot maker from Boston, when he asked the court in 1841 to allow him to take in a "common drunkard," to spare the man from being sentenced to prison (Augustus, 1852). (John Augustus is referred to as the "Father of Probation," who sought to rehabilitate first-time offenders and spare them the crime hardening experience of prison.) It has undergone many changes since that time and now is the most common sentencing response to crime as illustrated in Fig. 9.1. In 2008, there were over four million individuals on probation supervision (Glaze & Bonczar, 2009). That number increases to over five million when including parole. In the total 2008 correctional population, nearly 60% of all adult offenders under supervision were on probation (see Fig. 9.2). The supervision rate has been steadily increasing, with 2,201 adults under community supervision per 100,000 adult residents in 2008.

M. Carey (✉)
The Carey Group, White Bear Lake, MN 55110, USA
e-mail: mark@thecareygroup.com

C. Leukefeld et al. (eds.), *Handbook of Evidence-Based Substance Abuse Treatment in Criminal Justice Settings*, Issues in Children's and Families' Lives 11,
DOI 10.1007/978-1-4419-9470-7_9, © Springer Science+Business Media, LLC 2011

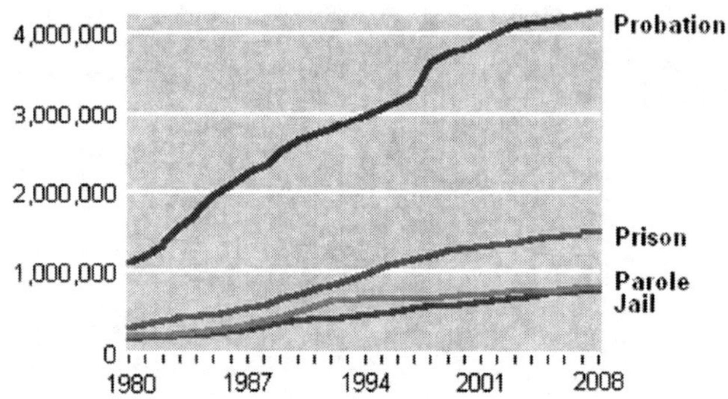


**Fig. 9.1** Adult correctional populations trends, 1980–2008
Source: Bureau of Justice Statistics (2008).

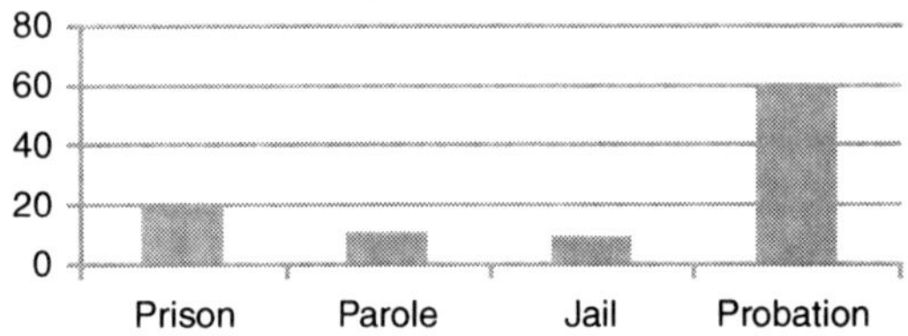


**Fig. 9.2** Percent of persons under correctional supervision, by supervision type, 2008
Source: Bureau of Justice Statistics (2006).

## Introduction

Policy makers often express one of two general views of probation: the first noting that probation as a response to crime has been ineffective. Rearrest rates are high, estimated at 30% (Bureau of Justice Statistics, n.d.), with unsuccessful discharge rates at 40% (Glaze & Palla, 2005). The caseloads of probation have increased to an average of approximately 127 adult offenders per supervision officer (Camp, 2003), resulting in recognition that probation can not be effective with caseloads that high. In addition, the number of mandates placed on probation agencies has increased over the years (ranging from the drawing of DNA samples to the completion of presentence investigations) reducing the amount of time the officers can spend on their primary duties (Pew Center on the States, 2009).

A second view celebrates the fact that probation is the preferred option of the courts. The Pew Center on the States (2009) notes that the cost of probation, at $3.42 per day, is a mere fraction of the cost of housing a prisoner, $78.95 per day. These policy makers further point out that incarceration is often criminogenic, meaning that the longer the period of incarceration, the greater the likelihood that the individual will commit a future crime (Smith, Goggin, & Gendreau, 2002). This view touts the fact that the criminal and juvenile justice probation systems have developed a wide range of intermediate sanctions and program interventions. These options allow the courts to impose community-based sanctions, thereby keeping the costs down and providing offenders with a chance to maintain productive relationships with their families, employers, and community.

One could argue that portions of both positions are correct. Probation has been expected to perform a myriad of tasks and objectives under extreme resource pressure, is under constant scrutiny and often is the target of blame when a probationer commits a serious crime. At the same time, legislatures and courts usually prefer community-based supervision as the solution to the problems of high correctional costs and prison crowding. Recent research results have provided guidance for managing probation's limited resources and producing more favorable results. This research that has developed consistently similar results is considered to be "evidence" and the commensurate policy and practice that are in alignment with this research have been described as "evidence-based practices (EBP) for purposes of risk reduction" (Bogue et al., 2004). Indeed, a growing number of agencies have implemented evidence-based practices in an effort to achieve reductions in recidivism.

Maryland's Division of Parole and Probation has adopted a series of evidence-based practices under a concept entitled Proactive Community Supervision. Evaluation showed lower rates of rearrest, warrants, and revocations than in the control group (Taxman, 2008; Taxman, Yancey, & Bilanin, 2006). In Texas, Travis County's Community Supervision and Corrections Department saw drops in numbers of felony revocations, absconders, and rearrest rates (17% decrease) when they compared 2005 results with those 3 years after they began implementing evidence-based practices. Furthermore, Travis County avoided $4.8 million in incarceration costs due to reduced revocations (Eisenberg, Bryl, & Fabelo, 2009). Other jurisdictions have reported similar results, making policy makers optimistic that probation can achieve significant public safety objectives if it follows the guidance indicated by the research. While many researchers state that a 10–12% recidivism reduction can be achieved, others assert that a 30% reduction in recidivism is possible (Andrews & Bonta, 2006) if current knowledge, regarding evidence that has resulted from empirical study is applied with fidelity (i.e., applied in accordance to the model). In response to this encouraging research, probation agencies are increasingly attempting to align their programs and services with these practices.

## Who Is on Probation?

Different forms of correctional supervision serve potentially different purposes. Goals ranging from punishment, incapacitation, and deterrence to rehabilitation and diversion can lead to different determinations of the best method to employ. As a general rule, courts use probation (also referred to as community corrections) when the punishment for illegal behavior can be achieved under community based supervision without unduly jeopardizing public safety. This case supervision and monitoring service is often combined with intermediate sanctions such as electronic monitoring, day reporting, and/or community service. Supervision can range in intensity, from multiple officer visits each week in the office, home, and on the job, to visiting an automated kiosk machine, or mailing in a reporting form to communicate any changes in living or legal status.

According to the Bureau of Justice Statistics (Glaze & Bonczar, 2009), three out of four probationers are male; approximately half are placed on probation for a felony conviction and half for a misdemeanor. Substance use and abuse are often key factors in probationers' legal difficulties, with at least 40% of probationers placed on probation for a drug or alcohol offense (29% for a drug violation and 15% for driving while intoxicated). An estimated 80% of incarcerated offenders in the United States have current substance abuse problems (National Center on Addiction and Substance Abuse [CASA], 1998).

## Evidence That Guides Probation Practice

Probation fulfills numerous roles, as reflected in varying mission statements from agency to agency. Some stress accountability; others support of the court, through investigations and assessments; and others victim restoration. Almost all make some mention of public safety. However, agencies can achieve public safety in many different ways. One agency could advocate for revocation of an offender's probation, leading to a prison term and thereby avoiding the possibility of a repeat crime; another could emphasize treatment services, working with an offender through increased programming and counseling. Both would be operating under the overall mission of public safety.

As a general rule, the two primary duties of probation are that of enforcer (i.e., enforcement of court orders and quick response to real or potential threats to public safety) and agent of change (i.e., provision of behavioral services to enhance offender motivation and ability to change behavior). Specific case circumstances, as well as organizational mission and policy, dictate which role to emphasize. Nonetheless, there is a perceived tension within the profession as to which is the dominant role.

Recent research, on long-term public safety (i.e., reduced rearrest rates over the long term), suggests a balanced approach that provides external controls, where and when reasonable given the risk conditions, and programming, for those who are most likely to respond favorably. This approach calls for certain probation officer traits (e.g., firmness, fairness, relationship orientation, and supportiveness regarding offender change) that, when applied strategically, will enhance the effectiveness of both accountability and behavioral change roles. Four areas will be examined to illustrate how this balanced approach is applied to probation agencies in an evidence-based probation (EBP) environment:

- Principles – Broad guidance based on research around effective risk reduction strategies.
- Policy and Practice – Specific agency actions that can be taken to improve the delivery of services that align with the research principles.
- Interventions – Activities and programs proven to reduce the likelihood that an offender with a particular profile will commit a new offense.
- Professional Traits and Skills – Specific staff qualities and abilities deemed to be effective at influencing behavioral change.

## Research-Based Principles That Guide Probation Practice

In 2003, the National Institute of Corrections (NIC), in collaboration with the Crime and Justice Institute, assembled leading scholars and practitioners from the fields of criminal justice and corrections, to define the core elements of EBP based upon the "what works" research (Bogue et al., 2004). The group identified eight, evidence-based principles for effectively intervening with offenders. These eight principles have served as the foundation for many agencies seeking to reduce recidivism. From these principles, a set of practical, cascading applications logically follows, including revisions to policy and practice, adoption of interventions that reduce future crime, and recruitment and training of a workforce that possesses a set of professional traits and skills that foster offender behavior change. These eight principles (Domurad & Carey, 2010) are listed below:

1. *Assess actuarial risk/needs*. Research demonstrates that aligning the intensity of intervention with the level of risk produces the best risk reduction outcomes. Empirically based, actuarial instruments enable professionals to assess the level of risk an individual offender is likely to pose. While these instruments cannot determine a specific individual's risk level with absolute certainty, they can – like the actuarial tools used to determine the probability that an adolescent male will get into a traffic accident as compared to a middle-aged man – identify the outcome of large groups of individuals with similar characteristics. Actuarial instruments assess both static risk factors (i.e., those that are unchangeable, such as age at first arrest, gender, and prior criminal history) and dynamic risk factors (i.e., those that are changeable, such as antisocial attitudes, stressful family circumstances, and lack of employment).

   Figure 9.3 offers an example of the predictive qualities of an actuarial tool. In this case, the Level of Service Inventory-Revised (LSI-R) was used to demonstrate the correlation between larger point totals on the risk assessment with higher recidivism rates, with a followup period of 1 year.

   There are generally three uses of risk assessments related to probation decisions regarding supervision, resources, and treatment. Each has a specific purpose and various limitations. Each should be validated with the local offender population, to ensure proper predictive qualities.

   *Brief screening*. Designed to quickly screen offenders' risk to reoffend. Uses risk factors such as, prior illegal behavior, previous supervision experience, and age, to determine whether additional, more thorough assessments are needed.

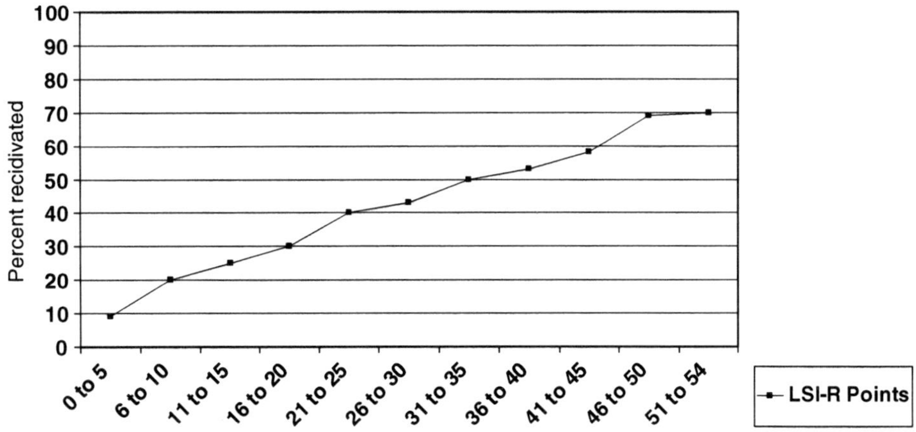


**Fig. 9.3** Recidivism change within one year
Source: Andrews and Bonta (2003b).

*General risk/need.* Designed, first, to more fully identify risk to reoffend by identifying what risk group the individual most closely emulates and categorizing by low, medium, or high risk; and, second, to identify criminogenic needs so that treatment targets can be established. Successful programming around these criminogenic needs reduces the overall risk of reoffense.

*Specialized assessments.* Designed to supplement the general risk/need assessment to provide a more comprehensive picture of risk and need, specialized assessments augment the information collected through the general risk/need tool by providing information about the offender's unique needs. The risk/need assessment may not adequately identify risk for certain illegal behaviors, such as domestic violence and sex offenses, and it may miss underlying factors like psychopathy, which are useful in determining how to manage and/or treat the offender. Additional tools are necessary to examine these unique factors. For example, The National Institute of Corrections has sponsored the development of specialized assessment tools for female offenders in an effort to better identify risk and need traits for women.

Specialized tools and assessments can be acquired through private companies and some are available in the public domain. Specialized assessments are sometimes developed through local universities or the community corrections research department and can be more cost effective than purchasing the assessment through a private provider.

2. *Enhance intrinsic motivation.* Motivation for change can be externally or internally driven. Many offenders are motivated to take action in order to avoid the penalties the justice system might impose. In some cases, their illegal acts may cause other negative consequences such as family conflict or financial loss, providing at least momentary motivation to change. The coercive power of the court and the threat of loss of liberty can provide effective initial incentives for offender cooperation. However, for the offender to stay motivated and truly embrace behavior change over time, something more impactful than external motivators is necessary; and research demonstrates that motivation can be influenced by corrections professionals' interactions with offenders (Castonguay & Beutler, 2006).
3. *Target interventions.* Matching the offender with the right kind of programming will enhance public safety results. Mismatching, assigning offenders to programs for which they are not well suited, will diminish positive results and, in some cases, increase the likelihood of rearrest. Use of the concept of responsivity – preplacement knowledge of offender traits, characteristics of the program,

and traits of individuals working with offenders – aligns the offender with the intervention with the greatest likelihood of success. The following considerations should influence the determination of the proper intervention for an individual offender:

*Risk.* Low-risk offenders do not require extensive programming or case management services and are more likely to succeed with less intense supervision and/or programming. Some research has indicated that extreme high-risk offenders (i.e., those that are psychopathic in nature and enmeshed in a criminal subculture) do not respond favorably to treatment and can be disruptive to a therapeutic environment. Targeting the extreme high-risk offender for programming should only be done with caution, using highly skilled practitioners in an intensive treatment environment. This type of offender is more likely to be appropriate for high-intensity supervision and surveillance techniques, such as frequent urinalysis, frequent field and office visits, electronic monitoring, GPS tracking, and/or curfew. Medium- and high-risk offenders are most likely to benefit from behavioral change programming and case management services, with risk reduction as the primary goal.

*Need.* Since the medium- and high-risk offenders are most likely to benefit from behavioral-change strategies, interventions should be specifically targeted based on assessed criminogenic needs (i.e., an attribute of an individual or an individual's environment that contributes to criminal behavior and can be changed). These offenders are likely to have multiple risk/need factors such as antisocial thinking, emotional regulation/antisocial personality, and antisocial peers, that can be changed with programming.

*Responsivity.* In addition to matching the offender's risk level to the appropriate interventions, it is important to address certain factors that influence the likelihood of a successful treatment experience. Although programming around these factors is not likely to reduce repeat offense rates by itself, these factors often require special consideration in order to ensure that the criminogenic intervention achieves its objectives. Some of these individual traits that need consideration, when matching the program with criminogenic needs, include the offender's mental health condition, gender, learning style, cultural and ethnic background, level of motivation, language or learning capacity, and intelligence level. Programs capable of dealing with these factors can achieve intended outcomes, while program interventions that fail to address these traits can hinder success (Andrews & Bonta, 2007; Cullen & Gendreau, 2000).

*Dosage.* The dosage and intensity of the interventions should increase commensurate with the offender risk level (Andrews & Bonta, 2007). Higher-risk offenders require significantly more structure than lower-risk offenders – at least until they begin to internalize motivation and prosocial behaviors. Higher-risk offenders should spend 40–70% of their free time in structured, prosocial activities over a 3–9-month period (Gendreau & Goggin, 1995). This structure can consist of a cluster of activities that both limit the offender's ability to engage in unlawful acts and maximize exposure to prosocial influences (e.g., structured recreation, probation supervision, meeting with a mentor, participating in treatment, attending AA, going to work, or participating in tutoring services). As a general rule, while higher-risk offenders need 200–300 hours over 6–12 months, medium-risk adult offenders need a total of 100 hours of intervention over the course of a 3–9-month period of time (Bourgon & Armstrong, 2005). Only programming that targets criminogenic needs should be considered as contributing toward this dosage target.

*Treatment.* Given the diversity of offender needs, probation needs to provide a wide assortment of treatment services. The most effective form of programming for most medium- and high-risk offenders is cognitive behavioral. Cognitive-behavioral programs address antisocial thinking patterns, build problem-solving skills, and teach behavioral techniques that equip the offender with new thinking and other skills, through repetitive skill practice increasing in difficulty as the offender masters each skill. These types of programs tend to most successfully address the criminogenic needs that are more likely to influence future crime.

4. *Skill train with directed practice*. The probation officer delivering programming and providing supervision should have the skills to communicate effectively and to influence behavior change and should understand social learning theory, which asserts that people learn and adopt new behaviors through positive and negative reinforcement, observation, and skill practice (Bandura, 1969, 1977). Probation staff seeking to reduce rearrest rates should be trained how to teach and reinforce skills. While programming offered in group settings tends to be more effective with higher-risk offenders, probation officers can teach offenders concrete skills through one-on-one practice sessions, where the offender learns, for example, how to regulate emotions or solve problems.
5. *Increase positive reinforcement*. Providing positive reinforcement is an important part of the offender change process. Providing frequent affirmations for prosocial acts and attitudes (e.g., four positive affirmations for every critical or disapproving message) is optimal for influencing behavioral change (Andrews & Bonta, 2006; Gendreau, 1996; Gendreau & Goggin, 1995; Gendreau, Little, & Goggin, 1996; Gendreau & Paparozzi, 1995). Probation agencies typically have clear expectations, policies, and practices around confronting and sanctioning unwanted behavior, but this is not sufficient. In addition to swift and proportional sanctioning to extinguish antisocial behavior, probation needs to systematically reward positive behavior. The use of incentives and rewards is a powerful tool in any probation agency's effort to motivate and encourage offenders along the path of prosocial change; however, focusing on positive reinforcement does not remove the need to sanction, or otherwise express disapproval, when negative behavior does occur. Both need to be administered when appropriate, but with a greater emphasis on positive messages when prosocial attitudes and behaviors are demonstrated.
6. *Engage ongoing support in natural communities*. Achievement of reductions in new criminal and delinquent behavior is more likely when offenders' significant others are engaged in the case plans and when offenders have meaningful connections to the prosocial community (Bonta, Wallace-Capretta, Rooney, & McAnoy, 2002; Clear & Sumter, 2002; Egelko, Galanter, Dermatis, & DeMaio,1998; Emrick, Tonigang, Montgomery, & Little, 1993; Galanter, 1993; Higgins & Silverman, 1999; Meyers, Miller, Smith, & Tonnigan, 2002; Meyers & Smith, 1997; O'Connor & Perryclear, 2002; Shapiro & Schwartz, 2001). Prosocial, community-based networks (both people and activities) provide opportunities for offenders to strengthen their own prosocial skills by engaging with others who model law-abiding attitudes and behavior. Prosocial family members and significant others (including employers, teachers, mentors, and spiritual leaders) can support programming and the skills offenders are attempting to adopt, by helping them practice these new skills in their natural environments and holding them accountable when their behavior is out of conformity. Probation officers who develop skills in brokering support and connections between offenders and those in their natural communities are best equipped to support long-term behavioral change.
7. *Measure relevant processes/practices*. Probation agencies need to collect and analyze data and information to provide a feedback loop to personnel to ascertain if the techniques used are having the intended impact.

This feedback cannot occur without a process in place that measures those activities deemed to be most important in achieving the goal(s). Measures might include activities (e.g., line staff trained on evidence-based principles and use of risk assessment instruments), intermediate outcomes (e.g., match between services delivered and criminogenic needs), and impact (e.g., decreases in technical violations, improvements in recidivism rates).

8. *Measurement feedback.* A wide variety of factors and actions can diminish the effectiveness of probation practices: extending an intervention designed for one population of offenders to another; committing errors in implementation; or failing to properly train staff. Measures of fidelity to design must be carefully constructed and put into place, with quality assurance oversight as a separate, but related, function. The value in measurement is not in the doing, but in the knowing. Once performance measurement data are collected and analyzed, findings should be shared widely. This information is useful at the individual offender level, staff level, program/agency level, and jurisdiction-wide (Rossman & Winterfield, 2009).

## Research-Based Policy That Guides Probation Practice

Application of the risk, need, and responsivity principles clearly influences recidivism. Results improve as more of the principles are integrated into practice. Applying just one principle will yield small results. For example, if probation uses an actuarial assessment tool to determine risk and criminogenic needs, but does not use this information to devise programming and supervision practices (such as increasing supervision levels as risk increases and applying programming that addresses the specific criminogenic needs), risk reduction will be diminished. Some agencies may effectively implement two principles, such as risk and need, yet lack the capacity to address the responsivity principle, and, thus, fail to ensure a continuum of treatment services that matches with individual offender characteristics (e.g., gender, mental health, intelligence, and culture). Placement of offenders in "generic" programs, without regard to responsivity, will diminish outcomes.

Figure 9.4 demonstrates how adherence to all three principles improves recidivism reduction results (nearly 30%) when compared to just two of the principles (approximately 20%). When one or no principle is applied, results are negligible.

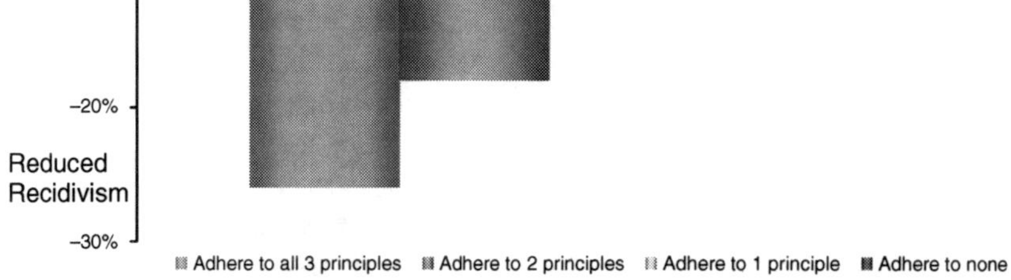


**Fig. 9.4** Impact of adhering to the core principles of effective intervention: Risks, needs, and responsivity
Source: Andrews, Dowden, and Gendreau (1999).

**Table 9.1** Central eight criminogenic needs

| Big Four Criminogenic Needs | | Other Four Criminogenic Needs | |
|---|---|---|---|
| **Need** | **Response** | **Need** | **Response** |
| Antisocial behavior | Build non-criminal alterative behaviors to risky situations, structure 40–70% of day | Family stressors | Reduce conflict, build positive relationships and communications |
| Antisocial attitudes | Reduce antisocial cognition, recognize high-risk thinking patterns and feelings, adopt alternative identity | Substance abuse | Reduce the supports for substance abusing behavior, enhance alternatives to substance abuse |
| Antisocial peers | Reduce association with antisocial peers, enhance contact with pro-social individuals | Lack of employment and education stability/achievement | Provide job readiness, pre-employment and job retention skills; enhance academic performance |
| Antisocial personality | Build problem solving and self management skills, develop anger management and coping skills | Poor use of leisure time | Enhance involvement and level of satisfaction with pro-social activities |

Source: Andrews et al. (2006).

It is important to note that not all criminogenic needs have equal influence on recidivism. While the literature has slightly different ways of expressing criminogenic needs, generally they fall into the "central eight" areas noted in Table 9.1. Of these eight, the "Big Four" (Andrews, Bonta, & Wormith, 2006), antisocial behavior, attitudes, peers, and personality, have the most significant impact on future recidivism and should be considered the primary intervention targets. Antisocial behavior or history is included in the "Big Four," even though it is technically a static risk factor. One cannot change the past. However, response to this risk factor is possible for the probation officer by teaching alternative ways of acting in high risk situations. The "other four" (family stressors, substance abuse, lack of employment and education stability/achievement, and poor use of leisure time) are also important, but they should generally be considered the secondary targets for intervention unless one of these four, such as addiction, is driving the antisocial behavior. An estimated 80% of incarcerated offenders in the United States have current substance abuse problems and sometimes this criminogenic need is the driver behind the antisocial behavior.

A higher-risk offender typically has a cluster of criminogenic needs that require attention. When the lesser four are attended to, while the offender continues to manifest attitudes and behaviors influenced by the top four criminogenic needs that support crime (e.g., uncontrolled anger, impulsivity, and poor problem-solving skills), intervention tends to be less effective or, in some cases, ineffective. For example, providing a job for offenders when they have significant problems with anger and impulsivity could just lead to them walking off the job or being fired.

The specific intervention strategy for an individual offender will depend upon the combination of the individual's needs and unique circumstances. For those offenders exhibiting recurring abuse of mood-altering substances, it may be necessary to address this criminogenic need before the others, as the use of chemicals will affect the manner in which they are able to receive, and comply with, other programming. For some offenders, the substance abuse is the primary influence that affects future criminal behavior and could even contribute to the presence of other criminogenic needs. For example, an individual who is law abiding might have a supportive family, good problem-solving skills, a functional temperament, prosocial friends, and prosocial attitudes. However, if this individual becomes addicted to drugs, he/she may soon experience subsequent stressors that would be criminogenic in nature. These might include interaction with antisocial others (e.g., drug dealers and other drug users), conflict with family members, and exhibition of mental health problems (e.g., anxiety, paranoia). For this individual, successful substance abuse treatment can simultaneously address most of these other factors. For other high-risk offenders, however, dealing with substance abuse without addressing the other risk factors will be insufficient by itself to significantly influence recidivism.

Figure 9.5 shows the effect of successfully addressing multiple criminogenic needs. The meta-analysis reflected here indicates that addressing six criminogenic needs had a significant impact on recidivism (approximately a 50% reduction), while addressing one criminogenic need resulted in minimal impact. Focusing exclusively on noncriminogenic needs resulted in no positive future crime impact and even a slightly elevated rate of recidivism.

The National Institute of Corrections, in cooperation with the Center for Effective Public Policy, produced *A Framework for Evidence-Based Decision Making in Local Criminal Justice Systems* (hereafter referred to as the Framework) in an effort to encourage entire justice systems to adopt evidence-based practices aimed at reducing harm and improving outcomes (National Institute of Corrections, 2010).

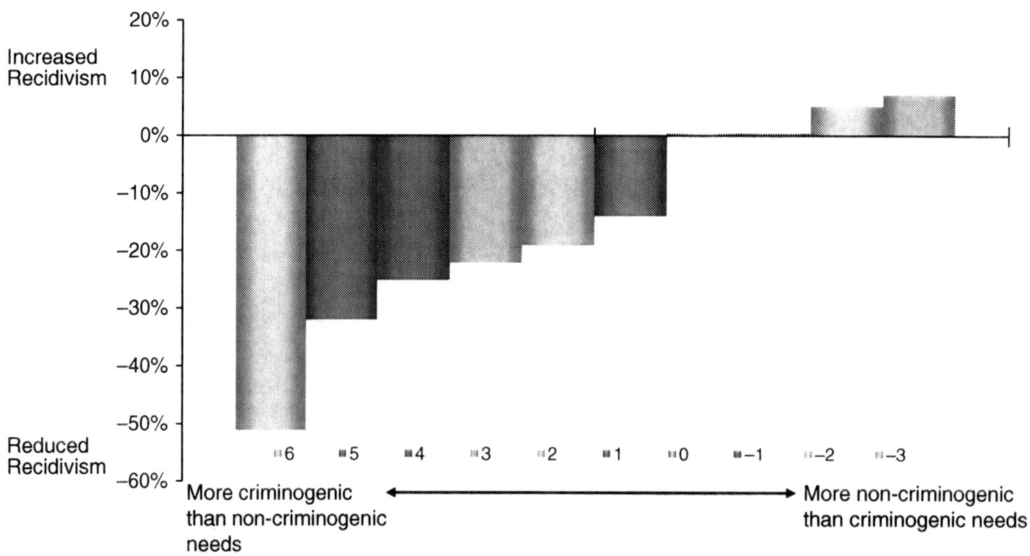


**Fig. 9.5** Recidivism reductions as a function of targeting multiple criminogenic vs non-criminogenic needs
Source: Andrews et al. (1999) and Dowden (1998).

Since probation partners with other system players from the point of pretrial release/supervision to discharge from supervision, its success is partly contingent on effective collaboration with the other justice entities. The framework was designed to give direction to policy makers on collaboration, specifically around the integration of evidence in all aspects of decision making. The project identified seven ways to reduce recidivism, all of them with policy implications for probation. Table 9.2 lists examples of how certain core research findings can affect the policy and practices in a probation system.

## Research-Based Structure for the Delivery of Probation Services

The principles of risk, need, and responsivity have affected how probation supervision is delivered, with some significant structural implications.

*Centralized intake*. Completion of actuarial risk tools requires special knowledge and skills. Individuals, without mental health or clinical certification, can conduct most of these assessments, but these must be done precisely or they will lose their validity and reliability. Quality control requires that the person applying the instrument be trained, receive ongoing guidance until mastery, and participate in quality assurance processes. Some jurisdictions limit the number of individuals assigned this duty, in order to concentrate on training and quality assurance services and reduce possible error. For these and other reasons, such as cost effectiveness, mid-size and larger urban agencies have created specialized intake units rather than spread the assessment responsibilities across the department.

*Specialized supervision based on risk*. Offender risk is a major consideration when selecting individuals on whom to spend limited probation resources. The greater the risk, the more restrictive supervision should be. The lower the risk, the less restrictive supervision should be. As a result, jurisdictions employ differential techniques.

*Low risk*: For offenders at low risk of recidivism, minimum supervision is the most effective strategy. In fact, over-supervision can increase their risk of recidivism, especially if it brings them into contact with higher-risk offenders. Treatment, if provided at all, should be one-on-one, educational in nature (e.g., classroom instruction), or in groups consisting of largely prosocial individuals.

*Medium and high risk*: The offenders in the medium- and high-risk categories are the most likely to benefit from a program designed to change behavior. These individuals should receive the majority of the risk reduction programming slots.

*Extreme high risk*: Offenders at extreme high risk to reoffend (perhaps 5% of the offenders at the top of the risk scale), and not likely to respond favorably to programming without highly specialized and intensive treatment, should receive supervision that focuses on monitoring and behavioral controls (e.g., frequent contacts, frequent urinalyses, home visits, curfews, restricted travel privileges, home confinement, electronic monitoring, intensive supervision, day reporting for monitoring purposes, and residential correctional centers). There is little evidence that traditional correctional treatment services will reduce their risk of recidivism; however, occupying their time, with interventions such as day programming, shows some promise in that their crime-prone hours are filled with structured activity.

*Caseload/workload targets*. State and local governments have increasingly relied on community corrections to address supervision and sanctioning objectives, given their comparatively lower costs than jails and prisons, but without the commensurate funding (Pew Center on the States, 2009). Most probation agencies have experienced burgeoning caseloads, with the average adult supervision caseload well over 100 cases per officer. As a result, probation has had to make difficult choices including, but not limited to, placing offenders on unsupervised probation. For example, in California many counties are "banking" half or more of the adult felons placed

**Table 9.2** Seven ways to reduce recidivism

| 7 Ways to Reduce Recidivism |
|---|
| 1 ***What works? Risk assessment tools are the gateway to risk reducing strategies.***<br>***Research finding:*** Structured assessment tools predict pretrial misconduct and risk of reoffense more effectively than professional judgment alone. Brief screening tools provide a quick assessment of risk; comprehensive tools provide information on risk to reoffend and effective targets of intervention to reduce future crime.<br>***Examples of policy implications:*** Assessments used by law enforcement, inform cite versus arrest decisions; by prosecutors and judges, inform plea and sentencing decisions; by jails, determine housing assignments and work release placements; and by community corrections, determine intensity of supervision.<br>***Examples of practice implications:*** Law enforcement officers administer brief assessments prior to making cite/release decisions; pre-trial services and community corrections conduct assessments prior to key decisions. |
| 2 ***What works? Effective programming can reduce recidivism for medium and higher-risk offenders, on average, by 30%.***<br>***Research finding:*** Recidivism rates are reduced when medium and high risk offenders receive appropriate behavior changing programming. Conversely, offenders assessed as low risk to reoffend do not benefit from behavior changing programming and are slightly more likely to recidivate when they are overly supervised or programmed.<br>***Examples of policy implications:*** For low-risk offenders, prosecutors use diversion programs, prosecutors and judges avoid excessive conditions; defense counsel advocates for low-intensity interventions; community corrections uses minimal supervision. Judges, prosecutors, and defense counsel target medium and high-risk offenders for programming designed to positively influence behavior.<br>***Examples of practice implications:*** Agencies performing assessments color code case files for easy identification by decision makers of high, medium, and low-risk offenders; community supervision agencies use call-in or kiosk reporting for low-risk offenders; treatment programs modify admission criteria to admit only medium and high risk offenders |
| 3 ***What works? The most effective programming for the majority of higher-risk offenders addresses criminal thinking and problem solving skills.***<br>***Research finding:*** Cognitive behavioral programs are generally the most effective programming interventions for higher-risk offenders. Furthermore, employing program interventions that influence the traits that lead to future crime (i.e., criminogenic needs) yield stronger reductions in recidivism (up to an average of 30% reduction). The net value (the cost of the program less the savings derived from preventing crime) of the average targeted, evidence-based cognitive-behavioral program, using a cost/benefit formula, is $10,299 per adult offender (Aos, Miller, & Drake, 2006b).<br>***Examples of policy implications:*** Judges ensure that sentencing conditions align with specific criminogenic needs; community corrections and treatment providers use assessment instruments to identify offenders' criminogenic traits; treatment providers avoid "one size fits all" programs; cognitive behavioral services are systematically utilized.<br>***Examples of practice implications:*** Treatment providers publish program listings that identify the criminogenic needs their services address; community corrections refers offenders to programs based upon the match between offenders' needs and programs' services; county executives/managers ensure that service contracts with treatment providers include accountability measures to make certain that the services provided include cognitive-behavioral interventions. |

**Table 9.2** (continued)

| 7 Ways to Reduce Recidivism |
|---|
| **4** ***What works? Swift, certain and proportional responses to misconduct improve compliance more effectively than severe responses.***<br>***Research finding:*** Graduated sanctions (i.e., sanctions that increase in severity based on the number and nature of acts of misconduct) increase compliance with supervision and treatment. Swift, certain and proportional actions that reflect disapproval of behavioral misconduct are more effective in reducing recidivism than actions that are disproportionate, delayed, or inconsistent.<br>***Example of policy implications:*** Court administrators develop policies to move cases swiftly through the court system; judges, prosecutors and community corrections agencies establish violation decision-making guidelines that take into account the risk of the offender and the severity of the violation behavior; all violation behavior is responded to in some fashion; judges and community corrections streamline procedures that allow for swift action following offender misbehavior.<br>***Example of practice implications:*** Court administrators manage dockets that streamline case processing; community corrections uses a decision-making tool to aid supervision officers in structuring their responses to violation behavior; community corrections provides administrative sanctioning processes to address misbehavior quickly. |
| **5** ***What works? Use more carrots than sticks.***<br>***Research finding:*** The use of incentives and positive reinforcement is effective in promoting behavioral change. Positive reinforcement should be provided at a rate of four reinforcers for every expression of disapproval (or sanction). Research demonstrates that this formula enhances offenders' motivation to continue exhibiting pro-social behaviors and attitudes.<br>***Examples of policy implications:*** Judges and community corrections develop policies around the structured and specific use of rewards to reinforce positive behavior.<br>***Examples of practice implications:*** Defense counsel requests review hearings when clients reach significant milestones; community corrections acknowledges progress through the posting of awards, writing letters of affirmation, providing complimentary bus passes, praising offenders' behavior to their families, or reducing reporting requirements; law enforcement acknowledges law abiding behavior of known offenders. |
| **6** ***What works? Deliver services in natural environments where possible.***<br>***Research finding:*** Although treatment services provided in structured (e.g., residential, institutional) settings are demonstrated to be effective, services delivered in natural environments (e.g., in offenders' immediate surroundings that most closely resemble pro-social, supportive environments) improve offenders' bonding to the pro-social community and aid in reducing recidivism).<br>***Examples of policy implications:*** Law enforcement refers to community-based service, crisis services are provided for offenders with mental health conditions; judges and prosecutors use community-based rather than residential or institutionally-based programs when the safety of the community is not in jeopardy; county executives/managers provide support for funding and zoning community-based programming options.<br>***Examples of practice implications:*** Judges, prosecutors, defense counsel, community corrections and others take inventory of available services to ensure a continuum of service options; resource directories are developed and shared among stakeholders. |

**Table 9.2** (continued)

| 7 Ways to Reduce Recidivism |
|---|
| **7** ***What works? Pair sanctions with interventions that address criminogenic needs.*** ***Research finding:*** Research demonstrates that sanctions alone (e.g., boot camps without a treatment component, electronic monitoring, intensive supervision, incarceration) do not contribute to reductions in reoffense rates. Modest increases in time served may even increase recidivism. ***Examples of policy implications:*** Prosecutors and judges employ a combination of sanctions and behavior changing programming for purposes of risk reduction; county executives/managers fund a balance of behavior changing programming and accountability measures; community corrections agencies address offender misbehavior with behavior changing, rather than solely punitive responses. |

Source: National Institute of Corrections (2010).

on probation just to keep the workload of the existing agents at a reasonable size and give the officers an opportunity to adequately perform key public safety functions. In some cases, innovative practices have been employed. In New York City, and other jurisdictions, low-risk offenders report to automated kiosks placed in the community or in probation offices, in order to verify their whereabouts and provide self-reported information (such as sentencing condition compliance, address changes, and rearrests).

The American Probation and Parole Association (APPA), in response to a growing constituent concern with these increased caseloads, compiled a policy paper to guide policy makers on proper caseload standards (Burrell, 2006). While workload is the preferred measure to quantify standards of work, APPA recognized that caseload is better understood by non-practitioners. In preparation for this policy paper, probation agencies employing evidence-based practices (EBP) were polled about how much time it takes for a probation officer to perform the kind of duties required (completing assessment instruments, using motivational interviewing techniques, teaching prosocial skills, etc.) in an EBP environment. Table 9.3 illustrates APPA suggested caseload standards for agencies seeking to implement EBP.

How a probation agency is structured, applies its limited resources, and communicates expectations of the staff is best based on caseload type. Table 9.4 provides an example of how Cook County Adult Probation structured its probation services based on offender risk. In this model, the caseload maximum target increases as the risk level decreases and the expectations of the probation officer differ based on the type of caseload. Officers, with large caseloads of low-risk offenders, do not engage in activities designed to change offender behavior; as low-risk individuals are likely to "self correct" and do not need much intervention. Officers who supervise the extreme high-risk group of offenders don't

**Table 9.3** APPA suggested caseload standards

| Case Type | Administrative | Low Risk | Moderate to High Risk | Extreme High Risk |
|---|---|---|---|---|
| Adult Cases | 1,000:1 | 200:1 | 50:1 | 20:1 |
| Juvenile Cases | Not recommended | 100:1 | 30:1 | 15:1 |

Source: Burrell (2006).

**Table 9.4** Circuit Court of Cook County adult probation department policy for standard, non-specialized supervision

| | Low Risk | Low-Med Risk | Med Risk | High-Med Risk | High Risk |
|---|---|---|---|---|---|
| **Supervision Standards** | Report by mail; in person every 3–6 months | Rotate monthly reporting: one in person and one by mail | Monthly in person; field visit every 6 months | Twice in person per month; field visit every 3 months | Weekly in person, field visits 2 per month; increase as needed |
| **Expectations** | Monitor court conditions using least amount of resources | Monitor court conditions using least amount of resources | Facilitate behavioral change with case plan addressing criminogenic needs, cog, MI, life skills | Facilitate behavioral change with case plan addressing criminogenic needs, cog, MI, life skills | Surveillance with treatment used sparingly if at all, enforcement and accountability is top priority |
| **Preferred Caseload Size** | 400 | 240 | 80 | 40 | 40 |

Source: Circuit Court of Cook County (2006).

focus on behavior change either, but for different reasons. For these individuals, the probation staff seeks to provide external controls and surveillance. Their caseloads are low because of the amount of time required for frequent visits and monitoring. On the other hand, probation officers with medium- and high-risk offenders are given caseloads of a size commensurate with intensive behavioral change techniques and case management. While these officers will likely use community resources for various treatment options, a great deal of intervention can occur during the individual officer-offender sessions.

## Research-Based Interventions for Probation

Research over the last 2 decades has provided clear and compelling guidance regarding the efficacy of programming. Some programs tend to reduce future risk of reoffense, others do not. Some programs work well with certain individuals but not others. For some populations (e.g., domestic violence) no program model has been consistently effective (Aos, Miller, & Drake, 2006a; Dutton & Sonkin, 2003). The National Institute of Corrections' Evidence-based Decision-Making Framework categorized the research findings as follows:

- *What does not work*: findings based on rigorous and methodologically sound research that repeatedly show (either through numerous single studies, or meta-analysis) that the intervention does not achieve the intended or desired results.
- *What works*: findings based on rigorous and methodologically sound research that consistently demonstrate significant positive results (either through numerous single studies, or meta-analysis studies).
- *What is promising*: findings that show promise but require more rigorous empirical study.
- *What is not clear*: findings that have conflicting results, i.e., one study shows something works while another study shows that it does not. These findings require additional empirical study.

From a cost effectiveness point of view, some programs work, but others work better. The

Washington State Institute for Public Policy examined a large sample of programs to determine the net present value, per participant, for commonly used correctional programs. The cost of the program, per participant, was deducted from the benefits of each program, described as reduced costs to the taxpayer as a result of fewer rearrests. Table 9.5 lists some of the programs that work and their relative benefit in dollars.

Effective program placement requires comprehensive knowledge of offender characteristics and program targets, criteria, and intervention techniques. Table 9.6 illustrates the process.

## Research-Based Knowledge That Guides Probation Skill Development

Even with the availability of risk assessments, the identification of criminogenic and responsivity factors, appropriate program placement, and appropriate levels of supervision, interventions will fall short of their promise, if the professional delivering the service does not have the knowledge, attitude, and skills to use them effectively. The importance of staff skill is demonstrated in a 2004 study conducted by the Washington State Institute for Public Policy (Barnoski, 2004). This study reviewed juvenile offender programs and found that the competency level of the staff working with the youth had a direct impact on the likelihood of recidivism, regardless of the intervention program in which the youth participated. Figure 9.6 shows felony recidivism rates 18 months after program completion comparing the skill level of different instructors delivering the same programming (in this case, Aggression Replacement Training, a cognitive behavioral program).

The importance of staff skill is evident across probation functions. Every interaction between justice personnel and offenders is an opportunity to positively influence behavior. In addition, since resource and other constraints limit the extent to which offenders can participate in risk-reducing programs and services, corrections professionals are often thrust into the role of primary service provider. Fairly brief exchanges (e.g., 15–60 minutes long) can have a positive outcome, as measured by rearrest rates. In one study, Trotter (2006) analyzed records of officers trained in a prosocial form of intervention, focused on modeling and reinforcing behaviors and teaching problem-solving skills. The study found that offenders, in the caseloads of these skilled officers, had lower recidivism rates than did offenders in the caseloads of officers who did not possess or use these skills.

Three key probation officer skills are required to positively shape offender behavior. They include the ability to

- focus on the right issues with the right offenders;
- use behavioral interventions to guide and redirect offenders; and
- exhibit effective relationship engagement and communication skills.

### Focus on the Right Issues with the Right Offenders

As noted earlier, most EBP probation agencies reserve behavioral intervention resources for the medium- and high-risk offender and utilize surveillance activities for the extreme high-risk offender. Programming targets, or criminogenic needs, must be carefully identified; they are dynamic in nature and can be changed over the long term through an intervention. It is, however, a fragile process. Effective staff skills will not likely compensate for wrong targeting, and proper targeting is not likely to overcome poor skills.

### Use Behavioral Interventions to Guide and Redirect Offenders

*Cognitive behavioral techniques.* The most effective interventions for offenders are behavioral (as opposed to other therapeutic approaches such as "talk therapy" or didactic, insight-oriented approaches). Behavioral approaches are rooted in social learning theory, which asserts that people learn best, and tend to adopt new behaviors, through positive and negative reinforcement, observation of role models, and skill practice. In 1998 Don Andrews and James Bonta stated (Andrews & Bonta, 1998), "There are virtually

**Table 9.5** Cost effectiveness of "What Works" programs. "n/e" means not estimated at this time. Prevention program costs are partial costs, prorated to match crime outcomes

| Program | Effect on Crime Outcomes (percent change in crime outcomes, and the number of evidence-based studies on which the estimate is based (in parentheses) | Benefits and Costs (Per Participant, Net Present Value, 2006 Dollars) | | | |
|---|---|---|---|---|---|
| | | Benefits to Crime Victims (of the reduction) | Benefits to Taxpayer (of the reduction) | Costs (marginal program cost, compared to the cost of alternative) | Benefits (total) Minus Costs (per participant) |
| Vocational education in prison | −9.0% (4) | $8,114 | $6,806 | $1,182 | $13,738 |
| Intensive supervision: treatment-oriented programs | −16.7% (11) | $9,318 | $9,369 | $7,124 | $11,563 |
| General education in prison (basic education or post-secondary) | −7.0% (17) | $6,325 | $5,306 | $962 | $10,669 |
| Cognitive-behavioral therapy in prison or community | −6.3% (25) | $5,658 | $4,746 | $105 | $10,299 |
| Drug treatment in community | −9.3% (6) | $5,133 | $5,495 | $574 | $10,054 |
| Correctional industries in prison | −5.9% (4) | $5,360 | $4,496 | $417 | $9,439 |
| Drug treatment in prison (therapeutic communities or outpatient) | −5.7% (20) | $5,133 | $4,306 | $1,604 | $7,835 |
| Adult drug courts | −8.0% (57) | $4,395 | $4,705 | $4,333 | $4,767 |
| Employment and job training in the community | −4.3% (16) | $2,373 | $2,386 | $400 | $4,359 |
| Electronic monitoring to offset jail time | 0% (9) | $0 | $0 | −$870 | $870 |
| Sex offender treatment in prison with aftercare | −7.0% (6) | $6,442 | $2,885 | $12,585 | −$3,258 |
| Intensive supervision: surveillance-oriented programs | 0% (23) | $0 | $0 | $3,747 | −$3,747 |
| Washington's Dangerously Mentally Ill Offender program | −20.0% (1) | $18,020 | $15,116 | n/e | n/e |
| Drug treatment in jail | −4.5% (9) | $2,481 | $2,656 | n/e | n/e |
| Adult boot camps | 0% (22) | $0 | $0 | n/e | n/e |

**Table 9.5** (continued)

| | | | | | |
|---|---|---|---|---|---|
| Domestic violence education/cognitive-behavioral treatment | 0% (9) | $0 | $0 | n/e | n/e |
| Jail diversion for mentally ill offenders | 0% (11) | $0 | $0 | n/e | n/e |
| Life Skills education programs for adults | 0% (4) | $0 | $0 | n/e | n/e |
| "n/e" means not estimated at this time. Prevention program costs are partial costs, prorated to match crime outcomes | | | | | |

Source: Aos et al. (2006b).

**Table 9.6** Program placement decision process

| Risk ⇒ | Criminogenic Need ⇒ | Program Identification ⇒ | Responsivity Factors ⇒ | Program Modification |
|---|---|---|---|---|
| Determine offender risk to identify medium to high-risk offenders for programming intervention | Identify the treatment targets for the medium and high risk (i.e., the specific traits and circumstances that influence future crime for that individual offender) | Identify the program that best targets the specific criminogenic needs for the individual medium and high-risk offender | Identify the unique offender traits that need attention to achieve success (e.g., learning disability, mental health, learning style, culture, gender, etc.) | Modify the program or program selection based on responsivity factors |

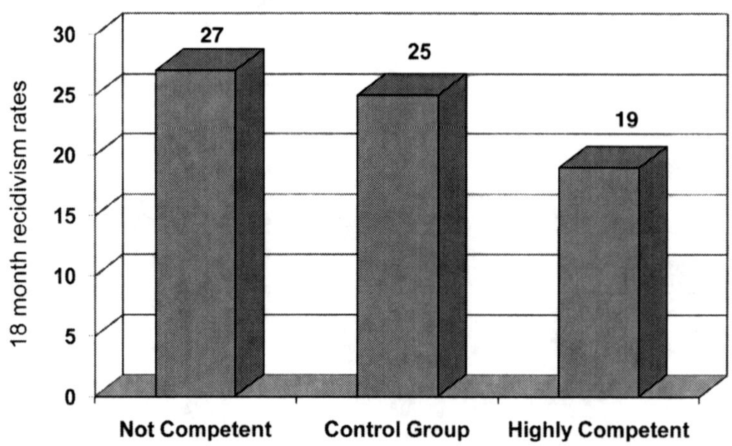


**Fig. 9.6** Staff skill level and offender recidivism
Source: Barnoski (2004).

no serious competitors for the following when it comes to changing criminal behavior" including

- Modeling: Demonstrating those behaviors we want to see in others;
- Reinforcement: Rewarding those behaviors we want to see repeated;
- Role-play: Creating opportunities for practice and providing corrective feedback;
- Graduated Practice: Unbundling complex behavior sets into their smaller components and practicing these smaller steps individually, building toward the complex behavior set; and
- Extinction: Assuring that antisocial styles of thinking, feeling, and acting are not inadvertently rewarded.

Insight alone is not enough to change behavior as those who have tried to lose weight or quit smoking can attest to. Most people tend to learn new ways of behaving through practice.

New ways of thinking occur as new ways of responding to situations occur. Sequential steps to skill practice include

- Observing others;
- Practicing new behavior;
- Receiving feedback on the practiced behavior; and
- Improving behavior, through increasingly difficult skill development, once a basic skill has been mastered.

Experts and professionals perfect their skills through repeated practice. It is no different with offenders. If they are going to adopt a new way of thinking and behaving they need to practice the desired behavior over and over again. Probation should refer higher-risk offenders to community programs where these techniques exist. In those areas where effective offender programs don't exist, the officer will need to use the supervision contact to demonstrate a skill, provide practice sessions with the offender, and give encouragement and feedback.

Higher-risk offenders tend to exhibit deficits in certain skills, which can lead to poor decision making. Skill deficits in the areas of conflict resolution, anger management, problem solving, and emotional regulation can result in frustration and poor decision making as the offender experiences life stressors, conflicts, and disappointments. Attending a class and listening to a counselor talk about problem solving is unlikely to help an offender build the kind of skills necessary to manage responses to challenging situations any more than listening to music will help a person become a musician. But when instruction in problem-solving techniques is followed by observation and practice, the offender is much more likely to master the desired behavior. When the skill is mastered, and when the offender sees positive results from the use of that skill, it is much more likely to be repeated.

*Rewards and sanctions.* Human behavior is shaped through a variety of social interactions. Rewards and sanctions can play a major role. If a child has a temper tantrum in the grocery store and acquires a desired treat, the behavior is more likely to happen again. If that child's behavior was disapproved and the child did not receive a treat, the behavior is less likely to be repeated.

Most probation professionals use sanctions as the primary method to respond to or control offenders' behavior. However, recent research indicates that positive reinforcement should be applied more frequently than negative responses when trying to change behavior. A ratio of four positive expressions (approval for a prosocial attitude or behavior) for every negative expression (disapproval for an antisocial attitude or behavior) should be the general approach (Andrews & Bonta, 2006; Gendreau & Goggin, 1995; Gendreau, Goggin, & Little, 1996). Higher-risk offenders tend to have long histories of punishment and disapproval, and many have learned to adapt to and dismiss the pain that accompanies them. In contrast, research has shown that antisocial individuals, just like the general population, are more likely to repeat behaviors and adopt attitudes that are recognized, acknowledged, and affirmed.

Simply put, rewards reinforce positive behaviors; sanctions express disapproval for negative behaviors. Rewards do not have to be costly or difficult to administer. A word of praise or encouragement can provoke a sense of pride and goodwill. Examples of rewards include

- Words of praise;
- The assignment of a task that demonstrates confidence in the individual's abilities and level of responsibility;
- A token of appreciation (e.g., a written note of acknowledgment or a certificate);
- Acknowledgment of accomplishment in front of others (e.g., praise in public, acknowledgment by a person in a position of authority);
- A more desirable housing or work assignment;
- A "pass" on a scheduled office visit;
- A bus voucher;
- A gift certificate (perhaps donated by a local merchant);
- Reduced drug testing; or
- Early discharge from supervision (Carey, 2010).

The failure to express disapproval when antisocial behaviors are exhibited conveys a neutral attitude or even implicit approval. It is an important opportunity lost. The procedural justice literature provides direction on how to express disapproval in the most efficacious manner, and has been used to craft responses to probation/parole violations (Taxman, 1999).

- Offenders should know what behaviors are desired and not desired and the consequences of negative behaviors should be clear and understood in advance (Tyler, 1990).
- Responses should be certain; every antisocial act should be responded to by some form of disapproval (Grasmack & Bryjak, 1980; Nichols & Ross, 1990; Paternoster, 1989).
- Level of punishment should be commensurate with the severity of the behavior (Von Hirsch, 1993).
- Responses should be as timely as possible in order to directly link the behavior to the response (Rhine, 1993).
- Responses should not be harsh or more punitive than necessary to change the behavior (Tonry, 1996).
- Responses should be fair and equitable (consider using structured decision-making instruments) (Paternoster, Brame, Bachman, & Sherman, 1997).
- Where possible, sanctions should be linked to the behavior.

*Role modeling.* In addition to skill practice, people learn new behaviors by observing others. The strength of this learning through observation is directly related to the extent to which the person respects, admires, and can relate to the individual. Given the amount of interaction higher-risk offenders have with criminal and juvenile justice officials there is significant opportunity to role model desired prosocial attitudes and behaviors. In a study conducted by James Bonta, parole officers were observed during their one-on-one supervision sessions with parolees. Each officer activity was recorded and tabulated. The frequency with which the officers utilized behavioral-changing activities in their supervision sessions is shown in Table 9.7 (Bonta, Rugge, Scott, Bourgon, & Yessine, 2008).

Probation agencies are in a better position to provide effective role modeling when they recruit individuals who mirror the culture and gender composition of the offender population. Offenders are most likely to relate to those who possess attributes similar to their own. However, reflecting the probationer characteristics is not sufficient by itself; proper behaviors need to be demonstrated and relationships need to be built.

## Utilize Effective Relationship Engagement and Communication Skills

*Effective relationship engagement.* Focusing on the right issues with the right offenders and using behavioral techniques, to guide and redirect offenders, are critical to changing offender behavior. Equally important is the ability of the probation officer to establish a relationship with the offender. This was demonstrated by a meta-analysis conducted by Dowden and Andrews (2004), in which they identified five key corrections professionals' skills, four of which positively shape offenders' behavior (see Table 9.8).

Relationship building requires many of the components listed in the Dowden and Andrews study (2004), including mutual respect and

**Table 9.7** Use of role modeling behavior by parole officers

| Behavior Modeled | Use by Parole Officer |
|---|---|
| Pro-social modeling | 16.5% |
| Practice skills | 22.3% |
| Pro-social reinforcement | 68.0% |
| Antisocial discouragement | 20.4% |
| Relapse prevention | 16.5% |
| Homework assignment | 28.2% |

Source: Bonta et al. (2008).

liking, warmth, the ability to engage the offender, flexibility, a sense of humor, trustworthiness, sincerity, openness, and a nonjudgmental approach. The establishment of a relationship does not diminish enforcement of the court order or protection of the public. An officer who communicates clear rules and expectations up front and aligns them with the offender's prosocial goals (e.g., to be successfully discharged from probation and obtain a well-paying job) has a relationship advantage when applying a sanction or otherwise holding the offender accountable. Most individuals do not want to disappoint someone who treats them respectfully and is working to assist them in meeting their goals, and offenders are more likely to comply with sanctions under these circumstances.

*Communication skills.* Effective interactions are supported by communication techniques that reduce defensiveness and increase engagement in dialogue around change, and an increasing number of probation agencies are training staff in motivational interviewing (MI) techniques. These techniques, popularized by William Miller and Stephen Rollnick (2002), provide a client-centered, directive method of communication that seeks to enhance intrinsic motivation to change, by exploring and resolving ambivalence toward change. Certain interviewing and communication skills (e.g., rolling with resistance, developing discrepancy, and supporting self-efficacy) are stressed in this training. It emphasizes using affirmations, reducing critical exchanges, deflecting defensive and resistive exchanges, and reducing direct confrontation. It seeks to enhance offender motivation by

- Engaging the offender in his/her own plan;
- Identifying and using offender strengths; and
- Emphasizing the offender's own motivation/goals in addressing barriers to change.

Staff trained in these relationship skills and interviewing techniques are likely to glean more information from offenders and assist them in marshaling the internal motivation that is at the core of long-lasting change (Ginsburg, Mann, Rotgers, & Weekes, 2002; Harper & Hardy, 2000; Miller & Mount, 2001; Miller & Rollnick, 2002; Ryan & Deci, 2000). These encounters offer an opportunity to increase offenders' motivation to change and reframe and redirect offenders' thinking and actions.

There are many opportunities for probation personnel or staff to use these communication skills regardless of their specific role within the agency. Presentence investigation officers need these skills when interviewing offenders for purpose of preparing a court report. Case managers need it when developing a treatment plan. Others need it when working with a victim. Use of good communication skills extracts better information, helps resolve conflict, and enhances motivation. Opportunities to apply and hone these skills – responding to a probation violation, addressing conflict among offender family members, or handling an angry citizen's call – present themselves on a daily basis.

**Table 9.8** Five dimensions of effective correctional treatment

| Five Dimensions of Effective Correctional Treatment | |
|---|---|
| ***Effective use of authority*** | Firm but fair approach<br>Make rules clear, visible, understandable<br>Compliance through positive reinforcement<br>Keep focus of message on behavior, not person<br>Use of normal voice<br>Give choices with consequences<br>Guide offender toward compliance |
| ***Modeling and reinforcing pro-social attitudes*** | Positive/negative reinforcement<br>Model and rehearse pro-social behavior in concrete and vivid way<br>Immediate feedback on why behavior is approved/disapproved<br>Offender encouraged to think about why certain behavior is desirable<br>Role playing with increasingly difficult scenarios |
| ***Teaching concrete problem-solving skills*** | Engage offender in activities that increase satisfaction and rewards for non-criminal pursuits<br>Help offender develop a plan, clarify goals, generate options/ alternatives, evaluate options |
| ***Advocacy/Brokerage of community resource*** | Arrange the most appropriate correctional service<br>Speak on behalf of client at home, school, work or other |
| ***Relationship factors*** | Open, warm, genuine, and enthusiastic communication<br>Self-confident<br>Empathetic<br>Flexible<br>Mutual respect and liking<br>Directive, solution focused, structured, non-blaming |

Source: Dowden and Andrews (2004).

## Recommendations

Recommendations for probation agencies address the principles, policy and practice, interventions, and professional traits and skills that have been discussed throughout this chapter. They are not intended to be all inclusive. Rather, they highlight some of the areas that need attention in any probation agency seeking to implement evidence-based practices, for the purpose of reducing rearrest rates for those under supervision long after their discharge from the court system.

### Principles

The following recommendations provide broad guidance to community corrections agencies around the research-based principles designed to reduce risk of reoffense.

*Provide evidence-based practices training.* Training of all staff on effective ways to reduce recidivism supports a collective understanding of the direction of the agency and provides a knowledge context for staff to understand and support subsequent changes in policy and practice.

*Provide booster training.* Initial training will not be sufficient. For learning to best occur, the foundational evidence-based practices training should be followed by short booster training that reinforces the initial training and provides opportunity to practice the corresponding skills.

*Conduct action planning.* Agencies need a roadmap that identifies the core strategies, activities, and timelines to achieve sustained practice around risk reduction. Providing staff an opportunity to have input on how these principles could be implemented will give them meaningful involvement, in light of the barriers and realities of day-to-day job responsibilities.

## Policy and Practice Implications

The specific, practical actions that can be taken to improve the delivery of services that align with research findings include the following:

*Use empirically based risk/need assessment tools.* Select risk/need assessment tools that are empirically based, validated on the local offender population, and user-friendly. This will identify the risk level of the offender (low, medium, high, extreme high), the criminogenic needs that become the target of case planning, and responsivity factors (offender traits to take into account when selecting criminogenic need programming). Ideally, the agency should consider selecting

1. A pretrial assessment to provide guidance to the court as to release pending trial;
2. A brief screening device (to quickly identify those offenders at low risk who are not in need of further assessment);
3. A general risk/need assessment to identity risk and need; and
4. Specialized tools which are assessments for special populations. Some of these unique populations include sex offenders, domestic violence offenders, and psychopathic personalities.

*Provide assessment information to the court and other justice system stakeholders.* The risk/need information is useful at many levels ranging from pretrial release, diversion, prepleas, sentencing, violations, programming placement, and discharge. It is critically important that the assessments be acted on once completed. They should not just become a part of the case file, not to be viewed or used again. Risk is dynamic in nature, changing as the offender and the offender's circumstances change. Therefore, the offender should periodically be reassessed and risk/need information provided to any of the stakeholders that are making decisions related to that offender.

*Align the case plan with the assessment information.* Probation should use case plans that tie the risk and criminogenic need to the expectations of the probationer. Each criminogenic need should have a corresponding intervention unless the offender is deemed to be low risk.

*Realign supervision caseloads and workload standards based on risk.* Low-risk offenders require minimal supervision, if any. Extreme high-risk offenders should be placed on high surveillance caseloads. Medium- and high-risk offenders should receive the majority of the programming offerings. Probation agencies should consider how to best use their staff resources, based on offender risk and specialized knowledge required. Workload should reflect the type and level of staff expectations. Setting up specialized units, such as low-risk units that use kiosks, group reporting, or administrative techniques to manage the low-risk offender, should be considered.

*Ensure that violation and revocation procedures are structured according to the research.* A large proportion of jails and prisons are filled with offenders who have violated the terms and conditions of their supervision. Many of these revocations could have been handled effectively at the local level using techniques described in the research such as certainty, swiftness, and proportionality. Probation agencies should have a structured decision-making process to take into account the effective means of handling violations with the goal of redirecting the offender toward the kind of programming that will decrease the likelihood of rearrest.

*Provide a balanced approach using incentives and sanctions*. Probation should use both rewards and incentives for good behavior and sanctions for antisocial behavior to maximize behavioral change results. Sanctions do not need to be severe in order to be effective, unless the harmful behavior is egregious. Furthermore, agencies should seek to use more rewards and incentives than sanctions (a four to one ratio) to improve offender motivation to change. The probation agency should establish policies that give staff direction on which rewards and sanctions are appropriate for different circumstances.

*Provide quality assurance mechanisms*. Failure in an agency's change initiative is more often the result of poor implementation rather than of poor design. Written policies should be established that reflect the agency's commitment to quality control. Each major activity that leads to a behavioral change initiative should have a quality control aspect. The failure to measure this will mean that the adherence to the behavioral change model will be suspect, potentially falling victim to quality slippage resulting in poor outcomes. Implementing a continuous quality improvement plan is often neglected and can jeopardize the recidivism reduction goal. Some of the areas in need of quality control include proper administration of assessment tools, case planning, cognitive behavioral programming, and individual communication and risk reduction techniques during the one-on-one supervision sessions.

*Measure performance*. Data should be collected on an ongoing basis to determine if the activities designed to drive down offender risk are being performed in the manner intended and if they are achieving the desired outcomes. An agency cannot know if it is successful if it does not establish performance benchmarks and measure progress toward those targets.

## Interventions

Interventions are activities, interventions, and programs proven to reduce the likelihood that an offender with a particular profile will commit a new offense.

*Provide an array of evidence-based programs*. Offenders need an individualized approach, not "one size fits all." They have different risk levels and these risk levels should not be combined in programs. They have different criminogenic needs and there should be programs designed to address each of these needs. Additionally, offenders have unique characteristics (responsivity factors such as culture, language, gender, age, intelligence, mental health, or a learning disability) that require programs that are specialized or can be adapted to the needs of the program participants. Probation programs should assess the nature and number of offenders with the differing responsivity and criminogenic needs and ensure that any program gaps are filled in the continuum of services that are provided. Furthermore, programs that do not align with evidence-based practice should be modified or replaced.

*Ensure a preponderance of cognitive behavioral programming*. While a wide spectrum of programs needs to be available to address the variety of offender traits and needs, higher-risk offenders will most likely benefit from cognitive behavioral programs. These programs tend to address the more influential criminogenic needs such as antisocial beliefs, antisocial peers, and temperament or self-regulation difficulties.

*Make the one-on-one supervision session a cognitive behavioral intervention*. The probation supervision session has increasingly become a method of monitoring court conditions and less a method of behavioral change. Little therapeutic value is added. This is partly due to growing caseloads and a shift, over the past 2 decades, from a rehabilitation mindset to one of supervision and accountability. Clearly, the interaction between the probation officer and offender can have an effect on future crime. However, in order for that to happen, the officer must use the right techniques and focus on the right issues (Bonta et al., 2008). In addition, the probation officer needs tools and aids to help the offender build critical skills such as problem solving, conflict resolution, anger management, and emotional regulation. Increasingly, probation agencies, in an evidence-based environment, are providing training in these tools.

## Professional Traits and Skills

The following steps help address the agency's need to ensure that its personnel possess specific traits and skills deemed to be effective at influencing behavioral change:

*Ensure staff members working with medium- and high-risk offenders have core correctional practice skills.* Medium- and high-risk offenders are more likely to adopt long-term behavioral change when they are exposed to effective behavioral, communication, and relationship techniques rather than an emphasis on rule compliance and monitoring. Some of these techniques include the use of motivational interviewing, relationship skills, role modeling, effective authority, expressing disapproval for antisocial attitudes and behaviors, rewarding prosocial behaviors, encouraging offender choice and problem solving, and skill practice in the key criminogenic need areas.

*Revise the agency's recruitment processes.* Many probation staff members respond favorably to skill-based training designed to increase the effectiveness of the supervision interaction. Others will struggle with the training due to disagreements around their expected role or, perhaps, an inability or unwillingness to change. Agencies need to design their hiring practices in order to recruit the kind of staff who naturally possess, or are able to acquire, the requisite attitudes and skills for an evidence-based environment.

*Distribute caseload assignments based on skills required.* Different offender risk levels require different sets of staff activities. These activities are better performed when the staff skill aligns with what is expected. For example, probation officers with large caseloads made up of low-risk offenders are not expected to change behavior. They are tasked with the responsibility of monitoring compliance with court conditions with little to no face-to-face contact with the offenders. Staff with this responsibility should possess certain skills and traits, such as being highly organized, able to work with automation and other forms of technology, and being comfortable with little personal contact. Officers working with the extreme high-risk offender typically receive small caseloads and are expected to closely supervise a group of offenders who live in a criminal subculture and who may be volatile or disruptive. These officers often work closely with law enforcement and may ride along with police on evening shifts, checking on offenders. They need to be street savvy, not easily manipulated, and willing to enter high-crime communities to monitor their caseload. They often carry weapons and/or other protection devices. Officers working with medium- and high-risk offenders are expected to engage in behavioral change techniques and should have the kind of traits identified by Dowden and Andrews (2004), such as good communication and relationship skills, effective behavioral techniques, and an ability to broker community resources. These officers will perform their jobs more effectively if they have the requisite skills for the specific roles they are asked to play. Probation agencies large enough to assign caseloads based on staff traits can best take advantage of natural human resources strengths.

*Equip first-line supervisors with evidence-based coaching skills.* Technical assistance consultants and agency heads have increasingly come to the realization that the front line supervisor holds a key position in agency alignment with evidence-based practices. Direct service staff is more likely to perform the duties required if they are comfortable with the required skills. An effective supervisor provides coaching, encouragement, and guidance to ensure that these activities are performed, and will require special training and attention to ensure that the coaching role is performed adequately.

*Align the agency's promotional and performance appraisal process to reflect its commitment to evidence-based practices.* An agency's reward system for its personnel should reflect the vision and mission of the organization. Staff should understand that, in an evidence-based environment that seeks to reduce offenders' risk to reoffend, the agency promotes and rewards the personnel that move the agency mission along.

## Conclusion

### The Changing Role of Probation in an EBP Environment

Research is providing a growing body of evidence that is changing the way probation is expected to operate. The American Probation and Parole Association, in partnership with the American Corrections Association, has promulgated guidelines for probation accreditation, but there is, as yet, no single definitive standard for modern-day probation that takes into account the research-based risk reduction strategies. As probation agencies apply the research there are also changing expectations of today's probation officer, who is increasingly expected to understand what is or is not effective. In some cases, the research demonstrates that a common correctional practice is ineffective or even increases the likelihood that an offender may commit a future crime. Since probation seeks to support public safety, the application of evidence-based practices is becoming a "moral mandate." A professional who possesses knowledge that, when applied with fidelity, reduces harm, decreases the likelihood of future victimization, and increases the possibility of offender success is obliged to apply that knowledge.

## Appendix: Additional On-line Resources and Tools

Campbell Collaboration, Crime and Justice Group (Web site). http://www.campbellcollaboration.org/crime_and_justice/index.php, accessed August 1, 2009.

Fixsen, D. L., Naoom, S. F., Blase, K. A., Friedman R. M., & Wallace, F. (2005). *Implementation research: A synthesis of the literature.* Tampa, FL: University of South Florida, 2005. Available at http://www.fpg.unc.edu/~nirn/resources/publications/Monograph/pdf/Monograph_full.pdf, accessed August 1, 2009.

Latessa, E. (2009). *What works and what doesn't in reducing recidivism: The principles of effective intervention* (PowerPoint Presentation). http://www.dsgonline.com/Program_Logic_Model/San_Diego_TM/Day%201-Lunch-Latessa.ppt, accessed August 1, 2009.

Motiuk, L. L., & Serin, R. C. (2007). *Compendium 2000 on effective correctional programming*. Ottawa, On: Correctional Service Canada. Available at http://www.csc-scc.gc.ca/text/rsrch/compendium/2000/index-eng.shtml, accessed August 1, 2009.

Taxman, F. S., Shepardson, E. S., & Byrne, J. M. (2006). *Tools of the trade: A guide to incorporating science into practice.* Washington, DC: U.S. Department of Justice, National Institute of Corrections. Available at http://www.nicic.org/pubs/2004/020095.pdf, accessed August 1, 2009.

Washington State Institute for Public Policy (Web site). http://www.wsipp.wa.gov/, accessed August 1, 2009.

## References

Andrews, D. A., & Bonta, J. (1998). *The psychology of criminal conduct* (2nd ed.). Cincinnati, OH: Anderson.

Andrews, D. A., & Bonta, J. L. (2003). *The level of service inventory-revised. U.S. norms manual supplement.* Toronto, ON: Multi-Health Systems.

Andrews, D. A., & Bonta, J. (2006). *The psychology of criminal conduct* (4th ed.). Newark, NJ: Anderson.

Andrews, D. A., & Bonta, J. (2007). *Risk-need-responsivity model for offender assessment and rehabilitation*. Ottawa, ON: Public Safety Canada.

Andrews, D. A., Bonta, J., & Wormith, S. (2006). The recent past and near future of risk and/or need assessment. *Crime and Delinquency, 52*(1), 7–27.

Andrews, D. A., Dowden, C., & Gendreau, P. (1999). *Clinically relevant and psychologically informed approaches to reduced reoffending: A meta-analytic study of human service, risk, need, responsivity, and other concerns in justice contexts*. Unpublished manuscript, Carleton University, Ottawa, ON.

Aos, S., Miller, M., & Drake, E. (2006a). *Evidence-based adult corrections programs: What works and what does not*. Olympia, WA: Washington State Institute for Public Policy.

Aos, S., Miller, M., & Drake, E. (2006b). *Evidence-based public policy options to reduce future prison construction, criminal justice costs, and crime rates*. Olympia, WA: Washington State Institute for Public Policy.

Augustus, J. (1852). *A report of the labors of John Augustus*. Boston: Wright & Hasty, Printers. (Republished in 1984 by the American Probation and Parole Association, Lexington, KY.)

Bandura, A. (1969). *Principles of behavior modification*. New York: Holt, Rinehart and Winston.

Bandura, A. (1977). *Social learning theory*. New York: General Learning Press.

Barnoski, R. (2004). *Outcome evaluation of Washington State's research-based programs for juvenile offenders*. Olympia, WA: Washington State Institute for Public Policy.

Bogue, B., Campbell, N., Carey, M., Clawson, E., Faust, D., Florio, K., et al. (2004). *Implementing evidence-based practice in community corrections: The principles of effective intervention*. Washington, DC: U.S. Department of Justice, National Institute of Corrections.

Bonta, J., Rugge, T., Scott, T., Bourgon, G., & Yessine, A. (2008). Exploring the black box of community supervision. *Journal of Offender Rehabilitation, 47*(3), 248–270.

Bonta, J., Wallace-Capretta, S., Rooney, J., & McAnoy, K. (2002). An outcome evaluation of a restorative justice alternative to incarceration. *Justice Review, 5*(4), 319–338.

Bourgon, G., & Armstrong, B. (2005). Transferring the principles of effective treatment into a "real world" prison setting. *Criminal Justice and Behavior, 32*(1), 3–25.

Bureau of Justice Statistics. (n.d.). Adults on probation, in jail or in prison, and on parole, United States, 1980–2006. *Sourcebook of Criminal Justice Statistics Online*. Accessed at http://www.albany.edu/sourcebook/pdf/t612006.pdf

Bureau of Justice Statistics. (2006). Adults on probation, in jail or in prison, and on parole, United States. 1980–2006. *Sourcebook of criminal justice statistics online*. Accessed at http://www.albany.edu/sourcebook/pdf/t612006.pdf, accessed on August 8, 2010.

Bureau of Justice Statistics. (2008). *Correctional surveys (The annual probation survey, National prisoner statistics program, Annual survey of jails, and Annual parole survey)* as presented in Correctional Populations in the United States, Prisoners in 2008, and Probation and Parole in the United States.

Burrell, W. D. (2006). Issue paper on caseload standards for probation and parole. *Perspectives, 31*(2), 37–41.

Camp, C. G. (2003). *The corrections yearbook—Adult corrections 2002*. Middletown, CT: The Criminal Justice Institute, Inc.

Carey, M. (2010). *Coaching packet: Shaping offender behavior. FY 2007 Presidential prisoner reentry initiative training and technical assistance program* (Vol. 8). Silver Spring, MD: Center for Effective Public Policy.

Castonguay, L. G., & Beutler, L. E. (2006). Common and unique principles of therapeutic change: What do we know and what do we need to know. In L. G. Castonguay & L. E. Beutler (Eds.), *Principles of therapeutic change that work* (pp. 353–369). New York: Oxford University Press.

Circuit Court of Cook County. (2006). Cook County adult probation supervision policy #09.16. *Circuit Court of Cook county adult probation policy manual*. Chicago: Author.

Clear, T. R., & Sumter, M. T. (2002). Prisoners, prison, and religion: Religion and adjustment to prison. *Journal of Offender Rehabilitation, 35*, 127–159.

Cullen, F. T., & Gendreau, P. (2000). Assessing correctional rehabilitation: Policy, practice, and prospects. In J. Horney (Ed.), *NIJ criminal justice 2000: Policies, processes, and decisions of the criminal justice system* (pp. 109–176). Washington, DC: U.S. Department of Justice.

Domurad, F., & Carey, M. (2010). *Coaching packet: Implementing evidence-based practices. FY 2007 Presidential prisoner reentry initiative training and technical assistance program* (Vols. 8–14). Silver Spring, MD: Center for Effective Public Policy.

Dowden, C. (1998). *A meta-analytic examination of the risk, need and responsivity principles and their importance within the rehabilitation debate*. Unpublished master's thesis, Carleton University, Ottawa, ON.

Dowden, C., & Andrews, D. A. (2004). The importance of staff practice in delivering effective correctional treatment: A meta-analytic review of core correctional practice. *International Journal of Offender Therapy and Comparative Criminology, 48*(2), 203–214.

Dutton, D., & Sonkin, D. (2003). *Intimate violence: Contemporary treatment innovations*. New York: Haworth Trauma and Maltreatment Press.

Egelko, S., Galanter, M., Dermatis, H., & DeMaio, C. (1998). Evaluation of a multisystems model for treating perinatal cocaine addiction. *Journal of Substance Abuse Treatment, 15*(3), 251–259.

Eisenberg, M., Bryl, J., & Fabelo, T. (2009). *Travis county community impact supervision project: Analyzing initial outcomes*. Austin, TX: Council of State Governments, Justice Center.

Emrick, C. D., Tonigang, J. S., Montgomery, H., & Little, L. (1993). *Alcoholics anonymous: Opportunities and alternatives*. New Brunswick, NJ: Alcohol Research Documentation, Inc., Rutgers Center of Alcohol Studies.

Galanter, M. (1993). *Network therapy for alcohol and drug abuse: A new approach in practice*. New York: Basic Books.

Gendreau, P. (1996). The principles of effective intervention with offenders. In A. T. Harland (Ed.), *Choosing correctional options that work: Defining the demand and evaluating the supply* (pp. 117–130). Newbury Park, CA: Sage.

Gendreau, P., & Goggin, C. (1995). *Principles of effective correctional programming with offenders*. St. John, NB: Center for Criminal Justice Studies and Department of Psychology, University of Brunswick (Monograph).

Gendreau, P., Goggin, C., & Little, T. (1996). *Predicting adult offender recidivism: What works!* (User Report No. 1996-07). Ottawa, ON: Solicitor General of Canada.

Gendreau, P., Little, T., & Goggin, C. (1996). A meta-analysis of adult offender recidivism: What works? *Criminology, 34*(4), 575–607.

Gendreau, P., & Paparozzi, M. A. (1995). Examining what works in community corrections. *Corrections Today, 57*(1), 28–31.

Ginsburg, J. I. D., Mann, R. E., Rotgers, F., & Weekes, J. R. (2002). Motivational Interviewing with criminal justice populations. In W. R. Miller & S. Rollnick (Eds.), *Motivational interviewing: Preparing people for change* (2nd ed.). New York: Guilford Press.

Glaze, L. E., & Bonczar, T. (2009). *Probation and parole in the United States, 2008*. Washington, DC: Bureau of Justice Statistics.

Glaze, L. E., & Palla, S. (2005). *Probation and parole in the United States, 2004* (Vol. 6). Washington, DC: Bureau of Justice Statistics.

Grasmack, H. G., & Bryjak, G. J. (1980). The deterrent effect of perceived severity of punishment. *Social Forces, 59*, 471–491.

Harper, R., & Hardy, S. (2000). An evaluation of motivational interviewing as a method of intervention with clients in a probation setting. *British Journal of Social Work, 30*, 393–400.

Higgins, S. T., & Silverman, K. (Eds.). (1999). *Motivating behavior change among illicit-drug abusers: Research on contingency management interventions*. Washington, DC: American Psychological Association.

Meyers, R. J., Miller, W. R., Smith, J. E., & Tonnigan, S. (2002). A randomized trial of two methods for engaging treatment refusing drug users through concerned significant others. *Journal of Consulting and Clinical Psychology, 70*(5), 1182–1185.

Meyers, R. J., & Smith, J. E. (1997). Getting off the fence: Procedures to engage treatment-resistant drinkers. *Journal of Substance Abuse Treatment, 14*, 467–472.

Miller, W. R., & Mount, K. A. (2001). A small study of training in motivational interviewing: Does one workshop change clinician and client behavior? *Behavioural and Cognitive Psychotherapy, 29*(4), 457–471.

Miller, W., & Rollnick, S. (2002). *Motivational interviewing: Preparing people for change*. New York: Guilford Press.

National Center on Addiction and Substance Abuse. (1998). *Behind bars: Substance abuse and America's prison population*. New York: Columbia University.

National Institute of Corrections. (2010). *A framework for evidence-based decision making in local criminal justice systems* (3rd ed.). Washington, DC: National Institute of Corrections.

Nichols, J., & Ross, H. L. (1990). Effectiveness of legal sanctions in dealing with drinking drivers. *Alcohol, Drugs, and Driving, 6*(2), 33–60.

O'Connor, T., & Perryclear, M. (2002). Prison religion in action and its influence on offender rehabilitation. *Journal of Offender Rehabilitation, 35*(3/4), 11–33.

Paternoster, R. (1989). Decisions to participate in and desist from four types of common delinquency: Deterrence and the rational choice perspective. *Law and Society Review, 23*(1), 7–40.

Paternoster, R., Brame, R., Bachman, R., & Sherman, L. W. (1997). Do fair procedures matter? The effect of procedural justice on spouse assault. *Law and Society Review, 31*, 163–204.

Pew Center on the States. (2009). *One in 31: The long reach of American corrections* (Vol. 2). Washington, DC: The Pew Charitable Trusts.

Rhine, E. (1993). *Reclaiming offender accountability: Intermediate sanctions for probation and parole violators*. Laurel, MD: American Correctional Association.

Rossman, S., & Winterfield, L. (2009). *Coaching packet: Measuring the impact of reentry effort,* 20. *FY 2007 Presidential prisoner reentry initiative training and technical assistance program*. Silver Spring, MD: Center for Effective Public Policy.

Ryan, R. M., & Deci, E. L. (2000). Self-determination theory and the facilitation of intrinsic motivation, social development, and well-being. *American Psychologist, 55*, 68–78.

Shapiro, C., & Schwartz, M. (2001). Coming home: Building on family connections. *Corrections Management Quarterly, 5*(3), 52–61.

Smith, P., Goggin, C., & Gendreau, P. (2002). *The effects of prison sentences and intermediate sanctions on recidivism: Age, gender and race*. Ottawa, ON: Solicitor General of Canada, Corrections Research Branch.

Taxman, F. S. (1999). Proactive supervision: Supervision as crime prevention. *The Journal of Offender Monitoring, 12*(2), 25–26.

Taxman, F. (2008). No illusions: Offender and organizational change in Maryland's proactive community supervision efforts. *Criminology and Public Policy, 7*(2), 275–302.

Taxman, F., Yancey, C., & Bilanin, J. (2006). *Proactive community supervision in Maryland: Changing offender outcomes*. Baltimore: Division of Parole and Probation.

Tonry, M. (1996). *Sentencing matters*. New York: Oxford University Press.

Trotter, C. (2006). *Working with involuntary clients: A guide to practice*. Thousand Oaks, CA: Sage.

Tyler, T. R. (1990). *Why people obey the law*. New Haven, CT: Yale University Press.

Von Hirsch, A. (1993). *Censure and sanctions*. Oxford, UK: Oxford University Press.

# Case Management for Substance Abusing Offenders

# 10

Pamela F. Rodriguez

**Abstract**

As many as 80% of offenders test positive for drug use while only 15% have access to treatment. Recidivism rates for drug involved offenders exceed 65%. Criminal justice system expectations for rehabilitation relative to drug use are high and consequences of treatment failure are even higher. Case management has been employed to increase offender access to treatment and improve retention in services. This chapter examines case management effectiveness in that context and specifically reviews the TASC model of offender case management. The chapter concludes with recommendations for practice and further research.

**Keywords**

Case management • Substance abusing offenders • Treatment access • Treatment retention • Recidivism • TASC

## Introduction

Between 50–80% of arrestees test positive for drug use (Office of National Drug Control Policy, 2009) while only 15% of those who need treatment actually have access to it (Substance Abuse and Mental Health Services Administration, 2007). In addition, only 50% of those eligible for treatment are admitted to treatment and attend their first treatment session (Ebener & Kilmer, 2003). While more than 40% of people in substance abuse treatment are involved in the justice system, only 41% of criminal justice participants complete treatment (Treatment Episode Data Set [TEDS], 2005). Furthermore, recidivism rates for drug involved offenders on probation or parole exceed 65% (OJP, BJS, Probation and Parole, 2009 cited in U.S. Department of Justice, 2009). These data clearly demonstrate the need for substance abuse treatment. It is also clear that getting into and completing treatment is not the norm. Consequently, our challenge is to ensure that substance abusing offenders have access to, enter, and complete treatment.

The single largest "user" of publicly funded substance abuse treatment is the justice system (TEDS, 2005). However, this use has been

P.F. Rodriguez (✉)
TASC, Inc., Chicago, IL 60642, USA
e-mail: prodriguez@tasc-il.org

C. Leukefeld et al. (eds.), *Handbook of Evidence-Based Substance Abuse Treatment in Criminal Justice Settings*, Issues in Children's and Families' Lives 11,
DOI 10.1007/978-1-4419-9470-7_10, © Springer Science+Business Media, LLC 2011

uneven. Policy changes have affected funding levels, service location (prison or community), and goals (treatment or rehabilitation). For over 40 years, researchers and practitioners have been working to "bridge" the treatment and justice systems, to increase the interface and integration of those two systems, and to improve outcomes of both systems for substance-using offenders (See Inciardi, McBride, & Rivers, 1996).

Case management is one of the approaches developed to improve the linkage between the justice system and the treatment system. People who need treatment are identified in jail or court, mandated to treatment and assigned a case manager (often a probation officer) who identifies a program and refers the client to services including substance abuse treatment. The presumptions underlying this approach are that mandated treatment referral provides access to treatment and treatment success reduces criminal activity. While participating in treatment, a client's compliance is monitored and reported to the court, enabling the court to respond to a client's behavior in a timely manner to reinforce treatment objectives and protect public safety.

Case management seeks to enhance treatment engagement and retention, primarily by removing barriers to participation and assisting in the management of client crises. Case managers, for example, can assist with housing, entitlements, transportation, and legal issues so clients are less distracted by challenges of daily living and can maintain a focus on treatment. This chapter examines case management in the context of the criminal justice system, with a particular focus on the Treatment Alternatives for Safe Communities (TASC) model of offender case management. The chapter concludes with recommendations for evidence-based practice and the further development of specialized case management for substance-abusing offenders.

## A Brief History of Case Management

The overall purpose of case management is to improve access to care and to ensure continuity of care (Encyclopedia of Mental Disorders, 2009 cited in Case Management, 2009). Case management is an important supplement to traditional substance abuse treatment since it provides "wrap around" support and services not generally available in a treatment program. The treatment system has generally embraced case management as a means to improve treatment retention and completion. Criminal justice expectations for case management include a decrease in drug use, criminal behaviors, and recidivism.

The roots of case management are found in social work, growing out of the movement to deinstitutionalize the mentally ill in the 1960s. The need to connect patients to community-based service agencies and monitor their participation in services is what guides case management functions including assessment, service planning, linking to community-based services, monitoring progress, and client advocacy (NASW Standards for Social Work Case Management, 2009). While case management was evolving for the mentally ill, courts and probation services were facing growing numbers of nonviolent substance abusers. At the federal level, the Nixon administration declared War on Drugs that focused on the growing number of heroin addicts in larger US cities. One goal of this effort was to divert nonviolent offenders into community-based drug treatment. In response, the community drug treatment system was expanding the number and type of programs in larger communities with methadone maintenance, inpatient residential, detoxification, and outpatient treatment. The increasing numbers of offenders, some with multiple and complex problems presented challenges for both the treatment system and the justice system. Case management was introduced to respond.

Substance abuse case management programs focus on improving a client's functioning as well as systems changes, including cost savings. When case managers intervene at the client level, effectiveness measures include accessing and retention in substance abuse treatment, decreased substance use, improved daily living skills, reduced criminal activity, and increased health and/or functioning. At the systems level, measures include access to care, service utilization, continuity of care within and among providers, systemic barriers to access, costs associated with hospitalizations or incarcerations, and recidivism.

Client level interventions include assessing the client's strengths as well as needs in major life areas including physical and emotional health, living environment, education/work, and family and other supports. Together with the client, the social worker develops an individualized service plan that "spells out" the roles and responsibilities of the client, social worker, family, and other service providers which can include an array of possible services needed by substance-abusing treatment clients.

It can be a daunting task to assess, organize, and address individual client needs. Most service systems are fragmented and many clients require services from separate systems. As a result, the social work case manager also intervenes at the systems level. In addition to advocacy to increase client service access, case management involves resource development, removing systemic barriers to care, agency policy formation, and social action (NASW Standards for Social Work Case Management, 2009). Core functions are generally consistent across case management models, although tailored to fit the specific client population served. For example, for substance-abusing offenders, case managers use standardized assessment tools such as the Addiction Severity Index (McLellan, Weinstein, Shen, Kendig, & Levine, 2005) and/or the American Society of Addiction Medicine's Patient Placement Criteria (Mee-Lee, 2001) to determine the needed level of care. Sanctions and incentives to enhance compliance can also be incorporated into supervision strategies to improve outcomes. Manual directed service delivery, quality assurance activities, and measures of fidelity are promising ways to providing needed structure and consistency to program delivery.

## Case Management Models for Substance Abusers

Vanderplasschen, Wolf, Rapp, and Broekaert (2007) describe four promising case management models for working with substance abusers: (1) the brokerage/generalist model, (2) the assertive community treatment/intensive case management model, (3) the clinical/rehabilitation model, and (4) the strengths-based case management model.

The brokerage model is a brief case management approach in which case managers help clients identify needs and broker supportive services usually during one or two sessions (Substance Abuse and Mental Health Services Administration [SAMHSA], 1998). This model is similar to an Employee Assistance Program (EAP). An expanded version of the brokerage model is called the generalist model in which the case manager supports additional client involvement. The focus of this model is care coordination. As services become more specialized and service systems more complex, the demand for coordination increases.

The assertive community treatment model can include a team of appropriate public safety and public health representatives including a case manager to provide assertive outreach and direct counseling services, skill building, and crisis interventions. Intensive case management incorporates these same principles but without a team and with slightly smaller case loads. A distinguishing characteristic of this model is comprehensive outreach. For example, as client problem severity increases and treatment resources decline, the demand for case management increases. Clinical and rehabilitation models combine case management functions, including accessing resources, with counseling and other rehabilitative activities. In this model, the case manager, serving as the primary caregiver, acts as a role model, problem solver, and therapist, reducing the number of interventions by others. Strengths-based case management (SBCM) focuses on client strengths, self-direction, and informal help networks rather than professional or agency services. Clients "lead" the process of assessment, goal setting, and service prioritization. This model focuses on client strengths and empowerment and reduces case manager's role by assuming that the client will take responsibility as primary decision maker.

Case management services can span a continuum from information and phone referrals to more formal service linkage such as counseling and training. Case management can be an adjunct service offered in addition to other services, or can compensate for the lack of appropriate services. Some case managers are imbedded in the criminal justice system or in the treatment systems as a provider. In these models, the case manager reports to the judge or the treatment provider with services as an adjunct to the agency's primary function. Other case management approaches are independent of both systems with all the case management functions provided outside the systems, often as a central intake unit or as an intermediary between systems, clients, and services. In these models, the case manager relies on advocacy and collaboration to negotiate access and influence treatment plans and definitions of success.

Case management caseloads can vary widely with intensive supervision caseloads ranging from 10 to 15 clients per case manager, while caseloads of 50–75 are not uncommon. Caseloads in excess of 100 cannot focus on service delivery and should not be used with high-risk populations such as substance abusers. The Assertive Community Treatment (ACT) model (Vanderplasschen et al., 2007) includes a team of 6 or more to serve no more than 15 clients. Caseload size drives decisions about the level of services and/or beliefs about the role and function of the case manager. Case managers can refer clients to programs and services using a list of community services or a case manager may work in the context of a formal negotiated memorandum of understanding which determines referrals, referral acceptance, and communication. Case managers may have control over financial resources and be able to purchase client services. Each of these case management characteristics parallels the type of services, protocol, and goals of the case management model. Goals are shaped by who purchases the service, the referral agency, the clients served, and/or the philosophy of the case management agency.

## Case Management with Substance Abusers

Research suggests two main areas of case management effectiveness: (1) increased service linkages and (2) treatment retention (SAMHSA, 1998). Treatment retention is associated with better outcomes and treatment is more likely to be successful when a client's other problems are addressed concurrently (SAMHSA, 1998). For example, it is easier to participate in treatment, if a client has a place to live and reasonable transportation to get to treatment.

Case management helps meet these needs by reducing barriers to access and participation. Results from a randomized trial of opiate abusers seeking treatment indicate that almost twice as many in the case-managed group accessed treatment than those in the comparison group (Mejta, Bokos, Mickenberg, Maslar, & Senay, 1997). Of those clients who entered treatment, the average length of time to enter treatment was 17 days for the case-managed group and 188 days for the comparison group. When case managers had vouchers to purchase treatment, linkages increased dramatically, suggesting that a primary barrier to treatment participation is limited resources rather than low client motivation. In another study which compared motivational interviewing and SBCM on service and treatment linkage, motivational interviewing was not effective in improving linkage rates (Rapp et al., 2008). However, SBCM was effective in improving service linkage compared to the usual standard of care. Specifically, service linkage for participants in the SBCM group was 55% compared to 38.7% in the standard care group. However, linkage rates by treatment modality varied within the SBCM group, with residential linkage at 46.3%, outpatient drug free at 41.2%, and methadone maintenance at 58.4.%.

In a meta-analysis of peer-reviewed case management research published between 1993 and 2003, Vanderplasschen et al. (2007) reported that the evidence for case management effectiveness is mixed with a differential effect for intensive case management and assertive community treatment for homeless and dually diagnosed substance abusers. Additionally, SBCM and the generalist model were found to be relatively effective with substance abusers. Positive effects were reported as reduced use of inpatient services, increased use of community-based services, higher treatment retention, improved quality of life, and higher client satisfaction, which is consistent with previous studies and with the purpose of case management. However, drug use and psychosocial functioning outcomes were less consistent, but mediated by treatment retention.

In a review of 15 randomized clinical case management trials, Hesse, Vanderplasschen, Rapp, Broekaert, and Fridell (2009) reported that case management effectively linked people with substance abuse treatment and other community services when compared with treatment as usual. However, the seven studies which included illicit drug use did not report a clear reduction in drug or alcohol use. Service linkages varied across studies, which was influenced by the availability of community services, the case management model, how effectively the model was applied, and the integration of case management into the local services network. When the effect sizes of intensive, brokerage, and SBCM were compared, the largest effect was found for SBCM, followed by brokerage and intensive case management.

Research on the effectiveness of case management has consistently reported a positive relationship between case management and treatment retention (Siegal, Li, & Rapp, 2002), although the impact on client recovery and recidivism rates might be indirect, through treatment access, retention, reengagement, and duration of aftercare. For example, a veterans study that focused on the extent to which treatment case management would improve treatment retention and whether continuing aftercare would reduce criminality, found that case-managed clients stayed longer in aftercare, which was associated with reduced self-reported criminal behaviors (Siegal et al., 2002). Similar results were found for the retention of pregnant substance-using women in treatment (Laken & Ager, 1996). Consequently, case management can help to keep people in treatment longer and can improve treatment and related client outcomes.

While the case management research literature is not large, services linkage and treatment retention are improved with case management. Effects are strongest when case management is manualized with well-trained staff and when fidelity to the model is monitored (Vanderplasschen, Rapp, Wolf, & Broekaert, 2004). If increasing access to and retention in treatment are treatment goals, case management is a viable strategy. When examining the effect case management has on changing drug use or criminal behavior, comparisons have generally focused on case management compared to substance abuse treatment. However, case management without treatment cannot replace treatment. Case management is an enhancement or adjunct to treatment which improves treatment. Case management is not primary treatment for substance users, but increases treatment access and treatment retention to enhance recovery. Case management also increases the probability of completing treatment and other services.

## TASC

Originally known as Treatment Alternatives to Street Crime, TASC is a case management intervention strategy focused on substance-abusing offenders in the justice system that links the coercive authority of the criminal justice system with community treatment interventions. The goal is to stop the revolving door of addiction, crime, arrest, incarceration, release, and return to drug use (Encyclopedia of Drugs, Alcohol, and Addictive Behavior, 2009 cited in Treatment Alternatives to Street Crime [TASC], 2009). Nonviolent offenders with substance use disorders are diverted from further penetration into the criminal justice system when TASC case management is used as the bridge to community provider systems.

The potential benefits of treatment for drug-using offenders have been supported, but achieving these benefits requires a strategy for ensuring that drug-using offenders are identified, receive appropriate treatment, are adequately supervised to detect drug use or crime, and appropriate interventions are used. The TASC model was developed in 1972 through the mutual efforts of the White House Special Action Office for Drug Abuse, the Law Enforcement Assistance

Administration, and the National Institute of Drug Abuse. The purpose of TASC is to stop the persistent and recurring criminality associated with drug or alcohol dependence, and to break the cycle of addiction for the nonviolent, substance-abusing offender (Inciardi et al., 1996). TASC emerged from an analysis of the criminal justice system which found that many drug-addicted arrestees were released on bail while awaiting trial and were likely to continue to commit crimes. The original focus was on pretrial diversion to reduce the drug use and criminal behavior of drug-using offenders, shift offenders from a system of deterrence and punishment to treatment and rehabilitation, and divert drug-involved offenders to community-based treatment to limit criminal labeling and avoid learning criminal behavior that occurs in prisons (Encyclopedia of Drugs, Alcohol, and Addictive Behavior, 2009 cited in TASC, 2009).

TASC provides an objective and effective bridge between differing philosophies of the justice system and the community treatment system. The justice system benefits with reduced incarceration costs and recidivism as well as increased access to rehabilitation services and behavior change. The treatment system benefits from the leverage of the criminal justice system to motivate and retain clients in treatment. TASC works with law enforcement as well as court and corrections officials to identify the substance-abusing offender and to help determine who enters the criminal justice system. TASC incorporates offender screening in jail or on bond to identify the seriousness of drug or alcohol dependence and to establish an objective process for determining the likelihood of rehabilitation with appropriate treatment. TASC reports assessment findings to the court, and the court, upon a review of the findings and considering the seriousness of the offense, may order the individual to TASC. TASC then assumes responsibility for making arrangements to procure medical, social, or psychological services. TASC also monitors client adherence to treatment plans and keeps the court and probation officials informed about client participation, to enhance community treatment retention. TASC case management and systems interventions can be provided at all points in the criminal justice process.

TASC's core criminal justice case management activities include engaging the client in the treatment process, assessing the client's needs, developing a service plan, linking the client with appropriate services, monitoring client progress, intervening with sanctions when necessary and advocating for the client as needed (Healey, 1999). TASC accomplishes these functions differently depending on local needs, resources, and system goals.

## The TASC Model

TASC, as an independent case management model, is separate from community treatment services and distinct from probation or parole supervision. It represents a fully defined broker/generalist case management model. A TASC case manager, as a member of the treatment and supervision team, is responsible for treatment access, retention, and recidivism reduction. As a member of multiple teams, the TASC case manager serves as the client advocate, by bridging system goals, language, and philosophy. At treatment team meetings, the TASC case manager ensures that concerns about public safety and accountability are considered. At criminal justice team meetings, treatment and other service-provider needs are addressed. Since a client can participate in many systems, it is clear that it is often impossible for one team meeting to include all the potential players involved in a client's life. The TASC case manager is the bridge to all those systems.

TASC is client centered. At the same time, it addresses barriers to access and increasing opportunities for offender substance abuse treatment. Clients generally volunteer to participate in developing their service plan, priorities, and strategies. Although mandated to participate in TASC, the court does not determine the treatment plan. The TASC case manager is the expert upon whom the court relies (Getty, 1989). Systems coordination provides the overarching support from the justice, treatment, and other social services systems to effectively manage substance-involved persons from the justice system (Robertson, 1989).

## Effectiveness of TASC: A Promising Case Management Intervention

A comprehensive study of TASC was conducted by Anglin, Longshore, and Turner (1999). At that time, more than 125 TASC programs were located in 25 states which differed by treatment, criminal justice systems, and clients. Five sites were selected for evaluation based on the size of the client pool, fidelity to TASC's Ten Critical Elements, and the number of high-risk offenders. Random assignment was used at two sites with a quasi-experimental design in the three other sites to compare TASC to an alternative probation intervention. Outcomes were assessed in three domains: treatment services received, drug use, and criminal recidivism. When compared to the other interventions to which control/comparison offenders were assigned, TASC provided more treatment services, suggesting that TASC is an effective strategy for improving treatment (Anglin et al., 1999). On one or more measures of drug use, TASC programs outperformed the other interventions at three of the five sites. Overall, TASC case management reduced drug use and drug-related crime. However, favorable outcomes for property crimes, new arrests, or technical violations were not reported by site (Anglin et al., 1999). While TASC outcomes across sites were consistently favorable, they were often modest or confined to high-risk offenders.

Another study which examined the effect of case management on risky sex among drug users included three sites with a quasi-experimental design (Longshore, Turner, & Anglin, 1998). Findings from this study were that TASC case management reduced risky sex among drug users with multiple problem behaviors. Additionally, when TASC was compared with probation as usual, a higher percentage of TASC clients accessed at least one type of service which was usually drug treatment. For example, in Chicago 70% of TASC clients received substance abuse treatment, compared to 28% on probation. A study in Toledo, Ohio, reported that subjects who successfully completed TASC were significantly less likely to be rearrested 12 months after discharge (Ventura & Lambert, 2004). However, an evaluation of Colorado's TASC program which served parolees found that TASC had no increased benefit to reduce recidivism (Owens et al., 1997). This finding is consistent with other studies which suggest that the major impact of TASC is on improving services linkage and reducing drug use. Consequently, the TASC case management model impact on recovery and rehabilitation is associated with the quality and nature of the treatment available.

With the experience of TASC in identifying substance-abusing justice system clients, bridging systems, linking clients to care, with changing demographics, and the increasing demands of the justice system, the TASC model has expanded to the mentally ill offender, veteran offenders, and other high-risk/high-need special populations. Initial results are encouraging. For example, one study which examined the TASC model combined with a mental health court reported significant reductions in arrests when compared to arrests in the previous year (Braude, 2005). Specifically, at baseline participants averaged 3.6 arrests, while in the year after enrollment 71% of the clients were not arrested, with an average of less than one arrest per participant. Days incarcerated were also reduced from an average of 107 days per participant to 10 days. The TASC model has also been used at post-incarceration community reentry, with similar reports of successful coordinated care, service linkage, and retention (Downey & Braude, 2005). Nissen and Kraft (2007) reported that, "The strength of the TASC model is that it laid the groundwork for a more widespread acceptance of a justice-centered systemic response to substance abuse problems, which if properly acknowledged and addressed concurrently with justice interventions could decrease recidivism for those who were able to access and complete alcohol and drug abuse treatment."

## Implications for Practice and Research

Treatment resources for publicly funded clients are scarce. There is neither a single system that triages and prioritizes criminal justice clients to enter substance abuse treatment nor are there standard criteria to determine what type of treatment a criminal justice client should receive. With a single gatekeeper for nonviolent criminal justice referrals to substance abuse treatment, costly fragmentation and inefficiencies could be reduced. Clients could be matched to appropriate treatment and other services, with funding "following" the client. This "network management" could further impact the recovery of, and reduce recidivism for, criminal justice clients.

Case management can increase access to care and retention in services, for substance abusers and reduces costly incarcerations and hospitalizations, and can positively affect recidivism (Braude, 2005). Current research is encouraging. However, additional research is needed, particularly research that better understands outcomes and implementation. Pressure continues to better manage substance-abusing offenders, increase recovery, reduce recidivism, and reduce costs. Case management programs, like TASC, can contribute to these objectives with clear protocols for client matching and service delivery, for staff training and supervision, for data collection, and for evaluation. Continued efforts to revise and refine service delivery models are essential and include the following:

1. Refining the definitions, goals, and expectations of case management models for substance-using offenders. Case management is currently a loosely defined term, which incorporates a broad range of activities in a variety of settings with different outcomes. This variation makes evaluations of client access, retention, recovery, and recidivism challenging.
2. Examining the impact of case management on systems integration including the number of clients served, decreased barriers to service access, increased service utilization, increased retention rates, improved recovery rates, decreased recidivism, improved collaborations, funding levels, and cross-system support for treatment goals and recovery.
3. Clarifying client types which are best suited for case management. Current evidence suggests a focus on high-risk and high-need clients.
4. Examining the impact of client/treatment matching. If case management increases access to and retention in well-matched substance abuse treatment, then case management is successful.
5. Clarifying differences between case management and treatment outcomes and evaluating case management in that context. If the goal of case management is to increase access to and retention in treatment, then outcomes should be measured in terms of access and retention.
6. Manualizing case management approaches to facilitate fidelity and make evaluation possible.
7. Defining and evaluating independent and "imbedded" case management by assessing the differences in treatment access, continuity of care, access to and use of ancillary services, use of sanctions/incentives, and criminal justice recidivism.
8. Considering the evolution of case management as "network management" with responsibility for aligning outcomes of different agencies, developing funding strategies, selecting providers, and improving system function.

## References

Anglin, M., Longshore, D., & Turner, S. (1999). Treatment alternatives to street crime: An evaluation of five programs. *Criminal Justice and Behavior, 26*(2), 168–195.

Braude, L. (2005, September/October). *The Cook County Mental Health Court: Development, implementation, and initial implications*. Offender Substance Abuse Report, Civic Research Institute, Vol. V, No. 5 pp. 67–76.

Downey, K., & Braude, L. (2005, January/February). *The case management role in clinical reentry management*. Offender Substance Abuse Report, Civic Research Institute, Vol. V, No. 1 pp. 3–7.

Ebener, P., & Kilmer, B. (2003). *Linking drug users with treatment: Admissions counselors describe the barriers*. Santa Monica, CA: Drug Policy Research Center, Rand Corporation.

Encyclopedia of Mental Disorders. (2009). *Case management*. Retrieved August 18, 2009, from www.minddisorders.com/Br-Del/Case-management.html

Getty, M. (1989). Alternative sentencing for the alcohol/drug defendant. *Southern Illinois University Law Journal, 14*, 1–26.

Healey, K. (1999, February). *Case management in the criminal justice system*. Washington, DC: U.S. Department of Justice, Office of Justice Programs, National Institute of Justice.

Hesse, M., Vanderplasschen, W., Rapp, R., Broekaert, E., & Fridell, M. (2009). *Case management for persons with substance use disorders. The Cochrane collaboration* [Issue 3]. Hoboken, NJ: Wiley.

Inciardi, J., McBride, D., & Rivers, J. (1996). *Drug control and the courts. Drugs, health, and social policy series* (Vol. 3). Thousand Oaks, CA: Sage.

Laken, M. P., & Ager, J. W. (1996, August). Effects of case management on retention in prenatal substance abuse treatment. *American Journal of Drug and Alcohol Abuse, 22*(3), 439–448.

Longshore, D., Turner, S., & Anglin, M. (1998). Effects of case management on drug users' risky sex. *The Prison Journal, 78*(1), 6–30.

McLellan, T., Weinstein, P. L., Shen, Q., Kendig, B. A., & Levine, M. (2005). Improving continuity of care in a public addiction treatment system with clinical case management. *The American Journal on Addictions, 14*, 426–440.

Mee-Lee, D., Dr. (2001, April). *American Society of Addiction Medicine, Patient placement criteria*. Annapolis Junction, MD: ASAM Publications Distribution.

Mejta, C. L., Bokos, P. J., Mickenberg, J., Maslar, M. E., & Senay, E. (1997). Improving substance abuse treatment access and retention using a case management approach. *Journal of Drug Issues, 27*(2), 329–340.

NASW Standards for Social Work Case Management. (2009). *National Association of Social Workers Board of Directors, 1992*. Washington, DC: NASW Press. Retrieved August 18, 2009, from www.socialworkers.org/practice/standards/sw_case_mgmt.asp

Nissen, L., & Kraft, M. (2007). The evolution of substance abuse treatment in juvenile justice. *Journal of Social Work Practice in the Addictions, 7*(3), 51–71.

Office of National Drug Control Policy. (2009). *2008 ADAM II report*. Retrieved August 20, 2009, from www.whitehousedrugpolicy.gov/new/press09/052809.html

Owens, S., Klebe, K., Arens, S., Durhan, R., Hughes, J., Moor, C., et al. (1997). The effectiveness of Colorado's TASC programs. *Journal of Offender Rehabilitation, 26*(1/2), 161–176.

Rapp, R., Otto, A., Lane, D., Redko, C., McGatha, S., & Carlson, R. (2008). Improving linkage with substance abuse treatment using brief case management and motivational interviewing. *Drug and Alcohol Dependence, 94*, 172–182.

Robertson, K. W. (1989). *Treatment alternatives to street crime (TASC)* (pp. 1–7). Washington, DC: U.S. Department of Justice, Office of Justice Programs, Bureau of Justice Assistance.

Siegal, H., Li, L., & Rapp, R. (2002). Case management as a therapeutic enhancement: Impact on post-treatment criminality. *Journal of Addictive Diseases, 21*(4), 37–46.

Substance Abuse and Mental Health Services Administration/Center for Substance Abuse Treatment. (1998). *Comprehensive case management for substance abuse treatment*. Treatment improvement protocols (TIP 27). Rockville, MD: Harvey A. Siegal, Ph.D., Consensus Panel Chair.

Substance Abuse and Mental Health Services Administration. (2007). *Results from the 2006 national survey on drug use and health: National findings* (NSDUH Series H-32, DHHS Publication No. SMA 07–4293). Washington, DC: Office of Applied Studies.

Treatment Alternatives to Street Crime. (2009). *Encyclopedia of drugs, alcohol, and addictive behavior*. Washington, DC: American. Psychological Association. Retrieved August 18, 2009, from www.enotes.com/drugs-alcohol-encyclopedia/treatment

Treatment Episode Data Set. (2005). *Discharges from substance abuse treatment*. Rockville, MD: U.S. Department of Health and Human Services, Substance Abuse and Mental Health Services Administration. Retrieved August 15, 2009, from http://wwwdasis.samhsa.gov/teds05/tedsd2k5indx.htm

U.S. Department of Justice. (2009). *Probation and Parole statistics, 2007*. Washington, DC: Office of Justice Programs, Bureau of Justice Statistics. Retrieved August 15, 2009, from www.ojp.usdoj.gov/bjs/crimeoff.recidivism

Vanderplasschen, W., Rapp, R., Wolf, J., & Broekaert, E. (2004). The development and implementation of case management for substance use disorders in North America and Europe. *Psychiatric Services, 55*(8), 913–922.

Vanderplasschen, W., Wolf, J., Rapp, R., & Broekaert, E. (2007, March). Effectiveness of different models of case management for substance-abusing populations. *Journal of Psychoactive Drugs, 39*(1), 81–95.

Ventura, L., & Lambert, E. (2004). Recidivism 12 months after TASC. *Journal of Offender Rehabilitation, 39*(1), 63–82.

# 11 The Impact of Drug Treatment Provided in Correctional Facilities

Doris Layton MacKenzie, Ojmarrh Mitchell, and David B. Wilson

**Abstract**

Over the past 40 years enormous changes have occurred in the philosophy and management of corrections and these changes had a dramatic impact correctional practice. The "War on Drugs" focused on the philosophies of incapacitation and deterrence. As a result the number of drug involved offenders entering correctional facilities greatly increased. Policy makers, correctional administrators and the public began to realize that many of these offenders had serious drug problems and that onerous punishment and longer prison sentences were not the answers to the drug-involved offenders' problems. A surprisingly large number of them returned to prison a relatively short time after release to the community. In response to this problem, many jurisdictions initiated drug treatment in correctional facilities so drug-involved inmates could receive treatment while incarcerated. This chapter reviews the research literature to examine whether these programs are effective in reducing the drug use and criminal activities of drug-involved offenders once they return to the community. We found some types of drug treatment programs are effective in reducing recidivism, although the research is disappointingly poor in terms of design quality and there are few randomized controlled trials.

**Keywords**

Drug treatment • Meta-analysis • Correctional programs • Treatment programs • Prison treatment

## Introduction

Changes in social conditions, leading to a transformation in the philosophy and management of corrections, have created dramatic changes in the United States criminal justice system, over the past 40 years. These changes have had a major

D.L. MacKenzie (✉)
Department of Sociology, Crime, Law and Justice Program, Justice Center for Research, College of the Liberal Arts, University Outreach, University Park, PA 16802, USA
e-mail: dlm69@psu.edu

C. Leukefeld et al. (eds.), *Handbook of Evidence-Based Substance Abuse Treatment in Criminal Justice Settings*, Issues in Children's and Families' Lives 11,
DOI 10.1007/978-1-4419-9470-7_11, © Springer Science+Business Media, LLC 2011

impact on the management and treatment of drug-involved offenders and delinquents in prisons, jails, and juvenile residential facilities. One result of these changes has been an increased commitment to drug treatment offered in facilities in response to the increasingly large number of drug-involved inmates, many of whom return to facilities after only a few years in the community.

Over 35 years ago, Martinson and his colleagues completed a study examining the effectiveness of treatment in the criminal justice system. According to their research, treatment programs were implemented so poorly and research was so deficient that it was impossible to determine whether treatment could reduce future criminal activities among offenders and delinquents. Since the time of Martinson's work, there have been numerous studies of the impact of drug treatment, provided in correctional facilities, on subsequent criminal activity and drug use. In this chapter, we examine these studies in order to determine the impact of these programs on participants' behavior after they are released to the community. We begin with a short discussion of the changes in correctional philosophy and the impact of these changes on the number of drug-involved inmates in facilities. The large increase in the number of offenders and delinquents entering facilities, combined with the knowledge that many of them will return to facilities in less than 3 years, led many jurisdictions to initiate or increase opportunities for drug treatment, during the period of incarceration.

## Changes in Correctional Philosophy and Management

For the first 7 decades of the twentieth century, corrections strongly emphasized rehabilitation (MacKenzie, 2006). Although the treatment programs were not necessarily implemented with integrity, rehabilitation was, at least in principle, the philosophy ascribed to by many decision makers. In line with this perspective, by the 1960s, all states employed indeterminate sentences. Correctional officials and parole boards were given wide discretion to determine a release date based on when the person was deemed sufficiently "rehabilitated." To further emphasize the focus on rehabilitation, prisons were called "correctional facilities" and guards were referred to as "correctional officers."

Several events occurred in the 1970s that led to major changes in the philosophy and practice of corrections. One of the most influential was Martinson's 1974 summary, of a more elaborate report by Lipton, Martinson, and Wilks (1975), in which he described the results of the research team's assessment of 231 evaluations of treatment programs conducted between 1945 and 1967. From this research, he concluded "with few and isolated exceptions the rehabilitative efforts that have been reported so far have had no appreciable effect on recidivism" (Martinson, 1974, p. 25). The report was widely interpreted as demonstrating that "nothing works" in correctional rehabilitation. This was not really what the report said. A more correct interpretation would be that the research methodology in the evaluations was so flawed, and the programs studied implemented so poorly, that it was impossible to tell whether something could work (Palmer, 1983, 1992).

At approximately the same time as Martinson's report, other factors had a major impact on corrections and explain, in part, why "nothing works" was so generally accepted. In the words of Cullen and Gilbert (1982), the historical times were ripe for a full-scale attack on rehabilitation and the indeterminate sentencing model (see also Cullen & Gendreau, 2000). Race, class, and gender inequities led to protests, riots, and bombings as did opposition to the war in Vietnam. Crime rates also increased during this time and, combined with the social turbulence of the times, profoundly affected the attitudes of many Americans. Societal events, along with the mantra "nothing works," led people to search for a new model for corrections.

Social conservatives began to have greater influence on politics and public policy in the 1970s and 1980s. "Law and order" advocates attacked rehabilitation as coddling criminals. They advocated "get tough" proposals such as mandatory minimums and lengthy determinate sentences as methods of deterring and incapacitating offenders. For corrections, this meant a movement away from a rehabilitation philosophy toward one of deterrence and incapacitation. In the opinion of many, increasing penalties for crime would deter people from criminal activities, and serious offenders would be locked up for long periods so they would not be able to continue to commit crimes. These changes were expected to reduce crime in the community.

## Impact on Drug-Involved Offenders

The change in policies toward crime and the criminal justice system had a dramatic impact on drug-involved offenders. In the early 1980s, the United States declared a "war on drugs." This "war" fit with the deterrence and incapacitation philosophy of corrections at the time. Increasingly severe penalties for drug-involved offenders were expected to reduce drug use and its related criminal activities. The policies resulted in a tremendous increase in the number of drug-involved offenders in prisons and jails and an overall increase in the incarcerated population. After a relatively stable incarceration rate of approximately 100 per 100,000 in the population from 1930 until the mid-1970s, the incarceration rate began to rapidly increase (Bureau of Justice Statistics, 2009). By 1990, there were 297 people incarcerated in state and federal prisons for every 100,000 in the population and, by 2007, the rate had increased to 506. The number of juveniles in residential facilities and offenders in jails also grew.

Much of the increase in prison and jail populations can be attributed to drug-related offenders. For example, in 1970 only 16.3% of the federal prison population were in for drug offenses. By 1990, this had grown to over 50% and this high percentage of drug offenders in federal prisons continues today. In 1986, only 9% of state prisoners were drug law violators. This figure increased to 20% in 1991 and remained at this level throughout the 1990s (Bureau of Justice Statistics, 2001). Furthermore, from 1990 until 2000, drug offenders accounted for 20% of the growth in state prisons (Office of National Drug Control Policy, 2003). The trend is the same for local jails where the percentage of drug offenders grew from 9% in 1983 to 24.7% in 2002 (Bureau of Justice Statistics, 2003).

## Need for Treatment

Many incarcerated offenders are drug-involved. In a survey of prisoners, Mumola (1999) found 80% of state prisoners and 70% of federal prisoners reported past drug use. Many reported being under the influence of alcohol (20–37%) or illicit drugs (22–33%) at the time of the offense. Additionally, 16, 19, and 16% of the inmates in federal and state prisons and jails, respectively, reported committing their offense to purchase drugs (Mumola, 1999; Wilson, 2000).

More evidence of the high level of drug involvement among criminal populations comes from studies testing the urine and hair of arrestees who are booked and charged in cities throughout the United States. A median of 67% of male arrestees tested positive for at least one illicit drug in 2000 (Taylor, Fitzgerald, Hunt, Reardon, & Brownstein, 2001); 23% of male arrestees and 24% of female arrestees tested positive for two or more (Taylor et al., 2001).

Many offenders released from prison return within 3 years. Langan and Levin (2002) examined nearly 300,000 prisoners released in 15 states in 1994. They found 67.5% were rearrested within 3 years and 51.8% were back in prison by then. Approximately half of those returned to prison were parole violators (e.g., failed a drug test, missed an appointment). The high rates of recidivism, combined with the realization that most offenders are drug-involved, led many to recognize the critical importance of providing drug treatment to drug-involved offenders and delinquents while they are incarcerated. The period of time when an individual is incarcerated represents a crucial opportunity to intervene in the cycle of drug abuse and crime.

By the late 1990s nearly all federal prisons (94%) and most state prisons provided substance abuse treatment of some kind (Substance Abuse and Mental Health Services Administration, 2002). However, jails and juvenile facilities lagged behind prisons, with only about a third providing treatment. A Bureau of Justice Statistics survey found that one-third of state prison inmates and one-fourth of federal prison inmates reported participating in drug treatment during incarceration. While many jurisdictions provide substance abuse treatment, many offenders who could benefit from such treatment do not participate while incarcerated. Furthermore, surveys may inflate the numbers of facilities with treatment because some respondents consider drug education, self-help groups, or peer counseling to be treatment. Considering the severity of many offender addictions, such programs are unlikely to effectively address the needs of offenders and delinquents (Belenko & Peugh, 2005).

Treatment provided in facilities has several advantages. First, access to drugs is more limited than in the community, fostering detoxification and abstinence during treatment. For some, the shock of incarceration may dispose them to change their lifestyle and take advantage of treatment opportunities (Zamble & Porporino, 1988). Furthermore, inmates often have an abundance of unstructured time available for introspection and treatment; and correctional facilities have the capacity to employ coercive force to encourage inmates to participate in treatment when they might not otherwise do so.

## Systematic Review and Meta-analysis of Treatment

The question is whether drug treatment can be provided, effectively, to inmates while they are in facilities. In other words, does such treatment reduce later drug use and criminal activity for these offenders and delinquents? We conducted a systematic review and meta-analysis of the research in order to answer this question (Mitchell, Wilson, & MacKenzie, 2007).

A meta-analysis is a quantitative analysis of a group of studies (Lipsey & Wilson, 1993, 2001). Studies included in the analysis must be clearly defined by specific eligibility criteria. An intensive search is conducted to identify all studies fitting the eligibility criteria. Once identified and located, each study is carefully coded so differences among the studies can be controlled and examined in the analyses. Outcomes are coded so they are consistent across studies. In this case, we were interested in outcomes of criminal recidivism and return to drug use, which may be measured with self-report data or official records. Data are analyzed to determine whether there are significant differences in outcomes between the treated group and the comparisons. That is, do those who receive treatment while incarcerated have lower recidivism rates and less drug use than the comparison groups once they are released? Followup analyses examine whether differences are consistent across interventions (e.g., Therapeutic Communities, counseling), participants (e.g., adults, juveniles), study designs (e.g., quasi-experimental, randomized trials), and intervention characteristics (e.g., length of program, followup, or aftercare).

The first step in our review was to carefully determine what studies we would include in the analysis. We only included studies of programs provided in facilities for offenders or adjudicated or detained juveniles that specifically targeted drug users. Interventions available to all offenders, regardless of drug history, such as cognitive skills programs were not included in the study. Through an examination of the research literature, we identified four different types of primary treatment interventions, with a sufficient number of studies, to include in the analysis: therapeutic communities (TCs), counseling, boot camps, and narcotic maintenance programs.

The community-based TC model (DeLeon, 1984, 1994) has been modified for in-prison treatment. While in-prison TCs vary greatly, there are several components common to most TCs. Inmates in TCs are housed in distinct treatment units, separated from the general population, where they spend time only with participating inmates. This environment isolates them from the rest of the prison population, away from drugs, violence, or other negative aspects of prison life that may inhibit rehabilitation.

Residents are involved in running community-based TCs. They help lead treatment sessions, monitor other residents, maintain the treatment unit, and resolve disputes. Participants and staff confront violators, when rule infractions occur. However, the role of participant-peers may be more limited in prison, when compared to community-based TCs, and there may be more use of clinically trained staff.

The guiding philosophy of TCs is that drug use is symptomatic of more general personal disorders and, thus, the focus is on these underlying disorders and not just drug abuse. Drug abuse is viewed as a disorder of the whole person – the problem is the person and not the drug, addiction is a symptom of the problem. The primary goal is to change the negative patterns that predispose the person to drug use.

Counseling programs provided in facilities are extremely varied so they are much more difficult to characterize. They usually incorporate some group sessions (e.g., 12-step, such as Alcoholics Anonymous or Narcotics Anonymous), life skills training, cognitive skills training, drug education, and, possibly, adult basic (academic) education. One commonality among these programs is their reliance on group-based therapies where substance abuse and other common problems are discussed among peers, in an effort to understand and solve problems.

Boot camps are short prison sentences, during which inmates participate in a program modeled after military basic training (MacKenzie & Armstrong, 2004). The daily schedule includes rigorous exercise regimens, military drill and ceremony, and challenge courses. Participants rise early in the morning and are constantly engaged in scheduled activities until "lights out" in the evening. Like TCs, boot camps involve considerable confrontation but, unlike TCs, confrontations most often occur between the correctional staff, called drill instructors, and inmates. While most boot camps include drug-involved participants, few are designed to specifically target drug users. In this analysis we included only the one study (two evaluations) of boot camps that was specifically geared toward drug users.

Narcotic maintenance programs (e.g., methadone, levo-alpha-acetyl-methadol [LAAM]) are very different from the other types of incarceration-based drug treatment programs. They attempt to reduce the harms associated with heroin dependency by prescribing synthetic opioid medication that does not produce a euphoric high. Methadone and LAAM block the high produced by heroin and suppress withdrawal symptoms. Some programs gradually reduce the amount of medication administered, until opiate dependence is relieved; others maintain clients indefinitely. The use of maintenance programs in facilities is relatively new.

## Previous Research

Each of the above described drug interventions has the potential to reduce drug use and other criminal behaviors. An earlier systematic review of 30 studies of corrections-based drug abuse programs by Pearson and Lipton (1999) examined the impact of TCs, boot camps, and group counseling on recidivism. They conducted an intensive search for quasi-experimental and experimental evaluations, of interventions in residential correctional facilities, completed between 1968 and 1996. Their synthesis indicated that TCs were effective in reducing recidivism. Of the seven TC studies, six produced substantial reductions in recidivism. Neither boot camp nor group counseling program studies yielded a statistically significant impact on recidivism. They found too few studies of other types of interventions to draw conclusions about effectiveness, although they characterized evidence of the effectiveness of methadone maintenance, drug education, cognitive-behavioral, and 12-step programs as promising.

Our systematic review can be viewed as an extension of the Pearson and Lipton work. As in the earlier work, we were interested in systematically and comprehensively reviewing the effects of incarceration-based drug interventions on post-treatment drug use and other types of criminal behaviors. The advantage to our study is that we use a more current time frame (studies had to be completed between 1980 and 2004). This is important, first, because more recent evaluations may be more generalizable to current correctional practices; and, second, because there have been numerous additional evaluations conducted since 1996, after Pearson's and Lipton's work.

## Eligible Studies

The first step in the analysis was to develop a list of eligibility criteria for the studies we would include in the analysis. In this meta-analysis, eligible studies had to be quasi-experimental or experimental evaluations of drug treatment programs provided within a correctional facility (e.g., jail or prison). The intervention had to specifically target substance users and had to include a no-treatment or minimal treatment comparison group. They had to report a post-release outcome measure of criminal behavior or drug use and they had to report enough information to permit us to calculate an effect size for the meta-analysis.

Studies had to be completed between 1980 and 2004 and could be either published or unpublished. It is important to include both published and unpublished studies because there may be a publication bias in favor of evaluations finding positive impacts. That is, more studies finding a positive impact of the program may be accepted for publication; therefore, if we used only published studies, we might find a significant effect although this would not be the case if all studies were included. For this reason, we included both published and unpublished studies in the review (Hunter & Schmidt, 2004; Lipsey & Wilson, 2001; Rothstein, Sutton & Borenstein, 2005).

We did not include studies that used a dropout versus completers design or those that compared participants who remained in treatment for various lengths of time. These types of studies are common in the drug treatment literature; however, they do not offer an adequate research design for determining whether a program has an impact on later behavior. Such designs introduce the internal validity problem of a selection effect. That is, almost assuredly, the groups (dropouts versus completers) differed prior to the treatment; therefore, the design cannot rule out the possibility that previously existing differences between the groups, and not the treatment given, led to any differences in outcomes.

The internal validity selection problem also exists in designs that compare completers of treatment with a comparison group. In these designs, researchers identify two groups – a comparison group and a treatment group. The problem is that some people in the treatment group drop out of treatment. The researcher is tempted to compare the outcomes for the comparison group and the treatment group completers without including the dropouts who may have been in the program for only a short time. Again, this introduces an internal validity problem, because the dropouts and the completers most likely differed, prior to treatment.

At times, drug treatment researchers call the completers the "motivated" group and they argue they are comparing the "motivated" to the "unmotivated"; however, this still introduces the internal validity problem of selection. The treatment completers would be expected to be more ready for treatment or more amenable to treatment. Comparing the completers to a comparison group, made up of the untreated and treatment dropouts, means those who are most ready, or most amenable to treatment, are being compared to a group that includes both the ready and amenable group (e.g., the untreated) and the unprepared, un-amenable group (e.g., the dropouts). Thus, any differences in outcomes are most likely because the "good" candidates (the ready, amenable group) are being compared to a group that includes the "good" treatment candidates and the "bad" treatment candidates (dropouts). Any differences in outcomes can easily be attributed to differences between groups that existed prior to treatment and, therefore, little can be said about the impact of the treatment.

Correctional facilities included in the study were jails or prisons or analogous facilities for juveniles. Interventions in half-way houses or community-based facilities were not included in the analysis.

## Search Strategy

The next step was to develop an intensive search strategy, in order to identify all studies meeting the above eligibility criteria (for a more detailed description of the search strategy see Mitchell et al., 2007). Key words such as drug treatment, substance abuse treatment, drug counseling, therapeutic community, methadone maintenance, boot camps, residential substance abuse treatment, and drunk driver were used to search a large number of databases. In addition, we searched for eligible studies, by examining the reference lists of existing studies and research syntheses and websites of prominent research organizations involved in substance abuse research. We also contacted researchers in the field to ask if they knew of any studies on the topic.

The titles and abstracts of studies were examined to identify potentially eligible studies. The potentially eligible studies were retrieved for further examination. In all, we identified 233 potentially eligible studies and we were able to obtain copies of 229 of these. Of these, we found 53 unique studies reporting the results of 66 independent evaluations. These 66 evaluations formed the unit of analysis of the meta-analysis.

## Coding of Studies

Each of the 66 independent evaluations was coded using structured coding forms. Coding included detailed information regarding the study, treatment provided, sample characteristics, outcome or outcomes measured, research design, and the direction and magnitude of the observed effect. This level of detail permitted us to examine whether the findings varied as a function of such factors as the measure of recidivism, the participants, the program characteristics, or the research design.

## Outcomes

Most of the studies were conducted in the United States ($n = 53$). The remaining were conducted in Australia ($n = 3$), Canada ($n = 3$), United Kingdom ($n = 1$), and Taiwan ($n = 1$). The studies were relatively recent, with well over half (66%) dated 1996 or later. Of these, 32 were published as journal articles or book chapters, the remaining 34 were unpublished technical reports and government documents. Pearson and Lipton's (1999) review included studies available before 1996 and so the vast majority of our studies were not included in their earlier review.

We examined five different outcomes: four measured criminal activity (i.e., general recidivism, rearrest, reconviction, and reincarceration) and one measured drug relapse. The "general recidivism" measure served as the main outcome measure in most of the analyses. This outcome was calculated by giving preference to measures that (1) were general instead of offense specific (i.e., covered all offense types not just violent or property offenses); (2) were based on arrests; (3) were dichotomous (yes or no and not time-to-failure); and (4) followed all the groups for at least 12 months. Thus general recidivism includes recidivism as measured by the 65 studies with recidivism outcomes, with rearrests as the measure for the 35 studies reporting rearrests. If the study did not record rearrests, then reconvictions were used as the outcome measure; and, if neither rearrests nor reconvictions were measured, then reincarcerations was used as the outcome. This permitted use to include all the studies in one analysis for the general recidivism analyses.

There were 65 effect sizes for the any-recidivism analyses (one study by Magura, Rosenblum, & Joseph, 1993 included only drug relapse as an outcome), 35 for rearrests, 17 for reconvictions, and 20 for drug relapse.[1] It is surprising that only 20 of the 66 independent evaluations assessed the effect of drug treatment on post-release drug use. One reason for the smaller number of studies investigating drug relapse may be the difficulty in collecting such data. Drug relapse results require researchers to obtain self-report or urinalysis data from the individual. In most cases, recidivism data are collected from existing official records, not requiring contact with the individuals.

As noted above, we classified programs into four types: therapeutic communities (TCs), counseling, boot camps, and narcotic maintenance. The descriptions of programs in three studies were ambiguous as to intervention type; although it was clear they provided treatment within facilities, the specific type of treatment was undefined. These programs were not included in analyses of program types (Darabi, 1992; Dowden & Blanchette, 2002; Oregon Department of Corrections, 1994).

The majority of the programs were TCs ($n$ = 30) or counseling ($n$ = 25); few were narcotic maintenance ($n$ = 5) or boot camps ($n$ = 2). It should be remembered that we only included studies where the major intervention was a drug treatment program; therefore, boot camp studies were only included in this meta-analysis if the program was designed as a drug treatment program.

Studies were evaluated on a four-point scale for the overall quality of the research methods. This scale was an ordinal measure of the internal validity of each evaluation and had previously been used in a University of Maryland study of crime prevention (Farrington, Gottfredson, Sherman, & Welsh, 2002; MacKenzie, 2006). The lowest level of method quality was a weak quasi-experimental design, using a comparison group that lacks comparability to the treatment group before the intervention. The next level was a "standard quasi-experimental" design, with a comparison group that was slightly different from the treatment group on some important observed variables. "Rigorous quasi-experiments" were designs with highly comparable treatment and comparison groups, or evaluations that employed slightly different groups but used multivariate analyses that controlled for the preexisting differences. The highest level designs were randomized trials.

As shown in Table 11.1, according to this scale, relatively few of the evaluations used methodologically strong research designs. Of the 66 evaluations 29% ($n$ = 19) were scored at the lowest level and 41% were scored as moderate. None of the narcotic maintenance and boot camps studies used randomized designs, and very few of the TCs and counseling programs did. Only 29% of the evaluations used strong quasi-experimental or randomized designs.

*Impact of treatment.* Studies varied in the type of recidivism measured (arrests, convictions, reincarcerations) and how drug use was measured (self-report, urinalysis). Effect sizes were used to determine differences between treatment and comparison groups. An effect size was calculated for each evaluation comparison, using the odds-ratio effect size for dichotomous outcomes (Lipsey & Wilson, 2001). Positive effect sizes indicated the treatment group had a more favorable outcome than the comparison (e.g., less recidivism or drug use).

We ran separate analyses with each of the 5 different outcomes: (1) general recidivism ($n$ = 65); (2) rearrest ($n$ = 35); (3) reconviction ($n$ = 17); (4) reincarceration ($n$ = 35); and (5) drug relapse ($n$ = 20). Overall, without controls in the analyses, we found the treated group (including all types of treatment) had significantly lower recidivism than the comparison groups on the four recidivism measures. No significant differences occurred between the treated group and the comparison, when drug relapse was the outcome measure. Using the results of the analyses, we estimated the recidivism rates for the treated groups, if the comparison groups' rates were set at 35%. For heuristic purposes, we assumed a 35% recidivism rate for the comparison group because this was the unweighted average rate of recidivism for all comparison groups. Given this assumption, the overall mean

[1] Note one study only reported a drug use outcome, so it is not included in the recidivism analyses.

**Table 11.1** Number and percent of studies rated at different research quality (on 4-point scale)

| Strength of design (comparison of treated/experimental group to comparison/control group) | TCs $n = 30$ | Counseling $n = 25$ | Narcotic maintenance $n = 5$ | Boot camps $n = 2$ | Other $n = 3$ | Total $n = 65$ |
|---|---|---|---|---|---|---|
| Weak quasi-experimental/comparison group only somewhat similar | $n = 6$ | 8 | 1 | 1 | 3 | 19 |
| | (20%) | (32%) | (20%) | (50%) | (100%) | (29%) |
| Moderate quasi-experimental/comparison group reasonably similar | $n = 13$ | 10 | 4 | 0 | 0 | 27 |
| | (43%) | (40%) | (80%) | | | (41%) |
| Strong quasi-experimental/comparison group similar to treated group | $n = 9$ | 5 | 0 | 1 | 0 | 15 |
| | (30%) | (20%) | | (50%) | | (23%) |
| Experimental design/randomized trial | $n = 2$ | 2 | 0 | 0 | 0 | 4 |
| | (7%) | (8%) | | | | (6%) |

One study had missing data on both type of treatment and methodological score.
Source: MacKenzie (2006) and Mitchell et al. (2007).

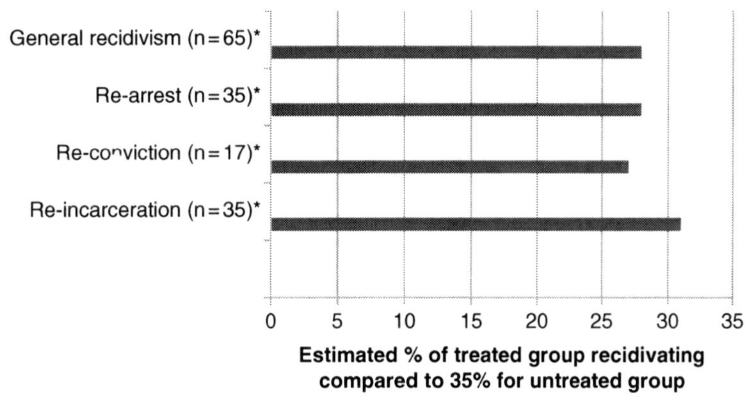


**Fig. 11.1** Estimated percent of treated group (any treatment) recidivating if the comparison group is assumed to recidivate at 35% (Mitchell et al., 2007; MacKenzie, 2006). *= significant difference between treatment and comparison groups

odds-ratio translates into a recidivism rate of approximately 28% for the treatment group, on the general recidivism measure. As shown in Fig. 11.1, the estimated recidivism rates (using four different measures) for the treated groups were generally well below the 35% recidivism of the control group. The effect of treatment was largest on rearrest and reconviction; smaller when measures of reincarceration or drug relapse were used.

Disappointingly, drug treatment during incarceration was not significantly associated with later drug relapse, although some programs appeared to significantly lower relapse rates. While only 20 studies examined drug relapse, our post hoc power analysis indicated the results were not due to a lack of statistical power. Shown in Table 11.2 are the studies that included a measure of drug relapse in their evaluation of programs. As can be seen, four of the six narcotic maintenance studies measured drug relapse. Most of the rest of the evaluations using relapse as an outcome studied TCs.

The results of the above analysis suggest that the drug treatment provided in prison is effective in reducing criminal behavior after release; however, this should be interpreted with caution because the analysis indicated that the effect size distributions displayed more variability than expected by chance alone. There may be important differences among studies in research methodology, sample, or intervention type that account for some of the differences. As noted above we attempted to code detailed information

**Table 11.2** Drug relapse results for 20 studies examined in the analysis showing estimated percent relapsing (if comparison is set to 35%), time frame of followup, and source of data (self-report, urinalysis)

| Study | *n* | Est. relapse (%) | Type of program | Data source | Time frame (months) |
|---|---|---|---|---|---|
| Inciardi, Martin, Butzin, Hooper, and Harrison (1997) – crest | 60 | 11 | TC | Official data | 18 |
| Crundall and Deacon (1997) | 654 | 13 | Counseling | Self-report | 3.5 |
| Prendergast, Podus, Chang, and Urada (2003) | 564 | 13 | TC | Self-report | 12 |
| Hume and Gorta (1989) | 671 | 14 | Methadone | Official data | 4 |
| Magura et al. (1993) (females) | 100 | 14 | Methadone | Self-report | 1 |
| Knight, Simpson, and Hiller (1999) | 479 | 16 | TC | Official data | 6 |
| Sealock, Gottfredson, and Gallagher (1997) | 220 | 26 | Counseling | Self-report | 2 |
| Magura et al. (1993) (males) | 149 | 27 | Methadone | Self-report | 1 |
| Pelissier et al. (2000) (males) | 1842 | 28 | TC | Official data | 36 |
| Pelissier et al. (2000) (females) | 473 | 28 | TC | Official data | 36 |
| Kinlock et al. (2005) | 646 | 28 | Methadone | Self-report | 9 |
| Hartmann, Wolk, Johnston, and Colyer (1997) | 557 | 29 | TC | Official data | 6 |
| Welsh (2002) | 572 | 31 | TC | Official data | 12.6 |
| Anglin, Prendergast, Farabee, and Cartier (2002) | 600 | 31 | TC | Self-report | 1 |
| Van Stelle and Moberg (2001) | 581 | 32 | TC | Official data | 3 |
| Prendergast, Wellisch, and Wong (1996) | 155 | 36 | TC | Self-report | 12 |
| Miller and Koons-Witt (2003) | 565 | 44 | TC | Official data | 12 |
| Zhang (2000) (1997 cohort) | 461 | 49 | Boot Camp | Self-report | 12 |
| Gordon (2002) | 576 | 52 | TC | Other | 12 or more |
| Vaughn, Deng, and Lee (2003) | 615 | 77 | Counseling | Official data | 12 |

Source: MacKenzie (2006) and Mitchell et al. (2007).

about methodology, sample, and intervention; however, our attempt to code this information was severely limited by the quality of the descriptions provided by the authors of the studies.

In the following analyses we used our general recidivism measure. As noted above, general recidivism was calculated from the reported study findings using a set of selection criteria. We used rearrest if this measure was given in the study. This was preferred because arrest is more proximate to offending than other outcome measures and because this was commonly reported. If no arrest effect size was available we selected reconvictions as preferable to reincarcerations. Each independent evaluation contributed one, and only one, effect size to the "general recidivism" data set.

*Overview of treatment outcomes*. The analysis above indicated that overall, for the four measures of criminal activities, treatment during incarceration reduces recidivism. The next question is whether these results are the same for the different types of interventions (i.e., TCs, counseling, boot camps, narcotic maintenance).

On average, TCs and counseling programs significantly reduced recidivism. If we assumed a 35% recidivism rate for the comparison groups (a reasonable assumption given the data from these studies), TC programs had a 28% recidivism rate for participants and counseling programs had a 26% recidivism rate for participants.

The odds-ratios for boot camps and narcotic maintenance programs were not statistically different, indicating that participation in these programs generally was not associated with significant reductions in recidivism. A post hoc power analysis indicated that the power of the boot camp analysis was appropriate to detect a small effect; thus, even though there were a small number of studies there appeared to be sufficient statistical power to detect differences. This was not true with the narcotic maintenance programs, where a post hoc analysis indicated that there was not sufficient power to detect differences. As a result, little can be said about the potential of incarceration-based narcotic maintenance programs other than that the limited existing evidence is discouraging.

In the next sections we separately examine the treatment interventions in more detail. Due to the small number of narcotic maintenance and boot camp programs, and because there were no significant outcomes, we describe the studies of these programs and outcomes but do not complete more statistical analyses. In contrast, we found sufficient numbers of studies examining TCs and counseling programs, and the analyses indicated they had a significant impact on later recidivism, so we continued our statistical analyses of these programs. We were interested in examining whether the impact of these programs differed depending upon aspects of the research design, the participants, or the program components.

## Therapeutic Communities

According to our analyses of outcomes for the 30 TC studies, treatment in TCs significantly reduced the recidivism of participants. Table 11.3 shows the recidivism rates calculated for the studies (if the comparison is set at 35%), the significance of these rates, and participant characteristics. We were now interested in examining whether the recidivism results differed, depending upon characteristics of the research methodology, the participants, or the programs.

In our discussion of the results it is important that the reader recognize three limitations to this research. First, we were unable to code many components, because the information was just not available in the studies. For example, we would have liked to examine whether treatment programs that relied on a cognitive-behavioral approach were more effective; however, many studies did not provide enough information about the treatment program to make such an assessment. A second limitation was that, since we begin with only 30 studies, these analyses have limited statistical power. (To combat the low statistical power we employ two strategies. First, we interpret as statistically significant any contrast that has a probability of occurring by chance alone of less than 10% (e.g., $p < 0.10$). Second, instead of relying solely on statistical significance we also discuss results that appear to be substantively large even if they are not statistically significant.) A third limitation was the sparseness of the information that could be coded, which meant that we were limited to bivariate analyses. Multivariate analyses would be highly problematic because the results would be very sensitive to small alternations. Given these three limitations, the results of the analyses of the characteristics of research methods, participants, and programs should be viewed as suggestive.

We began the examination of the TC studies, by examining whether the results of the meta-analyses differed depending on differences in research methods. Only two studies used randomized designs; most studies (63%) used weak or standard quasi-experimental designs (see Table 11.1). These analyses demonstrated that TC evaluations, with the lowest research quality score, yielded the smallest impacts, while those with highest quality scores (e.g., randomized trials) had the highest impacts. This finding suggests that more methodologically rigorous evaluations found stronger evidence of treatment effectiveness. In an analysis, such as this, the common fear is that poor designs will find stronger evidence of treatment effectiveness; and,

**Table 11.3** Evaluations of TCs showing estimated percent recidivating (if comparison recidivism is set to 35% recidivism) and participant characteristics

| Study | *n* | Est. recid (%) | Age group | Male (%) | Minority (%) | Violent included? |
|---|---|---|---|---|---|---|
| Van Stelle and Moberg (2001) | 96 | 11 | Adult | Approx. 50 | 51–70 | Yes |
| Prendergast et al. (1996) | 64 | 12 | Adult | 90+ | 51–70 | Yes |
| Prendergast et al. (2003) | 180 | 15 | Adult | 90+ | 51–70 | NA |
| Hartmann et al. (1997) | 244 | 19 | Adult | Approx. 50 | 50 or less | No |
| Pealer, Latessa, and Winesburg (2002) | 788 | 19 | Juvenile | Approx. 50 | 50 or less | Yes |
| Tunis, Austin, Morris, Hardyman, and Bolyard (1995) | 150 | 21 | Adult | Approx. 50 | 50 or less | No |
| Mosher and Phillips (2002) | 558 | 21 | Adult | 90+ | 50 or less | Yes |
| Wexler, Falkin, and Lipton (1990) – males | 594 | 21 | Adult | 90+ | 70+ | Yes |
| Inciardi et al. (1997) – crest | 359 | 22 | Adult | 60–90 | 70+ | Yes |
| Wexler, Melnick, Lowe, and Peters (1999) | 715 | 23 | Adult | Approx. 50 | 51–70 | Yes |
| Taxman and Spinner (1996) | 528 | 23 | Adult | 60–90 | 51–70 | Yes |
| Winesburg, Latessa, and Pealer (2002) | 399 | 23 | Adult | Approx. 50 | 50 or less | Yes |
| Knight et al. (1999) | 396 | 25 | Adult | Approx. 50 | 51–70 | No |
| Wexler et al. (1990) – females | 285 | 27 | Adult | Less than 10 | 70+ | Yes |
| Welsh (2002) | 551 | 28 | Adult | Approx. 50 | NA | NA |
| Eisenberg and Fabelo (1996) | 1067 | 29 | Adult | 60–90 | NA | Yes |
| Eisenberg, Riechers, and Arrigona (2001) prtc | 24017 | 29 | Adult | NA | NA | NA |
| Pelissier et al. (2000) – males | 1842 | 30 | Adult | 90+ | NA | No |
| Nash (2000) | 807 | 31 | Adult | Approx. 50 | 50 or less | NA |
| Pelissier et al. (2000) – females | 473 | 31 | Adult | Less than 10 | NA | No |
| Miller and Koons-Witt (2003) | 280 | 32 | Young adult (19–25) | Approx. 50 | 70+ | No |
| Tunis et al. (1995) – said | 374 | 32 | Adult | Approx. 50 | 70+ | No |
| Eisenberg et al. (2001) – prsap | 13968 | 33 | NA | NA | NA | NA |
| Klebe and O'Keefe (1998) | 778 | 33 | Adult | Approx. 50 | 50 or less | No |
| Gordon (2002) | 818 | 34 | Juvenile | Approx. 50 | 51–70 | Yes |
| Gransky and Jones (1997) | 415 | 34 | Adult | 90+ | 51–70 | Yes |
| Anglin et al. (2002) | 801 | 37 | Adult | Approx. 50 | 51–70 | Yes |
| Gransky and Jones (1997) | 8399 | 38 | Young adult (19–25) | Approx. 50 | 70+ | No |
| Porter (2002) | 513 | 41 | Adult | Approx. 50 | 70+ | Yes |
| Siegal, Wang, Falck, Rahman, and Carlson (1997) | 726 | 49 | Adult | 60–90 | 51–70 | NA |

NA = Data were not available because they were not reported by authors.
Source: MacKenzie (2006) and Mitchell et al. (2007).

in such cases, it will be unclear whether this is due to a selection effect or to the actual effect of treatment. The finding, that stronger designs provide stronger evidence of effectiveness, gives us more assurance that the finding of effectiveness is not due to selection problems in the research designs.

Other coded methodological features (e.g., random assignment, subject level matching, multivariate analyses controlling for subject differences) were not significantly associated with effect sizes suggesting that the results of the meta-analysis did not differ based on these methods. Thus, overall, the finding of the effectiveness of TCs was robust to methodological variations in studies.

Four sample characteristics were consistently reported by evaluators: age group (juvenile or adult), gender composition, racial composition, and type of offense (violent/nonviolent).[2] As shown in Table 11.3, most of the programs evaluated served adults ($n = 27$); only two addressed juveniles in the TCs. Similarly, most studies examined male programs ($n = 18$), only six examined programs for females and only four served both male and female. The racial composition of the samples varied from 50% or fewer non-white ($n = 7$), to 51–70% non-white ($n = 10$) to more than 70% non-white ($n = 7$). Fifteen of the TCs had only nonviolent offenders/delinquents, while nine included both violent and nonviolent. None of the sample characteristics displayed a statistically or substantively significant relationship with effect size. Therefore, we concluded that TC programs were effective with many different types of participants.

Next we examined whether the results varied depending on the characteristics of the TC programs (see Table 11.4). Sufficient data were reported in the evaluations to permit us to examine the impact of mandatory aftercare ($n = 9$ yes, $n = 14$ no), location of program ($n = 27$ prison, $n = 3$ jail), program maturity ($n = 14$ less than 1 year, $n = 4$ 1–3 years, $n = 11$ more than 3 years), short treatment ($n = 22$ not less than 90 days, $n = 3$ less than 3 years), and voluntariness ($n = 16$ yes, $n = 8$ no). Again, none of the coded characteristics of the programs were statistically or substantively related to effect size, suggesting the effectiveness of TCs was largely robust to coded variation in treatment features. Thus, although TC programs with mandated aftercare, or where participants spent more time in the program or programs that required participants to volunteer, produced somewhat larger effect sizes than other programs, these features were not significant. Therefore, the TCs appear to be effective in reducing recidivism rates regardless of several prominent program characteristics.

In conclusion, according to these results, TCs for drug-involved offenders and delinquents, provided within facilities, are effective in reducing later criminal activity. This appears to be true for the TCs studied despite differences in evaluation methodology, varied program characteristics, and diverse participants.

## Counseling Programs

According to our analyses, counseling programs significantly reduced recidivism. We followed up this finding with an examination of the impact of methodological features, and program and participant characteristics, as we did for the TCs. Shown in Table 11.5 are the estimates of the recidivism rates for the counseling studies (if the comparison samples are set at 35% recidivism) as well as participant characteristics. As with the TCs analyses, the limitations in the information presented in the reports (many characteristics we would have liked to study were not reported), and the limited statistical power due to the small number of studies resulted in our use of only bivariate analyses (we use $p < 0.10$ as the level of significance) of a limited number of characteristics.

Over two-thirds of the studies were rated as either "weak" or "standard" quasi-experiments and only two used randomized trials (see Table 11.1). The analysis of the quality of the methodology indicated that weaker studies may contribute the strongest evidence for the effectiveness of counseling programs in reducing reoffending. This is in contrast to the TC studies and suggests a problem with selection effect, because the weaker studies are more apt to have samples that differ prior to the treatment delivery. Also, in contrast with the TC analyses, is the finding of no differences between published and unpublished studies.

As shown in Table 11.5, most counseling program participants were adult ($n = 19$ adults, $n = 3$ juveniles), males ($n = 11$, $n = 3$ females, $n = 6$ mixed), in prison ($n = 16$ prison, $n = 9$ jail). Most programs were offered to a mix

[2] Data do not add up to 30 because many of the evaluations did not report some of the sample characteristics.

**Table 11.4** Characteristics of TC programs for evaluations included in the meta-analyses

| Author | Aftercare mandatory? | Location | Program maturity | Trt length (mos) | Voluntary? |
|---|---|---|---|---|---|
| Van Stelle and Moberg (2001) | NA | Prison | Less than 1 year | 8.5 | NA |
| Prendergast et al. (1996) | Yes | Prison | 3+ years | 4.0 | Yes |
| Prendergast et al. (2003) | Yes | Prison | 3+ years | 5.0 | Yes |
| Hartmann et al. (1997) | NA | Prison | Less than 1 year | NA | Yes |
| Pealer et al. (2002) | No | Prison | Less than 1 year | 6.8 | No |
| Tunis et al. (1995) – jet | No | Jail | 1–3 years | 3.4 | Yes |
| Mosher and Phillips (2002) | NA | Prison | Less than 1 year | 9.8 | No |
| Wexler et al. (1990) – males | No | Prison | 3+ years | 7.2 | Yes |
| Inciardi et al. (1997) – crest | Yes | Prison | Less than 1 year | 9.0 | Yes |
| Wexler et al. (1999) | Yes | Prison | 3+ years | 11.1 | Yes |
| Taxman and Spinner (1996) | No | Jail | Less than 1 year | 2.0 | Yes |
| Winesburg et al. (2002) | No | Prison | Less than 1 year | 7.3 | Yes |
| Knight et al. (1999) | Yes | Prison | 1–3 years | 9.0 | No |
| Wexler et al. (1990) – females | No | Prison | 3+ years | 7.2 | Yes |
| Welsh (2002) | No | Prison | NA | 11.6 | Yes |
| Eisenberg and Fabelo (1996) | Yes | Prison | Less than 1 year | 9.0 | No |
| Eisenberg et al. (2001) – prsap | No | Prison | Less than 1 year | 5.0 | No |
| Pelissier et al. (2000) – males | Yes | Prison | 3+ years | 10.5 | Yes |
| Nash (2000) | NA | Prison | 3+ years | NA | NA |
| Pelissier et al. (2000) – females | Yes | Prison | 3+ years | 10.5 | NA |
| Miller and Koons-Witt (2003) | No | Prison | Less than 1 year | 9.0 | Yes |
| Tunis et al. (1995) – said | No | Jail | 3+ years | 1.8 | Yes |
| Eisenberg et al. (2001) – prtc | No | Prison | Less than 1 year | NA | No |
| Klebe and O'Keefe (1998) | NA | Prison | 3+ years | 9.0 | No |
| Gordon (2002) | No | Prison | 3+ years | 12.0 | Yes |
| Gransky and Jones (1997) | No | Prison | 1–3 years | NA | Yes |
| Anglin et al. (2002) | NA | Prison | Less than 1 year | 10.2 | No |
| Gransky and Jones (1997) | NA | Prison | 1–3 years | 1.6 | NA |
| Porter (2002) | Yes | Prison | Less than 1 year | 12.0 | NA |
| Siegal et al. (1997) | No | Prison | Less than 1 year | NA | NA |

NA = Data were not available because they were not reported by authors.
Source: MacKenzie (2006) and Mitchell et al. (2007).

of races, with both males and females, who were convicted of both violent and nonviolent crimes. Our analyses found that programs were more effective with adult participants, when compared to those with juvenile participants, and female programs were more effective than male or mixed-gender programs. Counseling programs were effective in reducing reoffending in all racial categories and for nonviolent offenders and mixed groups.

What is offered to participants in counseling programs differs greatly. In our further assessment of the 25 counseling programs, we found five were primarily cognitive behavior therapy, three were primarily 12-step, seven were multifaceted (mixed), two were primarily drug education, and eight were other/unspecified. In general there was very limited information, about the specific characteristics of the programs, to use in examining the impact of various program characteristics (see Table 11.6). We could gather information from the reports on program maturity, mandatory aftercare, location, and program length. We found that both mandatory

**Table 11.5** Evaluations of counseling showing estimated percent recidivating (if comparison recidivism is set to 35%) and participant characteristics

| Authors | *n* | Est. recid (%) | Age group | Male (%) | Minority (%) | Violent included? |
|---|---|---|---|---|---|---|
| Voas and Tippetts (1990) | 2340 | 8 | NA | 90+ | NA | NA |
| Turley et al. (2004 ) | 70 | 13 | Adults | Approx. 50 | NA | No |
| Turley et al. (2004) | 67 | 16 | Adults | Approx. 50 | NA | No |
| Crundall and Deacon (1997) | 58 | 16 | Adults | Approx. 50 | 50 or less | NA |
| Tunis et al. (1995) – deuce | 264 | 20 | Adults | 60–90 | 50 or less | No |
| Tunis et al. (1995) – reach | 159 | 21 | Adults | Male (90+) | 51–70 | No |
| Turley et al. (2004) | 137 | 22 | Adults | Approx. 50 | NA | No |
| Finigan, Barron, and Carey (2003) – females | 196 | 22 | Adults | Less than 10 | NA | Yes |
| Daley et al. (2004) | 831 | 24 | Adults | Approx. 50 | 51–70 | Yes |
| Hanson (2000) | 271 | 24 | Adults | 60–90 | 50 or less | No |
| Martin, Butzin, Saum, and Inciardi (1999) | 1205 | 25 | Adults | Approx. 50 | 50 or less | Yes |
| Porporino, Robinson, Millson, and Weekes (2002) | 1572 | 26 | Adults | Approx. 50 | NA | Yes |
| Kunitz et al. (2002) | 6571 | 26 | NA | 60–90 | 70+ | No |
| Smith (1996) | 495 | 26 | Adults | Approx. 50 | 51–70 | Yes |
| Hughey and Klemke (1996) | 394 | 26 | Adults | NA | NA | Yes |
| WA State DOC (1988) | 676 | 27 | Adults | NA | NA | Yes |
| Finigan et al. (2003) – males | 190 | 28 | Adults | 90+ | NA | Yes |
| Kelly (2001) | 527 | 29 | Juvenile | Approx. 50 | 70+ | Yes |
| Aos (2004) | 273 | 30 | Juvenile | NA | NA | Yes |
| Peters, Kearns, Murrin, Dolente, and May (1993) | 420 | 30 | Adults | NA | 51–70 | No |
| Little, Robinson, and Burnette (1989) | 180 | 33 | Adults | Approx. 50 | 51–70 | Yes |
| Tunis et al. (1995) – new begin | 166 | 35 | Adults | 60–90 | 51–70 | No |
| Sealock et al. (1997) | 520 | 37 | Juvenile | NA | NA | No |
| Dugan and Everett (1998) | 117 | 43 | Adults | 60–90 | 50 or less | No |
| Vaughn et al. (2003) | 628 | 63 | NA | 60–90 | NA | No |

NA = Data were not available because they were not reported by authors.
Source: MacKenzie (2006) and Mitchell et al. (2007).

and voluntary counseling programs operating for longer than 3 years were more effective than new programs (less than 1 year) or developing programs (1–3 years). None of the other coded treatment characteristics (location, short term of treatment, mandatory aftercare) had any substantive or statistical relationship with general recidivism.

Overall, counseling programs appear to be effective in reducing recidivism. However, there may be a problem with the internal validity of the studies. In particular, the weak studies contributed the largest effect sizes to the analyses. If many of these studies had selection effect problems, the results could mean that counseling appears effective because those who participated in the programs studied differed from the comparison group prior to the treatment. Few studies ($n = 3$) evaluated counseling programs for juveniles and overall these did not appear to be effective. Similarly, counseling programs for women appear to be more effective than programs for males or mixed groups, although there were only a few female programs ($n = 3$). Programs in operation for longer than 3 years and

**Table 11.6** Characteristics of counseling programs for evaluations included in the meta-analyses

| Author | Aftercare mandatory? | Location | Program maturity | Trt Length (mos) | Voluntary? |
|---|---|---|---|---|---|
| Voas and Tippetts (1990) | Yes | Prison | NA | 1.0 | No |
| Turley et al. (2004) | No | Prison | 3+ years | 2.5 | Yes |
| Turley et al. (2004) | No | Prison | 3+ years | 2.5 | Yes |
| Crundall and Deacon (1997) | No | Prison | NA | 0.2 | Yes |
| Tunis et al. (1995) – deuce | No | Jail | 3+ years | 2.6 | Yes |
| Tunis et al. (1995) – reach | No | Jail | 1–3 years | 3.2 | Yes |
| Turley et al. (2004) | No | Prison | 3+ years | 2.5 | Yes |
| Finigan et al. (2003) – females | No | Jail | Less than 1 year | 0.5 | NA |
| Daley et al. (2004) | No | Prison | NA | 3.1 | Yes |
| Hanson (2000) | No | Prison | 3+ years | 3.3 | Yes |
| Martin et al. (1999) | No | Prison | 3+ years | NA | Yes |
| Porporino et al. (2002) | No | Prison | 3+ years | NA | Yes |
| Kunitz et al. (2002) | No | Jail | 3+ years | 1.0 | Yes |
| Smith (1996) | No | Prison | 3+ years | 6.0 | Yes |
| Hughey and Klemke (1996) | Yes | Jail | NA | 1.2 | NA |
| WA State DOC (1988) | No | Prison | Less than 1 year | NA | NA |
| Finigan et al. (2003) – males | No | Jail | Less than 1 year | 0.5 | NA |
| Kelly (2001) | NA | Prison | NA | NA | NA |
| Aos (2004) | Yes | Prison | Less than 1 year | 7.0 | NA |
| Peters et al. (1993) | No | Jail | Less than 1 year | 1.5 | NA |
| Little et al. (1989) | No | Prison | Less than 1 year | NA | Yes |
| Tunis et al. (1995) – new begin | No | Jail | 1–3 years | 3.8 | Yes |
| Sealock et al. (1997) | Yes | Prison | NA | 2.6 | No |
| Dugan and Everett (1998) | No | Jail | Less than 1 year | 0.9 | No |
| Vaughn et al. (2003) | No | Prison | Less than 1 year | 4.0 | No |

NA = Data were not available because they were not reported by authors.
Source: MacKenzie (2006) and Mitchell et al. (2007).

those that require participation are more effective than the comparisons.

## Boot Camps and Narcotic Maintenance

There were too few studies to permit us to draw any conclusions about boot camps for drug offenders and narcotic maintenance in prisons. We found only one study of boot camps for drug-involved offenders including two separate evaluations of the Los Angeles County Juvenile Drug Treatment Boot Camp (Zhang, 2000). Four studies evaluated narcotic maintenance programs (Hume & Gorta, 1989; Johnson, van de Ven, & Grant, 2001; Kinlock, Battjes, & Schwartz, 2005; Magura et al., 1993), but Magura et al. (1993) reported two effect sizes (separate effects by gender). All of the programs were either new or developing at the time of the evaluation. Evaluations typically measured both drug use and recidivism, but followed sample members for only a few months; the longest followup period was 9 months (Kinlock et al., 2005).

## Conclusions

The good news is incarceration-based drug treatment programs are effective in reducing recidivism! Eighty-three percent of the general recidivism odds-ratios favored the treated group over the comparison group. If the recidivism of the comparison group is set to 35%, the treated group would be estimated to recidivate at 28%. When we examined the different types of treatment, we found the most consistent evidence of treatment effectiveness came from evaluations of TC programs. These programs consistently showed post-release reductions in recidivism and drug use. This finding was robust to methodological variation and even the most rigorous evaluations demonstrated reductions in recidivism. TCs were effective with different groups of offenders suggesting that these programs can be applied to a wide range of offenders. In addition, the effectiveness of TCs was enhanced if they had mandatory post-release aftercare.

Similar to the TCs, counseling programs appear to be effective in reducing reoffending. Counseling programs appear to be most effective for females and adult offenders; however, the number of studies examining programs for females and juveniles were limited. Voluntary counseling programs were more effective than other types of counseling programs. However, the strongest evidence of the effectiveness of counseling comes from relatively weak research designs, raising the possibility that the findings may be due to selection effects. That is, it may be that subjects in these studies differed prior to the evaluation and therefore any differences between groups in drug use or recidivism are the result of these prior differences (i.e., a result of the poor research design) and not an effect caused by the treatment.

Extremely disappointing, in this body of research literature, is the generally poor to moderate research designs. Given the strong evidence of a drug-crime link, and the large number of drug-involved offenders and delinquents with serious drug problems who spend time in facilities and who return to facilities soon after release, it is surprising that more has not been done to understand how treatment could be effectively provided to those in need. Decision makers are clearly realizing the importance of providing drug treatment in facilities and this realization has brought about an increase in treatment. However, the amount of high quality research is limited. Recognition of need and the implementation of programs have not resulted in a recognition that more needs to be done to examine what type of treatment is successful, with whom, for how long, and in what context. We can only hope that the current emphasis on evidence-based corrections leads to more high quality research (MacKenzie, 2006, 2005, 2001).

It is important also to recognize that a meta-analysis, such as this, has limitations. One of the greatest limitations is our inability to say much about the implementation of the treatment programs (Latessa & Holsinger, 1998; Taxman & Friedmann, 2009). First, the evaluation reports provide limited information about the components of implementation such as program length, time spent in program, program content and credentials, skill and training of staff. Even if the reports included information on the planned implementation, we might still be left with questions about whether the programs were implemented as intended. That is, do participants really attend for the planned time, and are trained staff the ones who spend most of the time with the participants? This adherence, protocol fidelity, and implementation information is not available in these studies. Some research studies do include a process or implementation study as well as an outcome study; however, the difficulty is in finding both and being sure that the process study describes what was going on at the time of the outcome study.

Another important factor to consider in drawing conclusions about the results of these meta-analyses is that these studies examine programs at one point in time. The results may hold for these participants in this context, while outcomes may be very different in a new context with another group of participants.

In summary, the results of this research are encouraging. Drug treatment provided to juveniles and adults while they are incarcerated can reduce recidivism. Conversely, and disappointingly, the evidence does not demonstrate a reduction in relapse to substance use. Furthermore, the quality of research designs make some of the findings questionable (e.g., are the results from counseling due to design problems?). Future research should use stronger research designs (preferably more randomized trials), investigate implementation fidelity, and work on uncovering the details of what works for whom, and in what context.

## References


Anglin, M. D., Prendergast, M. L., Farabee, D., & Cartier, J. (2002). *Final report on the substance abuse program at the California Substance Abuse Treatment Facility and State Prison at Corcoran*. Los Angeles: The UCLA Integrated Substance Abuse Program.

Aos, S. (2004). *Washington State's family integrated transitions program for juvenile offenders: Outcome evaluation and benefit-cost analysis*. Olympia, WA: Washington State Institute for Public Policy.

Belenko, S., & Peugh, J. (2005). Estimating drug treatment needs among state prision inmates. *Drug and Alcohol Dependency, 77*, 269–281.

Bureau of Justice Statistics. (2001). *Key facts at a glance – Correctional populations, 1980–2000*. Washington, DC: U.S. Department of Justice. Retrieved 21 July, 2010, from http://www.albany.edu/sourcebook/toc_6.html

Bureau of Justice Stattistics. (2003). *Sourcebook of criminal justice statistics*. Retrieved July 21, 2010, from http://www.albany.edu/sourcebook/toc_6.html

Bureau of Justice Stattistics. (2009). *Sourcebook of criminal justice statistics*. Retrieved July 21, 2010, from http://www.albany.edu/sourcebook/toc_6.html

Crundall, I., & Deacon, K. (1997). A prison-based alcohol use education program: Evaluation of a pilot study. *Substance Use & Misuse, 32*(6), 767–777.

Cullen, F. T., & Gendreau, P. (2000). Assessing correctional rehabilitation: Policy, practice, and prospects. In J. Horney (Ed.), *Criminal justice 2000: Policies, processes, and decisions of the criminal justice system* (Vol. 3, pp. 109–176). Washington, DC: U.S. Department of Justice, National Institute of Justice.

Cullen, F. T., & Gilbert, K. E. (1982). *Reaffirming rehabilitation*. Cincinnati, OH: Anderson.

Daley, M., Love, C. T., Shepard, D. S., Petersen, C. B., White, K. L., & Hall, F. B. (2004). Cost effectiveness of Connecticut's in-prison substance abuse treatment. *Journal of Offender Rehabilitation, 39*(3), 69–92.

Darabi, G. A. (1992). *Psychological impact of tier programs: An outcome evaluation*. Tallahassee, FL: Bureau of Planning, Research, and Statistics.

DeLeon, G. (1984). Program based evaluation research in therapeutic communities. In F. M. Tims & J. P. Ludford (Eds.), *Drug abuse treatment evaluation: Strategies, progress and prospect* (Research Monograph No. 51) (pp. 69–87). Rockville, MD: National Institute on Drug Abuse.

DeLeon, G. (1994). Therapeutic communities. In M. Galanter & H. D. Kleber (Eds.), *The American Psychiatric Press Textbook of substance abuse treatment* (pp. 447–462). Washington, DC: American Psychiatric Press.

Dowden, C., & Blanchette, K. (2002). An evaluation of the effectiveness of substance abuse programming for female offenders. *International Journal of Offender Therapy and Comparative Criminology, 46*(2), 220–230.

Dugan, J. R., & Everett, R. S. (1998). An experimental test of chemical dependency therapy for jail inmates. *International Journal of Offender Therapy and Comparative Criminology, 42*(4), 360–368.

Eisenberg, M., & Fabelo, T. (1996). Evaluation of the Texas correctional substance abuse treatment initiative: The impact of policy research. *Crime & Delinquency, 42*(2), 296–308.

Eisenberg, M., Riechers, L., & Arrigona, N. (2001). *Evaluation of the performance of the Texas Department of Criminal Justice Rehabilitation Tier programs*. Austin, TX: Criminal Justice Policy Council.

Farrington, D. P., Gottfredson, D. C., Sherman, L. W., & Welsh, B. C. (2002). The Maryland scientific methods scale. In L. W. Sherman, D. P. Farrington, B. C. Welsh, & D. L. MacKenzie (Eds.), *Evidence-based crime prevention* (pp. 13–21). New York: Routledge.

Finigan, M. W., Barron, N., & Carey, S. (2003). Effectively assessing and preparing inmates for community substance abuse treatment: The Portland target cities project in-jail intervention. In R. C. Stephens, C. K. Scott, & R. D. Muck (Eds.), *Clinical assessment and substance abuse treatment: The target cities experience* (pp. 165–178). Albany, NY: State University of New York.

Gordon, J. A. (2002). *Barrett juvenile correctional center: Is it effective?* Richmond, VA: Virginia Commonwealth University.

Gransky, L. A., & Jones, R. J. (1997). *Evaluation of the post-release status of substance abuse program participants*. Chicago: Illinois Criminal Justice Information Authority.

Hanson, G. (2000). *Pine Lodge intensive inpatient treatment program*. Olympia, WA: Washington State Department of Corrections, Planning and Research Section.

Hartmann, D. J., Wolk, J. L., Johnston, L. S., & Colyer, C. J. (1997). Recidivism and substance abuse outcomes in a prison-based therapeutic community. *Federal Probation, 61*(4), 18–25.

Hughey, R., & Klemke, L. W. (1996). Evaluation of a jail-based substance abuse treatment program. *Federal Probation, 60*(4), 40–44.

Hume, S., & Gorta, A. (1989). *Results of community urinalyses for clients on the N.S.W. Prison Methadone program, Study 6*. New South Wales, Australia: New South Wales Department of Corrective Services.

Hunter, J. E., & Schmidt, F. L. (2004). *Methods of meta-analysis: Correcting error and bias in research findings*. Thousand Oaks, CA: Sage.

Inciardi, J. A., Martin, S. S., Butzin, C. A., Hooper, R. M., & Harrison, L. D. (1997). An effective model of prison-based treatment for drug-involved offenders. *Journal of Drug Issues, 27*(2), 261–279.

Johnson, S. L., van de Ven, J. T. C., & Grant, B. A. (2001). *Institutional Methadone maintenance treatment: Impact on release outcome and institutional behaviour* (No. 119). Ottawa, ON: Correctional Service of Canada, Research Branch.

Kelly, W. R. (2001). *An outcome evaluation of the Texas Youth Commission's Chemical dependency treatment program*. Austin, TX: University of Texas.

Kinlock, T. W., Battjes, R. J., & Schwartz, R. P. (2005). A novel opiod maintenance program for prisoners: Report of post-release outcomes. *American Journal of Drug and Alcohol Abuse, 31*, 433–454.

Klebe, K. J., & O'Keefe, M. (1998). *Outcome evaluation of the crossroads to freedom house and Peer I therapeutic communities*. Colorado Springs, CO: University of Colorado.

Knight, K., Simpson, D. D., & Hiller, M. (1999). Three-year reincarceration outcomes for in-prison therapeutic community treatment in Texas. *The Prison Journal, 79*(3), 337–351.

Kunitz, S. J., Woodall, W. G., Zhao, H., Wheeler, D. R., Lillis, R., & Rogers, E. (2002). Rearrest rates after incarceration for DWI: A comparative study in a Southwestern US County. *American Journal of Public Health, 92*(11), 1826–1831.

Langan, P. A., & Levin, D. J. (2002). *Recidivism of prisoners released in 1994* (No. NCJ-193427). Washington, DC: U.S. Department of Justice, Bureau of Justice Statistics.

Latessa, E. J., & Holsinger, A. M. (1998). The importance of evaluating correctional programs: Assessing outcome and quality. *Corrections Management Quarterly, 2*(4), 22–29.

Lipsey, M. W., & Wilson, D. B. (1993). The efficacy of psychological, educational, and behavioral treatment: Confirmation from meta-analysis. *American Psychologist, 48*(12), 1181–1209.

Lipsey, M. W., & Wilson, D. B. W. (2001). *Practical Meta-analysis*. Thousand Oaks, CA: Sage.

Lipton, D., Martinson, R., & Wilks, J. (1975). *The effectiveness of correctional treatment: A survey of treatment evaluation studies*. New York: Praeger.

Little, G. L., Robinson, K. D., & Burnette, K. D. (1989). Treating drug offenders with moral reconation therapy: A three-year recidivism report. *Psychological Reports, 69*(3), 1151–1154.

MacKenzie, D. L. (2001). Corrections and sentencing in the 21st century: Evidence-based corrections and sentencing. *The Prison Journal, 81*(3), 299–312.

MacKenzie, D. (2005). The importance of using scientific evidence to make decisions about correctional programming. *Criminology & Public Policy, 4*(2), 249–258.

MacKenzie, D. (2006). *What works in corrections*. New York: Cambridge University Press.

MacKenzie, D. L., & Armstrong, G. S. (Eds.). (2004). *Correctional boot camps: Military basic training as a model for corrections*. Thousand Oaks, CA: Sage.

Magura, S., Rosenblum, A. L. C., & Joseph, H. (1993). The effectiveness of in-jail methadone maintenance. *Journal of Drug Issues, 23*(1), 75–99.

Martin, S. S., Butzin, C. A., Saum, C. A., & Inciardi, J. A. (1999). Three-year outcomes of therapeutic community treatment for drug-involved offenders in Delaware: From prison to work release to aftercare. *Prison Journal, 79*(3), 294–320.

Martinson, R. (1974). What works? Questions and answers about prision reform. *Public Interest, 10*, 22–54.

Miller, J. M., & Koons-Witt, B. (2003). *Outcome evaluation of the South Caronlina residential substance abuse treatment program for state prisoners*. Columbia, SC: University of South Carolina.

Mitchell, O., Wilson, D. B., & MacKenzie, D. L. (2007). Does incaceration-based drug treatment reduce recidivism? A meta-analytic synthesis of the research. *Journal of Experimental Criminology, 3*(4), 353–375.

Mosher, C., & Phillips, D. M. (2002). *Final report on the program evaluation of the Pine Lodge pre-release residential therapeutic community for women offenders in Washington State*. Pullman, WA: Washington State University.

Mumola, C. J. (1999). *Substance abuse and treatment, state and federal prisioners, 1997*. Washington, DC: Bureau of Justice Stattistics.

Nash, J. E. (2000). *Final report of outcomes for Ozark Correctional Center Drug treatment program*. Springfield, MO: Center for Social Sciences and Public Policy Research.

Office of National Drug Control Policy. (2003). *Drugs and crime facts*. Retrieved January 15, 2010, from http://www.whitehouse-drugpolicy/gov/publications/factsht/drugdata/index.html

Oregon Department of Corrections. (1994). *Comparison of outcomes and costs residential and outpatient treatment programs for inmates alcohol and drug, mental health, sex offender, and social skills treatment*. Salem, Oregon: Oregon Department of Corrections.

Palmer, T. (1983). The "effectiveness" issue today: An overview. *Federal Probation, 47*, 3–10.

Palmer, T. (1992). *The re-emergence of correctional interventionism*. Newburry Park, CA: Sage.

Pealer, J. A., Latessa, E. J., & Winesburg, M. (2002). *Final report: Mohican Youth Center RSAT outcome evaluation*. Cincinnati, OH: University of Cincinnati, Center for Criminal Justice Research.

Pearson, F. S., & Lipton, D. S. (1999). A meta-analytic review of the effectiveness of corrections-based treatment for drug abuse. *The Prison Journal, 79*(4), 384–410.

Pelissier, B., Rhodes, W., Saylor, W., Gaes, G., Camp, S. D., Vanyur, S. D., et al. (2000). *TRIAD Drug treatment evaluation project final report of three-year outcomes: Part I*. Washington, DC: Federal Bureau of Prisons, Office of Research and Evaluation.

Peters, R. H., Kearns, W. D., Murrin, M. R., Dolente, A. S., & May, R. L., II. (1993). Examining the effectiveness of in-jail substance abuse treatment. *Journal of Offender Rehabilitation, 19*(3/4), 1–39.

Porporino, F. J., Robinson, D., Millson, B., & Weekes, J. R. (2002). An outcome evaluation of prison based treatment programming for substance users. *Substance Use & Misuse, 37*(8–10), 1047–1077.

Porter, R. (2002). *Breaking the cycle: Technical report*. New York: Vera Institute of Justice.

Prendergast, M. L., Podus, D., Chang, E., & Urada, D. (2003). *An outcome evaluation of the forever free substance abuse treatment program: One-year post-release outcomes*. Santa Monica, CA: Drug Abuse Research Center.

Prendergast, M. L., Wellisch, J., & Wong, M. M. (1996). Residential treatment for women parolees following prison-based drug treatment: Treatment experiences, needs and services, outcomes. *The Prison Journal, 76*(3), 253–274.

Rothstein, H. R., Sutton, A. J., & Borenstein, M. (Eds.). (2005). *Publication bias in meta-analysis: Prevention, assessment, and adjustments*. New York: Wiley.

Sealock, M. D., Gottfredson, D. C., & Gallagher, C. A. (1997). Drug treatment for juvenile offenders: Some good and bad news. *Journal of Research in Crime and Delinquency, 34*(2), 210–236.

Siegal, H. A., Wang, J., Falck, R. S., Rahman, A. M., & Carlson, R. G. (1997). *An evaluation of Ohio's prison-based therapeutic community treatment programs for substance abusers: Final report*. Dayton, OH: Wright State University, School of Medicine.

Smith, C. J. (1996). *The California civil addict program: An evaluation of implementation and effectiveness*. Unpublished doctoral dissertation, University of California, Irvine, CA and Ann Arbor, MI.

Substance Abuse and Mental Health Services Administration, Office of Applied Studies. (2002). *National survey of substance abuse treatment services (N-SSATS): 2000 Data on substance abuse treatment facilities* (DASIS Series: S-16, DHHS Publication No. (SMA) 02-3668). Rockville, MD: Department of Health and Human Services.

Taxman, F. S., & Friedmann, P. D. (2009). Fidelity and adherence at the transition point: Theoretically driven experiments. *Journal of Experimental Criminology, 5*, 219–226.

Taxman, F. S., & Spinner, D. L. (1996). *The jail addiction services (JAS) project in Montgomery County, Maryland*. College Park, MD: University of Maryland.

Taylor, B. G., Fitzgerald, N., Hunt, D., Reardon, J. A., & Brownstein, H. H. (2001). *ADAM preliminary 2000 findings on drug use and drug markets – Adult male arrestees* (No. NCJ-189101). Washington, DC: National Institute of Justice.

Tunis, S., Austin, J., Morris, M., Hardyman, P., & Bolyard, M. (1995). *Evaluation of drug treatment in local corrections: Final Report*. San Francisco: National Council on Crime and Delinquency.

Turley, A., Thornton, T. N., Johnson, C., & Azzolino, S. (2004). Jail drug and alcohol treatment program reduces recidivism in nonviolent offenders: A Longitudinal study of Monroe County, New York's jail treatment drug and alcohol program. *International Journal of Offender Therapy and Comparative Criminology, 48*(6), 721–728.

Van Stelle, K. R., & Moberg, D. P. (2001). *Outcome evaluation of the Wisconsin residential substance abuse program: The Mental illness-chemical abuse (MICA) program at Oshkosh Correctional Institution, 1998–2000*. Madison, WI: University of Wisconsin Medical School.

Vaughn, M. S., Deng, F., & Lee, L.-J. (2003). Evaluating a prison-based drug treatment program in Taiwan. *Journal of Drug Issues, 33*(2), 357–384.

Voas, R. B., & Tippetts, A. S. (1990). Evaluation of treatment and monitoring programs for drunken drivers. *Journal of Traffic Medicine, 18*, 15–26.

Washington State Department of Corrections. (1988). *Substance abuse treatment program evaluation of outcomes and management report*. Olympia, WA: Washington State Department of Corrections.

Welsh, W. N. (2002). *Evaluation of prison-based drug treatment in Pennsylvania*. Philadelphia: Temple University.

Wexler, H. K., Falkin, G. P., & Lipton, D. S. (1990). Outcome evaluation of a prison therapeutic community for substance abuse treatment. *Criminal Justice and Behavior, 17*(1), 71–92.

Wexler, H. K., Melnick, G., Lowe, L., & Peters, J. (1999). Three-year reincarceration outcomes for amity in-prison therapeutic community and aftercare in California. *Prison Journal, 79*(3), 321–336.

Wilson, D. J. (2000). *Drug use, testing and treatment in jails* (No. NCJ-179999). Washington, DC: U.S. Department of Justice, Bureau of Justice Statistics.

Winesburg, M., Latessa, E. J., & Pealer, J. A. (2002). *Final report: Noble Choices RSAT outcome evaluation*. Cincinnati, OH: Center for Criminal Justice Research, University of Cincinnati.

Zamble, E., & Porporino, F. J. (1988). *Coping, behavior, and adaptation in prision inmates*. New York: Springer.

Zhang, S. (2000). *An evaluation of the Los Angeles County juvenile drug treatment boot camp: Final report*. San Marcos, CA: California State University.

# Parole: "What Works" Is Still Under Construction

# 12

Faye S. Taxman

**Abstract**

Parole supervision serves three functions – to monitor offenders, to oversee the conditions of release, and to provide needed services – with an overarching goal of reducing criminal behavior. To assess the efficacy of parole, each function needs to be examined separately, and then all need to be considered collectively. The question of parole efficacy is dependent in part on the behavior to be influenced (e.g., criminal behavior, drug use, employment and social productivity, risky behaviors). Unfortunately, rigorous studies of parole supervision itself are lacking, limiting any conclusions about its overall effectiveness. Experimental studies have demonstrated that reduced caseload sizes (25 to 40) and intensive supervision (using various types of contact) do not reduce recidivism. Promising strategies include a behavioral management role for parole officers where the goal is to facilitate offender change and to reinforce treatment conditions. Most studies on parole have focused on specific treatment interventions, such as cognitive-behavioral therapy or therapeutic communities. We know much more about the interventions that work for offenders than we do about the role of parole officers and strategies that officers can use to affect offender outcomes. Future research should focus on the role of parole, and related activities of parole officers, to advance a greater appreciation for how to improve offender outcomes.

**Keywords**

Parole • Therapeutic alliance • Recidivism • Parole officers • Treatment • Behavioral Management

Parole supervision serves three functions – to monitor offenders, to oversee the conditions of release, and to provide needed services – with an overarching goal of reducing the risk of criminal behavior. To assess the efficacy of parole, each function needs to be examined separately, and then considered collectively. The question

F.S. Taxman (✉)
Criminology, Law & Society, Fairfax, VA 22030, USA
e-mail: ftaxman@gmu.edu

C. Leukefeld et al. (eds.), *Handbook of Evidence-Based Substance Abuse Treatment in Criminal Justice Settings*, Issues in Children's and Families' Lives 11,
DOI 10.1007/978-1-4419-9470-7_12, © Springer Science+Business Media, LLC 2011

of parole efficacy is dependent in part on the behavior to be influenced (e.g., criminal behavior, drug use, employment and social productivity, risky behaviors). Unfortunately, rigorous studies of parole itself are lacking, limiting any conclusions about its overall effectiveness. Studies have more commonly focused on specific treatment interventions, such as cognitive-behavioral therapy or therapeutic communities. We know much more about the interventions that work for offenders or addicts than we do about the effective use of parole and parole officers to impact overall outcomes. Most interventions that work, for probationers, drug court offenders, offenders in prison and jail settings, and those in community treatment who are not involved in the criminal justice system, are assumed to have a similar impact for parolees. However, research on parolees is lacking, and it is unclear how parole supervision may impact the outcomes from specific interventions.

We are in the early stages of evidence collection regarding how the parole officer can best facilitate parolees' involvement in, and compliance with, programs or interventions, as well as what evidence-based practices parole officers should employ. The following review outlines the available literature about the role of parole officers and provides a general roadmap for improving our knowledge about parole effectiveness. It is categorized into five main sections: (1) background on parole delivery systems and the needs of parolees; (2) overview of the theories guiding parole supervision; (3) effectiveness of parole, including parole-related services that have not been researched, parole-related services that are deemed ineffective, parole-related services that are promising, and parole-related services that are effective; (4) effectiveness of treatment services for offenders, including those that are not effective, promising, and effective; and (5) recommendations for improving parole. To classify a program or service as "effective," at least three well-designed studies that report similar findings are being used as the benchmark. This standard is slightly above other reviews of the literature but it serves to ensure that the findings are consistent across studies.

## Parole in the United States: Size of the Population

The estimated size of the parole population in the United States is around 800,000, but the actual size is unknown because parole is in a continuing state of change. Parole was once reserved for those released from incarceration before the completion of their sentence, and was offered to those offenders who exhibited good behavior while incarcerated. With the abolition of the parole release function by states and the federal government in the 1990s, release decisions changed markedly. Offenders could no longer earn early discharge based on good behavior or on the achievement of milestones, such as obtaining a high school diploma. Many states abolishing parole release recognized, however, that released offenders might require supervision in the community for a period of time: and, therefore, placed offenders on some form of mandatory supervision after release. Many jail sentences now include a post-incarceration period of probation, and the federal system treats many offenders in a similar manner. The size of the combined probation and parole population in the United States is estimated at over six million (Glaze & Bonczar, 2008).

Parole supervision is delivered through different state authorities. The majority of parolees are supervised by agencies that also administer the state prison system (69%); the rest are supervised by independent parole agencies (25%), or a mix of other types of agencies (7%). Over half of parolees are under supervision in five state agencies – California, Illinois, Texas, New York, and Pennsylvania. Parole agencies in California, Illinois, and Texas are administered by the state correctional department whereas the parole offices are independent agencies in New York and Pennsylvania. Probation and parole agencies are four times more likely to supervise probationers than parolees. Parole officers are generally required to meet with offenders under supervision on a fixed basis, ranging from once per week (14%), to once per month (54%), to less than once per month (17%). In some cases, only administrative reporting is required (13%). For a description of parole agencies, see Bonczar (2008).

Nearly all parole agencies have access to drug treatment services, yet the capacity of these programs is limited, with only around 11% of the offenders able to receive services (Glaze & Bonczar, 2008; Taxman, Perdoni, & Harrison, 2007). Other services provided include sex offender treatment (4%) and mental health programs (9%). Some agencies provide housing referrals (8%), while others have working relationships with state housing agencies (14%), or private rental agencies to refer parolees to landlords (12%). Some supervising agencies offer employment assistance through an in-house employment service (12%), a defined working relationship with a state employment agency (34%), or a private employment service (16%). However, a large portion of parole agencies do not have a formal arrangement with either a housing (60%) or an employment (50%) program (see Bonczar, 2008).

With the abolition of parole, offenders are more likely to be released on mandatory release (i.e., at the expiration of prison time) or on an early, discretionary release, based on good conduct. The average male offender released on discretionary parole serves 36 months as compared to 34 months for those on mandatory parole. The same pattern exists for female offenders; the average women released on discretionary parole serves 26 months, while those on mandatory parole serve 24 months. African Americans tend to have longer stays, with averages of 38 months (discretionary) and 37 months (mandatory).

While being supervised, parolees can be technically violated for failure to meet the conditions of release. Violations of parole are commonplace. About half of parolees return to incarceration for failure to complete parole successfully, and these returns represent a third of prison intakes. California (67.2%), Louisiana (53.1%), and Utah (55.3%) had the highest percentage of parole violators reenter state prisons, while the lowest portion of admissions were found in Florida (6.9%), Alabama (9.3%), and Indiana (9.6%). Parole revocations were most likely due to an arrest or conviction for a new offense (69.9%) but also include absconding (22.3%), drug-related violations (16.1%), and other violations, such as a possession of a firearm (3.5%), and failure to report for counseling (2.4%), or failure to maintain employment (1.2%). Drug offenders (i.e., drug possession, intent to distribute, or trafficking) and public order offenders (i.e., offenses that concern public order like urinating in public and loitering) are more often violators of parole than in the previous decades (Glaze & Bonczar, 2008).

## Theory of Parole Release Decisions and Parole Supervision

The release decision and community supervision operate under different theories. Typically parole refers to the supervision of offenders in the community, to monitor offenders, oversee conditions of release, and provide needed services. But the parole release decision, which was abolished in many states and federal agencies in the last two decades, offered another purpose.

The release decision is based on the concept of token economy or contingency management, where the goal is to incentivize good conduct by offering the prospect of earning early release from prison. The notion is that the offender's behavior can be shaped by the hope of serving less incarceration time. Offenders can demonstrate their commitment to changing behaviors, through participation in educational, work, or treatment programs designed to provide them with the skills needed to live crime free. Offenders can then present their accomplishments to an impartial board that can assess the progress made during incarceration. With the abolition of parole release decisions and the push to increase the minimum length of sentence served (the 1994 Truth in Sentencing Act encouraged that offenders serve 85% of their sentence), the incentive structure has diminished in value. To a large extent, correctional policies at the federal and state levels have removed these opportunities for "earned discharge" (Petersilia, 2006) and thus have diminished the ability to motivate incarcerated offenders to make positive changes in their behavior.

Parole supervision operates under a different theoretical framework. Three general theories define its purpose: to monitor behavior (law enforcement/surveillance), to acquire needed resources (resource broker), and to assist the offender in changing behavior (social worker) (Petersilia, 2006; Taxman, 2002, 2006). The law enforcement/surveillance premise is that supervision provides a form of external control that establishes and defines expected behaviors. The surveillance model of social control (specific deterrence theory) holds that the person will conform to expectations to avoid consequences. The resource broker model holds that parole agencies do not have the technical skills to address the psychological, social, or medical needs of the offender related to criminal behavior. The function of parole, therefore, should be to garner those needed services to ameliorate the conditions that contribute to criminal behavior. The social worker model considers the role of parole officer to be similar to that of a counselor, in providing the services that will reduce involvement in criminal behavior. A new theory of behavioral manager has evolved that is a hybrid of the law enforcement and social worker models (Taxman, 2008; Taxman, Shepardson, & Byrne, 2004). The behavioral manager model is based on the premise that compliance will occur when the parolee understands the expectations, is involved in the decisions regarding conditions of release and consequences for behavior, and is held responsible for his/her own behavior, and the parole officer illustrates a partnership in these shared decisions. The behavioral manager model is a relationship theory that emphasizes that the process for determining expectations should be a shared decision between the parole officer and the parolee, and that the emphasis should be on addressing the risk (historical behavior) and needs (psychosocial functioning) of the offender to improve outcomes. This theory builds on the risk-needs-responsivity model, with emphasis being placed on providing services that manage risk and need factors (Andrews & Bonta, 1998).

## Literature on Effective Parole Practices: The Core of Supervision

Under any theory of parole, face-to-face contacts between the parolee and the authority of the state (the parole officer) provide the mechanism for conducting parole: monitoring the offender in the community and overseeing the conditions of release established by the court or by the Parole Board, or, in some cases, by the parole officer. The conditions of release should be tied to the restrictions of movement or place that affect engagement in criminal behavior or to the services/programs that address the psychosocial functioning of offenders. The type of conditions varies, depending on the overriding theory of parole supervision employed. Most parole agencies have standard conditions of release for all parolees (i.e., inform the parole office of address changes, do not carry a weapon, remain crime free). Special conditions are generally tied to the offender's criminogenic factors that affect stability in the community, such as drug use, mental health problems, criminal peers, or negative social networks. Together, these standard and special conditions establish behavioral expectations for parolees and define the range of actions to be taken by the parole officer.

## Parole Supervision Areas That Lack Adequate Research

The core component of supervision has not been test empirically for efficacy. That is, there have been no experiments or studies addressing whether being on parole (i.e., having contact with the parole officer) has any impact on offender behavior. The unanswered question is whether an offender would perform just as well unsupervised. The answer to this basic question is needed to determine whether parole supervision has merit, or merely serves, through the use of technical violations, as an additional means of (re)entry into the justice system.

Another area that requires empirical testing is the working alliance or relationship between officer and parolee. Does it serve to monitor behavior, broker resources, provide social work services, or provide behavioral management services (Taxman & Ainsworth, 2009)? A recent review of the literature indicates that the working alliance is an important factor in that it fosters positive outcomes; however, it is unclear how this finding translates into a specific role for the parole officer. For example, the Petersilia and Turner (1993) large-scale, randomized, experiment on intensive supervision programs (ISP) seemed to indicate that, when the officer assumed a resource broker role (e.g., linked offenders with treatment and employment resources), there were fewer arrests and violations. However, the ISP experiment did not directly test one model of supervision against another. Therefore, it did not provide information such as whether the resource broker model of supervision model, with its many officer/parolee contacts, had a dosage effect.

## Practices That Are Ineffective

In the 1960s–1970s, a number of randomized trials were conducted to determine the optimal caseload size for a parole officer, the working hypothesis being that having too many cases would interfere with parole's effectiveness. The studies were designed to assess how many cases a parole officer could supervise and still achieve desired outcomes of fewer criminal behaviors, arrests, and/or technical violations (see Table 12.1). Unfortunately, none of the experiments generated findings that were useful in answering core questions about caseload size due to the large variation in tasks that officers performed and the failure of the studies to define the different theories of parole supervision. Within a parole office, some officers focused on controls and others focused on service provision. The studies were designed under the assumption that an officer could use a myriad of supervision strategies to be parolee-specific instead of just focusing on supervision. In the end, the studies did not document the supervision strategies but rather the size of the caseloads. While the studies indicate that caseload size does not matter, they are limited in that the dosage level, the number of parolees assigned to each officer, or the number of contacts that define supervision activities are not documented. These null effect experiments were reinforced by a later study that found that officers with reduced caseloads (around 40 offenders per officer) tended to spend more time on administrative duties rather than increasing the time spent on parole supervision duties with each parolee (Latessa, Travis, Fulton, & Stichman, 1998).

The caseload size research, while inconclusive, led to another set of studies on the frequency of contact between the officer and parolee. These "frequency of contact" or dosage-level studies paid attention to the amount of contacts, with an emphasis on the core set of a parole officer's activities. Intensive supervision, or increasing the frequency of contacts, was introduced as a mechanism to ensure that the officer had a minimum number of face-to-face contacts with the parolee and specific activities such as drug testing. This genre of research measured weekly contacts with the parole officer and drug testing regime. The largest multisite randomized trial (13 sites, of which 11 sites managed probationers and 2 managed parolees) found that intensive supervision services did not increase the average contacts between the officer and parolee but did increase the use of drug testing. The increased reporting resulted in heightened technical violations for those being observed more frequently (the experimental group) and had no impact on rearrest rates for criminal behavior compared to the comparison group (Petersilia & Turner, 1993). Not surprisingly, more frequent contact with the parole (probation) officer results in more oversight of the parolee, which provides more opportunities to observe compliance problems with parole requirements (technical violations). Even though no research has found a correlation between technical violations and criminal behavior, intensive supervision in several meta-analyses has been found to be ineffective in reducing criminal behavior and may actually increase technical violations (Aos, Miller, & Drake, 2006; MacKenzie, 2000; Petersilia & Turner, 1993). In summary, the existing research on caseload size and number

**Table 12.1** Primary studies examining caseload size and face-to-face contacts

| Intervention | Method | Findings |
|---|---|---|
| *Caseload size* | | |
| Adams, Welch, and Bonds (1958) | Randomized | NS |
| Eze (1962) | Randomized | NS |
| Havel and Sulk (1962) | Randomized | NS |
| CA Department of Corrections (1960, 1961) | Randomized | NS |
| Himelson and Margulies (1965) | Randomized | NS |
| Sing (1967) | Randomized | NS |
| Burkhart (1969) | Randomized | NS |
| *Intensive supervision* | | |
| Fallen, Apperson, Hall-Milligan, and Aos (1982) | Quasi-experimental | NS |
| Erwin (1986) | Quasi-experimental | NS |
| Mitchell and Butter (1986) | Quasi-experimental | NS |
| Pearson (1987) | Quasi-experimental | NS |
| Byrne and Kelly (1989) | Quasi-experimental | NS |
| Jolin and Stipack (1991) | Quasi-experimental | NS |
| Petersilia and Turner (1993) | Randomized (5) | NS |
| Austin and Hardyman (1991) (electronic monitor) | Quasi-experimental | NS |
| NCCD (1991) | Quasi-experimental | NS |
| Latessa (1992) | Quasi-experimental | NS |
| Latessa (1993a) | Quasi-experimental | NS |
| Moon and Latessa (1993) | Quasi-experimental | NS |
| Latessa (1993b) | Quasi-experimental | NS |
| Latessa et al. (1998) | Randomized | NS |

Adapted from Taxman (2002).
NS = not significant

of contacts fails to define the aspects of parole supervision that improve outcomes. Instead, the studies raise questions as to the efficacy of different models of parole supervision and its impact on rearrests or technical violations contributing to a growing concern that parole supervision is not valuable (Solomon, Johnson, Travis, & McBride, 2004).

## Promising Parole Services

A recent meta-analysis conducted by the Washington State Institute of Public Policy found that supervision combined with treatment (with the possibility that the parole officer is either a resource broker, social worker, or behavioral manager) was effective in reducing recidivism. The effect size was 0.07 for intensive supervision combined with community treatment which indicates a small, but significant effect (Aos et al., 2006). A number of quasi-experimental designs yielded similar findings (Paparozzi & DeMichele, 2008; Petersilia & Turner, 1993).

As noted above, parole supervision has started to test a new approach that involves the use of behavioral manager styles of supervision (Taxman, 2002). In the therapeutic literature, there is strong empirical evidence that the quality of the relationship between the counselor and the client is an important predictor of outcomes (see Castonguay & Beutler, 2005; Norcross, 2002). Taxman (2002) identified the counselor-client relationship as an important dimension of supervision and included it in the theoretical model of behavioral management supervision (see Taxman, 2008; Taxman & Ainsworth, 2009; Taxman et al., 2004). Skeem, Louden, Polaschek, and Camp (2007) developed the Dual-Role Relationships Inventory (DRI–R) instrument to measure relationship quality. Using this tool with probationers with mental health conditions, they found that relationship quality can be measured in terms of caring and fairness, trust, and an authoritative (not authoritarian) style. They concluded that the quality of dual-role relationships predicts compliance with the rules, as assessed by probation violations and revocation. Probationers (with mental health conditions) who perceived their officer to be tough had more failures and higher numbers of violations (Skeem et al., 2007). Thanner and Taxman (2003) found that, when offenders observed that they had a voice (i.e., the probation/parole officer allowed the offender to participate in deciding what type of sanctions to employ for failure to comply with requirements), reduced arrests and reduced positive drug tests resulted. Taxman (2008) found that a probation model that included this component was effective in reducing rearrest rates and approached statistical significance in terms of reducing violation rates.

A few prospective studies are examining the other roles that probation/parole officers could have in supervising offenders. These studies tend to be multisite trials that test the model of the parole officer as behavioral manager. Taxman, Byrne, and Thanner (2002) implemented a four-site, randomized study that involved placing a treatment counselor with a probation officer, to screen offenders for substance abuse disorders and place them in treatment as indicated. The probation/parole officer acted as both a resource broker, who worked with the counselor on treatment access, and a monitor who addressed compliance with drug test results and attendance records for treatment and supervision sessions. The trial resulted in increased access to treatment services and increased days in treatment, and reduced arrests and opiate drug use for high-risk offenders; but the seamless intervention was more costly to deliver and did not result in overall reduced recidivism (Alemi et al., 2006).

Another study examining the role transition of the parole officer from broker to behavioral manager is underway; and a similar randomized trial is underway, in three parole offices where offenders are provided cognitive-behavioral therapy on-site at the probation office (Effects of Manualized Treatment on a Seamless System of Care, see Taxman, Wilson, & Trotman, 2007). The latter study addresses the quality of the treatment services and also serves to refine the role of the parole officer as a behavioral manager. The parole officer conducts weekly progress reviews and determines the extent to which the parolee has established new goals. The goal-setting process occurs concurrently with weekly cognitive-behavioral therapy sessions for a total of 18 weeks. In this study, the working relationship between officer and offender is being measured using the Dual-Role Relationships Inventory (DRI–R) instrument (see Skeem et al., 2007). The control group receives the resource broker model of parole, with offenders referred to services in the community after being assessed by a clinician at the parole office. The preliminary findings from this study are that, after 3 months, those exposed to the seamless model, with manualized, on-site treatment, are more likely to be drug free and to access treatment than those receiving resource broker services (Taxman, Trotman, & Wilson, 2009).

The parole officer as a behavioral manager was also the focus of the six-site Step'n Out project. This study required the parole officer and treatment provider to work together on a collaborative behavioral management (CBM) process: accessing treatment needs; reviewing treatment progress; and using a structured reward schedule, to incentivize offenders for positive behavior. CBM has three major components. First, it explicitly articulates the roles of parole officer, treatment staff, and offenders, and conveys the expectations for each in the supervision process. Second, it employs a behavioral contract that defines the consequences if offenders fail to remain crime and drug free. The behavioral contract specifies, on a weekly basis, the concrete behaviors the offender is expected to engage in. These target behaviors include requirements for compliance with supervision and formal addiction treatment, and involvement in behaviors that compete with drug use (e.g., getting a job, enhancing a non-drug social network). This is known as behavioral targeting. Third, it regularly monitors adherence to the behavioral contract, and employs both reinforcers and sanctions to shape behavior. The project motto of "Catching People Doing Things Right" was based on a contingency management approach, creating, as part of normal supervision, the conditions to notice and reward offenders for achieving incremental, prosocial steps. CBM establishes a systematic, standardized, and progressive approach to reinforcement and sanctioning, thereby ensuring consistency and fairness. It was supported by a computer program, the Step'n Out Computerized Input Environment (SNOCONE). The weekly review of goals obtained was completed as part of standard parole conditions. The CBM contract was monitored weekly to expedite identification and reinforcement of compliance and sanction of noncompliance, and then renegotiated and printed for the following week. Compliance with the contract earned points for the parolee and, when preestablished milestones were reached, material and social rewards were given. The control group for this study received a resource broker style of parole. Study findings are yet to be published but it appears that the CBM approach had small, positive effects on drug use and criminal behaviors in some sites; implementation affected the overall outcomes (Friedmann, Rhodes, & Taxman, 2009).

The Proactive Community Supervision Study (PCS) (Taxman, 2008) tested the behavioral management style of parole compared to the monitoring style of parole. This was a place-based design where four parole/probation offices in Maryland used a behavioral manager supervision style, while the comparison group of four similar offices maintained their existing style of supervision. This quasi-experimental design matched offices based on characteristics such as the number of offenders supervised and the characteristics of the offenders (e.g., age, number of prior violations from supervision, number of incarcerations, types of arrests). The four PCS offices were involved in an organizational change process that spanned four years during which each office was converted to a learning laboratory. Supervisors were responsible, as mentors and coaches for the staff, and they were provided with specific training sessions to deliver to their staff during the conversion period. All staff was trained in three key skills: (1) building working relationships with offenders; (2) using risk and needs tools to develop outcome-driven case plans; and (3) motivating offenders. All three of these skills reinforced the behavioral management role of the parole officers and, since the offices were converting to this model, office leaders used these same skills to supervise staff and to promote implementation of the model. Findings from this study were impressive in that the degree of implementation of the overall model exceeded that of most other studies of altered practices. When controlling for length of time on supervision and prior criminal history, logistic regression results showed that offenders supervised in the behavioral management style were less likely to be rearrested (30% for the PCS and 42% of the non-PCS sample; $p < 0.01$) and less likely to have warrant issues for technical violations (34.7% of the PCS group and 40% for the non-PCS group; $p < 0.10$). Increased time on supervision without a violation occurred in the PCS offices, where the offender was on supervision for an average of 268 days, as compared with the non-PCS offices (mean = 210 days) ($t$-statistic: 2.69, $p \leq 0.05$). The reduction in rearrests and increase in time to violations indicate that the PCS intervention resulted in changed behaviors. The process yielded more time for officers to work with offenders on criminogenic needs. A replication of this study, conducted in Travis County, Texas, examined pre-post findings for a PCS-modeled intervention and found that revocations were reduced from 5.9% to 3.4% for felony offenders with reductions in recidivism noted for all three risk levels (Eisenberg, Bryle, & Fabelo, 2009; Sprow, 2009).

The body of literature on parole supervision is relatively small, especially given the size of the parole population and public concerns about the effectiveness of parole supervision. The majority of studies have been devoted to measuring the appropriate dosage level (i.e., number and length of contacts), with some recent attention paid to testing different theoretical frameworks for delivering supervision services. Studies with similar findings are not yet sufficient in number to conclusively establish a particular framework for supervising offenders in the field that would be most beneficial. Furthermore, researchers are just beginning to learn how to conduct intervention studies in parole environments. The techniques employed in clinical environments, where there are more unified goals, have also been used in correctional settings. But the multiple goals, and the tension between public safety and treatment objectives in these environments, create additional challenges in conducting field research studies and in implementing new practices (Taxman, Henderson, & Belenko, 2009). The PCS study techniques are instructive. First, the study involved a process of organizational change where sufficient time was devoted to training and preparing the staff as well as the supervisors. Attention was given to both educational and skill building training for staff (Taxman, 2008; Taxman et al., 2004).

Unfortunately, the more typical training for experimental studies, and the training employed by the CBM and seamless system studies, involves several two-day sessions that tend to be focused on more educational information. Second, the experiments were limited to a few staff in each office and the officers were frequently concerned that they were doing activities that were different from others in their office. In some cases they were ostracized for these activities; in most cases, where the experiment lasted over a year, the officers experienced study fatigue. Third, implementation oversight is often not vigorous. In the CBM study, the parole officers were taped and provided periodic feedback. In the seamless system study, the researchers held quarterly meetings to discuss the protocol and reviewed case files to confirm that the procedures were being followed. However, none of these procedures were used agency-wide; instead they were specific to the officers involved in the study. In the end, the focus on innovative ideas – balancing public safety and treatment objectives – is difficult in organizational cultures that have long histories of being focused on enforcement styles of supervision. In contrast, the PCS model included a process, by which the supervisors were responsible for monitoring adherence to the model, as part of their supervisory responsibility. This imbedded the protocol within the organization instead of it being a separate program. In the PCS project, the supervisors had a role in monitoring staff, and it became part of the process for improving their relationship. They had a specialized tool, the Quality Contact Standards, which was used to assess how well the staff was implementing the recommended protocol. The study had researchers use additional tools to measure adherence (Table 12.2).

## Effective Parole Practices That Work

The review did not reveal three or more studies examining the role of the parole officer that have the same positive findings. Therefore, we cannot identify parole practices that would be considered effective, at this time.

## Treatment Interventions for Parolees

Most of the available literature focuses on "what works," generally referring to programs and services designed to alter offender behavior. Clinical interventions such as cognitive-behavioral therapy, behavioral therapy, motivational interviewing, and moral reconation therapy have been directly tested on various populations, including substance abusers, offenders in various stages of the justice system, and individuals with mental health disorders. The general findings are that cognitive-behavioral therapies (Aos et al., 2006; Landenberger & Lipsey, 2005; Pearson, Lipton, Cleland, & Yee, 2002), motivational interviewing (McMurran, 2009), and therapeutic communities (Mitchell, Wilson, & MacKenzie, 2007) are effective in reducing recidivism. In community samples, cognitive-behavioral therapy (Dutra et al., 2008), contingency management (Prendergast, Podus, Finney, Greenwell, & Roll, 2006), motivational interviewing (Burke, Arkowitz, & Menchola, 2003), and relapse prevention (Dutra et al., 2008) have been found to reduce substance use. Cognitive-behavioral therapy (Pearson et al., 2002) and therapeutic communities (Mitchell et al., 2007) also reduce

**Table 12.2** Overview of existing studies

| Intervention | Setting | Outcome | No. of participants/ sites/studies | Significance |
|---|---|---|---|---|
| Intensive supervision programs (ISP) (Petersilia & Turner, 1993) | Probation/parole | No reduction in recidivism or prison crowding | 14 sites | NS |
| Evidence-based programming (Aos et al., 2006) | Adult and juvenile corrections, prevention programs | Reduction in crime | 571 studies | S, –7% |
| Intensive supervision with treatment-oriented programs (Aos et al., 2006) | Adult corrections | Reduction in crime | 11 studies | S, –16.7% |
| Cognitive-behavioral therapy (Aos et al., 2006) | Adult corrections | Reduction in crime | 25 studies | S, –6.3% |
| In-prison drug treatment (Aos et al., 2006) | Adult corrections | Reduction in crime | 20 studies | S, –5.7% |
| Adult drug courts (Aos et al., 2006) | Adult corrections | Reduction in crime | 57 studies | S, –8% |
| Intensive supervision with surveillance only (Aos et al., 2006) | Adult corrections | No reduction in crime | 23 studies | 0% |
| Therapeutic alliance (as assessed by DRI-R) (Skeem et al., 2007) | Mandated community treatment | Rule compliance | 2 studies | S |
| Risk and responsivity (Taxman & Thanner, 2006; Thanner & Taxman, 2003) | Substance abuse treatment | Treatment retention | 120 participants | S |
| Risk and responsivity (Taxman & Thanner, 2006; Thanner & Taxman, 2003) | Substance abuse treatment | Drug use<br>rearrest | 120 participants | S; $d = 0.54$<br>S; $d = 0.23$ |
| Risk-need-responsivity model (Taxman, 2008) | Community supervision | Rearrest, technical violation | 4 sites | S |
| Collaborative behavioral management (CBM) (Friedmann et al., 2009) | Adult parole | Parole and treatment utilization | 6 sites | NS |
| *Interventions for parolees* | | | | |
| Cognitive-behavioral programs (Pearson et al., 2002) | Any correctional setting | Recidivism | 68 studies | *S*; $r = 0.144$ |
| Behavioral reinforcement/incentive programs (Pearson et al., 2002) | Any correctional setting | Recidivism | 23 studies | *S*; $r = 0.066$ |
| Drug treatment (Mitchell et al., 2007) | Incarcerated populations | Recidivism | 65 studies | S |
| Drug treatment (Mitchell et al., 2007) | Incarcerated populations | Drug use | 20 studies | S |
| Contingency management (Dutra et al., 2008) | Substance abuse treatment | Abstinence | 14 studies | *S*; $d = 0.58$ |
| Cognitive-behavioral therapy (Dutra et al., 2008) | Substance abuse treatment | Abstinence | 13 studies | *S*, $d = 0.28$ |
| Relapse prevention (Dutra et al., 2008) | Substance abuse treatment | Abstinence | 5 studies | *S*, $d = 0.32$ |
| Contingency management (Prendergast et al., 2006) | Substance abuse treatment | Abstinence | 47 studies | *S*, $d = 0.42$ |

**Table 12.2** (continued)

| Intervention | Setting | Outcome | No. of participants/ sites/studies | Significance |
|---|---|---|---|---|
| Motivational interviewing (Burke et al., 2003) | Clinical treatment | Social impact measures | 8 studies | *S*, $d = 0.47$ |
| *Therapeutic communities with aftercare* | | | | |
| Therapeutic community (Wexler et al., 1992) | Parole (female) | Rearrest | 86 participants | S |
| Drug treatment (Mitchell et al., 2007) | Incarcerated populations | Recidivism | 65 studies | S |
| Cognitive thinking skills program (CTSP) (Gaes et al., 1999) | Offender populations | Recidivism | 14 studies | S |
| In-prison therapeutic community with aftercare (Knight et al., 1999) | Prison | Reincarceration | 394 participants | S |
| In-prison therapeutic community (CSATF) (Prendergast et al., 2001) | Prison | Prisoner custodial behavior | 28 participants | S |
| Therapeutic community with aftercare (Martin et al., 1999) | Prison reentry (work release) | Drug use | 428 participants | S |
| *Case management/reentry* | | | | |
| Transitional case management (TCM) (Prendergast, 2009) | Prison reentry | Case management session attendance | 787 participants | NS |
| Case management (Longshore et al., 2005) | Parole | Drug use | 519 participants | NS |
| *Medications for parolees* | | | | |
| Methadone maintenance (Kinlock et al., 2009) | Prison reentry | Drug use (opioid) | 211 participants | S |
| Egli et al. (2009) | Addicts | Drug use | 8 studies | S |
| Methadone maintenance (Schwartz et al., 2007) | Opioid treatment | Drug use (heroin) | 319 participants | S |
| Methadone maintenance (Gordon et al., 2008) | Prison reentry | Treatment retention | 211 participants | S |
| Methadone maintenance (Gordon et al., 2008) | Prison reentry | Drug use | 211 participants | S |
| *Risk principle (RNR)* | | | | |
| Risk principle (Lowenkamp et al., 2006) | Community corrections | Recidivism | 2 studies, 97 agencies | S |
| *Earned discharge* | | | | |
| Contingency management (Prendergast et al., 2006) | Substance abuse treatment | Abstinence | 47 studies | $D = 0.42$ |
| *Treatment–supervision balance* | | | | |
| Intensive supervision withtreatment-oriented programs (Aos et al., 2006) | Adult corrections | Reduction in crime | 11 studies | –16.7% |

NS = Nonsignificant at $p < .05$ level
S = Significant at $p < .05$ level

drug use among offenders, although research suggests that the impact of therapeutic communities on drug use is more variable. Few studies have directly tested these interventions with parolee populations. While there is no evidence to suggest that studies of clinical therapies are not relevant to those on parole with particular disorders (Prendergast, 2009), it should be recognized that being under the scrutiny of parole may either enhance or detract from the clinical intervention. As discussed above, it is unclear how the parole system impacts these findings.

Over the last decade, the focus of much research has been on three outcomes for parolees: recidivism through new crimes, drug use, and risky behaviors associated with HIV/AIDS. While few studies examine all three outcomes, a number of interventions focus on at least two. Interventions that work for these three areas apply to the majority of the parolee population, not including sex offenders. The following review does not include a discussion of boot camps or intensive supervision, which have largely been found to be ineffective (see Aos et al., 2006; MacKenzie, 2006). Rather, it focuses on the types of programs and interventions that have started to evolve, in trying to advance a better understanding of what works in parole supervision.

## Programs That Do Not Yet Have Sufficient Evidence: HIV Prevention

With the increased rate of risky behaviors among parolees and offenders and generalized findings that offenders returning home can have negative impact on the community, such as increased sexually transmitted diseases and increased pregnancies (Thomas & Torrone, 2008), more attention is being placed on reducing risky behaviors. A number of specialized programs, involving a structured release concept, have been attempted for offenders reentering the community. Built upon the therapeutic community literature, these programs provide some education and awareness in prison shortly before release and continue care in the community during parole supervision. One example, Project Start, is a Center for Disease Control (CDC) 6-session individual-level HIV, sexually transmitted diseases (STD), and hepatitis risk reduction intervention program for men. It includes two sessions in prison (about 69 days before release) and four individual sessions in the community after release (at 1, 3, 6, and 12 weeks). The intervention combines prevention case management, motivational interviewing, and incremental risk reduction. In the first in-prison session, the interventionist assesses the participant's knowledge of HIV/AIDS, STDs, and hepatitis; conducts a brief HIV risk assessment; and helps the participant develop a personal risk reduction plan. The goal is to provide information, skills training, and referrals as well as to identify incremental steps toward risk reduction. The second in-prison session focuses on community reentry needs and referrals for assistance with housing, employment, finances, substance abuse, mental illness, and any legal issues. This session also provides for the development of a plan to avoid reincarceration. The post-release sessions provide boosters from the prior sessions and involve discussion of the factors that facilitate, or impede, implementation of the risk reduction plan. The post-release sessions are generally conducted in community/private settings such as community-based organizations or parole offices. In a few instances the sessions are conducted by telephone. Those receiving Project Start's six sessions were compared to a group receiving a single-session education program prior to release, in eight state prisons in four states (California, Mississippi, Rhode Island, and Wisconsin). The unprotected sex rate was 68% for the Project Start group and 78% for the single-session group for 18–25-year-old men (OR = 0.40; 95% CI = 0.18, 0.88). There were no statistically significant differences in the self-reported reincarceration rate for the group; the study did not examine drug use rates.

Another study, examining the impact of an HIV/AIDS prevention program among parolees, was a four-site trial as part of the CJ-DATS initiative (Inciardi, Leukefeld, Martin, & O'Connell, 2008). The study tested the relative effectiveness of three brief interventions, of varying intensity, designed to change the risk behaviors of inmates reentering society. The interventions included a DVD-based, peer-delivered intervention with a workbook (see Inciardi et al., 2007, for a description of the video); the NIDA Standard HIV Intervention; and a standard practice condition (HIV educational video). The 343 study participants were assigned randomly to one of the interventions and were tested for HIV and HCV prior to release from custody. For those who completed the 90-day post-release interviews, there was a significant reduction in reported sexual risk behaviors for those participating in the DVD intervention, compared to the other two brief interventions. There were no reported differences in drug use among the three groups (Inciardi et al., 2008).

## Programs That Do Not Work: Case Management/Reentry

Reentry was coined as a term to refer to the transition from prison to the community, but it can have several meanings and interpretations. Taxman, Young, and Byrne (2002) discuss three transition processes: in-prison preparation, structured release, and supervised release. Parole supervision can occur within all of these processes, depending on the role and function of the parole officer; and, generally, structured release and supervised release can be consistent with resource broker, social worker, and behavioral manager strategies. The lessons learned, from the therapeutic community studies in the 1990s, have led to a renewed emphasis on transitioning offenders and providing needed services.

One new initiative that garnered a lot of attention was the Serious and Violent Offender Reentry Initiative (SVORI). This federally funded effort reflected a resource broker or case management approach, with the goal to provide services in the community for returning offenders. The services included housing, employment, vocational training, mental health treatment, substance abuse treatment, and health services. Funding was provided to over 69 sites, of which 16 agreed to participate in an impact study. The SVORI intervention was delivered by case managers, parole officers, or other actors, depending on the local site. It is difficult to ascertain a particular model since the underlying theory was simply that providing needed resources would help address crime-producing behavior. Few of the sites used standardized instruments to determine the risk or needs of the offender. The study design consisted of random assignment in two sites and a quasi-experimental design in the remaining 14 sites. In the 14 sites, offenders were assigned to SVORI reentry services or a comparison group. The comparison group consisted of those in another prison with like characteristics, on the waiting list, or those that had similar characteristics overall. Interviews were conducted with 2,391 offenders at baseline, 1,464 at 3 months, 1,527 at 9 months, and 1,637 at 18 months after release. The SVORI group received increased levels of services in all major categories; the comparison group did not. However, while improved access to services occurred, it did not have a significant impact on rearrest or reincarceration rates; the recidivism rates were similar across groups (see Lattimore, 2009). This review found that the SVORI model lacked a theoretical foundation for defining the activities of the case managers (e.g., advocate, resource broker, counselor) and the process did not encompass the well-documented RNR (risk-need-responsivity) model.

Another study on the transition of offenders from prison to the community was the Transitional Case Management (TCM) study conducted as part of the Criminal Justice Drug Abuse Treatment Studies (CJ-DATS) cooperative. The TCM study included two in-prison sessions and 12 weekly sessions with the case manager following release to parole. A total of 812 inmates (25% women) from four study sites were randomly assigned to the TCM group or to a Standard Referral (SR) group. TCM utilized a strengths-based model of case management (Prendergast et al., 2009; Siegal, Rapp, Li, Saha, & Kirk, 1997) as a theoretical framework. The goal was to focus on the strengths of the individual releasee as a means to engage him or her in continued care by (1) improving coordination and collaboration among correctional and treatment staff, community parole and treatment staff, and other health, mental health, and social service providers; and (2) working directly with the client, to develop specific goals and plans for transition to the community, to assist him or her during the crucial early months in the community. The intervention involved a strength assessment and a conference call to community providers (in lieu of an in-person meeting) conducted during the in-prison phase, with continued case management in the community. Those assigned to the comparison group received the standard services offered to parolees (see Prendergast & Cartier, 2008). TCM experienced a relatively large percentage of treatment-group "participants" who attended few or none of the scheduled sessions in the community. The intervention produced no impact on reincarceration rates or drug use, at the 9-month followup. This finding is consistent with other case management studies for parolees that have focused on trying to link parolees with services in the community (Aos et al., 2006; Longshore, Turner, & Fain, 2005), such as Project Greenlight (Wilson & Davis, 2006) that provided an array of services to offenders. These studies have not shown reductions in recidivism or drug use, nor have they produced other desired outcomes.

### Treatment Services That Work: Therapeutic Communities (with Aftercare) Effective for TC but Unknown for Aftercare

During the early 1990s, a number of experimental studies were conducted to assess the impact of the therapeutic community model for offenders. Stay'n Out (Wexler, Falkin, Lipton, & Rosenblum, 1992), the in-prison specialized treatment program with aftercare in the community, was found to reduce recidivism and findings were enhanced for those that attended aftercare in the community during their parole. The Stay'n Out program was based on a therapeutic community model, which included confrontation-based therapy. Participants lived in units separate from the general prison population and participated in group and individual counseling as well as educational and/or therapy sessions. The therapeutic community reestablishes strict norms for individual behavior and community responsibility. Through a highly structured process, the individual adopts mainstream values, by working through various stages of responsibility to the community, taking on job functions, and challenging his/her peers to fulfill their own potential. The goal is to build adherence to a moral code that counters the subculture of criminal behavior (and/or substance abuse).

Meta-analyses confirm the importance of studying the main effects of programs on recidivism, with generally positive findings for drug use (Mitchell et al., 2007). The three most well-known model programs – Key/Crest (Delaware), the Amity therapeutic prison (California), and Kyle New Vision (Texas) – demonstrate positive program outcomes but suffer from several methodological shortcomings, including incomparable treatment and control groups, inadequate controls for selection bias, and poor outcome measures (Gaes, Flanagan, Motiuk, & Stewart, 1999; Pearson & Lipton, 1999). The mean effect size on recidivism is 1.38; involvement in mandatory aftercare improves the effect size to a mean of 1.51 (Mitchell et al., 2007). The differential findings for several groups in the primary studies (Knight, Simpson, & Hiller, 1999; Martin, Butzin, Saum, & Inciardi, 1999; Prendergast, Farabee, & Cartier, 2001) – analyzing in-prison treatment with and without aftercare – demonstrate that there are measurable differences in program dropouts due to sample attrition and unique characteristics of the groups that self-select into different categories. Continued treatment in the community (aftercare) enhances the outcome, which suggests that beginning parole supervision in treatment and continuing treatment through the early period of parole is important to improved retention and other outcomes. More research is needed to better understand the type of community treatment that would reinforce the gains in prison-based treatment for offenders. Research is not sufficient to provide an understanding of how to improve treatment participation and retention for offenders in the community. For example, in the Amity program in California, 34% of in-prison program graduates who had a referral to community-based treatment entered treatment during parole, but nearly 45% dropped out within the first 90 days (Prendergast et al., 2001). No studies specifically examine the type of aftercare provided or the role of the parole officer in the treatment process.

### Programs That Work: Medications for Parolees

When a person is on parole, continued drug use can lead to increased parole violations and, potentially, reincarceration. Meta-analyses confirm that cognitive-behavioral therapies and therapeutic communities have an impact on recidivism and cognitive-behavioral therapy has been found to reduce drug use. Therapeutic communities have a positive but not significant impact on drug use. Medically assisted treatments have been developed to augment these traditional behavioral therapies, particularly for opiate addicts. A number of medications are available, including methadone, buprenorphine, naltrexone, and LAMM. Randomized trials are currently underway to examine the use of naltrexone in a probation population (O'Brien, McLellan, Childress, & Woody, 2009). Trials are also ongoing to examine the use of methadone during structured-release phases as well as during the early period of supervision (Kinlock, Gordon, Schwartz, Fitzgerald, & O'Grady, 2009). A recent systematic review by Egli, Pina, Skovbo, Christensen, Aebi, and Killias (2009) examined the efficacy of medically assisted treatments. This review included 46 studies with findings related to recidivism. Heroin substitution programs, where addicts are given daily doses of heroin, outperformed methadone maintenance and other behavioral therapies. Heroin substitution programs had the largest and most statistically significant mean effect size. The other medically assisted treatments (methadone maintenance, buprenorphine, and naltrexone) had no significant impact but had a more positive effect than behavioral therapies that did not include medication. The review did not examine drug use among the offender population. Some of the primary research studies have found that methadone maintenance reduces drug use (Schwartz, Jaffe, Highfield, Callaman, & O'Grady, 2007) and leads to continued treatment in the community (Gordon, Kinlock, Schwartz, & O'Grady, 2008). While these treatments are reported to be valuable, they have not been adequately tested during the period of parole supervision, and no studies have examined the role of the parole officer.

## Toward an Agenda to Better Understand Effective Parole Practices

As shown by this review, we know very little about parole supervision and the effectiveness of parole. The core component of parole – the nature of the interactions between the officer and the parolee – has not been adequately researched. The literature can be summarized based on general findings about offender and addict populations, but very little replication has occurred within parole settings. A need exists to replicate findings, within parole settings, given that the parole structure places certain demands on individuals as part of reintegrating into the community and reidentifying as a citizen. The rules of parole and behaviors of parole authorities affect offender outcomes, and they must be factored into the equation. That is, the general consensus is that what works for most offenders also works for parolees, but this cannot be empirically validated because there is insufficient research in parole settings and on parolees. More specifically, research that considers different theoretical models of parole is sorely lacking. It does appear that cognitive-behavioral therapy, motivational interviewing, working alliance between parole officer and parolee, therapeutic communities, and heroin substitution are useful means of improving outcomes, but the lack of studies on parolees limits the strength of that statement. Further, we cannot be sure about the size of the effect and the sustainability of the effect. A need exists to understand how different roles of parole officers affect outcomes and whether one theoretical approach yields stronger outcomes.

With over six million offenders on supervision and many spending periods of time, before and after supervision, incarcerated, the importance of understanding effective parole practices should not be understated. But the question is "What should be the research agenda?" First and foremost, we need evidence about the type of supervision that is likely to have an impact on proximal outcomes, such as drug use, attendance at supervision meetings, and attendance at treatment sessions. The current body of research cannot answer these basic questions. The theoretical models of enforcement, resource broker, social worker, and behavioral manager need to be tested, but, even more importantly, these models need to be developed into interventions that can be tested in the field. As shown, in the Step'n Out and Proactive Community Supervision studies, more work is needed to fully understand the mechanisms of action, and that work must be done with parole officers. Development beyond the level of theoretical models is imperative if the field is to move ahead.

To summarize the state of the art of parole supervision, insufficient evidence exists, and very few programs have yielded at least three studies that have drawn the same conclusions. Only one strategy – contingency management (Prendergast et al., 2006) – has sufficient evidence to confirm that it works for substance abusers. However, there is still insufficient evidence to determine that this approach works for parolees.

Nonetheless, a consensus panel convened to examine strategies to improve parole (Solomon et al., 2008) determined that 13 strategies have sufficient evidence, to conclude that they improve outcomes, and recommended their implementation. The following summarizes the basis for these determinations.

The first four focus on recommendations about the overall policies regarding the organization of services for offenders and all appear to have face validity. Furthermore, while little research has been conducted on whether these strategies are effective in reducing recidivism or drug use, each of them presents a testable hypothesis.

(1) Define success as recidivism reduction and measure performance of outcomes, both distal (long-term outcomes such as recidivism) and proximal (short-term outcomes such as drug use, employment, and treatment engagement).
The general management literature illustrates the importance of an organization stating its mission clearly and employing corresponding measures of effectiveness. Recent studies suggest that distal outcomes, like recidivism reduction, are sufficient for an organization to move forward. However, proximal outcomes are more likely to influence business processes, since they describe the immediate outcomes sought by core components of the operation. The Network for the Improvement of Addiction Treatment (NIATx) emphasizes process outcomes to help agencies organize their business around the engagement of addicts in treatment. Process improvements are designed to help clients gain access to treatment programs by changing how business is done. Examples of business process improvements are changes to clinic intake procedures so that clients did not need appointments but could rather appear at any time; and the training of all clinic staff to do intake procedures, thus reducing the need for set appointments. The impact on proximal outcomes is impressive, including reduced wait times and increased retention in treatment (Ford, Trestman, Wiesbrock, & Zhang, 2007; McCarty et al., 2007).

(2) Tailor the conditions of supervision to the parolee's criminogenic needs (i.e., have the court and/or parole board assign conditions of release based on criminogenic needs).
Little information is available regarding the matching of needs and conditions in this manner. How conditions of release would ultimately change is unclear. Research is urgently needed to determine the effectiveness of different treatment placement criteria.

(3) Focus resources on moderate- and high-risk parolees to provide them needed services.
A growing body of quasi-experimental research concludes that moderate- and high-risk offenders benefit from targeted interventions (Lowenkamp, Latessa, & Hoslinger, 2006; Marlowe, Festinger, Lee, Dugosh, & Benasutti, 2006; Taxman, 2006; Taxman & Marlowe, 2006). Formal experiments are needed to determine whether differential

outcomes will occur for high, moderate and low-risk offenders based on level of services provided.

(4) Front-load resources to provide services at the beginning of supervision.
Some preliminary findings suggest that, during the early period of release, offenders are more likely to fail. There is little research on whether front-loading supervision during the structured release period, or early supervision period (first 90 days), has an impact on outcomes. The Transitional Case Management (TCM) four-site study attempted to examine this but found that few offenders participated in strengths-based case management services. The position that front-loading or targeting specific needs will improve outcomes remains unproven.

UI's consensus panel also identified strategies to provide specific services to offenders. Most of these strategies offer testable hypotheses about mechanisms that could be used to alter offender behavior.

(1) Implement earned discharge, allowing an offender to be released from parole sooner.
*Recommend*: The earned release concept is a modified form of contingency management (CM) or token economy. CM has strong evidentiary support as an effective tool among substance abusers (Prendergast et al., 2006), but has not yet been tested within parole settings. The major difference between CM and earned release is that CM is based on short-term proximal outcomes – getting rewards for immediate results such as not testing positive for drug use. Earned discharge is based on the concept that the promise of parole release, or termination of supervision, will motivate parolees to be compliant. No research, yet, demonstrates that offenders will alter their behavior, over the long term, in hopes of getting a reward.

(2) Implement place-based supervision, to provide supervision and intervention services in the community where offenders reside.
*Recommend*: Recent evidence has shown that offenders living in certain neighborhoods are more likely to recidivate (Kubrin & Stewart, 2006; Mears, Wang, Hay, & Bales, 2008). However, there is no empirical evidence that targeted parole services in that area, or the physical concentration of parolees, affects recidivism rates. Nonetheless, the concept of providing place-based supervision where officers work in select neighborhoods, appears to have face validity as a tool for allocating parole resources.

(3) Engage partners and expand intervention capacities to provide needed educational, mental health, housing, vocational, and other services that address the stability of the parolee in the community.
*Recommend*: This strategy speaks to the need to study whether the resource broker model of supervision leads to improved services for parolees. Further, studies are needed to advance case management practices, where the role of the parole officer as a resource broker is compared to the role of an enforcer. This would contribute to a better understanding of what parole officer roles are likely to affect recidivism.

(4) Assess criminogenic risk and need factors to match them to services more likely to reduce recidivism.
*Recommend*: This behavioral manager model shows promise but has not yet been adequately researched. Under the Proactive Community Supervision (PCS) study, case plans were developed around criminogenic needs. Officers who complied with the protocol and placed targeted conditions of release on offenders tended to produce reduced violations and rearrests (Taxman, 2009). This study was conducted in four sites and this matching approach needs replication to establish it as an effective supervision strategy.

(5) Develop and implement case plans that balance surveillance and treatment, to ensure that the parolee is monitored while services are provided.
*Recommend*: This particular strategy addressed the core question of how external controls and treatment services can be used in balance. The meta-analysis findings of

Aos et al. (2006) demonstrate how supervision with treatment is effective. Yet this study did not define the nature of the surveillance techniques or the nature of the treatment, leaving the need to better understand the theoretical model of supervision under this model.

(6) Enhance parolee engagement in assessment, case planning, and supervision (shared decision making) to identify programs and services that are important to, and appropriate for, the parolee.
*Recommend*: The overriding premise is that when offenders participate in key supervision decisions, they will have a greater commitment to successful outcomes (Taxman, 2006). Available evidence is insufficient to support this claim.

(7) Engage informal social controls, such as family members or non-offending peers, to facilitate community reintegration.
*Recommend*: Taxman, Young, and Byrne (2003) argue that informal social controls or social networks are useful in helping parolees learn to be responsible citizens. Laub and Sampson (2001) suggest that marriage and positive social networks are useful in reducing negative peer influences. The role of family members in the supervision process has not been well defined. The Vera Institute's Family Justice Program (www.vera.org) offers some prototypes of family involvement, but these models have not yet been empirically tested.

(8) Incorporate incentives and rewards into the supervision process (i.e., contingency management).
*Recommend*: As stated above, contingency management (CM) is an evidence-based treatment for substance abusers. The model has not been researched for parolees, and it is unclear how supervision could interfere with reward-generating behaviors. Under parole supervision, a variety of offenders' behaviors is subject to critique. It is unclear how CM can be incorporated in a model where there may be many target behaviors that offenders must engage in or avoid. The use of rewards and incentives can, however, be included in a study of parole supervision strategies.

(9) Employ graduated, problem-solving responses to violations of parole conditions, in a swift and certain manner (i.e., a modified version of contingency management).
*Recommend*: Graduated sanctions seek to provide immediate responses to violations of the conditions of release. While punishing offenders has not generally been found effective (Lipsey & Cullen, 2007), this strategy is designed to ensure that negative reinforcement is used effectively to help parolees better manage their behavior.

## Advancing the Agenda: Recommendations for the Future

The above Urban Institute (2009) strategies reflect the practitioners' views of how parole *should* work. The collective knowledge is that parole is valuable, in terms of transitioning the offender from prison or jail to the community. Yet parole supervision is not well defined and the question of how to enable parole to contribute to better outcomes remains unanswered.

Our knowledge and understanding of parole supervision is still being developed. While it may be contended that general knowledge regarding treatment is applicable to parolees, this has not been adequately demonstrated. The first step, in providing a sound theory as to why parole can be a tool in reducing criminal behavior, will involve developing the theoretical models of different parole supervision methods to the point of concrete program elements. Such programs can then be evaluated regarding their impact on both proximal and distal outcomes for offenders. Right now, we are still trying to determine whether parole has any positive impact on behavior: not a good position to be in, given the growing number of evidence-based practices in other arenas.

The evidence-based practices literature has a role to play in defining how parole should be practiced. The behavioral management approach offers promise in that it equips the parole officer with the tools of evidence-based practices: a focus on rapport as the foundation of recidivism reduction; and on desistence (offender-driven decisions to cease criminal behavior) strategies. Of equal importance, it reaffirms that the individual, not the criminal justice system, makes choices that affect his/her liberty. Such a clinical approach places the power to control those decisions with the parolee, even though the parole system is viewed as a punishment agency. The lessons learned over the last several decades, from procedural justice experiments (see Tyler, 2010) which test the impact of equality and distributive justice, strongly suggest that more attention needs to be placed on creating environments in which the offender is given options; and that the consequences for nonresponsiveness and noncompliance (e.g., drug use, failure to attend treatment or supervision sessions) must be fairly applied to all offenders. Finally, the culture of the parole agency is important because it reinforces both the role of the officer and the manner in which key services are provided. Stated simply, the culture of parole agencies should reinforce a clinical approach coupled with procedural justice.

Parole agencies should adopt clinical approaches to working with parolees, where the environment supports individual decision making and fosters ownership in the successful completion of parole. To bring this about, the following must occur:

1. Legislative and executive officials must recognize that parole services should be focused on recidivism reduction and the importance of a clinical approach to reaching that end.
2. Parole agencies must adopt policies and procedures that focus on the components of the behavioral manager model: standardized screening tools for risk and need factors; the matching of conditions (requirements) to criminogenic factors; the use of contingency management protocols to incentivize parolees to comply with the conditions of release; and the establishment of a working relationship of trust, caring, and fairness within the justice setting.
3. The parole process must be seen as legitimate, by focusing on the issues of voice, neutrality, dignity in the delivery of services, and trust in authorities. As defined by Tyler (2010), a procedural justice framework can create legitimacy in the parole process. Voice is best achieved by giving the parolee input into decisions, such as types of controls and services and sanctions and rewards to be employed. Neutrality refers to the consistent application of rules without interference by the personal "styles" or actions of parole officers. Practices of humane care or dignity, in the delivery of services, reinforce the role of the parolee as a partner in the process. Finally, trust in authority is achieved through fair and equitable decisions by parole officers and other officials. These elements are embedded in the behavioral management approach, where the parolee is a partner in the decision making at all phases, and parole rules are reinforced by mutual action. Parolees should also involve their community support mechanisms; they provide positive support and protection, and guard against negative influences.
4. Parole agencies must use available technology to augment supervision. Technology can provide additional ways to reach and work with offenders. In the treatment field, cell phones with texting capabilities have been used to send messages about key appointments and motivational messages to enhance adherence to treatment protocols. These techniques are not yet being used in parole supervision, but offer promise.
5. The front-line supervision and assessment of parole officers' performance should be refined to reflect the goals of the organization. Measures of parolee short- and long-term outcomes (e.g., treatment attendance and completion, employment, compliance with conditions) that affect recidivism should be built into agency management information systems and used to assess officer performance.

Finally, parole should be recognized as a public health function. All evidence points to the advantages of adopting a public health mission, where the emphasis is on minimizing risks to the community, through the provision of appropriate services to address the psychosocial and medical needs of the parolee. A mission of punishment and monitoring has not served to enhance the quality of the interactions between the parolee and officer, the crux of the parole process; rather, it could be argued that the punishment emphasis has served to distance the parolee from the community to which he/she is returning. A public health approach alters the correctional mission to recognize that the health and well-being of the parolee are among the goals of parole. In the end, this advancement in parole practice may allow for easier adaptation of evidence-based practices (see Taxman & Ressler, 2009 for a proposal to advance the public health mission of corrections).

**Acknowledgments** This paper is partially based on work funded by the National Institute on Drug Abuse under grants R01DA10705, R01DA017729, and V01DA16213–CJ-DATS is funded by NIDA in collaboration with SAMHSA, CDC, NIAAA, and BJA. Funding was also received by the Maryland Division of Parole and Probation for a laboratory to test new concepts in supervision.

## References

Adams, S., Welch, A., & Bonds, J. (1958). *The specialized intensive parole unit: Supplementary report. No. 1*. Sacramento, CA: Bureau of Criminal Statistics, Research Section.

Alemi, F., Taxman, F. S., Baghi, H., Vang, J., Thanner, M., & Doyon, V. (2006). Costs and benefits of combining probation and substance abuse treatment. *Journal of Mental Health Policy and Economics, 9*(2), 57–70.

Andrews, D. A., & Bonta, J. (1998). *The psychology of criminal conduct*. Cincinnati, OH: Anderson Publishing Co.

Aos, S., Miller, M., & Drake, E. (2006). *Evidence-based public policy options to reduce future prison construction, criminal justice costs, and crime rates* (No. 06-10-1201) (p. 44). Olympia, WA: Washington State Institute for Public Policy.

Austin, J., & Hardyman, P. (1991). *The use of early parole with electronic monitoring to control prison crowding: Evaluation of the Oklahoma Department of Corrections pre-parole supervised release with electronic monitoring*. Washington, DC: National Institute of Justice.

Bonczar, T. (2008). *Characteristics of state parole supervising agencies, 2006* (NCJ 222180). Washington, DC: Bureau of Justice Statistics.

Burke, B. L., Arkowitz, H., & Menchola, M. (2003). The efficacy of motivational interviewing: A meta-analysis of controlled clinical trials. *Journal of Consulting and Clinical Psychology, 71*(5), 843–861.

Burkhart, W. R. (1969). The parole work unit programme: An evaluation report. *British Journal of Criminology, 9*, 125–147.

Byrne, J. M., & Kelly, L. M. (1989). *Restructuring probation as an intermediate sanction: An evaluation of the Massachusetts intensive probation supervision program*. Final Report to the National Institute of Justice. Lowell, MA: University of Lowell, Department of Criminal Justice.

California Department of Corrections. (1960). *Narcotics treatment–control project directive*. Sacramento, CA: California Department of Corrections, Adult Parole Division.

California Department of Corrections. (1961). *Narcotics treatment–control program*. Progress report – First year's program experience, October 1, 1959–September 30, 1960. Sacramento, CA: California Department of Corrections, Adult Parole Division.

Castonguay, L. G., & Beutler, L. E. (2005). *Principles of therapeutic change that work* (1st ed.). New York: Oxford University Press.

Dutra, L., Stathopoulou, G., Basden, S., Leyro, T., Powers, M., & Otto, M. (2008). A meta-analytic review of psychosocial interventions for substance use disorders. *The American Journal of Psychiatry, 165*(2), 179.

Egli, N., Pina, M., Skovbo Christensen, P., Aebi, M. F., & Killias, M. (2009). Effects of drug substitution programs on offending among drug-addicts. *Campbell Systematic Reviews*, 2009:3. Retrieved May 11, 2010, from http://www.campbellcollaboration.org/reviews_crime_justice/index.php

Eisenberg, M., Bryle, J., & Fabelo, T. (2009). *Travis County community impact supervision project: Analyzing initial outcomes*. New York: Council of State Government Center.

Erwin, B. S. (1986). Turning up the heat on probationers in Georgia. *Federal Probation, 50*(2), 17–24.

Eze, E. (1962). *Specialized intensive parole unit, Phase III*. Sacramento, CA: Bureau of Criminal Statistics, Research Section.

Fallen, D. L., Apperson, C. G., Hall-Milligan, J., & Aos, S. (1982). *Report: Intensive parole supervision*. Washington, DC: Department of Social and Health Services.

Ford, J. D., Trestman, R. L., Wiesbrock, V., & Zhang, W. (2007). Development and validation of a brief mental health screening instrument for newly incarcerated adults. *Assessment, 14*(3), 279–299.

Friedmann, P., Rhodes, A., & Taxman, F. S. (2009). Collaborative behavioral management: Integration and intensification of parole and outpatient addiction treatment services in the Step'n Out study.

*Journal of Experimental Criminology, 5*(3), 227–243.

Gaes, G. G., Flanagan, T. J., Motiuk, L. L., & Stewart, L. (1999). Adult correctional treatment. *Crime and Justice, 26*, 361–426.

Glaze, L., & Bonczar, T. (2008). *Probation and parole in the United States, 2007 – Statistical tables*. Washington, DC: Bureau of Justice Statistics. Retrieved May 11, 2010, from http://www.ojp.usdoj.gov/bjs/abstract/ppus07st.htm

Gordon, M. S., Kinlock, T. W., Schwartz, R. P., & O'Grady, K. E. (2008). A randomized clinical trial of methadone maintenance for prisoners: Findings at 6 months post-release. *Addiction, 103*(8), 1333–1342.

Havel, J., & Sulk, E. (1962). *Special intensive parole unit phase III* (Research Report No. 3). Sacramento, CA: Bureau of Criminal Statistics, Research Section.

Himelson, A. N., & Margulies, B. C. (1965). *Narcotics treatment control program phase III*. Sacramento, CA: Bureau of Criminal Statistics, Research Section.

Inciardi, J. A., Leukefeld, C. G., Martin, S. S., & O'Connell, D. J. (2008). Editors' introduction: HIV and other infectious diseases among drug-involved offenders. *Journal of Psychoactive Drugs, 40*(4), 423–426.

Inciardi, J. A., Surratt, H. L., Martin, S. S., O'Connell, D. J., Salandry, A. D., & Beard, R. A. (2007). Developing a multimedia HIV and hepatitis intervention for drug-involved offenders reentering the community. *The Prison Journal, 87*, 111–142.

Jolin, A., & Stipack, B. (1991). *Clackamas County community corrections intensive drug program: Program evaluation report*. Portland, OR: Portland State University, Department of Administration of Justice.

Kinlock, T. W., Gordon, M. S., Schwartz, R. P., Fitzgerald, T., & O'Grady, K. E. (2009). A randomized clinical trial of methadone maintenance for prisoners: Results at 12 months postrelease. *Journal of Substance Abuse Treatment, 37*(3), 277–285.

Knight, K., Simpson, D. D., & Hiller, M. L. (1999). Three-year reincarceration outcomes for in-prison therapeutic community treatment in Texas. *The Prison Journal, 79*(3), 337–351.

Kubrin, C. E., & Stewart, E. (2006). Predicting who reoffends: The neglected role of neighborhood context in recidivism rates. *Criminology, 44*(1), 165–197.

Landenberger, N. A., & Lipsey, M. W. (2005). The positive effects of cognitive-behavioral programs for offenders: A meta-analysis of factors associated with effective treatment. *Journal of Experimental Criminology, 1*(4), 435–450.

Latessa, E. J. (1992). *Intensive supervision and case management classification: An evaluation*. Unpublished manuscript, University of Cincinnati, Cincinnati, OH.

Latessa, E. J. (1993a). *An evaluation of the Lucas County adult probation department's IDU and high risk groups*. Unpublished manuscript, University of Cincinnati, Cincinnati, OH.

Latessa, E. J. (1993b). *Profile of the special units of the Lucas County adult probation department*. Unpublished manuscript, University of Cincinnati, Cincinnati, OH.

Latessa, E. J., Travis, L., Fulton, B., & Stichman, A. (1998). *Evaluating the prototypical ISP: Final report*. Cincinnati, OH: University of Cincinnati and American Probation and Parole Association.

Lattimore, P. K. (2009, September). *What works in reentry: Findings from the SVORI multi-site evaluation*. Paper presented at the National TASC conference in Charlotte, NC. Retrieved April 30, 2010, from http://www.svori-evaluation.org/documents/Presentations/2009_09_SVORI_NTASC.pdf

Laub, J. H., & Sampson, R. J. (2001). Understanding desistance from crime. *Crime and Justice, 28*, 1–69.

Lipsey, M., & Cullen, F. (2007). The effectiveness of correctional rehabilitation: A review of systematic reviews. *Annual Review of Law and Social Science, 3*, 297–320.

Longshore, D., Turner, S., & Fain, T. (2005). Effects of case management on parolee misconduct: The bay area services network. *Criminal Justice and Behavior, 32*(2), 205–222.

Lowenkamp, C. T., Latessa, E., & Hoslinger, A. (2006). Risk principle in action: What have we learned from 13,676 offenders and 97 correctional programs? *Crime and Delinquency, 52*, 77–93.

MacKenzie, D. L. (2000). Evidence-based corrections: Identifying what works. *Crime and Delinquency, 46*(4), 457–461.

MacKenzie, D. L. (2006). *What works in corrections? Reducing the criminal activities of offenders and delinquents*. Cambridge, UK: Cambridge Press.

Marlowe, D. B., Festinger, D. S., Lee, P. A., Dugosh, K. L., & Benasutti, K. M. (2006). Matching judicial supervision to clients' risk status in drug court. *Crime & Delinquency, 52*, 52–76.

Martin, S. S., Butzin, C. A., Saum, C. A., & Inciardi, J. A. (1999). Three year outcomes of therapeutic community treatment for drug involved offenders in Delaware: From prison to work release to aftercare. *The Prison Journal, 79*(3), 294–320.

McCarty, D., Gustafson, D. H., Wisdom, J. P., Ford, J., Choi, D., Molfenter, T., et al. (2007). The Network for the Improvement of Addiction Treatment (NIATx): Enhancing access and retention. *Drug and Alcohol Dependence, 88*(2–3), 138–145.

McMurran, M. (2009). Motivational interviewing with offenders: A systematic review. *Legal & Criminological Psychology, 14*, 83–100.

Mears, D. P., Wang, X., Hay, C., & Bales, W. D. (2008). Social ecology and recidivism: Implications for prisoner reentry. *Criminology, 46*(2), 301–340.

Mitchell, C. J. Z., & Butter, C. (1986). *Intensive supervision/early release parole*. Draper, UT: Utah Department of Corrections.

Mitchell, O., Wilson, D. B., & MacKenzie, D. L. (2007). Does incarceration-based drug treatment reduce recidivism? A meta-analytic synthesis of the research. *Journal of Experimental Criminology, 3*, 353–375.

Moon, M. M., & Latessa, E. J. (1993). *The effectiveness of an outpatient drug treatment program on felony probationers*. Paper presented at the annual meeting of the Academy of Criminal Justice Sciences, Kansas City, MO.

National Council on Crime and Delinquency. (1981). *The Wisconsin Case Classification/Staff Deployment Project: Two-year follow-up report*. Madison, WI: Wisconsin Division of Corrections.

Norcross, J. C. (2002). *Psychotherapy relationships that work. APA division of psychotherapy task force on empirically supported therapy relationships*. New York: Oxford University Press.

O'Brien, C. P., McLellan, A. T., Childress, A. R., & Woody, G. E. (2009). Penn/VA Center for studies of addiction. *Neuropharmacology, 56*(Supp. 1), 44–47.

Paparozzi, M., & DeMichele, M. T. (2008). Probation and parole: Overworked, misunderstood, and under-appreciated: But why? *The Howard Journal of Criminal Justice, 47*(3), 275–296.

Pearson, F. S. (1987). *Research on New Jersey's intensive supervision program*. Washington, DC: U.S. Department of Justice, National Institute of Justice.

Pearson, F. S., & Lipton, D. S. (1999). A meta-analytic review of the effectiveness of corrections-based treatments for drug abuse. *The Prison Journal, 79*(4), 384–410.

Pearson, F. S., Lipton, D. S., Cleland, C. M., & Yee, D. S. (2002). The effects of behavioral/cognitive-behavioral programs on recidivism. *Crime & Delinquency, 48*(3), 476–496.

Petersilia, J. (2006). *Understanding California corrections*. Berkeley, CA: California Policy Research Center.

Petersilia, J., & Turner, S. (1993). *Evaluating intensive supervision probation/parole: Results of a nationwide experiment*. Washington, DC: U.S. Department of Justice, National Institute of Justice.

Prendergast, M. A. (2009). Interventions to promote successful re-entry among drug-abusing parolees. *Addiction Science & Clinical Practice, 5*(1), 4–13.

Prendergast, M. A., & Cartier, J. (2008). Improving parolees' participation in drug treatment and other services through strengths case management. *Perspectives, 32*(1), 38–46.

Prendergast, M. A., Farabee, D., & Cartier, J. (2001). The impact of in-prison therapeutic community programs on prison management. *Journal of Offender Rehabilitation, 32*(3), 63.

Prendergast, M. A., Greenwell, L., Cartier, J., Sacks, J., Frisman, L., Rodis, E., et al. (2009). Adherence to scheduled sessions in a randomized field trial of case management: The Criminal Justice-Drug Abuse Treatment Studies Transitional Case Management Study. *Journal of Experimental Criminology, 5*(3), 273–297.

Prendergast, M. A., Podus, D., Finney, J., Greenwell, L., & Roll, J. (2006). Contingency management for treatment of substance use disorders: A meta-analysis. *Addiction, 101*(11), 1546–1560.

Schwartz, R. P., Jaffe, J., Highfield, D., Callaman, J., & O'Grady, K. E. (2007). A randomized controlled trial of methadone maintenance: 10-month follow-up. *Drug and Alcohol Dependence, 86*(1), 30–36.

Siegal, H. A., Rapp, R. C., Li, L., Saha, P., & Kirk, K. D. (1997). The role of case management in retaining clients in substance abuse treatment: An exploratory analysis. *Journal of Drug Issues, 27*(4), 821.

Sing, G. E. (1967). *The relationship between the average number of supervising agent-narcotic addict outpatient contacts and the number of successful weeks in the California narcotic addict outpatient program*. Corona, CA: California Rehabilitation Center, Research Division.

Skeem, J. L., Louden, J. E., Polaschek, D., & Camp, J. (2007). Assessing relationship quality in mandated community treatment: Blending care with control. *Psychological Assessment, 19*(4), 397–410.

Solomon, A. L., Johnson, K. D., Travis, J., & McBride, E. C. (2004). *From prison to work: The employment dimensions of prisoner reentry* (Reentry Roundtable Reports, p. 40). Washington, DC: Urban Institute.

Solomon, A. L., Osborne, J. L., Winterfield, L., Elderbroom, B., Burke, P., Stroker, R., et al. (2008). *Putting public safety first: 13 Parole supervision strategies to enhance reentry outcomes*. Washington, DC: Urban Institute.

Sprow, M. (2009). The probation experiment. *County, 21*(3), 24–28.

Taxman, F. S. (2002). Supervision – Exploring the dimensions of effectiveness. *Federal Probation, 66*(2), 14–27.

Taxman, F. S. (2006). What should we expect from parole (and probation) under a behavioral management approach? *Perspectives, 30*(2), 38–45.

Taxman, F. S. (2008). No illusion, offender and organizational change in Maryland's Proactive Community Supervision model. *Criminology and Public Policy, 7*(2), 275–302.

Taxman, F. S. (2009). Effective community punishments in the United States: Probation. *Criminal Justice Matters, 75*(1), 42–44.

Taxman, F. S., & Ainsworth, S. A. (2009). Correctional milieu: The key to quality outcomes. *Victims and Offenders, 4*(4), 334–340.

Taxman, F. S., Byrne, J. M., & Thanner, M. (2002). *Evaluating the implementation & impact of a seamless system of care for substance abusing offenders: The HIDTA model* (NCJ 197046). Washington, DC: National Institute of Justice.

Taxman, F. S., Henderson, C. E., & Belenko, S. (2009). Organizational context, systems change, and adopting treatment delivery systems in the criminal justice system. *Drug and Alcohol Dependence, 103*(Supp. 1), S1–S6.

Taxman, F. S., & Marlowe, D. (2006). Risk, needs, responsivity: In action or inaction? *Crime & Delinquency, 52*, 3–6.

Taxman, F. S., Perdoni, M., & Harrison, L. (2007). Drug treatment services for adult offenders: The state of the state. *Journal of Substance Abuse Treatment, 32*(3), 239–254.

Taxman, F. S., & Ressler, L. (2009). Public health is public safety: Revamping the correctional mission. In N. A. Frost, J. D. Freilich, & T. R. Clear (Eds.), *Contemporary issues in criminal justice policy: Policy proposals from the American Society of Criminology conference* (pp. 327–342). Belmont, CA: Cengage/Wadsworth.

Taxman, F. S., Shepardson, E., & Byrne, J. M. (2004). *Tools of the trade: A guide to implementing science into practice*. Washington, DC: National Institute of Corrections.

Taxman, F. S., & Thanner, M. (2006). Risk, need, & responsivity: It all depends. *Crime and Delinquency, 52*(1), 28–52.

Taxman, F. S., Trotman, A., & Wilson, M. (2009). *Curriculum for SOARING manualized treatment*. Fairfax, VA: George Mason University.

Taxman, F. S., Wilson, M., & Trotman, A. (2007). *Curriculum for SOARING: Seamless system of care*. Fairfax, VA: George Mason University.

Taxman, F. S., Young, D., & Byrne, J. M. (2002). *Offender's views of reentry: Implications for processes, programs, and services* (Reentry Partnership Initiatives). College Park, MD: Bureau of Governmental Research.

Taxman, F. S., Young, D., & Byrne, J. M. (2003). Transforming offender reentry into public safety: Lessons from OJP's Reentry Partnership Initiative. *Justice Research and Policy, 5*(2), 101–128.

Thanner, M., & Taxman, F. S. (2003). Responsivity: The value of providing intensive services to high-risk offenders. *Journal of Substance Abuse Treatment, 24*, 137–147.

Thomas, J. C., & Torrone, E. (2008). Incarceration as forced migration: Effects on selected community health outcomes. *American Journal of Public Health, 96*, 1762–1765.

Tyler, T. T. (2010). "Legitimacy in corrections": Policy implications. *Criminology and Public Policy, 9*(1), 127–134.

Wexler, H. K., Falkin, G. P., Lipton, D. S., & Rosenblum, A. B. (1992). Outcome evaluation of a prison therapeutic community for substance abuse treatment. *NIDA Research Monograph, 118*, 156–175.

Wilson, J. A., & Davis, R. C. (2006). Good intentions meet hard realities: An evaluation of the Project Greenlight reentry program. *Criminology & Public Policy, 5*(2), 303.

# Women's Treatment in Criminal Justice Settings

# 13

Joan E. Zweben

**Abstract**

This chapter looks at issues specific to women involved with the criminal justice system, examining characteristics that give rise to their distinctive needs. Factors are described that lead women into criminal behavior, as well as those that offer a pathway to a prosocial and productive life style. Treatment elements that have been shown to be important for women in general and those in criminal justice settings are discussed. The chapter offers guidelines for examining the evidence base and implementing evidence-based principles and practices successfully. Finally, recommendations are offered for improving treatment for women at this point in time.

**Keywords**

Women • Gender-responsive treatment • Substance abuse treatment • Criminal justice

## Introduction

This chapter looks at the issues specific to women involved with the criminal justice system. Characteristics are examined in an effort to get a picture of their distinctive needs. In particular, factors that lead women into criminal behavior, and when possible, give them a pathway to a prosocial and productive life style are presented. Elements that have been shown to be important in women's treatment in general, and for criminal justice populations in particular are also presented. Guidelines are offered for examining the evidence base and implementing evidence-based principles and practices successfully. Finally, recommendations for improving treatment for women at this point in time are considered.

## Epidemiology

In the early 1990s, it was recognized that women constitute the fastest growing segment of the criminal justice population, yet had the fewest services available to them (Wellisch, Anglin,

J.E. Zweben (✉)
Department of Psychiatry, University of California, San Francisco, CA 94143, USA
e-mail: joan.zweben@ucsf.edu

C. Leukefeld et al. (eds.), *Handbook of Evidence-Based Substance Abuse Treatment in Criminal Justice Settings*, Issues in Children's and Families' Lives 11,
DOI 10.1007/978-1-4419-9470-7_13, © Springer Science+Business Media, LLC 2011

& Prendergast, 1993). Data available from the Bureau of Justice Statistics (Greenfeld & Snell, 1999) indicated that population growth has continued since 1990, with a 48% growth in the number of women per capita involved in corrections, compared to a 27% increase in the number of men. This population growth occurred in each component of corrections: probation (up 40%), jail (up 60%), and parole supervision (up 80%). The most recent data available from the Bureau of Justice Statistics indicates a continuing growth in women offenders in custody (West & Sabol, 2009).

The majority (86%) of these women were nonviolent offenders, and among the 14% who did use violence, three out of four committed simple assault. In the federal prison system, only 7% are being held for a violent offense; 28% in state prison; and 12% in jails (Greenfeld & Snell, 1999; Harrison & Beck, 2005; Harrison & Karberg, 2003). Many treatment programs for women in the criminal justice system are located in highly restrictive settings, despite the fact that they are low-level offenders (Taxman & Cropsey, 2007). This limits the ability of treatment providers to offer effective services.

Women serving sentences in local jails, state, and federal prisons are largely minority, primarily black and Hispanic (Greenfeld & Snell, 1999). Younger women are more likely to be on probation or in jail; older women are more likely to be in prison. Prior to incarceration, they lived in difficult economic circumstances. Only about 40% reported having full-time jobs, and 30% reported receiving welfare assistance at the time of arrest.

Women offenders have a wide variety of medical problems, often more severe than their aged-matched counterparts, partly because of poor access to health services. They suffer from HIV/AIDS, TB, hepatitis, hypertension, diabetes, and asthma. They are particularly at risk for contracting sexually transmitted diseases due to their participation in prostitution (Pollock, 2002). Gynecological problems are common, partly due to women's complex reproductive system and partly due to their reluctance to seek intrusive medical procedures due to their trauma histories. African-American women who participated in prison treatment had particularly high perceived needs for health services (Grella & Greenwell, 2007).

Adult women in the criminal justice system are more likely than their counterparts to have never been married. However, most had minor children and a significant number of these had lived with their children prior to entering prison. Indeed, the BJA data indicate that 2.8% of children under the age of 18 have at least one incarcerated parent. Many barriers exist for women trying to maintain a relationship with their children, and services for these families are usually difficult to obtain.

## Women Offenders and Their Children

Most women offenders have children (Harrison & Beck, 2005). As of 2000, 1.5 million children in the United States or approximately 2% of minor children have a parent in state or federal prison. More than half of these children are under the age of 18 according to the Annie E. Casey Foundation (2009; http://www.fcnetwork.org/AECFChildren%20of%20Incarcerated%20Parents%20Factsheet.pdf).

This is disproportionately linked to race. African-American children are almost nine times more likely than white children to have a parent in prison; Hispanic children are three times more likely (The Sentencing Project, 2007). An incarcerated mother significantly increases her child's risk of being in foster care, compared to other children. They are less likely to be reunified with their parents or adopted, and are more likely to "age out" of the foster care system. However, in almost 75% of the cases, the children were placed in foster care prior to the mother's first period of incarceration (Moses, 2006). Thus, the mother's incarceration appears to be a marker for many other problems that have existed for some time.

These children are at high risk due to family disorganization, financial hardship, exposure to abuse and trauma, violence, and institutionalization (Campbell & Lewandowski, 1997; Greene, Haney, & Hurtado, 2000). They experience social stigma and shame. Interestingly, there is no reliable research to support the assertion that children with incarcerated parents are much more likely to be incarcerated as adults according to the Annie E. Casey Foundation (2009; http://www.fcnetwork.org/AECFChildren%20of%20Incarcerated%20Parents%20Factsheet.pdf). Indeed, one preliminary report on urban African-American adolescents reported that the majority were not especially deviant or maladjusted. All but a few avoided substance abuse. However, there were general indications of problematic school behavior and deviant peer influences, suggesting a focused target for prevention efforts (Hanlon, O'Grady, Bennett-Sears, & Callaman, 2005). The multiple risk factors are likely to lead to problems that will become visible if these children can be followed for a sufficient period of time.

Research also indicates that family contact in prison is associated with lower rates of post-release recidivism (Vigne, Naser, Brooks, & Castro, 2005). The authors recommend reducing the high cost of telephone calls and housing prisoners closer to their communities. Unfortunately, budget cuts have led many prisons to reduce visiting hours, creating additional barriers for families wishing to maintain contact. There are many promising programs in the United States that are focused on meeting the children's needs and reducing their risk for future problems, but there is little systematic study of short- or long-term effects.

## Women and Criminal Behavior

Criminogenic factors that affect recidivism are currently being targeted to improve outcomes (Taxman & Cropsey, 2007). Six major factors include antisocial values, criminal peers, dysfunctional families, substance abuse, criminal personality, and low self-control. In an older meta-analysis, the strongest predictors for treatment success for women were those focusing on interpersonal needs: family and peer (antisocial associates), relationships in general, and family process variables in particular (Dowden & Andrews, 1999). Although there is great overlap between "addictive thinking" and criminogenic thinking and behavior, specific emphasis on this element is likely to have a positive impact on treatment outcomes. This entails focus on specific areas of criminal thinking through a curriculum that explores and corrects the criminal thinking patterns utilized to justify, deflect blame, and continue criminal antisocial behavior.

## Substance Abuse

About half of women in state prisons were using alcohol and other drugs when they committed their offense. Drug use at the time of their offense was reported more often than alcohol use; 40% were under the influence of drugs when their crime occurred and on every measure of drug use, their problem was more severe. Women also reported higher usage over their lifetimes, during the month before the offense, and at the time of the offense. Almost one-third said they had committed the offense that brought them to prison in order to obtain money to buy drugs. Among women in federal prisons, 15% were consuming alcohol at the time of their offense (Greenfeld & Snell, 1999). Lifetime alcohol abuse or dependence was 38.6% (Teplin, Abram, & McClelland, 1996).

## Co-occurring Psychiatric Disorders

Women also have high rates of psychiatric disorders. Among jail detainees, 80% were found to meet criteria for one or more lifetime psychiatric disorders, and 70% were symptomatic within 6 months of the interview. Not surprisingly, major depressive episode (18.0%) and dysthymia (7.1%) were prevalent. This is of particular concern because suicide is the second most common cause of death for inmates. Most of these detainees were arrested for nonviolent crimes (Teplin et al., 1996; US Department of Justice, 1995). Rates for mood disorders were also high for convicted felons entering prison (Jordan, Schlenger, Fairbank, & Caddell, 1996; Teplin et al., 1996; US Department of Justice, 1995). Rates were elevated for antisocial and borderline personality disorders, compared to women in community samples. However, it is important to be cautious about diagnoses of antisocial personality disorder done in the early 1990s. Subsequent attention to PTSD has revealed that women who are high on the numbing cluster of PTSD symptoms can be mistakenly diagnosed as antisocial because they appeared to lack connection with others. Also, it was not until the publication of DSM IV in 1994 (American Psychiatric Association, 1994) that careful guidelines were given for distinguishing between borderline personality disorder and behaviors characteristic of active substance abuse.

Women inmates who have a psychiatric disorder are more likely to be physically victimized by another inmate while in prison (Blitz, Wolff, & Shi, 2008). However, a community-based study of men and women with severe mental illness and substance abuse concluded that effective treatment of substance abuse and stable housing appears to reduce arrests and incarcerations and concomitant costs (Clark, Ricketts, & McHugao, 1999).

Women in community samples are more than twice as likely as men to have PTSD (10.4% vs. 5.0%), and a third of those fail to recover even after many years. PTSD is strongly comorbid with other lifetime disorders (Kessler, Sonnega, Bromet, Hughes, & Nelson, 1995). Rates in correctional populations are much higher. A significant number (44%) of women in the corrections system report they were physically or sexually assaulted at some time in their lives, and most reported it occurred before age 18 (Greenfeld & Snell, 1999). Rates from other studies are even higher, ranging from 77–90% (Langan & Pelissier, 2001; Messina & Grella, 2006). In general, the higher the level of structure in treatment (outpatient, intensive outpatient, residential), the higher the frequency of abuse histories and PTSD.

## Relationships

Developmental psychologists have long stressed the importance of relationships for women, and how a sense of connection determines their behavior. For better and worse, much of a woman's addiction history is determined by her relationships. These influence her initiation to drugs and whether she seeks treatment and remains in it. Relationships are often the key relapse precipitant, whereas men have a wider variety of hazards. Many addicted women are introduced to drugs in their family of origin by a parent, sibling, or another relative, and their choice of an intimate partner is often a repeat of the past. Their way forward through treatment is also heavily dependent on forming positive relationships in the treatment program and in the wider recovering community.

Stephanie Covington has described the importance of gender awareness and how it influences many aspects of treatment (Covington, 2002, 2003, 2008). She stresses the importance of an integrated treatment that promotes healthy connections to children, significant others, and the community. Common themes in the lives of addicted women include shame and stigma, fear of losing a partner or children, and the sequelae of physical and sexual abuse. Women are most likely to be harmed by their lovers or partners, whereas males are more likely to be harmed by enemies or strangers. Covington notes that the standard management practices in the criminal justice system, such as searches, seclusion, and restraint, may traumatize women or elicit memories of earlier abuse. Early research on her model, Women's Integrated Treatment (WIT), and her manual, *Helping Women Recover*, are promising and client satisfaction is high (Messina, Grella, Cartier, & Torres, 2010).

## Treatment in Custody

Beneficial effects have been shown when treatment components which were oriented toward women's needs are integrated into prison programs for women. Women who were randomized to a gender-responsive treatment program had greater reductions in drug use, were more likely to remain in residential aftercare longer, and were less likely to be reincarcerated 12 months after parole (Messina et al., 2010). Women in this program participated in a program using manualized curricula, *Helping Women Recover* (Covington, 1999) and *Beyond Trauma* (Covington, 2003), and were compared to women who participated in a standard prison-based therapeutic community.

In-custody treatment alone is not likely to meet women's complex needs. In an outcomes study comparing 6- and 12-month return-to-custody data for treated and untreated female inmates in California, Messina and colleagues found no differences, except for those who participated in community-based aftercare (Messina, Burdon, & Prendergast, 2006). These women were significantly less likely to be returned to custody, compared with those who did not participate. Treatment in custody is much more successful when there is a relatively seamless connection to programs within the community that can support her in the transition and in continuing the recovery process.

Taxman (Taxman & Cropsey, 2007), Covington (Covington, 2000), and others have emphasized the importance of maintaining safety in the correctional environment. Women may be victimized by other inmates or custodial staff, exacerbating the impact of previous trauma in their lives. Custodial misconduct includes rape, sexual harassment, threats of force, or denying goods or privileges (Beck & Hughes, 2005). Although these things can occur in community programs, the mechanisms for accountability are stronger in the community.

## Treatment in the Community

The use of the reentry court as an alternative sanction has been implemented and is currently being studied in Los Angeles County (Messina & Chand, 2009). The Second Chance Women's Re-entry Court is a collaboration between the criminal justice system and PROTOTYPES comprehensive treatment program to provide early assessment of mental health and substance abuse disorders with appropriate community-based treatment and ancillary services. Based on the drug court model, it combines intensive supervision, mandatory drug testing, appropriate sanctions, positive reinforcement, and court-supervised treatment. The strength of the collaboration permitted targeting a population usually excluded from community treatment: women who have a current felony charge (sometimes violent) and are facing an imminent state prison sentence. These women have extensive addiction and criminal justice histories, and the majority met criteria for at least one mental health diagnosis. PROTOTYPES has a long history of integrating treatment for substance abuse, mental illness, HIV/AIDS, homelessness, domestic violence, trauma, and lack of life skills. *Seeking Safety* is used as the primary curriculum in this residential treatment program of a minimum of 6 months, followed by 6–12 months of outpatient services. Extensive evaluation is underway. When completed, this research will also look at women who would have been eligible for the reentry drug court program but went to prison instead.

Women emerging from prison onto parole have complex problems that must be addressed for them to succeed. These include early mental health problems, substance abuse, poor job skills and lack of employment, unstable housing, histories of abuse, and early entry into the criminal justice system (Grella & Greenwell, 2007). Study authors noted a high degree of problem recognition in many who volunteered for in-prison treatment, though their complex needs may not necessarily have been met. They suggested that many of the problems that lead women to enter treatment in prison and parole may influence treatment completion, and interventions to engage and retain women offenders in treatment are needed to reduce recidivism.

## Key Elements of Gender-Responsive Treatment

Specific treatment elements improve outcomes for women, through increasing access as well as improving engagement and retention (Greenfield et al., 2007; Grella, 2008). Specific barriers include lack of pregnancy or childcare services, fears of loss of custody or prosecution, and inadequate services for co-occurring disorders. Women-only programs are more likely to address these needs (Grella, Polinsky, Hser, & Perry, 1999). Services related to pregnancy and parenting include parenting classes, children's activities, and pediatric, prenatal, and postpartum services. In a UCLA study, the women-only programs (compared to mixed-gender programs) were more likely to assist with housing, transportation, job training, and acquisition of practical skills. In a study of eight community-based programs, women with great problem severity had better outcomes in women-only programs than in mixed-gender programs (Niv & Hser, 2007). Participants in these programs had what are generally considered poor prognostic signs: greater ASI severity scores in the areas of alcohol use, drug use, family, medical, and psychiatric domains. However, the effort to meet their specific needs led to better outcomes in the women-only programs. This is consistent with other findings that the tighter the fit between the client's problem profile and the services actually delivered, the better the outcomes (McLellan et al., 1997, 1998). For quality assurance, this can be measured with the Treatment Services Review described in these studies.

Very little experimental work has identified what is effective in women-only programs besides meeting practical needs. However, one study of group interaction is intriguing (Hodgins, el-Guebaly, & Addington, 1997). Women-only groups appear to foster greater interaction, emotional and behavioral expression, and more variability in interpersonal style than mixed groups. Women in mixed groups tended to engage in a more restricted type of behavior, while the behavior of the men showed greater variability. Gender-specific treatment is also associated with higher rates of continuing care, even when the women transfer from specialized, women-only programs to a mixed-gender program (Claus et al., 2007).

In selecting a treatment program for female offenders, it is important to probe claims of individualized treatment to determine if relevant services are actually available. It is common to find gaps between promotional materials (brochures and/or websites) and what is actually offered. Funding can change very rapidly, often for the worse, and programs may be slow to align their promotional materials. This may not necessarily represent an attempt to mislead, but can reflect the general instability in the treatment community during difficult economic times.

Another key element in the effort to engage and retain women is a program's willingness to start wherever the woman is prepared to begin and build the therapeutic alliance in preparation for tackling other issues. A woman may enter substance abuse treatment because it is available, but her primary goal may be relief from other situations that affect her current circumstances. Brown and her colleagues (Brown, Melchior, Panter, Slaughter, & Huba, 2000) have developed a Steps of Change Model that addresses four key areas: (1) domestic violence; (2) risky sexual behaviors; (3) addictive behaviors; and (4) emotional problems. For example, women in a domestic violence situation may enter residential substance abuse treatment because she needs safe housing and recognizes that her drug use puts her at risk, but she will be preoccupied with achieving greater safety and will be more able to address her substance use once safety is addressed. Substance abuse treatment programs are highly variable, and older, more traditional programs may insist that the substance abuse must be addressed first for other efforts to succeed. If a woman is labeled as "resistant," and her main concerns are minimized, the program will lose the opportunity to cultivate readiness in other areas by doing something useful in an area she views as a priority at the outset. Motivational enhancement strategies, which have been widely disseminated, emphasize the important of starting where the client wishes to begin and building from there (Miller, 1999).

It is important that the treatment culture is more supportive and less confrontational than older, male-dominated models of treatment. More traditional therapeutic communities utilized a model of relatively harsh confrontation that, despite the best intentions of staff, may persist into the present. Many who worked in those settings went on to other types of programs, bringing this style with them. It is likely that men succeeded in spite of this approach, rather than because of it, but most clinicians now view harsh confrontation as inappropriate for women with histories of trauma and co-occurring disorders. It contributes to premature dropout, and a treatment environment that replicates traumatic conditions and exacerbates a woman's sense of powerlessness. This is not conducive to revealing and exploring sensitive issues. A supportive environment includes forthright feedback; it is the attitude and tone that matters. Widespread dissemination of the motivational enhancement strategies has given counselors an alternative skill set, but they may still lapse back into punitive behavior when working with difficult clients. These challenges are even greater for programs within the prison setting, as a strong male-dominated culture sets the tone, even when women are in charge.

## Addressing PTSD

As has been noted earlier, rates of PTSD in criminal justice settings are even higher than in community samples. Treatment programs are largely dealing with complex PTSD, or abuse or exploitation that has taken place over many years (Herman, 1992) rather than a single traumatic episode. Recognition of this problem in the 1990s (Zweben, Clark, & Smith, 1994) has led to the development of specialized treatments that can be used in addiction treatment settings. However, even prior to the emergence of newer treatments, some success has been documented (Gil-Rivas, Fiorentine, Anglin, & Taylor, 1997). In this study, abused clients were just as likely as those who had not been abused to participate in counseling, complete treatment, and remain drug free up to 6 months later. Newer treatment models target emotions and behaviors that are usually problematic for women with PTSD, and will hopefully continue to improve outcomes.

Dissemination and implementation efforts are underway to encourage service systems to meet the needs of clients with histories of abuse and violence (Brown et al., 2007; Jennings, 2004). Substance abuse treatment programs are increasingly expected to be *trauma-informed*, or knowledgeable about and sensitive to trauma-related issues present in survivors. At minimum, services must be delivered in a way that avoids further traumatization and encourages consumer participation in treatment. Programs with more resources are encouraged to provide *trauma-specific services*, including appropriate assessment methods and specific interventions to address trauma issues.

Parenting classes offered to women should be trauma-informed, capable of acknowledging the impact of trauma in the life of both mother and her children. Children of battered mothers can experience trauma themselves. They are often subjected to ongoing marital conflict; family dysfunction; relocations of their home; and interactions with the police and court. Preschool children are more vulnerable to the effects of domestic violence than older children (Campbell & Lewandowski, 1997). Partnerships between substance abuse treatment programs and agencies focused on children can be excellent ways of bringing specialized services to enhance what can be offered in-house. Indeed, agencies can deploy staff directly to the substance abuse treatment program, utilizing federal (Medicaid) and other types of funding.

Among the newer treatments, *Seeking Safety* is the most thoroughly studied and widely disseminated in the treatment community (Brown et al., 2007; Najavits, 2002; Najavits, Weiss, Shaw, & Muenz, 1998). It is an integrated treatment approach designed for use in early stages of addiction recovery, to help clients better understand their feeling states and learn coping skills to manage their PTSD symptoms without resorting to substance use. It consists of 25 sessions, focusing on cognitive, behavioral, and interpersonal issues, including a case management component. It is manualized, but with an attractive flexibility that allows clients and clinical staff to select the sequence of sessions that they prefer.

Detailed feedback from a large number of clients and clinicians in diverse geographical areas outside the universities indicated an unusual level of enthusiasm for *Seeking Safety* (Brown et al., 2007).

Dr. Najavits is currently working on the next stage of trauma work, *Remembering and Resolution*. She has developed a readiness questionnaire to assess whether the client is ready to focus on past traumas in an effort to process some of the charged issues. The focus of this phase is exploring memories, expressing intense feelings, being vulnerable (vs. emphasis on being strong in the stabilization phase), and coming to terms with one's inner world. The emphasis is on seeing clearly, telling your story, and transforming pain into growth. *Seeking Safety* and *Creating Change* share many similarities. They are both integrated treatments for PTSD and substance abuse. The format is similar and flexible: the sequence of topics can vary, there is no set length or pacing, and they can be used with a wide variety of clients. Both address the cognitive, behavioral, and interpersonal domains. For more information, see www.seekingsafety.org.

The workforce in the substance abuse treatment system is very diverse, and although licensed clinicians work in this system, they are fewer in number than in the mental health system and more likely to be mostly in supervisory roles. Credentialing standards for substance abuse counselors have grown more rigorous and widespread (Zweben & Ries, 2009), but their role in addressing PTSD is circumscribed. Fortunately, counselors without advanced degrees can utilize a manualized treatment for early-stage stabilization (Najavits, 2002) that gives women excellent tools for symptom management and creates a foundation for future work.

## Staff Composition

Some clinicians believe that an all-female counseling staff is best for women participating in treatment (Bloom, Owen, & Covington, 2003). Others believe that while it is important to have women role models in positions of authority (Brown, Sanchez, Zweben, & Aly, 1996), both men and women have important contributions to make to treatment. Positive male role models are important to help women work through patterns of abusive relationships with men, and they are particularly important when children are present in the treatment facility. The concern that the presence of men creates thorny problems around sexual boundaries is legitimate, but reflects a naivete about the possibility of female staff violating these boundaries as well.

## Barriers to Effective Treatment in the Community

Specific barriers remain for programs trying to help women develop job skills that will take them beyond minimum wage. Over the years, the inmate composition has shifted from violent felons to nonviolent offenders, many in prison for drug-related charges. Nonetheless, laws and regulations devised to manage high-risk inmates tend to be applied, even in community corrections facilities for women who are low-level offenders. For example, it can be very difficult to get approval for a resident to obtain education in the community, despite the importance of job skills to reduce relapse potential and increase productivity. Corrections officials and contractors may refuse to take any level of risk that might expose them to adverse publicity. Residents may also be severely restricted in computer access to prevent them from engaging in unlawful activity. However, this prevents them from acquiring or improving the types of skills that will permit jobs that pay a living wage. It is likely that there is an inverse relationship between hourly pay and relapse rates, but this has not been systematically studied. Financial and other social rewards in the workplace can be a powerful motivator at high-risk times.

One of the most controversial issues is the requirement for inmates, even in community corrections settings to use collect call phones from one designated company. Many states use the prison phones as a profit center, allowing the companies to charge rates many times higher than those available using ordinary calling cards. In the state of New York alone, 57.5% of the profits were kicked back to the state in the form of commissions (Center for Constitutional Rights, 2009), totaling millions of dollars. Representatives from New York State argued the money was used to pay for basic prisoner services and release clothes. However, the families countered that they have not committed a crime and this amounts to a backdoor tax. In June 2007, the New York State Legislature required future contracts to offer the lowest costs to the consumer, but these exploitative practices remain in many other states.

Treatment providers in New York and elsewhere object because most of the families are from poor communities and their families are the least able to pay. The telephone is an important vehicle to maintain and develop family relationships. Maintaining contact with an incarcerated parent supports attachment and improves the child's emotional response (Vigne et al., 2005). Programs for women and their children are often required to reach out to family members. Prisoners with strong and healthy family ties are less likely to return to crime, and it is especially important for children to remain connected.

Nowhere is the resistance to evidence-based practices more evident than in opinions and practices about methadone. Four decades of research support the safety and efficacy of methadone maintenance, and its important role in reducing recidivism (Lowinson et al., 2005; Martin, Zweben, & Payte, 2009). It is the treatment of choice for opioid-addicted pregnant women and careful clinical management strategies have been developed for use during pregnancy and the postpartum period (Jones et al., 2008). Nonetheless, many probation and parole officers, drug court judges, and others associated with the criminal justice system refuse to allow opioid users to be placed on methadone, or require them to taper off the medication prematurely, sometimes with tragic results. Educational efforts have somewhat modified these practices, but much needs to be done to tip the balance from the stigma to the evidence (White, 2002).

The following summary checklist can be useful in identifying evidence-based practices for gender-specific treatment programming.

## Checklist for Gender-Specific Treatment

- Low threshold entry
- Pregnancy and postpartum services
- Childcare services, including activities and medical services
- Parenting classes (trauma informed)
- Family education and therapy
- Case management
- Legal services (custody and other issues)
- Psychiatric and specialized counseling services for co-occurring disorders
- Assistance with housing and transportation
- Organizational structure with positive female role models in authority
- Male role models who can promote healthy relationships
- Education and job skills training that allow women to support their families

## Appropriate Selection and Implementation of Evidence-Based Practices

The substance abuse treatment system was launched in response to the failure of the mental health model to produce good outcomes and developed through trial and error (Margolis & Zweben, 1998; Rawson & Obert, 2002). The founding of NIAAA and NIDA in the early 1970s added a research component that has borne fruit ever since. Concern about the failure to implement research findings led to the examination of obstacles and the publication of an Institute of Medicine report that interviewed a wide variety of stakeholders and made recommendations for disseminating and implementing research findings (Lamb, Greenlick, & McCarty, 1998). Since that time, federal, state, and local funders have encouraged the implementation of evidence-based interventions.

These efforts have focused the treatment system on outcomes and helped reduce or eliminate some ideologically based practices that do not contribute to positive outcomes. These include the following:

- Requiring abstinence as a condition of access to substance abuse or mental health treatment. On the substance abuse side, this practice evolved in part because programs did not have the resources to manage detoxification and in part as a test of motivation for treatment. On the mental health side, there was concern about using psychotropic medications with people who are drinking and using. Barriers in both settings have been reduced or eliminated as data emerged about the importance of rapid engagement and retention.
- Denying access to AOD treatment programs for people on prescribed medications. It used to be common for people to be denied access if they were on psychotropic medication, but this barrier has been greatly reduced. Programs that do not have medical staff can utilize a simple procedure to store medications safely and monitor to document that the client is taking them as prescribed. Unfortunately, some criminal justice organizations prevent women on psychotropic medications from participating in community programs by restricting eligibility criteria. Since over 20% of American women in community samples experience a major depressive episode during their lifetime (Kessler et al., 1994), this makes little sense. In practice, women in prison who want treatment often conceal their symptoms in order to enter the program. Staff then has the frustration of knowing that the woman's functioning would be enormously improved by medication, but they cannot risk having her sent back to prison by raising the issue.
- Arbitrary prohibitions against the use of certain prescribed medications (especially methadone). Nowhere is stigma-based decision making more apparent than in the use of methadone (White, 2002), as previously discussed. Buprenorphine, a partial agonist also used to treat opioid addiction, is sometimes more acceptable, but it is not always the best choice for the patient.
- Discharging clients for alcohol/drug use. The addiction treatment system is the only one that discharges patients for manifesting the problem for which they seek help. Unfortunately, some treatment programs, judges, probation and parole officers, and others in the criminal justice system still endorse some of these practices and return a woman to custody at any sign of relapse. Certainly, there are legitimate reasons for discharge which, for example, include violence or threats of violence or bringing drugs/alcohol into the treatment facility. But a growing consensus, based on an understanding that addiction is a chronic disorder characterized by at least some relapse, requires programs to have alternative practices.

It is also important to maintain a balanced perspective about the state of evidence and how it is implemented. To do this, it is useful to make a distinction between evidence-based *principles* and evidence-based *practices* (Miller, Zweben, & Johnson, 2005). The latter includes but is not limited to specific interventions. Evidence-based principles are often derived from services research using longitudinal, observational, or quasi-experimental studies. They shed important light on key issues. For example, repeated findings of a strong correlation between retention and desirable outcomes have led to challenging the practice of high-threshold admission requirements, or discharging clients for drug use. Instead, motivational enhancement strategies promote engagement and retention, and funders are instituting policies that discourage termination for alcohol and other drug use alone.

It is important to be inquisitive when researchers and others make a statement beginning with "There is no evidence for...." It is often assumed that the topic has been carefully examined and no evidence has been found. In fact, it often means that no one has conducted a careful study. This can be because of methodological difficulties in studying a particular topic (like psychodynamic psychotherapy) or because there simply aren't enough research dollars to evaluate every practice in the community. Clinicians have to make decisions every day on issues for which there is little or no data, and it is important to acknowledge the limitations of evidence. Greater respect for their insight can also be a pathway to innovative research.

Specific psychosocial interventions are usually investigated in random assignment studies using manualized treatments in carefully controlled trials. Samples and settings are homogenous and treatment is standardized. Specific procedures are used to assure fidelity to the model. Examples include the motivational enhancement strategies, contingency management, cognitive behavioral interventions for skill building, and the community reinforcement approach. Effectiveness trials examine how well these work in real-world settings, with diverse populations. There may be an insufficient number of trials to determine what will actually work with a criminal justice population.

Many problems can arise with the implementation of these interventions. In the past, most of the money has been spent on the research itself, and relatively little on implementation (Fixsen, Naoom, Blase, Friedman, & Wallace, 2005). Although this is changing, we do not know nearly enough about how to implement findings in the community with the limited resources at hand. Some funders adopt a "pick from this list" approach and refuse to fund anything but specific treatment interventions. This eliminates the possibility of providing the continuum of services that is associated with good outcomes. Community treatment providers are increasingly expected to include fidelity checks when they report using an evidence-based practice, but funding is often inadequate and methods for fidelity checks are often inappropriately adapted from research protocols. No one has yet figured out how to adapt interventions to specific cultural groups without losing the essential ingredients, but treatment providers are required to address this issue. In the enthusiasm to implement evidence-based treatment, the concept of individualizing treatment is sometimes a casualty. The following case example from a program with a criminal justice contract is summarized from a posting on the Center for Substance Abuse Treatment's Dual Diagnosis Listserve (CSAT, 2008).

The writer asks

*Is it possible that a rigid, very intensive 'evidence-based best practice' dual-diagnosis residential treatment program might be too stressful and even destructive for a person who is struggling with much stress from long-standing paranoid delusions?*

She describes a patient with longstanding psychotic symptoms. When referred to the residential program, he could converse normally for 10 min, but would then become delusional. He used naps to compensate for his sleep that was usually disturbed by his delusions. He was drinking "a little," and confessed it to his Probation Officer who sent him into a program with whom they had a contract. This program was very intense, with numerous groups and classes. The patient could not sleep at night and could no longer nap to compensate. He got no exercise and was cut off from support of old friends.

The deterioration over two months was "steady and hideous." He became more psychotic, his delusions expanded, and he was bolting from groups and classes. This was addressed as a disciplinary problem. He became hostile and aggressive, talking about "The Plot" by staff and residents.

When the writer expressed concern about what was happening, she was told, "We are an evidence-based best practice dual-diagnosis treatment facility so the program is appropriate for him and couldn't possibly be harmful for any dual-diagnosis person. They also say they can't make any adaptations to make it less stressful for him because county corrections contracts with them to do it exactly according to the evidence-based best practice model used. So he's just got to buck up, behave himself, go to all the groups and classes, etc."

This is a good example of how a lack of understanding of what constitutes an evidence-based practice leads to poor care. The literature on modified therapeutic communities for persons dually diagnosed describes the importance of an environment with lower stresses and demands than the usual residential treatment program (Sacks & Ries, 2005; Sacks, Sacks, & De Leon, 1999). In this example, it is quite possible that the program overstated its capability, and the contractor did not have sufficient research or clinical background to challenge their assertions. Emphasis on co-occurring disorders has led some programs to claim capabilities that are not supported by the specific services they offer. In their enthusiasm for positive findings, researchers may also promote overgeneralization of findings.

The literature does not support the idea that rigid devotion to the model at the expense of adaptations to address individual needs produces better results. Research studies look at what appears to work for a group of clients from a statistical perspective. There are always those who don't fit. Unfortunately, the term "fidelity" has become a buzzword, and if an individual does not benefit from a program, questions are raised about fidelity to a model rather than about whether treatment is being appropriately individualized. Criminal justice contractors often place a premium on "consistency" that restricts the scope for clinical judgment.

## Recommendations

The following recommendations are presented:

- Select appropriate evidence-based principles and practices to meet women's needs; avoid the "pick from this list approach."
- Carefully investigate whether necessary services are available; go beyond the program's promotional materials.
- Eliminate ideologically based constraints that have not been shown to work.
- Eliminate prohibitions against using medications for psychiatric conditions or addictive disorders.
- Acknowledge that treatment requires gradually building the client's capacity for independence; avoid excess restrictions that are not required for public safety.
- Make sure contract requirements are realistic and funding is adequate.
- Reduce barriers to maintaining telephone contact and visitation.
- Encourage research to clarify what types of intervention for the children of incarcerated mothers will reduce their risk of future problems.
- Assure that the placement of treatment services within the organizational structure of corrections gives it sufficient latitude to implement effective treatment.

### Conclusions

Much is now known about the characteristics of women in the criminal justice system over the last 2 decades that has brought progress in developing effective treatment for women in general and substance-abusing women in particular. However, much work remains to be done to refine treatment approaches to address what is distinctive about women in the criminal justice system, as well as to disseminate these interventions more broadly. Hopefully this will contribute to reducing recidivism, and result in enduring gains through interrupting the cycle of crime for these women and their children.

## References


American Psychiatric Association. (1994). *Diagnostic and statistical manual of mental disorders* (4th ed.). Washington, DC: American Psychiatric Association.

Annie E. Casey Foundation. (2009). *Children of incarcerated parents fact sheet.* Retrieved from http://www.fcnetwork.org/AECFChildren%20of%20Incarcerated%20Parents%20Factsheet.pdf. Accessed in November 30, 2009.

Beck, A. J., & Hughes, T. A. (2005). *Sexual violence reported by correctional authorities, 2004* (No. NCJ 210333). Washington, DC: Bureau of Justice Statistics, US Department of Justice.

Blitz, C. L., Wolff, N., & Shi, J. (2008). Physical victimization in prison: The role of mental illness. *International Journal of Law and Psychiatry, 31*(5), 385–393.

Bloom, B., Owen, B., & Covington, S. (2003). *Gender-responsive strategies: Research, practice, and guiding principles for women offenders.* Washington, DC: US Department of Justice, National Institute of Corrections.

Brown, V. B., Melchior, L. A., Panter, A. T., Slaughter, R., & Huba, G. J. (2000). Women's steps of change and entry into drug abuse treatment. A multidimensional stages of change model. *Journal of Substance Abuse Treatment, 18*(3), 231–240.

Brown, V. B., Najavits, L. M., Cadiz, S., Finkelstein, N., Heckman, J. P., & Rechberger, E. (2007). Implementing an evidence-based practice: Seeking safety group. *Journal of Psychoactive Drugs, 39*, 231–240.

Brown, V., Sanchez, S., Zweben, J. E., & Aly, T. (1996). Challenges in moving from a traditional therapeutic community to a women and children's TC model. *Journal of Psychoactive Drugs, 28*(1), 39–46.

Campbell, J. C., & Lewandowski, L. A. (1997). Mental and physical health effects of intimate partner violence on women and children. *Psychiatric Clinics of North America, 20*(2), 353–374.

Center for Constitutional Rights. (2009). *Factsheet: Corporate exploitation and the prison system.* Retrieved November 28, 2009, from http://ccrjustice.org/learn-more/faqs/factsheet%3A-corporate-exploitation-and-prison-system

Center for Substance Abuse Treatment's. (2008, February). *Psychosis in an intensive COD program.* CSAT Dual Diagnosis Listserve. Accessed February 19, 2008, from dualdx@treatment.org

Clark, R. E., Ricketts, S. K., & McHugao, G. J. (1999). Legal system involvement and costs for persons in treatment for severe mental illness and substance use disorders. *Psychiatric Services, 50*(5), 641–647.

Claus, R. E., Orwin, R. G., Kissin, W., Krupski, A., Campbell, K., & Stark, K. (2007). Does gender-specific substance abuse treatment for women promote continuity of care? *Journal of Substance Abuse Treament, 32*(1), 27–39.

Covington, S. (1999). *Helping women recover.* San Francisco: Jossey Bass.

Covington, S. (2000). Helping women recover: Creating gender-specific treatment for substance-abusing women and girls in community corrections. In M. McMahon (Ed.), *Assessment to assistance: Programs for women in community corrections* (pp. 171–233). Latham, MD: American Correctional Association.

Covington, S. (2002). Helping women recover: Creating gender-responsive treatment. In S. L. A. Straussner & S. Brown (Eds.), *Handbook of women's addiction treatment: Theory and practice* (pp. 52–72). San Francisco: Jossey Bass.

Covington, S. (2003). *Beyond trauma: A healing journey for women (Facilitator's guide).* Center City, MN: Hazelden Press.

Covington, S. (2008). Women and addiction: A trauma-informed approach. *Journal of Psychoactive Drugs, SARC Supplement, 5*, 377–385.

Dowden, C., & Andrews, D. A. (1999). What works for female offenders: A meta-analytic review. *Crime & Delinquency, 45*(4), 438–452.

Fixsen, D. L., Naoom, S. F., Blase, K. A., Friedman, R. M., & Wallace, F. (2005). *Implementation research: A synthesis of the literature* (No. Louis de la Parte Florida Mental Health Publication #231). Tampa, FL: University of South Florida.

Gil-Rivas, V., Fiorentine, R., Anglin, M. D., & Taylor, E. (1997). Sexual and physical abuse: Do they compromise drug treatment outcomes? *Journal of Substance Abuse Treatment, 14*(4), 351–358.

Greene, S., Haney, C., & Hurtado, A. (2000). Cycles of pain: Risk factors in the lives of incarcerated mothers and their children. *The Prison Journal, 80*(1), 3–23.

Greenfeld, L. A., & Snell, T. L. (1999). *Women offenders* (No. NCJ 175688). Washington, DC: Bureau of Justice Statistics, US Department of Justice.

Greenfield, S. F., Brooks, A. J., Gordon, S. M., Green, C. A., Kropp, F., McHugh, R. K., et al. (2007). Substance abuse treatment entry, retention, and outcome in women: A review of the literature. *Drug and Alcohol Dependence, 86*, 1–21.

Grella, C. E. (2008). From generic to gender-responsive treatment: Changes in social policies, treatment services, and outcomes of women in substance abuse treatment. *Journal of Psychoactive Drugs, Supplement, 5*, 327–343.

Grella, C. E., & Greenwell, L. (2007). Treatment needs and completion of community-based aftercare among substance-abusing women offenders. *Women's Health Issues, 17*(4), 244–255.

Grella, C. E., Polinsky, M. L., Hser, Y. I., & Perry, S. M. (1999). Characteristics of women-only and mixed-gender drug abuse treatment programs. *Journal of Substance Abuse Treatment, 17*(1–2), 37–44.

Hanlon, T. E., O'Grady, K. E., Bennett-Sears, T., & Callaman, J. M. (2005). Incarcerated drug-abusing mothers: Their characteristics and vulnerability. *American Journal of Drug and Alcohol Abuse, 31*(1), 59–77.

Harrison, P. M., & Beck, A. J. (2005). *Prisoners in 2004* (No. BJS Bulletin, NCJ 210677). Washington, DC: Bureau of Justice Statistics, US Department of Justice.

Harrison, P. A., & Karberg, J. C. (2003). *Prison and jail inmates at midyear 2002.* Washington, DC: Bureau of Justice Statistics, US Department of Justice.

Herman, J. (1992). *Trauma and recovery.* New York: Basic Books.

Hodgins, D. C., el-Guebaly, N., & Addington, J. (1997). Treatment of substance abusers: Single or mixed gender programs? *Addiction, 92*(7), 805–812.

Jennings, A. (2004). *Models for developing trauma-informed behavioral health systems and trauma specific services.* Rockville, MD: U.S. Department of Health and Human Services.

Jones, H. E., Martin, P. R., Heil, S. H., Kaltenbach, K., Selby, P., Coyle, M. G., et al. (2008). Treatment of opioid-dependent pregnant women: Clinical and research issues. *Journal of Substance Abuse Treatment, 35*, 245–259.

Jordan, K. B., Schlenger, W. E., Fairbank, J. A., & Caddell, J. M. (1996). Prevalence of psychiatric disorders in incarcerated women. II. Convicted felons entering prison. *Archives of General Psychiatry, 53*, 513–519.

Kessler, R. C., McGonagle, K. A., Zhao, S., Nelson, C. B., Hughes, M., Eshleman, S., et al. (1994). Lifetime and 12 month prevalence of DSM-III-R psychiatric

disorders in the United States. *Archives of General Psychiatry, 51*, 8–19.
Kessler, R. C., Sonnega, A., Bromet, E., Hughes, M., & Nelson, C. B. (1995). Posttraumatic stress disorder in the National Comorbidity Survey. *Archives of General Psychiatry, 52*(12), 1048–1060.
Lamb, S., Greenlick, M. R., & McCarty, D. (Eds.). (1998). *Bridging the gap between practice and research: Forging partnerships with community-based drug and alcohol treatment*. Washington, DC: National Academy Press.
Langan, N. P., & Pelissier, B. M. (2001). Gender differences among prisoners in drug treatment. *Journal of Substance Abuse, 13*(3), 291–301.
Lowinson, J., Marion, I., Joseph, H., Langrod, J., Salsitz, E. A., Payte, J. T., et al. (2005). Methadone maintenance. In J. H. Lowinson, P. Ruiz, R. B. Millman, & J. G. Langrod (Eds.), *Substance abuse: A comprehensive textbook* (4th ed., pp. 616–633). Baltimore: Williams and Wilkins.
Margolis, R. B., & Zweben, J. E. (1998). *Treating patients with alcohol and other drug problems: An integrated approach*. Washington, DC: American Psychological Association.
Martin, J., Zweben, J. E., & Payte, J. T. (2009). Opioid maintenance treatment. In R. K. Ries, S. C. Miller, D. A. Fiellin, & R. Saitz (Eds.), *Principles of addiction medicine* (pp. 671–687). Philadelphia: Lippincott, Williams & Wilkins.
McLellan, A. T., Grisson, G. R., Zanis, D., Randall, M., Brill, P., & O'Brien, C. P. (1997). Problem-service matching in addiction treatment. *Archives of General Psychiatry, 54*, 730–735.
McLellan, A. T., Hagan, T. A., Levine, M., Gould, F., Meyers, K., Bencivengo, M., et al. (1998). Supplemental social services improve outcomes in public addiction treatment. *Addiction, 93*(10), 1489–1499.
Messina, N., Burdon, W., & Prendergast, M. (2006). Prison-based treatment for drug-dependent women offenders: Treatment versus no treatment. *Journal of Psychoactive Drugs, Supplement 3*, 333–343.
Messina, N., & Chand, N. (2009). *Exemplary programs for women offenders with co-occurring disorders: Key recommendations for implementation and replication*. White Paper prepared for the Co-Occurring Joint Action Council (COJAC), the Department of Alcohol and Drug Programs (ADP), and Department of Mental Health, Sacramento, CA.
Messina, N., & Grella, C. (2006). Childhood trauma and women's health outcomes in a California prison population. *American Journal of Public Health, 96*(10), 1842–1848.
Messina, N., Grella, C. E., Cartier, J., & Torres, S. (2010). A randomized experimental study of gender-responsive substance abuse treatment for women in prison. *Journal of Substance Abuse Treatment, 38*(2), 97–107.
Miller, W. R. (1999). *Enhancing motivation for change in substance abuse treatment* (Vol. 35). Rockville, MD: U.S. Department of Health and Human Services.
Miller, W. R., Zweben, J. E., & Johnson, W. (2005). Evidence-based treatment: Why, what, where, when and how? *Journal of Substance Abuse Treatment, 29*, 267–276.
Moses, M. C. (2006). Does parental incarceration increase a child's risk for foster care placement? *National Institute of Justice Journal, 255*, 1–3.
Najavits, L. M. (2002). *Seeking safety: A treatment manual for PTSD and substance abuse*. New York: Guilford.
Najavits, L. M., Weiss, R. D., Shaw, S. R., & Muenz, L. R. (1998). "Seeking safety": Outcome of a new cognitive-behavioral psychotherapy for women with posttraumatic stress disorder and substance dependence. *Journal of Traumatic Stress, 11*(3), 437–456.
Niv, N., & Hser, Y. I. (2007). Women-only and mixed-gender drug abuse treatment programs: Service needs, utilization and outcomes. *Drug and Alcohol Dependence, 87*(2–3), 194–201.
Pollock, J. (2002). *Women, prison, and crime* (2nd ed.). Belmont, CA: Wadsworth Thomson Learning.
Rawson, R. A., & Obert, J. L. (2002). The substance abuse treatment system in the U.S.: What is it? What does it do? Myths and misconceptions. *Occupational Medicine: State of the Art Reviews, 17*(1), 27–39.
Sacks, S., & Ries, R. K. (2005). *Substance abuse treatment for persons with co-occurring disorders* (TIP 42). Rockville, MD: Department of Health and Human Services.
Sacks, S., Sacks, J. Y., & De Leon, G. (1999). Treatment for MICAs: Design and implementation of the modified TC. *Journal of Psychoactive Drugs, 31*(1), 19–30.
Taxman, F., & Cropsey, K. (2007). Women and the criminal justice system: Improving outcomes through criminal justice and non-criminal justice reponses. *Women and Criminal Justice, 17*(2–3), 5–26.
Teplin, L. A., Abram, K. M., & McClelland, G. M. (1996). Prevalence of psychiatric disorders among incarcerated women. I. Pretrial jail detainees [published erratum appears in *Archives of General Psychiatry* 1996 Aug; *53*(8), 664]. *Archives of General Psychiatry, 53*(6), 505–512.
The Sentencing Project. (2007). *Women in the criminal justice system: Briefing sheets*, Washington, DC. Accessed on November 10, 2009, from www.sentencingproject.org
US Department of Justice. (1995). *Jails and jail inmates 1993–94* (No. NCJ-151651). Washington, DC: Bureau of Justice Statistics, US Department of Justice.
Vigne, N. G. L., Naser, R. L., Brooks, L. E., & Castro, J. L. (2005). Examining the effect of incarceration and in-prison family contact on prisoners' family relationships. *Journal of Contemporary Criminal Justice, 21*(4), 314–335.

Wellisch, J., Anglin, M. D., & Prendergast, M. L. (1993). Numbers and characteristics of drug-using women in the criminal justice system: Implications for treatment. *Journal of Drug Issues, 23*, 7–30.

West, H. C., & Sabol, W. J. (2009). *Prison inmates at midyear 2008 – Statistical tables*. Washington, DC: Bureau of Justice Statistics, US Department of Justice.

White, W. L. (2002). *Long-term strategies to reduce the stigma attached to addiction, treatment, and recovery within the city of Philadelphia (with particular reference to medication-assisted treatment/recovery)*. Rockville, MD: Substance Abuse and Mental Health Services Administration (SAMHSA).

Zweben, J. E., Clark, H. W., & Smith, D. E. (1994). Traumatic experiences and substance abuse: Mapping the territory. *Journal of Psychoactive Drugs, 26*(4), 327–345.

Zweben, J. E., & Ries, R. K. (2009). Integrating psychosocial services with pharmacotherapies in the treatment of co-occurring disorders. In R. K. Ries, D. Fiellin, S. Miller, & R. Saitz (Eds.), *Principles of addiction medicine* (4th ed., pp. 1239–1247). New York: Lippincott, Williams & Wilkins.

# Self-Help

# 14

Philip R. Magaletta and Carl Leukefeld

**Abstract**

Self help approaches to addressing the needs of substance abusing offenders involved in the criminal justice system are frequently offered and understudied. This chapter collects, in one place, available information on self help 12-step approaches to substance abusing offenders, reviews the existing research, and recommends several strategies that criminal justice systems might consider when addressing 12-step approaches within their systems.

**Keywords**

Forensic • Corrections • Self help • 12-step • Offenders • Administrators

*What is needed is a method that works, not a philosophy about a method which can be very confusing.*
*Samuel L. Lewis (1990).*

If the past and present are indications of the future then the most frequently offered and used criminal justice substance abuse program will remain the least frequently studied approach. Over the past decade, self-help opportunities for substance-abusing offenders have experienced unprecedented growth in the criminal justice system. While the rates of prior drug use among state offenders remained stable between 1997 and 2004, the rate at which state offenders participated in self-help after admission to prison grew by over 60,000 (Mumola & Karberg, 2006).

P.R. Magaletta (✉)
Federal Bureau of Prisons, Psychology Services Branch, Washington, DC 20534, USA
e-mail: pmagaletta@bop.gov

Compared to outpatient and residential treatment for offenders, self-help is more likely to have been used during any stage of the criminal justice process. This includes prior to jail or prison, during incarceration, and after incarceration during parole or community supervision (Bonczar, 2008; Karberg & James, 2005; Mumola & Karberg, 2006; Mumola, 1999).

Beyond being the most frequently offered and used approach for offenders seeking relief from a substance use disorder, three other reasons highlight the importance of self-help. First, the message of hope that echoes through many of the substance abuse treatment techniques, curriculums, and communities in jails, prisons, and in community correction centers has a shared history with self-help programs (Hughes, Floyd, Norris, & Silva, 1970; Rapkin, 1971;

C. Leukefeld et al. (eds.), *Handbook of Evidence-Based Substance Abuse Treatment in Criminal Justice Settings*, Issues in Children's and Families' Lives 11,
DOI 10.1007/978-1-4419-9470-7_14, © Springer Science+Business Media, LLC 2011

Vogel, 1948). As an early example, in 1935 the self-help program Alcoholics Anonymous (AA; Alcoholics Anonymous, 1976) was forming among several members in Akron, Ohio. From that point, it is estimated to have taken just 3 years for the U.S. Public Health Service to introduce AA as part of its program menu at the secure Federal Narcotics Farm in Lexington, Kentucky and to recommend participation in AA as a component of aftercare upon release in the community (Magura, 2007; Vogel, 1948; White, 1998). DeLeon (2000, 2004) makes it clear that self-help programs were forerunners of contemporary Therapeutic Communities (TC). The modified TC method has received robust empirical support as an effective substance abuse service for criminal justice populations (Inciardi, Martin, & Butzin, 2004). Others too (DiClemente, 2007; McKay, 2009) have noted that many contemporary outpatient, residential, and medically oriented approaches to substance abuse treatment have borrowed heavily from self-help approaches. Next, the growing empirical base outside the criminal justice literature indicates that self-help programs generally, and 12-step programs specifically, lead to important substance abuse outcomes which include ceasing drug and alcohol use (Emrick & Tonigan, 2004; Fiorentine & Hillhouse, 2000a; Humphreys et al., 2004; Tonigan, Toscova, & Miller, 1996). Findings also suggest that program participation positively influences psychological health and promotes effective social support and coping. This is an important observation since substance-abusing offenders typically present with complex lifestyle disorders (DeLeon, 2000; Walters, 1999). Finally, research also demonstrates that clinicians can influence the process of entry into self-help programs. At the very least, an offender's belief about his/her prior self-help involvement represents an important clinical consideration among correctional practitioners for treatment planning and for change (Tonigan, Toscova, & Connors, 1999).

Before examining evidence that supports self-help approaches, several additional points are important. First, the exploration of self-help programs for substance-abusing offenders occurs against the backdrop of a larger offender self-help movement in criminal justice settings which includes mental health and reentry (Codd, 2002; Hamm, 1988; Maunder et al., 2009; McAnany & Tromanhauser, 1977). This chapter focuses on the 12-step approach for substance-disordered offenders as this approach to self-help is the most popular and frequently used in and out of criminal justice systems. Additionally, in community-based samples it has received the most extensive empirical review (Humphreys et al., 2004; Kessler et al., 1997; Magura, 2007; White, 2009). Although the focus is on 12-step approaches, it is noted by DeLeon (2004) that the distinctions and differences between self-help, 12-step, and therapeutic communities may exist only at the level of operationalization. There have also been no contemporary, randomized clinical trials of self-help programs with substance-disordered offenders who are actively involved in the criminal justice system (Lightfoot, 1999; McKenzie, 2006). This is not good news. The positive news is that self-help programs for offenders in criminal justice settings are used. Given that these programs are frequently offered within contemporary criminal justice settings the lack of research remains notable. It is particularly curious given the burgeoning self-help literature outside the criminal justice system which supports its use (White, 2009).

## Twelve-Step Interventions and Their Theoretical Grounding

Twelve-step self-help approaches include AA, Narcotics Anonymous (NA), and Cocaine Anonymous (CA). In 2009, it was estimated that over 2.1 million members were participating in AA, 40,000 of whom were inmates participating in over 1,500 groups registered as operating within correctional institutions (Alcoholics Anonymous, 2009). As cited in Magura (2007), NA is estimated to have 20,000 groups meeting with over 400,000 members and CA has 2,000 groups with 30,000 members. Within the United States 275 of the NA groups are registered as operating within institutions such as prisons and jails (NA World Service, Inc., personal communication, December 2, 2009). Criminal justice group and membership data are not regularly captured or reported by the CA organization. It should be noted that the reported number of AA and NA criminal justice groups is likely to be a conservative estimate for the number of meetings held in criminal justice settings. This is because the data do not include the various community members who, having completed all security procedures for a given setting, are invited into an institution to speak or provide other forms of 12-step service, such as workshops and retreats.

To begin organizing and describing 12-step interventions and their theoretical grounding, it is helpful to clarify what 12-step programs are not. This is the technique that Magura (2007) used in summarizing the work of Humphreys (2003). With standard substance abuse treatment as a point of contrast, the following elements were suggested: self-help programs rely on experiential knowledge, not professional expertise; they rely on mutual support between peers, not a role as a patient; they are always available, not time limited; and they are free, not fee-for-service.

Since 12-step approaches developed from the pragmatic framework of experience, a primary theoretical grounding is not clearly distinguishable (McCrady, 1994). In many ways this eclecticism remains a premier strength as it allows for the change process to be adapted to the whole person, across numerous types of people. However, it also remains a weakness because there is no clear theoretical base. Despite, or perhaps because of, this weakness many have described the 12-step approach using a theories of change framework. These theories are described next. A common thread is an emphasis on learning to promote recovery. To date, the most common types of learning are grounded in behavioral, cognitive-behavioral, social learning, and experiential orientations.

To organize and unify these common orientations of the 12-step approach, a definitional framework is useful. The most salient framework to date draws from Miller and Thoresen's (1999) definition of spirituality and the application of this definition to 12-step programs (Tonigan et al., 1999). In this framework, the 12-step approach is defined as an interrelated set of practices, beliefs, and experiences. Importantly, the framework is pragmatic enough to serve as an educational tool for criminal justice professionals who want to learn more about the 12-step approach (Leukefeld, Farabee, & Tims, 2002).

The practice component involves behaviors that can be quantified. It is therefore not surprising that many 12-step studies to date have been organized around this component. Twelve-step practices are rooted in behavioral learning principles (see Burt, 1975, for a review). They can be organized as distinct behaviors such as attending a meeting; participating in a meeting via listening, speaking or helping to set up or clean up after a meeting; talking with a sponsor; attempting to implement one or more of the 12-steps; praying or meditating; and providing service to other members in or out of the 12-step community. Other examples of practice interventions include recovery practices such as, reading and reflecting on basic 12-step program texts and/or daily meditation literature, attending meetings where literature is read and commenting upon it, and listening to audio recordings of speakers at meetings (Bergman et al., 2009). Many practices listed above occur in groups and when this is the case, it also becomes clear that social learning is operational.

Several authors have advanced the measurement literature for the 12-step practice. Among these measures are instruments including the Alcoholics Anonymous Involvement (AAI) Scale (Tonigan, Connors, & Miller, 1996) and the Recovery Interview (RI; Morgenstern, Kahler, Frey, & Labouvie, 1996). Studies with these and other instruments indicate that 12-step practices can be reliably measured through time and across samples. Unfortunately, not a single study within a criminal justice setting has used these measures or has received research support from a public safety funding agency.

Twelve-step beliefs highlight the role that cognition plays in maintaining an addiction, ceasing an addiction, and/or promoting recovery. Cognitive and cognitive-behavioral theoretical groundings are relevant. Typically there is a focus upon challenging, changing and/or adapting new beliefs, thoughts, attitudes, attributions, and expectations within the substance abuser (Bristow-Braitman, 1995; Steigerwald & Stone, 1997). Examples provided by McCrady (1994) include cognitive coping strategies such as pausing when faced with a desire to drink, and considering the negative consequences rather than the immediate desirable effects of drinking. She also highlights that 12-step approach participants are taught to identify negative thinking and beliefs that could lead to relapse. In addition, decreasing self-focus through the use of various cognitive techniques that challenge and alter thoughts, beliefs, and attitudes are delineated throughout the individual 12-steps (Beckman, 1990).

Finally, although it may appear to be the most empirically elusive component, experiences remain the quintessential feature of the 12-step approach. Typically linked to experiential, social learning and existential theoretical groundings, it is noted that the center of gravity in 12-step approaches is the spiritual experience. Several prominent mental health professionals have described the spiritual experience (James, 1902; Carl Jung, cited in Alcoholics Anonymous, 1984; Skinner, 1987) and more contemporary scholars are also focusing on operationalizing the spiritual experience (see Tonigan et al., 1999 for operationalizations of humility, serenity, and gratitude). In general however, the outcome of the spiritual experience is simply this: it allows the one who has the experience to take another point of view (Khan, 1997). For the substance abuser experiencing the 12-step approach this initially translates to finding oneself being able to do what he/she previously could not. The new point of view is to cease using drugs or alcohol. A simple concept, it has profound implications for altering not just substance abuse, but the substance-abusing lifestyle.

Moving out from the center of spiritual experience, a precise, summative explanation for the theoretical relevance of the experience component is described by DeLeon (1997) as

> ... the process of change is primarily understood by the participants themselves in subjective terms, through perceptions and experiences. Individuals not only must actively engage in the behaviors and attitudes to be changed but must feel the feelings associated with this engagement, understand the meaning or value of the change, and come to see themselves, others and the world differently. (p. 11).

White (2009) makes a similar point about the nature of the experience component and its definition. He presents process as a critical element in defining recovery and indicates that "Process implies that the assistance is not a single event or activity and is relational rather than mechanical, and that continuity of support over time is central to the desired outcome of long-term recovery." (p. 16). Tonigan et al. (1999) use the term "fellowship" to elucidate the experience component by stating, "Helping others, building relationships among other members, and the sharing of joys and hardships all belong to what is described as the fellowship. In short, the fellowship refers to the experiencing of a 12-step program." (p. 114).

It is important to note that these definitions of the experience component all refer to life – not just addiction. In this way, the whole individual and his/her behavior comes under review from vantage points that are internal and external to the individual with the addiction. For this reason, it is not unreasonable to expect that 12-step programs have, as a method, a high potential for addressing lifestyle disorders including the criminogenic risk factors that contribute to criminal lifestyles. Unfortunately, research has not explicitly linked the 12-step approach with criminogenic risk-need theories.

## Are There Specific Interventions for Specific Drugs?

Although there are no specific interventions for specific drugs, there are 12-step approaches for particular addictions. Sometimes overlooked, AA has remained organizationally buoyant for nearly 75 years. This stability is in sharp contrast to the iterative rise and fall of the national substance abuse treatment system (McLellan, Carise,

& Kleber, 2003; White, 1998). Some have noted that this is because as an organization, AA has focused itself on a single, primary purpose – to carry the message to still suffering alcoholics (Alcoholics Anonymous, 1953; Kurtz, 1991; Monahan, 2001; White, 1998).

For this reason, there are two types of AA meetings, open and closed. Open meetings are available to anyone to attend, whereas closed meetings are limited to individuals who have a desire to stop drinking. For other groups such as NA, closed meetings may also be attended by those who want to stop using drugs, regardless of the drug or combinations of drugs. The same holds true for CA groups which are organized around a primary purpose: "Our primary purpose is to stay free from cocaine and all other mind-altering substances and to help others achieve the same freedom." (Cocaine Anonymous, 2008).

## Twelve-Step Studies

To date, the only research on self-help substance abuse groups within criminal justice settings is survey research. The evaluative, empirical 12-step literature is on community samples where, at most, prior criminal justice involvement is mentioned. How self-help can and does influence substance use disorders among offenders is not available.

There are several categories of 12-step studies and findings which may have implications for the criminal justice setting. First there are studies which directly examine 12-step program participation. Second, there are treatment studies which evaluate the impact of treatments that blend 12-step principles into substance abuse professional treatment services. In these studies the goal is not to evaluate 12-step participation per se, but rather to explore the effect of the blended treatment compared to other treatments or to an outcome such as sustained remission. Third, there are studies which examine interventions proximal to participation in 12-step programs and seek to understand the degree to which participation in 12-step programs can be systematically influenced. Typically, these studies examine the impact of various approaches including phone contact, recovery coaches, and treatment curricula that specifically target encouraging, facilitating, or deepening 12-step program participation. A blended treatment study could also examine if the treatment approach enhances 12-step program participation.

## Interventions That Work

No studies using a randomized controlled design with substance-disordered offenders who were actively involved in the criminal justice system have been conducted (Lightfoot, 1999; McKenzie, 2006; White, 2009). Among the community randomized controlled trials with substance abusers, there is little debate that these studies were not conducted as direct outcome studies, but rather, proximal studies that have examined the impact of mandating AA meeting attendance (Humphreys et al., 2004; Miller, Andrews, Wilbourne, & Bennett, 1998). It should also be noted that some have questioned the desirability of random assignment to 12-step approaches. This debate concerning motivation, selection bias, and random assignment to 12-step approaches is outlined in Humphreys and Rappaport (1994), Martin, Inciardi, and O'Connell (2003), and Tonigan et al. (1996).

There are two "blended studies" that used random assignment to examine the effects of 12-step blended treatments compared to other substance abuse treatment. The first study examined 92 participants who sought outpatient community treatment for a cocaine abuse disorder (Wells, Peterson, Gainey, Hawkins, & Catalano, 1994). Within this sample, 87% of participants reported prior criminal justice involvement. The study compared a treatment approach that emphasized the 12 steps and the process of recovery to a treatment approach that emphasized skill training for relapse-prevention techniques. The implementation of each treatment was guided by a manual and each condition consisted of 17 2-hour sessions. Findings indicated there were few differences in the outcomes between groups. Specifically, in each condition participants were equally likely to be retained in treatment, to experience similar reductions in marijuana and cocaine use 6 months post-treatment, and to have similar increases in recovery skills. There was an effect for treatment adherence. Those attending and receiving more treatment sessions in either condition had the largest decreases in marijuana and cocaine use.

The National Institute of Alcohol Abuse and Alcoholism funded the second study, Project MATCH Research Group (1997). The overall aim of this project was to determine if specific patient characteristics would interact with treatment to yield different outcomes. The study used random assignment to one of three outpatient psychosocial treatment approaches for alcohol treatment. Subjects were recruited in two different arms of the study (outpatient, $n = 952$; aftercare, $n = 774$) and treated at one of nine US clinical research units. The arm with outpatient subjects included subjects recruited directly from the community. The arm with aftercare subjects was recruited after they completed inpatient addiction treatment.

Guided by manuals and extensive supervision, the three treatment approaches were (1) Motivational Enhancement Therapy (MET), a precursor to Motivational Interviewing (Miller, Zweben, DiClemente, & Rychtarik, 1992); (2) Cognitive Behavioral Therapy (CBT) (Kadden et al., 1992); and (3) Twelve Step Facilitation (TSF) (Nowinski, Baker, & Carroll, 1999). Both CBT and TSF were 12, weekly 1-hour sessions, and MET was four sessions over 12 weeks. The TSF treatment specifically blended the practices and beliefs of the 12-step approach generally and steps 1, 2, and 3 along with beliefs about denial and surrender specifically.

Consistent with the earlier findings (Wells et al., 1994), Project MATCH findings reported substantial reduction in drinking among participants, at 12 and 24 months followup, regardless of the treatment condition. In addition, outpatient arm participants with lower psychiatric severity had more days of abstinence in the TSF condition when compared to the CBT condition. Two specific characteristics by treatment interactions are of importance to criminal justice settings. First, among those who were high in measures of anger, the best drinking reduction outcomes were observed in the outpatient arm for those in the MET condition (Waldron, Miller, & Tonigan, 2001). Observed across time, 1- and 3-year followup, this matching to treatment was the most consistent study finding. Second, among participants living in environments where the social networks were highly supportive of drinking, TSF reduced drinking (Longabaugh, Wirtz, Zweben, & Stout, 2001). However, this finding emerged only in the 3-year followup. Specifically, participants in the TSF condition reported 83% days of abstinence, while MET participants reported 66% days of abstinence. These were the largest differences to emerge from Project MATCH. Importantly, this difference was described as TSF participants maintaining change, presumably through participation in 12-step meetings (Mattson, 1996). These findings may be important keys for treating substance-abusing offenders with histories of violence linked to anger, those high in the criminogenic deviant criminal associate networks, or those who are released back to neighborhoods with high substance involvement.

In summary, evidence from randomized clinical trials with community samples suggests that treatment approaches which blend 12-step principles are equally effective at reducing substance use when compared to other treatments. This suggests that there are commonalities across treatment approaches (DiClemente, 2003; Moos, 2003). It may also suggest that given the theoretical grounding noted earlier in the chapter, the 12-step approach is unique.

Although these findings remain hypothetical for those involved in the criminal justice system, they can provide a roadmap for discussion, exploration, and possible replication within criminal justice settings. It is important to note again that the 12-step approach literature includes a debate on the centrality of random assignment to determine evidence-based practice. Outside of the context of that debate however, naturalistic, longitudinal, and quasi-experimental and correlational direct 12-step studies have reported robust findings which are discussed in the next section.

## Interventions That Might Work

Compared to the very few random controlled studies, there are numerous correlational, quasi-experimental studies that examine 12-step participation. However, none of these studies examined substance-abusing offenders who were in the criminal justice system. These studies consider global and some specific aspects (i.e., practice frequency, practice duration, and beliefs) of 12-step participation as well as relationship to substance use and other psychosocial variables. Findings, including two meta-analyses, consistently report positive associations between 12-step involvement and abstinence (Dennis & Scott, 2007; Emrick & Tonigan, 2004; Emrick, Tonigan, Montgomery, & Little, 1993; Humphreys & Moos, 1996; Timko, Finney, Moos, & Moos, 1995; Tonigan et al., 1996). Other studies note increases in this association as practices and experiences increase (Kissin, McLeod, & McKay, 2003; Moos & Moos, 2004, 2007). Several studies have reported that there are independent, additive effects from 12-step participation as part of treatment (Fiorentine & Hillhouse, 2000a; Timko et al., 1995) and that weekly aftercare 12-step meeting attendance is associated with abstinence 24 months after completion of outpatient treatment (Fiorentine, 1999). McKay (2009) reviewed selected studies and noted that the lack of 12-step involvement post-treatment was consistently related to poorer treatment outcomes.

Fiorentine and Hillhouse (2000b) examined the impact of beliefs and recovery participation generally, and 12-step ideology specifically. Their findings revealed that acceptance of 12-step ideology generally and specifically with a belief to surrender to a higher power and frequent lifelong meeting attendance were the strongest predictors of attending weekly 12-step meetings. This effect was strong and independent of other mediating variables. Perhaps most important for the process of change was the belief that non-problematic drug use was not possible, which predicted abstinence from drug use among drug users who completed outpatient drug treatment. This effect was observed independent of weekly 12-step meeting attendance.

A Veterans Affairs sponsored "blended study" (Ouimette, Finney, & Moos, 1997), conducted with a large number of participants ($N = 3{,}018$), used salient analytic techniques with numerous covariates, and nearly two-thirds (63%) of the participants had a history of criminal justice system involvement. Using data from 15 inpatient facilities, the study examined the effectiveness of a 12-step (TS) inpatient approach ($n = 897$) that emphasized 12-step meeting attendance in the hospital and in the community as well as attending psychotherapy groups which emphasized practising the 12-steps and reading the 12-step literature. This group was compared to a Cognitive Behavioral (CB) approach ($n = 1{,}148$) that emphasized adaptive ways of coping in high-risk situations and modifying expectations of the effect of substances. A third condition categorized inpatient programs that provided elements of both approaches ($n = 973$).

Outcomes measured 12 months after inpatient treatment produced effects similar to the random assignment studies. Findings revealed that all conditions were equally effective in reducing substance use and psychological symptoms, although when the outcome was abstinence, 12-step patients were more likely to be abstinent then CB patients. However, the effect did not sustain in an analysis which compared only the most stringent TS and CB inpatient programs. The authors attribute this to limited statistical power. They also note that all conditions were equally effective at increasing the proportion of patients who avoided legal problems or incarceration post-discharge. Furthermore, in a subgroup which was court mandated to attend inpatient treatment, there were no differences for program type on any outcome measure. This contrasts with the studies in which coercion was used as a proximal mechanism for direct 12-step participation. Participants who received the most stringent 12-step or CB treatments were also compared on their affiliation with 12-step groups. Humphreys and Moos (2001) reported that findings suggest those treated in 12-step programs had substantially greater involvement in AA several months after treatment.

Another proximal study by Timko, DeBenedetti, and Billow (2006) compared standard and intensive 12-step group referral strategies in an outpatient setting for veterans. The intensive condition included providing lists of meetings where other veterans had benefited, directions to the meetings, and handouts that addressed typical questions and concerns. Although the overall size of the difference between conditions was not large, findings indicated that those in the intensive referral condition had higher rates of participation in meetings 6 months following outpatient treatment as well as better substance use outcomes.

Across these studies findings collectively suggest substance users who have fidelity with a 12-step approach have more favorable drug, alcohol, and lifestyle outcomes. In addition, these findings suggest that clinicians can influence the degree to which substance abusers can be encouraged to participate in 12-step programs. Just as motivation for treatment has emerged as a dynamic factor which is susceptible to influence (Velasquez, Maurer, Crouch, & DiClemente, 2001), clinicians can have a dynamic influence in encouraging 12-step participation (Humphreys et al., 2004; White, 2009). These are important observations for criminal justice practitioners, including clinicians.

## Interventions That Do Not Work

A literature search did not identify any studies reporting that direct or blended 12-step approaches or interventions are ineffective. It needs to be noted again that self-help programs have received limited research attention with criminal justice offenders. Future research which disaggregates self-help program practices, beliefs, and experiences among offenders in the criminal justice system could help to understand what works, what doesn't work, and why.

Community random controlled trials have been conducted which included coerced samples and focused on studying the impact of mandating AA attendance (Brandsma, Maultby, & Welsh, 1980; Ditman, Crawford, Forgy, Moskowitz, & Macandrew, 1967; Walsh et al., 1991). A general limitation of these proximal studies is selection bias before random assignment. In each of these studies one of the interventions was AA. However, this intervention assignment, while randomly assigned, was mediated with a referral mechanism proximal to the 12-step meeting attendance condition.

Ditman et al. (1967) examined the impact of a court order to attend five AA meetings as an intervention in comparison to a professional treatment program or no treatment. The outcome measure in this study was arrest for public drunkenness, and findings yielded no statistically significant differences between the intervention conditions and no intervention. Another study drew from a sample of employees who participated in an employee assistance program (EAP) for a drinking problem that interfered with their work (Walsh et al., 1991). These individuals would be terminated from their employment if their drinking continued. One of the randomly assigned referral possibilities was EAP counseling that encouraged AA attendance daily if possible but no less than three times per week for at least a year. However, participant intervention adherence was not discussed. Another assignment condition was inpatient hospitalization with a 12-step perspective, followed by attendance at AA meetings. A third condition allowed participants to choose an intervention from a menu of no intervention, inpatient followed by AA, or AA participation. For this study, possible job loss and referral may have been the conditions studied, not AA. This observation is mentioned by the authors, "our goal was to compare three distinct referral strategies and not to monitor the specific content of care in great detail." (p. 781). Findings from the study indicate that baseline drinking for those in the compulsory AA condition did improve. However, participants who had the greatest improvement were in the hospitalization condition followed by AA attendance. In summary, it appears that coerced AA attendance does not improve outcomes. That is, mandating attendance is not additive. This should not be surprising since coerced involvement can conflict directly with practices, beliefs, and experiences described in 12-step literature (Miller & Kurtz, 1994).

From a legal perspective, a growing body of case law, including a Supreme Court decision, has influenced self-help interventions. The rulings are that self-help 12-step programs are spiritual programs, and as such, are not the purview of government to deploy or mandate (see Moreland, 2004, 2007 for a review). More specifically, the dilemma in these cases is that offenders were not given an option to choose a self-help program other then a 12-step program.

## Treatment Recommendations

Three overarching themes emerge. First, survey research in the criminal justice setting makes it clear that criminal justice practitioners, including clinicians, probation and parole officers, and case managers, will encounter offenders with prior and current self-help experiences. Next, 12-step studies suggest the effectiveness of the 12-step approach. Third, it is likely that, much like their community colleagues, criminal justice practitioners can influence the degree to which offenders attempt a 12-step approach. From the nexus of these themes, the following recommendations are organized by training, accommodating meetings, and encouraging the 12-step approach.

*Recommendation one: Given the number of opportunities in the criminal justice system and the evidence that suggests clinicians can facilitate their clients' transition into 12-step programs, criminal justice practitioners should be helped to develop an understanding of 12-step practices, beliefs, and experiences in criminal justice organizations.*

- Training and education should include an orientation to what 12-step approaches are, and equally important, what they are not.
- Training manuals from many of the aforementioned studies remain available for training and this option should be explored. Manuals help to clarify treatment models and provide explicit and practical instructions on how to implement specific types of interventions. They provide a safe and effective place to begin understanding and practising the work. In addition, they establish clear treatment goals and clinical care standards, foster scientific replication of clinical trials to other settings, and facilitate transferring research to practice.

*Recommendation two: Participation in 12-step approaches directly is associated with positive outcomes in community samples, many of which included subjects with criminal justice involvement. Therefore, 12-step approaches generally and 12-step meetings specifically should be accommodated within the criminal justice setting itself.*

- There is evidence suggesting that the frequency of 12-step attendance is related to reductions in drug and alcohol use. Specifically, weekly attendance has been associated with significant changes compared to less than weekly attendance. Criminal justice settings might consider how many meetings it needs to "host" within institutional settings so that multiple offenders with multiple daily schedules could attend one meeting at least weekly.
- Accommodating activities can include criminal justice professionals helping to find a suitable location within the institution or serving as a liaison to facilitate bringing community-based 12-step members to sponsor a group or speaker at a meeting within the correctional facility. Haddock (1990) notes that increased use and acceptance of 12-step literature, brochures, and audiocassette tapes are also ways of introducing, implementing, enhancing, and expanding 12-step programs in criminal justice settings.

*Recommendation three: Helping offenders find prosocial peer communities such as a 12-step recovering community, a religious community, or the neighborhood community can provide the sustained context within which successful offender-based recovery careers can emerge. Because the literature suggests that community treatment which adopts 12-step principles is as effective as cognitive-behavior techniques, criminal justice practitioners should actively encourage offenders to engage in the 12-step approach both within the criminal justice setting and after release.*

- Practitioners should become proficient in encouraging and recommending 12-step programs as well as helping to locate meetings prior to release (Read, 1990). Miller (2004) suggests that three essential steps to encouraging participation include providing a rationale, exploring attitudes about 12-step approaches, and giving information about available groups.
- Studies support the recommendation to encourage at least weekly attendance during aftercare or reentry post-incarceration and supervision. However, those who encourage attendance should understand the distinction and difference between open and closed AA, NA, and CA meetings.
- Since there is evidence which suggests there are additive effects for 12-step participation and treatment, both treatment and 12-step participation should be pursued simultaneously. In addition, it appears that mapping 12-step practices, beliefs, and experiences with treatment is effective. Clinicians should also be aware that the more congruent the beliefs of treatment settings are with 12-step beliefs, the more likely it is that offenders will engage in this approach to recovery.
- Court rulings have determined that a menu of service beyond a 12-step meeting must be offered. Therefore, probation authorities should search and be prepared to make contact with meetings such as Rational Recovery and other fellowships. Clinicians and administrators should remain cognizant of these court rulings and develop alternatives if self-help attendance is made a condition of supervision.

### Conclusion

Anecdotally, practice-based evidence favors self-help. A large number of offenders in the criminal justice system are exposed to and participate in self-help programs. The frequency with which offenders are offered the opportunity to participate in self-help during and after incarceration continues to ascend. The ease with which 12-step programs can be found at community reentry is remarkable. This availability speaks to the observation that self-help programs seem impervious to fluctuations in the organizational, financial, and human resource structures of public safety and health systems. As an interesting example of such permanence, the Mill Creek AA Group at the Oregon State Penitentiary has been available to offenders for over 65 years (General Service Office of Alcoholics Anonymous, 2009). Conducted in a maximum-security setting, such stability might be considered remarkable.

Finally, further research is needed to continue developing evidence-based practices. This may allow criminal justice researchers, administrators, managers, and clinicians help offenders lead more integrated lives in the community. As the public health approach to substance use disorders continues to emphasize and develop models of sustained recovery management (DeLeon, 2007; Dennis & Scott, 2007; McKay, 2009; White, 2009) there is no better time to involve those models and approaches within public safety systems.

## References


Alcoholics Anonymous. (1953). *Twelve steps and twelve traditions*. New York: Alcoholics Anonymous World Services.

Alcoholics Anonymous. (1976). *The story of how thousands of men and women have recovered from Alcoholism*. New York: Alcoholics Anonymous World Services.

Alcoholics Anonymous. (1984). *Pass it on: The story of Bill Wilson and how the AA message reached the world*. New York: Alcoholics Anonymous World Services.

Alcoholics Anonymous. (2009). *Estimates of AA groups and members* [on-line]. Available at http://www.aa.org/lang/en/subpage.cfm?page=74, Downloaded August 25, 2009.

Beckman, L. J. (1990). An attributional analysis of Alcoholics Anonymous. *Journal of Studies on Alcohol, 41*, 714–726.

Bergman, B., Goddard, H. N., Lachiewicz, S. L., Bruder, L., Dougherty, M. C., Mantell, E. M., et al. (2009, August). *Recovery practices among long-term*

*members of Narcotics Anonymous*. Poster presented at the annual convention of the American Psychological Association, Toronto, ON.
Bonczar, T. P. (2008). *Characteristics of state parole supervising agencies, 2006*. Washington, DC: Department of Justice, Bureau of Justice Statistics.
Brandsma, J. M., Maultby, M. C., & Welsh, R. J. (1980). *Outpatient treatment of alcoholism: A review and comparative study*. Baltimore: University Park Press.
Bristow-Braitman, A. (1995). Addiction recovery: 12-step programs and cognitive behavioral psychology. *Journal of Counseling and Development, 73*, 414–418.
Burt, D. W. (1975). A behaviorist looks at AA. *Addictions, 22*, 56–59.
Cocaine Anonymous. (2008, January). *Public information fact file*. Retrieved April 1, 2010, from http://www.ca.org/pdf/conference/PI/WSCPI_factfile2007.pdf
Codd, H. (2002). "The ties that bind": Feminist perspectives on self-help groups for prisoners' partners. *The Howard Journal, 41(4)*, 334–347.
DeLeon, G. (Ed.). (1997). *Community as method: Therapeutic communities for special populations and special settings*. Westport, CT: Praeger Publishers.
DeLeon, G. (2000). *The therapeutic community*. New York: Springer.
DeLeon, G. (2004). Commentary on self-help organizations for alcohol and drug problems: Toward evidence-base practice and policy. *Journal of Substance Abuse Treatment, 26*(3), 163–165.
DeLeon, G. (2007). Therapeutic community treatment in correctional settings: Toward a recovery-oriented integrated system (ROIS). *Offender Substance Abuse Report, 7*(6), 81–88, 95.
Dennis, M. L., & Scott, C. K. (2007). Managing addiction as a chronic condition. *Addiction Science and Clinical Practice, 4*(1), 45–55.
DiClemente, C. (2003). *Addiction and change*. New York: Guilford Press.
DiClemente, C. (2007). Treatment matching in substance abuse. In G. P. Koocher, J. C. Norcross, & S. S. Hill (Eds.), *Psychologist's desk reference* (2nd ed., pp. 263–267). New York: Oxford University Press.
Ditman, K. S., Crawford, G. G., Forgy, E. W., Moskowitz, H., & Macandrew, C. (1967). A controlled experiment on the use of court probation for drunk arrests. *American Journal of Psychiatry, 124*(2), 64–67.
Emrick, C. D., & Tonigan, J. S. (2004). Alcoholics Anonymous and other 12-step groups. In M. Galanter & H. D. Kleber (Eds.), *Textbook of substance abuse treatment* (pp. 433–444). Washington, DC: American Psychiatric Association.
Emrick, C. D., Tonigan, J. S., Montgomery, H. A., & Little, L. (1993). Alcoholics Anonymous: What is currently known? In B. S. McCrady & W. R. Miller (Eds.), *Research on Alcoholics Anonymous: Opportunities and alternatives* (pp. 41–76). Piscataway, NJ: Rutgers Center for Alcohol Studies.
Fiorentine, R. (1999). After drug treatment: Are 12-step programs effective in maintaining abstinence? *American Journal of Drug and Alcohol Abuse, 25*, 93–116.
Fiorentine, R., & Hillhouse, M. P. (2000a). Drug treatment and 12-step program participation: The additive effects of integrated recovery activities. *Journal of Substance Abuse Treatment, 18*, 65–74.
Fiorentine, R., & Hillhouse, M. P. (2000b). Exploring the additive effects of drug misuse treatment and twelve-step involvement: Does twelve step ideology matter? *Substance Use and Misuse, 35*, 367–397.
General Service Office of Alcoholics Anonymous. (2009). Penitentiary AA meeting celebrates 65 years. *Box 459, 55(4)*, 10.
Haddock, B. D. (1990). Substance abuse counseling in community corrections: A primer. *Journal of Addictions and Offender Counseling, 11*, 2–12.
Hamm, M. S. (1988). Current perspectives on the prisoner self-help movement. *Federal Probation, 52*(2), 49–56.
Hughes, P. H., Floyd, C. M., Norris, G., & Silva, G. E. (1970). Organizing the therapeutic potential of an addict prisoner community. *The International Journal of the Addictions, 5*, 205–223.
Humphreys, K. (2003). *Circles of recovery: Self-help organizations for addiction*. Cambridge, UK: Cambridge University Press.
Humphreys, K., & Moos, R. H. (1996). Reduced substance-abuse related health care costs among voluntary participants in Alcoholics Anonymous. *Psychiatric Services, 47*, 709–713.
Humphreys, K., & Moos, R. H. (2001). Can encouraging substance abuse patients to participate in self-help groups reduce demand for health care? A quasi-experimental study. *Alcoholism: Clinical and Experimental Research, 25*, 711–716.
Humphreys, K., & Rappaport, J. (1994). Researching self-help/mututal help aid groups and organizations: Many roads, one journey. *Applied and Preventive Psychology, 3*, 217–231.
Humphreys, K., Wing, S., McCarty, D., Chappel, J., Gallant, L., Haberle, B., et al. (2004). Self-help organizations for alcohol and drug problems: Toward evidence-based practice and policy. *Journal of Substance Abuse Treatment, 26*, 151–158.
Inciardi, J. A., Martin, S. S., & Butzin, C. A. (2004). Five-year outcomes of therapeutic community treatment of drug-involved offenders after release from prison. *Crime and Delinquency, 50*, 88–107.
James, W. (1902). *The variety of religious experience*. New York: Modern Library.
Kadden, R. P., Carrol, K., Donovan, D., Cooney, N., Monti, P., Abrahams, D., et al. (1992). *Cognitive-behavioral coping skills therapy manual: A clinical research guide for therapists treating individuals with alcohol abuse and dependence* (Project MATCH Monograph Series, Vol. 3). Rockville, MD: National Institute on Alcohol Abuse and Alcoholism, National Institute of Health.

Karberg, J. C., & James, D. J. (2005). *Substance dependence, abuse, and treatment of jail inmates, 2002*. Washington, DC: Bureau of Justice Statistics, Department of Justice.

Kessler, R. C., Frank, R. G., Edmund, S. J., Katz, E., Lin, E., & Leaf, P. (1997). Differences in the use of psychiatric outpatient services between the United States and Ontario. *New England Journal of Medicine, 336*(8), 551–557.

Khan, H. I. (1997). *The inner life*. Boston: Shambhala.

Kissin, W., McLeod, C., & McKay, J. R. (2003). The longitudinal relationship between self-help attendance and course of recovery. *Evaluation and Program Planning, 26*, 311–324.

Kurtz, E. (1991). *Not God: A history of Alcoholics Anonymous*. Center City, MN: Hazelden Foundation.

Leukfeld, C. G., Farabee, D., & Tims, F. (2002). Clinical and policy opportunities. In C. G. Leukefeld, F. Tims, & D. Farabee (Eds.), *Treatment of drug offenders: Policies and issues* (pp. 3–8). New York: Springer.

Lewis, S. L. (1990). *Spiritual dance and walk*. Fairfax, CA: Peace Works Center for the Dances of Universal Peace.

Lightfoot, L. O. (1999). Treating substance abuse and dependence in offenders: A review of methods and outcomes. In E. Latessa (Ed.), *Strategic solutions: The international community corrections association examines substance abuse* (pp. 43–80). Lanham, MD: American Correctional Association.

Longabaugh, R., Wirtz, P. W., Zweben, A., & Stout, R. (2001). Network support for drinking. In R. Longabaugh & P. Wirtz (Eds.), *Project MATCH hypothesis: Results and causal chain analysis* (Project MATCH Monograph Series, Vol. 8) (pp. 260–275). Rockville, MD: National Institute on Alcohol Abuse and Alcoholism, National Institute of Health.

Magura, S. (2007). The relationship between substance user treatment and 12-step fellowships: Current knowledge and research questions. *Substance Use & Misuse, 42*, 343–360.

Martin, S. S., Inciardi, J. A., & O'Connell, D. J. (2003). Treatment research in Oz-Is randomization the ideal or just somewhere over the rainbow? *Federal Probation, 67*(2), 53–61.

Mattson, M. E. (1996). Finding the right approach. In W. R. Miller & N. Heather (Eds.), *Treating addictive behaviors* (2nd ed., pp. 163–172). New York: Plenum Press.

Maunder, L., Cameron, L., Moss, M., Muir, D., Evans, N., Paxton, R., et al. (2009). Effectiveness of self-help materials for anxiety adapted for use in prison – A pilot study. *Journal of Mental Health, 18*, 262–271.

McAnany, P. D., & Tromanhauser, E. (1977, January). Organizing the convicted: Self-help for prisoners and ex-prisoners. *Crime and Delinquency, 40*, 68–74.

McCrady, B. S. (1994). Alcoholics Anonymous and behavior therapy: Can habits be treated as diseases? Can diseases be treated as habits? *Journal of Consulting and Clinical Psychology, 62*, 1159–1166.

McKay, J. R. (2009). *Treating substance use disorders with adaptive continuing care*. Washington, DC: American Psychological Association.

McKenzie, D. L. (2006). *What works in corrections*. New York: Cambridge University Press.

McLellan, A. T., Carise, D., & Kleber, H. D. (2003). Can the national addiction treatment infrastructure support the public's demand for quality care? *Journal of Substance Abuse Treatment, 25*, 117–121.

Miller, W. R. (Ed.). (2004). *Combined behavioral intervention manual: A clinical research guide for therapists treating people with alcohol abuse and dependence* (DHHS Publication No (NIH) 04-5288) (COMBINE Monograph Series, Vol. 1). Bethesda, MD: National Institute of Alcohol Abuse and Alcoholism.

Miller, W. R., Andrews, N. R., Wilbourne, P., & Bennett, M. E. (1998). A wealth of alternatives: Effective treatments for alcohol problems. In W. R. Miller & N. Heather (Eds.), *Treating addictive behaviors* (2nd ed., pp. 203–216). New York: Plenum Press.

Miller, W. R., & Kurtz, E. (1994). Models of alcoholism used in treatment: Contrasting AA and other perspectives with which it is often confused. *Journal of Studies on Alcohol, 55*, 159–166.

Miller, W. R., & Thoresen, C. E. (1999). Spirituality and health. In W. R. Miller (Ed.), *Integrating spirituality into treatment* (pp. 3–18). Washington, DC: American Psychological Association.

Miller, W. R., Zweben, A., DiClemente, C., & Rychtarik, R. (1992). *Motivational enhancement therapy manual: A clinical research guide for therapists treating individuals with alcohol abuse and dependence* (Project MATCH Monograph Series, Vol. 2). Rockville, MD: National Institute on Alcohol Abuse and Alcoholism, National Institute of Health.

Monahan, S. M. (2001). *Seeds of grace: A nun's reflections on the spirituality of Alcoholics Anonymous*. New York: Riverhead Books.

Moos, R. H. (2003). Addictive disorders in context: Principles and puzzles of effective treatment and recovery. *Psychology of Addictive Behaviors, 17*, 3–12.

Moos, R. H., & Moos, B. S. (2004). Long-term influence of duration and frequency of participation in Alcoholics Anonymous on individuals with alcohol use disorders. *Journal of Consulting and Clinical Psychology, 72*, 81–90.

Moos, R. H., & Moos, B. S. (2007). Treated and untreated alcohol use disorders: Course and predictors of remission and relapse. *Evaluation Review: A Journal of Applied Social Research, 31*, 564–584.

Moreland, M. R. (2004). Legal issues. In K. Knight & D. Farabee (Eds.), *Treating addicted offenders: A continuum of effective practices* (pp. 1–31, appendix 1). Kingston, NJ: Civic Research Institute, Inc.

Moreland, M. R. (2007). Legal issues. In K. Knight & D. Farabee (Eds.), *Treating addicted offenders: A continuum of effective practices, Volume II* (pp. 1–42, appendix 1). Kingston, NJ: Civic Research Institute, Inc.

Morgenstern, J., Kahler, C. W., Frey, R. M., & Labouvie, E. (1996). Modeling therapeutic response to 12-step treatment: Optimal responders, nonresponders, and partial responders. *Journal of Substance Abuse, 8*, 45–59.

Mumola, C. J. (1999). *Substance abuse and treatment, state and federal prisoners, 1997*. Washington, DC: Bureau of Justice Statistics, Department of Justice.

Mumola, C. J., & Karberg, J. (2006). *Drug use and dependence, state and federal prisoners, 2004*. Washington, DC: Bureau of Justice Statistics, Department of Justice.

Nowinski, J., Baker, S., & Carroll, K. (1999). *Twelve step facilitation therapy manual: A clinical research guide for therapists treating individuals with alcohol abuse and dependence* (Project MATCH Monograph Series, Vol. 1). Rockville, MD: National Institute on Alcohol Abuse and Alcoholism, National Institute of Health.

Ouimette, P. C., Finney, J. W., & Moos, R. H. (1997). Twelve-step and cognitive behavioral treatment for substance abuse: A comparison of treatment effectiveness. *Journal of Consulting and Clinical Psychology, 65*, 230–240.

Project MATCH Research Group. (1997). Matching alcoholism treatments to client heterogeneity: Project MATHC posttreatment drinking outcomes. *Journal of Studies on Alcohol, 58*, 7–29.

Rapkin, R. M. (1971, March–April). The NARA unit at Danbury: A short history of a unique treatment program for heroin addicts. *American Journal of Correction*, 24–26.

Read, E. M. (1990). Twelve steps to sobriety: Probation officers "working the steps". *Federal Probation, 54*(4), 34–43.

Skinner, B. F. (1987). A humanist alternative to AA's twelve steps. *The Humanist, 47*, 5.

Steigerwald, F., & Stone, D. (1997). Cognitive restructuring and the 12-step program of Alcoholics Anonymous. *Journal of Substance Abuse Treatment, 16*, 321–327.

Timko, C., DeBenedetti, A., & Billow, R. (2006). Intensive referral to 12-step self-help groups and 6-month substance use disorder outcomes. *Addiction, 101*, 678–688.

Timko, C., Finney, J. W., Moos, R. H., & Moos, B. S. (1995). Short-term treatment careers and outcomes of previously untreated alcoholics. *Journal of Studies on Alcohol, 56*, 597–610.

Tonigan, J. S., Connors, G. J., & Miller, W. R. (1996). Alcoholics Anonymous Involvement (AAI) scale: Reliability and norms. *Psychology of Addictive Behaviors, 10*, 75–80.

Tonigan, J. S., Toscova, R. T., & Connors, G. J. (1999). Spirituality and the 12-step programs: A guide for clinicians. In W. R. Miller (Ed.), *Integrating spirituality into treatment* (pp. 111–131). Washington, DC: American Psychological Association.

Tonigan, J. S., Toscova, R. T., & Miller, W. R. (1996). Meta analysis of the Alcoholics Anonymous Literature: Sample and study characteristics moderate findings. *Journal of Studies on Alcohol, 57*, 65–72.

Velasquez, M. M., Maurer, G. G., Crouch, C. M., & DiClemente, C. C. (2001). *Group treatment for substance abuse*. New York: Guilford Press.

Vogel, V. H. (1948, June). Treatment of the narcotic addict by the U. S. Public Health Service. *Federal Probation, 12*(2), 45–50.

Waldron, H. B., Miller, W. R., & Tonigan, J. S. (2001). Client anger as a predictor of differential response to treatment. In R. Longabaugh & P. Wirtz (Eds.), *Project MATCH hypothesis: Results and causal chain analysis* (Project MATCH Monograph Series, Vol. 8) (pp. 134–148). Rockville, MD: National Institute on Alcohol Abuse and Alcoholism, National Institute of Health.

Walsh, D. C., Hingson, R. W., Merrigan, D. M., Levenson, S. M., Cupples, L. A., Heeren, T., et al. (1991). A randomized trial of treatment options for alcohol-abusing workers. *The New England Journal of Medicine, 325*, 775–782.

Walters, G. D. (1999). *The addictions concept*. Needham Heights, MA: Allyn & Bacon.

Wells, E. A., Peterson, P. L., Gainey, R. R., Hawkins, J. D., & Catalano, R. F. (1994). Outpatient treatment for cocaine abuse: A controlled comparison of relapse prevention and twelve-step approaches. *American Journal of Drug and Alcohol Abuse, 20*, 1–17.

White, W. L. (1998). *Slaying the dragon*. Bloomington, IL: Chestnut Health Systems.

White, W. L. (2009). *Peer-based addiction recovery support: History, theory, practice and scientific evaluation*. Chicago: Great Lakes Addiction Technology Center and Philadelphia Department of Behavioral Health and Mental Retardation Services.

# Pharmacotherapy

# 15

Robert P. Schwartz, Shannon Gwin Mitchell, Michael S. Gordon, and Timothy W. Kinlock

**Abstract**

The underutilization of pharmacotherapy for alcohol and drug withdrawal and dependence in the US criminal justice system undermines both public safety and public health. This chapter provides the reader with an overview of the use of medications in the treatment of opioid and alcohol dependence. Clinical research findings are first presented regarding the use of the opioid agonists methadone and buprenorphine and the opioid antagonist naltrexone. The use of these medications in community corrections as well as in jails and prisons is highlighted. Subsequent sections of the chapter include an overview of the pharmacology of the medications approved for the treatment of alcohol withdrawal and dependence as well as their use in the criminal justice system. The views of correction staff and patients under supervision are summarized and barriers to implementation of these effective treatments are discussed.

**Keywords**

Pharmacotherapy in criminal justice • Medications for alcohol dependence • Medications for drug dependence

## Introduction

The underutilization of pharmacotherapy for alcohol and drug dependence in the US criminal justice system is a lost opportunity for the staggering number of individuals with these disorders and for public safety and public health (Chandler, Fletcher, & Volkow, 2009). This chapter provides an overview of pharmacotherapy for opioid and alcohol dependence, summarizes the clinical research findings related to the treatment of opioid and alcohol dependence in the criminal justice system, and, closes with specific recommendations. Since there are no medications approved for the treatment of cocaine and methamphetamine dependence, clinical research in this area is not addressed.

There are two types of approved medications for the treatment of opioid dependence: opioid

R.P. Schwartz (✉)
Friends Research Institute, Baltimore, MD 21201, USA
e-mail: rschwartz@friendsresearch.org

C. Leukefeld et al. (eds.), *Handbook of Evidence-Based Substance Abuse Treatment in Criminal Justice Settings*, Issues in Children's and Families' Lives 11,
DOI 10.1007/978-1-4419-9470-7_15, © Springer Science+Business Media, LLC 2011

agonists and opioid antagonists. The former activates the opioid receptor and the latter occupies, but does not activate, it. The widely used opioid agonists, methadone and buprenorphine, are approved by the Food and Drug Administration (FDA) for the treatment of opioid dependence and are effective in treating opioid withdrawal, interrupting compulsive opioid use, and preventing relapse. Naltrexone, an opioid antagonist, is used for relapse prevention.

## Opioid Agonist Therapy

Although methadone, like heroin, is an opioid agonist, methadone has several pharmacological properties that distinguish it from heroin and make it an effective medication for treating opioid dependence: it can be taken by mouth, does not provide a euphoric "rush," and can be taken once daily. At the proper individualized methadone dose, patients do not experience opioid withdrawal or intoxication and can function normally in society. Importantly, at an adequate dose, methadone blocks the euphoric effects of heroin (Dole, Nyswander, & Kreek, 1966).

Buprenorphine is a partial opioid agonist with complex pharmacological properties (O'Brien, 2006). Although at lower doses buprenorphine is more potent than morphine, its opioid agonist effects plateau at higher doses. Thus, it is more difficult, although not impossible, to overdose on buprenorphine alone than on "full" agonists such as methadone or heroin (Johnson, Strain, & Amass, 2003). This superior safety profile contributed to the decision in the United States to permit buprenorphine to be prescribed by physicians through pharmacies for the treatment of opioid dependence, unlike methadone, which must be provided through specially licensed opioid treatment programs (Jaffe & O'Keeffe, 2003).

Buprenorphine is available for the treatment of opioid dependence in two sublingual (under the tongue) formulations in the United States. The combination product (Suboxone) combines buprenorphine and a low dose of the opioid antagonist naloxone (Narcan). Naloxone is poorly absorbed under the tongue and has little effect when Suboxone is taken properly. However, naloxone may serve to deter misuse by injection because its injection precipitates opioid withdrawal. For this reason, Suboxone is most widely recommended for use in community settings in the United States (Center for Substance Abuse Treatment, 2004). The mono-product (Subutex) consists of buprenorphine alone and is recommended for use only in the early induction phase for patients who may be sensitive to the presence of naloxone, such as those being switched from methadone to buprenorphine or who are allergic to naloxone. Internationally, the mono-product is widely used and in France it has been effective in reducing heroin use and drug-related overdose deaths (Fatseas & Auriacombe, 2007), although it has created its own problems of abuse in some countries (Jenkinson, Clark, Fry, & Dobbin, 2005).

## Research

### Withdrawal Treatment

Although opioid withdrawal is not life threatening in uncomplicated cases, untreated opioid withdrawal can contribute to morbidity and mortality in individuals with medical conditions that can be exacerbated by dehydration and hypertension, which may accompany withdrawal. Thus, deaths associated with opioid withdrawal have been reported in correctional settings and have sparked a number of lawsuits (Ladson, 2007).

In the United States, outpatient methadone detoxification for a period longer than 3 days must be provided through specially licensed opioid treatment programs (OTPs). In contrast, buprenorphine can be prescribed by specially licensed physicians outside of OTPs. In settings in which buprenorphine or methadone are not available, the antihypertensive medication, clonidine, a nonopioid, can be used in combination with over-the-counter medications to treat withdrawal. While clonidine has been shown to relieve some opioid withdrawal symptoms (Stine, Meandzija, & Kosten, 1998), it is not approved for opioid withdrawal and can cause hypotension.

Opioid detoxification alone is not considered "treatment" because by itself it is usually not sufficient to achieve sustained abstinence. It may serve as a precursor to residential treatment, naltrexone therapy, outpatient counseling without pharmacotherapy, and/or Narcotics Anonymous participation. Detoxification outcomes (whether provided in a freestanding residential program or outpatient setting) are generally poor (O'Brien, 1997). Importantly, it should be noted that opioid-dependent individuals who relapse after detoxification are subject to higher risk of overdose death because they are no longer tolerant to opioids. Patients considering detoxification should be informed that overdose is a risk of completing detoxification and offered opioid agonist maintenance as an alternative (Strang et al., 2003).

## Maintenance Treatment

Opioid maintenance therapy with methadone or buprenorphine is the most widely used treatment for opioid dependence throughout the world and is among the most researched of medical treatments for any disorder. There is unequivocal evidence from randomized controlled trials conducted by different research groups across several continents to support the efficacy of opioid maintenance treatments in increasing treatment retention and reducing heroin use (Mattick, Breen, Kimber, & Davoli, 2003). Based on a recent meta-analysis of 24 randomized clinical trials with 4,497 participants, it appears that methadone may have some advantage over buprenorphine for treatment retention and reduced heroin use (Mattick, Kimber, Breen, & Davoli, 2008).

Patients in maintenance therapy have significantly lower mortality rates as compared to out-of-treatment opioid-dependent individuals (Hulse, English, Milne, & Holman, 1999) and leaving opioid agonist treatment is associated with increased mortality (Zanis & Woody, 1998). Maintenance treatment is associated with reduced HIV-risk behavior (Ball & Ross, 1991) and lower rates of HIV sero-conversion (Metzger et al., 1993). Methadone maintenance has also been shown to reduce criminal behavior, as assessed by both patient self-reports and official arrest records (Ball & Ross, 1991; Cushman, 1972). A recent study of patients receiving methadone without counseling (termed "interim methadone"), as compared to patients on a waiting list, found that the former group had a significantly lower mean number of arrests at 6 months after starting methadone as compared to the waiting list group (Schwartz et al., 2009).

Given the strength of the evidence in favor of opioid agonist maintenance treatments, it is not surprising that these treatments are supported by the US Office of National Drug Control Policy (ONDCP, 2001), the Institute of Medicine (Institute of Medicine, 2006), the National Institutes of Health (NIH Consensus Conference, 1998), and the World Health Organization (WHO, 2005).

The choice of whether to use methadone or buprenorphine will depend on patient preference, local regulatory issues, cost, and funding structure. In the United States, except for select, highly stable, longer-term patients (Schwartz, Brooner, Montoya, Currens, & Hayes, 1999), methadone treatment must be provided through specially licensed opioid treatment programs (OTPs) which require initial daily attendance for medication administration, counseling attendance, urine testing, and other rules associated with treatment as provided under the US regulatory structure. Some patients may find adherence to this regimen burdensome and may drop out, while others may be discharged against their will for nonadherence to rules (Reisinger et al., 2009).

In contrast, qualified physicians can prescribe buprenorphine for the treatment of opioid dependence outside of OTPs and this medication can be retrieved from pharmacies by patients. Physicians wishing to prescribe buprenorphine in the United States for treatment must obtain a waiver from the Controlled Substance Act by completing an 8-hour continuing education training course (http://buprenorphine.samhsa.gov). There are expert guidelines regarding buprenorphine treatment in the community (CSAT, 2004) which provide more detail.

It is important to consider the patient's view, including attitudes and beliefs regarding treatment and medications, in determining treatment approach. Qualitative studies of drug abuse treatment provide insight into patient perspectives on treatment and can help providers and policy makers understand barriers and facilitators to treatment entry, adherence, and retention (Bourgois, 2000; Reisinger et al., 2009).

Attitudes regarding medications are present within drug-using communities and can influence an individual's willingness to enroll in treatment (Koester, Anderson, & Hoffer, 1999). For example, community folklore and negative beliefs regarding methadone are commonly reported by out-of-treatment heroin users throughout the world (Fischer, Chin, Kuo, Kirst, & Vlahov, 2002; Peterson et al., 2010). Even many individuals receiving methadone treatment express negative attitudes and beliefs concerning the physical and social effects of the methadone, such as the belief that it "rots your bones" (Zweben & Sorensen, 1988). There is some evidence that buprenorphine may be more favorably viewed than methadone by out-of-treatment opioid users in the United States (Schwartz et al., 2008).

Some patients drop-out in the first year of OTP enrollment because they enter with a preconceived idea of how long they are willing to remain in treatment (Reisinger et al., 2009). The reasons for setting these deadlines include fearing physical dependence on methadone and believing that they are not "abstinent" when taking methadone. Other patients may use treatment to take "time out" or to decrease (but not cease) their drug use, to try abstinence, or to reduce HIV risk (Koester, Anderson, & Hoffer, 1999). This self-imposed timeline may be countertherapeutic for some.

### Opioid Antagonist Treatment

Naltrexone is an opioid antagonist that is very effective when taken orally and has a strong attraction for the $\mu$-opioid receptor but has no opioid agonist effects of its own. Its ability to block opioids for about 24 hours in a 50-mg oral dose and 48 hours in 100-mg dose (Gonzalez & Brogden, 1988; O'Brien, Greenstein, Mintz, & Woody, 1975) permits its use as an opioid-dependence treatment when administered daily or every other day.

Naltrexone's effectiveness is hampered by frequent patient noncompliance which may, in part, be due to the lack of any opioid agonist effect to relieve craving during the post-detoxification period (O'Brien & Cornish, 2006). Literature reviews indicate that although oral naltrexone may have superior outcomes than placebo in terms of reducing opioid use, the results are modest (Johannson, Berglund, & Lindgren, 2006). Naltrexone's effectiveness can be increased when combined with special approaches to improve medication adherence. For example, health professionals with opioid addictions who are at risk of losing their licenses upon relapse may do well with monitored naltrexone dosing as part of a treatment and monitoring plan (Ling & Wesson, 1984). Behavioral incentives (Carroll, Sinha, Nich, Babuscio, & Rounsaville, 2002) may also potentially improve adherence and outcomes with oral naltrexone. In Russia, where opioid agonist medications are not approved for addiction therapy and where many heroin-addicted individuals are young adults living with their parents, the conditions seem favorable for family-monitored naltrexone administration. For example, one randomized trial in Russia reported that 44% of naltrexone patients as compared to 10% of placebo patients had not relapsed after 6 months (Krupitsky et al., 2004).

There is a now depot formulation of naltrexone (Vivitrol) delivered through intramuscular injection and approved by the FDA for the prevention of relapse to opioid dependence following detoxification. Depot naltrexone formulation provides opioid blockade for approximately 30 days (Comer et al., 2006). In several countries, a long-acting naltrexone implant which provides opioid blockade for several months has been used (Ngo, Tait, & Hulse, 2008).

To date, the most rigorous study in the United States of depot naltrexone for opioid dependence was a double-blind placebo-controlled study in which 60 heroin-dependent adults at two sites were randomly assigned to placebo injection or one of two doses of depot naltrexone (Comer et al., 2006). The first dose was provided during inpatient detoxification to ensure opioid blockade post-release. Weekly individual counseling was offered to all participants and a second dose was administered to the assigned group at 30 days post-discharge. The 2-month retention rates were dose-related as follows: 39% in placebo group, 60% in the low-dose group, and 68% in the high-dose group. When missing urine tests were considered positive, opioid-positive test results were significantly lower in the medication groups as compared to placebo. In a multi-site, double-blind placebo controlled trial conducted in Russia with 250 opioid dependent adults, Krupitsky and colleagues (2011) found that the group randomly assigned to long-acting injectable naltrexone as compared to placebo was more likely to be retained in treatment and to be opioid abstinent over the 24 weeks of the study.

## Pharmacotherapy in the Criminal Justice System

In the United States, opioid agonist therapy is seldom used in jails and prisons (Chandler, Fletcher, & Volkow, 2009) and opioid-dependent parolees, probationers, and drug court participants often do not have access to opioid agonist treatment (Hubbard, Collins, Rachal, & Cavanaugh, 1988). Indeed, the US Department of Justice's "Guide to Judiciary Policies and Procedures – Probation Manual" stated that "abstinence approaches are favored over those that use medication such as methadone as a treatment tool. Substituting one addicting drug for another is not a satisfactory approach to treating addiction" (Parrino, 2002).

Drawing on the voluminous data on the efficacy of community opioid agonist treatment, as well as the growing literature on agonist treatment in jails and prisons, the World Health Organization recommended the expansion of opioid agonist maintenance therapy in jails and prisons to (1) reduce drug-seeking behavior; (2) retain HIV-positive opioid-dependent individuals in Anti-Retroviral Therapy; (3) improve prison safety; (4) reduce mortality; and (5) increase entry into treatment post-release (Jürgens, 2007). The opioid antagonist naltrexone also has the potential to play a role in relapse prevention for prerelease inmates and individuals under community supervision (O'Brien & Cornish, 2006), although less is known about its effectiveness in these populations compared to opioid agonist treatment.

### Outpatient Pharmacotherapy for Patients on Community Supervision

In the early 1970s, in response to long waiting lists in community-based methadone programs, the New York City Office of Probation operated five methadone programs which treated nearly 1,000 probationers using probation officers as counselors and medical staff from area medical institutions (Joseph, 1988). The program was viewed as a success but eventually phased out as community treatment became more available. Since the 1970s, relatively few probationers and parolees have been treated in the United States with methadone maintenance treatment (Bureau of Justice Statistics, 2007; Leukefeld & Tims, 1988). Drug Courts, in particular, have been resistant to permitting participants to enroll in or to continue with methadone treatment – in some instances requiring patients to discontinue methadone treatment (Jaeger, 2003).

Although opioid agonist treatment is not widely available to patients under community supervision, there is evidence that when it is offered, it attracts patients with characteristics similar to those who enter treatment voluntarily on demographics, early risk factors, and drug use, criminal involvement, and employment histories (Anglin, Brecht, & Maddahian, 1989). Furthermore, regardless of their initial motivation for entering treatment, both coerced and voluntary patients show considerable reductions in their opioid use and criminal behavior during treatment (Desmond & Maddux, 1996). Nevertheless, probationers on methadone treatment may be more likely to be incarcerated than those patients not on supervision because of technical violations (Hiller, Knight, & Simpson, 1999).

There was also interest in the use of opioid antagonist treatment for probationers and parolees in the early 1970s, and placebo-controlled trials were conducted with the antagonist medications that were available at that time (Hanlon, McCabe, Savage, & Kurland, 1975). Starting in 1972, detoxified heroin-addicted inmates who wished to participate in a New York work release program were required to participate in oral naltrexone along with counseling and urine drug testing. Over 691 individuals were treated over a 10-year period and those with histories of heroin addiction performed as well as those without (Brahen, Henderson, Capone, & Kordal, 1984). This experience demonstrated that naltrexone could be used to facilitate program participation which had previously not been accessible to heroin-addicted inmates because of their high rate of relapse and recidivism.

After the mid-1970s, there was little research among criminal justice populations with naltrexone (Patapis & Nordstrom, 2006). One notable exception was a study of oral naltrexone in which 52 opioid-dependent federal probationers were randomly assigned on a 2:1 basis to either 6 months of oral naltrexone with counseling or counseling alone (Cornish et al., 1997). Study participation was voluntary and participants could discontinue medication without suffering any legal consequences. The naltrexone group, as compared to the control group, stayed in treatment at 6 months (52% vs. 33%) and had significantly fewer opioid-positive urine drug tests (8% vs. 30%). In addition, over twice as many participants assigned to the control group (56%) as compared to the naltrexone group (26%) returned to prison during the 6-month study period. Since federal parole is generally better resourced and staffed than state parole agencies, it is unknown whether this study's findings would generalize to state parole and probation agencies.

## Best Practices for Jail and Prison-Based Pharmacotherapy

Although an estimated 24–36% of all heroin-addicted individuals in the United States pass through the criminal justice system in 1 year (Rich et al., 2005), opioid agonist treatment is provided to less than 0.5% of US state and federal prisoners (Mumola & Karberg, 2006) and most US prison medical directors report using methadone only for limited circumstances, such as pregnancy (Nunn et al., 2009).

The situation outside the United States is quite different. In 1996, the provincial prisons in British Columbia, Canada, began continuing methadone treatment for arrestees who were enrolled in treatment before incarceration (Rothon, 1997–1998). In 1998, the Canadian federal prison system adopted the approach of British Columbia and in 2001 expanded access to methadone treatment for opioid-dependent individuals who were out of treatment at the time of incarceration (Sibbald, 2002). In the European Union, 17 nations provide methadone in prison and 10 nations provide buprenorphine (Commission of the European Communities, 2007). In France, buprenorphine and methadone treatment were made available in prisons in 1996 and 2002, respectively (Marzo et al., 2009). Beyond the European Union, methadone treatment is also provided in Australian and Iranian prisons (Stallwitz & Stover, 2007). Thus, it appears that there is a growing awareness of the benefits of opioid agonist treatments in correctional settings throughout the world (Dolan, Khoei, Brentari, & Stevens, 2007).

There are three best practices indications for providing pharmacotherapy for opioid use disorders among jail or prison inmates: (1) opioid withdrawal; (2) opioid maintenance for opioid-tolerant inmates; (3) opioid maintenance for inmates no longer tolerant to opioids.

### Opioid Withdrawal Treatment

Opioid withdrawal should be treated in the same manner as it is treated in the community, ideally with methadone or buprenorphine. Newly arrived inmates and inmates who are using opioids regularly while incarcerated may require detoxification. Unfortunately, a US national survey found that 49% of jails did not use methadone, other opioids, or clonidine to treat opioid detoxification (Fiscella, Moore, Engerman, & Meldrum, 2005).

Withholding withdrawal treatment in jails and prisons can lead to morbidity and mortality, unnecessary utilization of scarce medical services for avoidable sick calls, and violence with possible injury to correctional personnel or inmates. An increasing number of lawsuits against correctional systems throughout the world are being filed for denying human rights of prisoners who are deprived of appropriate detoxification (Boucher, 2003; Dolan, Khoei, Brentari, & Stevens, 2007). In the United States, the right to rehabilitation for alcohol and drug dependence has not been established by the courts, although the courts have ruled that inmates have a right to receive treatment for serious medical conditions, including alcohol and drug withdrawal syndromes (Weinstein, Kim, Mack, Lamavade, & Saraiya, 2005). The lack of detoxification treatment may also cause inmates to obtain illicit drugs or medications in the correctional institution, or to feign illness to receive other medications (Mitchell et al., 2009). Upon release, untreated former inmates often obtain diverted opioids, are reincarcerated, or overdose (Binswanger et al., 2007).

Out-of-treatment opioid-dependent individuals, as well as patients who are maintained on methadone in the community, often have negative experiences with untreated opioid withdrawal during incarceration, which can discourage them from seeking treatment upon release (Mitchell et al., 2009). To provide humane care and to increase treatment entry upon release, the New York City jail at Rikers Island offers a model of opioid detoxification (Tomasino, Swanson, Nolan, & Shuman, 2001). During 2000, the Rikers Island program provided heroin detoxification to 11,406 male and female detainees and short-term inmates. In addition, 6,052 men and women were afforded methadone treatment discontinuation through a gradual dose reduction because they received prison terms or preferred not to continue community methadone treatment. The heroin detoxification program typically reduces doses of methadone over a 12-day period while the tapered reduction from methadone for patients who wish to discontinue that treatment, depending on their dose, occurs over approximately 39 days.

### Opioid Maintenance for Opioid-Tolerant Individuals

As an alternative to detoxification, opioid maintenance (with either methadone or buprenorphine) can be offered to inmates in withdrawal who are either out of treatment or receiving agonist treatment at the time of arrest. In 1987, in recognition of the revolving door of relapse and recidivism associated with detoxification, Rikers Island started the Key Extended Entry Program (KEEP) during a period of overcrowding and unrest and the emerging AIDS epidemic (Magura, Rosenblum, & Joseph, 1992). This program was founded through the cooperation of the Department of Corrections, Correctional Health Services, and the New York State Division of Substance Abuse Services. Since its inception, KEEP has provided a high volume of methadone maintenance treatment, with 4,836 patients treated in 2007 (Magura et al., 2009).

Jail-based methadone maintenance provided by KEEP facilitates community treatment entry. Specifically, the rate of community-based drug treatment entry within 6.5 months from incarceration was significantly higher for patients maintained on methadone in jail compared to inmates who were detoxified (85% vs. 37%, respectively). Furthermore, the rate was higher for those KEEP patients who were enrolled in methadone treatment at the time of arrest as compared to those who were out of treatment and newly enrolled in methadone maintenance in jail. However, despite the encouraging findings regarding post-release treatment entry for the group that was in community treatment before arrest, that group's 6-month community treatment retention rate (27%) was relatively low compared to typical methadone patients, although it was three times higher than that of the detoxified group. Furthermore, there were no significant differences between the maintained and the detoxified groups on self-reported drug use and criminal behavior at followup, although treatment enrollment at followup was associated with decreased drug injection (Magura, Rosenblum, Lewis, & Joseph, 1993). Thus, even after continuity of care systems are in place, ongoing efforts to monitor and improve treatment outcomes are needed.

The availability of buprenorphine in the United States led to an effectiveness study at KEEP which compared in-jail and short-term post-release outcomes of methadone versus buprenorphine maintenance (Magura et al., 2009). In this study, 116 newly arrested individuals who experienced opioid withdrawal at the time of arrest were randomly assigned to buprenorphine or methadone treatment. Upon release, participants were referred to OTPs in the community to continue methadone or to buprenorphine providers. Completion rates in the jail were equally high for both groups; however, three times as many buprenorphine participants as compared to methadone participants reported a willingness to continue their treatment in the community. A significantly higher percentage of the group assigned to buprenorphine as compared to methadone (48% vs. 14%) reported to community treatment upon release. However, there were no significant group differences at 3-months post-release on self-reported heroin use, severity of crime, or arrest.

In France, buprenorphine (Subutex) has been offered in prisons since 1996 (Durand, 2001). In a nationwide prospective observational study in France of 507 opioid-dependent prisoners between June 2003 and September 2004, there was no difference in reincarceration rates over a 3-year period for individuals treated with maintenance therapy in prison with either buprenorphine or methadone as compared to opioid-addicted prisoners who did not receive medication (Marzo et al., 2009) which is in contrast to earlier retrospective findings (Levasseur, Marzo, Ross, & Blatier, 2002). However, the former study was somewhat limited by significant baseline differences between the study groups, including route of heroin use, prior overdose experiences, and suicide attempts.

Maintenance therapy in jails or prisons can reduce drug use within the institution. A study of the methadone program in a Puerto Rican prison showed a reduction in needle sharing during incarceration (Heimer et al., 2006). In Australia, inmates who received in-prison methadone treatment had lower rates of injection risk behavior compared to those who received counseling only or short-term methadone treatment, in a retrospective study of 185 injection drug users (Dolan, Wodak, & Hall, 1998).

The effectiveness of prison-based methadone treatment in Australia in reducing prison drug use was evaluated in a clinical trial in which 392 opioid-dependent prisoners were randomly assigned to receive methadone treatment in prison or to remain on a 4-month waiting list while in prison before initiating treatment (Dolan et al., 2003). The group treated with methadone, as compared to the waiting list group, showed significantly lower rates of heroin use (as measured by self-report and by hair testing), drug injecting, and needle sharing while in prison. Results at 4-year followup indicated that retention in treatment post-release was associated with lower mortality, reincarceration, and HCV conversion rates (Dolan et al., 2005). The study showed the benefits of providing methadone in an institution in which there is ongoing heroin abuse, and that treatment retention in the community post-release can continue to have important public health and public safety benefits.

## Opioid Maintenance for Inmates Who Are No Longer Tolerant to Opioids

A rarely used, but promising, strategy is to initiate opioid agonist therapy for inmates with a history of opioid dependence who were detoxified during incarceration but who are at high risk of relapse upon release. Such an approach was examined 40 years ago in a New York City jail in which 12 randomly selected prerelease inmates with a history of heroin dependence were offered an opportunity to initiate methadone 10 days before release (Dole et al., 1969). The initial dose was 10 mg of methadone (about half of the typical starting dose for a tolerant individual) which was gradually increased to 35 mg over 10 days before release. The dose started low and increased slowly because opioids such as methadone can cause overdose in nontolerant individuals, particularly in the first 2 weeks of dosing (Srivastava & Kahan, 2006). The randomly selected untreated control group was motivated to receive methadone treatment but not offered it during incarceration. During the 12-month post-release followup period, 15 of the 16 controls, as compared to only 3 of the 12 treated individuals, were reincarcerated. In addition, 15 of the 16 controls, as compared to none of the treated individuals, became readdicted.

The first randomized clinical trial of methadone treatment as a prison prerelease relapse prevention strategy was conducted recently in Baltimore (Kinlock, Gordon, Schwartz, & O'Grady, 2008). In this study, 211 opioid-dependent male prerelease prisoners who met the criteria for methadone treatment during the year prior to their incarceration volunteered to participate in the study. All participants were offered weekly group counseling over 12 weeks. In addition, participants were randomly assigned to one of three groups: (1) passive referral to community treatment (counseling only); (2) referral with a guaranteed admission to 1 year of free methadone community treatment; or (3) starting methadone maintenance approximately 3 months before release with guaranteed admission to free methadone community treatment. Because participants were not tolerant to opioids at the time of their dose induction, the starting methadone dose was 5 mg and the dose was increased slowly (5 mg per week to a 60 mg target, beyond which the dose was adjusted as needed). The most frequent side effect was constipation. At 12 months post-release, the prison-initiated methadone group, as compared to the community-initiated group and the counseling-only group, spent significantly more days in treatment (166, 91, 23 days, respectively) and had significantly lower rates of opioid-positive (25, 49, 66%, respectively) and cocaine-positive (43, 67, 72%, respectively) urine drug tests on urine samples (Kinlock, Gordon, Schwartz, Fitzgerald, & O'Grady, 2009). Approximately one-half of the total sample was arrested during the 12-month followup period without any significant differences among the groups. There were four opioid overdose deaths during the 12-month followup period, all of which occurred in the counseling-only group. Thus, this strategy appears promising as a relapse and overdose prevention approach, although pharmacotherapy had no impact at 12 months post-release on arrest status in Baltimore.

### Initiating Methadone Treatment Post-Release

Linking newly released inmates to community opioid agonist treatment for those who are not offered this treatment while incarcerated is another promising strategy to prevent relapse and recidivism. National surveys show that an increasing percentage of US correctional systems' medical directors report referring opioid-addicted prisoners to community OTPs, although no data are available regarding the number of referrals made (Nunn et al., 2009; Rich et al., 2005).

A program to encourage linkage between prerelease prisoners with preincarceration heroin addiction and community methadone treatment was recently developed and evaluated in Rhode Island (McKenzie, Macalino, McClung, Shield, & Rich, 2005). Inmates were provided information about OTPs, offered assistance to acquire documents required for admission (e.g., legal identification), and given appointments and transportation to their first clinic appointment. In addition, participants were provided free treatment for the first 12 weeks and a reduced fee for the next 12 weeks. Finally, several post-release case management visits were offered to provide assistance with job referrals and application for Medicaid.

Of the 175 participants who had completed 6 months in the project at the time of the report, 46% remained in treatment in the community. The two most frequent reasons for discharge were inability to pay fees (34%) and reincarceration (34%). Only 25% of the sample left treatment against medical advice. This study demonstrates the feasibility of increasing treatment entry in OTPs post-release even without initiating OTP treatment in the correctional institution. It also shows that barriers to treatment retention in community treatment are often related to nonclinical issues (e.g., reincarceration and fee payment). As with all nontolerant patients, individuals leaving jail or prison who are started on methadone or buprenorphine should receive lower than usual starting doses and their induction should proceed more slowly than usual practice for tolerant patients.

## Initiating Opioid Antagonist Treatment Prior to Release

Just before release from incarceration would seem an ideal time for initiating Naltrexone. Prior to release, many inmates are opioid free and thus likely to be able to start naltrexone without first undergoing detoxification and the required 7–10 days of opioid abstinence. Initiating naltrexone could afford protection from relapse and overdose death in the vulnerable time immediately following release and may permit newly released inmates to focus on reentry to the community. To date, there has been little research in this area (Lobmaier, Kunøe, & Waal, 2010; Shearer, Wodak, & Dolan, 2007).

In a study of Australian heroin-addicted male inmates, data were analyzed from a failed randomized clinical trial (Shearer, Wodak, & Dolan, 2007). Of the 68 participants randomly assigned to oral naltrexone therapy prior to release, only 13% agreed to start the medication and only 7% remained on naltrexone 6 months post-release. The 47 individuals who started opioid agonist therapy in prison as compared to naltrexone were significantly more likely to be retained in treatment.

Given the difficulty with adherence to oral naltrexone, a two-arm clinical trial was recently conducted in a Norwegian prison in which 46 adult opioid-dependent inmates were randomly assigned to 6-month naltrexone implants or methadone maintenance just prior to release (Lobmaier, Kunøe, & Waal, 2010). Of the 46 randomly assigned prisoners, only 27 actually received their assigned medication. The major reason for refusing participation ($n = 13$) was due to not being assigned to the medication that they desired. Preliminary findings indicated that 55% (6 of 11) of participants assigned to methadone and 25% (4 of 16) of those assigned to long-acting naltrexone relapsed at 6 months post-release. Long-acting naltrexone may have some utility in prerelease settings for those inmates who do not want to receive agonist therapy, although it appears that, as in the community, agonist therapy is preferred by many opioid-dependent individuals.

## Best Pharmacotherapy Practices for Alcohol Use Disorders

Despite the availability of three FDA-approved medications for the treatment of alcohol dependence, the proportion of patients receiving these pharmacotherapies in community-based alcohol and drug treatment programs is quite low (Ducharme, Knudsen, & Roman, 2006). Additionally, the more linkages providers have with criminal justice agencies, the less likely it is that these medications will be prescribed. As with the underutilization of pharmacotherapy for opioid dependence, the underutilization of medications for alcohol dependence can undermine both public health and public safety.

## Alcohol Dependence: Overview of Pharmacology

Although alcohol withdrawal may be mild, if inadequately treated it can manifest as grand mal seizures or life-threatening alcohol withdrawal delirium (Delirium Tremens or DTs). The treatment of choice for alcohol withdrawal is benzodiazepine given either in multiple daily doses over the course of 5–7 days or as a loading dose on an inpatient unit with careful monitoring in which the patient is given hourly 10-mg doses of Valium (or its equivalent) until the symptoms abate or the patient becomes sedated (Myrick & Anton, 1998).

## Alcohol Treatment with Pharmacotherapy

Naltrexone, the opioid antagonist described above, has been approved by the FDA for the treatment of alcohol dependence in its tablet formulation since 1994, and in its extended-release injectable formulation since 2006. It is believed that naltrexone's opioid antagonist effect and its action through the dopaminergic system lead to a reduction in the reinforcing effects of alcohol (Johnson, 2008). Alcohol-dependent patients who have a drink may have a reduced urge to continue drinking and therefore be less likely to relapse to binge or compulsive drinking. Thus, naltrexone seems to reduce relapse to heavy drinking rather than to increase complete abstinence (Bouza, Magro, Muoz, & Amate, 2004). Typically, 50 mg daily of naltrexone is taken orally, although it is also possible to take a double dose every other day. The most frequent side effects in clinical trials were nausea, dizziness, and weakness (Bouza, Magro, Muoz, & Amate, 2004). Physicians must ensure that a patient starting on naltrexone has not used opioids in the past 7–10 days, since its use can precipitate opioid withdrawal.

Several random assignment studies found that alcohol-dependent adults who achieved recent abstinence were less likely to resume heavy drinking while taking naltrexone 50 mg per day as compared to placebo (O'Malley et al., 1992; Volpicelli, Alterman, Hayashida, & O'Brien, 1992). A large, multisite placebo-controlled trial comparing naltrexone alone, acamprosate alone, or the two medications combined, found an advantage only for naltrexone (Anton et al., 2006). Results from randomized clinical trials which studied oral naltrexone for preventing short-term alcohol relapse have been summarized in meta-analyses, which indicate that patients treated with naltrexone had fewer relapses to heavy drinking, drank less alcohol, and were more likely to be abstinent as compared to patients receiving placebo (Srisurapanont & Jarusuraisin, 2005).

Unfortunately, as with opioid dependence treatment, oral naltrexone treatment for alcohol dependence has low adherence rates. The availability of injectable depot naltrexone may increase adherence since it can be administered monthly and produces less nausea early in treatment than oral naltrexone (Johnson, 2008). Several clinical trials comparing depot naltrexone to placebo injections found that the group receiving the active medication had significantly lower rates of heavy drinking days, as compared to the placebo group (Garbutt et al., 2005; Johnson et al., 2004) providing evidence that depot naltrexone can be effective in the treatment of alcohol dependence.

Disulfiram (Antabuse), an aversive agent used in the treatment of alcohol dependence for over 50 years, creates unpleasant symptoms when an individual drinks alcohol while taking this medication. By interfering with the metabolism of alcohol it causes an accumulation of acetaldehyde, which in turn causes nausea, vomiting, flushing, hypotension, dizziness, and shortness of breath.

Because of this aversive physical reaction, it is imperative that the patient abstain from drinking at least 12 hours before ingesting the first dose of disulfiram, usually 500 mg by mouth. Patient adherence with this medication can also be problematic; therefore, patients must be clearly informed that they can have a reaction to alcohol for a number of days after their last dose of disulfiram. There are some settings in which patient adherence can be monitored in order to increase medication adherence, including in methadone treatment programs (Bickel, Marion, & Lowinson, 1987) and within family settings (Keane, Foy, Nunn, & Rychtarik, 1984). Since disulfiram has no effect on alcohol craving, it is most effective in patients who are motivated to take it on a regular basis or who take it under observation (Johnson, 2008).

Acamprosate, approved for use in France in 1989 and in the United States in 2004, affects the glutamate receptors in the brain and may reduce the likelihood of relapse in individuals who have achieved abstinence (Kranzler & Gage, 2007). The medication is taken orally, usually as two 333-mg tablets three times per day. The main side effects in clinical trials were diarrhea, occasional headaches, dizziness, and itching (Bouza, Magro, Muoz, & Amate, 2004). The three successful European double blind placebo, controlled studies of acamprosate that were used by the FDA for the medication's approval in the United States included nearly 1,000 alcohol-dependent patients (Kranzler & Gage, 2007). These studies found that the acamprosate groups had three times the abstinence rates, as compared to the placebo groups, at 13-week followup. Over the course of 12 months, the patients who received acamprosate had double the abstinence rate of the placebo group. However, enthusiasm for using acamprosate in the United States is dampened by the lack of significant differences between acamprosate and placebo in two large US-based randomized trials (Johnson, 2008).

## Best Practices for Pharmacotherapy for Alcohol Dependence in the Criminal Justice System

### Pharmacotherapy During Community Supervision

There have been several small longitudinal studies of alcohol-dependent individuals who took disulfiram as part of jail diversion programs (Bourne, Alford, & Bowcock, 1966; Brewer & Smith, 1983; Haynes, 1973). In a Georgia study of alcohol-dependent individuals with repeat incarcerations, 71 of 132 agreed to take disulfiram as part of probation as an alternative to a 1-month prison sentence (Bourne, Alford, & Bowcock, 1966). The authors reported that several participants remained abstinent and gained steady employment. In another US longitudinal uncontrolled study, 66 of 141 alcohol-dependent repeat offenders agreed to take disulfiram under supervision at their probation office for 12 months in lieu of a 90-day jail term (Haynes, 1973). The authors reported a reduction in the average number of arrests from 3.8 to 0.3. Finally, prior to sentencing in England, 16 repeat offenders with alcohol dependence agreed to take supervised disulfiram as part of a presentencing agreement until their cases were heard (Brewer & Smith, 1983). Most participants tried to drink while on disulfiram early in their treatment. Nine were able to remain abstinent and comply with probation; two had a brief slip but were not rearrested and maintained abstinence at followup.

A more recent US prospective study followed two cohorts of alcohol-dependent veterans treated for 12 weeks as outpatients (Martin et al., 2003). One cohort consisted of 22 voluntary patients who requested disulfiram treatment and the second cohort of 19 patients was required by the criminal justice system to take disulfiram under supervision. The court-ordered group attended twice as many clinic visits (87%) as the voluntary group (42%). These findings on clinic visit adherence were sustained at 15-month followup, 61% versus 18% respectively (Martin, Clapp, Alfers, & Beresford, 2004). This non-random assignment study suggests that court-ordered supervision of disulfiram may enhance adherence. However, it has been noted that it is inappropriate for the criminal justice system to mandate a particular type of pharmacotherapy for addictive disorders (Marco & Marco, 1980; Ritson & Chick, 1992; Rossiter, 1992).

### Pharmacotherapy in Jails and Prisons

It has been estimated that only about 1 in 4 US jails offer alcohol or drug detoxification treatment, leaving approximately 750,000 arrestees per year at risk for untreated alcohol withdrawal (Fiscella, Pless, Meldrum, & Fiscella, 2004a). Withholding alcohol withdrawal treatment can lead to morbidity and mortality in correctional settings (Fiscella, Pless, Meldrum, & Fiscella, 2004b). Alcohol withdrawal in correctional facilities should be treated in the same manner as in the community (i.e., with benzodiazepines). Since benzodiazepines have abuse potential, their administration requires careful monitoring.

There is no research on naltrexone or other pharmacotherapies for treating alcohol dependence among incarcerated populations (Cropsey, Villalobos, & St. Clair, 2005). The extent to which alcohol abuse in jails and prisons is a problem is not known with certainty, however, as with opioids, it is likely that individuals with longstanding histories of alcohol dependence will relapse upon release. This is an area that clearly requires more systematic study.

## Inmate and Correction Staff Views on Pharmacotherapy

Correctional settings function within a culture of control in which inmates possess little ability to make decisions regarding the routine of their daily lives (Mahan, 1984). Despite this observation, drug use in correctional settings has been well documented (Crewe, 2005; Seal et al., 2007). Drug use in correctional institutions may serve different functions for different people (Mitchell et al., 2009; Strang et al., 2006). For example, drugs may be used to get high, to pass time, or to self-medicate withdrawal symptoms.

### Prisoner Views

Some prisoners view incarceration as an opportunity to stop all drug and alcohol use and they may not see the relevance or utility of taking medications, particularly if they are drug and alcohol abstinent when the opportunity for treatment occurs (Hartfree, Dearden, & Pound, 2008). Some prerelease inmates are overconfident and misjudge their ability to remain abstinent upon release (Lobmaier, Kunøe, & Waal, 2010). Others express a preference for detoxification using methadone, buprenorphine, or benzodiazepines rather than participating in maintenance treatment (Tompkins, Neale, Sheard, & Wright, 2007). When enrolled in a correctional institution treatment, inmates indicate that factors related to setting and staff issues (such as the quality and the type of intervention received) were important in determining their level of engagement with drug treatment (Ricketts, Bliss, Murphy, & Brooker, 2005). In addition, it is helpful if prisoners' participation in treatment counts toward earning time off their sentence. Thus, the structure and functioning of the program and its perceived value to prisoners can be influenced by the correctional staff and institution's rules.

### Staff Views

One study of corrections' staff attitudes, knowledge, and readiness to adopt methadone maintenance at a large metropolitan jail found that younger staff and those with less education had lower knowledge scores and often possessed more negative attitudes regarding the provision of drug treatment in correctional settings than did respondents who were at least 45 years old and were college graduates (McMillan & Lapham, 2005). Since line staff interact with prisoners on a daily basis, it is important to consider how staff attitudes regarding pharmacotherapy may influence program participation. In fact, at times peers or staff may try to influence patients to discontinue their medication (Lobmaier, Kunøe, & Waal, 2010).

### Barriers for Implementation of Pharmacotherapy

In the community, there are a number of barriers to implementing pharmacotherapy for individuals on probation, parole, or in drug courts. These barriers include negative attitudes about pharmacotherapy by potential patients (Schwartz et al., 2008), and some criminal justice staff as well as judges (Parrino, 2002). These negative attitudes may stem from misinformation about addiction and its treatment, or about the medications themselves. There are also structural barriers such as a lack of connection between drug treatment providers and criminal justice agencies, no health insurance or Medicaid coverage for addictive disorders, inadequate public grant funding support for services for newly released inmates or for individuals in community supervision, and the high cost of some medications, such as buprenorphine and depot naltrexone. Newly released inmates often lose their health benefits during incarceration and may not know how to regain them; they may lack transportation, and may not have a referral to treatment upon release (Rich et al., 2005). Some prison physicians indicated that they were in favor of opioid agonist treatment but that there were administrative and policy barriers to its implementation which required a huge cultural shift to remove (Nunn et al., 2009). Some examples of barriers that were successfully removed during the implementation of a prerelease opioid agonist program included prohibitions against the use of methadone or buprenorphine in halfway houses and in-home detention (Kinlock, Schwartz, & Gordon, 2005). These prohibitions were lifted after the OTP physician made presentations to the leadership and staff of the halfway houses and home detention units.

## Summary and Observations About Best Practices

Most US jails and prisons do not provide pharmacotherapy, despite the evidence of its effectiveness and its endorsement by the NIH (NIH Consensus Conference, 1998) and the Institute of Medicine (Institute of Medicine, 2006). Outside the United States, pharmacotherapy for drug dependence is more widespread and the World Health Organization includes both methadone and buprenorphine on its list of essential medications and recommends that all medications available in the community should also be available in prisons (Møller, Stöver, Jörgens, Gatherer, & Nikogosian, 2007).

There is strong evidence of the effectiveness of methadone and buprenorphine treatment for opioid-dependent individuals in the community. These treatments are associated with a reduction in heroin use, criminal behavior, arrests, HIV infection, and overdose. Hence, they should be made available to paroles, probationers, and individuals in drug courts. In terms of correctional settings, access to detoxification with methadone or buprenorphine for opioids, and benzodiazepines for alcohol, is humane and medically appropriate. US courts have concluded that access to detoxification for prisoners is a right, along with access to other types of essential healthcare. Individuals enrolled in methadone or buprenorphine treatments who become incarcerated should be permitted to remain on their medication and return to their community-based program upon release if they are in pretrial status or receive a short sentence. This continuity of care supports both public health and safety goals. Methadone and buprenorphine patients who receive long sentences in prisons without opioid agonist treatment should be slowly tapered off their medication. In prisons where there is a relatively high level of opioid use, opioid agonist treatments should be made available as in-prison maintenance therapy with an option to continue in treatment upon release.

For abstinent prerelease inmates with a history of severe opioid dependence, the opportunity to begin opioid agonist therapy before or immediately following release should be made available. In such cases, medical staff should start agonist medications at low doses and increase the dose more slowly than usual because these patients will not be tolerant to opioids at the time of treatment entry. This relapse-prevention approach should be studied further to determine more precisely its efficacy, to clarify for whom this treatment is best provided, and to examine the best approach to offering this service.

Now that long-acting depot naltrexone received FDA approval for the prevention of relapse to treatment of opioid dependence, it should play a role in treating select patients in the community and just before release from jail or prison. A multisite randomized clinical trial with depot naltrexone is now underway with probationers. Presently, only the oral naltrexone formulation is available, although it suffers from low adherence and is not likely to become an important strategy for prerelease prisoners, despite promising results in one outpatient trial with federal probations (Cornish et al., 1997).

All three approved pharmacotherapy medications for alcohol dependence are underused in the community and rarely used in correctional settings. This is a missed opportunity given the high prevalence of alcohol dependence and the risk of relapse. Disulfiram is likely to play a limited role because of poor adherence and its aversive mechanism of action. Acamprosate has suffered from a lack of efficacy in US trials, which has dampened enthusiasm for its use in the United States. Depot naltrexone has been shown in clinical trials to reduce alcohol relapse and it has promise as a prerelease relapse-prevention strategy, but it is yet to be studied in correctional settings. However, it should be offered to individuals under community supervision. Oral naltrexone is not widely used for alcohol dependence treatment because of poor adherence and is not likely to play a major role in the future.

As attitudes change regarding pharmacotherapy, and as more findings from research with these medications in criminal justice populations become available, and courts pressure public safety agencies to provide access to evidence-based treatments, this approach is likely to be more in use. Once medications are offered, the decision to enter or remain in pharmacotherapy may be only partly associated with the effectiveness of the medication. Patient beliefs, expectations, and aspects of the treatment structure may be also closely associated with entry and retention in treatment than the actual medication, and should be addressed at treatment initiation and periodically as treatment progresses.

## References

Anglin, M. D., Brecht, M. L., & Maddahian, E. (1989). Pretreatment characteristics and treatment performance of legally coerced versus voluntary methadone maintenance admissions. *Criminology, 27*(3), 537–557.

Anton, F. R., O'Malley, S. S., Ciraulo, D. A., Cisler, R. A., Couper, D., Donovan, D. M., et al. (2006). Combined pharmacotherapies and behavioral interventions for alcohol dependence: The COMBINE study – A randomized controlled trial. *Journal of the American Medical Association, 295*, 2003–2107.

Ball, J., & Ross, A. (1991). *The effectiveness of methadone maintenance Treatment*. New York: Springer.

Bickel, W. K., Marion, I., & Lowinson, J. H. (1987). The treatment of alcoholic methadone patients: A review. *Journal of Substance Abuse Treatment, 4*(1), 15–19.

Binswanger, I. A., Stern, M. F., Deyo, R. A., Heagerty, P. J., Cheadle, A., Elmore, J. G., et al. (2007). Release from prison – A high risk of death for former inmates. *New England Journal of Medicine, 356*(2), 157–165.

Boucher, R. (2003). The case for methadone maintenance treatment in prisons. *Vermont Law Review, 27*(2), 453–482.

Bourgois, P. (2000). Disciplining addictions: The biopolitics of methadone and heroin in the United States. *Culture, Medicine and Psychiatry, 24*(1), 131.

Bourne, P. G., Alford, J. A., & Bowcock, J. Z. (1966). Treatment of skid row alcoholics with disulfiram. *Quarterly Journal of Studies Alcohol, 27*, 42–48.

Bouza, C., Magro, A., Muoz, A., & Amate, J. M. (2004). Efficacy and safety of naltrexone and acamprosate in the treatment of alcohol dependence: A systematic review. *Addiction, 99*, 811–828.

Brahen, L. S., Henderson, R. K., Capone, T., & Kordal, N. (1984). Naltrexone treatment in a jail work-release program. *Journal of Clinical Psychiatry, 45*(9 Pt 2), 49–52.

Brewer, C., & Smith, J. (1983). Probation linked supervised disulfiram in the treatment of habitual drunken offenders: Results of a pilot study. *British Medical Journal, 287*, 1282–1283.

Bureau of Justice Statistics. (2007, December). *Bureau of Justice Statistics bulletin, probation and parole in the United States, 2006* (NCJ 220218). Retrieved May 1, 2009, from http://www.ojp.usdoj.gov/bjs/abstract/ppus06.htm

Carroll, K. M., Sinha, R., Nich, C., Babuscio, T., & Rounsaville, B. J. (2002). Contingency management to enhance naltrexone treatment of opioid dependence: A randomized clinical trial of reinforcement magnitude. *Experimental and Clinical Psychopharmacology, 10*(1), 54–63.

Center for Substance Abuse Treatment. (2004). *Clinical guidelines for the use of buprenorphine in the treatment of opioid addiction* (Treatment Improvement Protocol (TIP) Series 40. DHHS Publication No. (SMA) 04 -3939). Rockville, MD: Substance Abuse and Mental Health Services Administration.

Chandler, R. K., Fletcher, B. W., & Volkow, N. D. (2009). Treatment drug abuse and addiction in the criminal justice system. Improving public health and safety. *Journal of the American Medical Association, 301*(2), 183–190.

Comer, S. D., Sullivan, M. A., Rothernberg, J. L., Kleber, H. D., Kampman, K., Dackis, C., et al. (2006). Injectable, sustained-release naltrexone for the treatment of opioid dependence: A randomized placebo-controlled trial. *Archives of General Psychiatry, 63*(2), 210–218.

Commission of the European Communities. (2007). *Report from the Commission to the European Parliament and the Council on the implementation of the Council Recommendation of 18 June 2003 on the prevention and reduction of health-related harm associated with drug dependence*. Brussels, Belgium: Commission of the European Communities.

Cornish, J. W., Metzger, D., Woody, G. E., Wilson, D., McLellan, A. T., Vandergrift, B., et al. (1997). Naltrexone pharmacotherapy for opioid dependent

federal probationers. *Journal of Substance Abuse Treatment, 14*(6), 529–534.
Crewe, B. (2005). Prisoner society in the era of hard drugs. *Punishment & Society, 7*(4), 457–481.
Cropsey, K. L., Villalobos, G. C., & St. Clair, C. L. (2005). Pharmacotherapy treatment in substance-dependent correctional populations: A review. *Substance Use and Misuse, 40*, 1983– 1999.
Cushman, P. (1972). Methadone maintenance treatment of narcotic addiction. Analysis of police records of arrests before and during treatment. *New York State Journal of Medicine, 72*, 1752–1755.
Desmond, D. P., & Maddux, J. F. (1996). Compulsory supervision and methadone maintenance. *Journal of Substance Abuse Treatment, 13*(1), 79–83.
Dolan, K., Khoei, E. M., Brentari, C., & Stevens, A. (2007). Prisons and drugs: A global review of incarceration, drug use and drug services (Report 12). *The Beckley Foundation Drug Policy Programme* (pp. 1–9). Oxford: Beckley Foundation.
Dolan, K. A., Shearer, J., MacDonald, M., Mattick, R. P., Hall, W., & Wodak, A. D. (2003). A randomised controlled trial of methadone maintenance treatment versus wait list control in an Australian prison system. *Drug and Alcohol Dependence, 72*(1), 59–65.
Dolan, K. A., Shearer, J., White, B., Zhou, J., Kaldor, J., & Wodak, A. D. (2005). Four-year follow-up of imprisoned male heroin users and methadone treatment: Mortality, re-incarceration and hepatitis C infection. *Addiction, 100*(6), 820–828.
Dolan, K. A., Wodak, A. D., & Hall, W. D. (1998). Methadone maintenance treatment reduces heroin injection in New South Wales prisons. *Drug and Alcohol Review, 17*(2), 153–158.
Dole, V. P., Nyswander, M. E., & Kreek, M. J. (1966). Narcotic blockade. *Archives of Internal Medicine, 118*(4), 304–309.
Dole, V. P., Robinson, J. W., Orraca, J., Towns, E., Searcy, P., & Caine, E. (1969). Methadone treatment of randomly selected criminal addicts. *New England Journal of Medicine, 280*(25), 1372–1375.
Ducharme, L. J., Knudsen, H. K., & Roman, P. M. (2006). Trends in the adoption of medications for alcohol dependence. *Journal of Clinical Psychopharmacology, 26*(Suppl 1), S13–S19.
Durand, E. (2001). Changes in high-dose buprenorphine maintenance therapy at the Fleury-Merogis (France) prison since 1996. *Annales de Médecine Interne, 152*(Suppl 7), 9–14.
Fatseas, M., & Auriacombe, M. (2007). Why buprenorphine is so successful in treating opiate addiction in France. *Current Psychiatry Reports, 9*(5), 358–364.
Fiscella, K., Moore, A., Engerman, J., & Meldrum, S. (2005). Management of opiate detoxification in jails. *Journal of Addictive Diseases, 24*(1), 61–71.
Fiscella, K., Pless, N., Meldrum, S., & Fiscella, P. (2004a). Alcohol and Opiate withdrawal in US jails. *American Journal of Public Health, 94*(9), 1522–1524.
Fiscella, K., Pless, N., Meldrum, S., & Fiscella, P. (2004b). Benign neglect or neglected abuse: Drug and alcohol withdrawal in US. *Journal of Law, Medicine & Ethics, 32*(1), 129–136.
Fischer, B., Chin, A. T., Kuo, I., Kirst, M., & Vlahov, D. (2002). Canadian illicit opiate users' views on methadone and other opiate prescription treatment: An exploratory qualitative study. *Substance Use & Misuse, 37*(4), 495–522.
Garbutt, J. C., Kranzler, H. R., O'Malley, S. S., Gastfriend, D. R., Pettinati, H. M., & Silverman, H. (2005). Efficacy and tolerability of long-acting injectable naltrexone for alcohol dependence: A randomized controlled trial. *Journal of the American Medical Association, 293*, 1617–1625.
Gonzalez, J. P., & Brogden, R. N. (1988). Naltrexone. A review of its pharmacodynamic and pharmacokinetic properties and therapeutic efficacy in the management of opioid dependence. *Drugs, 35*(3), 192–213.
Hanlon, T. E., McCabe, O. L., Savage, C., & Kurland, A. A. (1975). A controlled comparison of cyclazocine and naloxone treatment of the paroled narcotic addict. *International Pharmacopsychiatry, 10*(4), 240–250.
Hartfree, Y., Dearden, C., & Pound, E. (2008). *High hopes: Supporting ex-prisoners in their lives after prison*. Norwich, UK: Centre for Research in Social Policy, Department for Work and Pensions.
Haynes, S. N. (1973). Contingency management in a municipally administered antabuse program for alcoholics. *Journal of Behavior Therapy and Experimental Psychiatry, 44*, 31–32.
Heimer, R., Catania, H., Newman, R. G., Zambrano, J., Brunet, A., & Ortiz, A. M. (2006). Methadone maintenance in prison: Evaluation of a pilot program in Puerto Rico. *Drug Alcohol Dependence, 83*(2), 122–129.
Hiller, M. L., Knight, K., & Simpson, D. D. (1999). Risk factors that predict drop out from corrections-based treatment for drug abuse. *The Prison Journal, 79*, 411–430.
Hubbard, R. L., Collins, J. J., Rachal, J. V., & Cavanaugh, E. R. (1988). The criminal justice client in drug abuse treatment. In C. G. Leukfeld & F. M. Tims (Eds.), *Compulsory treatment of drug abuse: Research and clinical practice* (NIDA Research Monograph 86, pp. 58–80). Rockville, MD: National Institute on Drug Abuse.
Hulse, G., English, D. R., Milne, E., & Holman, C. D. (1999). The quantification of mortality resulting from the regular use of illicit opioids. *Addiction, 94*(2), 221–229.
Institute of Medicine. (2006). *Preventing HIV infection among injecting drug users in high risk countries*. Washington, DC: National Academies Press.
Jaeger, G. A. (2003). Text of CSAM letter to drug court judges on methadone treatment and methadone detoxification for opioid-dependent offenders. *Journal of Maintenance in the Addictions, 2*, 81–83.

Jaffe, J. H., & O'Keeffe, C. (2003). From morphine clinics to buprenorphine: Regulating opioid agonist treatment of addiction in the United States. *Drug Alcohol Dependence, 70*(2 Suppl), S3–S11.

Jenkinson, R. A., Clark, N. C., Fry, C. L., & Dobbin, M. (2005). Buprenorphine diversion and injection in Melbourne, Australia: An emerging issue. *Addiction, 100*, 197–205.

Johannson, B. A., Berglund, M., & Lindgren, A. (2006). Efficacy of maintenance treatment with naltrexone for opioid dependence: A meta-analytical review. *Addiction, 101*(4), 491–503.

Johnson, B. A. (2008). Update on neuropharmacological treatments for alcoholism: Scientific basis and clinical findings. *Biochemical Pharmacology, 75*(1), 34–56.

Johnson, B. A., Ait-Daoud, N., Aubin, J. H., van den Brink, W., Guzzetta, R., & Loewy, J. (2004). A pilot evaluation of the safety and tolerability of repeat dose administration of long-acting injectable naltrexone in patients with alcohol dependence. *Alcoholism: Clinical and Experimental Research, 28*, 1356–1361.

Johnson, R. E., Strain, E. C., & Amass, L. (2003). Buprenorphine: How to use it right. *Drug and Alcohol Dependence, 70*, S59–S77.

Joseph, H. (1988). The criminal justice system and opiate addiction: A historical perspective. In C. G. Leukfeld & F. M. Tims (Eds.), *Compulsory treatment of drug abuse: Research and clinical practice* (NIDA Research Monograph 86, pp. 106–125). Rockville, MD: National Institute on Drug Abuse.

Jürgens, R. (2007). *Evidence for action technical papers. Interventions to address HIV in prisons*. Geneva, Switzerland: WHO, UNODC, UNAIDS.

Keane, T. M., Foy, D. W., Nunn, B., & Rychtarik, R. G. (1984). Spouse contracting to increase antabuse compliance in alcoholic veterans. *Journal of Clinical Psychology, 40*(1), 340–344.

Kinlock, T. W., Gordon, M. S., Schwartz, R. P., Fitzgerald, T. T., & O'Grady, K. E. (2009). A randomized clinical trial of methadone maintenance for prisoners: Results at 12 months post-release. *Journal of Substance Abuse Treatment, 37*(3), 277–285.

Kinlock, T. W., Gordon, M. S., Schwartz, R. P., & O'Grady, K. E. (2008). A study of methadone maintenance for male prisoners: 3-month post release outcomes. *Criminal Justice Behavior, 35*(1), 34–47.

Kinlock, T. W., Schwartz, R. P., & Gordon, M. S. (2005). The significance of interagency collaboration in developing opioid agonist programs for inmates. *Corrections Compendium, 30*(3), 6–30.

Koester, S., Anderson, K., & Hoffer, L. (1999). Active heroin injectors' perceptions and use of methadone maintenance treatment: Cynical performance or self-prescribed risk reduction? *Substance Use & Misuse, 34*(14), 2135–2153.

Kranzler, H. R., & Gage, A. (2007). Acamprosate efficacy in alcohol-dependent patients: Summary of results from three pivotal trials. *American Journal on Addictions, 17*, 70–76.

Krupitsky, E., Nunes, E. V., Ling, W., Illeperuma, A., Gastrfriend, D. R., Silverman, B. L. (2011). Injectable extended-release naltrexone for opioid dependence: a double-blind, placebo-controlled, multicentre randomised trial. *Lancet, 377*, 1506–1513.

Krupitsky, E. M., Zvartau, E. E., Masalov, D. V., Tsoy, M. V., Burakov, A. M., & Egorova, V. Y. (2004). Naltrexone for heroin dependence treatment in St. Petersburg, Russia. *Journal of Substance Abuse Treatment, 26*(4), 285–294.

Ladson, L. (2007, August 10). Settlement reached in lawsuit over inmate's death. *The Dallas Morning News*. Document ID: 11AF35DAEE3B9628.

Leukefeld, C. G., & Tims, F. M. (1988). An introduction to compulsory treatment for drug abuse: Clinical practice and research. In C. G. Leukefeld & F. M. Tims (Eds.), *Compulsory treatment of drug abuse: Research and clinical practice* (NIDA Research Monograph 86, pp. 1–7). Rockville, MD: National Institute on Drug Abuse.

Levasseur, L., Marzo, J., Ross, N., & Blatier, C. (2002). Frequency of re-incarcerations in the same detention center: Role of substitution therapy. A preliminary retrospective analysis. *Annales de Medecine Interne, 153*(3 Suppl), 1S14–IS19.

Ling, W., & Wesson, D. R. (1984). Naltrexone treatment for addicted health-care professionals: A collaborative private practice experience. *Journal Clinical Psychiatry, 45*, 46–48.

Lobmaier, P. P., Kunøe, N., & Waal, H. (2010). Treatment research in prison: Problems and solutions in a randomized trial. *Addiction Research and Theory, 18*(1), 1–13.

Magura, S., Lee, J. D., Hershberger, J., Joseph, H., Marsch, L., Shropshire, C., et al. (2009). Buprenorphine and methadone maintenance in-jail and post-release: A randomized clinical trial. *Drug and Alcohol Dependence, 99*(1–3), 222–230.

Magura, S., Rosenblum, A., & Joseph, H. (1992). Evaluation of in-jail methadone maintenance: Preliminary results. *NIDA Research Monograph, 118*, 192–210.

Magura, S., Rosenblum, A., Lewis, C., & Joseph, H. (1993). The effectiveness of in-jail methadone maintenance. *Journal of Drug Issues, 23*(1), 75–99.

Mahan, S. (1984). Imposition of despair: An ethnography of women in prison. *Justice Quarterly, 1*(3), 357–383 (27).

Marco, C. H., & Marco, J. M. (1980). Antabuse: Medication in exchange for limited freedom – Is it legal? *American Journal of Law & Medicine, 5*(4), 295–330.

Martin, B. K., Clapp, L., Alfers, J., & Beresford, T. P. (2004). Adherence to court-ordered disulfiram at fifteen months: A naturalistic study. *Journal of Substance Abuse Treatment, 26*(3), 233–236.

Martin, B., Clapp, L., Bialkowski, D., Bridgeford, D., Amponsah, A., Lyons, L., et al. (2003). Compliance to supervised disulfiram therapy: A comparison of voluntary and court-ordered patients. *The American Journal on Addictions, 12*, 137–143.

Marzo, J. N., Rotily, M., Meroueh, F., Varastet, M., Hunault, C., Obradovic, I., et al. (2009). Maintenance therapy and 3-year outcome of opioid dependent prisoners: A prospective study in France (2003–2006). *Addiction, 104*(7), 1233–1240.

Mattick, R. P., Breen, C., Kimber, J., & Davoli, M. (2003). Methadone maintenance therapy versus no opioid replacement therapy for opioid dependence. *The Cochrane Database of Systematic Review*, (2), CD002209. DOI: 10.1002/14651858.CD002209.

Mattick, R. P., Kimber, J., Breen, C., & Davoli, M. (2008). Buprenorphine maintenance versus placebo or methadone maintenance for opioid dependence. *Cochrane Database of Systematic Reviews*, (2), CD002207. DOI: 10.1002/14651858.CD002207.pub3.

McKenzie, M., Macalino, G., McClung, C., Shield, D. C., & Rich, J. D. (2005). Opiate replacement therapy at time of release from incarceration: Project MOD, a pilot program. *Journal of Opioid Management, 1*(3), 147–151.

McMillan, G. P., & Lapham, S. C. (2005). Staff perspectives on methadone maintenance therapy in a large southwestern jail. *Addiction Research and Theory, 13*(1), 53–63.

Metzger, D., Woody, G. E., McLellan, A. T., O'Brien, C. P., Druley, P., & Navaline, H. (1993). HIV seroconversion among intravenous drug users in- and out-of-treatment: An 18-month prospective follow-up. *Journal of Acquired Immunodeficiency Syndrome, 6*, 1049–1056.

Mitchell, S. G., Kelly, S. M., Brown, B. S., Reisinger, H. S., Peterson, J. A., Ruhf, A., et al. (2009). Incarceration and opioid withdrawal: The experiences of methadone patients and out-of-treatment heroin users. *Journal of Psychoactive Drugs, 41*, 2.

Møller, L., Stöver, H., Jörgens, R., Gatherer, A., & Nikogosian, H. (2007). *Health in prisons: A WHO guide to the essentials in prison health*. Geneva, Switzerland: WHO.

Mumola, C., & Karberg, J. (2006). *Drug use and dependence, state and federal prisoners*. Washington, DC: US Department of Justice, Office of Justice Programs.

Myrick, H., & Anton, R. F. (1998). Treatment of alcohol withdrawal. *Alcohol, Health & Research World, 22*(1), 38–43.

NIH Consensus Conference. (1998). Effective medical treatment of opiate addiction. *Journal of the American Medical Association, 280*(22), 1936–1943.

Ngo, H. T., Tait, R. J., & Hulse, G. K. (2008). Comparing drug-related hospital morbidity following heroin dependence treatment with methadone maintenance or naltrexone implantation. *Archives of General Psychiatry, 65*(4), 457–465.

Nunn, A., Zaller, N., Dickman, S., Trimbur, C., Nijhawan, A., & Rich, J. D. (2009). Methadone and buprenorphine prescribing referral practices in US prison systems: Results from a nationwide survey. *Drug and Alcohol Dependence, 105*(1–2), 82–88.

O'Brien, C. P. (1997). A range of research-based pharmacotherapies for addiction. *Science, 278*(5335), 66–70.

O'Brien, C. P. (2006). Drug addiction and drug abuse. In L. Brunton, J. Lazon, & K. Parker (Eds.), *Goodman and Gilman's the pharmacological basis of therapeutics* (11th ed.). New York: McGraw-Hill.

O'Brien, C. P., & Cornish, J. W. (2006). Naltrexone for probationers and parolees. *Journal of Substance Abuse Treatment, 31*, 107–111.

O'Brien, C. P., Greenstein, R., Mintz, J., & Woody, G. E. (1975). Clinical experience with naltrexone. *American Journal of Drug and Alcohol Abuse, 2*, 365–377.

Office of National Drug Control Policy. (2001). *The National Drug Control Strategy annual report*. Washington, DC: ONDCP.

O'Malley, S. S., Jaffe, A. J., Chang, G., Schottenfeld, R. S., Meyer, R. E., & Rounsavillle, B. (1992). Naltrexone and coping skills therapy for alcohol dependence: A controlled study. *Archives of General Psychiatry, 49*(11), 881–887.

Parrino, M. W. (2002). The renaissance of methadone treatment in America. *Journal of Maintenance in the Addictions, 2*(1), 5–17.

Patapis, N. S., & Nordstrom, B. R. (2006). Research on naltrexone in the criminal justice system. *Journal of Substance Abuse Treatment, 31*(2), 113–115.

Peterson, J. A., Schwartz, R. P., Mitchell, S. G., Reisinger, H. S., Kelly, S. M., O'Grady, K. E., et al. (2010). Why don't out-of-treatment individuals enter methadone treatment programs? *International Journal of Drug Policy, 21*, 36–42.

Reisinger, H. S., Schwartz, R. P., Mitchell, S. G., Peterson, J. A., Kelly, S. M., O'Grady, K. E., et al. (2009). Premature discharge from methadone treatment: Patient perspectives. *Journal of Psychoactive Drugs, 41*(3), 285–296.

Rich, J. D., Boutwell, A. E., Shield, D. C., Garret Key, R., McKenzie, M., & Clarke, J. G. (2005). Attitudes and practices regarding the use of methadone in US state and federal prisons. *Journal of Urban Health, 82*(3), 411–419.

Ricketts, T., Bliss, P., Murphy, K., & Brooker, C. (2005). Engagement with drug treatment and testing orders: A qualitative study. *Addiction Research and Theory, 13*(1), 65–78.

Ritson, B., & Chick, J. (1992). Letter to the editor. *British Medical Journal, 305*, 1155.

Rossiter, S. K. (1992). Psychosis with disulfiram prescribed under probation order. *British Medical Journal, 305*, 763.

Rothon, D. A. (1997–1998). Methadone in provincial prisons in British Columbia. *Canada HIV AIDS Policy Law Newsletter, 3–4*(4-1), 27–31.

Schwartz, R. P., Brooner, R. K., Montoya, I. D., Currens, M., & Hayes, M. (1999). A 12-year follow-up of a methadone medical maintenance program. *The American Journal on Addictions, 8*(4), 293–299.

Schwartz, R. P., Jaffe, J. H., O'Grady, K. E., Kinlock, T. W., Gordon, M. S., Kelly, S. M., et al. (2009). Interim methadone treatment: Impact on arrests. *Drug & Alcohol Dependence, 103*(3), 148–154.

Schwartz, R. P., Kelly, S. M., O'Grady, K. E., Mitchell, S. G., Peterson, J. A., Reisinger, H. S., et al. (2008). Attitudes toward buprenorphine and methadone among opioid-dependent individuals. *The American Journal on Addictions, 17*(5), 396–401.

Seal, D. W., Margolis, A. D., Morrow, K. M., Belcher, L., Sosman, J., Askew, J., et al. (2007). Substance use and sexual behavior during incarceration among 18–29-year old men: Prevalence and correlates. *AIDS and Behavior, 12*(1), 27–40.

Shearer, J., Wodak, A. D., & Dolan, K. A. (2007). Evaluation of a prison-based naltrexone program. *International Journal of Prisoner Health, 3*(3), 214–224.

Sibbald, B. (2002). Methadone maintenance expands inside federal prisons. *Canadian Medical Association Journal, 167*(10), 1154.

Srisurapanont, M., & Jarusuraisin, N. (2005, January 25). Opioid antagonists for alcohol dependence. *Cochrane Database Systematic Review,* (12), CD001867.

Srivastava, A., & Kahan, M. (2006). Methadone induction doses: Are our current practices safe? *Journal of Addictive Diseases, 25*(3), 5–13.

Stallwitz, A., & Stover, H. (2007). The impact of substitution treatment in prisons – A literature review. *International Journal of Drug Policy, 18*(6), 464–474.

Stine, S. M., Meandzija, B., & Kosten, T. R. (1998). Pharmacologic therapies for opioid addiction. In A. W. Graham, & T. K. Schultz (Eds.), B. Wilford (Assoc. Ed.), *Principles of addiction medicine* (2nd ed., pp. 545–555). Chevy Chase, MD: American Society of Addiction Medicine, Inc.

Strang, J., Gossop, M., Heuston, J., Green, J., Whitley, C., & Maden, A. (2006). Persistence of drug use during imprisonment: Relationship of drug type, recency of use and severity of dependence to use of heroin, cocaine and amphetamine in prison. *Addiction, 101*(8), 1125–1132.

Strang, J., McCambridge, J., Best, D., Beswick, T., Bearn, J., & Rees, S. (2003). Loss of tolerance and overdose mortality after inpatient opiate detoxification. *British Medical Journal, 326*(7396), 959–960.

Tomasino, V., Swanson, A. J., Nolan, J., & Shuman, H. I. (2001). The Key Extended Entry Program (KEEP): A methadone treatment program for opiate dependent inmates. *Mt. Sinai Journal of Medicine, 68*(1), 14–20.

Tompkins, C. N. E., Neale, J., Sheard, L., & Wright, N. M. J. (2007). Experiences of prison among injecting drug users in England: A qualitative study. *International Journal of Prisoner Health, 3*(3), 189–203.

Volpicelli, J. R., Alterman, A. I., Hayashida, M., & O'Brien, C. P. (1992). Naltrexone in the treatment of alcohol dependence. *Archives of General Psychiatry, 49*, 876–880.

WHO. (2005). *Status report on prisons: Drugs and harm reduction*. Geneva, Switzerland: WHO.

Weinstein, H. C., Kim, D., Mack, A., Lamavade, K., & Saraiya, A. U. (2005). Prevalence and assessment of mental disorders in correctional settings. In C. L. Scott& J. B. Gerbasi(Eds.), *Handbook of correctional mental health* (p. 54). Washington, DC: American Psychiatric Publishing, Inc.

Zanis, D. A., & Woody, G. E. (1998). One-year mortality rates following methadone treatment discharge. *Drug & Alcohol Dependence, 52*(3), 257–260.

Zweben, J. E., & Sorensen, J. L. (1988). Misunderstandings about methadone. *Journal of Psychoactive Drugs, 20*(3), 275–281.

# Co-occurring Disorders: Mental Health and Drug Misuse

# 16

Arthur J. Lurigio

**Abstract**

Numerous studies have demonstrated that people with serious mental illness also have high rates of substance use disorders. When such disorders are diagnosed in the same person, at the same time, they are referred as co-occurring or comorbid disorders. This chapter examines the prevalence, cause, and treatment of comorbid psychiatric and substance use disorders, which are each found on Axis I of the Diagnostic and Statistical Manual of the American Psychiatric Association. Co-occurring disorders are difficult to diagnose and treat and can co-occur in various combinations. Left untreated, people with comorbid disorders have poorer clinical outcomes than people with one type of disorder or the other. They are also more likely to be criminally involved, hospitalized, and imprisoned. The best treatments for comorbidity focus on both types disorders as primary and deliver services in a fully integrated model of care. Several prison-based programs for people with co-occurring disorders have been implemented and tested.

**Keywords**

Addiction • Substance use disorders • Psychiatric disorders • Integrated treatment

Numerous studies have demonstrated that people with serious psychiatric disorders (SPDs) have high rates of substance use disorders (SUDs) and vice versa (Mueser, Drake, & Wallach, 1998). These clinical conditions or syndromes are defined in Axis I of the Diagnostic and Statistical Manual (DSM-IV-TR) of the American Psychiatric Association, the widely used nomenclature for SPDs and SUDs (American Psychiatric Association, 2004). This chapter describes the causes, prevalence, consequences, and treatment of comorbid disorders, which refer to two or more co-occurring mental illnesses, including at least one SPD and at least one SUD (Mueser, Noordsy, Drake, & Fox, 2003). Comorbidity also refers to the interactions between two or more SPDs and SUDs that pertain

A.J. Lurigio (✉)
College of Arts and Sciences, Loyola University,
Chicago, IL 60656, USA
e-mail: alurigi@luc.edu

C. Leukefeld et al. (eds.), *Handbook of Evidence-Based Substance Abuse Treatment in Criminal Justice Settings*, Issues in Children's and Families' Lives 11,
DOI 10.1007/978-1-4419-9470-7_16, © Springer Science+Business Media, LLC 2011

to the effects of one on the other in terms of severity, course, treatment, and prognosis (National Institute on Drug Abuse, 2008). Finally, the current chapter discusses integrated treatment and other evidence-based practices for responding to comorbidity, especially among criminal offenders, who have co-occurring disorders at rates much higher than those found in the general population.

## Background

### Costs of Addiction

SUDs are chronic but treatable brain diseases involving compulsive drug-seeking and -using behaviors that persist despite immediate or potentially harmful consequences for users as well as their families and communities. Drug abuse and dependence are serious threats to public health and safety, costing hundreds of billions of dollars in annual healthcare expenditures, crime, poor work productivity, and job loss (Hoffman & Froemke, 2007). For example, in 2002, illegal drug use in the United States cost nearly 200 billion dollars. Approximately three-fourths of the costs (129 billion dollars) were economic losses attributable to people's inability to work because of drug-precipitated illness, premature death, or incarceration (Office of National Drug Control Policy, 2004). The treatment of healthcare problems among people with SUDs cost 16 billion dollars in 2002; meanwhile, drug-related criminal justice and welfare costs totaled 36 billion dollars that same year (Office of National Drug Control Policy, 2004). Addiction can also produce intangible costs, such as homelessness, academic failure, and troubled relationships. Indeed, it is one of the most pervasive and intransigent mental health disorders in the world, affecting the thoughts, feelings, and behaviors of millions of people annually (World Health Organization, 2004).

The most recent war on drugs in the United States, beginning with the passage of the Anti-Drug Abuse Act of 1988, placed an overwhelming emphasis on law enforcement strategies to combat the possession and sale of illegal drugs. Consequently, the number of arrests for such offenses increased dramatically. Although general population surveys reported declines in illegal drug use throughout the 1990s, rates of arrest for drug crimes continued at a record pace into the twenty-first century (Tonry, 1999). Drug offenses have been among the largest categories of arrests since the 1980s. From 1980 to 2000, for example, arrests for drug offenses more than doubled. In 2000 alone, more than 1.5 million persons were arrested for drug offenses – more than four-fifths of whom were arrested for drug possession (Bureau of Justice Statistics, 2002).

### Comorbidity

The war on drugs has also swelled this country's probation, jail, and prison populations with unprecedented numbers of drug-abusing and -dependent offenders, culminating in the implementation and evaluation of numerous drug treatment programs in correctional settings (Lurigio & Swartz, 2000). Often ignored in the design and implementation of such programs is the fact that drug-abusing and -dependent offenders have very high rates of comorbid psychiatric disorders, also known as co-occurring disorders (Kessler et al., 1994). The paucity of specific programs for offenders with co-occurring disorders has resulted in high rates of rearrests and reincarcerations and increased the likelihood of violent behavior within this population (Harris & Lurigio, 2007; Lurigio & Swartz, 2000).

Many descriptions of drug treatment programs in criminal justice settings acknowledge the presence of comorbid psychiatric disorders among offenders (Sacks, Sacks, DeLeon, Bernhardt, & Graham, 1997; Wexler, 1995). However, such descriptions usually present mental illness in the context of other problems, such as vocational and educational deficits, medical conditions, and family conflicts (e.g., Barthwell et al., 1995; Peters, 1993; Wexler, 1995). Only in the past 15 years have comorbid psychiatric disorders been conceptualized as unique or singular clinical entities that warrant specific interventions (El-Mallakh,

1998; Mueser, Drake, & Miles, 1997). In other words, the treatment of comorbid psychiatric disorders has been secondary to the treatment of alcohol or drug problems in criminal justice settings.

## Causes and Consequences of Co-occurring Disorders

### Genetic Vulnerability

Much research has been conducted to explain the co-occurrence of SUDs and SPDs. Family and twin studies support an inherited susceptibility to SPDs and SUDs; however, no investigations have found conclusive evidence of a specific genetic vulnerability for co-occurring disorders. Nonetheless, several studies indicate that diagnoses of antisocial personality disorder (ASPD) and its childhood precursor conduct disorder, increase the likelihood of being diagnosed with an SUD or SPD as well as the co-occurrence of those disorders. For example, among people with an SPD, the presence of ASPD is related to the early use of drugs and alcohol as well as severe drug or alcohol use problems (Mueser et al., 1998).

People with co-occurring disorders might have a shared genetic predisposition that places them at elevated risk for both types of illness. Genes can directly affect the development of addiction and mental illness or indirectly affect both by rendering an individual incapable of effectively coping or managing environmental stressors (National Institute on Drug Abuse, 2008). In addition, similar regions of the brain – especially those pathways that involve the neurotransmitter dopamine – might underlie the expression of SPDs and SUDs. Furthermore, drug use might trigger the onset of a psychiatric disorder by kindling the propensity toward mental illness, which is caused by abnormalities in the structure and functioning of the brain (National Institute on Drug Abuse, 2008). In short, drug and alcohol use can precipitate SPDs among people with a genetic vulnerability for such illnesses. Among those who already have SPDs, substance use can trigger psychiatric relapses. However, no data suggest that substance use invariably causes SPDs; rather, such use exacerbates or hastens the occurrence of symptoms in people who are genetically predisposed to psychiatric disorders (Goodwin & Jamison, 1990).

### Self-Medication Theory

Anecdotal evidence suggests that people with SPDs use particular substances to self-medicate, that is, they purposefully select drugs with the psychopharmacological properties that they expect will alleviate their symptoms. For example, if people with SPDs are depressed, they choose drugs that have stimulant effects (e.g., cocaine or amphetamines); if they are anxious, they choose drugs that have sedative effects (e.g., heroin or alcohol). However, studies have found little support for a self-medication theory that posits a direct match between a psychiatric disorder and drug choice. People with co-occurring disorders (PCDs) rarely report that they use specific substances to palliate the symptoms of particular psychiatric disorders. Instead, they use a variety of substances to relieve the dysphoria stemming from boredom, loneliness, and the side effects of psychiatric medications as well as the common symptoms of most serious mental illness, such as sleep disturbances, anxiety, depression, and paranoia (Mueser, 2005).

### Social Factors

Several risk factors are correlated with SPDs and contribute to SUDs, including poverty, poor interpersonal and cognitive skills, social isolation, lack of adult responsibilities, limited structured daily activities, and school/vocational failure. Many PCDs are motivated to continue using drugs as purchasing and sharing drugs provide them with a focus in their lives, an opportunity for social contacts, and a means to structure their time, which is empty because of school and work failure and estrangement from family members. Substance use also helps them dampen the painful memories of psychotic episodes ("sealing over") and the loss of life ambitions and self-esteem (Mueser et al., 2003).

## Brain Sensitivity

Research suggests that people with SPDs are hypersensitive to the effects of alcohol and drugs (substances). The use of alcohol and drugs is more likely to impair the performance of mentally ill adults on a variety of cognitive and motor tasks when compared to nonmentally ill adults. Indeed, even small amounts of substances can result in more abuse and dependence problems and other negative consequences for mentally ill adults when compared to non-mentally ill adults (Drake & Wallach, 1993).

## Adverse Consequences of Comorbidity

### Medical and Social Issues

PCDs experience a more extensive range of adverse medical, legal, and social consequences than those who have only one disorder or the other. For example, co-occurring disorders are associated with substantially higher rates of financial problems, family stressors, prostitution, morbidity, suicide, unemployment, homelessness, arrests, and incarcerations than are psychiatric and substance use disorders alone (Mueser et al., 2003). In addition, PCDs are more likely than those with no comorbidity to experience higher rates of infectious diseases (e.g., HIV, Hepatitis B and C) and premature death and to be hospitalized or use emergency rooms for psychiatric and other medical crises (Cournos & McKinnon, 1997; Woody, Metzger, Navaline, McLellan, & O'Brien, 1997).

People with only an SPD or SUD are significantly more likely than PCDs to adhere to medication regimes and significantly less likely to commit violent acts or have recurring episodes of SUDs or SPDs (Mueser, Drake, & Noordsy, 1998). Moreover, incarcerated PCDs are significantly more likely to be reincarcerated within 1 year of discharge than inmates with only an SUD (48% versus 31%). Hence, PCDs tend to return to prison sooner after release than those with only an SUD (Messina, Burdon, Hagopian, & Prendergast, 2004).

*Access to treatment.* Comorbid disorders differ from singular disorders in both their clinical courses and treatment regimes (Abram & Teplin, 1991). PCDs are generally more difficult to diagnose and treat, experience more psychotic symptoms, require more specialized and intensive treatment, and have poorer treatment outcomes than those with only an SPD or SUD (El-Mallakh, 1988; Osher & Drake, 1996; Ries & Comtois, 1997; Sacks et al., 1997; Woody et al., 1997). As Hills (2000) noted, the diagnoses, referral for services, and treatment of PCDs are all complicated by the varying nature and intensity of such disorders.

> Adding to the difficult task of diagnosis and treatment planning for [persons with comorbid disorders] is the awareness that [these] disorders vary in the degree to which they are disabling. One disorder may be more severe during a given period of time, they may both be continuous and chronic, or they may both be more intermittent and episodic... This instability in presentation poses a challenge to placement evaluators who feel the press of burgeoning inmate populations and are typically left with the decision to track an offender into either mental health or substance abuse services. (p. 3)

In addition, PCDs often encounter difficulties in accessing treatment. For example, only 19% of the PCDs participating in the National Comorbidity Survey reported that they had received treatment for both their psychiatric and substance use disorders, and 29% received no treatment for either disorder (Kessler et al., 1997). One national survey found that substance abuse treatment was a condition of probation for 41% of the country's adult probationers, whereas psychiatric treatment was a condition of probation for only 7% (Bureau of Justice Statistics, 1997). Compounding the issue, relatively few community-based drug treatment programs accept offenders with mental illness, and even fewer offer them integrated services for co-occurring disorders (Lurigio, 2004). For example, a study of 8,500 men and women in treatment in California found that only 26% of the state's drug treatment services were for co-occurring disorders; the rest were for SUDs alone (Messina et al., 2004).

## Prevalence of Substance Use and Co-occurring Disorders in Correctional Populations

### Drug Use in Correctional Populations

The prevalence of drug use and SUDs is significantly higher in criminal justice and correctional populations than in the general population. In 2003, the Arrestee Drug Abuse Monitoring (ADAM) Program found that nearly two-thirds (median among 39 sites) of male arrestees tested positive at arrest for one or more of five illicit drugs (i.e., marijuana, opiates, cocaine, methamphetamine, or PCP). For example, in Chicago, 86% of male arrestees participating in ADAM tested positive for one or more of these drugs – 53% tested positive for marijuana, 51% for powder cocaine, 25% for opiates, and 1% for methamphetamine. Approximately half were assessed as heavy drug users (52%) or at risk of substance dependence (49%) (Zhang, 2005).

In 2004, 83% of state prisoners reported lifetime use of illicit substances, while 78% reported marijuana use, 47% reported cocaine or crack cocaine use, 33% reported hallucinogen use, 29% reported amphetamine or other stimulant use, 23% reported heroin or other opiate use, and 21% reported barbiturate or other depressant use (Mumola & Karberg, 2006). The rates of drug use among jail detainees in 2002 were similar. Specifically, 82% reported lifetime use of any drug, 76% reported marijuana use, and 48% reported cocaine or crack cocaine use. More than two-thirds of jail detainees were diagnosed with an SUD; the highest rates occurred among detainees convicted of burglary (Karberg & James, 2005).

In 2004, much higher percentages of state prisoners than members of the general population reported past-month drug use. More than half of the inmates (56%) surveyed indicated that they had used drugs in the month before their current offense. The most commonly used drug was marijuana (40%), followed by cocaine (21%), methamphetamine (11%), heroin (8%), and hallucinogens (6%). Several national surveys of adult prison inmates, jail detainees, and probationers have all shown that many offenders were under the influence of drugs when they committed the crimes for which they were most recently arrested. For example, more than half of state and federal prisoners in the late 1990s indicated they had been under the influence of alcohol or drugs when they committed their offenses (Mumola, 1999; Mumola & Bonczar, 1998). In 2004, a combined total of 58% of state (32%) and federal (26%) prison inmates reported being under the influence of drugs when they committed the crime for which they had most recently been arrested. Being under the influence of drugs during the commission of a recent crime was most prevalent among state prison inmates convicted of drug and property offenses and among federal prison inmates convicted of drug and violent offenses (Mumola & Karberg, 2006).

### Comorbidity in General and Correctional Populations

SUDs are the most common and clinically severe disorders affecting people with SPDs such as, major depression, bipolar disorder, and schizophrenia. Co-occurring SUDs and SPDs afflict between 7 and 10 million adults in the United States annually (Substance Abuse and Mental Health Services Administration, 2002). Depending on the sampling procedures, definitions of disorders, and assessment tools used in various studies of comorbidity, estimates of the percentages of people with lifetime SUDs and comorbid SPDs vary from 20 to 65% (Mueser et al., 2003). For example, in the Epidemiological Catchment Area (ECA) Study, which interviewed more than 20,000 randomly selected adults, approximately half of those diagnosed with schizophrenia (48%) and more than half of those diagnosed with bipolar disorder (56%) had one or more SUDs (Kessler et al., 1994). The

ECA study found nearly a 60% overall comorbidity rate for substance use and psychiatric disorders (Chiles, Von Cleve, Jemelka, & Trupin, 1990). People with anxiety and mood disorders are twice as likely as those in the general population to suffer from a substance use disorder and vice versa (National Institute on Drug Abuse, 2008).

Comorbidity rates for major psychiatric disorders are high for untreated drug-dependent persons, higher for persons in drug treatment programs, and higher yet for offenders with SUDs (Lurigio & Swartz, 2000). For example, studies of male jail detainees have found high rates of comorbidity. One such investigation reported that 56% of the detainees in the Cook County (Chicago) Department of Corrections (CCDOC) – the largest single-site jail in the United States – who met the diagnostic criteria for schizophrenia also met the diagnostic criteria for an SUD (Abram & Teplin, 1991).

Similarly, a study of the prevalence of psychiatric and co-occurring disorders in a sample of pretrial detainees in the CCDOC's Day Reporting Center, which is a community-based program for low-risk detainees, indicated that more than half the sample had one or more lifetime psychiatric disorders (Swartz & Lurigio, 1999). The rates of SPDs in the sample were significantly higher than the lifetime prevalence rates of SPDs in the general population. The vast majority (89%) of detainees with a lifetime SPD (and ASPD) were comorbid for a current SUD. Conversely, nearly two-thirds (63%) of the detainees with a lifetime SUD were comorbid for a current SPD. The study further indicated that many offenders with SPDs were afflicted with other psychiatric disorders (e.g., post-traumatic stress disorder) (Swartz & Lurigio, 1999). Consistent with ECA findings, psychiatric problems tended to cluster among detainees with the most severe disorders (cf., Regier et al., 1990).

Another investigation examined comorbidity rates among adults in Illinois who were on probation, a sentence in lieu of incarceration in which offenders must adhere to conditions of release under the supervision of probation officers (Lurigio et al., 2003). The study found that 55% of probationers with SPDs were dependent on one or more drugs. The rate of polysubstance abuse among probationers with an SPD was nearly three times higher than the rate of polysubstance abuse among probationers who had no SPD (Lurigio et al., 2003). Jail detainees with mental health problems are more likely than those with no mental health problems to report drug use in the month before their recent arrests – 60% versus 40%, respectively (Mumola & Karberg, 2006). Likewise, a study of prison inmates showed that SUDs were more prevalent among those with mental health disorders than those with no mental health disorders – 74% versus 56%, respectively (Mumola & Karberg, 2006). The use of illegal drugs was also found to be more prevalent among prison inmates who reported a history of physical, emotional, or sexual abuse (Harlow, 1999). These results as well as findings from other studies described herein suggest that comorbidity is highly common in correctional populations.

## Treatment of Co-occurring Disorders

Corrections-based programs are typically the only treatment options for addicted offenders who would otherwise have no access to such services (Wexler, Williams, Early, & Trotman, 1996). Generally speaking, drug abuse programs in jails and prisons treat only offenders with the most serious SUDs; such programs offer several advantages over community-based treatment programs for addicted offenders (Peters, May, & Kearns, 1992; Wexler, 1995). For example, participants in jail- and prison-based drug treatment programs have relatively low drop-out rates and receive good-behavior incentives for their attendance in the program – a strong motivator for retention (Tunis, 1995).

Drug treatment programs in correctional settings are generally located in the safest and least-crowded areas in jails and prisons. As a result, even offenders with low motivation for drug treatment are likely to remain in these programs long enough to benefit from the experience. In addition, jail detainees and prison inmates are already being housed; hence, residential treatment – which is expensive in the outside community – costs much less per capita when implemented in jails or prisons. Finally, incarcerates in drug treatment are less likely to break rules or be involved in violent altercations than those in the general prison or jail population. Thus, jail and prison drug treatment programs help administrators better manage and control their populations (Early, 1998).

In 1997, slightly more than one-third of state prisoners nationwide reported previous participation in substance abuse treatment (e.g., detoxification, in-patient treatment, or professional counseling), while more than 40% reported previous participation in other types of substance abuse interventions (e.g., educational awareness sessions, self-help groups, or peer counseling activities). Nearly 60% indicated that they had previously participated in either one or both types of programs. Approximately half (48%) indicated that they had received drug treatment or other types of addiction-related services while under correctional supervision, and 32% indicated that they were participating in drug treatment or other types of services while currently incarcerated (Mumola, 1999).

Participation in drug-related interventions of any kind was higher among prison inmates who reported that they were under the influence of drugs or alcohol at the time of their most recent arrest as well as those who had 6 months or less to serve on their current prison sentence. Prison inmates with the highest percentages of participation in current drug treatment or other drug-related programs reported being under the influence of drugs or alcohol at the time they committed the offense for which they were imprisoned. Within this group, 18% were receiving treatment, 32% were receiving other drug-related services, and 39% were receiving either one or both services (Mumola, 1999).

From 1991 to 1999, the percentage of inmates who participated in prison-based treatment during their present incarceration declined significantly, from 24 to only 10%. Among state prisoners who reported regular drug use prior to incarceration, 34% indicated that they were currently participating in prison-based drug treatment in 1991; in 1997, that percentage dropped to 14%. However, from 1991 to 1997, the percentage of inmates who reported being presently involved in other types of drug programs increased slightly from 15 to 20% among all inmates and from 22 to 26% among inmates who regularly used drugs before their incarceration (Mumola, 1999). Furthermore, according to research, the effects of in-prison treatment greatly diminish when institutionally based services are not accompanied by post-release services. Thus, expanding offender treatment to include post-release services is critical for maintaining treatment benefits and increasing public safety (Sacks, 2004).

## Noneffective Treatment

Historically, treatment programs for people with SPDs or SUDs have each been administered through separate systems that rely on different selection criteria for clients and adhere to different training, education, and certification requirements for service providers. Within this framework, PCDs participate in sequential treatment during which they are expected to be free of their SPDs or SUDs before receiving treatment for one type of disorder or the other. Another option for PCDs is to receive parallel treatment, which involves participating in both treatments simultaneously, but with different practitioners who work in different agencies or clinics (Hills, 2000; Mueser et al., 2003).

Sequential and parallel treatments have produced fragmented and ineffective care for PCDs as such treatments force PCDs to navigate the mental health and substance abuse treatment systems separately while struggling with disparate messages from each about treatment goals and pathways to recovery. For example, many drug treatment programs prohibit PCDs from taking psychiatric medications, the mainstay of care for people with SPDs (Mueser et al., 1998). In addition, sequential programs in prison usually provide the bulk of treatment for either an SPD or SUD during incarceration, but address co-occurring disorders only in the time period immediately before release. Such programs have no empirical support and fail to meet the complicated needs of offenders with comorbidity (Chandler, Peters, Field, & Juliano-Bult, 2004).

## Promising Gender-Sensitive Approaches

The number of women involved in the criminal justice system has grown steadily in the past 20 years. However, treatment programs for offenders with co-occurring disorders have largely ignored women. SUDs play a critical role in women's criminality and complicate various aspects of their lives, especially those relating to parenting and family care. In one study of women in the criminal justice system, 86% had one or more SUDs (Sacks, 2004). Women with mental health problems are at a substantial risk for a co-occurring disorder. In addition, incarcerated women are more likely than incarcerated men to have an SPD and more severe psychiatric symptoms (Sacks, 2004).

In light of this situation, criminal justice agencies have started to attend to the special needs of women offenders (Sacks, 2004). However, very few treatment programs in prisons or the community effectively address the needs of women offenders with SUDs and SPDs and their co-occurrence. Gender-specific and responsive treatments are critical to the success of treating women offenders. In order to be effective and comprehensive, such treatments must focus on women's histories of physical, emotional, and sexual abuse; parenting issues; and reconciliation with their children and families (Sacks, 2004).

## Evidence-Based Approaches

Integrated treatments are the most effective, evidence-based interventions for PCDs. They are delivered by professionals who consider both SPDs and SUDs to be "primary" conditions, recognize the reciprocity between the symptoms of SPDs and SUDs, provide simultaneous care for co-occurring disorders, and adhere to consistent philosophies and treatment plans (Chandler et al., 2004; El-Mallakh, 1988; Mueser et al., 1997). The essential ingredients of integrated treatments for PCDs include assertive outreach procedures; case management models; comprehensive services; shared decision making among staff, clients, and clients' families; progressive stages that engage clients in treatment and help them avoid relapses; long-term commitment to services; cross-training for program staff; and the use of self-help groups and medications (Edens, Peters, & Hills, 1997; Hills, 2000; Mueser et al., 2003).

Integrated treatments for PCDs are more effective than sequential or parallel treatments. Studies show that PCDs in integrated treatment have remission rates from substance use that are two to four times higher than those of PCDs in nonintegrated treatment programs. Other benefits of integrated treatment for PCDs include longer retention in treatment, lower rates of victimization, and shorter hospital stays (Substance Abuse and Mental Health Services Administration, 2002).

A review of more than 30 studies of integrated treatment programs for PCDs found that "integrated treatment, especially when delivered for 18 months or longer, resulted in significant reductions of substance abuse and, in some cases, in substantial rates of remission, as well as in reductions in hospital use and/or improvements in other outcomes" (Drake, Mercer-McFadden, Mueser, McHugo, & Bond, 1998, p. 214). The most effective treatments for PCDs are tailored to match a consumer's stage of treatment (or motivation to change); address antisocial issues related to SPDs and SUDs; communicate information to consumers about the relationships between the symptoms of SPDs and SUDs (e.g., psychosis increases the brain's sensitivity to the effects of substances); enhance incentives for sobriety by linking them to the achievement of consumers' goals; use cognitive behavioral, relapse prevention, and skill-based techniques; draw on peer and family supports; assess the underlying psychological and social reasons for substance use; and teach PCDs alternative, safer strategies – other than substance use – for meeting their psychological needs (Chandler et al., 2004; Mueser, 2005).

The treatment dropout rates of PCDs are very high due to their low motivation, cognitive impairment, and disorganized lives. Therefore, clinicians in integrated programs concentrate their interventions in the community, bringing comprehensive services to clients rather than expecting clients to come to services. Comprehensive services encompass all areas of clients' lives and aim to improve their potential for jobs, stable housing, and independent living (Mueser et al., 2003). Treatment plans are more readily accepted and adhered to when PCDs and their families have a role in developing and modifying such plans. Moreover, a systematic or stage-wise approach to treatment emphasizes the notion that clients must be engaged in services, motivated to change, helped to achieve abstinence, and taught to prevent psychiatric and substance use relapses. Medications for SPDs and SUDs are instrumental in reducing and managing symptoms. If left untreated or treated with nonintegrated approaches, co-occurring SPDs and SUDs usually become more severe and chronic. PCDs require considerable time to recover; hence, integrated programs take a long-term view of success with such clients (Mueser et al., 2003).

## Evidence-Based Therapies for PCDs

Several effective therapies for PCDs have been identified (National Institute on Drug Abuse, 2008). For example, multisystemic therapy focuses on the attitudes and perceptions that lead to antisocial behavior and addiction among adolescents. Similarly, brief strategic family therapy incorporates techniques targeting the interactions among family members that exacerbate psychiatric and substance use problems as well as conduct disorders and risky sexual behaviors among troubled teenagers. Cognitive behavioral therapy is effective in confronting the irrational thoughts and self-defeating beliefs that can precipitate or worsen the symptoms of mental illness, drug use problems, and their co-occurrence.

Therapeutic communities (TC) have been a cornerstone of drug treatment for people in jail and prison. Although TC models vary in their implementation, most share a number of common principles and techniques, such as viewing the community as the therapeutic agent and demanding that participants adhere to a rigorous schedule of restorative activities and confrontative exercises. Beyond institutional settings, assertive community treatment (ACT) programs consist of teams that reach out to PCDs wherever (on the streets) and whenever (teams work 24/7) appropriate in order to serve their immediate treatment and habitation needs, which are quite formidable (National Institute on Drug Abuse, 2008).

Other interventions are designed to treat the symptoms of particular types of comorbidities. For example, dialectical behavior therapy is for people with addiction and borderline personality disorder, who are highly prone to suicidal gestures and other self-injurious behaviors. Exposure therapy, which helps individuals overcome traumatic experiences in controlled therapeutic settings, appears to be effective in the treatment of post-traumatic stress disorder and cocaine abuse and dependence. Finally, integrated group therapy has been suggested as an effective intervention for people with bipolar disorder and addiction (National Institute on Drug Abuse, 2008).

## Promising Prison-Based Treatment for Co-occurring Disorders

In many correctional settings, co-occurring disorders go undetected because few screening and assessment procedures are explicitly designed to identify both psychiatric and substance use disorders. Diagnosis is further complicated by the complex interactions among the symptoms of concurrent SPDs and SUDs (Edens et al., 1997). The improper or inadequate evaluation of inmates afflicted with comorbidity results in misdiagnosis and, in turn, inappropriate, inadequate, or no treatment, thereby producing even greater challenges in the institutional management of inmates with co-occurring conditions, who already have high rates of social, cognitive, and functional impairment (Edens et al., 1997).

A study of treatment programs for inmates with co-occurring disorders found that the most common psychiatric diagnoses were major depression, bipolar disorder, anxiety, and post-traumatic stress disorder (Peters, LeVasseu, & Chandler, 2004). A significant proportion was also diagnosed with schizophrenia. In addition, the study found that 38% of the general prison population included in the study had a co-occurring disorder, 36% had an SPD only, and 73% had an SUD only. The prevalence of SPDs found in these institutions was generally higher than those in other institutions because many of the treatment programs were housed in specialized prisons, where inmates are more likely to receive treatment services (Peters et al., 2004). Within these specialized prisons, 24% of the inmates were receiving substance abuse treatment, 15% were receiving mental health interventions, and 33% were receiving psychiatric medications – all likely higher percentages than those inmates receiving such services in other prisons (Peters et al., 2004).

Nonetheless, the demand for treatment in these institutions greatly exceeded the availability of services. Nearly every program for offenders with comorbidity had a waiting list for treatment. Similarly, all mandatory treatment programs had waiting lists, and many inmates had so little time left in their sentences that they were ineligible for the program (Peters et al., 2004). Negative stereotypes about mental illness, held by both inmates and staff, can also hinder the creation and implementation of such programs. Prisoners have several incentives to participate in treatment programs for co-occurring disorders, including the possibility of early release, desirable work assignments, safer housing, and other special privileges. Yet participants reported having less free time because of the requirements of treatment programs and were concerned about the stigmatization associated with program participation. Many inmates who participate in these programs are harassed by other inmates and misunderstood by correctional staff. Despite the negative repercussions of participating in such treatment programs, many inmates desire entry into these settings (Peters et al., 2004).

Prison programs for treating offenders with co-occurring disorders have implemented several modifications to improve their services (Edens et al., 1997; Peters et al., 2004), including the development of regimented schedules and routines for structuring the time spent in the program; stage-wise treatment interventions that focus on motivation and engagement issues; and collaboration and coordination among prison-based health services, such as psychiatry, psychology, and substance abuse treatment. Other adaptations of prison programs for inmates with comorbidity involve the cross-training of treatment staff, program administrations, case managers, and security staff as well as regular updates of treatment and case management plans that reflect progress in treatment and changing life circumstances. Another critical component has been the addition of outreach and case management staff, who provide prerelease and transition planning as well as track and assist program participants as they return to the community, and the implementation of system-wide coordination among mental health, correctional, and drug treatment agencies in order to ensure that case management and follow-up treatment services are in place to facilitate the reentry of inmates with comorbid disorders into the community (Chandler et al., 2004). Clinical modifications to treatment programs for inmates with co-occurring disorders have included the following (Edens et al., 1997; Peters et al., 2004):

- nonconfrontational and supportive activities for clients
- modules that contain information about medication and symptom management
- 12-step programs that focus on comorbidity
- interventions that challenge criminal thinking errors and patterns
- a combination of individual counseling and group role-playing sessions
- the use of peer mentors and support groups
- flexible, measured, and graduated responses to relapses and rule-breaking

- techniques that address memory and other cognitive impairments
- approaches that develop life-management and problem-solving skills
- a focus on symptom management rather than cures
- educational efforts to destigmatize mental illness and addiction.

The provision of treatment while in prison and subsequent followup care in the community is vital for inmates with co-occurring disorders, who are less likely to recidivate if they experience continuity of care. Recidivism is significantly lower for inmates who receive drug-related services after release (Messina et al., 2004). Decreased recidivism is attributable to the recovery skills learned in treatment as well as the assistance that they receive in their efforts to transition back into the community (Peters et al., 2004).

Although the tremendous need for programs treating inmates with co-occurring disorders has been well established, several barriers impede the development of such programs. Many prison systems simply lack the funding necessary to offer this kind of treatment. Another reason that inmates with co-occurring disorders receive inadequate treatment is the fundamental difference between the goals of the criminal justice and treatment systems. The purpose of the criminal justice system is largely to protect the public and punish the offender (Chandler et al., 2004). Treatment participation enhances public safety by reducing recidivism (Messina et al., 2004), but few prison staffs are aware of this benefit (Chandler et al., 2004). In addition, treatment requires the use of positive reinforcement, which is antithetical to the goal of punishment. Finally, whereas prison-based treatment for SPDs is often legally mandated, treatment for SUDs is not and is typically the first program to be cut under fiscal restraints (Chandler et al., 2004).

## Conclusions

PCDs are common in the mental health and substance abuse treatment systems as well as in the criminal justice system. They present significant challenges to treatment providers and place a tremendous drain on treatment resources. They also suffer from a wide range of public health problems and are unlikely to recover without long-term care. Co-occurring disorders generally go unnoticed in prison settings – a situation that increases the rate of recidivism among released prisoners and threatens community safety (Peters & Petrila, 2004). Offenders with comorbid SPDs and SUDs are more likely to recidivate, engage in violent behaviors, and have infectious diseases. Integrated programs have the best chance of helping such offenders achieve more satisfying and productive lives.

As the nation's correctional populations continue to grow, adequate and well-designed treatment programs will continue to be needed – and more urgently than ever – to address co-occurring disorders. Despite high rates of comorbidity among offender populations, drug treatment programs in criminal justice settings, like community-based programs in general, have concentrated on drug treatment and have failed to adequately address comorbidity (Edens et al., 1997). For an exception, see Sacks et al. (1997). Unfortunately, not enough programs for PCDs are available to meet the demand for such care. In general, existing programs are often underfunded, poorly operated, or inaccessible (Chandler et al., 2004). The provision of treatment and transitional services to inmates with comorbid disorders is also complicated and challenging due to the need for integrated services, which requires the coordination of treatment, security, and community supervision staff. Furthermore, followup and transitional programs that focus on integrated services are generally lacking in the community (Travis, Solomon, & Waul, 2001). Other obstacles to delivering and coordinating aftercare services for inmates with comorbid disorders include the paucity of resources for inmates returning to rural areas, the unwillingness of community agencies to provide services to people with criminal histories, the absence of medication and other psychiatric services in substance abuse treatment settings, the lack of mental health training among community supervision officers, and the resistance of formerly incarcerated people to continue their participation in treatment programs after release (Edens et al., 1997).

The presence of comorbid disorders are the expectation, not the exception, in the general and correctional population. PCDs are more difficult to treat and have a variety of sequelae that compound their recovery and complicate their responsiveness to interventions, when compared to people with an SPD or an SUD alone. Despite these impediments, research has demonstrated the effectiveness of numerous evidence-based practices, such as integrated programming, that can help control the symptoms of comorbidity and assist PCDs in leading satisfying lives while minimizing the likelihood of recidivism and relapse. The benefits of providing institutional treatment and contiguous care in the community greatly exceed the costs of such services and afford offenders with comorbid disorders a real chance to live productive and symptom-free lives.

## References

Abram, K. M., & Teplin, L. A. (1991). Co-occurring disorders among mentally ill detainees. *American Psychologist, 46*, 1036–1045.

American Psychiatric Association. (2004). *Diagnostic and statistical manual IV-TR*. Washington, DC: Author.

Barthwell, A. G., Bokos, J., Bailey, M., Nisenbaum, J., Devereux, J., & Senay, E. C. (1995). A continuum of care for substance abusers in the criminal justice system. *Journal of Psychoactive Drugs, 27*, 39–47.

Bureau of Justice Statistics. (1997). *Correctional populations in the United States, 1997*. Washington, DC: Author.

Bureau of Justice Statistics. (2002). *Drug law violations*. Washington, DC: United States Department of Justice.

Chandler, R., Peters, R., Field, G., & Juliano-Bult, D. (2004). Challenges in implementing evidence-based treatment practices for co-occurring disorders in the criminal justice system. *Behavioral Sciences and the Law, 22*, 431–448.

Chiles, J. A., Von Cleve, E., Jemelka, R. P., & Trupin, E. W. (1990). Substance abuse and psychiatric disorders in prison inmates. *Hospital and Community Psychiatry, 41*, 1132–1134.

Cournos, F., & McKinnon, K. (1997). HIV seroprevalence among people with severe mental illness in the United States: A critical review. *Clinical Psychology Review, 17*, 259–269.

Drake, R. E., Mercer-McFadden, C., Mueser, K. T., McHugo, G. J., & Bond, G. R. (1998). A review of integrated mental health and substance abuse treatment for patients with dual disorders. *Schizophrenia Bulletin, 24*, 589–608.

Drake, R. E., & Wallach, M. A. (1993). Moderate drinking among people with severe mental illness. *Hospital and Community Psychiatry, 44*, 780–782.

Early, K. E. (1998). *Correctional treatment: An effective model for Change*. Paper presented at the Office of the National Drug Control Policy's Conference of Scholars and Policy Makers, Washington, DC.

Edens, J. J., Peters, R. H., & Hills, H. A. (1997). Treating prison inmates with co-occurring disorders: An integrative approach of existing programs. *Behavioral Science and Law, 15*, 439–457.

El-Mallakh, P. (1998). Treatment models for clients with co-occurring addictive and mental disorders. *Archives of Psychiatric Nursing, 12*, 71–80.

Goodwin, F. W., & Jamison, K. R. (1990). *Manic-depressive illness*. New York: Oxford University Press.

Harlow, C. W. (1999). *Prior abuse reported by inmates and probationers*. Washington, DC: United States Department of Justice.

Harris, A., & Lurigio, A. J. (2007). The mentally ill as perpetrators of violence: A brief review of research and assessment strategies. *Aggression and Violent Behavior, 12*, 542–551.

Hills, H. A. (2000). *Creating effective treatment programs for persons with co-occurring disorders in the justice system*. Delmar, NY: The GAINS Center.

Hoffman, J., & Froemke, S. (2007). *Addiction: New knowledge, new treatments, new hope*. New York: Rodale.

Karberg, J. C., & James, D. J. (2005). *Substance dependence, abuse, and treatment of jail inmates, 2002*. Washington, DC: United States Department of Justice.

Kessler, R. C., Crum, R. M., Warner, L. A., Nelson, C. B., Schulenberg, J., & Anthony, J. C. (1997). Lifetime co-occurrence of DSM-III-R alcohol abuse and dependence with other psychiatric disorders in the National Comorbidity Survey. *Archives of General Psychiatry, 54*, 313–321.

Kessler, R. C., McGonagle, K. A., Zhao, S., Nelson, C. B., Hughes, M., Eshleman, S., et al. (1994). Lifetime and 12-month prevalence of DSM-III-R psychiatric disorders among persons aged 15–54 in the United States: Results from the National Comorbidity Survey. *Archives of General Psychiatry, 53*, 8–19.

Lurigio, A. J. (2004). The mentally ill offender initiative. *Executive Exchange, 20*, 2–9.

Lurigio, A. J., Cho, Y. I., Swartz, J. A., Graf, I., Johnson, T. P., & Pickup, L. (2003). Standardized assessment of substance-related, other psychiatric, and comorbid disorders among probationers. *International Journal of*

*Offender Therapy and Comparative Criminology, 47*, 630–652.
Lurigio, A. J., & Swartz, J. A. (2000). Criminal justice 2000: Changing the contours of the criminal justice system to meet the needs of persons with serious mental illness. In J. Horney, J. Martin, D. L. MacKenzie, R. Peterson, & D. P. Rosenbaum (Eds.), *Polices, processes, and decisions of the criminal justice system* (pp. 45–108). Washington, DC: National Institute of Justice.
Messina, N., Burdon, W., Hagopian, G., & Prendergast, M. (2004). One year returns to custody rates among co-disordered offenders. *Behavioral Sciences and the Law, 22*, 503–518.
Mueser, K. T. (2005). *Advances in the treatment and understanding of co-occurring disorders*. Hanover, NH: Dartmouth Medical School, NH-Dartmouth Psychiatric Research Center.
Mueser, K. T., Drake, R. E., & Miles, K. M. (1997). The course and treatment of substance use disorders in persons with severe mental illness. In L. S. Onken, J. D. Blaine, S. Genser, & A. M. Horton (Eds.), *Treatment of drug-dependent individuals with comorbid mental disorders* (pp. 236–251). Washington, DC: U.S. Department of Health and Human Services.
Mueser, K. T., Drake, R. E., & Noordsy, D. L. (1998). Integrated mental health and substance abuse treatment for severe psychiatric disorders. *Journal of Practical Psychiatry and Behavioral Health, 8*, 129–139.
Mueser, K. T., Drake, R. E., & Wallach, M. A. (1998). Dual diagnosis: A review of etiological theories. *Addictive Behaviors, 23*, 717–734.
Mueser, K. T., Noordsy, D. L., Drake, R. E., & Fox, L. (2003). *Integrated treatment for dual disorders: A guide to effective practice*. New York: Guildford Press.
Mumola, C. J. (1999). *Substance dependence, abuse, and treatment of state and federal prison inmates, 1997*. Washington, DC: United States Department of Justice.
Mumola, C. J., & Bonczar, T. P. (1998). *Substance abuse and treatment of adults on probation, 1995*. Washington, DC: U.S. Department of Justice, Office of Justice Programs, Bureau of Justice Statistics.
Mumola, C. J., & Karberg, J. C. (2006). *Drug use and dependence, state and federal prisoners, 2004*. Washington, DC: United States Department of Justice.
National Institute on Drug Abuse. (2008). *Comorbidity: Addiction and other mental illnesses*. Washington, DC: Author.
Office of National Drug Control Policy. (2004). *National drug control strategy: Update*. Washington, DC: White House.
Osher, F. C., & Drake, R. E. (1996). Reversing a history of unmet needs: Approaches to care for persons with co-occurring addictive and mental disorders. *American Journal of Orthopsychiatry, 66*, 4–11.
Peters, R. (1993). Drug treatment in jails and detention settings. In J. A. Inciardi (Ed.), *Drug treatment and criminal justice* (pp. 44–80). Beverly Hills, CA: Sage.
Peters, R., LeVasseu, M., & Chandler, R. (2004). Correctional treatment for co-occurring disorders: Results of a national survey. *Behavioral Sciences and the Law, 22*, 563–584.
Peters, R. H., May, R. L., & Kearns, W. D. (1992). Drug treatment in jail: Results of a nationwide survey. *Journal of Criminal Justice, 20*, 283–297.
Peters, R., & Petrila, J. (2004). Introduction to this issue: Co-occurring disorders in the criminal justice system. *Behavioral Sciences and the Law, 22*, 427–429.
Regier, D. A., Farmer, M. E., Rae, D. S., Locke, B. Z., Locke, S. J., Keith, S. J., et al. (1990). Comorbidity of mental disorders with alcohol and other drug abuse: Results from the Epidemiological Catchment Area (ECA) study. *Journal of the American Medical Association, 264*, 2511–2518.
Ries, R. K., & Comtois, K. A. (1997). Illness severity and treatment services for dually diagnosed severely mentally ill outpatients. *Schizophrenia Bulletin, 23*, 239–246.
Sacks, J. (2004). Women with co-occurring substance use and mental disorders (COD) in the criminal justice system: A research review. *Behavioral Sciences and the Law, 22*, 449–466.
Sacks, S., Sacks, J., DeLeon, G., Bernhardt, A. I., & Graham, G. L. (1997). Modified therapeutic community for mentally ill chemical abusers: Background, influences, program description and preliminary findings. *Journal of Substance Use and Misuse, 32*, 1217–1259.
Substance Abuse and Mental Health Services Administration. (2002). *Report to Congress on the prevention and treatment of co-occurring substance abuse disorders and mental disorders*. Rockville, MD: U.S. Department of Health and Human Services.
Swartz, J. A., & Lurigio, A. J. (1999). Psychiatric illness and comorbidity among adult male detainees in drug treatment. *Psychiatric Services, 50*, 1628–1630.
Tonry, M. (1999). Why are incarceration rates so high? *Overcrowded Times, 10*, 3–6.
Travis, J., Solomon, A. L., & Waul, M. (2001). *From prison to home: The dimensions and consequences of prisoner reentry*. Washington, DC: Urban Institute, Justice Policy Center.
Tunis, S. L. (1995). *Outcome evaluation of jail-based drug treatment: Effects of recidivism*. San Francisco: National Council on Crime and Delinquency.
Wexler, H. K. (1995). The success of therapeutic communities for substance abusers in American prisons. *Journal of Psychoactive Drugs, 27*, 57–66.
Wexler, H. K., Williams, R., Early, K. E., & Trotman, C. (1996). Prison treatment substance abusers: Stay'n out revisited. In K. E. Early (Ed.), *Drug treatment behind bars: Prison-based strategies for change* (pp. 17–34). New York: Praeger.
Woody, G. E., Metzger, D., Navaline, H., McLellan, T., & O'Brien, C. P. (1997). Psychiatric symptoms, risky behavior, and HIV infection. In L. S. Onken, J. D.

Blaine, S. Genser, & A. M. Horton (Eds.), *Treatment of drug-dependent individuals with comorbid mental disorders* (pp. 117–131). Washington, DC: United States Department of Health and Human Services.
World Health Organization. (2004). *Neuroscience of psychoactive substance use and dependence*. Geneva, Switzerland: Author.
Zhang, Z. (2005). *Drug and alcohol use and related matters among arrestees 2003*. Washington, DC: National Institute of Justice.

# Drug Abuse HIV/AIDS Interventions in Criminal Justice Settings

17

Carrie B. Oser, Kathi L. Harland Harp, and Michele Staton-Tindall

**Abstract**

The U.S. prison population is disproportionately affected by HIV/AIDS as compared to the general population. The high prevalence of HIV/AIDS among incarcerated individuals can be attributed to several risk factors both in their environments prior to incarceration and also within the prison environment. In particular, the large number of inmates with drug use and risky sexual behavior histories place this population at risk. This chapter provides an overview of the most effective HIV interventions that work in criminal justice setting to date and their theoretical underpinnings. Promising interventions for criminal justice populations and recommendations for improving them are also discussed. While many HIV interventions have demonstrated significant promise in reducing risk behaviors, the majority of correctional facilities in the U.S. have yet to implement such interventions.

**Keywords**

HIV Interventions • Theory • Prison • Probation

## Drug Abuse and HIV in Criminal Justice Settings

### Introduction

The World Health Organization reports that as of yearend 2007, 33 million people worldwide were living with HIV/AIDS (WHO, 2007a), with an estimated 1.2 million cases in the United States alone (WHO, 2008). Rates of HIV/AIDS vary by gender, region of the country, race, age, and many other factors; however, the HIV incidence rates among state prisoners is 3 times greater and the AIDS incidence rate is 10 times greater, than that of the general US population (Hammett, Maruschak, & Harmon, 1999; Maruschak, 2006). At yearend 2006, 1.7% of state and federal inmates were confirmed to have HIV or AIDS (Maruschak, 2008). Males account for 90.3% of these cases and females represent the remaining 9.7%. While a larger number of male than female

C.B. Oser (✉)
Department of Sociology, Center on Drug and Alcohol Research, University of Kentucky, Lexington, KY 40506, USA
e-mail: cboser0@uky.edu

C. Leukefeld et al. (eds.), *Handbook of Evidence-Based Substance Abuse Treatment in Criminal Justice Settings*, Issues in Children's and Families' Lives 11,
DOI 10.1007/978-1-4419-9470-7_17, © Springer Science+Business Media, LLC 2011

inmates have HIV/AIDS, the prevalence of HIV is greater for female inmates (2.4%) than for male inmates (1.6%) (Maruschak, 2008).

The high prevalence of HIV/AIDS among incarcerated individuals can be attributed to several risk factors both in their environments prior to incarceration and also within the prison environment. In particular, the large number of inmates with drug use and risky sexual behavior histories place this population at risk. The Centers for Disease Control and Prevention (CDC) report that risk for infection is increased among individuals who inject drugs, during which equipment and blood were shared with others; have unprotected vaginal, anal, or oral sex with men who have sex with men, multiple partners, or anonymous partners; exchange sex for drugs or money; have been diagnosed with hepatitis, tuberculosis, or a sexually transmitted disease; have unprotected sex with someone with any of the above listed risk factors (CDC, 2008a).

Concerning the leading causes of HIV transmission, 13% of all diagnosed HIV/AIDS cases in the United States in 2006 were attributed to injection drug use, 50% to male-to-male (MSM) sexual contact, and 33% to high-risk heterosexual contact (CDC, 2008b). When considering gender, the majority of HIV/AIDS cases diagnosed in males in 2006 were attributed to MSM contact (67%) while the majority of cases in women were attributed to high-risk heterosexual contact (80%) (CDC, 2008b). Of the incarcerated individuals with confirmed cases of HIV/AIDS, 5.1% reported having shared a needle (Maruschak, 2006). High-risk heterosexual contact, MSM contact, and injection drug use are consequently reported at much higher rates among incarcerated populations than the general United States and these risky behaviors are likely to account for their higher rate of HIV and AIDS.

The high prevalence of HIV/AIDS found in the incarcerated population is in part attributable to the disproportionately high percentage of African-Americans who are currently incarcerated, given that rates of HIV/AIDS are highest among African-Americans than any other ethnicity. While African-Americans comprise 13% of the total US population, they account for 40% of state and federal prisoners (West & Sabol, 2009), and 49% of diagnosed HIV/AIDS cases (CDC, 2008c).

While the prison environment is generally accepted to be free of most HIV-related risk behaviors, reports of in-prison sex, injection drug use, and tattooing are cause for concern (Zack, 2007). Given that condoms, bleach, and clean needles are not allowed (let alone provided) in most US prisons (Hammett et al., 1999), despite WHO recommendations, other interventions are needed to reduce inmates' risk of contracting and/or transmitting HIV. Inmates are at risk for HIV infection while incarcerated, but also post-release if they continue to engage in high-risk behaviors. This poses a danger not only to inmates post-release, but also others within the community with whom they might come into contact (Dean-Gaitor & Fleming, 1999; Grinstead, Zack, & Faigeles, 1999). Numerous researchers have noted the urgent need for effective prison-based HIV interventions targeting risk reduction (Braithwaite, Hammett, & Arriola, 2002; Bryan, Robbins, Ruiz, & O'Neill, 2006; Oser, Staton-Tindall, & Leukefeld, 2007). The World Health Organization has also advocated for the provision of HIV interventions in criminal justice settings (WHO, 2007b).

In the past 15 years, researchers have designed and implemented several HIV interventions in criminal justice settings across the United States with varying delivery formats and success. This chapter provides an overview of the most effective HIV interventions to date and their theoretical underpinnings, as well as a description of promising interventions and recommendations for improving them. While many HIV interventions have demonstrated significant promise in reducing risk behaviors, the majority of correctional facilities in the United States have yet to implement such interventions.

## Underlying Theories

Current HIV interventions are based on theoretical models derived from various disciplines including public health, psychology, and sociology. Only in the past decade researchers have come to agree that providing individuals with information about transmission and proper condom use, while important, is not sufficient for eliciting behavior change. Since this realization, a number of theories have grounded HIV interventions in criminal justice settings. Many of these theories emphasize the consideration of gender, ethnic, and cultural differences in designing effective interventions, instead of providing all individuals with a standardized format. Also central to many of these theories is the goal of empowering individuals to make important health-related behavior changes by increasing their self-efficacy. In addition, the context in which the HIV intervention is delivered should be considered. The primary and secondary goals of the criminal justice system are to ensure public safety and to provide rehabilitation opportunities for offenders, and while important, HIV interventions may be lower on the priority list. Thus, it is ideal for HIV interventions to be brief and cost effective because of the context in which they are delivered (e.g., prisons or jails). The following sections present brief descriptions of the underlying theories guiding interventions found to be most effective and promising for reducing the risk for HIV.

## Social Cognitive Theory

Bandura's social cognitive theory (1994) posits that information alone does not lead to behavior change. He writes, "To achieve self-directed change, people need to be given not only reasons to alter risky habits but also the behavioral means, resources, and social supports to do so" (1994, p. 25). In addition, a person's self-efficacy is seen as important to their ability to make concerted efforts toward behavioral change. Bandura defines self-efficacy as "the conviction that one can successfully execute the behavior required to produce the outcomes" (1977, p. 79). Social cognitive theory predicts that an individual low in self-efficacy can be more easily persuaded into risky behavior while someone high in self-efficacy and armed with adequate information is more likely to resist engaging in potentially harmful behaviors. According to Bandura, there are four components necessary for any intervention aimed at changing behavior and reducing risk: (1) the provision of information about health risks, (2) the development of "social and self-regulative" skills needed to make self-efficacious decisions that avert risks, (3) enhancing skills and self-efficacy by allowing individuals to practise skills and provide them with constructive feedback, and (4) providing the necessary social support for sustaining behavior changes (Bandura, 1994, p. 30). Interventions that implement components of social cognitive theory usually involve hands-on activities such as role playing and open discussions where positive feedback is given with the overall goal of increasing self-efficacy to promote behavior change.

## Harm Reduction

Harm reduction is a pragmatic public health approach to risky and harmful behaviors with success viewed more broadly than in abstinence. Whereas some models see success as the immediate cessation of any risky behavior (i.e. substance use, unprotected sex), the harm reduction approach focuses on alleviating some of the negative consequences associated with harmful behaviors when abstinence seems impractical (Marlatt, 1998). HIV harm reduction approaches focus on teaching participants how to properly clean injection equipment if stopping drug injection is not possible. Knowing that abstinence from sex and drugs is not a realistic goal, particularly for those in criminal justice settings who have few treatment options available and who may rely on sex work for income, a harm-reduction-based HIV intervention provides approaches to reduce the amount of potential harm from engaging in these behaviors. Consequently, emphasis is placed on using condoms, avoiding sharing needles with others, and cleaning needles that have been shared.

## Prevention Case Management

Prevention case management (PCM) has been defined by the CDC as "intensive, individualized support and prevention counseling to assist persons to remain seronegative or to reduce the risk for HIV transmission to others by those who are seropositive" (CDC, 1995, p. 32). PCM combines case management to address important needs faced by offenders (Rothman, 1992, 1998) with a prevention education component as well as risk reduction counseling (Purcell, DeGroff, & Wolitski, 1998). In 1992, the CDC funded a cooperative agreement with community-based organizations to examine PCM on the premise that addressing pressing needs (e.g., housing, food, and employment) may take precedence over protecting oneself from HIV (Falck, Carlson, Price, & Turner, 1994). Given the costly nature of providing one-on-one counseling, PCM is generally targeted at individuals who are likely to have a difficult time initiating or maintaining behavioral changes to reduce their HIV risk (CDC, 1997). As part of the CDC PCM guidelines, specific services must be provided by prevention case managers including an HIV risk, psychosocial, and medical assessment, the development and implementation of an individualized case plan with the active client involved, follow-up sessions to evaluate the plan, ongoing counseling to reduce HIV risk, and agency advocacy referrals (CDC, 1995).

## Motivational Interviewing

Motivational interviewing (MI) is a technique to evoke motivation for change from ambivalent clients by helping them to self-identify the discrepancy between their goals and the continuation of their current harmful behavior (Miller & Rollnick, 2002). Rather than using a confrontational approach or pressuring clients into changing, a skilled motivational interviewer helps a client uncover his or her own internal motivation for change. MI is a focused, goal-oriented technique in which the client, not the counselor, is charged with articulating and resolving his/her ambivalence about behavioral change. Only individuals who have been trained using Miller and Rollnick's (2002) motivational interviewing manual should be delivering HIV interventions with MI theoretical underpinnings. HIV interventions that incorporate motivational interviewing engage clients one-on-one and provide the support clients need to come to the decision that they want to take active steps to reduce their HIV risk by reducing their risky sex and drug-using behavior.

## Health Belief Model

The health belief model (HBM) is value-expectancy theory which proposes that an individual's actions are determined by his/her perceived vulnerability to contracting an illness (value), how severe the effects of that illness are perceived, and the perception of the benefits and obstacles to changing his/her behavior (expectation) (Rosenstock, Strecher, & Becker, 1994). There are four central components to the health belief model: (1) an individual's *perceived susceptibility* of contracting an illness or disease; (2) the *perceived severity* or threat of the illness; (3) the *perceived benefit* or belief that taking a given health action will be effective in reducing the disease threat; and (4) the *perceived barriers* or negative effects of taking an action to reduce one's risk (Janz & Becker, 1984; Rosenstock, 1974, 1990). The model proposes that individuals "go through" a cost-benefit analysis to determine if the potential effectiveness of taking a health action outweighs the barriers to or negative aspects of that action. This model was supplemented in 1990 to incorporate the importance of an individual's self-efficacy in their motivation for behavioral change (Rosenstock, 1990). HIV interventions based on the HBM emphasize the high risk of contracting the disease due to risky drug and sex behaviors and empower participants to make behavioral changes by increasing their sense of self-efficacy through skills training and supportive discussions.

## Gender and Culture-Based Theories of Empowerment and Cultural Competence/Sensitivity

Many theorists now acknowledge the importance of tailoring HIV interventions for participants. Gender-based theories focus on experiences unique to each gender. For instance, interventions based on Connell's theory of gender and power (1987) focus on the inequalities between men and women in society and in personal relationships that reduce women's control over their sexual decisions and therefore, personal safety. Interventions that incorporate theories of cultural competence (Martin, O'Connell, Inciardi, Surratt, & Maiden, 2008) or cultural sensitivity (Bryan et al., 2006) pay attention to the different prejudices, barriers, and experiences of individuals in different racial, ethnic, or cultural groups. It is important to note, however, that interventions based on cultural sensitivity may be structured quite differently from a framework of cultural competence. Specifically, interventions which incorporate tenets of cultural sensitivity (for example, Bryan et al., 2006). Generally do not separate participants by race or ethnicity and provide participants with the same broad information. HIV interventions using a cultural competence framework, however (see Martin et al., 2008), are more likely to tailor messages to specific racial/ethnic groups with interventions delivered by the same racial/ethnic group as participants. While the health-related content remains unchanged, the manner in which information is presented differs. Both gender and ethnic- or culture-based theories focus on empowering participants by presenting material in a way that is relevant to their lives and encourage talking through their questions and feelings with other groups.

## Interventions That Work in Criminal Justice Settings

The effectiveness of behavioral HIV interventions to reduce drug and sexual risk behaviors among at-risk populations has made large strides over the past decade; however, the focus on criminal justice populations is limited. An intervention is deemed to "work" if the intervention has demonstrated success in three experimental trials in criminal justice settings. A thorough review of the literature revealed no HIV interventions that "work" using this definition. Therefore, the definition for a Best Evidence HIV Intervention as outlined by the Centers for Disease Control and Prevention (CDC) is used here (Lyles, Crepaz, Herbst, & Kay, 2006; Lyles et al., 2007). Best Evidence HIV Interventions are scientifically rigorous and have provided evidence of efficacy. The efficacy criteria for a Best Evidence HIV Intervention evaluates HIV interventions on the intervention description, study design, quality of the study implementation, quality of the analytic approach, and strength of the evidence.

Specifically, the efficacy criteria for an intervention to be deemed a Best Evidence HIV Intervention includes (1) clear description of the key aspects of the intervention; (2) a concurrent comparison arm; (3) randomization or a minimally biased assignment of participants to study arms; (4) at least a 3-month post-intervention follow-up with participants in both arms; (5) at least a 70% follow-up rate for participants in both arms; (6) analysis must be based on post-intervention levels or pre-post changes in measures that are identical in both arms; (7) analysis must be based on at least an $\alpha = 0.05$ and a two-sided test; (8) in cases where there is non-randomized assignment, there should either be no significant baseline differences in the outcome measures of interest or differences must be controlled for in the analyses; (9) each arm must include at least 50 participants who are involved in the criminal justice system; (10) the intervention effects must include a positive and significant ($p \leq 0.05$) intervention effect for at least one relevant outcome measure; (11) no negative significant ($p \leq 0.05$) intervention effect for any relevant outcome measure (Lyles et al., 2006; Lyles et al., 2007).

After reviewing the most current literature, 12 HIV interventions conducted within criminal justice settings were identified. Based on the efficacy criteria, two HIV interventions were found to be Best Evidence HIV Interventions (Martin et al., 2008; Wolitski, 2006). There were five additional HIV interventions that do not meet all of the efficacy criteria but have shown significant positive effects and thus are discussed in the next section on promising interventions in criminal justice settings (Bryan et al., 2006; El-Bassel et al., 1995; Leukefeld et al., 2009; Martin, O'Connell, Inciardi, Surratt, & Beard, 2003; St. Lawrence et al., 1997). The remaining five did not qualify as either a Best Evidence HIV intervention or as a promising intervention because they did not meet the efficacy criteria in two or more areas (Bauserman, Ward, Eldred, & Swetz, 2001; Grinstead, Zack, & Faigeles, 2001; Rich et al., 2001; Richie, Freudenberg, & Page, 2001; Ross, Harzke, Scott, McCann, & Kelley, 2006).

## Targeted HIV/HCV Brief Intervention in Prisoner Reentry

The HIV/HCV Brief Intervention for Prisoner Reentry was developed as part of the NIDA-supported Criminal Justice Drug Abuse Treatment Studies (CJ-DATS) research cooperative. This "targeted" intervention was created to focus on reducing high-risk behaviors at the crucial time period after being released from prison when individuals face reentry challenges such as obtaining housing, seeking employment, and attending to medical needs (Petersilia, 2003; Travis & Visher, 2005). Thus, the intervention was conducted in the correctional institutions just before community reentry (Inciardi et al., 2007). The main goal was to produce an effective, generalizable, brief intervention (lasting about an hour) that incorporated the core elements of the NIDA Enhanced Standard Intervention into a peer-delivered DVD format. In addition, the targeted intervention was culturally competent and included gender- and race-specific tracks. Data was collected at baseline, 30-day follow-up interview, and 90-day follow-up interview.

A randomized controlled trial design was used which included three arms: (1) Standard Practice – HIV educational video, (2) NIDA Enhanced Standard Intervention (ESI), and (3) DVD Targeted intervention. An "urn" randomization process ensured race and gender balances in each of the study arms. The HIV educational video arm can be treated as the "control" because standard practice in correctional institutions usually involves an educational video (Martin et al., 2008). The NIDA ESI was developed as part of the AIDS Cooperative Agreement (Coyle, 1993) and a revised/augmented version was developed by the "New Cohort" site investigators (Wechsberg et al., 1997). In 2000, the revised NIDA ESI was further enhanced by the University of Delaware and the University of Kentucky (Leukefeld et al., 2003; Martin et al., 2003; Oser, Leukefeld, Cosentino-Boehm, & Havens, 2006). The NIDA ESI provides the most current information about HIV/AIDS, routes of infection, drug use and sexual risk behaviors, use of condoms and safe sex, cleaning needles, the benefits of drug treatment, and the HIV test.

The Targeted Intervention was designed to reduce harm by creating buy-in, making the message personally relevant, and actively engaging the participant. Focus groups with reentering offenders revealed that participants faced specific challenges upon reentry (e.g., meeting old friends who still engaged in drug use and unprotected sex) and that it would be helpful to see individuals on the DVD who are like themselves and who are living with HIV or HCV. Thus, the DVD Targeted intervention was designed to contain five main components including (1) an introduction segment featuring a former addict/offender; (2) a needle cleaning demonstration; (3) testimonials from people living with HIV and HCV; (4) scenarios that demonstrate condom negotiations and being offered drugs; and (5) both positive and negative commentaries that demonstrate what others have done in similar scenarios. The DVD includes real-life individuals who had experienced problems with drugs or been incarcerated. The content was minimally scripted and the individuals used their own language throughout in order to make the scenes believable. The Targeted Intervention was delivered by a peer interventionist (Martin et al., 2008).

Results are presented from preliminary data collected from the 343 participants (follow-up rate of 90% of the total 381 participants) from three states who had completed the 3-month follow-up interview. A multivariate model predicting the percentage of unprotected sex in the past 90 days, while controlling for other factors, was examined. Results indicate that being in the DVD Targeted Intervention group was associated with a statistically significant decrease in unprotected sex, as compared to the Standard Practice group (Martin et al., 2008). The Targeted Intervention has the potential for widespread adoption in correctional settings because it is a brief intervention that uses a DVD-based format. Future research should examine the effect of the DVD Targeted Intervention, as compared to the NIDA ESI and the Standard Practice Intervention, on both drug and high-risk sexual behaviors with the larger sample. In addition, future studies could adapt the DVD Targeted intervention to be delivered in a group setting or via a web-based application to make its use in a correctional setting more economical. Future research should also examine the feasibility of using the DVD format not only in correctional settings like jails and prisons, but also in probation and parole offices for community-supervised offenders.

## Project Start

Project START (Sexually Transmitted Disease and AIDS Risk-Reduction Trial) was a multisite behavioral HIV intervention designed for young male reentering offenders (Wolitski, 2006) to meet needs including housing, employment, reunification, and accessing healthcare (Petersilia, 2003; Travis & Visher, 2005). During the reentry period, these needs may distract individuals from practising safer sex. This transitional risk-reduction HIV intervention focused on reducing HIV, hepatitis, and other sexually transmitted infections as well as addressing community reentry needs. Project START was theoretically grounded in case management (CDC, 1997; Purcell et al., 1998), motivational interviewing (Miller & Rollnick, 2002), and harm reduction (Marlatt, 1998).

A single-session intervention (SSI) was compared to the enhanced intervention (EI). The SSI was a 60–90-minute session conducted before release. This session, led by an interventionist, consisted of a brief HIV-risk assessment and risk-reduction planning to develop a personalized risk reduction plan and provide information, skills training, and referrals (Wolitski, 2006).

The EI included six sessions, two of which occurred before release. The first session in the EI arm had the same content as the SSI. The second session, conducted in prison, included assessment, planning, problem solving, and referrals to address community reentry needs. These competing reentry needs included housing, employment, legal problems, substance abuse treatment, mental healthcare services, and social relationships. This session took about 60–90 minutes. The four community-based post-release sessions were about 30–60 minutes and focused on reviewing and revising the risk-reduction plan that was developed prior to release. In addition, barriers to implementing the risk reduction plan were addressed (Wolitski, 2006).

Between 2001 and 2002, 533 participants were recruited from eight state prisons in four states (California, Mississippi, Rhode Island, and Wisconsin). Eligibility criteria included being male, between the ages of 18 and 29, incarcerated at least 90 days, scheduled for release within the next 14–60 days, and willing to participate. Participants were assigned to the EI or SSI based on either the month of recruitment or month of release. There were no significant baseline differences in the outcome measures of interest. Follow-up interviews were conducted at 1 week, 12 weeks, and 24 weeks post-release. The follow-up rate at 24 weeks was 82.7%.

Intent to treat multivariate analyses included variables for the intervention arm, site, assessment visit, and two-way and three-way interactions while controlling for number of days on the street, and preincarceration levels of the outcome behavior. While there were no significant differences between the two groups at the 12-week follow-up interview, there were statistically significant differences between the SSI group and the EI group at the 24-week follow-up interview. Specifically, participants in the EI group were significantly less likely to report unprotected vaginal or anal sex during their most recent sexual encounter. Also, the men in EI, as compared to those in SSI, were less likely to report any unprotected intercourse (Wolitski, 2006). This intervention effect was specific to sexual practices with main partners; however it did not motivate behavior change with non-main sexual partners. While this finding was not expected, Wolitski (2006) suggests this differential finding could in part be explained by the relatively low rates of unprotected intercourse with non-main sexual partners. Future studies could examine the Project START intervention with other incarcerated populations (such as women or men aged 30 and older). In summary, many findings from Project START suggest that prevention case management approaches which incorporate individually tailored risk-reduction plans are effective in combating competing issues affecting young men's ability to successfully reenter the community.

## Promising Interventions in Criminal Justice Settings

In addition to the above evidence-based HIV interventions, a review of the literature revealed a number of promising HIV criminal justice interventions. These are interventions that meet many of the CDC's criteria for best-evidence qualification. The following section describes five promising interventions.

### Probationer Focused Intervention

The Probationer Focused Intervention (PFI) was developed in the late 1990s (Martin et al., 2003) and is theoretically grounded in the finding that knowledge alone is not a good predictor of behavioral change (DiClemente, Lanier, Horan, & Lodico, 1991). The PFI was designed to assist probationers in developing personalized strategies to protect against primary and secondary HIV transmission. Research indicates that the impact of a persuasive message is determined by whether it is personally relevant (e.g., developed by similar at-risk individuals) (Dees, Dansereau, Peel, & Knight, 1991; Sivacek & Crano, 1982) and whether active, rather than passive, participation occurs (Watts, 1967). Thus, the PFI was designed with input from probationers to target the HIV risk behaviors of probationers (i.e., making the intervention personally relevant) and includes thought mapping techniques (in order to facilitate active participation).

The PFI added a visual technique called Thought Mapping to the NIDA Enhanced Standard Intervention (ESI), an evidenced-based HIV intervention designed for substance users (Gordon, 1989; Wechsberg et al., 1997). Thought Mapping allows probationers to identify problems and possible solutions using a visual map that incorporates their own words. This approach enhances their thought processes and allows for rehearsals related to their own risky HIV problem situations, personalizing HIV risks while overcoming difficulties with literacy, cognition, and learning (Knight, Simpson, & Dansereau, 1994; Pitre, Dansereau, & Joe, 1996). In the PFI, an interventionist helped the participant focus personal issues using thought maps on drug use and risky sexual behaviors. The ESI was the comparison group (Martin et al., 2003).

Specifically, the PFI included a session at the baseline and a session at 3 months. Data was collected at the baseline, 3-month follow-up interview, and 6-month follow-up interview. The goals of the PFI were (1) to provide the most current information about HIV/AIDS, routes of infection, drug use and sexual risk behaviors, use of condoms and safe sex, cleaning needles, the benefits of drug treatment, and the HIV test; and (2) to help each participant individually examine two of his or her own HIV-related drug use and sexual risk behaviors, and develop personal action plans (Martin et al., 2003).

Session 1 included both education (e.g., the ESI) and the interventionist asking the participant questions about his/her HIV-related risk behaviors. The interventionist and participant completed a thought map together. The thought map uses nodes (boxes and ovals) to denote feelings, thoughts, and actions. Lines are used as a graphical depiction of the relationships between nodes. The thought map uses a problem-solving approach that is both personal and visually represented. This helps the participant understand how his/her HIV-risk behaviors interact with the actions and feelings of other people, as well as how these actions have consequences. The thought map concludes with a node on what positive behavior changes can be made to avoid this problem in the future (Martin et al., 2003).

Preliminary results are reported for the 426 participants who completed the 6-month follow-up interview. In this behavioral trial, preliminary results show statistically significant reductions for both the PFI and ESI from the baseline to the 6-month follow-up for heroin use, injection drug use, paying for sex, and having multiple sex partners. In addition, a gender-specific analysis revealed statistically significant reductions in the amount of unprotected sex for all groups with the exception of females in the PFI arm (Martin et al., 2003). These results suggest significant reductions in both drug use and high-risk sexual behaviors in both groups; however, there were no statistically significant differences between the ESI and PFI arms. Future studies could incorporate a "no intervention" control to examine efficacy. Martin et al. (2003) reported that the NIDA Scientific Review Committee felt that a true "no intervention" group would have been unethical.

## Social Cognitive Theory and Theory of Gender and Power

St. Lawrence et al. (1997) designed two HIV risk reduction interventions, one based on social cognitive theory (Bandura, 1994) and the other on the theory of gender and power (Connell, 1987). These two interventions were compared using a population of mostly African-American (80.7%), low-income, female prison inmates; 90 incarcerated women were recruited for the study and randomly assigned to one of the two intervention groups. For both interventions, 90-minute weekly group sessions were held for 6 weeks in prison. Female facilitators co-led the sessions. In both conditions, sessions one and two were identical, providing information about how HIV/AIDS and other sexually transmitted diseases are contracted and spread. The final four sessions covered identical content using different formats.

The first intervention was derived from Bandura's (1994) social cognitive theory (SCT) which emphasizes that information alone is not adequate for behavior change. In addition to receiving information, individuals also need to observe and practise skills hands-on to foster their self-efficacy and elicit behavior change (Bandura, 1994). This change is thought to come from practise, role playing, and group social support (McDermott, 1998). In session three, participants were trained to correctly use condoms. Sessions four and five provided training on how to refuse unprotected sex or negotiate condom use with an intimate partner. The final session addressed the drug use/risky sexual behavior connection, and participants were taught drug refusal techniques and how to correctly clean needles (St. Lawrence et al., 1997).

The comparison intervention, based on the theory of gender and power (TGP), focused on sexual inequality as well as gender and power imbalances (Connell, 1987). During sessions three through six of the TGP intervention, group leaders facilitated discussions among participants using open-ended questions that focused on gender and power issues related to reducing one's risk for contracting HIV (St. Lawrence et al., 1997). Session three targeted women and condoms (St. Lawrence et al., 1997). Sessions four and five focused on sexual communication. The final session targeted the connection between using drugs and engaging in risky sexual behavior. No skill training or practising of risk-reduction skills were included in the TGP intervention (St. Lawrence et al., 1997).

At baseline, after completing the intervention, and at the 6-month follow-up, all participants completed a self-administered questionnaire. At baseline and post-intervention, all participants also role-played high-risk situations one-on-one with a group leader and practiced properly putting a condom on a model.

No baseline between-group differences were found between women assigned to the two intervention groups. Post-intervention, women in both conditions displayed increases in positive attitudes toward prevention, self-esteem, AIDS knowledge, stage of change, and frequency of discussions about using condoms (St. Lawrence et al., 1997). These increases remained unchanged at the 6-month follow-up for women in both groups. The SCT group showed greater improvement than the TGP group in condom application skills, and the TGP group exhibited greater commitment to behavior change than the SCT group ($p < 0.05$).

In order for either of these two interventions to be classified as "best evidence", a more refined research design is needed. Specifically, future research should include a control group that receives only the first two sessions of the intervention (identical to the other groups) but no additional information. This design could determine if changes in HIV risk-reduction behaviors and attitudes are significantly greater for participants in the intervention groups than for those in the control condition. Although 90 participants were recruited for this study, the CDC requires at least 50 participants per study arm to qualify for best-evidence classification, so a larger-scale study would be recommended.

## Skill Building and Social Support Enhancement

El-Bassel et al. (1995) designed an AIDS prevention intervention that focused on skill building and social support enhancement as paths to behavioral change. Participants were 145 female jail inmates who reported recent heavy drug use. Most of the women in the study were African American (93%), unemployed, single mothers with a criminal history. Women were randomly assigned to either the skill-building and social support enhancement (SBSSE) intervention group ($n = 67$) or to the AIDS information comparison ($n = 78$) group.

Participants in the SBSSE intervention attended two 1-hour sessions that met twice weekly for 8 weeks in the prison facility and six group-booster sessions held in the community post-release. Two facilitators from similar ethnic backgrounds and with experience in substance abuse led groups of 10. The intervention was derived from a number of theories, including social cognitive theory, self-efficacy (Bandura, 1989), the health belief model (Janz & Becker, 1984; Rosenstock, 1974), behavioral and cognitive skills training (Lazarus, 1971; Meichenbaum, 1972), problem solving (D'Zurilla & Goldfried, 1971; Nezu & D'Zurilla, 1981; Platt, Taube, Metzger, & Duome, 1988), social support and health seeking (Fraser & Hawkins, 1984; Froland, Pancoast, Chapman, & Kimboko, 1981; Wills, 1982), and empowerment (Levine et al., 1993; Simon, 1994).

The intervention included both improving cognitive-behavioral skills such as problem-solving and social skills, and developing technical skills such as proper condom use and needle cleansing (El-Bassel et al., 1995). Skills were discussed and modeled for participants before participants were asked to role-play skills. Participants were also encouraged to identify and establish contact with drug-free, supporting people in their friend or family networks who could provide recovery support. Participants also completed homework assignments which were reviewed at the following session.

The AIDS education comparison intervention group met for three 2-hour sessions. During these sessions participants were given information about how HIV/AIDS is transmitted and safer drug and sex behaviors were explained (El-Bassel et al., 1995). Open discussions provided a forum for participants' questions and concerns (El-Bassel et al., 1995).

Participants were interviewed seven times: at pretest, within a week before release, 1–2 days after their release, and at 1, 3, 6, and 12 months following release. Many of these interviews were used to stay in contact with participants and remind them of the community sessions and follow-up interviews. At the pretest interview and

1-month post-release follow-up interview, participants completed a questionnaire. Of the initial 145 participants, 69.7% ($n = 101$) participated in the post-release follow-up interview.

No significant differences were found between women in the two groups at baseline or between the women in each group who dropped out of the study. At the 1-month follow-up, both intervention groups reduced their HIV risk behaviors; however, the SBSSE group demonstrated significantly better outcomes than the AIDS information group on measures of safer sex behavior, coping skills, and direct emotional support. No significant differences were found for perceived vulnerability to HIV infection, sexual self-efficacy, or AIDS knowledge.

The addition of a true control group in future studies would eliminate confounding variables. In addition, future research could incorporate follow-up interviews at least 3 months post-intervention as specified by the CDC's best-evidence guidelines.

## Beyond Fear

Another promising HIV intervention is the Beyond Fear program, an ongoing intervention program in 19 correctional facilities in Connecticut (Bryan et al., 2006). This intervention was developed based on selected theoretical models including social cognitive theory (Bandura, 1994, 1997), the health belief model (Rosenstock, 1990), problem solving (D'Zurilla & Goldfried, 1971; Nezu & D'Zurilla, 1981; Platt et al., 1988), and cultural sensitivity (Ramirez, 1999; Sue & Sue, 1999). A total of 196 inmates (90% male) participated in the Beyond Fear study. There is no comparison group. The program is offered to all eligible inmates. At the time of the study, certified HIV educators led 37 groups with a median group size of six (Bryan et al., 2006).

Inmates in the Beyond Fear program attend 90-minute weekly sessions for 6 weeks. During these sessions, HIV educators addressed five objectives: (1) provide inmates with education about the transmission and prevention of HIV; (2) discuss myths about HIV antibody counseling and testing; (3) enable inmates to anticipate and identify potentially high-risk situations and discuss personal strategies they have used to navigate these situations; (4) increase each participant's self-efficacy for HIV prevention by reducing the psychosocial barriers to making healthy decisions; and (5) encourage inmate peer-educator behaviors by teaching inmates that effective peer educators can be instrumental in reducing the anxieties and fears about HIV that other inmates might have by providing support and HIV-related information (Bryan et al., 2006). Homework and role-playing identify, address, and overcome barriers to practise effective, positive communication skills. Referral sources are provided in case participants would like to be tested for HIV.

Bryan et al. (2006) assessed pre- and post-intervention changes in attitudes toward HIV prevention, norm-supporting behaviors, self-efficacy/perceived behavioral control for HIV prevention behaviors, and intentions to engage in HIV prevention behaviors post-release. Significant increases were found for HIV knowledge, condom attitudes, condom self-efficacy, condom intentions, self-efficacy for not sharing needles, peer education self-efficacy, peer education intentions, and peer education behavior (all $p$-values $\leq 0.05$). Racial differences in these increases were observed. Specifically, Caucasians showed the greatest increase in intentions to use condoms and Caucasians and African Americans showed a greater increase in condom use self-efficacy than Hispanic participants (Bryan et al., 2006). In fact, Hispanics showed a small *decrease* in condom use self-efficacy following the intervention, with lower gains in positive attitudes about not sharing needles/tattooing equipment. After the study, Beyond Fear administrators held focus groups with Hispanic inmates who emphasized the important role of their families in health-related decisions. The intervention has been modified to include discussion and is now offered in Spanish.

Bryan et al. (2006) noted many of the limitations that prevent this study from meeting best-evidence criteria and point to the restrictions in these specific correctional institutions that did not allow for a control group, random assignment, or a post-release follow-up. An implementation and evaluation of this intervention in a jurisdiction with less restrictive policies is suggested. In addition, a study of the current Beyond Fear intervention would be warranted to determine if the post-evaluation study changes have addressed racial differences in post-intervention outcomes. This intervention could also be evaluated with a smaller ratio of male to female inmates.

## Reducing Risky Relationships for HIV

The final promising HIV/AIDS intervention is the Reducing Risky Relationships for HIV (RRR) (Leukefeld et al., 2009) which was developed through the NIDA-funded CJ-DATS cooperative agreement (www.cjdats.org). Using information gained from four focus groups conducted with incarcerated women and women on work release or in substance abuse treatment, researchers designed the RRR intervention to target seven "Risky Relationship Thinking Myths" – defined as errors in thinking about relationships that may increase women's risk for HIV. The intervention design is based on the idea that relationships are very important to women and women who believe these myths may adapt their behavior in intimate relationships, potentially putting themselves at risk.

Eligible women who were scheduled for parole within 6 weeks of the initial contact were recruited from prisons in four US states. The 442 women recruited were randomized into one of the two intervention groups: the RRR-HIV group, or the HIV awareness video comparison group. Face-to-face interviews were conducted by trained interviewers preintervention, 30 days post-release, and 90 days post-release.

The RRR intervention is based on Carroll and Johnson's (1990) decision-making model which describes the stages an individual goes through when making a decision. The goal of this intervention was to recognize common myths that women often experience in relationships that have the potential to influence their risky behaviors. The association between the relationship thinking myths and risky sexual behavior was seen as the first step in changing those thinking myths in order to protect themselves from HIV (Staton-Tindall et al., 2007). The intervention was comprised of five, 90-minute in-prison sessions conducted on a daily basis, and a sixth session held in the community 30 days post-release. The seven thinking myths targeted in the intervention were (1) "Having sex without protection will strengthen my relationship" (Fear of Rejection); (2) "I only think good things about myself when I am in a relationship, even if it is a risky relationship" (Self-worth); (3) "I can use drugs and always make healthy choices about protection" (Drug Use); (4) "I know my partner is safe by the way my partner looks, talks, and/or acts" (Safety); (5) "I will not get HIV because I'm not really at risk" (Invincibility); (6) "I've been with this partner for a long time so there's no need to practice safe sex" (Trust); (7) "I have to use sex as a way to get what I want in a relationship" (Strategy/Power) (Staton-Tindall et al., 2007).

In each session, female facilitators who were certified HIV counselors focused on one or more of these thinking myths and held open discussions about the connections between falling in love, using drugs, and making risky sexual decisions; triggers to risky behavior; the importance of social support; and general information about HIV/AIDS transmission (Staton-Tindall et al., 2007). At the end of sessions 2, 3, and 4, the women created a safety plan related to the topics covered that day. During the final community session, the interviewer reviewed the safety plans with the participants.

Women in the comparison group viewed a gender-specific HIV awareness video that contained a portion of the content from the NIDA Standard Intervention. Both groups were tested for HIV and HCV during the intervention and received post-test counseling 2 weeks after completing the intervention. The researchers were interested in differences between the two intervention groups in terms of participants' attitudes, knowledge, and HIV risk behaviors. Post-release interviews assessed the effectiveness of the intervention on the behavior of women after being released from prison.

The retention rate from baseline to 90-day follow-up was 91%. At the 30-day follow-up, participants in the RRR group reported significantly greater knowledge of HIV risk behaviors, greater levels of sexual relationship power, higher self-esteem, and increased knowledge about safe and risky sexual behaviors and HIV transmission than women in the comparison group (Leukefeld et al., 2009). Women in the RRR group, when compared to those in the comparison group, were also significantly more likely to recognize four of the seven thinking myths as false (Leukefeld et al., 2009).

The RRR intervention is promising and particularly beneficial to the literature on HIV/AIDS interventions in criminal justice settings because it evaluates intervention effects post-release and specifically targets women. Future research should be implemented in other prisons to examine its effectiveness. The primary reason this intervention appears in the promising, rather than evidence-based section, is that data from the 90-day follow-up interviews are yet to be published.

## Best Practices and Future Directions

The delivery of HIV interventions in criminal justice settings is beneficial from both primary and secondary prevention perspectives. Providing HIV interventions in criminal justice settings is an excellent public health opportunity in which to reduce the HIV risk behaviors of an otherwise hard-to-reach and high-risk population. Prisons and jails provide an audience of individuals who engage in high-risk behaviors such as injection drug use and commercial sex work (Braithwaite et al., 2002; Oser et al., 2006; Oser et al., 2007). Prison-based HIV interventions are needed because the majority of inmates are released to the community (Harrison & Beck, 2006). Moreover, the majority of individuals involved in the criminal justice system are under community supervision (69.8% are on probation or parole while 30.2% are incarcerated in prison or jail) (Glaze & Bonczar, 2009). Thus, there may be an even greater need for HIV interventions among nonincarcerated criminal justice populations because these offenders have more opportunities to engage in HIV risk behaviors. Prevention, early identification, and treatment are critical to reducing infectious disease transmission (see the National Institute on Drug Abuse [NIDA], 2006) Principles of Drug Abuse Treatment for Criminal Justice Populations.

Despite the substantiated need for HIV interventions in criminal justice settings, there are few interventions that meet the efficacy criteria for a Best Evidence HIV Intervention. In fact, only two interventions (Targeted HIV/HCV Brief Intervention in Prisoner Reentry and Project Start) meet these criteria. Both of these Best Evidence HIV Interventions targeted reentering offenders; however, future HIV interventions are needed for offenders in other segments of the criminal justice system such as jails and probation. In addition, efforts are needed to ensure that criminal justice agencies are adopting and implementing these Best Evidence HIV Interventions to improve offender outcomes. Too often, evidence-based interventions are not adopted (Guydish, Turcotte Manser, Jessup, Tajima, & Sears, 2005; McCarty, Edmundson, & Hartnett, 2006; Roman, Ducharme, & Knudsen, 2006; Sorenson, Guydish, Rawson, & Zweben, 2003), thereby limiting the public health impact of research (Simpson & Flynn, 2007). The majority of studies focus on implementing Best Evidence HIV Interventions in community-based organizations (Peterson & Randall, 2006; Shea, Callis, Cassidy-Stewart, Cranston, & Tomoyasu, 2006; Wingood & DiClemente, 2006) despite the higher prevalence of HIV among criminal offenders. In fact, there are no known studies which examine the effective transfer of Best Evidence HIV Interventions into criminal justice settings.

Due to the limited research on the organizational-level processes associated with the adoption and implementation of evidence-based practices, the National Institute on Drug Abuse (NIDA) funded a cooperative agreement titled the Criminal Justice Drug Abuse Treatment Studies (CJ-DATS 2) in 2008. This research cooperative is charged with the task of developing and testing systems-level and organizational-level models that integrate public health and public safety approaches for criminal justice involved adults with substance use disorders. CJ-DATS is based upon researcher/criminal justice agency partnerships and focuses on improving the adoption of evidenced-based practices in three areas: assessment, treatment, and HIV. It is expected that within the next 5 years CJ-DATS will identify organizational factors that influence the adoption, implementation, and sustainability of Best Evidence HIV Interventions.

There are several interventions that are promising but do not meet CDC's efficacy criteria. Four avenues for future research could improve promising HIV interventions. This future area of inquiry could move promising HIV interventions to best-evidence qualification. First, one promising HIV intervention has not had the opportunity to publish findings. Specifically, preliminary RRR-HIV study results are promising; however, the data collection was completed in 2008; thus, manuscripts reporting the effectiveness of the intervention are underway (Leukefeld, personal correspondence, 2009). If published results of the RRR-HIV meet the CDC's Best Evidence HIV Intervention criteria, this intervention can be categorized as the best practice.

Second, another intervention has not published results for 3-month post-intervention follow-up. The only study published by El-Bassel and colleagues in 1995 on the effectiveness of the Skills Building and Social Support Enhancement (SBSSE) intervention reported findings at the 1-month post-release period.

Third, the Social Cognitive Theory and the Theory of Gender and Power HIV interventions did not have sufficient sample sizes. This study included 90 participants; however, 50 participants who are involved in the criminal justice system are needed for each arm.

Fourth, several studies (PFI, SCT/TGP, and Beyond Fear) do not have a "true no-intervention" control group. It has been noted that there is an ethical dilemma in regard to providing a true "no intervention" control group (Martin et al., 2003). A possible lag-time in which the control group received the intervention at a later time point could address some of these ethical concerns.

Despite these limitations in meeting the CDC's efficacy criteria as Best Evidence HIV intervention, there is promise for expanding the availability of HIV interventions in criminal justice settings. In addition, administrators in US criminal justice agencies have become more aware of the HIV problem in the last decade (Braithwaite, Hammett, & Mayberry, 1996; Hammett & Harmon, 1999). Since more than one-fourth of people living with HIV cycle through the criminal justice system (Hammett, Harmon, & Rhodes, 2002), there is a clear need to provide Best Evidence HIV interventions in criminal justice settings.

## References

Bandura, A. (1977). *Social learning theory*. Englewood Cliffs, NJ: Prentice-Hall.

Bandura, A. (1989). Perceived self-efficacy in the exercise of control over AIDS infection. In V. M. Mays, G. W. Albee, & S. F. Schneider (Eds.), *Primary prevention of AIDS* (pp. 128–141). Newbury Park, CA: Sage.

Bandura, A. (1994). Social cognitive theory and exercise of control over HIV infection. In R. J. DiClemente & J. Peterson (Eds.), *Preventing AIDS* (pp. 25–59). New York: Plenum.

Bandura, A. (1997). *Self-efficacy: The exercise of control*. New York: Freeman.

Bauserman, R. L., Ward, M. A., Eldred, L., & Swetz, A. (2001). Increasing voluntary HIV testing by offering oral tests in incarcerated populations. *American Journal of Public Health, 91*, 1226–1229.

Braithwaite, R. L., Hammett, T., & Arriola, K. J. (2002). Introduction to the special issue: HIV/AIDS in correctional settings. *AIDS Education and Prevention, 14*, 1–6.

Braithwaite, R. L., Hammett, T., & Mayberry, R. (1996). *Prisons and AIDS: A public health challenge*. San Francisco: Jossey-Bass.

Bryan, A., Robbins, R. N., Ruiz, M. S., & O'Neill, D. (2006). Effectiveness of an HIV prevention intervention in prison among African Americans, Hispanics, and Caucasians. *Health Education & Behavior, 33*, 154–177.

Carroll, J. S., & Johnson, E. J. (1990). *Decision research: A field guide. Applied social research methods series.* Thousand Oaks, CA: Sage.

Centers for Disease Control and Prevention. (1995). HIV prevention case management. *Guidelines for health education and risk reduction activities* (pp. 32–35). Atlanta, GA: Author.

Centers for Disease Control and Prevention. (1997). *HIV prevention case management.* Atlanta, GA: US Department of Health and Human Services. Available at http://www.cdc.gov/hiv/topics/prev_prog/CRCS/resources/PCMG/pdf/hivpcmg.pdf. Accessed August 17, 2009.

Centers for Disease Control and Prevention. (2008a). *HIV/AIDS basic information.* Available at http://www.cdc.gov/hiv/topics/basic/index.htm. Accessed August 16, 2009.

Centers for Disease Control and Prevention. (2008b). *HIV/AIDS in the United States, factsheet.* Available at http://www.cdc.gov/hiv/resources/factsheets/PDF/us.pdf. Accessed August 18, 2009.

Centers for Disease Control and Prevention. (2008c). *HIV/AIDS and African Americans, factsheet.* Available at http://www.cdc.gov/hiv/topics/aa/index.htm. Accessed August 18, 2009.

Connell, R. W. (1987). *Gender and power.* Stanford, CA: Stanford University Press.

Coyle, S. (1993). *The NIDA HIV counseling and education intervention model* (NIH Pub. No. 93-3508). Rockville, MD: National Institute on Drug Abuse.

Dean-Gaitor, H. D., & Fleming, P. L. (1999). Epidemiology of AIDS in incarcerated persons in the United States, 1994–1996. *AIDS, 13*, 2429–2435.

Dees, S. M., Dansereau, D. F., Peel, J. L., & Knight, K. (1991). Using conceptual matrices, knowledge maps, and scripted cooperation to improve personal management strategies. *Journal of Drug Education, 21*, 211–228.

DiClemente, R. J., Lanier, M. M., Horan, P. F., & Lodico, M. (1991). Comparison of AIDS knowledge, attitudes, and behaviors among incarcerated adolescents and a public school sample in San Francisco. *American Journal of Public Health, 81*, 628–630.

D'Zurilla, T. J., & Goldfried, M. R. (1971). Problem solving and behavior modification. *Journal of Abnormal Psychology, 78*, 107–126.

El-Bassel, N., Ivanoff, A., Schilling, R. F., Gilbert, L., Borne, D., & Chen, D. (1995). Preventing HIV/AIDS in drug-abusing incarcerated women through skills building and social support enhancement: Preliminary outcomes. *Social Work Research, 19*, 131–141.

Falck, R., Carlson, R. G., Price, S. K., & Turner, J. A. (1994). Case management to enhance HIV risk reduction among users of injection drugs and crack cocaine. *Journal of Case Management, 3*, 162–166.

Fraser, M., & Hawkins, J. D. (1984). Social network analysis and drug misuse. *Social Service Review, 58*, 81–97.

Froland, C., Pancoast, D., Chapman, N., & Kimboko, P. (1981). *Helping networks and human services.* Beverly Hills, CA: Sage.

Glaze, L. E., & Bonczar, T. P. (2009). *Probation and Parole in the United States, 2007 Statistical tables* (Publication No. NCJ 224707). Washington, DC: U.S. Department of Justice, Bureau of Justice Statistics.

Gordon, R. S. (1989). An operational classification of disease prevention. *Public Health Reports, 98*, 107–109.

Grinstead, O. A., Zack, B., & Faigeles, B. (1999). Collaborative research to prevent HIV among male prison inmates and their female partners. *Health Education & Behavior, 26*, 225–238.

Grinstead, O., Zack, B., & Faigeles, B. (2001). Reducing postrelease risk behavior among HIV seropositive prison inmates: The health promotion program. *AIDS Education and Prevention, 13*, 109–119.

Guydish, J., Turcotte Manser, S., Jessup, M., Tajima, B., & Sears, C. (2005). Multi-level assessment protocol (MAP) for adoption in multi-site clinical trials. *Journal of Drug Issues, 35*, 529–546.

Hammett, T. M., & Harmon, P. (1999). Sexually transmitted diseases and hepatitis: Burden of disease among inmates. In T. M. Hammett, P. Harmon, & L. M. Maruschak (Eds.), *1996–1997 Update: HIV/AIDS, STDs, and TB in correctional facilities* (pp. 132–146) (Publication No. NCJ 176344). Washington, DC: U.S. Department of Justice, Office of Justice Programs, National Institute of Justice.

Hammett, T. M., Harmon, P., & Rhodes, W. (2002). The burden of infectious disease among inmates and releases from US correctional facilities, 1997. *American Journal of Public Health, 92*, 189–194.

Hammett, T. M., Maruschak, L., & Harmon, P. (1999). *1996–1997 update: HIV/AIDS, STDs, and TB in correctional facilities.* Available at http://www.ncjrs.org/txtfiles1/176344.txt. Accessed August 16, 2009.

Harrison, P. M., & Beck, A. J. (2006). *Prison and jail inmates at midyear 2005* (Publication No. NCJ 213133). Washington, DC: U.S. Department of Justice, Bureau of Justice Statistics.

Inciardi, J. A., Surratt, H. L., Martin, S. S., O'Connell, D. J., Salandy, A. D., & Beard, R. A. (2007). Developing a multimedia HIV and Hepatitis intervention for drug-involved offenders reentering the community. *The Prison Journal, 87*, 111–142.

Janz, N. K., & Becker, M. H. (1984). The health belief model: A decade later. *Health Education Quarterly, 11*, 1–47.

Knight, K., Simpson, D. D., & Dansereau, D. F. (1994). A psychoeducational tool in drug abuse relapse prevention training. *Journal of Offender Rehabilitation, 20*, 187–205.

Lazarus, A. A. (1971). *Behavior therapy and beyond.* New York: McGraw-Hill.

Leukefeld, C., Havens, J., Oser, C., Staton-Tindall, M., Knudsen, H., Palmer, J., et al. (2009, June). *Thirty day outcomes of a randomized controlled trial of women's relationship characteristics, HIV risk behaviors, and knowledge*. Paper presented at the meeting of the College on Problems of Drug Dependence, Reno, NV.

Leukefeld, C. G., Roberto, H., Hiller, M., Webster, M., Logan, T. K., & Staton Tindall, M. (2003). HIV prevention among high-risk and hard-to-reach rural residents. *Journal of Psychoactive Drugs, 35*(4), 427–434.

Levine, O. H., Britton, P. J., James, T. C., Jackson, A. P., Hobfoll, S. E., & Lavin, J. P. (1993). The empowerment of women: A key to HIV prevention. *Journal of Community Psychology, 21*, 320–334.

Lyles, C. M., Crepaz, N., Herbst, J. H., & Kay, L. S. (2006). Evidence-based HIV behavioral prevention from the perspective of the CDC's HIV/AIDS prevention research synthesis team. *AIDS Education and Prevention, 18*(Supplement A), 21–31.

Lyles, C. M., Kay, L. S., Crepaz, N., Herbst, J. H., Passin, W. F., Kim, A. S., et al. (2007). Best-evidence interventions: Findings from a systematic review of HIV behavioral interventions for US populations at high risk, 2000–2004. *American Journal of Public Health, 97*, 133–143.

Marlatt, G. A. (1998). *Harm reduction: Pragmatic strategies for managing high-risk behaviors*. New York: The Guilford Press.

Martin, S. S., O'Connell, D. J., Inciardi, J. A., Surratt, H. L., & Beard, R. A. (2003). HIV/AIDS among probationers: An assessment of risk and results from a brief intervention. *Journal of Psychoactive Drugs, 35*, 435–443.

Martin, S. S., O'Connell, D. J., Inciardi, J. A., Surratt, H. I., & Maiden, K. M. (2008). Integrating and HIV/HCV brief intervention in prisoner reentry: Results of a multisite prospective study. *Journal of Psychoactive Drugs, 40*, 427–436.

Maruschak, L. M. (2006). *HIV in prisons, 2004* (Publication No. NCJ 213897). Washington, DC: U.S. Department of Justice, Bureau of Justice Statistics.

Maruschak, L. M. (2008). *HIV in Prisons, 2006* (Publication No. NCJ 222179). Washington, DC: U.S. Department of Justice, Bureau of Justice Statistics.

McCarty, D., Edmundson, E., & Hartnett, T. (2006). Charting a path between research and practice in alcoholism treatment. *Alcohol, Research & Health, 29*, 5–10.

McDermott, R. (1998). Adolescent HIV prevention and intervention: A prospect theory analysis. *Psychology, Health, & Medicine, 3*, 371–386.

Meichenbaum, D. H. (1972). Cognitive modification of test-anxious college students. *Journal of Consulting and Clinical Psychology, 39*, 370–380.

Miller, W. R., & Rollnick, S. (2002). *Motivational interviewing: Preparing people for change*. New York: The Guilford Press.

National Institute on Drug Abuse. (2006). *Principles of drug abuse treatment for criminal justice populations: A research-based guide* (Publication No. 06-5316). Bethesda, MD: National Institutes of Health, U.S. Department of Health and Human Services.

Nezu, A., & D'Zurilla, T. (1981). Effects of problem and formulation of the generation of alternatives in the social problem-solving process. *Cognitive Therapy and Research, 5*, 265–271.

Oser, C., Leukefeld, C., Cosentino-Boehm, A., & Havens, J. (2006). Rural HIV: Brief interventions for felony probationers. *American Journal of Criminal Justice, 31(1)*, 125–143.

Oser, C., Staton-Tindall, M., & Leukefeld, C. (2007). HIV/AIDS testing in correctional agencies and community treatment programs: The impact of internal organizational structure. *Journal of Substance Abuse Treatment, 32*, 301–310.

Petersilia, J. (2003). *When prisoners come home: Parole and prisoner reentry*. New York: Oxford University Press.

Peterson, A. S., & Randall, L. M. (2006). Utilizing multilevel partnerships to build the capacity of community-based organizations to implement effective HIV prevention interventions in Michigan. *AIDS Education and Prevention, 18*(Suppl. A), 83–95.

Pitre, U., Dansereau, D. F., & Joe, G. W. (1996). Client education levels and the effectiveness of node-link maps. *Journal of Addictive Diseases, 15*, 27–44.

Platt, J., Taube, D. O., Metzger, D. S., & Duome, M. J. (1988). Training in interpersonal problem solving (TIPS). *Journal of Community Psychology, 2*, 5–34.

Purcell, D. W., DeGroff, A. S., & Wolitski, R. J. (1998). HIV prevention case management: Current practice and future directions. *Health and Social Work, 23*, 282–289.

Ramirez, M., III. (1999). *Multicultural psychotherapy: An approach to individual and cultural differences*. Needham Heights, MA: Allyn & Bacon.

Rich, J. D., Holmes, L., Salas, C., Macalino, G., Davis, D., Ryczek, J., et al. (2001). Successful linkage of medical care and community services for HIV-positive offenders being released from prison. *Journal of Urban Health, 78*, 279–289.

Richie, B. E., Freudenberg, N., & Page, J. (2001). Reintegrating women leaving jail into urban communities: A description of a model program. *Journal of Urban Health, 78*, 290–303.

Roman, P. M., Ducharme, L. J., & Knudsen, H. K. (2006). Patterns of organization and management in private and public substance abuse treatment programs. *Journal of Substance Abuse Treatment, 31*, 235–243.

Rosenstock, I. M. (1974). Historical origins of the health belief model. *Health Education Monograph, 2*, 328–335.

Rosenstock, I. M. (1990). The health belief model: Health beliefs, decisions, and behaviors among adults. In K. Glanz, F. Lewis, & B. Rimer (Eds.), *Health behavior and health education: Theory, research, and practice* (pp. 39–62). San Francisco: Jossey-Bass.

Rosenstock, I. M., Strecher, V. J., & Becker, M. H. (1994). The health belief model and HIV risk behavior change. In R. DiClemente & J. Peterson (Eds.),

*Preventing AIDS: Theories and methods of behavioral interventions* (pp. 5–24). New York: Springer.

Ross, M. W., Harzke, A. J., Scott, D. P., McCann, K., & Kelley, M. (2006). Outcomes of Project Wall Talk: An HIV AIDS peer education program implemented within the Texas state prison system. *AIDS Education and Prevention, 18*, 504–517.

Rothman, J. (1992). *Guidelines for case management: Putting research to professional use*. Itasca, IL: F.E. Peacock Publishers, Inc.

Rothman, J. (1998). *Case management: Integrating individual and community practice*. Boston: Allyn and Bacon.

Shea, M. A., Callis, B. P., Cassidy-Stewart, H., Cranston, K., & Tomoyasu, N. (2006). Diffusion of effective HIV prevention interventions – Lessons from Maryland and Massachusetts. *AIDS Education and Prevention, 18*(Suppl. A), 96–107.

Simon, B. L. (1994). *The empowerment tradition in American social work*. New York: Columbia University Press.

Simpson, D. D., & Flynn, P. M. (2007). Moving innovations into treatment: A stage-based approach to program change. *Journal of Substance Abuse Treatment, 33*, 111–120.

Sivacek, J., & Crano, W. D. (1982). Vested interest as a moderator of attitude-behavior consistency. *Journal of Personality and Social Psychology, 43*, 210–221.

Sorenson, J. L., Guydish, J., Rawson, R. A., & Zweben, J. E. (2003). Introduction: The need for research-practice collaboration. In J. L. Sorenson, R. A. Rawson, J. Guydish, & J. E. Zweben (Eds.), *Drug abuse treatment through collaboration: Practice and research partnerships that work* (pp. 3–10). Washington, DC: American Psychological Association.

St. Lawrence, J. S., Eldridge, G. D., Shelby, M. C., Little, C. E., Brasfield, T. L., & O'Bannon, R. E. (1997). HIV risk reduction for incarcerated women: A comparison of brief interventions based on two theoretical models. *Journal of Consulting and Clinical Psychology, 65*, 504–509.

Staton-Tindall, M., Leukefeld, C., Palmer, J., Oser, C., Kaplan, A., Krietemeyer, J., et al. (2007). Relationships and HIV risk among incarcerated women. *The Prison Journal, 87*, 143–165.

Sue, D. W., & Sue, D. (1999). *Counseling the culturally different: Theory and practice* (3rd ed.). New York: John Wiley.

Travis, J., & Visher, C. (Eds.) (2005). *Prisoner reentry and crime in America*. New York: Cambridge University Press.

Watts, W. A. (1967). Relative persistence of opinion change induced by active compared to passive participation. *Journal of Personality and Social Psychology, 5*, 4–15.

Wechsberg, W., MacDonald, B., Inciardi, J. A., Surratt, H., Leukefeld, C., Farabee, D., et al. (1997). *The NIDA cooperative agreement standard intervention: Protocol changes suggested by the continuing HIV/AIDS epidemic*. Bloomington, IL: Lighthouse Institute Publications.

West, H. C., & Sabol, W. J. (2009). *Prison inmates at Midyear, 2008* (Publication No. NCJ 225619). Washington, DC: U.S. Department of Justice, Bureau of Justice Statistics.

Wills, T. A. (1982). *Basic processes in helping relationships*. New York: Academic.

Wingood, G. M., & DiClemente, R. J. (2006). Enhancing adoption of evidence-based HIV interventions: Promotion of a suite of HIV prevention interventions for African American women. *AIDS Education and Prevention, 18*(Suppl. A), 161–170.

Wolitski, R. J. (2006). Relative efficacy of a multisession sexual risk-reduction intervention for young men released from prisons in 4 states. *American Journal of Public Health, 96*, 1854–1861.

World Health Organization. (2007a). *Global summary of the AIDS epidemic*. Available at http://www.who.int/hiv/data/2008_global_summary_AIDS_ep.png. Accessed August 16, 2009.

World Health Organization. (2007b). *Effectiveness of interventions to address HIV in prisons*. Available at http://whqlibdoc.who.int/publications/2007/9789241596190_eng.pdf. Accessed August 18, 2009.

World Health Organization. (2008). *UNAIDS/WHO epidemiological fact sheet on HIV and AIDS: Core data on epidemiology and response, 2008 update*. Available at http://apps.who.int/globalatlas/predefinedReports/EFS2008/full/EFS2008_US.pdf. Accessed August 16, 2009.

Zack, B. (2007). HIV prevention: Behavioral interventions in correctional settings. In R. Greifinger (Ed.), *Health behind bars: From prisons to communities* (pp. 156–173). New York: Springer.

# Epilogue: The Enduring Litany

**18**

John Gregrich

**Abstract**

Many criminal justice programs have become prohibitively expensive, due to the cumulative consequences of past policy decisions, notably the incarceration of a large, aging population resulting from the harsh sentencing laws of recent decades. The current and anticipated economic situation will require that all state criminal justice policies be reviewed and many sharply revised. A wholesale move from incarceration to community-based programs is one likely outcome. Such a move will require a level of long-term discipline seldom seen in the past. Fortunately, effective structures are offered by Treatment Alternatives To Street Crime (TASC) and some drug court and probation programs. In addition, program delivery knowledge and techniques have improved markedly and a large body of "what works" research now exists. A Federal commitment, to make the research available and assist with its application, combined with a young, technologically sophisticated labor force can make significant reforms possible, even during difficult economic times.

**Keywords**

Community-based programs • Treatment Alternatives to Street Crime (TASC) • "what works" • Drug courts • Probation • State policy

The old adage, "the more things change the more they stay the same," seems an apt summary of The National Criminal Justice Commission Act of 2010 (S. 714)[1], which is awaiting Senate floor action. It highlights the following decades-old, intractable problems:

J. Gregrich (✉)
Retired from Office of National Drug Control Policy (ONDCP), Washington, DC 20503, USA
e-mail: jbgregrich@comcast.net

[1] The National Criminal Justice Commission Act of 2010 (S. 714) was placed on the Senate Legislative Calendar, under General Orders, on May 6, 2010. The act establishes the National Criminal Justice Commission to undertake a

C. Leukefeld et al. (eds.), *Handbook of Evidence-Based Substance Abuse Treatment in Criminal Justice Settings*, Issues in Children's and Families' Lives 11,
DOI 10.1007/978-1-4419-9470-7_18, © Springer Science+Business Media, LLC 2011

The United States has an incarceration rate five times the world's average; black males have a 32% chance of serving time in prison at some point in their lives; Hispanic males have a 17% chance; white males have a 6% chance; 1 in every 31 American adults is incarcerated or on probation or parole; of the ex-offenders returning to their communities, an average of two out of every three will be rearrested and half will return to prison within 3 years of release; over the past 20 years, inflation-adjusted state spending on corrections rose 127% while higher education expenditures rose just 21%, according to an analysis by the Pew Charitable Trusts:

> Despite high incarceration rates for drug-related offenses, illicit drug availability remains consistent. Eighty-six percent of high school students report that it is "very easy" or "fairly easy" to obtain marijuana, 47 percent report the same for cocaine, 39 percent for crack, and 27 percent for heroin; there has been a twelve-fold increase in the number of drug offenders in prisons and jails, since 1980. A significant percentage of these offenders have no history of violence or high-level drug selling activity; prisons and jails nationwide have become holding facilities for the mentally ill, mentally ill people in prisons outnumbering those mental health hospitals by a four to one margin and roughly three-quarters of mentally ill inmates suffer from a substance abuse disorder;
>
> prisons present significant public health risks, cases of HIV and hepatitis C occurring at two and a half and nine times, respectively, the rate for the general population; and prison administration is uneven, lacking clear, affirmative standards of training and performance, varying greatly from institution to institution, locality to locality, and among Federal, state and local jurisdictions.

This is a sadly familiar list. Innovative programs have arisen episodically, to tackle one or more of the problems; however, few have become ingrained as permanent solutions. Resources have always been a challenge. Ironically, the current period of severe economic difficulty might afford the impetus for the long-postponed change required. Just as necessity is forcing the world to "go green," the combination of necessity and knowledge can spur the criminal justice "system" to jettison outdated policies and procedures in favor of more effective and efficient ways to keep our communities safe. The solutions are actually simple, but they are not easy.

## The Overarching Economic Problem

On July 31, 2010, the US Chamber of Commerce hosted a national meeting, in Washington D.C., to discuss state pension and healthcare plans. Among the expert presenters was Raymond Scheppach, Executive Director of the National Governors Association. Mr. Scheppach outlined the impact on state governments of slow economic growth and stubbornly persistent, high unemployment (National Governors Association Center for Best Practices, 2010). It was not a pretty picture. In response to declining tax revenue, governors were continuing to make draconian budget cuts; some had borrowed from pension and healthcare trust funds and all were dreading the end of federal stimulus money. During this period, which he characterized as "survival mode," there had been little maintenance of infrastructure and "rainy day" funds had been depleted.

Mr. Scheppach then turned to the future and predicted a decade of slow growth, with higher taxes, higher interest rates, and increased regulation. He noted that we could no longer afford the operational consequences of past policy decisions; a prime example, "three strikes" and other harsh sentencing laws, which have turned our state prisons into expensive, long-term care facilities.

comprehensive review of all areas of the criminal justice system, including federal, state, local, and tribal governments' criminal justice costs, practices, and policies. The act directs the commission to (1) make findings regarding its review and recommendations for changes in oversight, policies, practices, and laws designed to prevent, deter, and reduce crime and violence, improve cost effectiveness, and ensure the interests of justice; (2) conduct public hearings in various locations around the United States; (3) consult with federal, state, local, and tribal governmental and nongovernmental leaders and other stakeholders in the criminal justice system, including the US Sentencing Commission; and (4) submit a final report, within 18 months after its formation, to Congress, the President, and state, local, and tribal governments, and make such report available to the public.

Given the demand that pension and healthcare plans will be making on state treasuries, Mr. Scheppach called for a wholesale redesign of state service delivery systems. Alternatives to incarceration and expanded use of monitoring in the community must be emphasized in the future.

## Wholesale Redesign – Back to the Future

There is virtual unanimous agreement among practitioners that offenders and drug abusers require structure to be able to successfully complete a program of treatment or rehabilitation. However, the need for structure in the design and delivery of a program, which is easily as important, is not so respected. The failure to proceed with the necessary structure and infrastructure markedly limits the ability to monitor and evaluate a program and to share information with, or otherwise communicate with, others.

Over 20 years ago, the Federal Bureau of Justice Assistance (BJA) sought to address this challenge with the publication of program briefs, to guide the use of block grant funds (Federal Bureau of Justice Assistance, 1988). These documents were developed in collaboration with practitioners and other experts.

They took programs that had experienced some success (e.g., Treatment Alternatives to Street Crime [TASC], Juror Utilization and Management, Victim/Witness Assistance) and broke them down into their essential, severable pieces. Whenever possible, an operating standard was established for each. For example, the operating standard for the "Setting the Term of Service" piece under the juror program was one day-one trial. Not all grantees adhered to that standard: but all did sufficient analysis to establish the standard (e.g., two days-one trial) that best fit their jurisdiction. These pieces, called critical elements, were then placed into their optimal order for phased implementation. For example, the program brief for TASC identified organizational elements that created the infrastructure necessary to start a program and operational elements that identified the program's action areas. Finally, flow charts presented each of the critical elements with a suggested timetable for completion.

The benefits that accrue to such an approach are multiple: the elements of the program are visible to funders, implementers, and others; the common structure offers different jurisdictions an easy means for communicating with one another and for comparing their relative progress; the operating standards offer a common way to evaluate performance; and the phased implementation assures that the program development is cumulative and, if interrupted, can resume without having to return to square one.

This book offers a number of effective techniques and program models that, if applied with fidelity, can reduce both incarceration and recidivism. However, over the years, criminal justice agencies have adopted many workable programs only to see them atrophy, due to a lack of phased and faithful implementation, training, quality control, and systematic program review to maintain fidelity. To overcome these shortfalls, structure is essential and can become virtually permanent, while advances in research and practice will lead to continuing changes within the elements of a program (Tables 18.1 and 18.2).

## Cardinal Advances

On September 19, 2010, National Public Radio devoted an early morning hour to a discussion of the power of language, highlighting research by Barnard College into the role of sign language for the deaf. Part of this research involved the screening of animated short subjects for two deaf groups that employ sign language – one made up of elementary school students, the other of adults – and asking them questions about what they had seen. One of the screenings was about two brothers playing in their bedroom. The older brother was playing with a toy train, while the younger one watched. The older brother then put the train under the bed, admonished the younger one not to touch it, and left the room. The younger one immediately took the train from under the bed and placed it in a toy box, which was also

**Table 18.1** TASC program elements: Organizational

| *Organizational* |
|---|
| 1. *Support of justice*: A broad base of support within the justice system with a protocol for continued and effective communication |
| 2. *Support of treatment*: A broad base of support within the treatment system with a protocol for continued and effective communication |
| 3. *TASC unit administration*: An independent TASC unit with a designated administrator |
| 4. *Staff training*: Policies and procedures for required staff training |
| 5. *Data collection/evaluation*: A data collection system to be used in program management and evaluation |
| 6. *Eligibility criteria*: A number of agreed-upon offender eligibility criteria |
| 7. *Client identification*: Procedures for the identification of eligible offenders that stress early justice and treatment intervention |
| 8. *Assessment/Referral*: Documented procedures for assessment and referral |
| 9. *Urinalysis/Testing*: Documented policies and procedures for urinalysis and other physical tests |
| 10. *Monitoring/Case management/Reporting/Termination*: Procedures for offender monitoring that include criteria for success/failure, required frequency of contact, schedule of reporting and notification of termination to the justice system |

Source: Federal Bureau of Justice Assistance (1988).

**Table 18.2** TASC program elements: Operational/Clinical

| *Operational elements* |
|---|
| *Element 1*<br>*Community as method* – Staff and inmates model behaviors that are expected when living in a prosocial community setting |
| *Element 2*<br>*Unit appearance* – The physical appearance of the unit reflects the values and goals of the community. Treatment is conducted on the unit with the expectation of participants working together to build a safe community with prosocial values and goals |
| *Element 3*<br>*Rules and norms* – Stated and specific rules create and affirm a prosocial community |
| *Element 4*<br>*Staff roles* – Staff serve as role models to participants, demonstrating community responsibility and positive behaviors |
| *Element 5*<br>*Supervision and training* – Program coordinators are responsible for the growth of the community and the staff |
| *Clinical elements* |
| *Element 6*<br>*Transition* – A modified therapeutic community requires participants to transition through a series of levels as they demonstrate increasingly positive behaviors |
| *Element 7*<br>*Community activities* – A daily regimen of activities within a community milieu is designed to facilitate healing, social learning, and changes in behaviors |
| *Element 8*<br>*Community Service Crews* – As in any community, community service is the key to a functioning community by building responsibility and a sense of personal achievement |
| *Element 9*<br>*Treatment phases through journals* – Interactive journal groups focus on the language, replicability, and permanency of the bureau's psychology treatment programs. Movement through program phases is earned by demonstrating behavior change |
| *Element 10*<br>*Small therapy groups* – Participants focus on feelings and relationships in a prosocial manner |

Source: Federal Bureau of Prisons (2010).

in the room. The two groups were asked, "On returning to the bedroom, where do you think the older brother will look, first, for the toy train?" All of the elementary school students responded, correctly, that he would look under the bed, while virtually all of the adults responded that he would look in the toy box.

Thorough examination of this discrepancy led to the realization that the young group had 8–11 word variations for the concept "think," while the adults, who had learned sign language much earlier, had but one word or sign. In short (as Schumacher (1977) taught us decades ago) ideas are not simply the result of thought; rather, they are the very elements of thought. The young group could easily ask itself what the older brother was, or would be, thinking; the adult group could not. A rich vocabulary spurs the intellect on to the discovery of nuances and relationships that are not available to those with no or limited language. And this book is rife with examples of such advancement.

The recently acquired ability to formally assess offender risk, need, and responsivity is also the ability to provide cost-effective community safety. Assessment of risk, need, and responsivity will allow us to keep more offenders safely in the community, avoid the provision of treatment services to those who do not need them and steer clear of the waste associated with providing services that are not a match to the offender.

Our understanding of "Your brain on drugs" has matured. Brain chemistry research continues to shed light on why and how effective programs work, guiding service providers to focus on and emphasize areas critical to success. On another front, medications in use, and under development, are providing a way to manage addiction like any other chronic disease.

Evaluations of residential and institutional treatment are yielding the strong suggestion of a symbiotic relationship between the structure of the therapeutic community and the operating philosophy of cognitive behavioral therapy.

## The Near Future

Federal leadership, when coupled with funding, can enforce the implementation of critical program elements and operating standards, buttressed by solid management information systems. However, the looming deficit will likely keep major funding efforts at a minimum. The best we can hope for is federal publication of solid "what works" documents and the provision of implementation technical assistance to states and localities.

Fortunately, young people who are taking jobs in criminal justice agencies, given their experience with computers and social networking sites, will be more likely to be collaborative and technically proficient than their predecessors. Therefore, there is reason to believe that they will be more likely to access "what works" sites and sources of technical assistance and apply this knowledge and skill in making informed rehabilitation and placement decisions.

## References

Federal Bureau of Justice Assistance. (1988). *Guidelines for implementing and operating treatment alternatives to street crime (TASC) programs*. U.S. Department of Justice, Washington, DC.

Federal Bureau of Prisons. (2010). *Challenge program training*. U.S. Department of Justice, Washington, DC.

National Governors Association Center for Best Practices. (2010). *The big reset: State government after the great recession*. A non-profit organization of governers, Washington, DC.

The National Criminal Justice Commission Act of 2010 (S. 714). (2010). Retrieved 25 October, 2010, from www.thomas.loc.gov

Schumacher, E. F. (1977). *A guide for the perplexed*. New York: Harper & Row.

# Index



C. Leukefeld et al. (eds.), *Handbook of Evidence-Based Substance Abuse Treatment in Criminal Justice Settings*, Issues in Children's and Families' Lives 11,
DOI 10.1007/978-1-4419-9470-7, © Springer Science+Business Media, LLC 2011

**D**

# About the Editors

**John Gregrich** is retired from the Office of National Drug Control Policy (ONDCP) where he served as Chief of the Treatment Branch in the Office of Demand Reduction. From this position he had oversight over, and developed interagency working groups involving, agencies from the Departments of Health and Human Services, Justice, and Education. He annually drafted sections of the National Drug Control Strategy, and developed white papers addressing needle exchange, drug-dependent offenders, and drug treatment principles. He developed and oversaw a major Institute of Medicine study of marijuana and a national conference on drug-dependent offenders; and served on review panels for, and occasionally contributed to publications of, the National Institute of Justice, the National Institute on Drug Abuse, the Center for Substance Abuse Treatment, and the Institute of Medicine. He achieved parity for drug treatment in federal employee health benefit plans and initiated efforts to establish linkages between primary healthcare providers and drug treatment and prevention programs. John came to ONDCP from the Department of Justice, where he developed, documented, and conducted national demonstrations of the Treatment Alternatives to Street Crime, Drug Abuse Resistance Education, Juror Utilization and Management, and Victim/Witness programs.

**Thomas P. Gullotta** is the C.E.O. of Child and Family Agency and a member of the psychology and education departments at Eastern Connecticut State University. He is the senior author of the 4th edition of The Adolescent Experience, co-editor of The Encyclopedia of Primary Prevention and Health Promotion, and editor emeritus of the Journal of Primary Prevention. He is the senior book series editor for Issues in Children's and Families' Lives. Tom holds editorial appointments on the Journal of Early Adolescence, The Journal of Adolescent Research, and the Journal of Educational and Psychological Consultation. He has published extensively on adolescents and primary prevention. Tom was honored in 1999 by the Society for Community Research and Action, Division 27 of the American Psychological Association with their Distinguished Contributions to Practice in Community Psychology Award.

**Carl Leukefeld** is Professor and Chair of the Department of Behavioral Science and founding Director of the Center on Drug and Alcohol Research at the University of Kentucky. He is also the Bell Alcohol and Addictions Endowed Chair. He came to the University of Kentucky in 1990 to establish the Center on Drug and Alcohol Research from the National Institute on Drug Abuse (NIDA) where he filled administrative and research positions. He was also the Chief Health Services Officer of the United States Public Health Service. Dr. Leukefeld has published over 200 articles, chapters, books, and monographs. He has taught the undergraduate Alcohol and Problem Drinking Course, the Dependency Behavior graduate course, and the Introduction to Clinical Medicine course for medical students. He currently is a reviewer and consulting editor for five journals, grant reviewer, and has been a member of the NIH Community-Level Health Promotion Study Section and the NIH/NIDA Health Services Initial Review Group. His research interests include treatment interventions, HIV prevention, criminal justice sanctions, and health services.

# About the Authors

**Shanna Babalonis, M.A.,** is a doctoral candidate in the Behavioral Neuroscience and Psychopharmacology division of the Experimental Psychology Ph.D. Program in the Psychology Department at the University of Kentucky. Specific research interests include: hormonal modulation of drug effects as it relates to women's vulnerability to drug abuse; laboratory measures of impulsivity and their relation to drug use and abuse; behavioral economics and mathematical models of behavior; and individual differences in vulnerability to drug abuse.

**Steven Belenko, Ph.D.,** is Professor in the Department of Criminal Justice at Temple University, and is affiliated with the University of Pennsylvania Department of Psychiatry and the Rutgers University Center for Behavior Health Services and Criminal Justice Research. His research and policy interests involve drug abuse and crime, substance abuse treatment and health services for adult and juvenile offenders, HIV service needs for offenders, and drug courts. In addition to numerous journal articles, book chapters, and technical reports, he has published two books: *Crack and the Evolution of Anti-Drug Policy* (recipient of an Outstanding Academic Book Award from the American Library Association's Choice Magazine), and *Drugs and Drug Policy in America: A Documentary History*.

**Mary Carroll Burnett** has an M.S degree from Oklahoma State University and is a certified rehabilitation counselor. She is currently a full-time MSW student at University of Kentucky. She has a number of years experience with the Veteran's Administration and currently works with Dr. Staton-Tindall and the Criminal Justice Kentucky Treatment Outcome Study.

**Mark Carey** has served as the Deputy Commissioner of Community and Juvenile Services in the Minnesota Department of Corrections from 1999 to 2003, Director of Dakota County Community Corrections, Director of Dodge-Fillmore-Olmsted County Community Corrections and warden of MCF-Shakopee, the only state women's prison in Minnesota. He has over thirty years of experience in the correctional field serving as a counselor, probation/parole officer, planner, administrator, and consultant. He is currently the President of The Carey Group (TCG), a national consulting firm that provides training and technical assistance for justice and correctional professional and community groups. Mr. Carey was President of the American Probation and Parole Association from 2005 to 2007 and has been on the American Probation and Parole Association (APPA) Board of Directors since 1997.

**Brian Chodrow's** primary responsibility is for implementing strategies, programs, materials and information for use by national prosecutorial, court and judicial organizations promoting the highway safety issues of interest to the National Highway Traffic Safety Administration (NHTSA). After a career as a police officer, he also worked as a probation and parole officer for the Department of Corrections. He has a Bachelor of Science degree in Law Enforcement and Corrections from the Pennsylvania State

University and is a graduate of the Mississippi College School of Law where he received his Juris Doctorate (J.D.) and is admitted to the Virginia Bar. This work was written by the author in his individual capacity and is not a work of the U.S. Government, Department of Transportation or the National Highway Traffic Safety Administration. It represents his views alone.

**Dr. Michael S. Gordon's** research is focused on drug abuse treatment for criminal justice populations, including opioid maintenance treatment for prisoners with heroin addiction histories. Dr. Gordon has been involved with numerous federally funded studies including Methadone for Prisoners, Buprenorphine for Prisoners, Prevention of Relapse to Opioid Addiction Using Long-acting Injectable Naltrexone, and Evaluation of an Outpatient Substance Abuse Treatment Program for Adolescents. In addition, his research interests include correctional administration and justice-system policy.

**Roger Guy,** is an assistant professor of sociology and criminal justice at the University of North Carolina at Pembroke. He began his research in criminology with a spatial analysis of the patterns of stranger rape in Charlotte while working with the Charlotte Police Department. His work has appeared in the *Journal Contemporary Criminal Justice*, *Applied Social Science*, and *International Social Work*. His recent research interests include evidence-based practices in community corrections, and prisoner reentry.

**Kathi L. Harland Harp, MA,** is a research assistant for the Center on Drug and Alcohol Research at the University of Kentucky where she is currently pursuing a Ph.D in sociology. Her research interests include mothers with alcohol or other drug problems, the relationship between social support and substance use, and criminological theory.

**Jennifer R. Havens** has a PhD in epidemiology as well as a Masters in Public Health (MPH) from the Johns Hopkins School of Public Health. Her research interests include the epidemiology of prescription drug abuse, rural health disparities specific to substance use, and the infectious complications of injection drug use, namely HIV and hepatitis C. Dr. Havens is currently funded through the National Institutes of Health to examine social networks and HIV risk among rural drug users.

**William M. Heffron, M.D.,** is an Associate professor of Psychiatry at the University of Kentucky. Since July of 1997, he has been working as Chief of Mental Health Services for the Kentucky Department of Juvenile Justice (DJJ). He oversees the development of Mental Health treatment programs in DJJ and monitors their quality. He has been a member of the Work Group on Community Systems of Care for Children and Adolescents with Serious Emotional Disturbance of the American Academy of Child and Adolescent Psychiatry. Currently he is a justice fellow in the Reclaiming Futures Project.

**Matthew L. Hiller, Ph.D.,** is an Associate Professor in the Department of Criminal Justice at Temple University. He received his PhD in experimental psychology from Texas Christian University in 1996 and previously held research positions at the Institute of Behavioral Research at Texas Christian University and the Center on Drug and Alcohol Research at the University of Kentucky. He has served as principal investigator on several projects with funding from the Bureau of Justice Assistance, National Institute of Justice, State Justice Institute, and the Center for Substance Abuse Treatment. He also has served as a co-principal investigator on several studies funded through the National Institute on Drug Abuse. He has authored numerous articles on corrections-based substance abuse treatment, drug courts, mental health, HIV risk behaviors, motivation, health services utilization, and treatment engagement.

**Hon. Peggy Fulton Hora, Judge of the Superior Court of California (Ret.).** Judge Peggy Fulton Hora has 25 years of judicial experience including presiding over the Drug Treatment Court. She is a former dean of the B.E. Witkin Judicial College of California and is a long-term faculty member of the National Judicial College. Judge Hora is a Senior Judicial Fellow for the National Drug Court Institute and is the 2009/2010 Thinker in Residence appointed by the Premier of South Australia. She is the first "Justice Thinker" and is working on therapeutic jurisprudence and restorative justice issues for the government in Adelaide.

**Katie House, M.S.,** is a Research Assistant for the Department of Psychiatry Research Center at the University of Kentucky as is involved in 2 NIH funded studies involving pharmacological interventions involving smoking cessation and Adult Attention Deficit Disorder. She received her MS in Health Promotion from the University of Kentucky. Previous research experiences include serving as the Health Promotion Coordinator in an NIH-funded pediatric diabetes prevention program.

**Alessandra N. Kazura, MD** is Director of the Pediatric Psychiatry Consultation Service at Maine Medical Center and Medical Director, Center for Tobacco Independence of Maine Health. She received her MD in 1982 from Brown University and is board certified in pediatrics, psychiatry, and child and adolescent psychiatry. She completed a K award from the American Academy of Child and Adolescent Psychiatry (AACAP) and National Institute on Drug Abuse to study family socialization influences on child tobacco use. In addition, she has received funding from the National Cancer Institute, National Institute on Drug Abuse, and several private foundations to study adolescent smoking uptake and parent smoking cessation.

**Dr. Timothy W. Kinlock** received his Ph.D. in criminology and criminal justice from the University of Maryland. He has been a Senior Research Scientist at Friends Research Institute since that time. He has collaborated closely with correctional agencies and substance abuse treatment programs in creating, implementing, and evaluating innovative medicated-assisted interventions for offenders with histories of opioid addiction. These studies include a recently completed clinical trial examining the benefits of prison-initiated methadone maintenance continued in the community and an ongoing study that examines the effectiveness of buprenorphine treatment provided to pre-release prison inmates with prior heroin dependence.

**Karen M. Lommel, D.O., M.H.A.** is the Director of the Pediatric Psychiatry Consultation Liaison Service at Kentucky Children's Hospital with the University of Kentucky. She completed the combined residency program in Pediatrics, Adult Psychiatry and Child/Adolescent Psychiatry prior to joining the faculty at the University of Kentucky. She is currently supported by a Building Interdisciplinary Research Careers in Women's Health (K12) award. Her research interests include fertility issues and body image issues in adolescent and young female cancer survivors and juvenile primary fibromyalgia syndrome.

**Dr. Arthur J. Lurigio,** a psychologist, is Associate Dean for Faculty in the College of Arts and Sciences and a Professor of Criminal Justice and Psychology at Loyola University Chicago. He is also the Director of the Center for the Advancement of Research, Training, and Education (CARTE) at Loyola University Chicago, and a Senior Research Advisor at Illinois Treatment Alternatives for Safe Communities (TASC). In 2003, Dr. Lurigio was named a faculty scholar, the highest honor bestowed on senior faculty at Loyola University Chicago. In recognition of his outstanding contributions to criminology and criminal justice practices, Dr. Lurigio was conferred the University of Cincinnati Award in 1996, the Hans W. Mattick Award in 2003, and the Champions for Recovery: Excellence in Research Award in 2009. Dr. Lurigio's research lies in the areas of offender drug abuse and dependence problems, mental disorders and crime, community corrections, police-community relations, criminal victimization, and victim services.

**Doris Layton MacKenzie, Ph.D.,** Professor, Department of Criminology and Criminal Justice at the University of Maryland. Prior to this position she earned her doctorate from Pennsylvania State University, was on the faculty of the Louisiana State University where she was honored as a "Researcher of Distinction," and was awarded a Visiting Scientist position at the National Institute of Justice. As an expert in criminal justice, Dr. MacKenzie has consulted with State and Local jurisdictions, and has testified before U.S. Senate and House Committees. She has an extensive publication record on such topics as examining what works to reduce crime in the community, inmate adjustment to prison, the impact of intermediate sanctions on recidivism, long-term offenders, methods of predicting prison populations, self-report criminal activities of probationers and boot camp prisons. She recently completed, "What Works in Corrections: Examining the Criminal Activities of Offenders and Delinquents (Cambridge University Press, 2006)."

**Philip R. Magaletta** has administered and practiced correctional psychology for over a decade with the Federal Bureau of Prisons. He currently serves the agency as the Clinical Training Coordinator for the Psychology Services Branch and is a faculty associate at the Johns Hopkins University. A graduate of University of Scranton, Magaletta earned his Master's degree in 1992 from Loyola College in Maryland and his doctorate in Clinical Psychology in 1996 from St. Louis University. He is an active member of several professional associations and his research and work have been published in several journals and books. His areas of research include mental health services delivery to incarcerated populations, addictions counseling, spirituality, telehealth, and organizational approaches to behavioral sciences research in prisons.

**Douglas B. Marlowe, J.D., Ph.D.** is the Chief of Science, Policy & Law for the National Association of Drug Court Professionals, a Senior Scientist at the Treatment Research Institute, and an Adjunct Associate Professor of Psychiatry at the University of Pennsylvania School of Medicine. A lawyer and clinical psychologist, Dr. Marlowe has received numerous state and federal research grants to study coercion in drug abuse treatment, the effects of drug courts and other diversion programs for drug abusers involved in the criminal justice system, and behavioral treatments for drug abusers and criminal offenders. He is a Fellow of the American Psychological Association (APA) and has received proficiency certification in the treatment of psychoactive substance use disorders from the APA College of Professional Psychology. Dr. Marlowe has published over 125 professional articles and chapters on the topics of crime and substance abuse. He is the Editor-in-Chief of the *Drug Court Review* and is on the editorial board of *Criminal Justice & Behavior.*

**Catherine A. Martin, M.D.** is Professor and Vice Chair for Research and E.A. Edwards Professor in the Department of Psychiatry. She currently has NIH funding for research in medications for smoking cessation and ADHD. She is also investigating individual differences in drug effects of drugs of abuse and is collaborating on a rural based Contingency Management smoking cessation intervention. She is concluding the pilot work with lung cancer patients and their families to investigate a novel family intervention for smoking cessation. She is involved in the training of clinical researchers locally and nationally through NIH funded BIRCWH program and the NIDA: AACAP K12 programs.

**Ojmarrh Mitchell** is an assistant professor in the Department of Criminology at the University of South Florida. Professor Mitchell earned his PhD in Criminal Justice and Criminology from the University of Maryland with a doctoral minor in Measurement, Statistics, and Evaluation. His research interests include drugs and crime, corrections and sentencing, and meta-analysis.

**Shannon Gwin Mitchell** is a Research Scientist at Friends Research Institute in Baltimore, Maryland, where she specializes in qualitative and mixed methods research. She received her

M.A. in Clinical Psychology and her Ph.D. in Community and Applied Social Psychology. Dr. Mitchell was at Johns Hopkins University, Bloomberg School of Public Health from 1998 to 2006, where she worked as an ethnographer on numerous federally-funded HIV-related interventions with injection drug users. In 2006 she joined Friends Research Institute to assume primary responsibility for the ethnographic component of a NIDA-funded study of entry and engagement in methadone treatment.

**Lori Molenaar, ARNP, CS** is a psychiatric nurse practitioner in the University Health Service Student Behavioral Health Clinic at the University of Kentucky. She is an adjunct faculty member of the University of Kentucky College of Nursing. She is certified by the American Nurses Credentialing Center as a clinical specialist in child and adolescent psychiatry.

**Carrie B. Oser** received her Ph.D. from the University of Georgia in 2004. She is currently an Associate Professor of Sociology at the University of Kentucky, with a faculty appointment in the Center on Drug and Alcohol Research. Dr. Oser has National Institute on Drug Abuse funded projects which are examining health disparities among African American women across criminal justice status as well as exploring the counselor contextual and organizational contributions to rural and urban treatment outcomes in public substance abuse treatment facilities. Her research interests include HIV and substance use among criminal justice and rural populations. She has recently published in *Drug and Alcohol Dependence, the Journal of Substance abuse Treatment*, and *AIDS Care Journal.*

**Dr. Mario A. Paparozzi** is a Chair of the Department of Sociology and Criminal Justice at University of North Carolina at Pembroke. Over the past 35 years, Dr. Paparozzi has served as President of the American Probation and Parole Association, President of the International Association of Reentry, Assistant Corrections Commissioner and State Parole Board Chair for the State of New Jersey. Dr. Paparozzi has published extensively on a variety of issues related to probation, parole, and community corrections. As well, has provided numerous keynote addresses, seminars, and professional training in 46 states, the District of Columbia, Singapore, the United Kingdom, Canada, Bermuda, Poland, Germany, and The Council of Europe in Strasbourg, France. He has served as an international judge for the United Kingdom's International Community Justice Awards Conference hosted by Her Royal Highness Princess Anne and the British Home Office.

**Roger H. Peters, Ph.D.,** serves as Chair and Professor in the Department of Mental Health Law and Policy at the Louis de la Parte Florida Mental Health Institute (FMHI), University of South Florida (USF), where he has been a faculty member since 1986. He received his Ph.D. in clinical psychology from the Florida State University, following completion of a pre-doctoral internship at the University of North Carolina, School of Medicine. Dr. Peters has served as Principal Investigator and Director for several grant projects, including the recently established NIDA Research Core Center – USF's Center on Co-Occurring Disorders, Justice, and Multidisciplinary Research. He served as Chair and Co-Editor of the SAMHSA/CSAT Treatment Improvement Protocol (TIP) #44 on "Substance Abuse Treatment for Adults in the Criminal Justice System". On March 20, 2007, Dr. Peters provided testimony to the U.S. House Judiciary Committee on the "Second Chance Act of 2007" legislation.

**Jessica M. Ramos** received her B.A. in Psychology from Eastern Connecticut State University. She is a Research Assistant at Child and Family Agency of Southeastern Connecticut. Jessica has assisted in the editorial process of books on primary prevention, prevention and treatment of behavioral problems in childhood and adolescents, Asperger Syndrome, promotion of prosocial behavior, and interpersonal violence in the African American community. She is involved in agency research and reviews cases for Quality Assurance.

**Pamela F. Rodriguez** is president of TASC, Inc. of Illinois, a statewide, nonprofit case management agency that serves adults and youth with substance use and mental health disorders. Ms. Rodriguez oversees TASC's service delivery to nearly 30,000 individuals each year who are referred to TASC by Illinois courts, corrections, and child welfare systems. She was appointed in 2007 to serve as a practitioner member of the Coordinating Council on Juvenile Justice and Delinquency Prevention, an independent organization in the U.S. executive branch that coordinates all federal juvenile delinquency prevention and detention programs. Ms. Rodriguez earned her master's degree in Social Service Administration from the University of Chicago.

**Stanton E. Samenow, Ph.D.** is a clinical psychologist in Alexandria, Virginia. He specializes in evaluating and treating juvenile and adult offenders. He has been an expert witness, a member of Presidential Task Forces dealing with crime, a consultant to federal, state, and local correctional, educational, and law enforcement agencies. Dr. Samenow is the author of a number of books the subject matter of which is criminal behavior. His best known book is "Inside the Criminal Mind" (NY: Random House, 2004). His most recent book, available in paperback, is titled "The Myth of the Out of Character Crime."

**Robert P. Schwartz, M.D.** is the Medical Director of Friends Research Institute. Dr. Schwartz is the author or co-author of over 50 peer reviewed journal articles. He has been Principal Investigator or Co-Investigator on numerous research grants funded by the National Institute on Drug Abuse (NIDA). His work has included randomized trials of methadone without counseling as compared to waiting list, methadone and buprenorphine in prison, role induction as an adjunct to buprenorphine detoxification and a mixed methods longitudinal study on entry and engagement in methadone treatment. He served as the former Director of the Division of Alcohol and Drug Abuse of the University of Maryland School of Medicine and has been a member of the NIDA Health Services Grant Review Committee for the past three years.

**Michele Staton-Tindall** received her Ph.D. from the University of Kentucky in 2004. She is currently an Assistant Professor of Social Work at the University of Kentucky, with faculty appointments in the Center on Drug and Alcohol Research and the Center on the Study of Violence Against Children. Dr. Staton-Tindall is the Principal Investigator of the state funded Criminal Justice Kentucky Treatment Outcome Study (CJKTOS). She is also the lead evaluator for five projects funded by the Center on Substance Abuse Treatment to expand and enhance substance abuse treatment programs. Her research interests include substance use among women and related problems, behavioral health service utilization, and treatment outcomes for offenders paroling to rural areas.

**Faye S. Taxman, Ph.D.** is a University Professor in the Administration of Justice Department and Director of the Advancing Correctional Excellence Center at George Mason University. Dr. Taxman is recognized for her work in the development of the seamless systems of care models that link the criminal justice with other service delivery systems as well as reengineering probation and parole supervision services. She has active "laboratories" with her nearly 20 year agreement with the Maryland Department of Public Safety and Correctional Services; she has been a PI of one of the National Institute on Drug Abuse's research centers in the Criminal Justice Drug Abuse Treatment Studies (CJ-DATS) network. She has received numerous awards including a Fellow of the Academy of Experimental Criminology and the Distinguished Scholar from the American Society of Criminology's Division on Sentencing and Corrections.

**Beth Weinman** is the Bureau of Prisons National Drug Abuse Programs Coordinator in the Psychology Services Branch of the Correctional

Programs Division. In her capacity, she is responsible for the design, implementation, oversight and evaluation of all drug abuse treatment programming in the Bureau. Before coming to the Bureau in 1991, Ms. Weinman worked with state and local criminal justice components and community treatment providers to shape linkages between these systems to improve the treatment and supervision of the drug offender population. Ms. Weinman has also worked with juvenile offenders, crime victims, and has provided direct treatment services to drug offenders. She has written extensively on the management and treatment of the drug offender. Ms. Weinman received her M.A. from John Jay College of Criminal Justice in 1988.

**Wayne N. Welsh, Ph.D.,** Dr. Welsh's areas of expertise include substance abuse treatment in criminal justice settings, corrections, violence, and organizational theory. Dr. Welsh has collaborated with state correctional agencies on several large, multisite studies of prison-based drug treatment. Projects included a NIJ-funded project to develop a model academic/justice research partnership with a state correctional agency. Dr. Welsh subsequently led a quasi-experimental, multisite study that examined individual and programmatic factors associated with drug treatment outcomes. Dr. Welsh also conducted a randomized experiment examining drug treatment programs at a specialized drug treatment prison. A three-year follow-up study of recidivism and drug relapse is currently underway. Books include *Criminal Violence: Patterns, Causes and Prevention*, co-authored with Marc Riedel (Oxford University Press, 2008), and *Criminal Justice Policy and Planning* (LexisNexis/Anderson, 2008).

**David B. Wilson, Ph.D.,** is Professor and Chair of the Department of Criminology, Law and Society, at George Mason University. His Ph.D. is in applied social psychology from Claremont Graduate University. His research interests are the effectiveness of offender rehabilitation and crime prevention efforts, program evaluation methodology, and meta-analysis. His researched has included a broad range of topics, including the effectiveness of juvenile delinquency interventions, school-based prevention programs, correctional boot-camps, court-mandated batterer intervention programs, and drug-courts; the effects of sugar on children's behavior; and the effects of alcohol on violent behavior. He is an associate editor of the Journal of Experimental Criminology, a consulting editor for Psychological Bulletin, and was awarded the Marcia Guttentag Award for Early Promise as an Evaluator by the American Evaluation Association.

**Dr. Gary Zajac** is Managing Director of the Justice Center for Research and Senior Research Associate at Penn State University, and a member of the graduate faculty. Prior to joining the Justice Center in 2010, Dr. Zajac was Chief of Research and Evaluation in the Pennsylvania Department of Corrections for nearly thirteen years, where he initiated and oversaw an ambitious program evaluation agenda. While at the PADOC, he initiated and lead numerous studies and evaluations of PADOC programs and related topics, partnering with external researchers and securing third party grants. The research partnership model that Dr. Zajac developed within the PADOC won a 2008 *Innovations Award* from the Council of State Governments, being recognized as a model for knowledge creation and transfer. His scholarly work has appeared in many journals and books, including *Criminology and Public Policy* and *Crime and Delinquency*. He has advised dozens of state, local and international corrections agencies and organizations on the development of research capacity and the implementation of research-based practice.

**Joan E. Zweben, Ph.D.,** is a clinical psychologist with over 35 years' experience in treatment, training and research. She is the founder and Executive Director of the East Bay Community Recovery Project in Oakland, California (1989-present). Since 1994, she is Clinical Professor of Psychiatry; University of California, San Francisco. She has collaborated with researchers locally and nationally since 1981, and since

2002, she has been in several leadership roles in NIDA's Clinical Trials Network. Her activities as a treatment provider, author, teacher, and consultant keep her informed of new developments in the field. She is the author of over 60 articles or book chapters and editor of 15 monographs on treating addiction. Her books include: Washton & Zweben, *Treating Alcohol and Drug Problems in Psychotherapy Practice* and *Cocaine and Methamphetamine Dependence: Treatment, Recovery and Relapse Prevention*; Margolis & Zweben, *Treating Patients with Alcohol and Other Drug Problems: An Integrated Approach*.

CPSIA information can be obtained at www.ICGtesting.com
Printed in the USA
LVOW09*0219040815

448655LV00002BA/2/P

9 781441 994691